THE NEW WITTGENSTEIN

"This collection provides an accessible and stimulating introduction to a radically different way of interpreting the philosophical significance of Wittgenstein's work (both early and late) that is becoming increasingly influential. The editors and their contributors manage to illuminate the widely ramifying implications of this interpretation without underplaying its highly controversial status. Their work opens up an important and potentially fruitful field for future debate."

Stephen Mulhall, New College, Oxford

The New Wittgenstein offers a major re-evaluation of Wittgenstein's thinking. This book is a stellar collection of essays that present a significantly different portrait of Wittgenstein. The essays clarify Wittgenstein's modes of philosophical criticism and shed light on the relation between his thought and different philosophical traditions and areas of human concern. With essays by Stanley Cavell, James Conant, Cora Diamond, Hilary Putnam and John McDowell, we see the emergence of a new way of understanding Wittgenstein's thought.

This is a controversial collection, with essays by the most highly regarded Wittgenstein scholars that will change the way we look at Wittgenstein's body of work. Anyone interested in gaining a new and fresh understanding of Wittgenstein's work will find this a fascinating read.

Contributors: Stanley Cavell, David R. Cerbone, James Conant, Alice Crary, Cora Diamond, David H. Finkelstein, Juliet Floyd, P.M.S. Hacker, John McDowell, Hilary Putnam, Rupert Read, Martin Stone, Edward Witherspoon.

Alice Crary is a Tutor in Philosophy at Harvard University. **Rupert Read** is a Lecturer in Philosophy at The University of East Anglia.

THE NEW WITTGENSTEIN

Edited by
Alice Crary and Rupert Read

London and New York

First published 2000
by Routledge
2 Park Square, Milton Park, Abingdon, Oxon, OX14 4RN

Simultaneously published in the USA and Canada
by Routledge
270 Madison Ave, New York NY 10016

Reprinted 2000, 2001

Transferred to Digital Printing 2005

Routledge is an imprint of the Taylor & Francis Group

Typeset in Times New Roman by Florence Production Ltd,
Stoodleigh, Devon

British Library Cataloguing in Publication Data
A catalogue record for this book is available
from the British Library

Library of Congress Cataloguing in Publication Data

The new Wittgenstein / edited by Alice Crary and Rupert Read.
p. cm.
Includes bibliographical references and index.
1. Wittgenstein, Ludwig, 1889–1951. I. Crary, Alice Marguerite,
1967–II. Read, Rupert J., 1966–
B3376.W564 N49 2000
192–dc21
99–048803

ISBN 0–415–17318–3 (hbk)
ISBN 0–415–17319–1 (pbk)

CONTENTS

CONTENTS

CONTRIBUTORS

Stanley Cavell is Walter M. Cabot Professor Emeritus of Aesthetics and the General Theory of Value, at Harvard University. He is the author of *Must We Mean What We Say? A Book of Essays* (Cambridge University Press, 1969; reprinted 1976), *The Claim of Reason: Wittgenstein, Skepticism, Morality and Tragedy* (Oxford University Press, 1979), *In Quest of the Ordinary: Lines of Skepticism and Romanticism* (University of Chicago Press, 1988), *This New yet Unapproachable America: Lectures after Emerson after Wittgenstein* (The Living Batch Press, 1989), *Conditions Handsome and Unhandsome: The Constitution of Emersonian Perfectionism* (University of Chicago Press, 1990), *A Pitch of Philosophy* (Harvard University Press, 1994) and *Philosophical Passages: Wittgenstein, Emerson, Austin, Derrida* (Blackwell, 1995).

David R. Cerbone is Assistant Professor of Philosophy at West Virginia University. He has published articles on Wittgenstein, Heidegger and the analytic and phenomenological traditions more generally.

Alice Crary is a Tutor in Philosophy at Harvard University. Her interests include ethics, moral psychology and philosophy and literature.

James Conant is Professor of Philosophy at the University of Chicago. He has published articles on Kant, Kierkegaard, Nietzsche, Frege, William James, Wittgenstein, Carnap and others.

Cora Diamond is Kenan Professor Philosophy and Professor of Law at the University of Virginia. She has also taught at Princeton University, Aberdeen University and the University of Sussex. She is the author of *The Realistic Spirit: Wittgenstein, Philosophy, and the Mind* (MIT Press, 1991) and the editor of *Wittgenstein's Lectures on the Foundations of Mathematics, Cambridge 1939* (University of Chicago Press, 1976).

David H. Finkelstein is Assistant Professor of Philosophy, Indiana University. His interests include topics in epistemology and the philosophy of mind. He has written about Wittgenstein on expression, the idea of inner sense and the distinction between conscious and unconscious mental states.

Juliet Floyd is Associate Professor of Philosophy at Boston University. She has published papers on Kant, Frege, Moore, Wittgenstein (early and late) and Gödel.

She is the editor of *Future Pasts: Perspectives on the Place of the Analytic Tradition in Twentieth Century Philosophy* (with Sanford Shieh; Oxford University Press, 2000).

P.M.S. Hacker is Fellow and Tutor in Philosophy at St.John's College, Oxford. He is the author of *Insight and Illusion: Themes in the Philosophy of Wittgenstein* (Oxford University Press, 1972; revised edition, 1986), *An Analytic Commentary on Wittgenstein's Philosophical Investigations* in 4 volumes (vols 1 and 2 with G.P. Baker; Blackwell, 1984), *Scepticism, Rules and Language* (with G.P. Baker; Blackwell, 1984), *Frege: Logical Excavations* (with G.P. Baker; Blackwell, 1984), *Appearance and Reality* (Blackwell, 1987) and *Wittgenstein's Place in 20th Century Analytic Philosophy* (Blackwell, 1996).

John McDowell is University Professor of Philosophy at the University of Pittsburgh. His recent publications include *Mind and World* (Harvard University Press, 1994; second edition, 1996), *Mind, Value and Reality* (Harvard University Press, 1998) and *Meaning, Knowledge and Reality* (Harvard University Press, 1998).

Hilary W. Putnam is Cogan University Professor at Harvard University. His books include *Reason, Truth and History* (Cambridge University Press, 1981), *Realism With A Human Face* (Harvard University Press, 1990), *Renewing Philosophy* (Harvard University Press, 1992), *Words and Life* (Harvard University Press, 1994) and *Pragmatism* (Blackwell, 1995).

Rupert Read is Lecturer in Philosophy at the University of East Anglia (Norwich, England). He has published articles in *Philosophical Papers, Philosophical Investigations* and *The Philosophical Forum*. He is the editor of *The New Hume Debate* (Routledge, 2000) and *Thomas Kuhn* (Polity, 2000).

Martin Stone is Professor of Law and Associate Professor of Philosophy at Duke University. He also teaches in the Graduate Program in Literature at Duke. His previously published essays are on the philosophy of law and on Wittgenstein.

Edward Witherspoon is Assistant Professor of Philosophy at Colgate University. His interests include the history of analytic philosophy, epistemological skepticism and twentieth-century continental philosophy.

ACKNOWLEDGEMENTS

We would like here to thank the many individuals who at different stages made useful suggestions about this project and who in various ways helped to bring it to completion. Our thanks are due, in particular, to Stanley Cavell, James Conant, Tobyn DeMarco, Anne DeVivo, Cora Diamond, James Guetti, Nathaniel Hupert, Kelly Dean Jolley, John McDowell, Hilary Putnam, Wes Sharrock and Emma Willmer. We are indebted also to Adrian Driscoll, Anna Gerber and Ruth Jeavons, at Routledge, for their support and suggestions.

Stanley Cavell, 'Excursus on Wittgenstein's vision of language' is reprinted from *The Claim of Reason: Wittgenstein, Skepticism, Morality and Tragedy*, copyright © 1979 by Oxford University Press, Inc. Used by permission of Oxford University Press, Inc., Oxford. John McDowell, 'Non-cognitivism and rule-following' is reprinted from *Wittgenstein: to Follow a Rule*, S.H. Holtzman and C.M. Leich (eds), London, Routledge and Kegan Paul, 1981, pp. 141–62. Hilary Putnam, 'Rethinking mathematical necessity' is reprinted by permission of the publisher from *Words and Life*, Cambridge, Mass., Harvard University Press. Copyright © 1994 by the President and Fellows of Harvard College. Cora Diamond, 'Ethics, imagination and the method of Wittgenstein's *Tractatus*' is reprinted from *Bilder der Philosophie*, R. Heinrich and H. Vetter (eds), *Wiener Reihe: Themen der Philosophie*, Vienna and Munich, Oldenbourg, 1991, pp. 55–90.

INTRODUCTION

Alice Crary

This volume contains papers on Wittgenstein which (with one exception which I will mention below) share certain fundamental and – with respect to received views about Wittgenstein's thought – quite unorthodox assumptions about his conception of the aim of philosophy. This is not to say that the papers form a homogeneous body of work. They are concerned with different periods and regions of his thought, and they diverge from each other to various extents in their emphases and styles, and in the views they attribute to him. Nevertheless, without regard to the period (or periods) of his work with which they are concerned, they agree in suggesting that Wittgenstein's primary aim in philosophy is – to use a word he himself employs in characterizing his later philosophical procedures – a *therapeutic* one. These papers have in common an understanding of Wittgenstein as aspiring, not to advance metaphysical theories, but rather to help us work ourselves out of confusions we become entangled in when philosophizing. More specifically, they agree in representing him as tracing the sources of our philosophical confusions to our tendency, in the midst of philosophizing, to think that we need to survey language from an external point of view. They invite us to understand him as wishing to get us to see that our need to grasp the essence of thought and language will be met – not, as we are inclined to think in philosophy, by metaphysical theories expounded from such a point of view, but – by attention to our everyday forms of expression and to the world those forms of expression serve to reveal.

This description of what unites the papers in this volume may seem to fall short of a description of an unorthodoxy about *both* Wittgenstein's early and later thought. It is extremely irregular to speak of a therapeutic aim in connection with the *Tractatus*. But some of the most widely accepted interpretations of Wittgenstein's *later* thought characterize his main philosophical aspiration, in roughly the terms used above, as a therapeutic one. If these familiar characterizations are taken at face-value, it will seem as though accounts of Wittgenstein's later thought as having a therapeutic aim, of the sort developed in some of the papers in this volume, are anything but unorthodox. And, further, it will seem as though a volume like this one which represents his thought as having a therapeutic aim both early and late is groundbreaking only in its suggestion that the *Tractatus* anticipates his later thought in more significant ways than is ordinarily assumed.

It would not be wrong to say that what is most striking about the papers in this volume has to do with their suggestion of significant *continuity* in Wittgenstein's thought. These papers criticize more standard interpretations of his work in so far as such interpretations furnish a narrative about the development of his thought which, while it leaves room for important similarities between the views he holds at different times, accents the idea of a *decisive break* in his mode of philosophizing between the *Tractatus* and his later writings. But what is most striking about these papers cannot be captured *simply* by saying that they challenge the idea of a decisive break in his thought. The way in which the papers challenge this idea is a function of the manner in which they depart, in their therapeutic understanding of Wittgenstein's conception of the aim of philosophy, from standard interpretations of the *Tractatus and* from standard interpretations of Wittgenstein's later writings. It is necessary to appreciate how this understanding of Wittgenstein's conception of the aim of philosophy places them at odds with standard interpretations of *both* periods in order to grasp the distinctive kind of continuity they suggest.

The narrative about the development of Wittgenstein's thought told within standard interpretations, sketched broadly enough to abstract from local disagreements, proceeds as follows. It begins with Wittgenstein, in the *Tractatus*, giving an account of the connection between language and the world. The main tenet of the account is that the form of language and the form of the world reflect each other. The world is made up of simple objects which can combine into facts, and language is made up of names which can combine into propositions. These two types of combination mirror each other, and the fact that they do so is what ensures that propositions have meaning. The meaning of a name, on this allegedly Tractarian theory, is determined by an act which ties it to a particular simple object. Simple objects have logical forms which are their possibilities of combination with other objects, and names have logical forms – or possibilities of combination with other names – derivatively. What a name means determines what can be said with it in the sense that the logical form of a name reflects the logical form of the object it denotes.

The standard narrative proceeds by telling us that in his post-*Tractatus* writings Wittgenstein turns on this theory of meaning and rejects it in favor of a very different kind of theory. Now the meaning of a word is fixed not by an act which serves to connect it to particular features of reality but rather by the ways in which we use it – by its place in the *language-game* or by its *grammar*. Further, the grammar of a word fixes not only its meaning but also its logical character in the sense of its possibilities of combination with other words in specific circumstances. So, according to standard interpretations of Wittgenstein's later writings, questions about whether or not a given bit of language makes sense are questions about whether or not an utterance (i.e., a combination of words used in particular circumstances) is intelligible, and the answers to such questions are determined by grammar.

This gives us an outline of the standard narrative about the development of Wittgenstein's thought. Its centerpiece is a dramatic rupture between Tractarian and post-Tractarian periods which allegedly comes as Wittgenstein moves from one kind of theory of meaning to another kind of theory. The most well-known version of this narrative runs as follows: in the *Tractatus* Wittgenstein advocates a *truth-conditional* theory of meaning which has the characteristic features of *realism*, and later on he rejects it and embraces a theory of meaning as consisting in *assertibility-conditions* which has the characteristic features of *anti-realism*.[1]

This narrative about the development of Wittgenstein's thought is often glossed as a story about how Wittgenstein makes a transition from developing a metaphysical account of the relation between language and the world in the *Tractatus* to relinquishing the project of developing such an account later on and limiting himself to non-metaphysical descriptions of our linguistic practices. It is this conception of Wittgenstein as rejecting any concern with traditional metaphysical theorizing which, within standard interpretations, is sometimes taken to accommodate an understanding of his philosophy as having a therapeutic aim. The idea is that he has given up any ambition of providing a metaphysical explanation of how language hooks on to the world and has turned instead to presenting therapies, in the form of ordinary descriptions of language, intended to "cure" us of the belief that we require such an explanation. In this way, standard interpretations of Wittgenstein's later thought seem to make room for the idea of a therapeutic aim. So it appears that here the idea is by no means a surprising or unorthodox one.

This appearance is, however, fundamentally misleading. In the sense in which the papers in this volume champion the idea of a therapeutic aim in connection with both the *Tractatus* and Wittgenstein's later philosophy, standard interpretations of his later philosophy *utterly fail to capture its therapeutic character*. These papers agree in at least implicitly offering a deep criticism of standard interpretations of Wittgenstein's later philosophy. They charge that standard interpretations in effect represent Wittgenstein as undertaking the very type of metaphysical project which, even according to the interpretations themselves, he is repudiating. The result is that such interpretations entirely fail to locate the therapeutic nature of his philosophical procedures.

This criticism is developed, roughly, along the following lines. It takes as its point of departure the fact that standard interpretations of Wittgenstein's later philosophy assume both that Wittgenstein abandons the idea of an external standpoint on language and also that he construes the abandonment of this idea as having important consequences for our entitlement to certain basic epistemic ideals. Within standard interpretations, Wittgenstein is portrayed as holding that it follows from the abandonment of the idea of such a standpoint that what counts as agreement between the use of a sign and its meaning is fixed (not by objective reality, but) by grammar – and that there can therefore be no such thing as fully *objective* agreement. There is, according to the criticism developed here, something essentially unsatisfactory about this picture of Wittgenstein's philosophical concerns. The difficulty is that abandoning the idea of an external standpoint on language only appears to threaten our entitlement to talk about full-blooded objectivity if it is assumed that we depend for any entitlement we enjoy on the existence of features of reality which transcend our forms of thought and speech and determine their correctness – features of reality which (we imagine) are only discernible from an external standpoint – and if it is assumed, further, that in abandoning the idea of such a standpoint we have tacitly admitted that there are *no* such features of reality. It follows that to the extent that Wittgenstein is taken to be drawing the conclusion that full-blooded objectivity is out of reach, he is, at the same time, understood as preserving the idea of an external standpoint. He is understood as holding that it is possible to occupy such a standpoint and to detect from there that nothing external underwrites our ways of thinking and talking – and that something else (say, our language-games themselves) must provide a standard of correctness. Thus, standard interpretations, even though they claim to be depicting Wittgenstein as rejecting the idea of an external standpoint, offer representations of his thought which keep the idea in play. This is the upshot of the criticism which is spelled out in these papers. Standard interpretations portray Wittgenstein's thought as governed by traditional metaphysical presuppositions in a way which totally distorts its therapeutic character.

This criticism of standard interpretations of Wittgenstein's later philosophy provides a framework within which it is possible more fully to characterize the unorthodoxy which unites the papers in this volume. These papers claim that one of Wittgenstein's main aims throughout his work is getting us to see that the idea of an external standpoint on language is thoroughly confused and that its abandonment is accordingly *without consequences* for our entitlement to our basic epistemic ideals. Our willingness to insist that abandoning the idea does have such consequences is, by the lights of these papers, a sign that we are still participating in the confusion Wittgenstein seeks to address. This understanding of Wittgenstein as trying to free us in a quite radical manner from the idea of an external standpoint is what licenses talk, in reference to the papers, of a therapeutic aspiration. It is in so far as the papers represent Wittgenstein's philosophy as therapeutic in *this* sense – in a sense which, importantly, constitutes a divergence from standard interpretations of his work at both periods – that they suggest a fundamentally different kind of continuity in his thought and thus make a novel contribution to Wittgenstein scholarship.

There is a further respect in which it may seem strange to speak of novelty in connection with the papers in the volume which are specifically concerned with Wittgenstein's *later* philosophy. Readings of his later work on which its main aim is therapeutic in the particular sense at issue in this volume were already available back in the 1960s. Indeed, although such readings have never occupied a central place within mainstream philosophical conversations about Wittgenstein, they have nevertheless achieved a respectable level of recognition.

By the same token, it may seem more appropriate to speak of novelty in connection with the writings on the *Tractatus* included here. Although some of the original papers defending the view that Wittgenstein's early book should be read as having a therapeutic aim are now several decades old, this unorthodoxy about the *Tractatus* has only very recently received anything like the same amount of attention as the corresponding unorthodoxy about Wittgenstein's later thought.

The sense in which this volume represents a novel contribution to conversations about Wittgenstein is, however, *not* a function of these sorts of comparative judgments about what is new and what is familiar in Wittgenstein scholarship. Its novelty is a function of the fact that the papers in it, taken together, represent his thought as characterized by a novel kind of continuity.

Any reasonable defense of this kind of continuity claim needs to address ways in which standard interpretations of the *Tractatus* and standard interpretations of Wittgenstein's later writings inform each other. On standard interpretations, Wittgenstein is depicted as favoring certain metaphysical theses about the nature of logic and language in the *Tractatus* and then turning on them later on and rejecting them in favor of something like their negations. This means that, within such interpretations, a basic understanding of the *Tractatus* shapes and delimits the space available for developing an interpretation of Wittgenstein's later philosophy.

It is a consequence of this interdependence that unorthodox approaches to Wittgenstein's later philosophy, without regard to whether or not they explicitly take up questions about how to read the *Tractatus*, at least implicitly make way for radically revising standard interpretations of it. The possibility of a radically revised reading of the *Tractatus* is in a sense already contained in "therapeutic" readings of Wittgenstein's later writings.

The structure of the volume is designed to underline this fact. Part I contains a set of papers which are primarily concerned with Wittgenstein's later writings, and Part II contains a set which are in the first instance concerned with Wittgenstein's early writings. The papers in Part I, although only a few of them explicitly touch on the fact that they make possible a new approach to thinking about the *Tractatus*, can none the less be seen as developing an understanding of Wittgenstein's later philosophy which calls for the sort of reassessment of the *Tractatus* carried out in the papers in Part II. The papers in Part II, in turn, recognize and explicitly theorize the fact that they anticipate the central lines of thought in Wittgenstein's later philosophy accented in the papers in Part I.

There is one paper in the volume which represents an exception to the principle which otherwise guided the volume's composition and which therefore deserves special mention here. P.M.S. Hacker's paper, placed at the end of the volume (after Part II), is a defense of a traditional interpretation of the *Tractatus* (it is an interpretation he himself helped to make famous) against the heterodox reading developed by two other contributors to the volume – Cora Diamond and James Conant. Since the reading of the *Tractatus* Diamond and Conant lay out in their respective contributions to this volume has received relatively little critical attention, it seemed that, with regard to it, the best strategy for fostering discussion would involve including a voice dissenting from their dissenting voices and thus making way for the reader to decide for herself.

These remarks enable me to describe the main aim of this volume more succinctly: its aim is, by bringing together for the first time discussions of Wittgenstein's later writings and discussions of the *Tractatus* which agree in representing his primary philosophical aim as therapeutic, to create a space in which it is at last possible to gauge the philosophical significance of these unorthodox approaches to both his early and later work.

This introduction is devoted to an overview of how the specific papers included in Parts I and II of the volume contribute to telling a narrative about the development of Wittgenstein's thought suggestive of a distinctive kind of continuity in his conception of the aim of philosophy. It also contains a few comments about P.M.S. Hacker's paper.

Part I: Wittgenstein's later writings: the illusory comfort of an external standpoint

Before turning to any of the specific papers in Part I (i.e., those that focus primarily on Wittgenstein's later philosophy), it will be helpful to have a slightly more expansive description of the understanding of Wittgenstein's conception of the aim of philosophy which they have in common – a description which encompasses the understanding they share of the modes of criticism and methods he employs in pursuing his aim. The description which follows initially applies to the papers in Part I, but it does not *only* apply to these papers. This volume is distinguished by the fact that all the papers in it, both those that focus primarily on Wittgenstein's later philosophy and those that focus primarily on the *Tractatus*, agree in attributing to him the same fundamental conception of the aim of philosophy. So the description that follows, in as far as it bears on the papers in Part I, also has a bearing on those in Part II (i.e., those that focus at least in the first instance on Wittgenstein's early thought). Indeed, as it will emerge below, even the part of the description having to do with the method Wittgenstein employs in later writings for pursuing his main philosophical aim has a bearing on some of the research on the *Tractatus* contained in Part II.

It is possible to describe the understanding of Wittgenstein's conception of the aim of philosophy which unites these papers by saying that, on their terms, his fundamental aim is to get us to see that the point of view on language we aspire to or think we need to assume when philosophizing – a point of view on language as if outside from which we imagine we can get a clear view of the relation between language and the world – is no more than the *illusion* of a point of view. To speak of "illusion" here is to signal that these papers, without regard to whether or not they actually use the language of illusion, represent Wittgenstein as telling us that when we envision ourselves occupying such a point of view we don't wind up saying anything coherent about the way things stand. That is, their suggestion is not that Wittgenstein hopes to get us to acknowledge that when we envision ourselves occupying such a point of view we are led to make claims which are false or in some way misleading – as if he believed our difficulty were to find a true or appropriate description of how things look from there. Nor is it that he hopes to get us to acknowledge that when we envision ourselves occupying such a point of view we are led to come out with sentences which express thoughts the logical structure of language prohibits us from saying – as if he believed our difficulty were that the kinds of thoughts we are attracted to in philosophy are thoughts which, due to the nature of language, are forever out of our reach. Their suggestion is, rather, that he hopes to get us to see that when we envision ourselves occupying an external point of view on language we don't succeed in articulating *any* thoughts – and that he sees our difficulty as one of coming to recognize that the idea of such a point of view creates the *illusion* of understanding the sentences we want to utter in philosophy.

This basic understanding of Wittgenstein's conception of the aim of philosophy has important implications – implications taken up in all the papers in this volume – for how we should conceive his modes of philosophical criticism. It follows from it that we should take the gestures in which Wittgenstein distances himself from this or that metaphysical sentence (i.e., from this or that sentence presented as if from an external point of view on language) as indicating – not that he thinks the sentence is false or that it expresses an impermissible thought, but rather – that he thinks it fails to make any claim at all.

Many of the papers in this volume make this general point about Wittgenstein's modes of philosophical criticism in connection with his use of "nonsense" as a term of philosophical appraisal. (This includes all of the papers in Part II and Martin Stone's and my own in Part I.) The idea is that when Wittgenstein says that a combination of words we are tempted to utter in philosophy is nonsense, he is saying, not that we know what the words attempt to say and that *that* cannot properly be put into words, but instead that those words do not say anything, that they haven't (yet) been given any significant use. Now it is perhaps useful to observe that if we appeal to this way of characterizing (what here are taken as) Wittgenstein's characteristic modes of philosophical criticism, it is possible to give a rough indication of the kinds of considerations which make these modes of philosophical criticism, together with the conception of the aim of philosophy they underwrite, seem attractive. In endorsing these modes of philosophical criticism, we thereby distance ourselves from the idea, as we might now put it, that we can survey the logical structure of language from outside meaningful uses of language and determine that some nonsensical sentences express impermissible thoughts. One consideration which seems to speak in favor of distancing ourselves from this idea – and at the same time in favor of endorsing these modes of philosophical criticism – is that if we retain the idea we thereby retain an image of ourselves as somehow capable of identifying the logical roles played by the parts of nonsensical (and hence presumably logically defunct) sentences. (Cora Diamond was the first philosopher to underscore the interest of Wittgenstein's use of "nonsense" as a term of philosophical appraisal in connection with the above general point about his characteristic modes of philosophical criticism.[2])

This view of Wittgenstein's characteristic modes of philosophical criticism, whether or not it is specifically developed with reference to his use of "nonsense" as a term of philosophical appraisal, is reflected in the exegetical strategies of all the papers in Part I – in their tacit assumptions about the *method* of Wittgenstein's later writings. These papers assume that the exchanges in Wittgenstein's later writings between different "interlocutory voices" should be understood as realizing his modes of philosophical criticism as these modes of criticism are conceived here. More precisely, they assume that some of these voices describe, as if from within the sorts of illusions that tempt us in philosophy, the attractions of metaphysical forms of words and, further, that others endeavor to show us – by giving expression to various plain renderings of the words in question and inviting the recognition that *no* construal of them satisfies us – that we have conflicting desires with regard to our own words and that our sense that we understand what we want to say in our efforts to philosophize is merely illusory. Thus, by the lights of these papers, the dialectical structure of Wittgenstein's writing makes an internal contribution to the philosophical instruction it contains. The success of his writing depends on its leading us to identify, successively, with the images of ourselves expressed by the different voices at play in it and on its thereby bringing us to the recognition that certain words we are tempted to utter in philosophy are nonsense, that they fail to say anything we want to say. (Stanley Cavell's writings contain the earliest descriptions, in this basic vein, of the method of Wittgenstein's later writings.[3])

It will be convenient to have a label for readings of Wittgenstein's later philosophy which attribute to him the closely interwoven set of views just described – i.e., the above set of views about his conception of the aim of philosophy, his characteristic modes of criticism and his distinctive method – since such readings are developed in all of the papers in Part I of this volume. I will hereafter refer to them as "therapeutic readings" of Wittgenstein's later philosophy.

The goals of Part I of this volume are two-fold. It is designed both to give a modest road-map of the original emergence of therapeutic readings of Wittgenstein's later philosophy and, in addition, to provide a selection of some of the most interesting and insightful recent research which further elaborates and defends such readings. It is with an eye towards the first of these goals that Part I reprints influential papers by two philosophers whose work helped to introduce therapeutic readings of Wittgenstein's later philosophy – Stanley Cavell and John McDowell. (There are others whose work on Wittgenstein's later philosophy might also have been presented in this context – e.g., G.E.M. Anscombe and Rush Rhees.)

Cavell was one of the first philosophers to develop a therapeutic reading of Wittgenstein's later thought. The section of *The Claim of Reason* included here ("Excursus on Wittgenstein's vision of language") was selected for the forcefulness with which it describes such a reading. Here Cavell claims that, for Wittgenstein, what leads us into philosophical confusion is our attraction to explanations of projections of words which seem to *insure* agreement in so far as they appear to go beyond or cut deeper than our ordinary practices with words. Wittgenstein's ambition in philosophy, as Cavell evokes it here, is to facilitate the recognition that the demand for reflective understanding that drives us to philosophize will be met, not by explanations of our lives with language which thus seem to proceed from outside, but rather by explanations grounded in the ordinary circumstances of those lives.

Cavell's therapeutic understanding of Wittgenstein shapes his sense of the importance of Wittgenstein's emphasis throughout his later writings on situations of *instruction* – an emphasis Cavell inherits in this section of the *Claim of Reason* with his own investigations of situations of teaching and learning a word.[4] What is of interest about such investigations, from the perspective of this understanding, is that they return us to our human natures. Cavell's investigations bring out with great clarity that our ability to follow those who teach us is "no more than natural" in the sense that it is not somehow propped up by features of reality perceptible from outside our natural reactions. His investigations remind us that someone who did not share our sense of what is funny and what sad, who did not try to make the sounds and gestures we make, who couldn't recognize the similarities our ways of projecting words track (and so on) "would not grow into our world."

A recurring theme in Cavell's writing about Wittgenstein is that, for Wittgenstein, our tendency to become entangled in philosophical confusion is the product of a natural disappointment with the conditions of human knowledge. Cavell sounds this theme here when he suggests that, confronted with Wittgenstein's "vision of language," we will be inclined to think that we are being asked to believe our language "rests upon very shaky foundations" and to go in search, once again, of explanations which somehow reach beyond – or outside – our ordinary forms of thought and speech and which can (we imagine) therefore furnish them with "solid foundations." What Wittgenstein wishes to get us to see, according to Cavell, is that the demand for such foundations is inherently confused and will inevitably lead to frustration.

Like Cavell, John McDowell contributed significantly to the initial development of a therapeutic reading of Wittgenstein's later writings. Now it is a striking feature of recent philosophical conversations about Wittgenstein that, although Cavell and McDowell are often both mentioned as favoring unorthodox readings of

Wittgenstein, it is rare that the existence of any philosophically interesting points of convergence between their work is registered. One consideration which weighed heavily in the choice of the particular paper of McDowell's which appears here ("Non-cognitivism and Rule-Following") was the desire to remedy this neglect of affinities between their work. What spoke in favor of this paper was the fact that in it McDowell appeals to a passage in one of Cavell's early discussions of Wittgenstein ("The availability of Wittgenstein's later philosophy") at a central juncture in his own description of a therapeutic reading of Wittgenstein.

The moment in Wittgenstein's thought which particularly concerns McDowell in this paper is the moment at which Wittgenstein considers a picture of a rule as an infinitely long and ideally rigid rail. What makes the picture attractive to us, while we are philosophizing, is the idea that our practices of rule-following depend for their stability on being underwritten by features of reality which transcend them in the sense of being discernible from a standpoint external to the reactions which characterize us as participants in the practices. The picture of a rule-as-rail incorporates this idea in its suggestion that the meaning of a rule reaches out in front of its application and determines correct linguistic behavior in the same brute way that the tracks of an infinitely long rail determine its extension. If we conceive of our practices in terms of the picture, we will, however, be unable to locate the grounds of our confidence in their stability. *This*, according to McDowell, is the lesson Wittgenstein's treatment of the picture is intended to impart. In contrast to what the picture suggests to us "there is nothing that keeps our practices in line except the reactions and responses we learn in learning them." It is just at this point in his discussion that McDowell makes the connection with Cavell's reading of Wittgenstein.

A conception of our practices as resting on nothing external may, McDowell acknowledges, strike us as too flimsy to accommodate talk of objectivity, and it may lead us to "recoil" into insistence that, if our practices in fact accommodate such talk, the picture of rules as rails must capture an important truth about them. But any tendency towards "recoil" simply repeats the confusion of thinking that we need a glimpse of language from outside in order to determine whether or not it is built on secure foundations. On McDowell's reading, the dialectic of Wittgenstein's treatment of rule-following comes to rest in a naïve realism which does not present itself, in the way traditional realism does, as furnishing an answer to a philosophical question raised from an external standpoint. (The sort of naïve realism in question here is no less at odds with anti-realism than with traditional realism in so far as both positions return answers, albeit opposing ones, to such a philosophical question.)[5]

Over the last couple of decades, therapeutic approaches to Wittgenstein's later philosophy – approaches which can be seen as developing the work of philosophers like Cavell and McDowell – have figured more prominently in philosophical discussions of Wittgenstein's later philosophy. These approaches have been defended against traditionally dominant interpretations, and their distinctiveness has been brought to light. The interest of the remaining papers in Part I of this volume should be seen within this general framework.

Consider, for instance, David Finkelstein's discussion of the sense in which Wittgenstein is attacking *platonism*. The idea that Wittgenstein distances himself from platonistic modes of thought is familiar from standard interpretations of his later philosophy. What the idea typically amounts to, within such interpretations, is an understanding of Wittgenstein as both pointing out that there is a kind of gulf between any spoken or written rule and the behavior which is said to satisfy it and also denying that an appeal to a rule's meaning can bridge such a gulf. This understanding speaks in favor of a portrait of Wittgenstein as a sort of "anti-realist" who maintains that there can be no fully objective answer to the question whether or not some activity is in accord with a particular rule. What is noteworthy about Finkelstein's discussion of platonism, viewed in this larger interpretative context, is his claim that, while there is a sense in which it is correct to speak of Wittgenstein as repudiating platonism, this familiar portrait not only fails to capture the relevant sense but is, moreover, itself platonistic. On the therapeutic reading of Wittgenstein Finkelstein defends, if we want to understand "platonism" as the name of a position Wittgenstein criticizes, we need to understand it in terms of the assumption that there is an external standpoint on language from which we can perceive a gulf between any rule and the behavior it calls for. Where Wittgenstein's "resistance to platonism" is thus taken to center on his rejection of the idea of such a standpoint, it leaves in place the possibility of objectivity in the relation between the rules and their applications (while implying that realizing the possibility doesn't require somehow "getting outside language"). The sort of "resistance to platonism" Finkelstein thinks is at issue is thus consistent with a position we might yet describe as innocently platonistic. There is an important point of contact here with McDowell's talk of a naïve realism in connection with his reading of Wittgenstein.

One of Finkelstein's concerns in his discussion of Wittgenstein and platonism is questioning the merits of Crispin Wright's well-known anti-realist interpretation of Wittgenstein's later philosophy. Rupert Read's paper deserves mention here, since it explores a similar set of issues – now with an eye towards discrediting central tenets of Saul Kripke's famous 'skeptical' interpretation of Wittgenstein's later philosophy.

Therapeutic approaches to Wittgenstein's later work have implications for how we understand the relation between his philosophy and other intellectual traditions. Standard ('anti-realist') interpretations of his later work invite its alignment with contemporary skeptical or relativistic intellectual trends. It is, for instance, a sign of the enormous influence of such interpretations that it is widely accepted that there are deep and thorough-going parallels between Wittgenstein's philosophy and the style of philosophical criticism Jacques Derrida dubs *deconstruction*. But this assimilation to deconstruction depends for its apparent plausibility on the acceptance of standard interpretations of Wittgenstein's later philosophy. Viewed from the perspective of a therapeutic reading, the assimilation appears to obscure precisely what is distinctive about Wittgenstein's philosophical procedures.

Martin Stone's recent work develops an insightful defense of a therapeutic reading of Wittgenstein's later philosophy against an assimilation to Derridean deconstruction. In his paper for this volume, Stone tries to account for the appeal of deconstructive readings of Wittgenstein by noting that there is what might aptly be called a "deconstructive moment" in Wittgenstein's later philosophy. The moment Stone identifies as deconstructive is, he points out, one which is central not only to deconstruction but also to standard interpretations of Wittgenstein's later philosophy – and, in particular, to Kripke's interpretation. What Stone has in mind is the moment at which an interlocutory voice insists that it is impossible to rule out *all* possible misunderstandings of signs and that the stability of our concourse with signs must therefore depend on a "ubiquitous interpretative activity." Stone argues that this moment should be understood as one at which Wittgenstein expresses a view he ultimately rejects. Wittgenstein's exploration of the view represents a preliminary stage in his treatment of rules, not its end-stage. His aim is to show that there is something inherently confused about the idea of a pure standpoint on language from which our inability to rule out *all* misunderstandings might be experienced as a lack. It follows that he should not be read as recommending a "deconstructive" view of meaning which draws conclusions about our epistemic condition from our inability to demonstrate that no misunderstandings are possible. Such a reading would err, Stone maintains, in representing him as entangled in the very form of confusion he aspires to illuminate.

My own paper, like Stone's, questions the assimilation of Wittgenstein's later philosophy to relativistic intellectual trends – in particular, in so far as such an assimilation informs an on-going debate about the bearing of Wittgenstein's philosophy on political thought.

The papers mentioned thus far – those included in Part I – share a concern with defending therapeutic readings of Wittgenstein's later philosophy against the claims of more standard interpretations. In challenging standard interpretations, these papers implicitly criticize the narrative about the development of Wittgenstein's thought to which such interpretations belong, and they thus in effect call for an exploration of the possibility of a new narrative about that development – an exploration of the sort undertaken in the papers in Part II.

Part II: the *Tractatus* as forerunner of Wittgenstein's later writings

There is a small body of secondary literature on the *Tractatus*, dating back to the 1960s, which argues that various parts of the book should be understood, not – as they traditionally are – as putting forward metaphysical doctrines about how language hooks onto the world, but instead as attacking the assumption that we require any such doctrines. Within this body of literature, passages of the *Tractatus* are represented as characterized by what I am calling a therapeutic aim. (The original contributors to this body of literature include Hidé Ishiguro, Rush Rhees and Peter Winch.) There is a sense in which this body of literature, in spite of the fact that it represents different passages of the *Tractatus* as therapeutic, falls short of delivering a full-fledged therapeutic *reading* of the book. What is at issue has to do with the most notoriously perplexing feature of the *Tractatus* – namely, its closing claim that its sentences are nonsense and that as readers we should treat them as the rungs of the ladder which we have now ascended. Although this body of literature describes various remarks in the *Tractatus* as therapeutic in intent, it nevertheless does not explain how these instructions for reading the book can be understood in therapeutic terms. It thus falls short of furnishing a therapeutic reading of Wittgenstein's early book in failing to provide an account of how the peculiar *method* of the book serves a therapeutic aim.

Until very recently, this body of literature on Wittgenstein's early thought was routinely overlooked in mainstream philosophical discussions of Wittgenstein. But over the last decade or so, there has been greater interest in questions about whether the *Tractatus* can be read as having a therapeutic aspiration. One reason for this new interest is Cora Diamond's and James Conant's development of a therapeutic *reading* of Wittgenstein's early book – a reading which includes an account of how its enigmatic ladder-structure promotes a therapeutic aim. Diamond and Conant explicitly align their reading of the *Tractatus* with what they see as congenial lines of thought in Wittgenstein's later philosophy. What emerges in their work on the *Tractatus* is thus the most forceful and direct case for a reading of Wittgenstein on which there is significant continuity in his philosophical ambitions. The suggestiveness of the case they make has contributed to creating interest in research into affinities between Wittgenstein's early and later philosophical procedures.

Part II of this volume has two main goals. It aspires both to make available some of Diamond's and Conant's central writings on the method of the *Tractatus* and also to provide an exemplary selection of some of the other recent research on Wittgenstein's philosophy which is concerned with emphasizing the continuity of his early and later thought.

Conant's paper and one of the two papers by Diamond ("Ethics, imagination and the method of the *Tractatus*") are both devoted primarily to the question of how to read the *Tractatus*. Their reading places emphasis on Wittgenstein's statements in the Preface and in the concluding remarks that the book's sentences are nonsense, and it does so in a manner which draws on the understanding of his use of "nonsense" as a term of philosophical appraisal outlined above. Diamond and Conant argue that when Wittgenstein describes his sentences as nonsense, he does not mean they are improperly formed but we can still make out what they are trying to say. Rather, he means that they are not logically distinct from gibberish – i.e., to use one of Diamond's examples, not logically distinct from "piggly wiggle tiggle" – and that we should give up the idea that they are trying to say *anything*. (Diamond and Conant refer to this as an *austere* view of nonsense.)

This account of the significance of the 'framing statements' of the *Tractatus* stands in direct opposition to standard interpretations on which the book's sentences advance genuine claims which make up the steps of an argument about the representational character of language and on which its framing description of its sentences as nonsense is a conclusion which follows from that argument. Within such interpretations, the frame of the *Tractatus* refers to the very sorts of logical distinctions among kinds of nonsense which, according to Diamond and Conant, the book as a whole invites us to question. The guiding idea of the interpretations is that the book's metaphysical sentences, although officially nonsensical by Wittgenstein's lights, nevertheless somehow succeed in gesturing at what they fail to say. Such sentences are accordingly treated as logically distinct from "piggly wiggle tiggle."

Diamond's and Conant's basic account of the method of the *Tractatus* presupposes that, while it excludes as confused *logical* distinctions among types of nonsense, it is nevertheless happy to acknowledge that there are *psychological* distinctions among nonsensical sentences – i.e., distinctions with respect to the tendencies of different nonsensical sentences to lead us to imagine that we can make sense of them. As they understand it, the method of the book involves the employment of nonsensical forms of words psychologically distinguished by how they produce illusions of sense. Their thought is that the *Tractatus* combats as illusory the idea of an external standpoint on language from which we can offer a metaphysical account of linkages between language and the world, and they take the book's nonsense-sentences to be composed to explode that illusion from within. These sentences serve as a sort of metaphysical lure – first encouraging the reader to envision herself occupying an external standpoint and then, by inviting her fully to articulate the things she imagines she can say once she has occupied it, placing her in a position in which she can recognize that she is putting inconsistent pressures on her words and that *no* rendering of them will satisfy her. Thus the *Tractatus* delivers us from the illusion that we can do philosophy in a traditional vein through its presentation of nonsensical sentences which, to the extent that they seduce us, equip us to lead ourselves out of our state of illusion.

Both Diamond and Conant note that at the close of the *Tractatus* Wittgenstein writes that the person who understands *him* recognizes the sentences of the book as nonsense (*Tractatus*, 6.54). They take it to be of philosophical moment that he stresses that recognition of the nonsensicality of the book's sentences reflects an understanding of the book's author and not, as we might have expected, of those sentences themselves. This remark signals that he has written a book which consists, not in a line of *argument* which would require us to understand its premises, but rather in a form of *activity* designed to lead us to a point at which we come to see that the appearance that the book is advancing metaphysical claims is an illusion.

This gives us a rough outline of Diamond's and Conant's account of the method of the *Tractatus*: the book presents us with metaphysical sentences which lead us to participate in an imaginative activity of articulating the structure of the illusion of an external standpoint on language – an imaginative activity through which we can come to recognize that illusion *as* an illusion.

Diamond and Conant accent the fact that, on their reading, the method of the *Tractatus* is similar in important respects to the method of Wittgenstein's later writings (which they understand roughly along the lines I traced out above in discussing therapeutic readings of his later writings). They argue that, although the *Tractatus* lacks the particular kind of dialectical structure his later writings have (since it does not contain dialogues between different interlocutory voices), its method nevertheless anticipates the method of the later writings in a fundamental respect. It is designed to lead its reader to the recognition that certain words she is inclined to utter in philosophy fail to express anything she wants to say – to teach her "to pass from a piece of disguised nonsense to something that is patent nonsense" (*Investigations*, §464). Thus Diamond and Conant give us a picture of the philosophy of Wittgenstein, early and late, on which it is unified in its fundamental aim, in its characteristic modes of criticism and even, to some degree, in its methods.

Diamond's and Conant's work on the *Tractatus* has contributed to an increase in interest in research on the question of the continuity of Wittgenstein's thought. Some of this research is concerned with reassessing the main intellectual influences that shaped the *Tractatus* – above all, Frege and Russell – and asking whether an understanding of these influences speaks in favor of a reading of the book which enables us to align it with therapeutic readings of his later work.

This volume contains three papers which count among their central concerns reassessing, in this basic spirit, Wittgenstein's inheritance from Frege – viz., the papers by Conant, Hilary Putnam and David Cerbone. These papers converge on a view of the relation between Frege and Wittgenstein which is noteworthy, not only for its embodiment of a philosophically unorthodox understanding of Wittgenstein as favoring early and late a view of logic consistent with the idea of a therapeutic aim in philosophy, but also for its embodiment of a no less philosophically unorthodox understanding of Frege as an important source for this view.

Putnam's and Cerbone's papers form a natural grouping together with a previously published paper of Conant's which does not appear here – viz., "The search for logically alien thought: Descartes, Kant, Frege and the *Tractatus*."[6] These three papers agree in making the following claims about the relation between Frege and Wittgenstein. (i) Frege holds that logic is internal to thought, and there is therefore, for him, no such thing as illogical thought. This first claim merits a comment. It is worth noting that what is in question here is not the claim that Frege holds that we never contradict ourselves. It would not be unreasonable to speak of illogical thought in connection with our tendency to come out with contradictory statements or espouse contradictory beliefs, but this tendency has nothing to do with the putatively Fregean doctrine in question. What is in question is a claim to the effect that, for Frege, logical notions represent a condition of the possibility of thought so that there can be no such thing as recognizing something as an episode of thought without seeing it as logically articulated – and hence no such thing as recognizing something as illogical thought. (This philosophically radical claim about Frege was originally defended in writings on Frege by Cora Diamond, Thomas Ricketts, Hans Sluga and Joan Weiner.) (ii) Frege is also committed to another view of logic, a view on which the laws of logic stand in some normative relation to thought and furnish constraints that we can run up against – and transgress – in our thinking. (iii) These two views of logic are in tension with each other. (iv) Wittgenstein is, both early and late, concerned to show that Frege's formulations of a view of logic which leaves no room for illogical thought is undermined by his tendency to construe logic as supplying normative constraints on thought. And (v) Wittgenstein's early and later writings explore different approaches to rescuing a view of logic which leaves no room for illogical thought from ways of conceiving logic that come into conflict with it.

Conant's paper for this volume considers this same basic picture of Wittgenstein's relation to Frege – only now in connection with Frege's explorations of the idea of "illogical thought" at the level of the proposition. The analogue to (i), above, within this new paper of Conant's, is the following claim: Frege holds that the logical segmentation of a sentence takes for granted a grasp of its sense, and therefore there is for him no such thing as the logical segmentation of a nonsensical sentence – and hence no such thing as concatenating words so that they express an illegitimate (or illogical) thought in virtue of their logical categories. Conant's concern with Wittgenstein's relationship to Frege's work is central to the account he gives, in this paper, of the method of the *Tractatus*. He believes that "the neglect of Frege" – i.e., the neglect of this unfamiliar picture of Frege – has left most readers of the *Tractatus* ill-prepared to appreciate the directions Wittgenstein gives us for reading his book. The main device the *Tractatus* uses to engage its reader is, Conant suggests, helpfully understood in terms of Wittgenstein's working through of what he sees as a tension in Frege's thought. Conant's specific proposal is that the *Tractatus* tries to deliver us from the illusion of an external point of view on language by taking us through the following sequence of steps: (a) leading us to imagine ourselves occupying a standpoint from which we can identify illogical thought, (b) offering a corrective in the form of the Fregean idea that illogical thought is impossible, (c) encouraging us to participate in what Wittgenstein sees as Frege's internally inconsistent formulation of this idea by inviting us to imagine that, while the structure of language prohibits us from saying that there is some particular thing – namely, illogical thought – which is impossible, we can nevertheless somehow gesture at what we cannot say; and, finally, (d) placing the inconsistency before our eyes and bringing us to the point of throwing all the preceeding "rungs" of the ladder cleanly away.

In the paper of his reprinted here ("Rethinking mathematical necessity"), Hilary Putnam takes up the same basic set of claims about Wittgenstein's relation to Frege (i.e., (i)–(v), above) – only now primarily out of an interest in bringing into focus Wittgenstein's later view of logic. Like Conant, Putnam holds that in the *Tractatus* Wittgenstein is responding to a tension in Frege's view of logic. Further, he wants to show that the view of logic which emerges from this conversation with Frege importantly prefigures (in spite of what Putnam sees as some "metaphysical excess baggage") Wittgenstein's later view – a view Putnam describes as one on which there is no such thing as an external standpoint from which we can theorize about logic and hence no such thing as a standpoint from which we can answer a question about whether or not the laws of logic are revisable.

To the extent that a significant portion of the interest of Conant's and Putnam's discussions of Frege and early Wittgenstein in their papers for this volume thus turns on the idea that Wittgenstein's early relationship to Frege has implications for his later view of logic, the paper of David Cerbone's included here forms a helpful complement to both. Cerbone in effect tries to vindicate the suggestion that Wittgensten's later view of logic bears the imprint of his inheritance from Frege by drawing attention to and underlining the importance of a passage in the *Remarks on the Foundations of Mathematics* in which Wittgenstein specifically describes his view of logic in terms of the resolution of the sort of tension in Frege's thought which, according to Putnam and Conant, exercises him in the *Tractatus*.

The project of demonstrating continuity in Wittgenstein's thought is one which needs to involve, not only the sort of reassessment of influences on his work with which these papers on his relationship to Frege are concerned, but also some sort of explanatory account of the original reception of his work. Edward Witherspoon's paper on Wittgenstein's relationship to Rudolf Carnap is of note in this context. Witherspoon attempts to show that the reception of Wittgenstein's work, from the *Tractatus* to later writings, has mirrored stages of Carnap's work, from his "logical syntax phase" to his "linguistic frameworks phase." Witherspoon argues that the appearance of convergence between Wittgenstein's thought and Carnap's is deeply misleading. He attempts to show that the theories of meaning Carnap champions at different times, in spite of their apparently great differences, are similar in drawing on the presupposition that it is possible logically to partition a nonsensical sentence – a presupposition which, on the terms of the therapeutic understanding of Wittgenstein Witherspoon favors, is at odds with Wittgenstein's thought both early and late.

An important way of investigating the idea of continuity in Wittgenstein's thought involves examining his approach to specific problems which engaged him throughout his life. Any adequate account of the most important recent research along these lines would need to mention Juliet Floyd's work on Wittgenstein's philosophy of mathematics. In the paper of hers included here, Floyd examines Wittgenstein's life-long fascination with classical impossibility proofs and above all with the proof of the impossibility of trisecting the angle. She argues that Wittgenstein's interest in this proof reflects his thought that demonstrations of impossibility in mathematics produce a form of understanding which, on the therapeutic understanding of Wittgenstein Floyd defends here and elsewhere, his philosophical investigations are likewise intended to produce: viz., a form of understanding issuing from the recognition that there is nothing of the sort we took ourselves to want and that we were laboring under an illusion of understanding.

In the second of her papers for this volume ("Does Bismarck have a beetle in his box? The private language argument in the *Tractatus*"), Cora Diamond is similarly concerned with tracing Wittgenstein's approach throughout his life to certain specific issues – in particular, to issues of privacy. She discusses a line of thought in the *Tractatus* which she maintains its author thinks should be brought to bear on Russell's views of knowledge by acquaintance and knowledge by description and on the view of quantifiers that comes with those views. What is troubling about these views from the perspective of the *Tractatus*, according to Diamond, is that they seem to make room for us to talk about "judgments I cannot make" (e.g., to mention the Russellian example Diamond considers, judgments directly about someone else's private sensations) and to represent such judgments as standing in logical relations with judgments I can make. Russell's views come into conflict with the Tractarian idea that grasping what a sentence says just is grasping the inferential relations in which it stands with other meaningful sentences or placing it in "logical space." On Diamond's reading, the *Tractatus* develops a line of thought which shows that "judgments I cannot make about someone's private objects" have no place in logical space and drop out as nonsensical or irrelevant. Her quite arresting conclusion is that there is a basic similarity between this line of thought and an important moment in the *Investigations* discussion of the idea of a "private language": namely, the moment at which Wittgenstein suggests that if we use the metaphor of a beetle in a box for what we think we want when we cling to the idea of "items in our mind which no one else can know," the beetle has no place in the language-game and drops out as nonsensical or irrelevant.

This ends this introductory overview of the way in which the papers in Parts I and II of this volume challenge the suggestion, internal to standard interpretations of Wittgenstein's philosophy, of a sharp break in his mode of philosophizing between the *Tractatus* and later writings. The overview emphasizes the tendency of the papers to highlight similarities in the views Wittgenstein holds in the *Tractatus* and in later writings, but its point is not that they do not flag or theorize *differences*. The papers which are explicitly concerned with continuity claims (i.e., those in Part II) are also concerned, albeit in different ways and to different degrees, with such differences. Further, many of the differences the papers accent bespeak metaphysical views Wittgenstein holds at the time of the *Tractatus* which are in conflict with the therapeutic aspirations the papers themselves claim to identify as distinctive of the book. (In this connection, see, especially, Putnam's paper and the second of Diamond's papers.) The principle uniting these papers is *not* that we would be wrong to understand Wittgenstein as having any metaphysical commitments in the *Tractatus* from which he frees himself later on. The principle is rather that the *Tractatus* shares with his later writings a therapeutic aim and that, although it may have certain metaphysical commitments, these metaphysical commitments are largely unselfconscious and don't essentially qualify that aim.

A dissenting voice

It remains to say a word about P.M.S. Hacker's paper. His paper is anomalous in this volume in its defense of a standard interpretation of the *Tractatus* against the therapeutic account of its aim and method laid out in the work of Diamond and Conant. What recommends its inclusion here is this volume's aim of fostering discussion about the merits of therapeutic accounts of both the *Tractatus* and of Wittgenstein's later work.

The title of Hacker's paper – "Was he trying to whistle it?" – is taken from a remark of Frank Ramsey's: "But what we can't say, we can't say, and we can't whistle it either." Ramsey took the *Tractatus* to contain a metaphysical argument intended to show that all metaphysical arguments are nonsense, and his point was that only intellectually suspicious maneuvering could make it appear that the argument of the book somehow succeeded in hinting at – or whistling – what, by its own lights, could not be said. In adopting Ramsey's quip as his title, Hacker signals that, like Ramsey, he thinks Wittgenstein was "trying to whistle it." (His answer to his titular question turns out to be: "Yes!") His main criticisms of Diamond's and Conant's therapeutic reading of the *Tractatus* include the following three: (i) he charges that the passages they mention in favor of attributing an "austere" view of nonsense to Wittgenstein fail to support such an attribution; (ii) he argues that in so far as they represent Wittgenstein both as favoring an austere view of nonsense and also as trying to engage and teach his readers by means of nonsense-sentences, they represent him as employing an inconsistent method; and (iii) he claims that a great deal of external evidence – in particular, material from Wittgenstein's correspondence and conversations as well as from various published and unpublished manuscripts – indicates that Wittgenstein *consciously* holds various metaphysical doctrines in the *Tractatus* and thus flies in the face of the suggestion that the book has a therapeutic aim. Where we are left is with the task of determining whether Hacker's charges hit their mark and whether, to the extent that they do so, an account of the *Tractatus* as possessing a therapeutic aim and method can nevertheless survive them.[7]

Notes

1   This description of Wittgenstein's philosophy originates with Michael Dummett. (See, e.g., *The Logical Basis of Metaphysics*, Cambridge, Mass., Harvard University Press, 1991, esp. chapters 14 and 15.) Dummett's description has been taken up and elaborated by a number of prominent commentators – such as, e.g., Saul Kripke and David Pears.

2   See the essays in *The Realistic Spirit: Wittgenstein, Philosophy and the Mind*, Cambridge, Mass., MIT Press, 1991.

3   See especially "The availability of Wittgenstein's later philosophy," in *Must We Mean What We Say? A Book of Essays*, Oxford, Oxford University Press, 1976, pp. 70–2.

4   See also "The argument of the ordinary: scenes of instruction in Wittgenstein and Kripke," in *Conditions Handsome and Unhandsome: The Constitution of Emersonian Perfectionism*, Chicago, University of Chicago Press, 1990.

5   Elsewhere McDowell explicitly frames his reading of Wittgenstein in terms of the contemporary debate between realism and anti-realism. See, e.g., *Mind, Value and Reality*, Cambridge, Mass., Harvard University Press, 1998, chapters 11, 12 and 14.

6   This paper of Conant's was written in response to the paper of Putnam's included here. Cerbone's paper for this volume is, in turn, a response to this paper of Conant's.

7   I am indebted to Nathaniel Hupert, John McDowell and Rupert Read for comments on a previous draft, and I am indebted to James Conant, Cora Diamond and Kelly Dean Jolley for discussing this introduction with me and making a number of helpful suggestions.

Part I

WITTGENSTEIN'S LATER WRITINGS

The illusory comfort of an
external standpoint

1

EXCURSUS ON WITTGENSTEIN'S VISION OF LANGUAGE

Stanley Cavell

Now I want to say something more specific about what it is Wittgenstein has discovered, or detailed, about language (i.e., about the entire body and spirit of human conduct and feeling which goes into the capacity for speech) which raises the sorts of problems I have so crudely and vaguely characterized in terms of "normality" and "our world".

What I wish to say at this point can be taken as glossing Wittgenstein's remark that "we learn words in *certain* contexts" (e.g., *Blue Book*, p. 9). This means, I take it, both that we do not learn words in *all* the contexts in which they could be used (what, indeed, would that mean?) and that not every context in which a word is used is one in which the word *can* be learned (e.g., contexts in which the word is used metaphorically). And after a while we are expected to know when the words are appropriately used in further contexts. This is obvious enough, and philosophers have always asked for an explanation of it: "How do words acquire that generality upon which thought depends?" As Locke put it:

All things that exist being particulars, it may perhaps be thought reasonable that words, which ought to be conformed to things, should be so too, I mean in their signification: but yet we find quite the contrary. The far greatest part of words that make all languages are general terms; which has not been the effect of neglect or chance, but of reason and necessity. ... The next thing to be considered is, how general words come to be made. For since all things that exist are only particulars, how come we by general terms, or where find we those general natures they are supposed to stand for?

[*An Essay Concerning Human Understanding*, Book III; Chapter III; Sections I and VI]

This is one of the questions to which philosophers have given the answer, "Because there are universals"; and the "problem of universals" has been one of assigning, or denying, an ontological status to such things and of explaining, or denying, our knowledge of them. What Wittgenstein wishes us to see, if I understand, is that no such answers could provide an explanation of the questions which lead to them.

"We learn words in certain contexts and after a while we are expected to know when they are appropriately used in (= can appropriately be projected into) further contexts" (and, of course, our ability to project appropriately is a criterion for our having learned a word). Now I want to ask: (1) What is (do we call) "learning a word", and in particular (to keep to the simplest case) "learning the general name of something"?; and (2) what makes a projection an appropriate or correct one? (Again, traditionally, the answer to (1) is: "Grasping a universal", and to (2): "The recognition of another instance of the same universal", or "the fact that the new object is *similar* to the old".)

Learning a word

Suppose we ask: "When a child learns the name of something (e.g., 'cat', 'star', 'pumpkin'), obviously he doesn't learn merely that *this* (particular) sound goes with *that* (particular) object; so what does he learn?" We might answer: "He learns that sounds *like* this name objects *like* that." We can quickly become very dissatisfied with that answer. Suppose we reflected that that answer seems to describe more exactly a situation in which learning that "cat" is the name of *that* means learning that "rat" (a sound *like* "cat") is the name of *that* (an object *like* a cat). That obviously is not what we meant to say (because that obviously is not what happens?). How is what we meant to say different? We might try: "He learns that sounds *exactly* similar to this name objects *exactly* similar to that." But that is either false or obviously empty. For what does it mean to say that one cat is exactly similar to another cat? We do not want to mean that you can not tell them apart (for that obviously would not explain what we are trying to explain). What we *want* to say is that the child learns that a sound that *is* (counts as) this *word* names objects which *are* cats. But isn't that just what we thought we needed, and were trying to give, an *explanation* for?

Suppose we change the point of view of the question and ask: What do we teach or tell a child when we point to a pumpkin and say, "Pumpkin"? Do we tell him what a pumpkin is or what the word "pumpkin" means? I was surprised to find that my first response to this question was, "You can say either". (Cf. "Must We Mean What We Say?", p. 21.) And that led me to appreciate, and to want to investigate, how much a matter knowing what something *is* is a matter of knowing what something is *called*; and to recognize how limited or special a truth is expressed in the motto, "We may change the names of things, but their nature and their operation on the understanding never change" (Hume, *Treatise*, Book II, Part III, Section I).

At the moment I will say just this: That response ("You can say either") is true, at best, only for those who have already mastered a language. In the case of a child still coming to a mastery of its language it may be (fully) true *neither* that what we teach them is (the meaning of) a word *nor* that we tell them what a thing is. It looks very like one or the other, so of course it is very natural to say that it is one or the other; but so does malicious gossip often look like honesty, and so we very often call it honesty.

How might saying "Pumpkin" and pointing to a pumpkin not be "telling the child what a word means"? There are many sorts of answers to that. One might be: it takes two to *tell* someone something; you can't give someone a piece of information unless he knows how to *ask* for that (or comparable) information. (Cf. *Investigations*, §31.) And this is no more true of learning language than it is true of learning any of the forms of life which grow language. You can't tell a child what a word means when the child has yet to learn what "asking for a meaning" is (i.e., how to ask for a meaning), in the way you can't lend a rattle to a child who has yet to learn what "being lent (or borrowing) something" means. Grownups like to think of children (especially their own) as small grownups, midgets. So they say to their child, "Let Sister use your shovel", and then nudge the child over towards Sister, wrest the shovel from the child's hand, and are later impatient and disappointed when the child beats Sister with a pail and Sister rages not to "return" the shovel. We learn from suffering.

Nor, in saying "Pumpkin" to the child, are we telling the child what a pumpkin is, i.e., the child does not then know what a pumpkin is. For to "know what a pumpkin is" is to know, e.g., that it is a kind of fruit; that it is used to make pies; that it has many forms and sizes and colors; that this one is misshapen and old; that inside every tame pumpkin there is a wild man named Jack, screaming to get out.

So what are we telling the child if we are telling him neither what a word means nor what a thing is? We might feel: "If you can't tell a child a simple thing like what a pumpkin is or what the word 'pumpkin' means, then how does learning ever *begin*?" But why assume we are telling him anything at all? Why assume that we are *teaching* him anything? Well, because obviously he has learned something. But perhaps we are too quick to suppose we know what it is in such situations that makes us say the child is learning something. In particular, too quick to suppose we know what the child is learning. To say we are teaching them language obscures both how different what they learn may be from anything we think we are teaching, or mean to be teaching; and how vastly more they learn than the thing we should say we had "taught". Different and more, not because we are bad or good teachers, but because "learning" is not as academic a matter as academics are apt to suppose.

First, reconsider the obvious fact that there is not the *clear* difference between learning and maturation that we sometimes suppose there is. Take this example: Suppose my daughter now knows two dozen words. (Books on child development must say things like: At age 15 months the average child *will have a vocabulary of* so many words.) One of the words she knows, as her Baby Book will testify, is "kitty". What does it mean to say she "knows the word"? What does it mean to say she "learned it"? Take the day on which, after I said "Kitty" and pointed to a kitty, she repeated the word and pointed to the kitty. What does "repeating the word" mean here? and what did she point to? All I know is (and does she know more?) that she made the sound I made and pointed to what I pointed at. Or rather, I know less (or more) than that. For what is "her making the sound I made"? She produced a sound (imitated me?) which *I accepted, responded to* (with smiles, hugs, words of encouragement, etc.) as *what I had said*. The next time a cat came by, on the prowl or in a picture book, she did it again. A new entry for the Baby Book under "Vocabulary".

Now take the day, some weeks later, when she smiled at a fur piece, stroked it, and said "kitty". My first reaction was surprise, and, I suppose, disappointment: she doesn't really know what "kitty" means. But my second reaction was happier: she means by "kitty" what I mean by "fur". Or was it what I mean by "soft", or perhaps "nice to stroke"? Or perhaps she didn't mean at all what in my syntax would be recorded as "That is an X". After all, when she sees real kittens she not only utters her allophonic version of "kitty", she usually squeals the word over and over, squats down near it, stretches out her arm towards it and opens and closes her fingers (an allomorphic version of "petting the kitten"?), purses her lips, and squints with pleasure. All she did with the fur piece was, smiling, to say "kitty" once and stroke it. Perhaps the syntax of that performance should be transcribed as "This is like a kitty", or "Look at the funny kitty", or "Aren't soft things nice?", or "See, I remember how pleased you are when I say 'kitty'", or "I like to be petted". Can we decide this? Is it a *choice* between these definite alternatives? In each case her word was produced about a soft, warm, furry object of a certain size, shape, and weight. What did she learn in order to do that? *What did she learn from having done it?* If she had never made such leaps she would never have walked into speech. Having made it, meadows of communication can grow for us. Where you can leap to depends on where you stand. When, later, she picks up a gas bill and says "Here's a letter", or when, hearing a piece of music we've listened to together many times, she asks "Who's Beethoven?", or when she points to the television coverage of the Democratic National Convention and asks "What are you watching?", I may realize we are not ready to walk certain places together.

But although I didn't tell her, and she didn't learn, either what the word "kitty" means or what a kitty is, if she keeps leaping and I keep looking and smiling, she will learn both. I have wanted to say: Kittens – what we call "kittens" – do not exist in her world yet, she has not acquired the forms of life which contain them. They do not exist in something like the way cities and mayors will not exist in her world until long after pumpkins and kittens do; or like the way God or love or responsibility or beauty do not exist in our world; we have not mastered, or we have forgotten, or we have distorted, or learned through fragmented models, the forms of life which could make utterances like "God exists" or "God is dead" or "I love you" or "I cannot do otherwise" or "Beauty is but the beginning of terror" bear all the weight they could carry, express all they could take from us. We do not know the meaning of the words. We look away and leap around.

"Why be so difficult? Why perversely deny that the child has learned a word, and insist, with what must be calculated provocativeness, that your objects are 'not in her world'? Anyone will grant that she can't do everything we do with the word, nor know everything we do about kitties – I mean kittens; but when she says 'Kitty's nice' and evinces the appropriate behavior, then she's learned the name of an object, learned to name an object, and the *same* object we name. The differences between what she does and what you do are obvious, and any sensible person will take them for granted."

What I am afraid of is that we take too much for granted about what the learning and the sharing of language implies. What's *wrong* with thinking of learning language as being taught or told the names of things? Why did Wittgenstein call sharp attention to Augustine's having said or implied that it is, and speak of a particular "picture" of language underlying it, as though Augustine was writing from a particular, arbitrary perspective, and that the judgment was snap?

There is more than one "picture" Wittgenstein wishes to develop: one of them concerns the idea that all words are names, a second concerns the idea that learning a name (or any word) is being told what it means, a third is the idea

24

that learning a language is a matter of learning (new) words. The first of these ideas, and Wittgenstein's criticism of it, has, I believe, received wider attention than the other two, which are the ones which concern us here. (The ideas are obviously related to one another, and I may say that I find the second two to give the best sense of what Wittgenstein finds "wrong" with the first. It isn't as I think it is usually taken, merely that "language has many functions" besides naming things; it is also that the ways philosophers account for naming make it incomprehensible how language can so much as perform *that* function.)

Against the dominant idea of the dominant Empiricism, that what is basic to language (basic to the way it joins the world, basic to its supply of meaning, basic to the way it is taught and learned) are basic *words*, words which can (only) be learned and taught through "ostensive definitions", Wittgenstein says, among other things, that to be *told* what a word means (e.g., to know that when someone forms a sound and moves his arm he is *pointing to* something and *saying its name*, and to know *what* he is pointing to) we have to be able to ask what it means (*what* it refers to); and he says further: "One has already to know (or be able to do) something in order to be capable of asking a thing's name. But what does one have to know?" (*Investigations*, §30). I want to bring out two facts about this question of Wittgenstein's: that it is not because naming and asking are peculiarly mental or linguistic phenomena that a problem is created; and that the question is not an experimental but a conceptual one, or as one might put it, that the question "What do we call 'learning or asking for a name'?" had better be clear before we start experimenting to find out "how" "it" is done.

It will help to ask: Can a child attach a label to a thing? (Wittgenstein says that giving a thing a name is like attaching a label to something (§15). Other philosophers have said that too, and taken that as imagining the essential function of language. But what I take Wittgenstein to be suggesting is: Take the label analogy seriously; and then you'll see how *little* of language is like that. Let us see.) We might reply: "One already has to know (or be able to do) something in order to be capable of attaching a label to a thing. But what does one have to know?" Well, for example, one has to know what the thing in question is; what a label is; what the point of attaching a label to a thing is. Would we say that the child is attaching a label to a thing if he was pasting (the *way* a child pastes) bits of paper on various objects? Suppose, even, that he can say: "These are my labels" (i.e., that he says ⟨ɣyzir may leybils⟩). (Here one begins to sense the force of a question like: What makes "These are labels" *say that* these are labels?) And that he says: "I am putting labels on my jars." *Is* he?

Mightn't we wish to say *either* Yes or No? Is it a matter of *deciding* which to say? What is it a decision about? Should we say, "Yes and No"? But what makes us want to say this? Or suppose we ask: In what sense does a child *pay* for something (cp. say something) (e.g., for groceries, or tickets to a puppet show)? Suppose he says "Let me pay" (and takes the money, handing it to the clerk (putting it on the counter?)). *What* did he do?

Perhaps we can say this: If you say "No, he is not putting labels on things, paying money (repeating names)", you are thinking: He doesn't know the significance of his behaviors; or, he doesn't know what labels or money or names are; or, he isn't intending to do these things, and you can't do them without intending to (but is that true?); anyway, he doesn't know what doing those things really would be (and what would be "doing them really"? Is he only pretending to?). If you say "Yes, he is pasting labels on", etc., then won't you want to follow this with: "only not the way *we* do that"? But how is it different?

Maybe you feel: "What else would you say he's doing? It's not wrong to say 'He's pasting labels, paying money, learning names', even though everyone knows that he isn't quite or fully *doing* those things. You see the sense in which that is meant." But what has begun to emerge is how far from clear that "sense" is, how little any of the ways we *express* that sense really satisfy us when we articulate them.

That the justifications and explanations we give of our language and conduct, that our ways of trying to intellectualize our lives, do not really satisfy us, is what, as I read him, Wittgenstein wishes us above all to grasp. This is what his "methods" are designed to get us to see. What directly falls under his criticism are not the results of philosophical argument but those unnoticed turns of mind, casts of phrase, which comprise what intellectual historians call "climates of opinion", or "cultural style", and which, unnoticed and therefore unassessed, defend conclusions from direct access – fragments, as it were, of our critical super-egos which one generation passes to the next along with, perhaps as the price of, its positive and permanent achievements: such fragments as "To be clear about our meaning we must define our terms", "The meaning of a word is the experience or behavior it causes", "We may change the names of things but their operation on the understanding never changes", "Language is merely conventional", "Belief is a (particular) feeling", "Belief is a disposition caused by words (or signs)", "If what I say proves false then I didn't (don't?) know it", "We know our own minds directly", "Moral judgments express approval or disapproval", "Moral judgments are meant to get others to *do* something, or to change their attitudes", "All rationally settleable questions are questions of language or questions of fact", "Knowledge is increased only by reasoning or by collecting evidence", "Taste is relative, and people might like, or get pleasure from anything" ... If philosophy is the criticism a culture produces of itself, and proceeds essentially by criticizing past efforts at this criticism, then Wittgenstein's originality lies in having developed modes of criticism that are not moralistic, that is, that do not leave the critic imagining himself free of the faults he sees around him, and which proceed not by trying to argue a given statement false or wrong, but by showing that the person making an assertion does not really know what he means, has not really said what he wished. But since self-scrutiny, the full examination and defense of one's own position, has always been part of the impulse to philosophy, Wittgenstein's originality lies not in the creation of the impulse, but in finding ways to prevent it from defeating itself so easily, ways to make it methodical. That is Freud's advance over the insights of his predecessors at self-knowledge, e.g., Kierkegaard, Nietzsche, and the poets and novelists he said anticipated him.

Now let me respond, in two ways, to the statement: "It's not *wrong* to say the child is pasting labels, repeating names; everyone *sees the sense* in which that is meant."

First of all, it is not true that everybody knew that he wasn't *quite* "learning a thing's name" when Augustine said that in learning language he learned the names of things, and that we all "knew the sense" in which he meant what he said. (We do picture the mind as having inexplicable powers, without really knowing what these powers are, what we expect of them, nor in *what* sense they are inexplicable.)

Again, neither Wittgenstein nor I said it was *wrong to say* the child was "learning the names of things", or "paying for the tickets", or "pasting labels on her jars". One thing we have heard Wittgenstein say about "learning names" was: ". . . Augustine describes the learning of human language as if the child came into a strange country and did not understand the language of the country; that is, as if it already had a language, only not this one" (§32). And, in the same spirit, we could say: To describe the child as "pasting labels on his jars" or "paying for the tickets" is to describe the child as if he were an adult (or anyway, master of the adult activity). That is, we say about a child "She is pasting labels on jars" or "He paid for the tickets", when we should also say "She's a mommy" or "He was Uncle Croesus today". No one will say it's wrong (because untrue?) to say *those* things. And here we do begin more clearly to see the "sense" in which they are meant. You *and* the child know that you are really playing – which does not mean that what you are doing isn't serious. Nothing is more serious business for a child than knowing it *will* be an adult – and *wanting* to be, i.e., *wanting to do the things we do* – and knowing that it can't really do them yet. What is wrong is to say what a child is doing as though the child were an adult, and not recognise that he is still a child playing, above all growing. About "putting on labels", "playing school", "cooking supper", "sending out invitations", etc., that is, perhaps, easy to see. But elsewhere perhaps not.

Consider the older child, one ignorant of, but ripe for a pumpkin (knows how to ask for a name, what a fruit is, etc.). When you say "That is a pumpkin" we can comfortably say that this child learns what the word "pumpkin" means and what a pumpkin is. There may still be something different about the pumpkins in his world; they may, for example, have some unknown relation to pumps (the contrivance or the kind of shoe) and some intimate association with Mr. Popkin (who lives next door), since he obviously has the same name they do. But that probably won't lead to trouble, and one day the person that was this child may, for some reason, remember that he believed these things, had these associations, when he was a child. (And does he, then, stop believing or having them?)

And we can also say: When you say "I love my love" the child learns the meaning of the word "love" and what love is. *That* (*what you do*) will *be* love in the child's world; and if it is mixed with resentment and intimidation, then love is a mixture of resentment and intimidation, and when love is sought *that* will be sought. When you say "I'll take you tomorrow, I promise", the child begins to learn what temporal durations are, and what *trust* is, and what you do will show what trust is worth. When you say "Put on your sweater", the child learns what commands are and what *authority* is, and if giving orders is something that creates anxiety for you, then authorities are anxious, authority itself uncertain.

Of course the person, growing, will learn other things about these concepts and "objects" also. They will grow gradually as the child's world grows. But all he or she knows about them is what he or she has learned, and *all* they have learned will be part of what they are. And what will the day be like when the person "realizes" what he "believed" about what love and trust and authority are? And how will he stop believing it? What we learn is not just what we have studied; and what we have been taught is not just what we were intended to learn. What we have in our memories is not just what we have memorized.

What is important in failing to recognize "the spirit" in which we say "The child, in learning language, is learning the names of things" is that we imagine that we have explained the nature of language when we have only avoided a recognition of its nature; and we fail to recognize how (what it really means to say that) children learn language *from* us.

To summarize what has been said about this: In "learning language" you learn not merely what the names of things are, but what a name is; not merely what the form of expression is for expressing a wish, but what expressing a wish is; not merely what the word for "father" is, but what a father is; not merely what the word for "love" is, but what love is. In learning language, you do not merely learn the pronunciation of sounds, and their grammatical orders, but the "forms of life" which make those sounds the words they are, do what they do – e.g., name, call, point, express a wish or affection, indicate a choice or an aversion, etc. And Wittgenstein sees the relations among *these* forms as "grammatical" also.

Instead, then, of saying either that we *tell* beginners what words mean, or that we *teach* them what objects are, I will say: We initiate them, into the relevant forms of life held in language and gathered around the objects and persons of our world. For that to be possible, we must make ourselves exemplary and take responsibility for that assumption of authority; and the initiate must be able to follow us, in however rudimentary a way, *naturally* (look where our finger points, laugh at what we laugh at, comfort what we comfort, notice what we notice, find alike or remarkable or ordinary what we find alike or remarkable or ordinary, feel pain at what we feel pain at, enjoy the weather or the notion we enjoy, make the sounds we make); and he must *want* to follow us (care about our approval, like a smile better than a frown, a croon better than a croak, a pat better than a slap). "Teaching" here would mean something like "showing them what we say and do", and "accepting what they say and do as what we say and do", etc.; and this will be more than we know, or can say.

In what sense is the child's ability to "follow" us, his caring what we do, and his knowing when we have and have not accepted the identity of his words and deeds, *learned?* If I say that all of this is natural, I mean it is nothing more than natural. Most people do descend from apes into authorities, but it is not inevitable. There is no reason why they don't continue crawling, or walk on all fours, or slide their feet instead of lifting them; no reason why they don't laugh where they (most) now cry; no reason why they make (or "try" to make) the sounds and gestures we make; no reason why they see, if they do, a curving lake as like a carousel; no reason why, having learned to use the phrase "turn down the light" they will accept the phrase "turn down the phonograph" to mean what it means, recognizing that the factor "turn down" is the same, or almost the same, in both; and then accept the phrases "turn down the bed" and "turn down the awning" and "turn down the offer" to mean what they mean, while recognizing that the common factor has less, if any, relation to its former occurrences. If they couldn't do these things they would not grow into our world; but is the avoidance of that consequence the *reason* they do them?

We begin to feel, or ought to, terrified that maybe language (and understanding, and knowledge) rests upon very shaky foundations – a thin net over an abyss. (No doubt that is part of the reason philosophers offer absolute "explanations" for it.) Suppose the child doesn't grasp what we mean? Suppose he doesn't respond differently to a shout and a song, so that what *we* "call" disapproval *encourages* him? Is it an accident that this doesn't normally happen? Perhaps we feel the foundations of language to be shaky when we look for, and miss, foundations of a particular sort, and look upon our shared commitments and responses – as moral philosophers in our liberal tradition have come to do – as more like particular agreements than they are. Such an idea can give us a sense that whether our words will go on meaning what they do depends upon whether other people find it worth their while to continue to understand us – that, seeing a better bargain elsewhere they might decide that we are no longer of their world; as though our sanity depended upon their approval of us, finding us to their liking.

This vision of our relation to the child prompts me – in addition to my suggestions in the early essays of *Must We Mean What We Say?*, along with the suggestions listed in Chapter VI [of *The Claim of Reason* – editor's note] (at the end of the section "The Appeal to Projective Imagination") – to a further characterization of the kind of claims made by philosophers who proceed from an examination of ordinary language, about the kind of validity appealed to when a philosopher says things like "When we say . . . we are implying . . ." or "We wouldn't call that (say) 'recounting'". In such appeals such a philosopher is voicing (reminding us of) *statements of initiation*; telling himself or herself, and us, how in fact we (must) go about things, not predicting this or that performance. He is not claiming something as true of the world, for which he is prepared to offer a basis – such statements are not synthetic; he is claiming something as true of himself (of his "world", I keep wanting to say) for which he is offering himself, the details of his feeling and conduct, as authority. In making such claims, which cannot be countered by evidence or formal logic, he is not being dogmatic; any more than someone who says "I didn't promise to . . .", or "I intend to . . .", "I wish . . .", or "I have to . . ." is being dogmatic, though what he says cannot be countered, in the usual way, by evidence. The authority one has, or assumes, in expressing statements of initiation, in saying "We", is related to the authority one has in expressing or declaring one's promises or intentions. Such declarations cannot be countered by evidence because they are not supported by evidence. We may, of course, be wrong about what we say and do or will say and do. But that failure is not one which can be corrected with a more favorable position of observation or a fuller mastery in the recognition of objects; it requires a new look at oneself and a fuller realization of what one is doing or feeling. An expression of intention is not a specific claim about the world, but an utterance (outerance) of oneself; it is countered not by saying that a fact about the world is otherwise than you supposed, but by showing that your world is otherwise than you see. When you are wrong here, you are not in fact mistaken but in soul muddled.

Projecting a word

I said that in trying to sketch the vision of language underlying the appeals to ordinary language I would have to discuss both what it meant to say that "a word is learned in certain contexts" and what I had in mind in speaking of "appropriate projections into further contexts". It is the second of these topics which is most directly relevant to what more I shall have to say about the limitations of the appeal to ordinary language as a direct criticism of traditional philosophy; but a discussion of the first was necessary to give a concrete sense of the nature of this problem.

If what can be said in a language is not everywhere determined by rules, nor its understanding anywhere secured through universals, and if there are always new contexts to be met, new needs, new relationships, new objects, new perceptions to be recorded and shared, then perhaps it is as true of a master of a language as of his apprentice that though "in a sense" we learn the meaning of words and what objects are, the learning is never over, and we keep finding new potencies in words and new ways in which objects are disclosed. The "routes of initiation" are never closed. But *who* is the authority when all masters? Who initiates us into new projections? Why haven't we arranged to *limit* words to *certain* contexts, and then coin new ones for new eventualities? The fact that we do not behave this way must be at the root of the fierce ambiguity of ordinary language, and that we won't behave this way means that for real precision we are going to have to get words *pinned* to a meaning through explicit definition and limitation of context. Anyway, for *some* sorts of precision, for some purposes, we will need definitions. But maybe the very ambiguity of ordinary language, though sometimes, some places, a liability, is just what gives it the power, of illumination, of enriching perception, its partisans are partial to. Besides, to say that a word "is" ambiguous may only be to say that it "can" mean various things, can, like a knife, be used in various ways; it doesn't mean that on any given occasion it *is* being used various ways, nor that on the whole we have trouble in knowing which way it is being used. And in that case, the *more* uses words "can" have, then the *more* precise, or exact, that very possibility might allow us to be, as occasion arises. But let's move closer.

We learn the use of "feed the kitty", "feed the lion", "feed the swans", and one day one of us says "feed the meter", or "feed in the film", or "feed the machine", or "feed his pride", of "feed wire", and we understand, we are not troubled. Of course we could, in most of these cases, use a different word, not attempt to project or transfer "feed" from contexts like "feed the monkey" into contexts like "feed the machine". But what should be gained if we did? And what would be lost?

What are our choices? We could use a more general verb, like "put", and say merely "Put the money in the meter", "Put new material into the machine", "Put film into the camera", etc. But first, that merely deprives us of a way of speaking which can discriminate differences which, in some instances, will be of importance; e.g., it does not discriminate between putting a flow of material into a machine and putting a part made of some new material into the construction of the machine. And it would begin to deprive us of the concept we have of the emotions. Is the idea of feeding pride or hope or anxiety any more metaphorical, any less essential to the concept of an emotion, than the idea that pride and hope, etc., grow and, moreover, grow on certain circumstances? Knowing what sorts of circumstances these are and what the consequences and marks of overfeeding are, is part of knowing what pride is. And what other way is there of knowing? Experiments? But those are the very concepts an experiment would itself be constructed from.

Second, to use a more general verb does not reduce the range of transfer or projection, but increases it. For in order that "put" be a relevant candidate for this function, it must be the same word we use in contexts like "Put the cup on the saucer", "Put your hands over your head", "Put out the cat", "Put on your best armor", "Put on your best manner", "Put out the light and then put out the light".

We could, alternatively, use a more specific verb than "feed". There would be two ways of doing this, either (a) to use a word already in use elsewhere, or (b) to use a new word. In (a) we have the same case as before, In (b) we might "feed eels", "fod lions", "fawd swans", "fide pride", "fad machines". . . . Suppose we find a culture which in fact does "change the verb" in this way. Won't we want to ask: *Why* are these forms different in the different cases? What differences are these people seeing and attaching importance to, in the way these things are (as we say, but they cannot say) "fed"? (I leave open the question whether the "f – d" form is morphemic; I assume merely that we have gathered from the contexts in which it is used that it can always be translated by *our* word "feed".) We could try to answer that by seeing what else the natives would and would not accept as "feeding", "fodding", "fawding", etc. What other animals or things or abstractions they would say they were "fiding" or "fadding". . . . (I am also assuming that we can tell there is no reason in superficial grammar why the forms are as they are, e.g., no agreement in number, gender, etc.) Could we imagine that there were *no* other contexts in which these forms were used; that for *every* case in which we have to translate their verb as "feed" they use a different form of (the "morpheme") "f – d"? This would be a language in which forms were perfectly intolerant of projection, one in which the natives would simply look puzzled if we asked whether you could feed a lion or fod an eel. What would we have to assume about them, their forms of life, in order to "imagine" that? Presumably, that they saw no connection between giving food to eels, to lions, and to swans, that these were just different actions, as different as feeding an eel, hunting it, killing it, eating it. If we had to assume that, that might indeed be enough to make us call them "primitive". And wouldn't we, in addition, have to assume, not only that they saw them as different, but that these activities *were* markedly different; and not different in the way it is different for *us* to feed swans and lions (we don't hold bread crumbs to a lion's mouth, we don't spear whole loaves with a pitchfork and shovel them at swans) but different in some regularized way, e.g., in the preparations gone through in gathering the "food", in the clothes worn for the occasion, in the time of day at which it was done, in the songs sung on each occasion . . .? And then don't we have to imagine that these preparations, clothes, times, songs are never used for other purposes, or if they are, that no connection between *these* activities and those of "feeding" are noticed or noted in the language? And hence further imagine that the way these clothes, times, songs are used are simply different again, different the way wearing clothes is from washing them or rending or mending them? Can everything be just different?

But though language – what we call language – is tolerant, allows projection, not just any projection will be acceptable, i.e., will communicate. Language is equally, definitively, intolerant – as love is tolerant and intolerant of differences, as materials or organisms are of stress, as communities are of deviation, as arts or sciences are of variation.

While it is true that we must use the same word in, project a word into, various contexts (must be *willing* to call some contexts the *same*), it is equally true that what will *count* as a legitimate projection is deeply controlled. You can "feed peanuts to a monkey" and "feed pennies to a meter", but you cannot feed a monkey by stuffing pennies in its mouth, and if you mash peanuts into a coin slot you won't *be* feeding the meter. Would you be feeding a lion if you put a bushel of carrots in his cage? That he in fact does not eat them would not be enough to show that you weren't; he *may* not eat his *meat*. But in the latter case "may not eat" means "isn't hungry then" or "refuses to eat it". And not every case of "not eating" is "refusing food". The swan who glides past the easter egg on the shore, or over a school of minnows, or under the pitchfork of meat the keeper is carrying for the lion cage, is not refusing to eat the egg, the fish, or the meat. What will be, or count as, "being fed" is related to what will count as "refusing to eat", and thence related to "refusing to mate", "refusing to obey", etc. What can a lion or a swan refuse? Well, what can they be offered? (If we say "The battery refuses to respond" are we thinking of the battery as stubborn?)

I might say: An object or activity or event onto or into which a concept is projected, must *invite* or *allow* that projection; in the way in which, for an object to be (called) an art object, it must allow or invite the experience and behavior which are appropriate or necessary to our concepts of the appreciation or contemplation or absorption ... of an art object. What kind of object will allow or invite or be fit for that contemplation, etc., is no more accidental or arbitrary than what kind of object will be fit to serve as (what we call) a "shoe". Of course there are variations possible; because there are various ways, and purposes, for being shod. On a given occasion one may fail to recognize a given object as a shoe – perhaps all we see is a twist of leather thong, or several blocks of wood. But what kind of failure is this? It may help to say: What we fail to see here is not *that* the object in question is a shoe (that would be the case where, say, we failed to notice what it was the hostess shoved under the sofa, or where we had been distracted from our inventory of the objects in a painting and later seem to remember a cat's being where you say a shoe lies on its side), but rather we fail to see *how* the object in question is a shoe (how it would be donned, and worn, and for what kind of activities or occasions).

The question "How do we use the word 'shoe' (or 'see' or 'voluntary' or 'anger' or 'feed' or 'imagine' or 'language')?" is like the question a child once asked me, looking up from the paper on which she was drawing and handing me her crayon, "How do you make trees?"; and perhaps she also asked, "How do you make a house or people or people smiling or walking or dancing or the sun or a ship or the waves ...?". Each of these questions can be answered in two or three strokes, as the former questions can each be answered in two or three examples. Answered, that is, for the moment, for that question then. We haven't said or shown everything about making trees or using the expression "But now imagine ...". But then there is no "everything" to be said. For we haven't been asked, or asked ourselves, *everything* either; nor *could* we, however often we wish that were possible.

That there are no explanations which are, as it were, complete in themselves, is part of what Wittgenstein means when he says, "In giving explanations I already have to use language full-blown ...; this by itself shows that I can adduce only exterior facts about language" (*Investigations,* §120). And what goes for explaining my words goes for giving directions and for citing rules in a game and for justifying my behavior or excusing my child's or for making requests . . . or for the thousands of things I do in talking. You cannot use words to do what we do with them until you are initiate of the forms of life which give those words the point and shape they have in our lives. When I give you directions, I can adduce only exterior facts about directions, e.g., I can say, "Not that road, the other, the one passing the clapboard houses; and be sure to bear left at the railroad crossing". But I cannot *say* what directions *are* in order to get you to go the way I am pointing, nor *say* what my direction *is,* if that means saying something which is not a further *specification* of my direction, but as it were, cuts below the actual pointing to something which makes my pointing finger point. When I cite or teach you a rule, I can adduce only exterior facts about rules, e.g., say that it applies only when such-and-such is the case, or that it is inoperative when another rule applies, etc. But I cannot *say* what following rules is *überhaupt,* nor say how to obey a rule in a way which doesn't presuppose that you already know what it is to follow them.

For our strokes or examples to be the explanations we proffer, to serve the need we see expressed, the child must, we may say, see *how* those few strokes are a tree or a house ("There is the door, there is the window, there's the chimney with smoke coming out. . . ."); the person must see how the object is a shoe ("There is the sole, that's for the toe . . ."); how the action was – why you call it one, say it was – done in anger ("He was angry at . . .", "He knew that would hurt", "That gesture was no accident", "He doesn't usually speak sharply to his cat". . .). Those strokes are not the only way to make a house (that is not the only instance of what we call a shoe; that is not the only kind of action we call an affront, or one performed voluntarily) but if you didn't see that and how *they* made a house, you probably wouldn't find or recognize any other ways. "How much do we have to imagine?" is like the question, "How many strokes do we have to use?"; and mustn't the answer be, "It depends"? "How do we know these ten strokes make a house?" is like the question, "How do we know that those ten words make that question?". It is at this level that the answer "Because we know the grammar of visual or verbal representation" is meant to operate.

Things, and things imagined, are not on a par. Six imagined rabbits plus one real rabbit in your hat do not total either seven imagined or seven real rabbits. But the very ability to draw a rabbit, like the ability to imagine one, or to imagine what we would feel or do or say in certain circumstances, depends upon the mastery of a form of representation (e.g., knowing what "That is a pumpkin" says) *and* on the general knowledge of the thing represented (e.g., knowing what a pumpkin is). That language can be represented in language is a discovery about language, one which shows the kind of stability language has (viz., the kind of stability an art has, the kind of stability a continuing culture has) and the kind of general knowledge we have about the expressions we use (viz., the kind we have about houses, faces, battles, visitations, colors, examples . . .) in order to represent or plan or use or explain them. To know how to use the word "anger" is to know what *anger* is. ("The world is my representation.")

I am trying to bring out, and keep in balance, two fundamental facts about human forms of life, and about the concepts formed in those forms: that any form of life and every concept integral to it has an indefinite number of instances and directions of projection; and that this variation is not arbitrary. *Both* the "outer" variance and the "inner" constancy are necessary if a concept is to accomplish its tasks – of meaning, understanding, communicating, etc., and in general, guiding us through the world, and relating thought and action and feeling to the world. However many instances or kinds of instances of a concept there are – however many kinds of objects we call shoes – the word "shoe" *can* be (verbally) defined, and in that sense has *a* meaning (cf. Berkeley, *Principles*, Introduction, section 18). The aspect of meaning I am trying to get at, that condition of stability and tolerance I have described as essential to the function of a concept (the use of a word), can perhaps be brought out again this way: to say that a word or concept has a (stable) meaning is to say that new and the most various instances can be recognized as falling under or failing to fall under that concept; to say that a concept must be tolerant is to say that were we to assign a new word to "every" new instance, no word would have the kind of meaning or power a word like "shoe" has. Or: there would *be* no *instances*, and hence no concepts either.

It is one thing to say that words have both connotation and denotation and that these are not the same; it is something else to try to say *how* these are related to one another – beyond remarks at the level of "on the whole (with obvious exceptions) they vary inversely". The level at which I could wish an answer to this question would be the level at which we could answer the questions: How do we know that an instance "falls under" a concept?; or: How, having a word "defined" ostensively, do we know *what* point or points of the displayed object the ostension is to strike? (Is that even a fair formulation of the problem? For upon *what specific* point or *definite* set of points does the "ostensive definition" of, e.g., a monkey or an organ grinder turn? There would be definite points only where there are definite alternatives – e.g., the difference between an Old World and a New World monkey.) Or: What is the difference between regarding an object now as an individual, now as an example? One way of putting the problem about examples (and hence one problem of universals) is: How is the question "Of *what* is this object (say what we call a shoe) an example?" to be answered? One wants to answer it by holding up the shoe and crying out, "Why, an example of this!". Would it help to hold up a different shoe? If you did, and someone then replies, "*Now* I see what it (the first shoe) is an example of", what would he have seen? (This seems to be what Berkeley's idea of a particular idea (or object) representing others of "the same sort" amounts to.)

I might summarize the vision I have been trying to convey of the tempering of speech – the simultaneous tolerance and intolerance of words – by remarking that when Wittgenstein says "*Essence* is expressed by grammar" (§371), he is not denying the importance, or significance, of the concept of essence, but retrieving it. The need for essence is satisfied by grammar, if we see our real need. Yet at an early critical juncture of the *Investigations*, the point at which Wittgenstein raises the "great question that lies behind all these considerations" (§65), he imagines someone complaining that he has "nowhere said what the essence of a language-game, and hence of language, is: what is common to all these activities, and what makes them into language. . . ."; and he replies: ". . . this is true. – Instead of producing something common to all that we call language, I am saying that these phenomena have no one thing in common which makes us use the same word for all." He then goes on to discuss the notion of "what is common" to all things called by the same name, obviously alluding to one familiar candidate philosophers have made to bear the name "universal" or "essence"; and he enjoins us, instead of saying "there *must* be something in common" – which would betray our possession by a philosophical "picture" – to "*look and see*" whether there is. He says that what we will actually find will be "a complicated network of similarities overlapping and criss-crossing: sometimes overall similarities, sometimes similarities of detail. . . . I can think of no better expression to characterize these similarities than 'family resemblances'" (§66, §67); and it looks as if he is here offering the notion of "family resemblances" as an alternative to the idea of "essence". But if this is so, his idea is empty, it explains nothing. For a philosopher who feels the need of universals to explain meaning or naming will certainly still feel their need to explain the notion of "family resemblance". That idea would counter the idea of universals only if it had been shown that family resemblance is all we need to explain the fact of naming *and* that objects may bear a family resemblance to one another and may have *nothing* in common; which is either false or trivial. It is false if it is supposed to mean that, asked if these brothers have anything in common and we cannot say what, we will say "Nothing at all". (We may not be able to *say* very well what it is, but we needn't, as Wittgenstein imagines to be our alternative, merely "play with words" and say "There is something common to all . . .– namely the disjunction of all their common properties" (§67). For that would not even *seem* to say, if we see something in common among them, what we see. We might come up with, "They all have that unmistakeable Karamazov quality". That may not tell you what they have in common, but only because you don't know the Karamazovs; haven't grasped their essence, as it were.) Or else it is trivial, carries no obvious philosophical implication; for "They have nothing in common" has as specific and ordinary a use as "They have something in common" and just as Wittgenstein goes on to show ordinary uses of "what is common" which do not lead us to the idea of universals (cf. §72), so we can show ordinary uses of "there is nothing common to all" (which we *may* say about a set of triplets) which will equally not lead us *away* from the idea of universals.

But I think that all that the idea of "family resemblances" is meant to do, or need do, is to make us dissatisfied with the idea of universals as explanations of language, of how a word can refer to this and that and that other thing, to suggest that it fails to meet "our real need". Once we see that the expression "what is common" *has* ordinary uses, and that these are different from what universals are meant to cover; and, more importantly, see that concepts do not usually have, and do not need "rigid limits", so that universals are neither necessary nor even useful in explaining how words and concepts apply to different things (cf. §68); and again, see that the grasping of a universal cannot perform the function it is imagined to have, for a new application of a word or concept will still have to be *made out, explained*, in the particular case, and then the explanations themselves will be sufficient to explain the projection; and see, finally, that I *know* no more about the application of a word or concept than the explanations I can give, so that no universal or definition would, as it were, *represent* my knowledge (cf. §73) – once we see all this, the idea of a universal no longer has its *obvious* appeal, it no longer carries a *sense* of explaining something profound. (Obviously the drive to universals has more behind it than the sense that the generality of words must be explained. Another source of its power is the familiar fact that subjects and predicates function differently. Another is the idea that all we can know of an object is its intersection of essences.)

I think that what Wittgenstein ultimately wishes to show is that it *makes no sense* at all to give a general explanation for the generality of language, because it makes no sense at all to suppose words in general might *not* recur, that we might possess a name for a thing (say "chair" or "feeding") and yet be willing to call *nothing* (else) "the same thing". And even if you say, with Berkeley, that "an idea [or word] which considered in itself is particular, becomes general by being made to represent or stand for all other particular ideas of the same sort" (*Principles*, Introduction, section 12) you still haven't explained *how* this word gets used for these various "particulars", nor what the significance is if it doesn't. This suggests that the effort to explain the generality of words is initiated by a prior step which produces the idea of a word as a "particular", a step of "considering it in itself". And what *is* that like? We learn words in certain contexts. . . . What are we to take as the "particular" present here? Being willing to call other ideas (or objects) "the same sort" and being willing to use "the same word" for them is one and the same thing. The former does not explain the latter.

There is a Karamazov essence, but you will not find it if you look for *a* quality (look, that is, with the wrong "picture" of a quality in mind); you will find it by learning the grammar of "Karamazov": it is part of its grammar that *that* is what "an intellectual Karamazov" is, and *that* is what "a spiritual Karamazov" is, and *that* is what "Karamazov authority" is, . . . Each is too much, and irresistible.

To ask for a general explanation for the generality of language would be like asking for an explanation of why children acquiring language take what is said to them as consequential, as expressing intention, as projecting expectations which may or may not be satisfied by the world. But do we imagine that we know why we (non-children) take what is said and what is written as inconsequential, as without implication, as not mattering? It seems to me that growing up (in modern culture? in capitalist culture?) is learning that most of what is said is only more or less meant – as if words were stuffs of fabric and we saw no difference between shirts and sails and ribbons and rags. This could be because we have too little of something or too much, or because we are either slobs or saints. Driven by philosophy outside language-games, and in *this* way repudiating our criteria, is a different way to live, but it depends on the same fact of language as do the other lives within it – that it is an endless field of possibility and that it cannot dictate what is said *now*, can no more assure the sense of what is said, its depth, its helpfulness, its accuracy, its wit, than it can insure its truth to the world. Which is to say that language is not only an acquirement but a bequest; and it is to say that we are stingy in what we attempt to inherit. One might think of poetry as the second inheritance of language. Or, if learning a first language is thought of as the child's acquiring of it, then poetry can be thought of as the adult's acquiring of it, as coming into possession of his or her own language, full citizenship. (Thoreau distinguishes along these lines between what he calls the mother tongue and the father tongue.) Poetry thereby celebrates its language by making it a return on its birth, by reciprocating.

36

It is of immediate relevance to what I have been asking about Wittgenstein's view of language, and indicates one general and important limitation in my account, to notice that in moving, in Part II of the *Investigations*, to "figurative" or "secondary" senses of a word (which Wittgenstein explicitly says are not "metaphorical senses", cf. *Investigations*, p. 216), Wittgenstein is moving more concentratedly to regions of a word's use which cannot be assured or explained by an appeal to its ordinary language games (in this, these uses are *like* metaphorical ones). Such uses have consequences in the kind of understanding and communication they make possible. I want to say: It is such shades of sense, intimations of meaning, which allow certain kinds of subtlety or delicacy of communication; the connection is intimate, but fragile. Persons who cannot use words, or gestures, in these ways with you may yet be in your world, but perhaps not of your flesh. The phenomenon I am calling "projecting a word" is the fact of language which, I take it, is sometimes responded to by saying that "All language is metaphorical". Perhaps one could say: the possibility of metaphor is the same as the possibility of language generally, but what is essential to the projection of a word is that it proceeds, or can be made to proceed, *naturally*; what is essential to a functioning metaphor is that its "transfer" is *unnatural* – it breaks up the established, normal directions of projection.

2

NON-COGNITIVISM AND
RULE-FOLLOWING

John McDowell

1 Non-cognitivists hold that ascriptions of value should not be conceived as propositions of the sort whose correctness, or acceptability, consists in their being true descriptions of the world; and, correlatively, that values are not found in the world, as genuine properties of things are. Such a position should embody a reasoned restriction on the sort of proposition that does count as a description (or at worst misdescription) of reality: not merely to justify the exclusion of value-ascriptions, but also to give content to the exclusion – to explain what it is that value judgements are being said not to be. In fact presentations of non-cognitivist positions tend to take some suitable conception of the descriptive, and of the world, simply for granted. In this paper, if only to provoke non-cognitivists to explain how I have missed their point, I want to bring out into the open the nature of a conception that might seem to serve their purpose, and to suggest that there is room for doubt about its serviceability in this context.

According to the conception I have in mind, how things really are is how things are in themselves – that is, independently of how they strike the occupants of this or that particular point of view. With a literal interpretation of the notion of a point of view, this idea underpins our correcting for perspective when we determine the true shapes of observed objects. But the idea lends itself naturally to various extensions.

One such extension figures in the thought, familiar in philosophy, that secondary qualities as we experience them are not genuine features of reality. If, for instance, someone with normal human colour vision accepts that the world is as his visual experience (perhaps corrected for the effects of poor light and so forth) presents it to him, then the familiar thought has it that he is falling into error. This is not merely because the appropriate sensory equipment is not universally shared. That would leave open the possibility that the sensory equipment enables us to detect something that is really there anyway, independently of how things appear to us. But the familiar thought aims to exclude this possibility with the claim that the appearances can be satisfyingly explained away. If, that is, we suppose that how things really are can be exhaustively characterized in primary-quality terms, then we can explain why our colour experience is as it is without representing it as strictly veridical: the explanation reveals the extent to which the world as colour experience presents it to us is mere appearance – the extent to which colour vision fails to be a transparent mode of access to something that is there anyway.[1]

Now an analogy between colour experience and (so to speak) value experience seems natural. We can learn to make colour classifications only because our sensory equipment happens to be such as to give us the right sort of visual experience. Somewhat similarly, we can learn to see the world in terms of some specific set of evaluative classifications, aesthetic or moral, only because our affective and attitudinative propensities are such that we can be brought to care in appropriate ways about the things we learn to see as collected together by the classifications. And this might constitute the starting-point of a parallel argument against a naive realism about the values we find ourselves impelled to attribute to things.[2]

There is an extra ingredient that threatens to enter the argument about values and spoil the parallel. In the argument about colours, we are led to appeal to the explanatory power of a description of the world in primary-quality terms, in order to exclude the suggestion that colour vision is a mode of awareness of something that is there anyway. The parallel suggestion, in the case of values, would be that the members of some specific set of values are genuine features of the world, which we are enabled to detect by virtue of our special affective and attitudinative propensities. And it might be thought that this suggestion can be dismissed out of hand by an appeal to something with no analogue in the argument about secondary qualities; namely, a philosophy of mind which insists on a strict separation between cognitive capacities and their exercise, on the one hand, and what eighteenth-century writers would classify as passions or sentiments, on the other.[3] The suggestion involves thinking of exercises of our affective or conative natures either as themselves in some way percipient, or at least as expanding our sensitivity to how things are; and the eighteenth-century philosophy of mind would purport to exclude this *a priori*.

But perhaps this gets things the wrong way round. Do we actually have any reason to accept the eighteenth-century philosophy of mind, apart from a prior conviction of the truth of non-cognitivism?[4] The question is at least awkward enough to confer some attractions on the idea of a route to non-cognitivism that bypasses appeal to the eighteenth-century philosophy of mind, and proceeds on a parallel with the argument about secondary qualities, claiming that the character of our value experience can be satisfyingly explained on the basis of the assumption that the world – that is, the world as it is anyway (independently of value experience, at any rate[5]) – does not contain values. (I shall return to a version of the eighteenth-century philosophy of mind later: § 4 below.)

How is the explanatory claim made out? Typically, non-cognitivists hold that when we feel impelled to ascribe value to something, what is actually happening can be disentangled into two components. Competence with an evaluative concept involves, first, a sensitivity to an aspect of the world as it really is (as it is independently of value experience), and, second, a propensity to a certain attitude – a non-cognitive state which constitutes the special perspective from which items in the world seem to be endowed with the value in question. Given the disentangling, we could construct explanations of the character of value experience on the same general lines as the explanations of colour experience that we have in mind when we are tempted by the argument about secondary qualities: occupants of the special perspective, in making value judgements, register the presence in objects of some property they authentically have, but enrich their conception of this property with the reflection of an attitude.[6]

2 Now it seems reasonable to be skeptical about whether the disentangling manoeuvre here envisaged can always be effected: specifically, about whether, corresponding to any value concept, one can always isolate a genuine feature of the world – by the appropriate standard of genuineness: that is, a feature that is there anyway, independently of anyone's value experience being as it is – to be that to which competent users of the concept are to be regarded as responding when they use it; that which is left in the world when one peels off the reflection of the appropriate attitude.

Consider, for instance, a specific conception of some moral virtue: the conception current in a reasonably cohesive moral community. If the disentangling manoeuvre is always possible, that implies that the extension of the associated term, as it would be used by someone who belonged to the community, could be mastered independently of the special concerns which, in the community, would show themselves in admiration or emulation of actions seen as falling under the concept. That is: one could know which actions the term would be applied to, so that one would be able to predict applications and withholdings of it in new cases – not merely without oneself sharing the community's admiration (there need be no difficulty about that), but without even embarking on an attempt to make sense of their admiration. That would be an attempt to comprehend their special perspective; whereas, according to the position I am considering, the genuine feature to which the term is applied should be graspable without benefit of understanding the special perspective, since sensitivity to it is singled out as an independent ingredient in a purported explanation of why occupants of the perspective see things as they do. But is it at all plausible that this singling out can always be brought off?

Notice that the thesis I am skeptical about cannot be established by appealing to the plausible idea that evaluative classifications are supervenient on non-evaluative classifications. Supervenience requires only that one be able to find differences expressible in terms of the level supervened upon whenever one wants to make different judgements in terms of the supervening level.[7] It does not follow from the satisfaction of this requirement that the set of items to which a supervening term is correctly applied need constitute a kind recognizable as such at the level supervened upon. In fact supervenience leaves open this possibility, which is just the possibility my skepticism envisages: however long a list we give of items to which a supervening term applies, described in terms of the level supervened upon, there may be no way, expressible at the level supervened upon, of grouping just such items together. Hence there need be no possibility of mastering, in a way that would enable one to go on to new cases, a term which is to function at the level supervened upon, but which is to group together exactly the items to which competent users would apply the supervening term.[8] Understanding why just those things belong together may essentially require understanding the supervening term.

I shall reserve till later (§ 5) the question whether there may be a kind of non-cognitivist who can happily concede this possibility. Meanwhile it is clear that the concession would at any rate preclude explaining the relation between value experience and the world as it is independently of value experience in the manner I described above (§ 1). And actual non-cognitivists typically assume that they must disallow the possibility I have envisaged.[9] They may admit that it is often difficult to characterize the authentic property (according to their standards of authenticity)

40

that corresponds to an evaluative concept; but they tend to suppose that there must be such a thing, even if it cannot be easily pinned down in words. Now there is a profoundly tempting complex of ideas about the relation between thought and reality which would make this "must" seem obvious; but one strand in Wittgenstein's thought about "following a rule" is that the source of the temptation is the desire for a security which is actually quite illusory.

3 A succession of judgements or utterances, to be intelligible as applications of a single concept to different objects, must belong to a practice of going on doing the same thing. We tend to be tempted by a picture of what that amounts to, on the following lines. What counts as doing the same thing, within the practice in question, is fixed by its rules. The rules mark out rails along which correct activity within the practice must run. These rails are there anyway, independently of the responses and reactions a propensity to which one acquires when one learns the practice itself; or, to put the idea less metaphorically, it is in principle discernible, from a standpoint independent of the responses that characterize a participant in the practice, that a series of correct moves in the practice is really a case of going on doing the same thing. Acquiring mastery of the practice is pictured as something like engaging mental wheels with these objectively existing rails.

The picture comes in two versions. In one, the rules can be formulated, as a codification of the practice in independently accessible terms. Mastery of the practice is conceived as knowledge, perhaps implicit, of what is expressed by these formulations; and running along the rails is a matter of having one's actions dictated by proofs of their correctness within the practice, with these formulations as major premises. Sometimes, however, a practice of concept-application resists codification other than trivially (as in "It is correct to call all and only red things 'red'"), and in such cases we tend to resort to the other version of the picture. Here we appeal to grasp of a universal, conceiving this as a mechanism of an analogous sort: one which, like knowledge of an explicitly stateable rule, constitutes a capacity to run along a rail that is independently there.

Extending a number series is an example of going on doing the same thing which should constitute an ideal case for the application of this picture. Each correct move in a series of responses to the order "Add 2" is provably correct, as in what seems the clearest version of the picture. But in fact the idea that the rules of a practice mark out rails traceable independently of the reactions of participants is suspect even in this apparently ideal case; and insistence that wherever there is going on in the same way there must be rules that can be conceived as marking out such independently traceable rails involves a misconception of the sort of case in which correctness within a practice can be given the kind of demonstration we count as proof.

We can begin working up to this conclusion by coming to appreciate the emptiness, even in what should be the ideal case, of the psychological component of the picture: that is, the idea that grasp of a rule is a matter of having one's mental wheels engaged with an independently traceable rail. The picture represents understanding of, for instance, the instruction "Add 2" – command of the rule for extending the series 2, 4, 6, 8, . . . – as a psychological mechanism which, apart from mistakes, churns out the appropriate behaviour with the sort of reliability which, say, a clockwork mechanism might have. If someone is extending the series correctly, and one takes this to be because he has understood the instruction and is complying with it, then, according to the picture, one has hypothesized that the appropriate psychological mechanism, the engagement with the rails, underlies his behaviour. (This would be an inference analogous to that whereby one might postulate a physical mechanism underlying the behaviour of an inanimate object.)

But what manifests understanding of the instruction, so pictured? Suppose we ask the person what he is doing, and he says "Look, I'm adding 2 each time". This apparent manifestation of understanding will have been accompanied, whenever it occurs, by at most a finite fragment of the potentially infinite range of behaviour which we want to say the rule dictates. The same goes for any other apparent manifestation of understanding. Thus the evidence we have at any point for the presence of the pictured state is compatible with the supposition that, on some future occasion for its exercise, the behaviour elicited by the occasion will diverge from what we would count as correct, and not simply because of a mistake. Wittgenstein dramatizes this "possibility" with the example of the person who continues the series, after 1000, with 1004, 1008, ... (§ 185). Suppose a divergence of the 1004, 1008, ... type turned up, and we could not get the person to admit that he was simply making a mistake; that would show that his behaviour hitherto was not guided by the psychological conformation we were picturing as guiding it. The pictured state, then, always transcends any grounds there may be for postulating it.

There may be a temptation to protest as follows: "This is nothing but a familiar inductive skepticism about other minds. After all, one knows in one's own case that one's behaviour will not come adrift like that." But this objection is mistaken in itself, and it misses the point of the argument.

First, if what it is for one's behaviour to come adrift is for it suddenly to seem that everyone else is out of step, then any skeptical conclusion the argument were to recommend would apply in one's own case just as much as in the case of others. (Imagine the person who goes on with 1004, 1008, ... saying in advance "I know in my own case that my behaviour will not come adrift".) If there is any skepticism involved, it is not especially about *other* minds.

Second, it is anyway a mistake to construe the argument as making a skeptical point: that one does not know that others' behaviour (or one's own, once we have made the first correction) will not come adrift. The aim is not to suggest that we should be in trepidation lest "possibilities" of the 1004, 1008, ... type be realized.[10] We are in fact confident that they will not, and the argument aims, not to undermine this confidence, but to change our conception of its ground and nature. Our picture represents the confident expectation as based on whatever grounds we have *via* the mediation of the postulated psychological mechanism. But we can no more find the putatively mediating state manifested in the grounds for our expectation (say about what someone else will do) than we can find manifested there the very future occurrences we expect. Postulation of the mediating state is an idle intervening step; it does nothing to underwrite the confidence of our expectation.

(Postulation of a mediating brain state might indeed figure in a scientifically respectable argument, vulnerable only to ordinary inductive skepticism, that some specifically envisaged train of behaviour of the 1004, 1008, ... type will not occur; and our picture tends to trade on assimilating the postulation of the psychological mechanism to this. But the assimilation is misleading. Consider this variant of Wittgenstein's case: on reaching 1000, the person goes on as we expect, with 1002, 1004, . . ., but with a sense of dissociation from what he finds himself doing; it feels as if something like blind habit has usurped his reason in controlling his behaviour. Here the behaviour is kept in line, no doubt, by a brain state; but the person's sense of how to extend the series correctly shows a divergence from ours, of the 1004, 1008, . . . type. Of course we confidently expect this sort of thing not to happen, just as in the simpler kind of case. But a physically described mechanism cannot underwrite confidence in the future operations of someone's sense of what is called for; and once again postulation of a psychological mechanism would be an idle intervening step.[11])

What, then, is the ground and nature of our confidence? Stanley Cavell has described the view Wittgenstein wants to recommend as follows:

> We learn and teach words in certain contexts, and then we are expected, and expect others, to be able to project them into further contexts. Nothing insures that this projection will take place (in particular, not the grasping of universals nor the grasping of books of rules), just as nothing insures that we will make, and understand, the same projections. That on the whole we do is a matter of our sharing routes of interest and feeling, senses of humour and of significance and of fulfilment, of what is outrageous, of what is similar to what else, what a rebuke, what forgiveness, of when an utterance is an assertion, when an appeal, when an explanation – all the whirl of organism Wittgenstein calls "forms of life". Human speech and activity, sanity and community, rest upon nothing more, but nothing less, than this. It is a vision as simple as it is difficult, and as difficult as it is (and because it is) terrifying.[12]

The terror of which Cavell writes at the end of this marvellous passage is a sort of vertigo, induced by the thought that there is nothing that keeps our practices in line except the reactions and responses we learn in learning them. The ground seems to have been removed from under our feet. In this mood, we are inclined to feel that the sort of thing Cavell describes is insufficient foundation for a conviction that some practice really is a case of going on in the same way. What Cavell offers looks, rather, like a congruence of subjectivities, not grounded as it would need to be to amount to the sort of objectivity we want if we are to be convinced that we are *really* going on in the same way.

It is natural to recoil from this vertigo into the picture of rules as rails. But the picture is only a consoling myth elicited from us by our inability to endure the vertigo. It consoles by seeming to put the ground back under our feet; but we see that it is a myth by seeing, as we did above, that the pictured psychological mechanism gives only an illusory security. (Escaping from the vertigo would require seeing that this does not matter; I shall return to this.)

The picture has two interlocking components: the idea of the psychological mechanism correlates with the idea that the tracks we follow are objectively there to be followed, in a way that transcends the reactions and responses of participants in our practices. If the first component is suspect, the second component should be suspect too. And it is.

In the numerical case, the second component is a kind of platonism. The idea is that the relation of our arithmetical thought and language to the reality it characterizes can be contemplated, not only from the midst of our mathematical practices, but also, so to speak, from sideways on – from a standpoint independent of all the human activities and reactions that locate those practices in our "whirl of organism"; and that it would be recognizable from the sideways perspective that a given move is the correct move at a given point in the practice: that, say, 1002 really does come after 1000 in the series determined by the instruction "Add 2". It is clear how this platonistic picture might promise to reassure us if we suffered from the vertigo, fearing that the Wittgensteinian vision threatens to dissolve the independent truth of arithmetic into a collection of mere contingencies about the natural history of man. But the picture has no real content.

We tend, confusedly, to suppose that we occupy the external standpoint envisaged by platonism, when we say things we need to say in order to reject the reduction of mathematical truth to human natural history. For instance, we deny that what it is for the square of 13 to be 169 is for it to be possible to train human beings so that they find such and such calculations compelling. Rather, it is because the square of 13 really *is* 169 that we can be brought to find the calculations compelling. Moved by the vertigo, we are liable to think of remarks like this as expressions of platonism. But this is an illusion. To suppose that such a remark is an expression of platonism is to suppose that when we utter the words "the square of 13 is 169", in the context "It is because . . . that we can be brought to find the calculations compelling", we are speaking not from the midst of our merely human mathematical competence but from the envisaged independent perspective instead. (As if, by a special emphasis, one could somehow manage to speak otherwise than out of one's own mouth.) We cannot occupy the independent perspective that platonism envisages; and it is only because we confusedly think we can that we think we can make any sense of it.

If one is wedded to the picture of rules as rails, one will be inclined to think that to reject it is to suggest that, say, in mathematics, anything goes: that we are free to make it up as we go along.[13] But none of what I have said casts any doubt on the idea that the correctness of a move, in a mathematical case of going on doing the same thing, can be proved – so that it is compulsory to go on like that. The point is just that we should not misidentify the perspective from which this necessity is discernible. What is wrong is to suppose that when we describe someone as following a rule in extending a series, we characterize the output of his mathematical competence as the inexorable workings of a machine: something that could be seen to be operating from the platonist's standpoint, the standpoint independent of the activities and responses that make up our mathematical practice. The fact is that it is only because of our own involvement in our "whirl of organism" that we can understand a form of words as conferring, on the judgement that some move is the correct one at a given point, the special compellingness possessed by the conclusion of a proof. So if dependence on the "whirl of organism" induces vertigo, then we should feel vertigo about the mathematical cases as much as any other. No security is gained by trying to assimilate other sorts of case to the sort of case in which a hard-edged proof of correctness is available.

Consider, for instance, concepts whose application gives rise to hard cases, in this sense: there are disagreements, which resist resolution by argument, as to whether or not a concept applies.[14] If one is convinced that one is in the right on a hard case, one will find oneself saying, as one's arguments tail off without securing acceptance, "You simply aren't seeing it", or "But don't you see?" (cf. § 231). One will then be liable to think oneself confronted by a dilemma.

On the first horn, the inconclusiveness of the arguments results merely from a failure to get something across. This idea has two versions, which correspond to the two versions of the picture of rules as rails. According to the first version, it is possible, in principle, to spell out a universal formula that specifies, in unproblematic terms, the conditions under which the concept one intends is correctly applied. If one could only find the words, one could turn one's arguments into hard-edged proofs. (If the opponent refused to accept the major premiss, that would show that he had not mastered the concept one intended; in that case his inclination not to accept one's words would reveal no substantive disagreement.) According to the second version, the concept is not codifiable (except trivially), and one's problem is to use words as hints and pointers, in order to get one's opponent to divine the right universal. (This is really only a variant of the first version. The idea is that if one could only convey which universal was at issue, the opponent would have a sort of non-discursive counterpart to the formulable proof envisaged in the first version; and as before, if he grasped what one was trying to get across and still refused to accept one's conclusion, that would show that there was no substantive disagreement.)

If neither of these alternatives seems acceptable, then one is pushed on to the second horn of the dilemma by this thought: if there is nothing such that to get it across would either secure agreement or show that there was no substantive disagreement in the first place, then one's conviction that one is genuinely making an application of a concept (genuinely going on in some same way) is a mere illusion. The case is one which calls, not for finding the right answer to some genuine question, but rather for a freely creative decision as to what to say.

In a hard case, the issue seems to turn on that appreciation of the particular instance whose absence is deplored, in "You simply aren't seeing it", or which is (possibly without success) appealed to, in "But don't you see?" The dilemma reflects a refusal to accept that a genuine issue can really turn on no more than that; it reflects the view that a putative judgement that is grounded in nothing firmer than that cannot really be a case of going on as before. This is a manifestation of our vertigo: the idea is that there is not enough there to constitute the rails on which a genuine series of applications of a concept must run. But it is an illusion to suppose one is safe from vertigo on the first horn. The illusion is the misconception of the mathematical case: the idea that provable correctness characterizes exercises of reason in which it is, as it were, automatically compelling, without dependence on our partially shared "whirl of organism". The dilemma reflects a refusal to accept that when the dependence that induces vertigo is out in the open, in the appeal to appreciation, we can genuinely be going on in the same way; but the paradigm with which the rejected case is unfavourably compared has the same dependence, only less obviously. Once we see this, we should see that we make no headway, in face of the discouraging effects of the vertigo, by trying to assimilate all cases to the sort of case where proofs are available. We should accept that sometimes there may be nothing better to do than explicitly to appeal to a hoped-for community of human response. This is what we do when we say "Don't you see?" (though there is a constant temptation to misconceive this as a nudge towards grasp of the unversal).

Once we have felt the vertigo, then, the picture of rules as rails is only an illusory comfort. What is needed is not so much reassurance – the thought that after all there is solid ground under us – as not to have felt the vertigo in the first place. Now if we are simply and normally immersed in our practices, we do not wonder how their relation to the world would look from outside them, and feel the need for a solid foundation discernible from an external point of view. So we would be protected against the vertigo if we could stop supposing that the relation to reality of some area of our thought and language needs to be contemplated from a standpoint independent of that anchoring in our human life that makes the thoughts what they are for us.[15]

At any rate, it is a bad move to allow oneself to conceive some area of thought from the extraneous perspective at which vertigo threatens, but then suppose one can make oneself safe from vertigo with the idea that rules mark out rails discernible from that external point of view. Just such a move – seeing the anthropocentricity or ethnocentricity of an evaluative outlook as generating a threat of vertigo, but seeking to escape the threat by finding a solid, externally recognizable foundation – would account for insistence (cf. § 2 above) that any respectable evaluative concept must correspond to a classification intelligible from outside the evaluative outlook within which the concept functions.[16]

The idea that consideration of the relation between thought and reality requires the notion of an external standpoint is characteristic of a philosophical realism often considered in a different, more epistemologically oriented context, and in areas where we are not inclined to question whether there are facts of the matter at all. This realism chafes at the fallibility and inconclusiveness of all our ways of finding out how things are, and purports to confer a sense on "But is it *really* so?" in which the question does not call for a maximally careful assessment by our lights, but is asked from a perspective transcending the limitations of our cognitive powers. Thus this realism purports to conceive our understanding of what it is for things to be thus and so as independent of our limited abilities to find out whether they are. An adherent of this sort of realism will tend to be impressed by the line of thought sketched in § 1 above, and hence to fail to find room for values in his conception of the world; whereas opposition to this kind of realism about the relation, in general, between thought and reality, makes a space for realism, in a different sense, about values.[17]

4 I want now to revert to the eighteenth-century philosophy of mind, mentioned and shelved in § 1 above, and consider one way in which it connects with the line of thought I have been discussing.

What I have in mind is an argument for non-cognitivism that goes back at least to Hume (though I shall formulate it in rather un-Humean terms).[18] It has two premisses. The first is to the effect that ascriptions of moral value are action-guiding, in something like this sense: someone who accepts such an ascription may (depending on his opportunities for action) *eo ipso* have a reason for acting in a certain way, independently of anything else being true about him. The second premiss is this: to cite a cognitive propositional attitude – an attitude whose content is expressed by the sort of proposition for which acceptability consists in truth – is to give at most a partial specification of a reason for acting; to be fully explicit, one would need to add a mention of something non-cognitive, a state of the will or a volitional event. Clearly, it would follow that ascriptions of value, however acceptable, can be at most in part descriptive of the world.

The key premiss, for my purposes, is the second. Notice that if this premiss is suspect, that casts doubt not only on the non-cognitivism to which one would be committed if one accepted both premisses, but also on a different position which rejects the non-cognitivist conclusion, and, keeping the second premiss as a fulcrum, dislodges the first. This different position might merit Hare's label "descriptivism", meant as he means it – something that is not true of the anti-non-cognitivism I would defend, which retains the first premiss.[19] (A version of descriptivism, without general insistence on the second premiss – exceptions are allowed in the case of reasons that relate to the agent's interest – but with a restricted form of it used to overturn the first premiss, is found in some of the writings of Philippa Foot.[20])

I suspect that one reason why people find the second premiss of the Humean argument obvious lies in their inexplicit adherence to a quasi-hydraulic conception of how reason explanations account for action. The will is pictured as the source of the forces that issue in the behaviour such explanations explain. This idea seems to me a radical misconception of the sort of explanation a reason explanation is; but it is not my present concern.

A different justification for the second premiss might seem to be afforded by a line of thought obviously akin to what I have been considering; one might put it as follows. The rationality that a reason explanation reveals in the action it explains ought, if the explanation is a good one, to be genuinely there; that is, recognizable from an objective standpoint, conceived (cf. § 3) in terms of the notion of the view from sideways on – from outside any practices or forms of life partly constituted by local or parochial modes of response to the world. This putative requirement is not met if we conceive value judgements in the way I would recommend: the ascription of value that one cites in giving an agent's reason for an action, so far from revealing the rationality in the action to an imagined occupier of the external standpoint, need not even be intelligible from there. By contrast, insistence on the second premiss might seem to ensure that the requirement can be met. For on this view an explanation of an action in terms of a value judgement operates by revealing the action as the outcome of an unproblematically cognitive state plus a non-cognitive state – a desire, in some suitably broad sense[21]; and if we think someone's possession of the desires in question could be recognized from a standpoint external to the agent's moral outlook, then it might seem that those desires would confer an obvious rationality, recognizable from that objective standpoint, on actions undertaken with a view to gratifying them.

I shall make two remarks about this line of thought.

First, I expressed skepticism (in § 2) about the possibility of mastering the extension of a value concept from the external standpoint (so that one could move to understanding the value concept by tacking on an evaluative extra). The skepticism obviously recurs here, about the possibility of grasping, from the external standpoint, the content of the envisaged desires. On this view there is a set of desires, a propensity to which constitutes the embracing of a particular moral outlook; if the content of this set can be grasped from the external standpoint, then the actions required by that moral stance are in theory classifiable as such by a sheer outsider. This amounts to the assumption that a moral stance can be captured in a set of externally formulable principles – principles such that there could in principle be a mechanical (non-comprehending) application of them which would duplicate the actions of someone who puts the moral stance into practice. This assumption strikes me as merely fantastic.[22]

Second, the underlying line of thought inherits whatever dubiousness is possessed by its relatives in, say, the philosophy of mathematics. (See § 3, but I shall add a little here.)

Consider the hardness of the logical "must". One is apt to suppose that the only options are, on the one hand, to conceive the hardness platonistically (as something to be found in the world as it is anyway: that is, the world as characterized from a standpoint external to our mathematical practices); or, on the other (if one recoils from platonism), to confine oneself to a catalogue of how human beings act and feel when they engage in deductive reasoning. (Taking this second option, one might encourage oneself with the thought: at least all of this is objectively there.) On the second option, the hardness of the logical "must" has no place in one's account of how things really are; and there must be a problem about making room for genuine rationality in deductive practice, since we conceive that as a matter of conforming our thought and action to the dictates of the logical "must". If one recoils from platonism into this second position, one has passed over a fully satisfying intermediate position, according to which the logical "must" is indeed hard (in the only sense we can give to that idea), and the ordinary conception of deductive rationality is perfectly acceptable; it is simply that we must avoid a mistake about the perspective from which the demands of the logical "must" are perceptible. (As long as the mistake is definitely avoided, there is something to be said for calling the intermediate position a species of platonism.)[23]

Now it is an analogue to this intermediate position that seems to me to be most satisfying in the case of ethics. The analogue involves insisting that moral values are there in the world, and make demands on our reason. This is not a platonism about values (except in a sense analogous to that in which the intermediate position about the logical "must" might be called a species of platonism); the world in which moral values are said to be is not the externally characterizable world that a moral platonism would envisage.[24] Non-cognitivism and descriptivism appear, from this point of view, as different ways of succumbing to a quite dubious demand for a more objective conception of rationality. If we accept the demand, then they will indeed seem the only alternatives to a full-blown moral platonism. But in the logical case, we should not suppose that recoiling from platonism commits us to some kind of reduction of the felt hardness of the logical "must" to the urging of our own desires.[25] In the ethical case too, we should not allow the different option that the intermediate position affords to disappear.[26]

5 Non-cognitivism, as I see it, invites us to be exercised over the question how value experience relates to the world, with the world conceived as how things are anyway – independently, as least, of our value experience being as it is. The non-cognitivism I have been concerned with assumes that evaluative classifications correspond to kinds into which things can in principle be seen to fall independently of an evaluative outlook, and thereby permits itself to return an answer to the question which clearly does not undermine the appearance that evaluative thinking is a matter of the genuine application of concepts. As one's use of an evaluative term unfolds through time, one is genuinely (by the non-cognitivist's lights) going on in the same way. Admittedly, the non-cognitive ingredient in what happens makes the case more complex than our usual paradigms of concept-application. But the non-cognitive extra, repeated as the practice unfolds, is seen as a repeated response to some genuinely same thing (something capturable in a paradigmatic concept-application): namely, membership in some genuine kind. To put it picturesquely, the non-cognitive ingredient (an attitude, say) can, without illusion by the non-cognitivist's lights, see itself as going on in the same way. Given that, the whole picture looks sufficiently close to the usual paradigms of concept-application to count as a complex variant of them. But I have suggested that the assumption on which the possibility of this partial assimilation depends is a prejudice, without intrinsic plausibility.

Might non-cognitivism simply disown the assumption?[27] If what I have just written is on the right track, it can do so only at a price: that of making it problematic whether evaluative language is close enough to the usual paradigms of concept-application to count as expressive of judgements at all (as opposed to a kind of sounding off). Failing the assumption, there need be no genuine same thing (by the non-cognitivist's lights) to which the successive occurrences of the non-cognitive extra are responses. Of course the items to which the term in question is applied have, as something genuinely in common, the fact that they elicit the non-cognitive extra (the attitude, if that is what it is). But that is not a property to which the attitude can coherently be seen as a response. The attitude can see itself as going on in the same way, then, only by falling into a peculiarly grotesque form of the alleged illusion: projecting itself on to the objects, and then mistaking the projection for something it finds and responds to in them. So it seems that, if it disowns the assumption, non-cognitivism must regard the attitude as something which is simply felt (causally, perhaps, but not rationally explicable); and uses of evaluative language seem appropriately assimilated to certain sorts of exclamation, rather than to the paradigm cases of concept-application.

Of course there are some who will not find this conclusion awkward.[28] But anyone who finds it unacceptable, and is sympathetic to the suggestion that the disputed assumption is only a prejudice, has reason to suspect that the non-cognitivist is not asking the right question. It is not that we cannot make sense of the non-cognitivist's conception of a value-free world; nor that we cannot find plausible some account of how value experience relates to it (causally, no doubt). But if we resist both the disputed assumption and the irrationalistic upshot of trying to read an account of the relation between value experience and the world so conceived, not based on the disputed assumption, as an account of the real truth about the conceptual content of the experience, then we must wonder about the credentials of the non-cognitivist's question. If we continue to find it plausible that asking how value experience relates to the world should yield a palatable account of the content of value experience, we must wonder whether the world that figures in the right construal of the question should not be differently conceived, without the non-cognitivist's insistence on independence from evaluative outlooks.[29] In that case the non-cognitivist's anxiety to maintain that value judgements are not descriptive of *his* world will seem, not wrong indeed, but curiously beside the point.

Notes

Much of § 3 of this paper is adapted from my 'Virtue and reason', the *Monist*, 62, No. 3 (July 1979); I am grateful to the Editor and Publisher of the *Monist* for permission to use the material here. I first delivered a version of this paper at a conference in Oxford, and Simon Blackburn commented (a version of his comments was published as "Rule-Following and Moral Realism"). In revising the paper I read at the conference, I have been unable to resist trying to benefit from some of Simon Blackburn's thoughtful comments; but most of the changes are merely cosmetic.

1 There is an excellent discussion of this line of thought (though more sympathetic to it than I should want to be myself) in Bernard Williams, *Descartes: The Project of Pure Enquiry*, Penguin, Harmondsworth, 1978, Chapter 8. (I shall not pause to criticize the application to secondary qualities.)
2 The parallel is suggested by Williams, *ibid.*, when (p. 245) he writes of "concepts . . . which reflect merely a local interest, taste or sensory peculiarity".
3 Cf. J. L. Mackie, *Ethics: Inventing Right and Wrong*, Penguin, Harmondsworth, 1977, p. 22.
4 Cf. Mackie, *ibid.*, pp. 40–1.
5 The non-cognitivist's conception of the world is not exhausted by primary-quality characterizations. (See David Wiggins, "Truth, invention, and the meaning of life", *Proceedings of the British Academy*, 62 (1976), pp. 361–3.) So his notion of the world as it is anyway is not the one that figures in the argument about secondary qualities. What is wanted, and what my parenthesis is intended to suggest, is an analogy, rather than an addition, to the secondary-quality argument.
6 This formulation fits Mackie's error theory, rather than the different sort of non-cognitivism exemplified by R. M. Hare's prescriptivism (see, e.g., *Freedom and Reason*, Clarendon Press, Oxford, 1963), in which ordinary evaluative thinking has enough philosophical sophistication not to be enticed into the projective error of which Mackie accuses it. But the idea could easily be reformulated to suit Hare's position; this difference between Hare and Mackie is not relevant to my concerns in this paper.
7 Cf. Hare, *ibid.*, p. 33 (on the thesis of universalizability): "What the thesis does forbid us to do is to make different moral judgements about actions which we admit to be exactly or relevantly similar". In Chapter 2, Hare claims that this thesis of universalizability just is the thesis that evaluative concepts have "descriptive" meaning (which is Hare's version of the thesis I am skeptical about): see p. 15. The identification is undermined by my remarks about supervenience.
8 The point is not merely that the language may lack such a term: a gap that might perhaps be filled by coining one. (See Hare, "Descriptivism", *Proceedings of the British Academy*, 49 (1963).) What I am suggesting is that such a coinage might not be learnable except parasitically upon a mastery of the full-blown evaluation expression.
9 See Hare, *op. cit.*, Chapter 2. Mackie (*op. cit.*, p. 86) objects to the idea that a corresponding value-neutral classification is (as in Hare's position) part of the meaning of an evaluative term, but evidently in the context of an assumption that there must be such a corresponding classification.
10 Nor even that we really understand the supposition that such a thing might happen; see Barry Stroud, "Wittgenstein and logical necessity", *Philosophical Review*, 74 (1965), pp. 504–18.
11 In the context of a physicalistic conception of mind, this paragraph will be quite unconvincing; this is one of the points at which a great deal more argument is necessary.

12 *Must We Mean What We Say?*, Charles Scribner's Sons, New York, 1969, p. 52.
13 See Michael Dummett, "Wittgenstein's philosophy of mathematics", *Philosophical Review*, 68 (1959), pp. 324–48. (For a corrective, see Stroud, *op. cit.*)
14 Simon Blackburn objected that the central "rule-following" passages in Wittgenstein discuss cases where following the rule is a matter of course. (There are no hard cases in mathematics.) In the end I do not mind if my remarks about hard cases correspond to nothing in Wittgenstein; they indicate (at least) a natural way to extend some of Wittgenstein's thoughts. (Where hard cases occur, the agreement that constitutes the background against which we can see what happens as, e.g., disputes about genuine questions cannot be agreement in judgements as to the application of the concepts themselves: cf. § 242. What matters is, for instance, agreement about what counts as a reasonable argument; consider how lawyers recognize competence in their fellows, in spite of disagreement over hard cases.)
15 This is not an easy recipe. Perhaps finding out how to stop being tempted by the picture of the external standpoint would be the discovery that enables one to stop doing philosophy when one wants to (cf. § 133).
16 The idea of rules as rails seems to pervade chapter 2 of Hare's *Freedom and Reason* (cf. notes 7 and 9 above). Hare argues there that evaluative words, if used with "that consistency of practice in the use of an expression which is the condition of its intelligibility" (p. 7), must be governed by principles connecting their correct application to features of value-independent reality (that which can be "descriptively" characterized, in Hare's sense of "descriptively"). Hare mentions Wittgenstein, but only as having introduced " 'family resemblance' and 'open texture' and all that" (p. 26) into "the patter of the up-to-date philosophical conjurer" (p. 7). It is hard to resist the impression that Hare thinks we can respect everything useful that Wittgenstein said, even while retaining the essentials of the picture of rules as rails, simply by thinking of the mechanism as incompletely rigid and difficult to characterize in precise terms.
17 I distinguish opposition to the realism that involves the idea of the external standpoint from anti-realism in the sense of Michael Dummett (see, e.g., *Truth and Other Enigmas*, Duckworth, London, 1978, *passim*), which is the positive doctrine that linguistic competence consists in dispositions to respond to circumstances recognizable whenever they obtain. (See my "Anti-realism and the epistemology of understanding", in Jacques Bouveresse and Herman Parret (eds), *Meaning and Understanding*, De Gruyter, Berlin and New York, 1981.)
18 See *A Treatise of Human Nature*, III. I. I, in the edition of L. A. Selby-Bigge, Clarendon Press, Oxford, 1896, p. 457.
19 As Hare uses the word "descriptive", a descriptive judgement is, by definition, not action-guiding. Hare does not consider a resistance to non-cognitivism that accepts the first premiss of the Humean argument.
20 See especially *Virtues and Vices*, Blackwell, Oxford, 1978, p. 156. From the point of view of a resistance to non-cognitivism that accepts the first premiss of the Humean argument, the difference between non-cognitivism and descriptivism tends to pale into insignificance, by comparison with the striking fact that they share the disputable conception of the world as such that knowing how things are in it cannot by itself move us to moral action.
21 Either, as in non-cognitivism, acceptance of a moral judgement really is a composite state including a desire; or, as in descriptivism, the moral judgement is itself strictly cognitive, but it makes the behaviour intelligible only in conjunction with a desire.
22 See my "Virtue and reason" (cited in the remarks that precede the notes for this paper).
23 The following passage seems to be an expression of the intermediate position:

What you say seems to amount to this, that logic belongs to the natural history of man.
 And that is not combinable with the hardness of the logical "must".
 But the logical 'must' is a component part of the propositions of logic, and these are not propositions of human natural history.

(RFM VI, 49)

24 Hence Mackie's error is not committed. (It is a fascinating question whether Plato himself was a moral platonist in the sense here envisaged: I am myself inclined to think he was not.)

25 On these lines: to "perceive" that a proposition is, say, a conclusion by *modus ponens* from premisses one has already accepted, since it constitutes having a reason to accept the proposition, is really an amalgam of a neutral perception and a desire (cf. non-cognitivism); or the perception constitutes having a reason only in conjunction with a desire (cf. descriptivism). I am indebted to Susan Hurley here.

26 For the suggestion that Wittgenstein's philosophy of mathematics yields a model for a satisfactory conception of the metaphysics of value, see Wiggins, *op. cit.*, pp. 369–71.

27 Simon Blackburn pressed this question, and what follows corresponds to nothing in the paper I read at the conference.

28 I mean those who are content with a view of values on the lines of, e.g., A. J. Ayer, *Language, Truth and Logic*, Gollancz, London, 1936, Chapter VI.

29 The pressure towards a conception of reality as objective, transcending how things appear to particular points of view, is not something to which it is clearly compulsory to succumb in all contexts, for all its necessity in the natural sciences. See Thomas Nagel, "Subjective and objective", in his *Mortal Questions*, Cambridge University Press, 1979.

3

WITTGENSTEIN ON RULES AND PLATONISM

David H. Finkelstein

A rule or an instruction provides a standard against which a person trying to follow it may be judged – as either behaving in accord with it or not. For example, my copy of the *Better Homes and Gardens New Cookbook* includes a recipe for chocolate soufflé that begins with the following instruction: "Beat 3 egg yolks till thick and lemon-colored; set aside." Imagine that you are helping me make a chocolate soufflé. I read this instruction aloud to you, and you proceed to engage in various activities around my kitchen. You locate a heavy porcelain bowl and place it on the counter; you find a wire whisk and set it next to the bowl; you open the refrigerator and pull out a carton of eggs. . . . Your activities may, in the end, satisfy – i.e., be in accord with – the instruction I've given you.

Here, a philosopher might ask: "How is it that, in a situation like this, you come to grasp which of your activities would accord, or fail to accord, with a sequence of noises that you've heard? How, for that matter, is it that a sequence of activities *can* accord, or fail to accord, with a sequence of noises or marks?" Especially since the publication of Saul Kripke's enormously influential book on Wittgenstein in 1982,[1] questions such as these have been taken to lie at the heart of Wittgenstein's concerns in his later writings. Nonetheless, confusion still surrounds what he has to say about them. In what follows I shall discuss Wittgenstein's dissatisfaction with one approach to answering these questions. The approach that I have in mind – a kind of platonism about meaning and understanding – is taken up by Wittgenstein's interlocutor in passages such as the following:

> How does it come about this arrow ›››——› *points*? Doesn't it seem to carry in it something besides itself? – "No, not the dead line on paper; only the psychical thing, the meaning, can do that."[2]

In this passage, Wittgenstein's interlocutor is struck by the thought that a written sign is just an ink mark, just a "dead line on paper." In order to explain how such a thing could have a kind of significance that random squiggles lack, he imagines something *behind* the line on paper – something hidden – which, as it were, infuses it with significance.

Let us say, provisionally, that a platonist about meaning is someone who, in an effort to explain how mere noises and marks can have semantic significance, is driven to posit self-standing *sources* of significance – items which stand to the significance of our dead marks and noises as the sun stands to the light of the moon.[3] While Wittgenstein's commentators agree that some such view figures as an important target of criticism in his discussions of rule-following, I believe that most of them badly misunderstand the character – the depth, as it were – of this criticism: they read Wittgenstein as endorsing one or another position that participates in the very thing to which he objects in platonism. (In what follows, Crispin Wright will serve as an example of such a commentator.) The aim of this paper is to elucidate Wittgenstein's response to platonism. I believe that we can understand a good deal of what seems most opaque in his later writings by coming to appreciate just what it is that he does and does not find objectionable in platonism.

1 Rules and platonism: some preliminary remarks

In this section, I shall briefly describe the way in which platonism emerges as a temptation in Wittgenstein's discussions of rule-following. I'll go on to say a little bit about what's unsatisfactory in the platonist's understanding of rule-following. The deep problem that Wittgenstein sees in platonism – the one shared by platonists and anti-platonists alike – will come to light only later in the paper.

At *Investigations*, §185, Wittgenstein asks us to imagine a pupil who has been taught to write out various mathematical series when given instructions of the form "+n." His teacher says, "+2," and he writes, "2, 4, 6," etc. But when the pupil is asked to continue the +2 series beyond 1000, he writes, "1000, 1004, 1008." Two questions arise: first, how is the pupil supposed to know what the order calls for him to do after he's written "1000"? (He has not been *explicitly* trained to write "1002" immediately after "1000.") And second, what determines that "1002" is in fact what he's supposed to write at that point; what fixes it that writing "1002" after "1000" would be in accord with the teacher's instruction?

One kind of answer to these questions would appeal to the notion of interpretation. We might say that what determines that the teacher's utterance – "+2" – calls for the pupil to write "1002" immediately after "1000" is that the teacher attaches a particular interpretation to it. We might say, moreover, that the pupil's understanding the utterance requires that he attach the same, or a suitably similar, interpretation to it.

But here we run into a problem. For let us allow that the teacher and the pupil *do* attach an interpretation – the same interpretation – to what the teacher says. Let's say that they both take "+2" to mean: *write "2,4,6," and just continue to write the next but one number after every number that you've written.* How is the pupil to know that *this* sentence requires him to write "1002" after "1000"? And what determines that this sentence does indeed call for "1002" to be written at that point?

If we say that what a rule requires or means is determined by its interpretation, we are left wondering how the interpretation gets *its* meaning. If we say that the interpretation requires its *own* interpretation, an infinite regress threatens: each interpretation that we introduce requires the support of another. Thus at *Investigations*, §198, Wittgenstein writes: "[A]ny interpretation still hangs in the air along with what it interprets, and cannot give it any support. Interpretations by themselves do not determine meaning." This conclusion gives rise to the famous "paradox" of *Investigations*, §201:

> This was our paradox: no course of action could be determined by a rule, because every course of action can be made out to accord with the rule. The answer was: if everything can be made out to accord with the rule, then it can also be made out to conflict with it. And so there would be neither accord nor conflict here.

Now, we can think of platonism as a desperate attempt to block the infinite regress of interpretations that gives rise to the paradox of §201. The platonist posits special items which – unlike noises, marks and gestures – are, as it were, intrinsically significant: they neither need nor brook interpretation. According to the platonist, what saves our words from emptiness is that such items stand behind them. The regress of interpretations doesn't arise as a problem because these intrinsically significant items neither need be, nor can be, interpreted. We should read Wittgenstein as describing the impulse toward such a position when he writes: "What one wishes to say is: 'Every sign is capable of interpretation; but the *meaning* mustn't be capable of interpretation. It is the last interpretation.'"[4]

* * *

I want to mention two reasons why we ought to be dissatisfied with a platonistic account of meaning and understanding. One is: if we say that all of our words and gestures derive their semantic significance from items that lie hidden behind them, communication comes to look deeply problematic. How is it that when I say something to you, you not only hear my words – you generally grasp my meaning? A platonist might say: "My words and gestures can be interpreted any which way, but the thing behind them – the meaning – needs no interpretation. Now, I can't convey this item directly to my interlocutor. All that I can do is talk to him, or gesture to him, and all my words and gestures can be interpreted in various ways. But if he's lucky, he'll guess what I have in mind and understand me."[5]

On this picture of things, if you and I are to successfully communicate, we must be fortunate enough to guess each other's meanings correctly. Not only must we correctly guess the meanings of each other's words; there is no way for us to determine that any of our guesses have been correct. You can't tell me whether I've guessed your meaning correctly because you can only guess at what I have guessed. Given this picture of communication, a *conversation* might be modeled by the following game. You draw a picture on a piece of paper that is blocked from my view. Although I can't see your drawing, I try to produce a copy of it on a piece of paper that *you* can't see. We go back and forth like this without ever showing each other our drawings.[6]

I said that I would mention two problems with platonism, with the picture of meaning as "the last interpretation." One of these is that platonism makes communication look miraculous. Another is that the platonist really has no idea how anything *could* block the regress of interpretations and so be "the last interpretation" – no idea how something could be a fount from which our dead noises and marks derive their significance, rather than just another intrinsically contentless item awaiting interpretation. The platonist is driven in the course of his theorizing to say that there are – there *must* be – such items, but they seem mysterious even to him.

* * *

In summary, we can think of platonism as entering Wittgenstein's discussion of rule-following as a desperate and unsatisfactory attempt to avoid the regress of interpretations which gives rise to the paradox of *Investigations*, §201. In his efforts to explain how rule-following is possible at all, the platonist finds himself driven to posit mysterious, regress-stopping items – items from which significance flows into all our signs and gestures, but which themselves neither need nor brook interpretation. The platonist himself has no real idea of how there could be such items nor of how they might be communicated.

2 Wright's "flat-footed response" to Kripke's skeptic

According to Kripke, what's at issue in Wittgenstein's discussions of rule-following is a form of skepticism according to which there are no facts concerning what our words mean. Kripke tries to illustrate the line of thought that leads to this remarkable conclusion by asking us to imagine a skeptic who challenges his interlocutor to show that, given what he'd always meant by the term "plus" in the past, the correct answer to the question, "What is 68 plus 57?" is "125" rather than "5." In other words, the skeptic challenges his interlocutor to prove that in the past he'd meant *plus* by "plus" rather than some function (the "quus" function) whose value is 5 when its arguments are 68 and 57. The interlocutor is to meet this skeptical challenge by citing facts about his own past life that his meaning *plus* by "plus" had consisted in. A range of facts are adduced – facts not only about how the interlocutor has interpreted the word "plus," but also about the circumstances under which he's used it, about his dispositions to use it and about occurrent mental episodes he's undergone in connection with it. The skeptic argues persuasively that none of these could have determined, for an infinity of possible applications of "plus," which ones would accord with what the interlocutor had meant by the word. The skeptic concludes that there is no fact about what his interlocutor had meant by "plus." From here, he argues that there are, in general, no facts about what our signs mean.

The problem raised by Kripke's skeptic threatens more than the idea that there are facts about what we mean when we speak and write. It is as much a problem about how there could be contentful *mental* states. Kripke's skeptic might have challenged his interlocutor to show that he'd ever had an *intention* to add (rather than to "quadd") with similar results. (Indeed, Kripke sometimes puts the point this way.) Just as a person's having meant something determinate by "plus" requires that there be facts about whether an infinity of possible uses of the word would accord with what she meant, someone's having had a determinate intention (or desire or wish) requires that there be facts about whether an infinity of possible states of affairs would accord with what she'd intended (or desired or wished). The conclusion reached by Kripke's skeptic amounts to the claim that there are no content-facts at all, and so no facts about what someone intends or wishes, any more than facts about what she means when she speaks.

According to Kripke, Wittgenstein recommends a "skeptical solution" to the problem that is posed by the skeptic, i.e., a response to skepticism which concedes "that the skeptic's negative assertions are unanswerable."[7] Precisely *which* negative assertions does Kripke take Wittgenstein to concede to the skeptic? Because Kripke's text invites more than one answer to this question, I find it difficult to get into clear focus the skeptical solution that he means to attribute to Wittgenstein.[8] There is, however, a prevailing interpretation of Kripke's Wittgenstein, and, for present purposes, it will suffice for me to summarize it. According to this interpretation, Kripke's Wittgenstein concedes to the skeptic that a sentence like "Jones means *plus* by 'plus'" (or "Jones intends to add") cannot be used to state a fact because there is nothing about Jones's behavior or state of mind for such a fact to consist in. What saves assertions about meaning from being pointless is that such talk may be used for purposes other than that of stating facts.[9] While a sentence like "Jones means *plus*" cannot be true, it may yet have a kind of correctness: its utterance may be justified within a communal language-game. Such a sentence may be used to register our acceptance of Jones into the linguistic community. We, as it were, pin a membership badge on him when we say, "He means *plus* by 'plus'"; we accept him as one of us.

* * *

At least as he is widely understood, then, Kripke takes the central conclusion of Wittgenstein's *Investigations* to be that there can be no fact of the matter concerning what it is that someone means, intends, or wishes. In a pair of papers by Crispin Wright to which I'll refer in what follows, Wright rejects this conclusion; moreover, he rejects the reading of the *Investigations* according to which Wittgenstein endorses it. Wright follows a number of other commentators[10] in noting that Kripke's skeptic unjustifiably assumes that if there are facts about content, they must reduce to facts that can be characterized in terms of contentless states and events·

> [T]here is an explicit and unacceptable reductionism involved at the stage at which the Sceptic challenges his interlocutor to recall some aspect of his former mental life which might constitute his, for example, having meant addition by 'plus'. It is not acceptable, apparently, if the interlocutor claims to recall precisely that.[11]

Wright says that the correct answer to the challenge raised by Kripke's skeptic is what he calls a "flat-footed response"[12] along the following lines: "The fact about my past usage of 'plus' that fixes it that I am now acting in accord with what I then meant by 'plus' is just that I meant *plus* by 'plus'." Wright, moreover, thinks that Wittgenstein would have endorsed such a response. But, he says, this leaves us with a real problem – that "of seeing how and why the correct answer just given can *be* correct."[13]

Wright begins his explanation of how and why the flat-footed response to Kripke's skeptic can be correct by describing a temptation which, he points out, Wittgenstein is concerned to undermine – the temptation to think that when I give someone a rule to follow, e.g., a rule governing an arithmetical series, I must somehow bring him to guess what I have in mind. I might say, "Continue the series that begins 2, 4, 6, 8, 10." Or I might say, "Start with 2 and just keep adding 2." But I can't name *all* the numbers in the series, and *whatever* words I say to my interlocutor, they will be amenable to various interpretations, e.g., interpretations under which the series that I have in mind includes a segment that goes: 1000, 1004. So we are tempted to think that my interlocutor's coming to understand me aright requires that he guess at the essential thing *behind* my words – my meaning or intention – where this is understood to transcend any description or explanation that I can give of it. We are tempted, Wright says, toward platonism.

What does Wright think we should say about rule-following if we are not satisfied with platonism? He puts what he takes to be one of the central lessons of Wittgenstein's discussions of rule-following as follows: "It might be preferable, in describing our most basic rule-governed responses, to think of them not as informed by an *intuition* (of the requirements of the rule) but as a kind of *decision*."[14] The platonist thinks that a rule (or anyway, the meaning that lies behind the statement of a rule) autonomously calls for a course of action, and that when we set out to follow a rule, we intuit or perceive what it requires us to do. According to Wright's Wittgenstein, this must be rejected: when we follow rules, we don't perceive their requirements; we *decide* them.

A problem with saying that we decide a rule's requirements is that this suggests a rule-follower is free to decide that anything she happens to do is what the rule calls for. Wright is aware of this problem, describing it as follows:

> The rule-following considerations attack the idea that judgments about the requirements of a rule on a particular occasion have a 'tracking' epistemology, answer to states of affairs constituted altogether independently of our inclination to make those judgments. How can judgments lack a substantial epistemology in this way, and yet still be *objective* – still have to answer to something distinct from our actual dispositions of judgment?[15]

Wright's answer to the question raised in this passage is to say that it is only our "best" judgments (i.e., our best decisions) about the statement of a rule that determine what it means or requires – where a judgment is a best judgment if it is arrived at under certain ideal conditions, which Wright calls "C-conditions." Judgments made about the requirements of rules have what Wright calls a "substantial epistemology" by virtue of the fact that when the C-conditions are *not* satisfied, such judgments are constrained by the characteristics of rules that are determined by judgments made under the C-conditions.[16]

On the view that Wright puts forward, when the C-conditions are satisfied, a person's judgments about a rule determine (rather than reflect) what it requires – determine, in other words, what the words that make up the statement of the rule *mean*. Now, what are these C-conditions? Although Wright is less forthcoming about this than we might have hoped, he does say that under most *ordinary* circumstances, if I form an opinion about what *I myself* mean or meant in saying something, such an opinion determines rather than reflects its subject matter. Typically, in judging that I meant X, I make it the case – I determine – that X was what I meant. (Wright notes that this determination is defeasible. What a subject says about his own meanings and intentional states is generally allowed to stand, but subsequent events occasionally overturn his judgment.) In other words, for judgments or opinions that may be expressed in the form of avowals of meaning, the C-conditions are usually satisfied.[17]

Recall that in Kripke's discussion of Wittgenstein, a skeptic asks his interlocutor, "What is 68 plus 57?" The interlocutor answers, "125," whereupon the skeptic suggests that – given what the interlocutor had always meant by "plus" in the past – the correct answer is "5." The skeptic challenges his interlocutor to cite a fact or facts about his past in which his previously meaning *plus* by "plus" might have consisted. When the interlocutor fails to meet this challenge satisfactorily, the skeptic concludes that there is no fact of the matter concerning what his interlocutor meant. We saw that Wright endorses a flat-footed response to Kripke's skeptic – one that goes: "The fact about my past usage of 'plus' that fixes it that I am now acting in accord with what I then meant by the word is just that I meant *plus* by 'plus'." We also saw that Wright wants to provide an explanation of *how* such a response could be the correct one. We're now in a position to consider Wright's explanation:

> It will be ... a perfect answer to Kripke's Sceptic to explain how judgments concerning one's own meanings, both past and present, are ... provisionally extension-determining in the most ordinary circumstances. Challenged to justify the claim that I formerly meant addition by 'plus', it will not be necessary to locate some meaning-constitutive fact in my former behaviour or mental life. A sufficient answer need only advert to my present opinion, that addition is what I formerly meant, and still mean, and to the *a priori* reasonableness of the supposition, failing evidence to the contrary, that this opinion is best.[18]

Kripke's skeptic challenges his interlocutor to cite some fact or facts *about his former life* that his meaning *plus* by "plus" consisted in. The skeptic presupposes that if his interlocutor meant anything determinate in the past by "plus," there must be such facts. Wright rejects this presupposition. On his view, what someone meant in the past can be constituted by judgments he makes in the present.[19] According to Wright, when I answer the skeptic in the flat-footed fashion – when I issue the avowal, "I meant *plus* by 'plus'" – I express the sort of "best" opinion that determines rather than reflects what is true; I *make* it the case that, in the past, I meant *plus* by "plus." We could say that I now make it the case that the rule I always attached to the word "plus" calls for me to answer, "125" (rather than, say, "5") in response to the question, "What is 68 plus 57?"

What does it mean to say that I *make* it the case that a rule calls for a particular activity? Ordinarily, when someone makes it the case that a stated rule calls for one activity rather than another, we describe him as "stipulating" what the rule requires. Imagine, for example, that a pamphlet entitled *Rules for Students* is issued to seventh-graders on the first day of school. The pamphlet includes the following sentence: "While in class, students shall conduct themselves in an orderly fashion." A teacher might stipulate that following this rule requires that students in his classroom sit in alphabetical order. It seems a fair characterization of Wright's position to say that he thinks every rule gets its content by a kind of stipulation.

* * *

Kripke's skeptic demands a *constitutive* account of that by virtue of which his interlocutor could have meant anything determinate in his past usage of "plus": he asks in what his interlocutor's meaning *plus* might have *consisted*. Wright offers such an account, though not of a sort that Kripke's skeptic envisages. Kripke's skeptic assumes that if his interlocutor meant anything determinate in the past by "plus," his meaning what he did must be constituted by facts about his life *as it was in the past*. As we've seen, Wright claims that what a person meant in the past can be stipulated here and now, and so be constituted by facts about his *present* life. In §3, I'll argue that this sort of "stipulativism" about rules is neither a viable position nor one that Wittgenstein would have us accept, and I'll present what I take to be a better reading of Wittgenstein on rules. Before I come to that, I want to comment briefly on another approach to dealing with Kripke's skeptic – an approach that Wright calls "official" Wittgensteinianism.[20]

According to "official" Wittgensteinianism, we should accept that there are facts about what our words mean (what our rules call for, etc.), while rejecting the demand for a constitutive account of that by virtue of which they mean what they do: "Asked what constitutes the truth of rule-informed judgment of the kind we isolated, the official Wittgensteinian will reply: 'Bad question, leading to bad philosophy – platonism, for instance, or Kripkean scepticism.'"[21] The problem with taking up this stance, according to Wright, is that it requires us to turn our faces away from a question that might, after all, yield a philosophically illuminating answer. To Wright, "official" Wittgensteinianism seems to amount to a kind of *avoidance* of philosophy. According to the "official" readings of him, Wittgenstein refuses to answer constitutive questions about meaning. As Wright sees things, the "official" Wittgenstein thereby fails to rise to "the challenge posed by his own thought."[22] Thus, when Wright is introducing his own non-"official," stipulativist reading of Wittgenstein, he writes:

> I want to canvass a third possibility: an account of the central insight of Wittgenstein's discussion of rule-following which is neither Kripkean nor 'official'. It may be that the 'official' view is exegetically correct, and that I do here part company with the intentions of the actual, historical Wittgenstein. But it seems to me that it is an important methodological precept that we do not despair of giving answers to constitutive questions too soon; if the accomplishments of analysis in philosophy often seem meagre, that may be because it is difficult, not impossible.[23]

Soon, I shall claim that Wright does indeed "part company with the intentions of the actual, historical Wittgenstein." As the quoted passage makes clear, Wright recognizes this as a real possibility. But although he sees that the actual Wittgenstein might reject constitutive questions about meaning, Wright never gets in view the *kind* of rejection that is actually at issue in Wittgenstein's texts. To Wright, it appears that when we become dissatisfied with platonism, we have just two options: we must try to articulate that in which meaning one thing rather than another consists, or we must (with the "official" Wittgenstein) opt for "quietism"[24] and refuse to engage with what is, after all, a gripping question. By the end of this paper, I hope to have shown that to understand Wittgenstein's response to platonism is to see that we are not, after all, faced with this dilemma.

3 The gulf between an order and its execution

At *Investigations*, §431, Wittgenstein has an interlocutor say: "There is a gulf between an order and its execution. It has to be filled by the act of understanding." In saying that there's "a gulf between an order and its execution," Wittgenstein's interlocutor means that a sequence of written or spoken words cannot be understood without some "act" to serve as a bridge between the words themselves and what they mean. What sort of act could perform this function? Imagine that an American who speaks little Italian is traveling in Rome. A local police officer approaches her in the street and shouts something at her. The policeman's tone of voice and his facial expression suggest that he is issuing an order – as indeed, he is – but our traveler can't make out *what* he wants her to do. Here, it would be natural to say that there was a gulf between the policeman's saying what he did and the traveler's understanding him. It would be equally natural to say that if the traveler managed to interpret the policeman's order into English (perhaps with the aid of a dictionary), the gulf would be bridged. So it seems that an act of *interpretation* can bridge the gulf between an order and its execution.

This conclusion, however, begins to wobble under the weight of the following line of thought: "We need not imagine the meeting of different languages (e.g., English and Italian) if all that we want is an example of a case in which there's a gulf between an order and its execution. There's a gulf between *any* order and its execution. Any order could, conceivably, be misunderstood. Imagine that someone approaches you and says, 'Hands up!' He wants you to put your hands above your head, but you *might* misunderstand him; you might think that he wants you to, e.g., turn your hands palms up directly in front of you. There's a gulf between even this simple an order and its execution: unless you interpret it properly, you won't know how to execute it as it was intended." This line of thought may sound innocuous, but it leads to a problem. Once we have come to think that there's a gulf between *any* order and its execution, interpretation no longer looks like a way to bridge such a gulf. Any interpretation that I attach to "Hands up!" will, itself, be such that it *could* be misunderstood. *It* will seem to stand in as much need of interpretation as "Hands up!" It will, as it were, come with its *own* gulf.[25] Once we take there to be a gulf between every order and its execution, we can't seem to find anything to bridge the gulfs.

The apparently innocuous thought – that there is a gulf between any order and its execution – might be argued for in a slightly different way. Someone might say: "An order, recipe, or instruction is, in itself, nothing but sounds or ink marks. Interpretation, or something like interpretation – some 'act of understanding' – is needed if the sounds or ink-marks are to strike anyone as more than empty noises or squiggles. This goes for *any* order, recipe, or rule; there is a gap between any such item and what it requires." A thought like this is expressed in the second paragraph of *Investigations*, §431. (I began this section by quoting its first paragraph.) Wittgenstein's interlocutor says: "Only in the act of understanding is it meant that we are to do THIS. The *order* – why, that is nothing but sounds, ink-marks. –" When we consider an order as mere ink-marks, it seems dead, inert. It seems to us that a bridge is needed to link it with any determinate set of requirements. Interpretation is an obvious candidate to play the role of bridge, but – under the pressure of an insistence that there's a gulf between *any* string of words and what it calls for – every interpretation seems inert as well.

The paradox of *Investigations*, §201 has its roots in the thought that there is always a gulf between the statement of a rule – a string of words – and the rule's execution or application. Let's look again at the first paragraph of §201:

> This was our paradox: no course of action could be determined by a rule, because every course of action can be made out to accord with the rule. The answer was: if everything can be made out to accord with the rule, then it can also be made out to conflict with it. And so there would be neither accord nor conflict here.

In what sense *can* every course of action be made out to accord with a rule? Imagine that a line in a recipe book reads, "Beat six egg whites until stiff peaks form." If, in trying to follow this instruction, I were to beat six egg *yolks*, how could my action be made out to accord with the recipe? The paradox comes into view only under the illumination of a thought like this: "The words 'Beat six egg whites' are just ink-marks in a book. They call for one activity rather than another only on a particular interpretation, and ink-marks can be interpreted *any* which way." Once we are in the grip of such a thought, we cannot escape the conclusion that "any interpretation still hangs in the air along with what it interprets, and cannot give it any support."[26]

Soon, I'm going to claim that Wittgenstein's response to the paradox of §201 is to question the thought that there is a gulf between every rule and what it requires. For now, notice that this is not the course Wright recommends. Wright suggests, in effect, that an appeal to stipulation can solve the problem that we had hoped to address by appealing to interpretation; he argues that even though interpretation cannot bridge the gulf between a rule and its application, stipulation can.

How might stipulation bridge the gulf between a rule and what it requires? Recall the example in which a pamphlet of rules for students has a line reading, "While in class, students shall conduct themselves in an orderly fashion." A teacher stipulates that this rule calls for his students to sit in alphabetical order. Here we could say that by stipulating what the rule requires, the teacher bridges a gulf between the rule as it appears in the pamphlet and its application in his classroom. As it appears in the pamphlet, the rule is imprecise. With his stipulation, the teacher clarifies what sort of behavior would accord with it – at least in his classroom. Now, does it make sense to suggest – as Wright, in effect, does – that this is how rules (and intentional states) quite generally acquire their content?

No. Once we are in the grip of the thought that there is a gulf between *any* rule and its application, stipulation looks as powerless as interpretation to bridge such a gulf. A stipulation, like an interpretation, is made up of *words* – sounds or ink-marks – and being so constituted, it will seem to us to "hang in the air" unless *it* is interpreted (or until a *further* stipulation is made). We've already seen where this goes: we wind up with an infinite regress of inert signs standing behind each other. Wright thinks that our best *opinions* about the requirements of a rule (rather than our interpretations of it) determine what would accord with it. The problem with this view is that any *expression* of such an opinion will seem to stand in need of interpretation or stipulation, and any such interpretation or stipulation will seem to stand in need of a further interpretation or stipulation, *ad infinitum*. Wright's view is subject to the same objection as the view that interpretations determine the requirements of rules: it leads to an infinite regress of meaningless signs.

In order to accept a position like Wright's, we'd have to think that stipulations are regress-stoppers – that although rules and orders, in themselves, have no content, stipulations *do*. We'd have to think that while an order stands in need of a stipulation if it is to be contentful, a meaningful stipulation requires nothing outside itself. Such a view amounts to a (non-standard) form of platonism. According to this sort of platonism, content stipulations are able to do what mere words (that is, all words other than those that make up content-stipulations) cannot; although recipes, instructions, and orders are, in themselves, strings of empty noises, stipulations are (somehow) intrinsically meaningful.

Wright thinks that we can steer clear of both the regress of interpretations and platonism – and thus avoid the paradox of *Investigations*, §201 – by recourse to the idea that we *decide* the requirements of rules. I have argued that he is mistaken. Someone might reply to my argument as follows: "Wright says that our best judgments or opinions determine the requirements of rules. Now, if we think only of judgments rendered *in language*, there *is* a problem with this position – a problem about how the expression of such a judgment could be understood without interpretation or further stipulation. But I might express my best judgment about what, e.g., a particular soufflé recipe requires, by reading the recipe and – without uttering a word – preparing a soufflé. In such a case, I would not generate any sounds or ink-marks, so my decision about what the recipe requires would not stand in need of interpretation or further stipulation. Why not say that what determines the requirements of rules are such wordless expressions of opinion? This would allow us to preserve Wright's basic idea: that we don't intuit the requirements of rules; rather, we decide them."

This attempt to save something like Wright's position fails. The problem is that once we are insisting that words are nothing more than sounds or ink-marks, we'll view my activities, e.g., my examining a page in a book and preparing a soufflé, as meaningless *movements*. There will seem to be a gulf between these movements and any determinate judgment or opinion that they might express (just as – once one has reached this point in the dialectic – there seems to be a gulf between the movements made by a speaker's mouth and any determinate judgment). My movements around the kitchen will seem open to a variety of interpretations – interpretations according to which they express quite various opinions about what the recipe that I'm following requires (or about anything else). And any interpretation of them will stand in need of another. Wright's position cannot be saved. Stipulation – whether it is understood as linguistic or not – provides no better way to avoid the paradox of *Investigations*, §201 than interpretation.

* * *

What moral are we supposed to draw from the *Investigations'* discussion of rule-following? In response to Kripke's commentary – which has often been read as suggesting that the first paragraph of §201 summarizes the main conclusion of the book – a number of writers[27] have pointed out that the *second* paragraph of §201 rejects the line of thought expressed in the first paragraph:

> It can be seen that there is a misunderstanding here from the mere fact that in the course of our argument we give one interpretation after another; as if each one contented us at least for a moment, until we thought of yet another standing behind it. What this shews is that there is a way of grasping a rule which is *not* an *interpretation*, but which is exhibited in what we call "obeying the rule" and "going against it" in actual cases.

The second paragraph of §201 indicates that, according to Wittgenstein, the paradox mentioned in the first paragraph reflects a misunderstanding. The paradox depends upon our thinking that the grasping of *any* rule requires that it first be interpreted. On the reading of Wittgenstein that Wright recommends, one grasps a rule without interpreting it by stipulating what it requires. I take it that Wittgenstein would have us avoid the paradox of *Investigations*, §201 – not by finding a non-interpretative way to bridge a gulf between a rule and its meaning, but – by coming to question the idea that every rule comes with such a gulf. We are led to this idea by a pair of related arguments:

(1) Where it is possible to misapply a rule – and this is always possible – understanding requires that the rule be supplemented. An "act of understanding" is needed in order to insure that there will be no mistakes in the application of the rule. We see, e.g., that the teacher's order (in *Investigations*, §185) *might* be interpreted to mean that one should write "1004" after "1000," and we infer that the order can be grasped only by someone who gives it an adequate *interpretation*, or something like an interpretation – a *stipulation*, perhaps.

(2) In itself, any rule is just a sequence of meaningless noises or ink-marks (or bodily movements). Something must be added to such items if they are to *call for* one activity rather than another. So (once again), an act of understanding is needed in order to bridge the gulf between a rule – viewed as noises or ink-marks – and any determinate set of requirements.

As I read Wittgenstein, both of these arguments are under attack. Let's begin with (1). At *Investigations*, §85, Wittgenstein writes:

> A rule stands there like a sign-post. – Does the sign post leave no doubt open about the way I have to go? ... But where is it said which way I am to follow it; whether in the direction of its finger or (e.g.) in the opposite one?

It is *possible* that on seeing a sign-post in the road, someone with no experience of sign-posts would take it to be pointing in the direction opposite to its finger. But this doesn't mean that for most of us, such a sign-post needs to be supplemented by an interpretation or an explanation in order for it to be understood. For most of us, a sign-post is clear enough:

> Suppose I give this explanation: "I take 'Moses' to mean the man, if there was such a man, who led the Israelites out of Egypt, whatever he was called

then and whatever he may or may not have done besides." – But similar doubts to those about "Moses" are possible about the words of this explanation (what are you calling "Egypt", whom the "Israelites" etc.?). Nor would these questions come to an end when we got down to words like "red", "dark", "sweet". – "But then how does an explanation help me to understand, if after all it is not the final one? In that case the explanation is never completed; so I still don't understand what he means, and never shall!" – As though an explanation as it were hung in the air unless supported by another one. Whereas an explanation may indeed rest on another one that has been given, but none stands in need of another – unless *we* require it to prevent a misunderstanding. One might say: an explanation serves to remove or to avert a misunderstanding — one, that is, that would occur but for the explanation; not every one that I can imagine.

It may easily look as if every doubt merely *revealed* an existing gap in the foundations; so that secure understanding is only possible if we first doubt everything that *can* be doubted, and then remove all these doubts.

The sign-post is in order – if, under normal circumstances, it fulfills its purpose.[28] An interpretation is a kind of explanation. It makes sense to provide an interpretation of a sentence (or a sign-post) when someone has misunderstood it or when there's a real danger that someone will misunderstand it. This is where interpretation has, as it were, its home. When doing philosophy, however, we find ourselves insisting that interpretation is called for wherever we can *imagine* a misunderstanding. An adequate interpretation, we think, is one that would eliminate all chance of anyone's misapplying a sentence or rule. This reflects a misunderstanding about the purpose of interpretation. Once we have succumbed to this misunderstanding, interpretation stops making sense to us. It looks pointless.

A child might misunderstand the instruction, "Beat six egg whites until stiff peaks form." (She might have no idea that eggs can be separated. She might think "stiff" means *stiff as a board*.) It doesn't follow that *I* need an interpretation in order to understand these words when I encounter them in a cookbook. For me, there is no gulf between such an instruction and what it requires; I see what it calls for – without the need for interpretation or explanation.

At this point, someone might introduce a version of argument (2) from above: "But isn't the instruction in your recipe book really just a series of dead ink-marks? Don't you need to interpret the marks in order to bring them to life? Or if it isn't interpretation that brings a sign to life, mustn't it then be an assignment of meaning – a stipulation?"

At *Investigations*, §432, Wittgenstein writes: "Every sign *by itself* seems dead. *What* gives it life? – In use it is *alive*." Wittgenstein does not agree that signs are dead until we interpret them or stipulate what they mean. A sign only *seems* dead if we consider it *by itself* – i.e., apart from the use that we make of it. In its use, a sign is *alive*. The following passage (part of which we've already seen) has a similar moral: "How does it come about this arrow ››——› *points*? . . . The arrow points only in the application that a living being makes of it."[29] If we view the arrow as cut off from the activities of human beings, it *will* seem that only an interpretation or a stipulation could give it life – could make it point. (There's nothing special about arrows; this is true of any sign.) As we've seen, we cannot provide a general account of how signs get their meaning by appealing to interpretation or stipulation. The conclusion that Wittgenstein draws from this is not that we must succumb to skepticism about meaning – succumb, that is, to the view that signs are in fact dead. Rather, Wittgenstein would have us realize that we need not view the arrow as cut off from the activities of living beings. "In use it is *alive*."

Are our signs – arrows, words, etc. – really just dead ink-marks, squiggles on the page? I've noticed that if I stare at written English words for a long time, they begin to *seem* like squiggles. (It helps to squint a little.) But it makes sense for me to say this only thanks to the *distinction* between squiggles and English words. My copy of *The Joy of Cooking* does contain ink-marks, but ink-marks of *that* sort figure in our lives in all sorts of ways that meaningless squiggles don't. If a book contained *mere* ink-marks – empty squiggles – it would be very odd to suggest that someone should try to *follow* some of them.

Wittgenstein is continually reminding us that the phenomena in which he is interested – e.g., providing interpretations, ostensively defining, reading, making a move in a game of chess, feeling pain – make sense only when "surrounded by certain normal manifestations of life."[30] As long as we try to mentally undress words – to strip away the context and understand them as squiggles – we will be unable to make sense of the suggestion that "there is a way of grasping a rule which is *not* an *interpretation*." How could someone understand a squiggle unless he first attached some interpretation to it? By stipulation? If someone merely *stipulates* that a squiggle means, e.g., *dice three medium onions*, he isn't *understanding* a recipe; he's making one up. (And if *these* words are just noises, he's not even managing that.) When I open a cookbook and see "Beat six egg whites," I don't encounter a squiggle; in the context of the way we live with words, recipes, food, kitchens and each other, that sentence calls for a quite specific activity.[31] Strip away the context, however, and you won't be able to make sense of the idea that the ink-marks that remain call for me to do anything.

The thought that, in reality, words are no more than squiggles has come to seem innocuous (and indeed goes unnoticed) by many contemporary philosophers.[32] But the thought is *not* innocuous; it causes us to lose our grip on important and obvious distinctions – such as that between vague, imperspicuous rules, like the one calling for "orderly" behavior from students, and clear, precise ones, such as are found in good cookbooks. While the former stand in need of supplementation – interpretation or stipulation – the latter generally do not. We might say that a cookbook's instructions autonomously call for quite specific activities in the kitchen.

4 Wittgenstein's response to platonism

Wright's Wittgenstein hears any talk of a rule autonomously calling for one activity rather than another as an expression of platonism:

> Platonism is, precisely, the view that the correctness of a rule-informed judgment is a matter quite independent of any opinion of ours, whether the states of affairs which confer correctness are thought of as man-made –

constituted by over-and-done-with episodes of explanation and linguistic behaviour – or truly platonic and constituted in heaven.[33]

[W]e have no model of what constitutes the direction taken by a rule . . . once the direction is conceived, after the fashion of platonism, as determined autonomously . . . .[34]

These passages express a misunderstanding of the role that the platonist plays in Wittgenstein's dialectic. The 'platonist' – in so far as this term is supposed to name someone who figures as a target in the dialectic – is not merely someone who allows himself to say that a rule autonomously calls for this or that. Wittgenstein's platonist is someone who, first, unthinkingly agrees that there is a gulf between any rule and its application, and then imagines items that have a mysterious power to bridge the gulf. (Moreover the platonist imagines that he *explains* something by saying that certain items have this power. He claims to explain the connection between a rule and its application by saying, in effect: "Certain items have the power to reach out to all of their applications." The problem with saying this is *not* that there are no items which reach out to their applications (rules *are* such items!), but that the platonist has done nothing more than describe what he promised to explain – adding, misleadingly, that what's going on is mysterious.)

Let us consider again *Investigations*, §454 – the section about the arrow's pointing – this time looking at a bit more of it:

> How does it come about that this arrow ››»——› *points*? Doesn't it seem to carry in it something besides itself? – "No, not the dead line on paper; only the psychical thing, the meaning, can do that." – That is both true and false. The arrow points only in the application that a living being makes of it.
>
> This pointing is *not* a hocus-pocus which can be performed only by the soul.

As we saw above, the question about how the arrow manages to point arises only because we are inclined to view it as a dead mark on paper; we forget that such marks have a life in the activities of human beings. The platonist is someone who – seeing the arrow as dead – supposes that it manages to point thanks to some "psychical thing" associated with it. This account of how the arrow points looks spooky even to the platonist himself. In viewing our words as dead noises and marks, the platonist imagines them divorced from the practices in which they participate and the states of mind that they express. This leaves both words *and* states of mind seeming unconnected to anything. What Wittgenstein calls "the weave of our life"[35] comes to seem unraveled, and its strands – whether they be items encountered on the page or in the mind – seem incapable of meaning anything. The platonist maintains that even so, words and thoughts somehow manage to have content, but it seems mind-boggling to him that they should.

According to Wittgenstein, the platonist isn't wrong in thinking that our words and thoughts have content; he's wrong to find it mind-boggling that they should. Consider the following passage from *Investigations*, §195:

"But I don't mean that what I do now (in grasping a sense) determines the future use *causally* and as a matter of experience, but that in a *queer* way, the use itself is in some sense present." – But of course it is, 'in some sense'! Really the only thing wrong with what you say is the expression "in a queer way".

Typically, Wittgenstein's response to platonism is not, "What you're saying is *false*," but rather, "What you say is all right; only there's nothing queer or magical about it." Wittgenstein doesn't deny that when I grasp the sense of a rule, the steps that I'm supposed to take are, in some sense, already present to my mind. (He doesn't think – as Wright thinks – that the question of which steps I'm supposed to take awaits determination by decision.) The platonist's problem is not that he wants to say that the steps are present, but that he imagines that *in* saying this, he's remarking on a mind-boggling fact.

Most of the platonist's words can be uttered innocently by someone who doesn't try to view signs apart from the applications that living beings make of them – apart, that is, from "the weave of our life." At *Investigations*, §218, an interlocutor says, "The rule, once stamped with a particular meaning, traces the lines along which it is to be followed through the whole of space." An utterance of these words *might* be an expression of platonism, but it might be an innocent example of what Wittgenstein calls a "grammatical remark" about rules. Wittgenstein is not denying that rules reach out to their infinity of applications; he's urging us to free ourselves from a conception of what rules are in themselves according to which a rule's "reaching out to its applications" can be understood only as a sort of magical gulf-bridging.[36]

Wright's response to platonism fails to address it at the right depth. The platonist's crucial mistake is one that he shares with both Kripke's skeptic and with Wright, namely, imagining that there's a gulf between every rule and its application. We overcome the impulse toward platonism only by coming to recognize this mistake as a mistake.

According to Wright and Wright's Wittgenstein, to say that a rule autonomously calls for this or that activity is to commit oneself to platonism. I've been arguing that this is not Wittgenstein's view. The platonist who figures in Wittgenstein's texts is someone who first imagines that there's a gulf between every rule and its application, and only then thinks that somehow, mysteriously, the rule (or its meaning, or something) autonomously manages to call for one activity rather than another. Once we stop thinking of words in isolation from the human lives in which they are embedded – once we give up imagining that there's a gulf between every rule and its application – we can say, innocently, that a particular rule autonomously called for this or that.[37]

* * *

"So what you're saying is that, while Wright's Wittgenstein thinks stipulation is what connects a rule with its correct applications, your Wittgenstein thinks it's 'the weave of our life'?"

The point is *not* that "the weave of our life" (or customs or institutions[38]) – rather than stipulation or interpretation – is what bridges the gulf between the statement of a rule and what would satisfy it. It would be better to say that when rules are seen as situated *within* our lives, such gulfs are exceptional. In general, *nothing* bridges a gulf between a rule and its application because no gulf opens up. It makes sense to speak of such a gulf only against a backdrop of cases in which there is no difficulty about what the statement of a rule means. *Sometimes*, I come upon an instruction that I don't understand. In such a situation, an interpretation might be what I need, but in general, I need *nothing* of the sort. A philosopher who asks, "How is it that the statement of a rule is connected to its meaning?" has – even before she's offered any answer to the question – already succumbed to the idea that some link is needed if our words are to have significance; she presupposes that there is always a gulf between words and their meanings. Wittgenstein is not offering another account of the connection between words and their meanings. He is urging us to question our inclination to search for any such account: "If it is asked: 'How do sentences manage to represent?', – the answer might be: 'Don't you know? You certainly see it, when you use them.' For nothing is concealed."[39]

Wright claims that the best answer to Kripke's skeptic is flat-footed (i.e., one that goes, "The fact about my past usage of 'plus' that fixes it that I am now acting in accord with what I then meant by 'plus' is just that I meant *plus* by 'plus'"). This is exactly right; the flat-footed response to Kripke's skeptic embodies a refusal to accept the skeptic's implicit insistence that *something* must link a person's words with what he means by them. Wright fails, however, to understand the significance of the flat-footed response. He *says* that it's the correct response, but in his attempt to justify it, he recommends a response that is anything but flat-footed – one that says, in effect: "What fixes it that in the past I meant *plus* by 'plus' is that I now judge that I meant *plus* by 'plus'." To Wright, the flat-footed response *by itself* appears to avoid a genuine question – a question that he formulates as follows: "[W]hat constitutes the truth of rule-informed judgment"?[40] But to understand Wittgenstein is to see that he thinks there is no real question here. The point is not that Wright's words express a question which Wittgenstein thinks we must "quietistically" avoid. According to Wittgenstein, it is only when we conceive of words as cut off from the applications that living beings make of them that there even appears to be a question concerning how, in general, rule-informed judgments – e.g., the judgment that a particular recipe calls for the beating of egg whites – can be true. Freed from such a picture of words, we can meet a query like: "What constitutes the truth of your judgment that the recipe calls for the beating of egg whites (rather than yolks or heavy cream)?" with a genuinely flat-footed response: "It *says* to beat egg whites. You can look for yourself."[41]

Notes

1 *Wittgenstein on Rules and Private Language*, Cambridge, MA, Harvard University Press, 1982.
2 *Philosophical Investigations*, §454.
3 This characterization should be understood as provisional in that how *it* is to be understood – how, e.g., we should hear the term "self-standing" in this context – will be part of what's at issue in what follows.
4 *The Blue and Brown Books*, p. 34.

5 Wittgenstein depicts the platonist's sense that communication requires guessing in passages such as the following:

> "But do you really explain to the other person what you yourself understand? Don't you get him to *guess* the essential thing? You give examples, – but he has to guess their drift . . . ."
>
> *(Investigations*, §210)

> "Once he has seen the right thing, seen the one of infinitely many references which I am trying to push him towards – once he has got hold of it, he will continue the series right without further ado. I grant that he can only guess (intuitively guess) the reference that I mean – but once he has managed that the game is won."
>
> *(Zettel*, §304)

6 Compare the game just described with a well-known example that Wittgenstein presents in the context of a discussion of pain: "Suppose everyone had a box with something in it: we call it a 'beetle'. No one can look into anyone else's box, and everyone says he knows what a beetle is only by looking at *his* beetle" *(Investigations*, §293). Although I can't take up the issue in this paper, I'd argue that according to Wittgenstein, the same philosophical pressures that underlie platonism about meaning also underlie a picture of sensations as mind-bogglingly private.

7 Kripke, *Wittgenstein on Rules and Private Language*, op. cit., p. 66.

8 On the one hand, Kripke says that although Wittgenstein might resist admitting it in so many words, he concedes to the skeptic that there are no facts of the matter concerning what we mean:

> Wittgenstein, perhaps cagily, might well disapprove of the straightforward formulation [of his response to skepticism] given here. Nevertheless I choose to be so bold as to say: Wittgenstein holds, with the sceptic, that there is no fact as to whether I mean plus or quus.
>
> (ibid., pp. 70–71)

On the other hand, Kripke ascribes a deflationist view of facts to Wittgenstein:

> Like many others, Wittgenstein accepts the 'redundancy' theory of truth: to affirm that a statement is true (or presumably, to precede it with 'It is a fact that . . .') is simply to affirm the statement itself, and to say it is not true is to deny it: ('*p*' is true = *p*).
>
> (ibid., p. 86)

Moreover, he suggests that Wittgenstein would not "wish to deny the propriety of an ordinary use of the phrase 'the fact that Jones meant addition by such-and-such symbol'" (ibid., p. 69). There is a tension between these two strands in Kripke's reading of Wittgenstein – a tension that makes it hard to see just what the "skeptical solution" is supposed to come to.

9 See, e.g., C. Wright, "Wittgenstein's rule-following considerations and the central project of theoretical linguistics," in *Reflections on Chomsky*, A. George (ed.), Oxford, Basil Blackwell, 1989, pp. 233–264:

> According to Kripke's Wittgenstein, all our discourse concerning meaning, understanding, content, and cognate notions, fails of strict factuality – says nothing literally true or false – and is saved from vacuity only by a 'Sceptical Solution', a set of proposals for rehabilitating meaning-talk in ways that prescind from the assignment to it of any fact-stating role.
>
> (p. 234)

For other readings of Kripke that more or less agree with this characterization of the skeptical solution, see, e.g., G. Baker and P. Hacker, *Scepticism, Rules and Language*, Oxford, Basil Blackwell, 1984, p. 4; P. A. Boghossian, "The rule-following considerations," *Mind*, vol. 98, 1989, pp. 508–549 (see p. 518); and J. McDowell, "Meaning and intentionality in Wittgenstein's later philosophy," *Midwest Studies in Philosophy*, vol. 17, 1992, pp. 40–52 (see p. 43). I'm familiar with two commentators who argue that, contrary to the received reading of Kripke, Kripke's Wittgenstein does *not* concede that attributions of meaning must be non-factual. See A. Byrne, "On misinterpreting Kripke's Wittgenstein," *Philosophy and Phenomenological Research*, vol. 56 (2), June 1996, and G. M. Wilson, "Semantic realism and Kripke's Wittgenstein," *Philosophy and Phenomenological Research*, vol. 58 (1), March 1998, pp. 99–122.

10 E.g., J. McDowell, "Wittgenstein on following a rule," *Synthese*, vol. 58 (3), 1984, pp. 325–363; C. McGinn, *Wittgenstein on Meaning*, Oxford, Basil Blackwell, 1984; and W. Goldfarb, "Kripke on Wittgenstein and rules," *Journal of Philosophy*, vol. 82, 1985, pp. 471–488.

11 Wright, "Wittgenstein's rule-following considerations," op. cit., p. 236; cf. C. Wright, "Critical notice," *Mind*, vol. 98, 1989, pp. 289–305, especially p. 292.

12 Wright, "Wittgenstein's rule-following considerations," op. cit., p. 236.

13 Ibid., p. 237.

14 Ibid., p. 240; Wright, "Critical notice," op. cit., p. 300.

15 Wright, "Wittgenstein's rule-following considerations," op. cit., p. 246.

16 See ibid., p. 262, fn. 28.

17 Wright recommends the same sort of story in connection with intentional states. He suggests that "subjects' best opinions determine, rather than reflect what it is true to say about their intentional states" (ibid., p. 250); moreover, he takes it that intentional state *avowals* are, generally, expressions of a subject's best opinions. Typically, according to this view, when I say that I, e.g., intend to bake a cake, I make it the case that baking a cake is what I intend to do:

> [W]hy is it *a priori* reasonable to believe that, provided Jones has the relevant concepts and is attentive to the matter, he will believe that he intends to phi if and only if he does? ... [T]he matter will be nicely explained if the concept of intention works in such a way that Jones's opinions, formed under the restricted set of C-conditions, play [an] extension-determining role ....
>
> (ibid., p. 252)

18 Ibid., p. 254.

19 He suggests that "subjects' best opinions about their intentions, *both past and present*, are properly conceived as provisionally extension-determining" (ibid., p. 254, Wright's emphasis).

20 In a footnote to his "Wittgenstein's rule-following considerations," op. cit., Wright identifies G. Baker and P. Hacker, *Wittgenstein: Understanding and Meaning*, Oxford, Basil Blackwell, 1980 as a paradigmatic expression of "official" Wittgensteinianism, noting that McDowell's "Wittgenstein on following a rule," op. cit., might be one as well.

21 Wright, "Wittgenstein's rule-following considerations," op. cit., p. 257.

22 Wright, "Critical notice," op. cit., p. 305.

23 Wright, "Wittgenstein's rule-following considerations," op. cit., p. 246.

24 See Wright, "Critical notice," op. cit., p. 305.

25 Compare *Investigations*, §433:

> When we give an order, it can look as if the ultimate thing sought by the order had to remain unexpressed, as there is always a gulf between an order and its execution. Say I want someone to make a particular movement, say to raise his arm. To make it quite clear, I do the movement. This picture seems unambiguous till we ask: how does he know that *he is to make that movement?* – How does he know at all what use he is to make of the signs I give him, whatever they are? – Perhaps I shall

now try to supplement the order by means of further signs, by pointing from myself to him, making encouraging gestures, etc. Here it looks as if the order were beginning to stammer.

26 *Investigations*, §198.
27 E.g., McDowell, "Wittgenstein on following a rule," op. cit., and McGinn, *Wittgenstein on Meaning*, op. cit.
28 *Investigations*, §87.
29 *Investigations*, §454.
30 *Zettel*, §534.
31 This is not to deny that there is a *subpersonal* story to be told by cognitive psychology about how my visual system processes patterns of light and dark when I read a book. But when I peruse *The Joy of Cooking*, *I* don't interpret patterns of light and dark. *I* see instructions. (My seeing instructions is made possible by – among other things – my visual system's processing patterns of light and dark.)
32 *Why* such a thought has come to seem innocuous – what additional assumptions contribute to making it seem irresistible – is a topic that would take us beyond the scope of this paper. In order to address it, we would have to explore the way in which modern science has left us with what John McDowell calls a "disenchanted" conception of nature (in his *Mind and World*, Cambridge, MA., Harvard University Press, 1994).
33 Wright, "Wittgenstein's rule-following considerations," op. cit., p. 257.
34 Wright, "Critical notice," op. cit., p. 301.
35 The phrase is from *Investigations*, p. 174:

> "Grief" describes a pattern which recurs, with different variations, in the weave of our life. If a man's bodily expression of sorrow and of joy alternated, say with the ticking of a clock, here we should not have the characteristic formation of the pattern of sorrow or of the pattern of joy.

36 John McDowell suggests that "we can *always* frame threats of platonistic mythology, as they figure in Wittgenstein's landscape, on the pattern of *Investigations* §195." He continues:

> The following is not a Wittgensteinian exchange, though on Wright's reading it ought to be: 'An intention determines what counts as conformity to it autonomously and independently of any subsequent judgements of its author' – 'Platonism! Anathema!' The following is: 'An intention in some sense determines, in a *queer* way, what counts as conformity to it autonomously and independently of any subsequent judgements of its author.' – 'But of course it does, "in *some* sense"! Really the only thing wrong with what you say is the expression "in a queer way".'
> (p. 54 of "Response to Wright," in *Knowing Our Own Minds*, C. Wright, B.C. Smith, and C. Macdonald (eds.), Oxford, Oxford University Press, 1998, pp. 47-62)

37 We should not let the various ways in which the term "platonism" may be deployed obscure the crucial point here – that, according to Wittgenstein, someone might utter most of the platonist's words without falling into a conception of rules as mind-boggling. Indeed, although I won't speak this way, I would not object much to saying that what Wittgenstein is recommending is an innocent *kind* of platonism. In other words, we might grant Wright that *anyone* who affirms that a rule can autonomously call for one thing rather than another is to be called a "platonist," and then say that according to Wittgenstein there is a truistic, unmetaphysical kind of platonism which does not commit one to seeing rules (or their meanings) as mind-boggling. McDowell speaks this way about Wittgenstein and platonism in his *Mind and World*, op. cit. McDowell distinguishes what he calls "naturalized platonism" – a position he endorses and that he reads Wittgenstein as recommending – from a problematic kind of platonism that he calls "rampant platonism":

[N]aturalized platonism is quite distinct from rampant platonism. In rampant platonism, the rational structure within which meaning comes into view is independent of anything merely human, so that the capacity of our minds to resonate to it looks occult or magical. Naturalized platonism is platonistic in that the structure of the space of reasons has a sort of autonomy; it is not derivative from, or reflective of, truths about human beings that are capturable independently of having that structure in view. But this platonism is not rampant: the structure of the space of reasons is not constituted in splendid isolation from anything merely human.

(p. 92)

If I understand McDowell, his "rampant platonism" is what I have been referring to as "platonism," and what he calls "naturalized platonism" is close to the approach to these issues that I've been attributing to Wittgenstein.

McDowell is not the only commentator who characterizes Wittgenstein as an innocent sort of platonist. Writing about platonism in the philosophy of mathematics, W.W. Tait distinguishes between an "unintelligible" kind of platonism according to which there is a mathematical reality that is wholly "independent of our practice and which adjudicates its correctness" (p. 361 of "Truth and proof: the Platonism of mathematics," *Synthese*, vol. 69, 1986, pp. 341–370), and an innocent sort of platonism which appears "not as a substantive philosophy or foundation of mathematics, but as a *truism*" (p. 342). According to Tait, what Wittgenstein attacks is "a particular picture of Platonism" (p. 348) and what he defends is a "version of Platonism" (p. 348) – where this latter version of platonism is to be equated with "our ordinary conception of mathematics" (p. 353).

My reason for not wanting to say that Wittgenstein endorses an innocent kind of platonism is that this way of describing what he's up to is liable to give the impression that he is playing the same game as his interlocutors – that he is trying to explain what it is that links a rule with its applications. As will become clear in the remainder of this paper, I take this to be a serious misreading of Wittgenstein's intentions.

38 At *Investigations*, §198, Wittgenstein writes, "To obey a rule, to make a report, to give an order, to play a game of chess, are *customs* (uses, institutions)." One will misunderstand Wittgenstein if one takes passages such as this one to be offering an answer to a question like, "What bridges the gulf between a rule and what it requires?" (For a reading along these lines, see D. Bloor, *Wittgenstein: A Social Theory of Knowledge*, New York, Columbia University Press, 1983.) Wittgenstein speaks of the customs and institutions in which our words have a life for the same reason that he speaks of the weave of our life – not to answer such questions, but to bring out what is wrong with them.

39 *Investigations*, §435.
40 Wright, "Wittgenstein's rule-following considerations," op. cit., p. 257.
41 This paper owes obvious debts to writings on Wittgenstein by Cora Diamond and John McDowell. In addition, I'm grateful to Annette Baier, Alice Crary, Cora Diamond, Samantha Fenno, Kimberly Keller, Michael Morgan, and Rupert Read for helpful comments on earlier drafts. Finally, I am especially indebted to James Conant and John McDowell for many illuminating conversations about this material.

4

WHAT 'THERE CAN BE NO SUCH THING AS MEANING ANYTHING BY ANY WORD' COULD POSSIBLY MEAN

Rupert Read

'There can be no such thing as meaning anything by any word.'[1]

This sentence, if such it is, has rightly been taken to be the conclusion of Saul Kripke's famous line of argument beginning with his 'quus' thought-experiment. That is, the thought-experiment which has us doubt whether we have any grounds for denying that by the word 'plus' we might in fact *mean* 'quus', where 'quus' yields the same as 'plus' for sums with answers up to 125, but for sums with notionally higher answers it simply and always yields 5.[2] As W.W. Tait and many others have made clear, after Kripke, the meaning-nihilism induced by this 'sceptical paradox' 'would apply equally well to all meaningful uses of language',[3] not just to contexts such as arithmetic where the rules concerned are typically made explicit.

And Kripke's conclusion has rightly been taken also to be completely unacceptable; for one thing, because it is self-refuting – as *Kripke himself* observes.[4]

What do I mean here by 'rightly been taken'? I mean that, if we allow that Kripke's thought-experiment can so much as be coherently stated,[5] we are bound to take the argument's conclusion as not being merely about 'facts about individuals'. That is, the conclusion is not merely that individuals alone cannot succeed in meaning things but require the presence of a community to do so.[6] No. As Kripke makes clear at a couple of points,[7] the correct conclusion to draw from his argument, if it could be coherently stated, would be simply and drastically that the idea of words having meaning at all entirely evaporates.

Whatever *that* could possibly mean. . . . For let us be absolutely clear: according to Kripke's argument, it's not just that there are no facts about (say) me to ground meaning, it's supposedly that there are *no* meaning-facts, no facts about meaning, at all.[8] Thus the term 'meaning' in the context of Kripke's argument need not be thought of as a full-blown theoretical notion but only in a fairly 'minimal' sense. That is, simply as what is meant and understood in instances of language use. Meaning as use, meaning-in-use, or meaning as *immanent in* use (not meaning merely as mention, nor meaning as static, nor as the subject of some museum-myth) – *that* is the inevitable target of Kripke's argument, as he intended it.

Am I *equivocating* between public meaning and so-called 'speaker meaning', between the meaning of a word and what a speaker means by a word at a given time? I think not – for the latter is conceptually dependent upon the former. I follow Wittgenstein in taking use to be paramount, such that 'speaker meaning' (and also 'conversational implicature', *etc. etc.*) is only a special case of (public) meaning, of meaning *in* use. Kripke's subject-matter – intention, 'speaker' meaning, and so on – is only a special (or even parasitic) case of ordinary common-or-garden linguistic meaning.

Or am I *omitting an interpretive possibility*, the option that Kripke may indeed be arguing for a 'non-factualist' thesis about meaning (or 'content'), but that this is something short of a complete meaning-nihilism? [9] That, rather, 'non-factualism' may be a way of preserving meaning-talk, albeit at the cost of its having an inferior status to what we might have wished? Again I think not, for the following reasons.

Either non-factualism is the same as meaning-nihilism, or it is less severe than it. If the two are the same, then clearly the pro-'non-factualism' objection to my argument thus far is nullified. If it is less severe, then what *is* it? One supposes that it is the view that we can without impropriety carry on talking about meanings even though there are no facts about meanings. But here two difficulties are encountered.

Firstly, if one is a deflationist about truth, as Kripke's Wittgenstein, drawing on Wittgenstein's approval of a 'redundancy' view of truth, is,[10] then one cannot have non-factualism *as opposed to* something else. But non-factualism only works for one domain if it does not work for some other domain which can function as a contrast-class, if one requires there a factualist picture of discourse. Deflationism about truth undercuts this contrast. Deflationism leaves no role for the purported possibility of talk about meanings without facts about meanings, because it is deflationist about fact-talk, about truth-talk. If, like Kripke's Wittgenstein, one endorses deflationism about truth, then one cannot be accurately described as a non-factualist about meaning!

Secondly, even if there were some way to have Kripke's Wittgenstein emerge coherently from that desperate quandary, and we then had in our possession some account of how it is that non-factualism can be a coherent possibility for how to read Kripke, we would be faced with the following awkward fact: that such a putative 'moderate' non-factualism, less severe than meaning-nihilism, fails to capture the letter of Kripke's text. For Kripke does not write, when telling us what his arguments have shown, that 'There is no fact about me, or about you, for meaning ascriptions to correspond to'. Nor does he even write, 'There is no fact for meaning ascriptions to correspond to', though that would be drastic enough. He writes, simply and plainly, 'There can be no such thing as meaning anything by any word'! That he sometimes gives the weaker formulations elsewhere in his text should not distract us from that fact that at the most crucial moments it is meaning-nihilism which is claimed to have been proven by 'Kripke's Wittgenstein'. A putative moderate non-factualist thesis could be discussed philosophically – but it would not accurately capture the extremity of the would-be position apparently enunciated in Kripke's text.

Finally, I take Paul Boghossian to have proven in 'The status of content' that in any case non-factualism, *considered as a thesis,* is incoherent, self-refuting in much the same manner that 'There can be no such thing as meaning anything by any word' is.[11] In which case, the resort to a non-factualist reading of Kripke does not help to moderate Kripke's claims at all!

So then, what I mean to say is this: that the would-be Kripkean evaporation of meaning, this meaning-nihilism, is not to be restricted to one area of language (e.g. maths), but is putatively fully general, and would undermine the truism that there is something more than a merely psychological difference between apparently mean-ingful linguistic strings, on the one hand, and plain nonsense, mere noise, on the other. And I mean that this clearly is an intolerable would-be conclusion, that a *modus tollens* is in order, and that the evisceration of meaning of even 'There can be no such thing as meaning anything by any word' by itself might be the clearest of all indications of this.[12]

But wait. Can it really be right to take a major philosopher of logic to have entertained such a peculiar, such a fantastically extreme 'scepticism', let alone to have attributed it to Wittgenstein? For Wittgenstein would surely have undercut its very imagining, as several commentators interested in the accuracy of Kripke's interpretation have since made plain. Here is Tait, for instance: 'Wittgenstein intended no sceptical paradox or sceptical solution: rather, he was attempting, successfully in my opinion, to clarify confusions which underlie the appearance of paradox.'[13]

So could mine possibly be the right way to take 'Wittgenstein's argument as it struck Kripke'? Especially, furthermore, when a number of commentators on Kripke have apparently not found such extreme (self-defeating) consequences to follow inevitably from the sceptical argument?[14] Well, of course, these cautionary consid-erations are hardly decisive; these folks, and Kripke in particular, *might* all be somewhat confused. But at the very least – even were one to hold that this were so – one ought to try to explain a little bit *why.* I want to essay an account of why it is philosophically attractive – and dangerous – to equivocate on what the conclu-sion of Kripke's argument *is.* And to suggest how such equivocation can appear for example to avert the necessity of choosing, as I shall endeavour to force one to choose, between a true (but unoriginal) conclusion, on the one hand, and some-thing deeply confused, incoherent, on the other.

Here is a possible partial explanation of where the confusion comes from here: Kripke's 'quus' idea, focused as it is on bizarre renditions or interpretations of *indi-vidual* words (viz. 'plus', 'green'), discourages one from bearing in mind what the units of linguistic meaning normally *are.* That is, one focuses on individual words, forgetting Frege's dictum that, as we might put it, the minimum unit of linguistic significance is properly the sentence. Let alone Wittgenstein's 'dictum' that in a certain sense the minimum unit of linguistic significance is properly the whole language-game – that, just as words normally mean only in the context of sentences, so sentences normally mean only in the context of languages.[15] (I should perhaps add that, following Cora Diamond,[16] I would actually read Frege's dictum as being much more strongly anticipative of Wittgenstein's than the conventional wisdom teaches. Because, for example, if one wants to distinguish between whether a word in a given sentence means a concept or an object, as Frege does, one will need from the very start to consider inferential relations between the judgements expressed by that sentence and by other sentences. But I cannot go into this interpretive question further here.)

Frege's dictum, his injunction 'never to ask for the meaning of a word in isolation, but only in the context of a proposition',[17] is, I take it, a basic tool for understanding what it makes sense to say about language and thought, and moreover is putatively widely accepted. It might even be argued to be a philosophical principle, if there are any, of the 'Analytic' tradition – unlike Wittgenstein's more controversial Holistic 'extension' of it (even if all Wittgenstein was actually doing was spelling out what Frege's dictum implies). One has to take a strongly psychologistic stance or uphold some other version of a 'museum-myth' of meaning in order to object to it as a methodological principle. (At any rate, I shall assume its basic viability henceforth – while recognizing that I have not offered a *defence* of it, and that, as with anything in philosophy, some people would object to it. The most common cry the objectors make is that Frege's context principle is irreconcilable with compositionality, that it makes our understanding of new sentences completely mysterious. Diamond, Palmer and other philosophers have I think offered an effective defence of Frege against this objection and others.[18])

Of course, there are apparent exceptions to Frege's dictum. As Wittgenstein wrote,

> *For a large class of cases – though not for all –* in which we employ the word 'meaning' it can be defined thus: the meaning of a word is its use in the language.
> And the meaning of a name is sometimes explained by pointing to its bearer.[19]

Thus the name 'Saul Kripke' on a door in a Philosophy Department, or on a name tag at a conference, can be quite reasonably said to have a meaning, even though there is no sentence involved. Similarly with cases like the appearance of words on a shopping-list, labels on bottles; even the shout, 'Saul!' when one espies a certain figure in the distance. And dictionaries do tell one what single words mean.

It would be quite unnecessarily forced to treat all these cases as involving condensed 'sentences', but not unreasonable to treat them all as involving linguistic meaning – *so long as* one is not then fooled into thinking that the meanings of sentences are simply compounds of such meanings, or that all words are 'really' names.[20]

So, Frege's dictum is not to be treated as a thesis, a philosophical straitjacket, into which every case must be fitted. To give a close analogy: Wittgenstein's deflationary discussion of the claim that we must say that 'Slab!' in the Builders' language-game is elliptical for our sentence 'Bring me a slab!' strongly resists the urge to theorize here, the urge to give an all-purpose account of when we must say something is a sentence, or is elliptical, *etc.*[21] The point of my discussion is in a way simply the trivial grammatical point, the reminder, that words have meaning *in use*. And by far the most contexts of use are contexts essentially involving sentences.

Having refreshed our memories as to the importance for Frege and Wittgenstein of resisting an 'additive' conception of linguistic meaning, let us look again at that memorable, hyperbolic string of Kripke's: 'There can be no such thing as meaning anything by any word.' Perhaps we can now start to see how there *may* in fact be an interpretation of this set of words available such that it need not be the apex of an extreme, self-refuting, incoherent 'scepticism'. Let us, that is, be as charitable as we can be in reading Kripke. Let us try to find something that this linguistic string could mean, some sentence that it could actually be.

THERE CAN BE NO SUCH THING AS MEANING ANYTHING BY ANY *PARTICULAR* WORD, *CONSIDERED INDIVIDUALLY.*[22] If Frege is right, then this is right; Kripke's conclusion even comes out as *true*, when read as being strictly about *isolated* words! Certain special exceptions such as those discussed above aside, it is only in the context of a sentence – that is, a linguistic string having meaning in a language, and being used to do something – that one can truly speak of something being meant by a word. For example, one means addition by 'plus' only in the context of a sentence. Not if one is just staring at a '+' symbol, or lumping it together with some other symbols.

We might venture the following: that Kripke is still too much in the same boat as those who in general one might dub 'semantic theorists', for he covertly holds something in common with them, something I'll come to in a moment. Granted, he sees (albeit darkly) that they're wrong-headed in, for example, holding out hope for a combinatorial semantics to *ground* meaning, to vouchsafe facts of the matter on which to *found* assertions *etc.*, and thus his arguments in Section 2 of his book, when read purely negatively, have rightly been widely understood to present a powerful challenge to certain philosophical *theories* (of meaning, reference, *etc.*); i.e., if the question is not 'Do our words mean anything?' but rather, 'Are there metaphysical arguments available to provide philosophical foundations for meaning?' then Kripke's Wittgenstein indeed poses a challenge. Semantic theorists and philosophers of language are anxious to respond to this substantial challenge – so they tend to pass over the self-refuting nature (let alone the unstatability) of the form of the challenge which we actually find in Kripke's text, and instead they engage their own substantive theses directly with 'Kripkenstein's' supposed 'thesis' of non-factualism about meaning. Meanwhile, Kripke himself wrongly draws a 'sceptical' moral from his powerful negative challenge, a moral along the following lines: *if a word means nothing individually, how can it possibly do so compositionally either?* '[T]he entire idea of meaning vanishes into thin air.'[23]

No. All that vanishes is *a tempting but ultimately wholly worthless picture* of sentence-meanings being the result of 'adding together' the meanings of individual words.[24] But that picture has not been thoroughly extirpated from semantics, from the philosophy of language. Regrettably, it retains some attraction to *both* Kripke (as evidenced by his being tempted by the 'sceptical' moral) *and* his 'Meaning-Realist' opponents. We need to truly realize the primacy of sentential meaning, if we are not to oscillate endlessly between meaning-nihilism on the one hand and an (endless) 'research programme' of constructive/systematic efforts to refute it (through semantic compositionality, through 'dispositional' accounts, *etc. etc.*) on the other.

The mistake made by (psychologistic, *etc.*) semanticists and the like is, I am claiming, the implicit rejection of Frege's context principle. Kripke's argument, I have just argued, depends upon *just such* an implicit rejection of Frege, in order to get going (and in order to seem exciting). But Kripke is then in a rather absurd – indeed, incoherent – 'position' when he attacks the positions of those (the semanticists) with whom he has such an important thing in common, when he attacks them with his negative arguments against the dispositional theory of meaning, *etc.*

etc. . . . and when furthermore he ends up enunciating a conclusion that can only be meaningful at all if it is read as an implicit *affirmation* of the context principle!

What I have presented in the above discussion is one way of understanding why Kripke's summary presentation of 'the Kripkensteinian paradox', at the opening of Section 3 (the culminative section) of his book, is so misleading:

[i] The sceptical argument, then, remains unanswered.
[ii] There can be no such thing as meaning anything by any word.
[iii] Each new application we make is a leap in the dark . . .

On the charitable 'reading' of the crucial claim [ii], the reading of it that we have essayed in this paper, claim [iii] is much more obviously a *non-sequitur* than it was on the meaning-nihilistic 'reading' of [ii].[25] For just because a word normally only has meaning in the context (minimally) of a sentence *is no reason for thinking that every new application is a leap in the dark.* Indeed, it is normally *only* in sentences (old and new) that the use of a word can so much as *count* as the application of a rule! (There would be no rules here, and no rule-following, if there were only isolated words, not sentences. If 'There can be no such thing as meaning anything by any word' is a sentence, then there are sentences, there are rules.) What have been taken to be Kripke's claims may work for single words, but they simply do not work for words in use, for sentences.

We have shown, then, that even on a reading of Kripke's conclusion that tries to be charitable, that attempts to find a way in which something – perhaps some putative novel scepticism he wants us to entertain – can be stated, or asserted, *a way in which the climactic words of his famous and influential text can be saved* – that on such a reading, there is actually no generation of any thing worth calling meaning-scepticism or meaning-nihilism. And in the fairly extensive 'literature', there are no further alternative interpretations of the 'conclusive' claim of Kripke's text.[26]

That is as much as to say that no reason whatsoever has been presented to us for believing, on any interpretation of 'There can be no such thing as meaning anything by any word' that we can rightly be thought coherently to entertain, that any 'content-scepticism' follows. What follows can only be the grammatical point that we are all as it were supposed to have learnt at Frege's knee, but which is so very easy for us to forget in the heat of a philosophical moment. Frege's context principle (let alone Wittgenstein's 'expansion' of it) is something we may take ourselves to understand and agree with, but often without really absorbing it. Thus we can get drawn into thinking, for instance, of Kripke's line of thought as coherent – without noting that it actually goes way beyond (indeed, against) anything licensed by Frege and Wittgenstein. (*Unless*, of course, it is (mis-)read in the 'charitable' direction ventured above, as being a rather misleading presentation of a point which is not original (because it was established long ago, by Frege), and in fact is in a certain sense arguably 'trivial', and obvious (because one can make no serious moves whatsoever in 'the philosophy of language' without it).)

But perhaps this short piece has helped at least to clarify why it could be that this has arguably escaped notice for so long, through what is now fifteen years or more of commentary and research on and inspired by Kripke's book.[27]

Notes

1 Saul Kripke, *Wittgenstein on Rules and Private Language*, Cambridge, Mass., Harvard University Press, 1982, p.55. See also p.62 and p.21 for similar formulations. The question I am trying to answer in the present piece is: what could formulations such as this *possibly* (intelligibly) mean? How might they begin to make sense? (How can they be anything other (ultimately) than *plain nonsense?*)

2 Ibid., pp.7–9.

3 W.W. Tait, 'Wittgenstein and the "sceptical paradoxes"', *Journal of Philosophy*, 1986, vol. 83, p.475. The term 'meaning-nihilist', less potentially misleading than 'meaning-sceptic' (which might suggest a *paramountcy* of epistemic over constitutive doubts), is from T. Shogenji, 'Boomerang defense of rule following', *Southern Journal of Philosophy*, 1992, vol.30, pp. 115–22.

4 On p.55 of Kripke, op. cit., and on p.71, where he describes the conclusion he has reached on Wittgenstein's behalf quite plainly, as '. . . the incredible and self-defeating conclusion, that all language is meaningless'. Kripke's admitting this ought not to be obscured by the fancy footwork of his novel 'community sceptical solution', expounded later in the book (see below, especially n.12; and Shogenji, op. cit., especially n.3 on p.122 of his paper). As argued below, Kripke's conclusion stands if any of his argument in Section 2 of his book does – and any 'sceptical solution' is in actuality at best a palliative to help us to deal with the psychological consequences of this (as I argue in my 'Kripke's Hume' (forthcoming in the *Journal of Philosophical Research*) and in more detail in Part 2 of my Ph.D. thesis, *Practices without foundations? Sceptical readings of Wittgenstein and Goodman* (Rutgers University, 1995)). It is surprising how many commentators – either due to the presence of the sceptical solution, or due to their *interest* in the meaning/content scepticism for its own sake – do not accept Kripke's own admission that the conclusion to his argument is self-refuting. See for instance pp.766–7 of C. Wright, 'Kripke's account of the argument against private language', *Journal of Philosophy*, 1984, vol.81, and p.120 of David Oderberg, 'Kripke and "quus"', *Theoria*, 1987, vol. 53.

5 I have a minority opinion here; I do not allow this. See my 'The unstatability of Kripkean Scepticisms', *Philosophical Papers*, 1995, vol.24, pp.67–74, and my 'In what sense is "Kripke's Scepticism" a *Scepticism?* On the essential tension between its epistemic and metaphysical aspects', *De Philosophia*, 1996, vol.12, pp.117–32) – in which I argue that Kripke's argument cannot even get so far as to refute itself, that it actually only gives the appearance of being an argument, that Kripke's words (ironically) simply cannot mean what *he* evidently (if inchoately) wants them to mean.

6 This is an influential suggestion which Kripke makes later at op. cit., pp.69f.

7 See n.1, above; and Kripke, op. cit., p.71.

8 As Kripke writes for example at op. cit., p.21: 'There can be no fact [period] as to what I mean by "plus", or any other word at any time.'

9 Crispin Wright famously argues for the non-factualist view, for instance in *Truth and Objectivity*, Cambridge, Mass., Harvard University Press, 1992, chapter 6.

10 See Kripke, op. cit., p.86. For discussion, see Alex Byrne, 'On misinterpreting Kripke's Wittgenstein', *Philosophy and Phenomenological Research*, 1996, vol.56, pp.339–43; and Paul Boghossian, 'The status of content', *Philosophical Review*, 1990, vol.99, pp.157–84.

11 Ibid., pp.174–6 and pp.182–4.

12 Though see n.5, above: I would actually assert the sheer *unstatability* or *unassertability* or *non-propositionality* of Kripke's would-be position (such that it is in fact not accurate to say that Kripke's enunciated 'position' refutes itself). Though all three of these terms *still* run the risk of striking one as a little too 'static', too 'logical', in character – one must think of them as use-oriented, of there being no way of Kripke (or anyone else!) meaningfully accomplishing the extended linguistic act(s) of enunciating a coherent position starting as he does with 'quus' and ending up with 'There can be no such thing as meaning anything by any word', with all the consequences that that ought to have.

(It should be perhaps added that the putative power of Kripke's Wittgenstein's scepticism is such that, *were* it coherently assertible, it would completely eviscerate of content his own 'communitarian sceptical solution' too, as has been demonstrated by (e.g.) Baker and Hacker, and C. McGinn.)

13 Tait, op. cit., p.475. Detailed defence of this thought, that Wittgenstein raised doubts about whether any general sceptical paradox or nihilism as to meaning (or understanding) are or can be generated at all, can be found also in Baker and Hacker (especially *Scepticism, Rules and Language*, Oxford, Blackwell, 1984), in Arthur Collins, 'On the paradox Kripke finds in Wittgenstein', *Midwest Studies in Philosophy*, 1992, vol.17, pp.74–89, and in G.E.M. Anscombe, 'Critical Notice: Wittgenstein on rules and private language', *Canadian Journal of Philosophy*, 1985, vol.15, pp.103–9.

14 I am thinking of those who take Kripke's argument to have at least some implications, such as, again, Crispin Wright ('Kripke's account', op. cit.; on Wright, see David Finkelstein's response to Wright's 'constitutive scepticism', this volume), and Ian Hacking (who in 'On Kripke's and Goodman's use of "grue"', *Philosophy*, 1993, 68, pp.269–95) takes it to have certain effects in the philosophy of maths); *and* of those who find the argument meaningful and threatening but ultimately rebuttable in the philosophy of mind (e.g. Oderberg, op. cit.; Paul Coates, 'Kripke's sceptical paradox: normativeness and meaning', *Mind*, 1986, vol.95, pp.77–80; C. McGinn, *Wittgenstein on Meaning*, Oxford, Blackwell, 1984; and Ruth Millikan, 'Truth rules, hoverflies, and the Kripke-Wittgenstein paradox', in her *White Queen Psychology and Other Essays for Alice*, Cambridge, Mass., MIT Press, 1993, pp.211–46).

15 For further explication, see J. Coulter, 'Is contextualising necessarily interpretive?', *Journal of Pragmatics*, 1994, vol.21, pp.689–98.

16 Personal communication; and see the essays on Frege in her *The Realistic Spirit*, Cambridge, Mass., MIT Press, 1991.

17 *The Foundations of Arithmetic*, J. Austin (trans.), Evanston, IL, Northwestern, 1980, p.x.

18 Cora Diamond, 'What nonsense might be', in *The Realistic Spirit*, op. cit., pp.107–11; Anthony Palmer, *Concept and Object: The Unity of the Proposition in Logic and Psychology*, London, Routledge, 1988; John Cook, 'Wittgenstein on privacy', in G. Pitcher (ed.), *Wittgenstein: The Philosophical Investigations*, Englewood Cliffs, NJ, Prentice Hall, 1974, pp.286–323; Jeff Coulter, 'Is the new sentence problem a genuine problem?', *Theory and Psychology*, 1991, vol.1:3, pp.317–36.

19 L. Wittgenstein, *Philosophical Investigations*, para. 43 (emphasis mine). Cf. also para. 421.

20 *Ibid.*, para. 49.

21 *Ibid.*, paras 19f.

22 Amusingly, this point suggests itself as a superficial analogue of Kripke's 'communitarian sceptical solution' to rule-scepticism (the 'solution' being that it is the community's correction which enables any individual to be said to be following rules): words *considered in isolation* do not effectuate a 'solution' to the problem posed, but (roughly speaking) words taken (always already) *collectively* DO . . . .

23 Kripke, op. cit., p.22.

24 A would-be claim such as 'There is no such thing as meaning anything by any word' (or, somewhat similarly, C. McGinn's claim that 'The mind-body problem is of course soluble, only absolutely not by us'), read as it 'rightly' should be, as the conclusion of Kripke's argument, is thought by some philosophers to be statable, to be propositional, simply because of its surface grammar, because we can claim to understand all the (individual) words out of which it is composed, and can recognize their grammatical categories. But arguably, we do not so much as *understand* their combination – except under the kind of interpretation which I have put forward as being a charitable (mis-)reading. (This again provides a reason for thinking (see n.5, above) that, strictly speaking, one ought not allow that, 'rightly taken', Kripke's string is self-refuting. For, 'rightly taken', this string is mere noise, and noises *qua* noises cannot self-refute. As explained earlier, the only significant respect in which (rightly taken) it is not mere noise is in its psychological effects, in the temptations toward confusion it presents that, e.g., 'Spfh aqaaaazzzzzzzzz sffhoo' does not.)

25 And thus [i], the claim that 'the sceptical argument remains unanswered', is pretty misleading, at best – for there *is* no such argument, on the charitable reading of [ii].

26 Except of course, again, for the perhaps-more-'natural' reading of 'There is no such thing as meaning anything by any word' as simply incoherent, because *self-annihilating*. But as such, it's important to be clear that it is not even a *claim*.

27 The inspiration for and idea of this paper came from James Guetti, whom I here thank very heartily. Sincerest thanks also to Cora Diamond, Chrys Gitsoulis, Peter Hacker, Anne Jacobson, Kelly Dean Jolley, Nigel Pleasants, Louis Sass, and (especially) Alice Crary for very useful comments and suggestions.

5

WITTGENSTEIN ON DECONSTRUCTION

Martin Stone

Introduction

These terms [*differance*, supplement, trace, etc.] can be related with the entire thematics of active interpretation, which substitutes an incessant deciphering for the disclosure of truth as a presentation of the thing itself in its presence, etc. What results is a cipher without truth, or at least a system of ciphers that is not dominated by truth value. . . .

(Derrida[1])

[A]s Dummett says, 'the *Investigations* contains implicitly a rejection of the classical . . . view that the general form of explanation of meaning is a statement of the truth conditions'. In the place of this view, Wittgenstein proposes an alternative. . . . There is no objective fact [about the meaning of a sign]. . . . In fact, it seems that no matter what is in my mind at a given time, I am free in the future to interpret it in different ways.

(Kripke[2])

All that philosophy can do is to destroy idols. And that means not creating a new one – for instance as in "absence of an idol."

(Wittgenstein[3])

1 "All that philosophy can do is to destroy idols." Wittgenstein is speaking here of his philosophy – of the subject of philosophy, that is, as he claims to continue it. I think we can gain a sharper sense of Wittgenstein's originality if we compare his sense of philosophy's appropriate destructiveness with the form of philosophical criticism which Derrida first called for in criticizing Husserl's account of how a sign expresses meaning – *viz.*, "deconstruction." One of my aims in pursuing this comparison will be to show that "deconstruction," taken in a roughly Derridian sense, names a variety of views which cut across the post-Kantian philosophical "divide." As will emerge, I take the quotations from *both* Derrida and Kripke above to be expressive of "deconstruction" in this Derridian sense, and I take the third quotation from Wittgenstein to indicate why it is he could not have regarded deconstruction as his philosophical aim. One mark of Wittgenstein's originality is that the differences between the instances of "continental" and "analytic" philosophy represented by the quotations from Derrida and Kripke come to look unimportant; measured by their distance from Wittgenstein, these instances of the two traditions look surprisingly harmonious.

Wittgenstein and Derrida resemble each other in a number of ways. Both take metaphysical philosophy as their primary target (both are, in this respect, heirs of Kant). More specifically, both identify a main region of this target with a suspect notion of the mental self-presence of meanings (something which in both Derrida's reading of Husserl and in contemporary readings of Wittgenstein's *Investigations* goes under the name of "platonism");[4] and both locate the source of this suspect notion in the attempt to account for the possibility of representing meaning in linguistic signs given the premise that what could account for this must be found in the mind, conceived as a region of reality left over for investigation after one brackets the world and its empirical circumstances. Given these resemblances, it is understandable that a growing number of commentators should suggest that we might come to appreciate Wittgenstein's discussion of meaning and understanding in terms drawn from Derrida. Wittgenstein, it is said, "achieved a consistently deconstructive standpoint."[5]

There is an accurate perception in this suggestion, to be sure, but there is also a significant misconception. In the *Investigations* Wittgenstein mentions his formal procedures – his "form of account" (§122)[6] – as something he thinks is distinctive about his thought. Notwithstanding themes and characteristic gestures which align him with Derrida, Wittgenstein could not have been satisfied with "deconstruction" as a description of his formal procedures. The perception that Wittgenstein's response to "platonism" is an endeavor at deconstruction arises from the fact that one of his aims is, as I shall argue, to *give voice* to deconstruction. However, to give voice to deconstruction is not, for Wittgenstein, to adopt its standpoint; it is only to give expression to a way of thinking to which (Wittgenstein thinks) someone attracted to a philosophical investigation of meaning is apt to be attracted.

Why should Wittgenstein do this? And why should some of his readers misunderstand it? My answer to these questions will proceed in three stages: first, by sketching the relevant notion of deconstruction; second, by locating that notion in Wittgenstein's discussion of rule-following; and third, by claiming that a central aim of Wittgenstein's discussion is to suggest that if (1) a certain metaphysical idea of meaning and (2) the deconstruction of that idea seem to exhaust the philosophical options, that is owing to our failure to see another possibility – namely, a return to the ordinary or everyday: "What *we* do [*i.e., in contrast to other philosophers – my note*] is to bring words back from their metaphysical to their everyday use" (§116). Wittgenstein identifies philosophy's metaphysical voice as his critical target. But this alone would hardly distinguish him from any number of other philosophers within the huge Kantian wake of philosophy's self-criticism. So it would be a mistake to infer, from such a common metaphysical target, that the contrast Wittgenstein wishes to draw (between himself and others) should not embrace – or even refer most especially to – those philosophers who set their face *against* metaphysics. "We bring words back" – Wittgenstein is to be read as saying – "in contrast to the way other philosophers criticize metaphysics; in their form of criticism, words remain metaphysically astray." In fact, as I will try to show, the meaning of

Wittgenstein's claim for the philosophical pertinence of "everyday use" comes into sharp focus against the background of the deconstructive voice in his text.

Part I Deconstruction

2 There is today a widespread notion that to understand the meaning of any text is to put some interpretation on it. As a general thesis about meaning, this is apt to seem puzzling. Suppose the master chef says: "Now add two cups of water and stir." The *sous*-chef correctly carries out this instruction by adding, of all things, two cups of water and stirring. That the uttered words (or the same words found in a recipe book) can be understood to call for *this* only by way of interpretation would hardly seem obvious. What would this mean? Perhaps the *sous*-chef felt uncertain about what to do until he recalled a definition of "water" or a picture of "stirring." But of course, if he has gotten this far, that is not likely. One wants to say that in a situation of this sort, and in a great many others, a person may simply *hear* the meaning in another's words; and that unless the situation is distinguished by the presence of some misunderstanding needing to be averted or cleared up, the meaning of words is available without interpretive mediation.

The contemporary proponent of a general requirement of interpretation (henceforth "the interpretivist") is not, however, likely to be deterred by such examples. Indeed, he is likely to feel that a deep point of his is being missed (or repressed) entirely. It would be a mistake, he says, to distinguish situations in which some misunderstanding needs to be averted or cleared up from situations in which the meaning of words is altogether plain, and then to suppose that interpretation is called for only in a remedial way, in order to turn situations of the first sort into situations of the second (untroubled) sort. For misunderstandings, the interpretivist will point out, are *possible* in every situation; they are an "essential" or "necessary" possibility."[7] To fully grasp the implications of this, the interpretivist claims, would be to see that what one takes to be cases of plain meaning are really special cases of interpretation. That is, given that "misunderstandings" are always possible, the phenomena of "plain meaning" exhibits the success or hegemony of a particular interpretation, not the absence or superfluity of interpretation as such. *Not* to see this would accordingly be to fall prey to a quite suspect notion of the way meaning is present in the best of cases – a notion of "absolutely meaningful speech."[8]

That is not all. That suspect notion of meaning – the interpretivist will continue – might fairly be seen as part of a familiar metaphysical picture concerning a peculiar sort of relationship that a mind can have to its own contents: a Cartesian picture of the undoubtable presence of consciousness to itself at the present moment of speaking. According to this Cartesian picture: at least in one exemplary case, in the intimacy of my relation to my own voice, I must know, beyond a doubt, what I mean; and if *I* know, then another might hear these spoken signs as I do and so know as well. Of course communication, like any movement across the world or visible space, is beset by possible failure and uncertainty. But it is so, on this picture, in relation to the fact that meaning – in the inward communion that occurs when I hear *myself* speak – is not.[9] Now such a picture of self-present meanings animating the signs which carry meaning, the interpretivist suggests, is part of the intellectual environment in which our notion of "plain meaning" thrives. So it matters little that common sense should tell, in the foregoing sort of example, against the ubiquity of interpretation. That only shows, the interpretivist will say, that common sense is unwittingly caught up in this metaphysical environment.

3 A view of this sort is available in Derrida's work. Its general structure may be seen in the idea of "deconstruction" conceived as an endeavor to replace certain classical philosophical notions of the origins (or "general space of possibility")[10] of sense and presence with other notions or functions (e.g., *differance*, arche-writing, active interpretation), which, in accounting for untroubled cases, would thereby exhibit apparent deviations – e.g., the whole family of "mis's" (misunderstanding, misapplication, misconception, etc.) – as "essential possibilities." Derrida finds the classical paradigm in Husserl's conception of "the use of signs in solitary mental life" as "pure expression," in contrast to the physical sign (which appears in discourse) as merely "indicating" the presence of inner, sense-giving experiences. Given this dichotomy, Husserl is apparently forced to ground the identity of meaning (i.e., the possibility of repeated uses of signs in accord with their grasped meaning) in acts of "meaning-intention" which present "ideal unities" having "no necessary connection [to] . . . the signs to which they are tied."[11] Such a conception is "metaphysical," in Derrida's view, in so far as it presents the sign-involving behavioral events of speech and writing as merely "secondary" or external to the purely or ideally grasped meanings which give linguistic behavior a normative shape. Hence, in criticism of such a conception, the deconstructive task is to think, as Derrida remarks, "*at once* both the rule and the event, concept and singularity."[12]

To see more clearly how the interpretivist thesis serves to articulate this general idea of deconstruction, consider the following remark from a recent discussion by Derrida of legal judgment: "Each case is other, each decision is different and requires an absolutely unique interpretation which no existing, coded rule can or ought to guarantee absolutely."[13] If we think of "an interpretation" in a familiar sense as something that determines or explains the meaning of a text (here, the meaning of a rule), then a sufficient motivation for this remark may be characterized precisely as "the necessity of thinking *at once* both the rule and the event." This means: the singular, datable behavioral "event" of judging according to a rule is to be thought of as essential to the meaning of the rule – as somehow determining and not merely following from the rule's meaning what it does. (Ditto for the relation between one's grasp of a "concept" and the eventful bits of linguistic behavior which apply that concept in determinate judgements.) Since such behavioral events are extended across time and circumstance, to say that every such event "requires an interpretation" (i.e., a determination of meaning) is thus to imply that the meaning of the rule cannot be simply "present"; it is critically to limit the self-presence of meaning.

Lawyers and laymen are apt to fall in with the previous bit of common sense (section 2). They are apt to suppose: (1) that there are "easy cases" in which the plain meaning of a rule demands a certain decision; (2) that such cases leave no room for judicial discretion, at least if the judge endeavors to apply rather than to revise the rule; (3) that there are other cases in which discretion is required, for instance when an otherwise clear rule must be applied in circumstances which are unusual or unforseen; and (4) that in such "hard cases" the judge may interpret the rule – he may reformulate it, for example – so as to make clear what it requires in the particular case. The burden of Derrida's remark, however, is to suggest that this weave of conceptual distinctions – *viz.*, between easy and hard cases, ordinary and novel circumstances, required and discretionary judgment, etc. – rests on a suspect notion of the presence of meaning and thus lacks the substance we are inclined to credit it with. Just as the phenomenon of "plain meaning" exhibits the success of a particular interpretation, so paradigmatically "easy cases," rather than providing a stay against interpretive activity, are to be seen as its result.[14] Each decision requires an interpretation "as if ultimately nothing previously existed of the law, as if the judge himself invented the law in every case." For otherwise, Derrida remarks, "the judge is a calculating machine . . . and we will not say that he is just, free and responsible."[15]

The contrast Derrida draws here – between the judge as interpreter and as a machine – helps to locate the general region of the present problem. Unless we locate the judge within a space of interpretive freedom, Derrida implies, we shall not be able to see him *as a judge*: as someone who exercises responsible agency, who takes the rule as a *reason* for his decision and not merely (consider that an electric current compels him to tick the "guilty" box) as an excuse. The "necessity of interpretation"[16] thus appears here as an implication of the thought that judgment involves *normative* or rational constraint, not purely natural pressures.[17] But thus motivated, the need for interpretation is not any special feature of the endeavor to subject human conduct to legal (or other) rules.[18] For any judgment at all presents an example of the "normative reach" of meaning: i.e., of a general relation between the notion of grasping a meaning and that of appropriate behavior undertaken in circumstances which bring that meaning into play.[19] Intuitively, the idea is that someone who grasps the meaning of an expression is obliged, if he is to remain faithful to what he grasps, to judge in certain determinate ways when the appropriate circumstances arise. Since, in the case of an expression used to describe the world, this amounts to the thought that a judgment ("p") lays down the conditions the world must meet if it can correctly be said that p, to make "interpretation" a condition of the normative reach of meaning is, in the broadest terms, to say something about how thought gets a purchase on the world. Thought draws a draft which the world may fulfill – but only under some interpretation. This very general form of interpretivism is offered in numerous remarks of Derrida's – for example, in the one quoted at the beginning of this paper (presenting "active interpretation" as a "substitute" for "truth as a presentation of the thing itself"), or in his characterization of deconstruction as affording the insight that one "cannot refer to [the] 'real' except in an interpretive experience."[20]

If to deconstruct the normative – or as Derrida says "nonnatural"[21] – realm of meaning is to exhibit misunderstanding as an "essential possibility," it seems apparent why the notion of interpretation should strike the deconstructivist as well equipped for service in this endeavor. The thought which mediates between the requirement of interpretation and the "essential possibility of misunderstanding" is evidently this. To say that an interpretation is required in order to determine the normative reach, and hence the meaning, of a sign, is to say that there could have been, and may be in the future, some other interpretation. Interpretations function in a space of other *possible* interpretations. So if we manage to embrace the thesis that to understand is to interpret, then, in such an account of what understanding is, we shall be exhibiting the possibility of "misunderstanding" as essential. To give "interpretation" a constitutive (and not merely remedial: section 2) role is to locate "understanding" as an achievement within the space of interpretive *possibility*.

4 The general idea of deconstruction I have begun to sketch is that of an account of meaning which replaces a classical conception which is "metaphysical" in a specific sense of the word (section 3, paragraph 1). However, I am choosing to focus on just one articulation of this general idea, that which involves a strikingly broad application of the term "interpretation." There are two reasons for this. First, the term "interpretation" (unlike, e.g, "*differance*" or "arche-writing") appears in a similar philosophical role in Wittgenstein's discussion of meaning, so such a focus best suits my present limited purpose. Second (and more generally), the term "interpretation" (again unlike the other terms) plays a significant role in a variety of everyday contexts. The "necessity of interpretation" thereby becomes the sort of expression to which it is natural to have recourse in explaining what is meant by "*differance*" or "arche-writing" – terms which find gainful employment only in deconstructive philosophy. The relative everydayness of "interpretation" is a reason to give it special attention in a consideration of deconstruction. It is also, as will emerge when I turn to Wittgenstein, a source of special difficulties. For while a neologism like "*differance*" has its uselessness outside of philosophy graphically inscribed on its face ("it is literally neither a word nor a concept" Derrida points out),[22] the term "interpretation" (which clearly functions as a word and a concept) is bound to carry associations from its significant use in other contexts. And these associations are at once the source of its attractiveness for philosophical purposes and an impediment to seeing clearly what someone who is thus attracted to the word, and who uses it to characterize the "general space of possibility" of meaning, might mean.[23]

Before turning to Wittgenstein, however, it will be useful first to clarify a few points in the preceding sketch of a strand of deconstructive thought by considering how the response might go to two objections which are sometimes raised against it. The first objection takes Derrida to be saying something obviously wrong (section 5); the second sees his point as innocuously correct (section 6). In different ways, both of these objections construe Derrida as advancing a simple interpretivist thesis, something intended to be sufficiently unproblematic in sense to be pronounced either right or wrong. Both thereby miss Derrida's own view of the matter which is that in characterizing the "general space of possibility" of meaning by means of such terms as "active interpretation" or "*differance*," he is not advancing any simple thesis – indeed, he is, strictly speaking, not *saying* anything – at all. I will turn to Derrida's view in section 7.

5 According to one recent critic, deconstruction purports to recognize, in a pyrrhonic spirit, that "texts have no decidable meaning."[24] This view (which is also the popular, hearsay view) takes deconstruction to be directed against any form of distinction between cases of plain meaning and cases (as Derrida might say) of "undecidability." And that of course makes Derrida look like a maniac, for, as everyone knows, we do successfully traffic in plain meanings everyday. (Many practical conflicts, for example, never become official "cases" at all because their appropriate legal resolution is beyond question.) However, it is clear that the target of deconstruction is not the notion of plain meaning just *as such*, but rather only what might be called a naive as opposed to a properly thoughtful version of it. Here is Derrida:

> [T]he value of truth . . . is never contested or destroyed in my writings, but only reinscribed in more powerful, larger, more stratified contexts. . . . [W]ithin interpretive contexts . . . that are relatively stable, sometimes apparently almost unshakeable, it should be possible to invoke rules of competence, criteria of discussion and of consensus. . . . I take into account and believe that it is necessary to account for this stability [of interpretive contexts], as well as for all the norms, rules, contractual possibilities, that depend upon it. But . . . to account for a certain stability . . . is precisely not to speak of eternity or of absolute solidity; it is to take into account a historicity, a nonnaturalness, of ethics, of politics, of institutionality, etc. . . . I say that there is no stability that is absolute, eternal, intangible, natural, etc. But that is implied in the very concept of stability. A stability is not an immutability; it is by definition always destabilizable.[25]

Whether this defense of deconstruction ultimately joins issue with its critics may not be easy to tell, for presumably those who worry that "truth" is coming under threat in Derrida's writings may not wish (any more than Derrida) to "speak of eternity or absolute solidity." But if to say "there is no stability which is absolute, eternal . . ." is to say something significant, it must be that there are people who believe that there *are* the relevant sort of rock-solid immutable, structures standing surety for our concourse with meanings. Then what has happened, we might imagine the deconstructivist to say, is this. The numbing everydayness of the human traffic in meaning has blinded people to the fact that their entitlement to make ascriptions of meaning is held only by positive license from a ("relatively stable") interpretive regime. That is what deconstruction exposes. It does not contest the entitlement. But it seeks to bring us into responsible recognition of the way our entitlement to use notions such as "plain meaning" requires some account of how such a thing is possible. And properly conceived, the aim of deconstruction would not be to destroy such a notion but to replace the naive (and metaphysically inflected) version of it with a version which takes proper account of its conditions of possibility.

So conceived, deconstructive criticism would involve what Derrida sometimes calls a "quasi-transcendental" point.[26] The word "quasi" is no doubt meant to insist on a difference between deconstructive and more traditional recountings of our conceptual entitlements – and hence also to register the difficulty deconstruction faces of making that difference legible.[27] But however this difference is to be seen or heard, it seems clear that deconstruction is bound to be unrecognizable outside the context in which it is understood or assumed that philosophy's problem is not to assert or deny the existence of meaning but to answer a question of the form: "How is meaning *as such* possible?" So Derrida does not say, as the hearsay charges would require, that a text has no decidable meaning; he characteristically says that "it is *always possible* that it has no decidable meaning."[28] That is a remark not about whether you should expect to find plain meanings, but about what it is, when you find them, you may intelligibly think you have found. What goes missing in the hearsay account, then, is evidently just the philosophical context of Derrida's remarks – the context in which one could so much as conceive of "accounting for" the stability of meaning in a way which, as Derrida puts it, reoccupies the very place of metaphysics, "replaces" it.[29]

Thinking about what goes missing in the hearsay charges against deconstruction is instructive. It serves to bring out the extent to which Derrida takes philosophy – its history and its institutions – to provide a context of the significant use of expressions like "guarantee absolutely" or "a stability which is absolute and eternal." If this reliance on philosophy and its institutions should seem to be natural or inevitable (at least in philosophical writing), it will require something like Wittgenstein's *Investigations* to bring its significance, its remarkableness, into view. The distinctiveness of Wittgenstein's thought about meaning is largely unavailable, I shall suggest later on, if one ignores his contrasting view of this matter.

6 The second objection to deconstruction is more sophisticated. It says not that its claims are absurd but that such "quasi-transcendental" claims – as that "misunderstanding is always possible"[30] – are sufficiently benign as to have, at least in Anglo-American philosophy, no live target. Even if such claims are considered to pose a problem for early modern notions of intentionality, the thought goes, and even if those notions remain invidiously active, as Derrida wishes to show, in Husserl's distinction between expression and indication, such notions appear also to be so unremittingly (and agreeably) under criticism in mid-twentieth century Anglo-American philosophy (in Austin and Ryle, to leave Wittgenstein aside for the moment) that someone might wonder – e.g., whenever Derrida says "there cannot be any absolute such-and-such" – who, exactly, is supposed to be thinking otherwise.

This second objection flows from the answer to the first. It says that once you understand to whom Derrida is speaking and to what purpose, then you understand that, at least in philosophy, there isn't anyone, any longer, in this interlocutor's place.

Derrida's encounter with Austin provides a helpful context for pursuing this matter. It brings certain aspects of deconstruction into sharp focus precisely because Austin would have seemed to be an unlikely candidate for the interlocutor which deconstruction requires. Doesn't Austin's *How To Do Things With Words* explicitly call attention to the way intentional speech acts are vulnerable to all manner of circumstantial mishap and failure?[31] And doesn't Austin elsewhere recommend to philosophers the study of excuses precisely on the grounds that "to examine excuses is to examine cases where there has been some abnormality or failure," and that examination of such cases throws light on "the mechanisms of the natural successful act"?[32] What Derrida says is this. Austin acknowledges, but does not "ponder the consequences issuing from the fact that a possibility – a possible risk [*i.e., of mishap and failure – my note*] – is always possible, and is in some sense a necessary possibility."[33] The deconstructive aim, then, is sufficiently "to ponder" this rather than merely to acknowledge it or to add it – as Derrida suggests Austin does – on second thought.[34]

The general picture gripping Derrida here might be spelled out like this. In "reaching out" into the world, human intentionality is vulnerable to its circumstances, at risk of failure. The upshots and consequences of every action may exceed its intended and foreseeable aspects; and no explanation of the meaning of a word, it seems, can insure against the possibility of a "misapplication" of the word in circumstances not yet present. Now Derrida's complaint against traditional philosophy is that in endeavoring to explain how intentionality is possible – how, for example, certain states of affairs can be in accord with what someone says or intends – such philosophy regards the worldly circumstancing of speech and action as "external" and "accidental" to its subject when it ought really, on reflection, to regard this as internal and essential to it. Hence, the mark of metaphysical accounts of intentionality is that they continuously recreate, even when they declare impossible, an ideal of pure thought reaching out to "the thing itself."

Austin, for Derrida, is someone still naively captive to metaphysics so conceived. Recreating such an ideal of purity, he "excludes" the risk of circumstantial failure as "accidental, exterior." He does not "ponder" the consequences of what he acknowledges. But what would it be properly to ponder this? What would evince the right kind of thoughtfulness? Once this question is squarely posed, Derrida's answer seems hard to miss:

> We must account for the essential possibility of deviant cases . . . the essential and irreducible *possibility* of *mis*-understanding . . . must be taken into account in the description of those values said to be positive . . . what must be recognized is how a structure called normal or ideal can render possible or necessary . . . all these 'accidents' . . . This structural possibility must be taken into account when describing so-called ideal normality. . . . In the description of the structure called normal . . . this possibility must be integrated as an essential possibility. The possibility cannot be treated as if it were a simple accident.[35]

What is needed, this says, beyond Austin's acknowledgment of the possibility of accidents, is an *account* of this possibility. "Anomalies," then, must be represented as not anomalous at all, as falling, rather, under an integrating "law."[36] Hence, concerning the question of "how signs express meaning," proper pondering would require that one represent the possibility of various mishaps (misunderstanding, misconception, misapplication, etc.) as an "internal" condition of the possibility of all those "ideal" cases involving no such mishap. Otherwise expressed, the requirement of pondering is that of a certain form of representation: the requirement is satisfied, as it happens, just when the conditions of the possibility of something in the realm of meaning are represented as simultaneously conditions of the thing's *impossibility* – the impossibility, that is, of its "rigorous purity."[37] Such a paradox evidently earmarks the form of account deconstruction gives, its way of looking at things.[38]

That the deconstructive use of the classical philosophical idiom of "possibility conditions" is in the service of exposing a paradox, and that deconstructive criticism is to be understood, on Derrida's suggestion, as "quasi-transcendental" – hence as something both continuous and discontinuous with the traditional philosophical search for origins or grounds – are related points. Both points may be expressed as a distinction between a "deconstructive" and a "simple" interpretivism. The latter presents "interpretation" as the central notion in the right answer to a question about "how signs express meaning," an answer that is thus without further problematic consequences (save perhaps for some other philosophers in the business of theorizing about meaning).[39] In contrast, Derrida stresses that interpretivism has quite paradoxical and revisionary consequences, not just for the way we think about meaning but for any number of related concepts (e.g., understanding, truth, sign, representation, etc.) as well. Moreover, it is important, in Derrida's view, that one ponder these consequences to see to what new conceptions they may lead. For if one doesn't – if one cuts these consequences short – then, despite the fact that one affirms an interpretivist thesis, one is bound to remain unwittingly in the grip of the metaphysical picture one meant to oppose: one will simply have turned "interpretation" into another name for self-present mental acts of meaning. Derrida does not wish to give his readers the impression that his philosophical aims would be accomplished if one were simply to affirm this or that thesis, like the thesis that "to understand is to interpret." What is needed is to follow out – even to as yet "unheard-of thoughts"[40] – the paradoxical implications of such a thesis.

7 Implicit in these matters concerning Austin is a point which deserves special emphasis. I have followed Derrida in speaking of what Austin failed to ponder as a "paradox." Yet here one perhaps ought more cautiously to say "*apparent* paradox." For in Derrida's way of representing things, what is said to be possible (meaning) and what is said to be impossible (absolute purity of meaning) are, someone might wish to say, not exactly the same. The difference between the two might be described, from Austin's point of view, as the difference between an expression ("meaning") which plays a role in various everyday contexts and an expression ("absolute purity of meaning") which apparently finds employment only in philosophy – i.e., in the context of a question about the "general space of possibility" of meaning. Indeed, it looks like these two notions could appear to be the same (and there could appear to be a paradox here) only on the assumption that our entitlement to make use of such everyday notions as "meaning" requires *some* philosophical account of their possibility, so that absent a deconstructive account, talk of "meaning" must, by general default, rely upon ideas of metaphysical presence. In fact, this is just what Derrida often suggests: the need for deconstruction arises from the fact that the conceptual commitments manifest in our everyday ways of speaking "belong to" the metaphysics of presence.[41] Hence, on Derrida's view, there is no further alternative to naive involvement in metaphysics and proper (deconstructive) pondering of it. Metaphysics is invidious. That is why, without the appropriate critical vigilance, it can take hold of a philosopher like Austin despite his efforts to be free of it.[42]

The sense that there are just these two options, and hence of deconstruction as philosophically compulsory, can be sharply felt in a programmatic passage appearing in the wind-up of Derrida's discussion of Husserl:

> In order to conceive of this age, in order to "speak" about it, we will have to have other names than those of sign or representation. New names will have to be used if we are to conceive as "normal" and preprimordial what Husserl believed he could isolate as a particular and accidental experience, something dependent and secondary – that is, the indefinite drift of signs,

as errance and change of scene, linking re-presentations one to another without beginning or end. ... And contrary ... to what our desire cannot fail to be tempted into believing, the thing itself always escapes.[43]

Derrida describes an endeavor to conceive of the present age, the age that is both tempted to believe in – and attempting to criticize its belief in – the presentability of "the thing itself." Two options appear. The first is the kind of thinking which runs along in the metaphysical grooves of the age. The second is an endeavor to "speak" about the age, not simply from within it, by giving primary place to drift and change – phenomena which Husserl puts into mere second place. This second option involves deconstructive criticism: that which Husserl presents as primordial bedrock (the self-presentation of meanings as ideal unities) is to be represented as dependent on an even deeper (or "pre-primordial") stratum. It is to be so represented even though what is said to be deepest – an original temporal drift of signs – is no longer aptly called an origin or ground in the classical sense at all, since, properly conceived, it betokens the impossibility of any such foundation.

Why represent things in this way? Doesn't such an account inherit the weaknesses of just the sort of metaphysical "first philosophy" it seeks to criticize?[44] The need for an account of this form might be thought of as the way out of a dilemma which takes hold once it is assumed that our entitlement to use such notions as "meaning" and "understanding" requires that we have some account of how such things are possible. The first horn of the dilemma – a commonplace of post-Kantian philosophy – is that the various terms employed in criticism of metaphysics ("representation," for example) function to preserve the very notion (the presence of "the thing itself") which they are employed to limit. The commonplace reflects the sense that there is something confused about the idea of criticizing metaphysics by drawing a limit to thought; for in order to think of a limit, it seems we need to station ourselves along both sides – the cognitively legitimate and the metaphysically illegitimate side – of it. Thus as Derrida remarks "the whole history and meaning" of such concepts as sign and representation "belongs to the adventure of the metaphysics of presence."[45] Concepts which "belong to metaphysics" are not what we need in order to conceive of an age which thinks metaphysically. For to conceive of the age, in the relevant sense, is to be able to conceive of what is beyond it; to conceive, as Derrida puts it, "of what stands opposed to the text of Western metaphysics."[46] Hence, "new names will need to be used."

But now the second horn of the dilemma is that there are, in the present age, no available names of the required sort. That is what makes the present age, for Derrida, the *present age*. "For us, *differance* remains a metaphysical name; and all the names that it receives from our language are still, so far as they are names, metaphysical."[47] But why is this? Why can't we talk about *differance*, under any name, without participating in the sort of talk we are trying to criticize?[48] The answer might be spelled out as a requirement of relevancy which applies to any concept employed in criticism of metaphysics. To be relevant, such a concept must be a candidate answer to the question: "How are sense and presence as such possible?" Metaphysical philosophy, as Derrida represents it, has an autonomous existence – the only critique it is obliged to listen to is a self-critique. So the only way to work with it is in its own terms: *viz.*, by showing that what is taken as prior or

93

primordial is rather to be thought of as conditioned in such-and-such ways; as having such-and-such as its still more profound ground of possibility.[49]

So the dilemma, now, is this: to conceive of the age, one needs terms that both *must* and *cannot* "belong to" metaphysical philosophy, which both must and cannot be answers to its "how possible" question, its demand for grounds.[50] And from this arises both the idea of and need for deconstruction, conceived as the self-criticism of metaphysics. "The movements of deconstruction do not destroy structures from the outside. ... They inhabit those structures."[51] Deconstruction is an internally destructive, but therefore essentially transitional, inhabitation of metaphysical structures – in effect, like sawing off the branch on which one is sitting. Such discourse is in fact obliged to employ the "old signs" of metaphysics,[52] to proceed *as if* it were exposing the profound basis of the notions which structure our thinking. But this is not to continue the metaphysical adventure. For the deconstructivist is knowing about all this; as Derrida emphasizes, his use of metaphysical language is a "strategic" one,[53] part of an endeavor, as Derrida suggests, "to think [an] *unheard-of* thought"[54] by thinking the old signs (placeholders for the "origins" of sense and presence) in radically new ways. (An "unheard-of thought" is also evidently an unspeakable one; but that one may still contemplate that which one cannot properly "speak" about would seem to be the implication of Derrida's putting scare quotes around the word "speak" – but not around, e.g., "conceive" – in the wind-up passage quoted above.)

These difficult remarks of Derrida's offer a picture of four closely related matters. First, of the *necessity* of deconstruction: to get a proper grip on the most fundamental notions which structure our thinking, we must approach these notions neither from the inside nor destructively from the outside, but, as it were, deconstructively – strategically attempting to straddle "two sides of a limit."[55] Second, of the *difficulty* of this endeavor: it necessarily proceeds in resistance to the very language it must use and may even at times appear indistinguishable from "the metaphysical text" it seeks to criticize. Third, of how *philosophy ends*: in "unheard-of" thoughts, in thoughts for which there are at present no words or concepts, only "quasi-concepts" like *differance* which gesture toward an original temporal drift ("*differance* is neither a word nor a concept"). Fourth, of what philosophical muteness or nonsense might be: that which results from such a strategic employment of "quasi-concepts" for the purpose of at least contemplating what it is that one is not yet managing properly to conceive – for the purpose of glimpsing, then, the limits of the present age *as limits*. Deconstruction's question concerning the metaphysics of presence, Derrida says, "will legitimately be understood as *meaning* nothing, as no longer belonging to the system of meaning."[56] This of course is not meant to say that deconstructive discourse is mere gibberish; the implication, rather, is that it falls into meaninglessness precisely on account of what it is trying to say; on account, then, of its meaning something all right, but something "illegitimate." And *this* – this "not-in-the-present-age-legitimately-expressible thing" – is what we are to grasp.[57]

In the following sections of this essay I will try to show: (1) that a significant point of intimacy between Wittgenstein and Derrida is that Wittgenstein too does not regard interpretivism as any kind of simple thesis – he too stresses its paradoxical implications; (2) that Wittgenstein's discussion of meaning and

understanding proceeds from a deep sense of the attractions of the foregoing deconstructive line of thought; and (3) that one of Wittgenstein's aims is to dissipate its
attractions by showing the reader that there is nothing compulsory about it. The
efficacy of such a remedy presupposes, of course, that our attraction to deconstruction is owing to a false sense of options – the attraction would wither away
if one were to pierce the sense of necessity that goes with deconstruction. Of course,
that can fail to be the case. But the only help Wittgenstein thinks he can offer his
reader is related to the terms in which he wishes to criticize the deconstructive
account of meaning: *viz.*, not as an erroneous account of how things are, but as the
expression of an understandable inclination to insist on how things *must* be. This
leaves the deconstructivist free to insist on what he says as much as he likes, for
nothing in Wittgenstein's criticism implies that what the deconstructivist says (or
means to say) is to be denied.

Part II Deconstruction in *Philosophical Investigations*

8 As my introduction indicated, the interest in placing Wittgenstein in relation
to deconstruction is not limited to the interest in comparing him to Derrida; the
issues raised by this comparison bear on a range of contemporary readings of
Wittgenstein's work. A number of commentators have suggested that we might
appreciate Wittgenstein's aims in terms drawn from Derrida.[58] But a number of
Anglo-American commentators who lack this specifically comparative interest
would seem to give the comparison in question some solid support. For in these
readings, Wittgenstein is said to be: (1) criticizing a metaphysical account of
meaning (one which portrays the meaning of what someone says as a matter of the
conditions under which it would be true); (2) "replacing" such an account with an
alternative account (one which explains how ascriptions of meaning are possible
even though "there are no objective facts" for those ascriptions to represent);[59] and
(3) criticizing the metaphysical account and replacing it with this alternative
precisely on the basis of – or in order to accommodate – the following point: that
whatever someone may be said to grasp when they grasp the meaning of a sign is
such that it can always be interpreted in different ways. So in readings of
Wittgenstein stemming from both sides of philosophy's self-divide, Wittgenstein
appears committed not only to the general idea of a substitutive account, but also
to the specific articulation of this idea which involves the thesis that the meaning
of a sign is available only by way of interpretation. On the reading of the
Investigations I want now to sketch, this "deconstructive" reading, as I propose to
call it, is not without considerable textual basis. But it essentially mistakes for the
Investigations' own doctrine the very ideas Wittgenstein means to criticize.

9 Given this situation, a good way to grasp the general structure of Wittgenstein's
discussion will be first to describe the elements of his text which lend themselves
to a deconstructive reading. I will set out two main building blocks of this reading.
After that, I will complete the structure. And only then will I come to the way
Wittgenstein means to reject the entire edifice as a "misunderstanding."

First block. A main ingredient of Wittgenstein's discussion is a criticism of a
certain picture of meaning, a picture which gets characteristically expressed in terms

of a notion of *presence* and which is felt to be mysterious or queer. Thus in one vivid version of this picture, grasping the meaning of an expression is represented as a kind of mental engagement with a super-rigid mechanism, the future movements of which are not simply empirically or causally determined in advance but are "really – in a mysterious sense – already *present*."[60] One might call this, in a rather literal sense, a "meta-physical" notion of presence. For the imagery which serves to convey this notion uses a picture of a physical mechanism in order to represent a kind of determination which is supposed to be in principle harder or more secure than any actual physical movement through space and time. In so far as there is a view quoted in the *Investigations* which might be called "platonism," it is expressed by such imagery.

Second block. The so-called platonistic interlocutor in the *Investigations* is someone who feels that such a notion of presence, though admittedly mysterious, is virtually forced upon us if we want to retain a secure grip on the commonplace about meaning which I earlier called its normative reach (section 3). The *Investigations* gives the following mathematical example. Suppose someone endeavors to carry out a series according to the instruction "add two." If her previous training in arithmetic has brought about a correct understanding of the instruction, then she *must*, it seems, continue on to 1,002 after reaching 1,000; no other number would be in *accord* with her understanding as manifested in her performance so far. Obviously, if a grasped meaning is to have this sort of bearing on bits of future behavior, the platonist reasons, it must be that to grasp the meaning of a sign is to present oneself, in some sense, with its future use. And that is what the platonist's imagery is meant to capture: to grasp the meaning of a sign is mentally to hitch oneself to an indefinitely long rail that traverses the future career of the sign and thus determines, for any of one's future linguistic performances, whether it keeps faith with the meaning one has grasped.

10 So much for the building blocks.[61] Now for the deconstructive reading. On this reading, Wittgenstein finds something amiss in the platonist's talk of presence and he opposes it in roughly the following terms.

First, it is absurd to suppose that one could, in grasping the meaning of a sign, literally bring the whole eventful use of the sign to mind. But short of that, neither anything that does come to mind nor anything about one's previous applications of a sign could be conceived as a plausible candidate for the role of the platonist's rail. For take anything you like that *does* come to mind or any number of applications of the sign: these remain discrete items, like the sign itself, which can always be projected, in future circumstances, in different ways. An image for the impotence of any mental representative of a sign to constrain its future application might be found in a simple sign-post, considered as a mere inscribed block of wood. So considered, the post clearly does not determine the direction in which it is to be followed, whether, say, in the direction of the finger or in the opposite one (cf. §85). It determines this only when it is *interpreted* as an object that points *this* way rather than *that*. And that is how it must be with any sign: to determine a distinction between applications of it which are in accord with its meaning and those which are not must be to give the sign a particular interpretation. So the right picture of meaning is as much one of rail-like fixity as one of immeasurable drift.

Platonism is the myth that meaning takes care of itself. In fact, the reach of meaning into the world – according to the deconstructive reading of Wittgenstein – requires ubiquitous interpretive activity.

Now someone might object – rather along the lines of the hearsay objection to deconstruction (section 5) – that what is depicted here is nothing less than the ruin of meaning. For if to understand a sign is to interpret it, and if "interpreting" a sign is not simply another (metaphysical) name for making mental contact with the platonist's fantastic rail, then "an interpretation" could only be one more discrete item which itself requires an interpretation before *it* determines a particular use of the sign:

> This was our paradox: no course of action could be determined by a rule, because every course of action can be made out [i.e., on some interpretation of it: cf. §198] to accord with the rule. The answer was: if everything can be made out to accord with the rule then it can also be made out to conflict with it. And so there would be neither accord nor conflict here.
>
> (§201)

Of course, the difficulty described here pertains not just to "rules" but to any meaningful items (statements, orders, promises, expectations – in general thoughts: cf. §§437–8) which reach out into the world in the sense that certain states of affairs may (or may fail to) be in accord with them. If the reach of meaning is possible only if some interpretation is placed on the relevant item, then, according to this passage, the very idea of accord goes missing. For, by a regress of interpretations, any action can be made to accord with any interpretation of the item. Where the item is a rule, the requirement of interpretation would thus amount to the thesis that a "fresh decision" has to be made in each case. But now, unless some further account is provided, this says not just that rules do not provide "absolute guarantees;" it says that talk of *rules* is fictional.

Despite this skeptical threat, Wittgenstein's criticism of platonism, according to the deconstructive reading, hinges on the thesis that no matter what mental item someone might acquire in coming to understand a sign, their linguistic performances keep faith with that item only under one possible interpretation of it. So a defining feature of this reading would be the following thought. Opposition to the platonist's notion of a grasped meaning as predetermining specific performances cannot but incur a commitment to a paradox. The paradox at §201 has two components. First, it is assumed that some applications of a rule are in accord with it. That is, there is undoubtedly *such a thing* as following a rule, creating an exception to a rule, and so on. Such everyday things are not fictions. Second, what makes such phenomena *possible* (*viz.*, interpretive activity) appears at once as the condition of their *impossibility* – the impossibility, that is, of any action being, as a matter of simple fact, in accord with the rule. Now given the centrality of such paradoxes to deconstruction, the controlling thought in this reading of Wittgenstein may be put like this. If, starting with the conceptual commitments manifest in our everyday talk of "accord," one asks – "How it is possible for us to employ such notions?" – then one will either profess a dogmatic form of platonism ("meaning *must* run on rails") or, short of that, incur a commitment – in so far as one cannot but persist in using such notions – to a *deconstructive* paradox.

But still: how *could* one accept the ensuing paradox without destroying the notion of meaning? Clearly, such destruction is no more Wittgenstein's aim than Derrida's. At the same time, it looks as if the interpretivist thesis which Wittgenstein is supposed to be deploying against platonism itself provides a powerful motivation for embracing the platonist's imagery, regarded now as a paradox-escaping answer to the question of what someone's *interpreting* a sign could consist in, if it is to have the requisite normative bearing on future linguistic behavior. If the deconstructive reading of Wittgenstein is to hold up, there must be some way of passing between the Scylla of a paradox which seems to destroy all meaning and the Charybdis of a platonism which, in light of the reasoning producing the paradox, now looks like a desperate way to reassure ourselves about the possibility of meaning.

The thought needed here, according to this reading of Wittgenstein, is that the impression of skeptical consequences attendant on the paradox arises only because we have not sufficiently disabused ourselves of a longing for the platonistic ideal, by comparison with which the available notions of meaning and truth seem disappointing. To take counsel against immodest metaphysical hope, however, can be at once to take arms against the fear of nihilism. For the right way to sufficiently disabuse ourselves of platonism is to recognize that while there indeed are no facts in which the correctness of ascriptions of meaning consists, there is available, instead of such facts, a close substitute: namely, a story about our membership in communities of mutual correction and accreditation, about how we achieve good standing in such communities, about the sanctions that attach to deviance and so on. Essentially, someone who fails to "go on" as the community does (e.g., 1000, *1002*) is in violation of one of its norms and may justifiably be said to misunderstand the relevant concept. So by means of such a story, the thought goes, we can both establish title to the notion of accord (i.e., after it seemed clouded by the requirement of interpretation) and, indeed, account for whatever stability our judgements have always had. But, as Derrida puts it, "to account for a certain stability . . . is precisely not to speak of eternity or absolute solidity;" it is not to provide any "absolute guarantees." Compare Kripke, to whom this reading of Wittgenstein is, on the Anglo-American side, substantially indebted:

> There is no objective fact – that we all mean addition by '+', or even that a given individual does – that explains our agreement in particular cases. Rather our license to say of each other that we mean addition by '+' is part of a 'language game' that sustains itself only because of the brute fact that we generally agree. (Nothing about 'grasping concepts' guarantees that it will not break down tomorrow).[62]

If we forget this, the paradox is there to set us straight. The paradox kicks in if we lapse into thinking that, beyond socially convergent behavior, there must be some "objective fact" corresponding to someone's correctly understanding a rule, such that he is thereby compelled to reach the appropriate outcomes. "There really is no accord (and therefore no meaning)," Wittgenstein would be saying, "in *that* sense." But the lesson to be learned is that we ought to stop demanding such track-guaranteeing facts. We ought instead to look and see how meaning and truth are – by a kind of groundless self-enactment of the community – socially constructed and maintained.

11 The deconstructive reading of Wittgenstein is an example of how to miss Wittgenstein's originality. Kripke brushes up against the originality of Wittgenstein's thought when he correctly senses that Wittgenstein would probably not approve of such "straightforward" Kripkean formulations as that "there is no objective fact" as to what someone means by "plus."[63] Kripke is more sensitive on this score than many other commentators. He realizes that the way Wittgenstein chose to formulate matters is internally connected to what Wittgenstein took those matters to be.[64] But Kripke nonetheless has trouble crediting Wittgenstein's claim that the distinctiveness of his thought lies exactly in his formal procedures and not, independently of this, in any substantive views or theses he is advancing (cf. §128). Hence Kripke does not appreciate the extent to which Wittgenstein's own formulations are determined, in part, as a response to the following sort of difficulty in the kind of "straightforward" thesis which Kripke puts forward. If there is something amiss – some cause for philosophy – in talk of "facts" about meaning, how could denying the proposition that such facts exist be any less problematic than asserting it? Wittgenstein writes out of a sense that the philosophical attempt to exorcize illusion is continuously – one might say internally – at risk of giving the following impression: that to rid oneself of a false notion of presence (e.g., a mental act of meaning that traverses the future use) must be to embrace a substantial notion of absence ("there are no facts"). But to embrace such a notion is, on Wittgenstein's view, to embrace a kindred philosophical illusion, and indeed, an illusion that is not significantly different from the one that was to be exorcized. If there is something confused about the statement "p," then one moves no closer to the truth if one reverses its direction; one merely perpetuates the philosophical problem. Now the negation of a metaphysical notion of presence has the form of a representation of absence. It is what Wittgenstein calls "the absence of an idol." When Wittgenstein says that to create the "absence of an idol" is to create a new idol, he means that one of the characteristic ways in which we frustrate our philosophical aims is by representing matters as if metaphysical philosophy had produced intelligible but substantially mistaken notions of how things are, such that overcoming these notions requires asserting their negation. The result is to preserve, by means of an intellectual recoil, the "idol" which one had wanted to destroy.[65]

But doesn't Wittgenstein in fact regard the platonist's talk of "presence" as substantially mistaken? In fact, if one confines Wittgenstein to the options of either affirming or denying a platonistic thesis about meaning, one is bound to misunderstand him. Wittgenstein clearly finds something amiss in the platonist's talk of "presence;" and this gets expressed by the thought that whatever item someone's present grasp of a "meaning" might consist in can always be interpreted in different ways. But if one takes this to mean that Wittgenstein wishes to counter what the platonist says by endorsing a deconstructive paradox, it becomes impossible to fathom why Wittgenstein should add (in a statement Kripke himself ignores) just after stating the paradox: "It can be seen that there is a misunderstanding here" (§201). Suppose we try to take Wittgenstein at his word.[66]

Part III How to read §201

12 As a number of commentators point out, §201 gives no hint that Wittgenstein regards the alleged paradoxicality of meaning as making it necessary to "account for the stability of meaning" after using the paradox to twist free of platonistic guarantees. On the contrary, it looks as if Wittgenstein thinks he can rightfully decline to be troubled by the paradox. Indeed, the very language in which he presents the paradox suggests that to have stated the paradox is already to have drained it of significance;[67] or, more precisely, that to recognize the interpretivist thesis as harboring a paradox is thereby already to have "answered" the paradox by undermining the attractiveness of that thesis. The second paragraph of §201 explicitly draws the moral like this: "[T]his shews . . . there is a way of grasping a rule which is *not* an *interpretation*. . . ." No *ersatz* notion of correctness in ascriptions of meaning is needed to address the skeptical consequences of a paradox which would arise *if* one accepted the idea that every application of a rule requires an interpretation of it; for we cannot, this says, accept that idea. Wittgenstein's easy continuation after the paradox – "It can be seen that there is a misunderstanding here . . ." – thus presents a structure of *latency* characteristic of his thought: the paradox represents the flowering into recognizable or patent nonsense of a line of thought which *looked* compelling because previously it contained only unrecognizable or latent nonsense. "Here, with the paradox," §201 is to be read as saying, "it can be seen that it was nonsense from the beginning."

This should be put together with what Wittgenstein says at the end of §201: "Hence there is an inclination to say: every action according to the rule is an interpretation. But we ought to restrict the term 'interpretation' to the substitution of one expression of the rule for another." After dismissing the paradox-inducing thought as a "misunderstanding," Wittgenstein goes on to give expression to the temptation to say – in order to show us how to avoid saying – what Derrida says. Wittgenstein says there is an *inclination* to say it. He *frames* what Derrida says, calls attention to it as a form of expression to which someone, in a philosophical investigation of the concept of meaning, might be attracted.[68] Wittgenstein's point comes into sharper focus if we ask: why does he go on like this? Why does he proceed from (1) the instruction "there is a way of grasping a rule which is *not* an *interpretation*" to (2), the framing of words implying that this instruction is mistaken? Doesn't (1) sound more like a proper conclusion? The answer, I shall suggest, is that Wittgenstein takes the crucial point of the passage to be the framing of a form of words, not an instruction about how one ought to conceive of following a rule.

13 "*Hence* there is an inclination. . . ." Why – just after drawing the conclusion that interpretivism is a misunderstanding – "hence"? To spell out the inference involved here, I shall first summarize one main strand of Wittgenstein's discussion leading up to and motivating §201, starting with the thought that a sign, considered by itself, does not determine what is in accord with it and what is not. The inference introduced by the word "hence" at the end of §201 becomes clear when we see it as a continuation of this strand.

(A) Suppose we ask: why should it be thought that an item called "an interpretation" can create the determinacy of meaning that goes missing when a sign is considered by itself? The motivation for appealing to interpretation in this context seems clear enough if we remember the everyday sense of the word in which "an interpretation" consists of a linguistic reformulation – "the substitution of one expression for another" (§201). Interpretations in this sense are often called for in cases involving doubt or unclarity, for reformulation is an effective way of clarifying or resolving what, in any expression, may be unclear. To interpret, in this familiar sense, is to give an explanation where an explanation is needed to remove or avert a doubt about meaning – not, of course, every possible doubt (whatever that might mean), but such doubts or misunderstandings, as may, under the circumstances, arise. But now, of course, there is a problem if we seek to make a quite general use of this notion of interpretation. If every sign, considered by itself, is unfixed in meaning, then it is obvious that no further linguistic item is going to help. If *that* is what an interpretation is supposed to be, then interpretations are signs themselves, and they shall stand in need of further interpretations to fix *their* meanings, and so on. Rather than animating the normative reach of signs, talk of interpretation, in this sense, merely redoubles the problem of their impotence.

(B) Once interpretation becomes a general requirement, we can no longer appeal, on pain of a hopeless regress, to the idea of interpretation as linguistic substitution. But if interpretations are not linguistic items, what are they? It may be tempting to think that the idea needed here is that of some essentially mental act of thinking or intending the sign one way rather than another. But this looks no more promising. Indeed, it looks like a relapse into those platonistic notions which interpretivism was meant to parry.[69] For it involves a commitment to the intelligibility of the notion that an item in the mind – say, the thought "Add water and stir" – can be such as to be more determinate, or less in need of interpretation, than a text representing that thought. Against this, the interpretivist thesis was meant to say that we cannot really understand what it would be for there to be an item in the mind that had the requisite normative properties of meaning but that was not, from the get go, subject to the conditions or requirements of representability (or communicability) in signs.

(C) Given (A) and (B) above, someone might understandably think that the idea of "interpretation" needed here is just that of a remarkable spiritual power to make signs mean *this* rather than *that* (rather like the power to give life to dead matter). Perhaps "the Mind" is just that unique kind of thing that has such spiritual powers. A grasped meaning, on this suggestion, would be a very special kind of entity – a universal form which sorts out, for all occasions, what is in accord with it and what is not; and to "interpret" would be to perform an extraordinary act of mind in which one presents oneself with such an entity. But here the meaning-endowing power of "interpretation" begins to seem magical or occult;[70] and it is this alternative which deserves, if anything does, the name "platonism."

Leaving this occult alternative aside, from the premises (1) that a sign, considered by itself, is indeterminate in meaning, and (2) that interpretations are representable in signs, it would follow, as Wittgenstein remarks, that "interpretations by themselves do not determine meaning" (§198). The sense of "by themselves," as §201 indicates, is roughly: "in logical independence of applicative behavior" – e.g., "of following a rule or going against it in actual cases." The paradox of §201 appears at this point as a vivid illustration of the absurdity of supposing otherwise: i.e., of supposing that, given the normative impotence of a sign considered by itself, some general application of "interpretation" can get the notion of accord – and thereby some more modest notion of meaning – back into play.

14 Now the inclination voiced at the end of §201 is one which arises *after* this point has been accepted. Wittgenstein's thought may be put like this: it is precisely once one sees that "interpretations," considered as linguistic substitutions or analogous mental items, do not *by themselves* – i.e., apart from applicative behavior – determine meaning that one may be inclined to say: "every *action* according to the rule is an interpretation." The thought framed here is thus continuous and not in conflict with the instructions issued at §198 and §201 ("interpretations by themselves do not determine meaning," "there is a way of grasping a rule which is *not* an *interpretation*"). For the intelligibility of these instructions depends on taking the word "interpretation" in the sense of linguistic substitution. Against this, the framed assertion at the end of §201 expresses a philosophical inclination to conclude, on the basis of the fact that the interpretivist thesis is an obvious absurdity when "interpretation" is taken in *that* familiar sense, that what one means to say in putting forward that thesis must be something else. The relevant "inclination" arises, in short, as an attempt to hold onto an interpretivism which had seemed serviceable in wording one's rejection of platonism, even after accepting the lesson of the discussion up to this point, *viz.,* that interpretations – *qua* garden variety linguistic items – do not determine meaning.

Given Derrida's conception of deconstruction as involving a radically insightful type of nonsense, it would be accurate to say that the assertion Wittgenstein wishes to frame – after reaching the conclusion that the interpretivist thesis is a bit of plain, uninsightful nonsense – involves a *deconstructive* use of the term "interpretation." Someone who makes such a use of the term is clearly depending on our familiarity with – even as they are rejecting the implications of – its more restricted everyday use. And this is what interests Wittgenstein about such a philosophical use of the term. In framing that use, he records the fact that there is an inclination to continue putting forward "interpretation" as a condition of the possibility of meaning even after recognizing that one's point will be lost by various available clarifications of what one might mean. Now, I suggested that the main point of §201 lies in this framing of a form of words, not in an instruction about the possibility of a non-interpretive grasp of a rule. In fact, since an instruction of this kind would be pointless if there were no inclination to make interpretation a general requirement (compare instructing someone who had never heard of sylphs that there are no sylphs), there is a sense in which the instruction (i.e., that there need not be an interpretation) is no more asserted here, or no less framed, than the requirement (i.e., that there must always be an interpretation). Such parity would flow from recognizing the requirement of interpretation, in light of the paradox, as nonsensical. If we so recognize it, it can't be any more intelligible to negate it. (The negation of nonsense is not something distinguishable in sense.) Contrapositively, if we *can* conceive of "a way of grasping a rule which is *not* an *interpretation*," it must be that we are giving the word "interpretation" a sense which would not have satisfied the proponent of the interpretive requirement – for example, the "substitution of one expression for another." In that familiar sense, we can easily conceive of a non-interpretive grasp of a rule. Nor are we likely to encounter disagreement. For clearly, no one inclined to make interpretation a general requirement ever meant to say – or would feel understood if construed as saying – that every rule must have an additional linguistic rider. In thus juxtaposing the interpretivist's paradox-inducing use of the word "interpretation" with a felicitous sense which might be given to the word ("the substitution of one expression for another"),[71] §201 should lead us to ask whether there is *anything* which the interpretivist would exactly be satisfied to be construed as saying; or whether, on the contrary, his philosophical purposes are such as to be frustrated when the word "interpretation" is made fathomable.

Thus construed, §201 does not (as it must on the deconstructive reading) depart from one of Wittgenstein's main points about his own philosophical procedures: "If one tried to advance *theses* in philosophy, it would never be possible to debate them, because everyone would agree to them" (§128). Tailored to the present context, the point would be that what might be said about the need for "interpretation" in "grasping a rule" (i.e., upon giving the word "interpretation" a clear or fathomable sense) is something to which the present parties would in fact agree. To say that they would agree is to say that the opponent of platonism would not wish to be construed as *denying* the instruction that "there is a way of grasping a rule which is not ... the substitution of one expression for another." She would not want to say that we must always interpret in *that* sense. And beyond this, §201 merely frames the form of expression which would seem to be saying something philosophically disagreeable. So by way of (1) drawing attention to something to which "everyone would agree," and (2) framing the rest as something "there is an inclination to say," §201 ends by not saying (asserting or denying) anything; it ends, one might venture to say, in silence.

Why, if this is so, is §201 sometimes thought to contain one of the book's most important theses? The answer is evidently that it can be difficult to see how Wittgenstein *could* be untroubled by the paradox given that the reasoning leading to it does play a role in combating a suspect notion of the "presence" of meaning.[72] But that rejecting the paradox does not depend, for Wittgenstein, on the availability of a substantive alternative to the platonist's notion of "presence" is suggested by the non-adversarial response to that notion in a passage like this:

> "But I don't mean that what I do now (in grasping a sense) determines the future use causally and as a matter of experience, but that in a queer way, the use itself is in some sense present." – But of course it is, 'in some sense'! Really the only thing wrong with what you say is the expression "in a queer way." The rest is all right ...
>
> (§195)[73]

According to this remark, there is nothing wrong with what the platonist *says*; the problem lies only in his sense that there is something *queer* about what he says. Now this response to the platonist – viz., that his feeling of queerness need be no part of his otherwise all-right thought – is connected to the view of §201 I have sketched in the following way: to emerge from the latent misunderstanding identified at §201 is not to incur any commitment to *platonism* (i.e., to meanings as mysterious entities) but to be able to return the platonist's words to their everyday, unmysterious use, and so to redeem them. To make this plausible, an account is needed – not of the stability of meaning, but of why, in the platonist's attempt to explain this, his own words should come to strike him as so strange.

15 To bring out the connections between the latent misunderstanding identified at §201 and the non-adversarial response to the platonist at §195, consider first how the platonist gives expression to his feeling of "queerness." The sense of what he means to say has been missed, he declares, in so far as he is taken to be speaking of the determination of future use "causally and as a matter of experience." His difficulty is evidently this. In attempting to account for the reach of meaning, he was tempted to speak of a tracking mechanism, the mind's engagement with an infinite rail. But he has been brought to see that such a mechanism, if it is to so much as seem serviceable in explaining a *normative* relation, must be rather unique. For ordinary machines are subject to empirical mishap; they can break, bend, crash, melt or otherwise jump track. In the present case, however, the very identification of a mechanical glitch (e.g., 998, 1000, *1004*) presupposes the applicability of a prior notion of the results that *must* be reached when the mechanism is functioning properly. So if mechanical operations are really to give us a purchase on how someone is compelled to reach just *these* results, the mechanism in question needs to be imagined as somehow invulnerable to mishap, as ideally rigid. But now what is it to imagine an ideally rigid mechanism? Is it not just to think of its movements as in accord with a rule?

One might conclude from this that talk of a mechanism is at best a pseudo-explanation, a "mythological description" as Wittgenstein says (§221), of following a rule. Since the normative relation of "accord" must already figure in its conception, to appeal to a mechanism in this context is to do little more than redescribe the very relation, the possibility of which one wishes to explain. However, the platonist at §195 takes a different tack. Seeing that ordinary mechanical determination in the realm of experience cannot serve as an account of the way meaning is "already present," he is inclined to think that the grasped meaning of an expression must determine its future use in some ghostly *para*-mechanical way. Essentially, the platonist represented here is someone who (1) thinks that the normative aspect of meaning must be metaphysically queer if it cannot be rendered intelligible on the model successfully employed in explaining bits of nature (conceived as the realm of experience under causal laws), (2) finds that it cannot be thus rendered intelligible, and (3) concludes that it is therefore metaphysically queer.[74]

Now the explanatory futility of the platonist's imagery is clearly an important point in Wittgenstein's discussion. But to see why the point carries no commitment, for Wittgenstein, to an interpretivist alternative (and, vice versa, why the rejection of interpretivism incurs no commitment to platonism), we need properly to locate platonism within the general shape of the dialectic informing this region of Wittgenstein's thought. Briefly recapitulating, the other pieces of the dialectic – the pieces which comprised the textual basis of the deconstructive reading – were as follows:

(1) A sign, considered just by itself, is normatively inert: like any bit of nature (e.g., sounds, ink marks), it does not sort behavior into that which accords with it and that which does not.

(2) The same is true of any mental items in which one's present grasp of the meaning of a sign might be said to consist.

(3) There is thus always a gap between the present contents of the mind and bits of the world which might be said to be in accord with those contents. Interpretation is needed to close the gap, bringing mind and world together.

(4) But this is paradoxical. Since any action can be brought into accord with any interpretation of a sign (i.e., on some interpretation of *it*), there can be no accord or conflict.

(5) This paradox, however, destroys not the possibility of meaning, but only the classical conception of it. For we can account for our talk of meaning and understanding through a social-pragmatic story featuring convergent behavior.

The question is: where in this dialectic does platonism belong? The deconstructive reading makes it the critical point of departure for an argument, which, starting with (1) and (2), would culminate in an alternative account of meaning along the lines of (5). And this is not entirely wrong: given the platonist's talk of ghostly mental acts, (1) and (2) are a natural corrective response. But neither is this the whole story. For without more, this is to allow Wittgenstein no interest in how the question which the platonist takes himself to be answering – *viz.,* "how is meaning possible" – arises; it is to assume that the question expresses, for Wittgenstein, an autonomous problem which philosophy is naturally obliged to address. The *Investigations* gives contrary indications: "Thought does not strike us as mysterious while we are thinking, but only when we say, as it were retrospectively: 'How was that possible?' How was it possible for thought to deal with the very object *itself*?" (§428). We get a deeper sense of Wittgenstein's purposes when we recognize that it is precisely the kind of thinking made explicit in the progression from (1) to the paradox at (4) – i.e., a kind of thinking latently carrying the suggestion that meaning is in fact *impossible* – which can make the platonist's question ("how is meaning possible") seem urgent and compelling.[75] Rather than initiating the philosophical dialectic, the platonist's words may thus be seen as arising *after* the paradox at (4) and as comprising, in this position, an understandable response to an interpretivist line of thought. The thought which mediates between the paradox and the platonist's image of rails would be this: given that an interpretation is needed to fix the meaning of a sign, there must, on pain of a paradoxical regress, be some last or final interpretation – i.e., an interpretation not in need of any further interpretation – which is what we call "the meaning."[76] In other words, the interpretivist line of thought leading up to the paradox makes it urgent to find some item in which a meaning-constituting "interpretation" might consist, but an item which, unlike ordinary linguistic signs, can function as a *regress-stopper*; and it is in this intellectual environment that so-called "platonism" intelligibly takes hold.

On this reading, platonism is to be seen as arising from an interpretivist premise about meaning, albeit one which may go unnoticed until it becomes explicit, and explicitly paradoxical, under the pressure of a recoil from the platonism it spawns. The opening step of the dialectic is that which introduces the notion of a sign "considered by itself." If one takes that step unquestioningly, then it will be natural to accept the thesis that to grasp the meaning of a sign is to interpret it; and if one accepts that thesis, then it may come to seem that one's only alternatives are "platonism," on the one hand, and some alternative account of meaning to be wrought from whatever materials are available without presupposing the applicability of such normative notions as accord with a rule. But in saying that the paradox (4) arises on account of a latent misunderstanding, Wittgenstein means to bring into view another way – a non-philosophical way, as it were (cf. §85) – in which this dialectic might end. On this alternative, we might work our way free of the interpretivist thesis by coming to see that an abstraction such as "a sign by itself" comes to seem useful only if we have the idea of giving ourselves a particular *kind* of account of what a sign means – *viz.*, a *philosophical* account. Such abstraction from the circumstances that surround our actual concourse with signs is wanted just when our idea is to give ourselves an account of the meaning of a sign that is not to be dependent on the contingencies of the practical world in which such signs normally operate. Such an account, in other words, is not addressed to someone on whose responses we are relying. For the burden of such an account is not simply to rule out such doubts as might, under the circumstances, arise, but to specify the meaning of a sign absolutely, say, from among *all* the possibilities.[77] Let me explain.

If we regard the use of a sign as an event which, appropriately specified, *includes* the surrounding circumstances, then we are bound to see that from the fact that a doubt about meaning is *possible*, it does not follow that anyone does, or even intelligibly could (under the circumstances) actually doubt (cf. §213). Hence we should want to ask: is there really any clear sense in which doubts and misunderstandings about the meaning of a sign are, as Derrida insists, a "necessary possibility"? Whence such necessity? The necessity appears only on the basis of the assumption that we can intelligibly consider a bit of sign-involving behavior in abstraction from its surrounding circumstances and nonetheless still have *sign*-involving behavior in view. By means of the expression "a sign by itself," we thus precisely manage to represent a doubt which is merely notionally possible as *already present*, just as if any doubt which actually (i.e., in certain circumstances) arises somehow merely *reveals* an indeterminacy that was present in any grasp of meaning *all along.* Clearly this describes the exact mirror image of the platonistic thought that a grasped meaning must be present in such a way as already to determine the resolution of any doubt which might, in future circumstances, arise. The idea of a "philosophical account" which interpretivism and platonism share in common becomes plain if we ask: from what point of view, if not of the circumstantially placed user of language, can it appear, in light of the "necessary possibility" of doubt and misunderstanding, that "to understand is always to interpret"? The answer is: this appears from the point of view of a being who can see (in a timeless present) *all* the possibilities. Of course, it is hardly clear what "all the possibilities" refers to when it figures in the description of such a philosophical account. So the matter might perhaps best be put like this: the notion "a sign by itself" expresses the same metaphysical demand as the demand for an account of what a sign means *absolutely.*

The alternative which Wittgenstein wishes to bring into view involves freeing ourselves of the very idea of such an account. Were we to do so, it seems clear that we should have no use for considering signs "by themselves" –

i.e., independently of our natural responses to them or the way they function in our practical activities. And if we had no use for this abstraction, we should also have no use for the thought (which never seemed very intuitive anyway) that there must always be an interpretation of signs that fixes their meaning. Moreover, our rejection of interpretivism, by this route, would not incur any commitment to platonistic doctrines of meaning. To the contrary, it would indicate nothing more than that we no longer feel obliged to reconstruct an adequate notion of the meaning of a sign out of whatever materials still remain in view after bestowing an abstract attention on signs "by themselves."[78] Our need for such an abstract conception disappears once we no longer feel compelled to try to conceive either the contents of the mind or the linguistic behavior in which such contents are manifest in a way which would especially suit the explanatory purposes of someone undertaking to give "an account" of the very possibility of meaning – an account, that is, from outside (or from beneath) our everyday use of such normative notions as "accord."[79]

On this reading, the problem with the imagery of platonism is simply that it comes too late. Set forth in the context of a deconstructive dialectic in which the question "how is meaning possible" has become urgent, the platonist's various images of presence provide no genuine reassurance. But to say that the imagery is useless in this dialectical context is not to say that there is anything wrong with it just as such. To the contrary, if, following §201, we manage to give up the idea that to understand is to interpret, then the rail-imagery can be taken on board as simply a colorful way of redescribing the commonplace, everyday phenomena of following a rule. Freed from the "misunderstanding" which makes the question "how is meaning possible?" seem urgent, there is simply no cause to take the platonist's images of "presence" in any other way. And that is Wittgenstein's point at §195. The intelligible content of what the platonist says is unobjectionable, something no more philosophically fraught than saying – rather less colorfully and in an everyday tone of voice – that a rule is the sort of thing which provides a standard of correctness for a future series of instances. When Wittgenstein replies non-adversarially to the platonist – "of course [the use is present] in *some* sense" – he is inviting us to affirm the platonist's words in the sense they have before (1), before the philosophical dialectic takes hold, rather than after (4), where, in the environment of interpretivism, the need for an account of meaning has become urgent and the very same words are apt to seem queer.

Could the platonist be satisfied to find himself making sense in such an agreeable, everyday way? Not as long as the idea of a "philosophical account" of meaning persists. If it does, the platonist will reject this rendition of what he might mean, just as he understandably rejects the suggestion that he is talking about the causal determination of future use. The result will be the following dilemma. (1) On the one hand, talk of a causal mechanism seems unsuited – too vulnerable or soft – for explaining the normative possibility of "accord." (2) But to recognize his own imagery as a merely colorful but innocuous way of redescribing a normative relation would be to give up any claim to be accounting for that relation. The platonist represented at §195 is essentially someone who tries to resolve this dilemma by imagining an "ideally rigid" tracking mechanism to be just like a real physical mechanism except (because also ideally rigid) strangely unworldly.[80] And this produces the sense of metaphysical difficulty which gets expressed as a "queer" idea of presence because: (1) in an innocuous sense (the dilemma's second horn), future applications of a rule *are* present (i.e., there is such a thing as grasping a *rule*); (2) in a no less straightforward sense, future applications are *not* present (i.e., they are not spatio-temporally present, physically present before they take place); and finally (3) the "platonist" is someone who is determined to reject both (1) and (2) as an account of what *he* means by "present," on the grounds that if *that* were what he meant, he would too obviously be making an agreeable kind of sense. In short, his philosophical purpose would be frustrated by anything other than a *metaphysical* idea of presence, for example – a phrase from Derrida's account of Husserl might win his assent – "a self-proximity that would in fact be the absolute reduction of space in general."[81] Of course, that *is* queer, nay spooky.

Conclusion: notes on aligning Wittgenstein and Derrida

16 From Wittgenstein's perspective, we can see the proponent of the deconstructive paradox as joining league with his platonistic interlocutor in two important ways.

First, as I have argued, to assert (against the implications of the everyday use of the term "interpretation") that "an interpretation is always required because no text is immune to *possible* doubt," is to commit oneself to the idea of an account of how meaning is fixed in view of "all the possibilities." Just as we should be able (by freeing ourselves from the idea of such an account) to return the platonist's words to their agreeable, everyday use, so too we would be able to bring the word "interpretation" back to its ordinary use, whereby interpretation is sometimes needed (i.e., in cases of real doubt or uncertainty) and sometimes not (cf. §85). Conceived as an everyday form of words gone astray, platonism and its deconstructive criticism are, for Wittgenstein, two sides of the same philosophical coin.

Second, both the platonist and the deconstructivist appear as figures who would rather pursue a "philosophical account" of meaning to the point of nonsense than be taken to mean anything they could easily say. The difficulty in making sense of what they say belongs to their very intention in speaking; if it made sense, it wouldn't satisfy them and they would reject it.[82]

This last point might be expressed in Derrida's terms by saying that the deconstructivist's intention is to speak outside of the "system of meaning"; it might be expressed in Wittgenstein's terms by saying that the intention is to speak outside of "language games." However, these notions, exhibiting a basis of intimacy between Wittgenstein and Derrida, also enter into a number of systematic contrasts between them. To indicate the level of difficulty involved in aligning Wittgenstein's and Derrida's thought, I shall now propose, somewhat summarily, two main points of contrast between them.

First, concerning how philosophy ends and what its necessity is. If implicit in Derrida's picture of philosophical self-criticism is the suggestion that deconstructive thinking is compulsory for anyone who would not be spoken for by the metaphysical commitments of the age, then a strong point of contrast between Wittgenstein and Derrida might be marked by saying that while, on Derrida's conception, philosophical investigation must end (if it is ever to end or satisfy itself) in "unheard-of thoughts," on Wittgenstein's conception, it ends in thoughts heard everyday (which is to say, it ends both more often and less finally): "What *we* do is to bring words back from their metaphysical to their everyday use" (§128). This is explicitly to refuse the idea that any words (including "sign," "representation," "intention," "meaning," etc.) are, in themselves, lost to metaphysics, that any words, just as such, "belong" to metaphysics. Indeed, the idea that philosophy's destruction of metaphysical notions consists in returning words to their everyday employments, in redeeming them in the available currency, is part of the account in the *Investigations* of how it comes to look as if metaphysics has (or ever had) any words, anything to speak of, at all: somehow our words have gone astray. Since this is a picture of metaphysics as dependent, for its apparent intelligibility, on the sense our words have in their everyday employments, it is no exaggeration to say that while for Derrida metaphysics appears to exist autonomously and invidiously, conditioning our every effort to think something else, for Wittgenstein there simply is no such thing as a metaphysical word or thought in the traditional sense.[83] Rather, our attraction to certain forms of words which seem to express great philosophical difficulties arises from our imagining that there is.

Second, concerning the experience of philosophical muteness. It is sometimes said that the *Investigations'* attention to "everyday use" represents a shift in Wittgenstein's "account" of meaning. On the reading I have proposed, however, the philosophical pertinence which Wittgenstein claims for the everyday use of words is simply the heuristic pertinence of reminding ourselves of the contexts of the significant use of various expressions when such reminders are needed in order to carry out the philosophical procedure which is already described in the *Tractatus* as "the only strictly correct" one: "to say nothing [philosophical] and then, whenever someone else wanted to say something metaphysical, to demonstrate to him that he had failed to give a meaning to certain signs in his sentences."[84] The motivation of Wittgenstein's appeal to the "everyday" in the *Investigations* becomes clearer if one asks: how can one demonstrate this? How can one demonstrate to someone who insists that what they want to say is terribly queer (and even impossible to express) that the difficulty lies not in the *sense* of what they say but in the lack of it? One method, pursued in the *Investigations*, is to try to bring one's interlocutor to see, by reference to various contexts of the significant use of expressions, that their purpose in speaking – their "wish to say something metaphysical" – requires that they refuse such accounts of what they might mean on the grounds that what they say would then make perfect sense (i.e., they would be saying something obviously right or obviously wrong). There is no suggestion in the *Investigations* that such a procedure has any natural end (cf. §133) because there is no suggestion that any combination of words, just *as such*, does not have (or could not be given) a sense. Thus conceived, our expressive frustration in philosophy is not a problem with our words at all, but rather with our relation to our words, for example, our conflictually both wanting and not wanting them to make sense. The difference is crucial for Wittgenstein. In the first case, we are apt to regard our muteness as the mark of our wanting to express an inexpressible content; in the second case, we would come to see our problem as owing to there being *no* content which we (unconflictually) want to express.[85] With this proviso, it may be said that the deconstructive theme of philosophical muteness is, for Wittgenstein, just as it is for Derrida, something like the last philosophical straw, or the last rung of the philosophical ladder:

– So in the end when one is doing philosophy one gets to the point where one would like just to emit an inarticulate sound. – But such a sound is an expression only as it occurs in a particular language-game, which should now be described.

(§261)

17 In conclusion, a note on philosophy's destructiveness. Wittgenstein is sometimes remembered as saying that his philosophy is essentially negative or destructive – and of course, in some sense, it is. But if we look closely at remarks which address the matter directly, we find Wittgenstein trying to dispel a false impression. The following remark from the *Investigations* appears originally near Wittgenstein's remark about destroying "idols":

Where does our investigation get its importance from, since it seems only to destroy everything interesting, that is, all that is great and important? (As it were all the buildings, leaving behind only bits of stone and rubble.) What we are destroying is nothing but houses of cards [*Luftgebäude*] ...

(§118)

The *Investigations* are destroying something all right, this says, but not anything that had any substance to begin with, not any dwelling that a human being could – were he to recognize it for what it is – wish to inhabit. What is destroyed is a non-structure, an airy nothing. But that is a strange sort of destruction. It betokens a movement toward greater philosophical self-recognition, such that once matters are seen aright – once the destruction has been successful – part of what will be seen is that there was no real destruction at all. I take it that Wittgenstein is saying something here about what it would be for his way of continuing philosophy to be successful: such a philosophical destruction must destroy, among other things, the impression of its own destructiveness. By the same token, Wittgenstein is drawing attention to one way in which his *Investigations* might *fail* to achieve their aim – namely, by leaving behind in the reader an impression of substantial destructiveness.

That idea of philosophical failure is also the central idea in Wittgenstein's remark about destroying idols. That remark, an emblem of the form of Wittgenstein's thought, builds upon two commonplaces about the history and nature of philosophy.

First, it recalls the commonplace that philosophy sets its face against great errors – errors, that is, not about this or that item in the world, but about the world as a whole. "Philosophy destroys idols." This means: philosophy sets its face against false representations of the absolute, false ideas of human being's relation to Being as such. Philosophy shows the way out of the cave of fundamental illusion.

Second, after recalling this commonplace, Wittgenstein's remark goes on to suggest that in setting its face against fundamental illusions, philosophy is apt to produce new ones. This too is a commonplace. What philosopher has not wanted to stand on the side of reality? And what philosopher has not thereby brought against himself the charge of creating new dogmas? When Nietzsche, for example, announces the twilight of the idols ("I erect no new idols")[86] he means specifically to say that Plato's picture of a fundamental illusion affecting humanity creates a

110

new idol; and Nietzsche suggests, against what he takes Plato to be saying, that the very idea of humanity as a "condition" – analogous to the condition of being blind – that handicaps one's efforts to make contact with the Real, is itself human kind's "longest error."[87] Nietzsche proposes to philosophize against such an idol "with a hammer." But now what about Nietzsche himself? Nietzsche's way of representing things has left many readers with the impression that what is to be grasped when one emerges from the long night of platonistic error is that there are no facts, only the appearance or "interpretation" of facts. But it seems we could hardly get any grip on what "apparentness" or "interpretation" means here unless we make room for the possibility of judgments concerning that which appearances or interpretations may fall short of; unless, that is, we find some application (if only one reserved for a divine being) for the notion of judgments which do not stop short of the facts. The understandable inclination to put apparentness or interpretation in place of a suspiciously metaphysical notion of the Real thus seems bound to self-disappointment because it remains essentially a recoil from a platonistic adversary: such a thesis seems intelligible only insofar as it incorporates and preserves the position it means to oppose.

Suppose, then, that we recognize such idol-preserving recoils as characteristic of philosophy's self-criticism, its still uncompleted Copernican revolution. Then it should be possible to see Wittgenstein's remark about "destroying idols" as an internal characterization of philosophical thought in terms of the way such thought tends to go wrong. Philosophical thought, Wittgenstein is saying, characteristically preserves what it intelligibly wishes to destroy; it does so by creating "its absence." So a philosophical destruction that proved satisfying – i.e., that succeeded in satisfying its own aim – would be in part a self-destruction, or a destruction, at least, of one characteristic idea of philosophy's destructiveness, the one that creates the idol of substantial absence in place of substantial presence.

To remove the Zen-like sound of paradox in this, it might be useful to state the matter in terms of a distinction between two kinds of negativity – theoretical and practical. One way philosophy goes wrong, Wittgenstein would be saying, is by giving the impression that what is required is a theoretical negation, something that has the effect of a denial (cf. §305). Philosophy's appropriate destructiveness is practical: its aim, as Rush Rhees remembers Wittgenstein to have said, is not to get the reader to believe something but to do something he is so far unwilling to do.[88] To succeed, it must therefore challenge the reader's prior sense of what is "great and important."

Such a distinction (between practical and theoretical negativity) can help us to see how the third sentence of §118 ("What we are destroying is nothing but *Luftgebäude*") answers the question (concerning the source of philosophy's importance) posed in the first. This third sentence ("nothing but *Luftgebäude*") challenges an impression of philosophy's theoretical destructiveness precisely by challenging – by destroying – a prior notion of what is supposed to be important about philosophy. The passage as a whole is addressed to a reader who is attracted to philosophical investigation as something "great and important" and who looks for its greatness and importance in its revelation of the grounds of that which, in everyday activity, is merely taken for granted. The first two sentences record the disappointment such a reader is apt to feel in reading the *Investigations*. But then the third sentence – cast as an answer to the question of philosophy's importance – goes on to suggest that the disappointed reader was not exactly wrong when he took up philosophical investigation thinking it would put him in touch with something great and important. His mistake lies in where he was looking for philosophy's greatness and importance. He expected to find this in philosophy's theoretical results, in its substantive constructions and deconstructions, its insight into the world as a whole. He is disappointed because he is looking in the wrong place. Philosophy's importance, Wittgenstein suggests, lies in its showing such a reader that philosophy doesn't have *that* kind of importance.[89] And to show him this is not nothing. For it is to show him something quite important about *himself*, about his own attraction to philosophical investigation. Philosophy's importance lies in its holding up a mirror, as it were, in which the reader, seeing his own disappointment, may come to see that his attraction to philosophical investigation involved a false sense of importance. This idea of philosophical success – at once deeply practical and negative – may seem to spell the end of philosophy. But one ought to remember that in so far as the philosophical problem involves a false sense of philosophy's importance, the structure of the problem is such that it is philosophy which is needed to solve it.

Notes

I am grateful to Jim Conant, Alice Crary, Emilie Gonand and Toril Moi for comments on previous drafts of this essay. The essay also benefited from conversations with David Finkelstein, Richard Moran, George Wilson and Walter Benn Michaels. Among those from whose work I have learned most about Wittgenstein, the influence of Stanley Cavell, Cora Diamond and John McDowell is, I believe, deep and pervasive in this essay.

1 J. Derrida, *"Differance"* in *Speech and Phenomena and Other Essays on Husserl's Theory of Signs*, D. Allison (trans.) Evanston, Northwestern University Press, 1973, p. 149.

2 S. Kripke, *Wittgenstein on Rules and Private Language*, Cambridge, Massachusetts, Harvard University Press, 1982, pp. 73, 77, 107.

3 L. Wittgenstein, "Big Typescript Sections 86–93" in *Philosophical Occasions*, §88.

4 See Derrida, *Speech and Phenomena*, op. cit., pp. 108, 53, 128.

5 H. Staten, *Wittgenstein and Derrida*, Lincoln, University of Nebraska Press, 1984, p. 1. Another perceptive Derridean appreciation of Wittgenstein is S. Glendinning, *On Being With Others*, London, Routledge, 1998.

6 "§" refers to Wittgenstein's *Philosophical Investigations*.

7 See J. Derrida, *Limited Inc*, S. Weber (trans.) Evanston, Northwestern University Press, 1988, pp. 15, 126, 133, 147.

8 Ibid., p. 15.

9 See Derrida, *Speech and Phenomena*, op. cit., pp. 76–81.

10 Derrida, *Limited Inc*, op. cit., p. 19.

11 E. Husserl, *Logical Investigations I*, J. Findlay (trans.) London, Routledge, 1970, §35, p. 333.

12 Derrida, *Limited Inc*, op. cit., p. 119.

13 J. Derrida, "Force of Law: The 'Mystical Foundation of Authority'" in D. Cornell, M. Rosenfeld and D. Carlson (eds) *Deconstruction and the Possibility of Justice*, New York, Routledge, 1992, p. 23.

14 Cf. S. Fish, "Force" in *Doing What Comes Naturally*, Durham, Duke University Press, 1989, p. 153 (mentioned approvingly in "Force of Law," op. cit., pp. 14, 23).

15 Ibid., p. 23.

16 The phrase is from Derrida, *Writing and Difference*, Chicago, University of Chicago Press, 1978, p. 292.

17 This motivation of interpretivism is not unique to Derrida. Compare Richard Rorty, *Objectivism, Relativism, and Truth*, Cambridge, Cambridge University Press, 1991, p. 81.
18 Derrida's claim should be distinguished from a more restricted interpretivist thesis, according to which our interest in having *authoritative* standards of decision entails that the proper role of a judge is *to interpret* the rules – i.e., to conserve their meaning in applying them – rather than to substitute his own judgment. See e.g., J. Raz, "Intention in Interpretation" in A. Marmor (ed.) *Law and Interpretation: Essays in Legal Philosophy*, Oxford, Oxford University Press, 1995. This use of "interpretation" is not what Derrida has in mind; his attraction to the term evidently depends on the implication of innovation it carries in other contexts. At the same time, however, there is no reason to take Derrida to be asserting that it *cannot* be a rational exercise of judgment to decline, on grounds of the law's authority, to engage in innovative (as opposed to meaning-conserving) application of the rules. Derrida's quarrel is with a philosophical picture of what any such meaning-conserving application must involve: a picture of the rule as providing, in the face of possible disputes, "an absolute guarantee" of the faithfulness of one or another judgment.
19 My formulation here is indebted to J. McDowell, "Meaning and Intentionality in Wittgenstein's Later Philosophy," *Midwest Studies in Philosophy*, 1992, vol. 17, pp. 40–52.
20 Derrida, *Limited Inc*, op. cit., p. 148; see also ibid., p. 137 and "Structure, Sign and Play," op. cit., p. 292.
21 See, e.g., Derrida, *Limited Inc*, op. cit., pp. 151, 134, 136, 147.
22 Derrida, *"Differance,"* op. cit., p. 131; see also pp. 130, 136.
23 The philosophical use of "interpretation" contrasts not only with its use in contexts where there is some actual doubt about meaning, but also with such related uses as (1) "interpretations of literature," (2) interpreting as opposed to innovating (see note 18) and (3) performing interpretations, e.g., "Olivier's interpretation of Hamlet." It would be instructive to consider the analogies between these and the philosophical use of the term "interpretation."
24 M. Nussbaum, "Skepticism About Practical Reason in Literature and the Law," *Harvard Law Review*, 1994, vol. 107, pp. 723–32.
25 Derrida, *Limited Inc*, op. cit., pp. 146, 151.
26 See, e.g., ibid., pp. 127, 152.
27 The depth of this difficulty may be gauged by what Rodolphe Gasché says in response to the charge that Derrida's use of such notions as "interpretation" and *"differance"* as "conditions of possibility" simply continues philosophy's traditional quest for what is prior or older. Gasché's response is that such notions are only "older in a ... very strange way," for if they are conditions of possibility "they are at the same time *conditions of impossibility"* (*Inventions of Difference*, Cambridge, Massachusetts, Harvard University Press, 1995, p. 4). But how would this make such notions discontinuous with Kantian philosophy? Kant himself summarizes the First Critique by saying that the conditions of the possibility of knowledge (viz., its relation to possible experience) are at once the conditions of its impossibility – i.e., the impossibility of its rational "purity." See, e.g., *Critique of Practical Reason*, L.W. Beck (trans.) Indianapolis, Bobbs-Merrill, 1956, p. 56.
28 J. Derrida, *Spurs: Nietzsche's Styles*, B. Harlow (trans.) Chicago, University of Chicago Press, 1979, p. 133.
29 J. Derrida, *Of Grammatology*, G. Spivak (trans.) Baltimore, Johns Hopkins University Press, 1976, p. 41.
30 Derrida, *Limited Inc*, op. cit., p. 147.
31 Cf. Ryle, speaking of "operations of reason": "Where success is possible, failure is possible..." *Aspects of Mind*, Oxford, Blackwell, 1993, p. 72.
32 J. L. Austin, "A Plea for Excuses" in *Philosophical Papers* (third edition), Oxford, Oxford University Press, 1979, pp. 179–80.
33 Derrida, *Limited Inc*, op. cit., p. 15.

34 Stanley Cavell's rich exploration of Derrida's reading of Austin has been helpful to me in this and the following paragraph. See *A Pitch of Philosophy: Autobiographical Exercises*, Cambridge, Massachusetts, Harvard University Press, 1994, chapter 2.

35 Derrida, *Limited Inc*, op. cit., pp. 126, 147, 127, 157, 133.

36 Ibid., p. 15. Cf. p. 118.

37 Ibid., p. 20.

38 I mean for this sentence to recall *Investigations*, §122. Derrida notes that such a paradox "recurs almost everywhere" in his work. *Aporias*, T. Dutoit (trans.) Stanford, Stanford University Press, 1993, p. 15.

39 Stanley Fish ("Force," op. cit.) would be an example of a simple interpretivist.

40 Derrida, *Speech and Phenomena*, op. cit., p. 102.

41 See ibid., p. 51.

42 Cf. Derrida, *Limited Inc*, op. cit., p. 15.

43 Derrida, *Speech and Phenomena*, op. cit., pp. 103, 104.

44 Cf. J. Habermas's criticism of Derrida in *The Philosophical Discourse of Modernity*, F. Lawrence (trans.) Cambridge, Massachusetts, MIT Press, 1987, p. 187.

45 Derrida, *Speech and Phenomena*, op. cit., p. 51.

46 Derrida, "*Differance*," op. cit., p. 158. Cf. p. 153.

47 Ibid.

48 Cf. Derrida, *Speech and Phenomena*, op. cit., pp. 51–2: "For the present and for some time to come, [deconstruction] will only be capable of working over the language of metaphysics from within, from a certain sphere of problems inside that language."

49 Cf. one of Derrida's glosses on "quasi-transcendental": a discourse that up to a point "respects the rules of that which it deconstructs," *Limited Inc*, op. cit., p. 152.

50 Cf. ibid., p. 127.

51 Derrida, *Of Grammatology*, op. cit., p. 41.

52 Derrida, *Speech and Phenomena*, op. cit., p. 102.

53 See, e.g., Derrida, "*Differance*," op. cit., pp. 142, 147.

54 Ibid., p. 153; cf. Derrida, *Speech and Phenomena*, op. cit., pp. 102, 103.

55 Cf. Derrida, *Limited Inc*, op. cit., p. 152.

56 Derrida, *Speech and Phenomena*, op. cit., p. 103.

57 The four points mentioned in this paragraph may all be found in *Of Grammatology*, op. cit., p. 14.

58 See note 5 above.

59 On "replacing," see Kripke, *Wittgenstein on Rules and Private Language*, op. cit., pp. 73, 75, 77; on "objective facts," see ibid., pp. 71, 72, 77–8, 86, 97, 108.

60 §193; cf. §§195, 197.

61 It might be added that many of Wittgenstein's elaborations of "platonism" present a version of the picture of meaning that Derrida finds in Husserl; and that, like Derrida, Wittgenstein draws attention to how, given such a picture, it becomes tempting to privilege phonetic over graphic embodiments of meaning: i.e., to treat speech (and especially speaking to oneself) as the locus of self-present life, spirit or breath; and correlatively, to associate the graphic sign with death. Cf. §432; *Zettel*, §§143, 236 and 36; *Speech and Phenomena*, op. cit., pp. 77–8, 81. A thought that tempts us, according to both Wittgenstein and Derrida, is that our words are more than inert marks or sounds in virtue of some "inner" mental act of meaning or intending. But since meaning and intending also reach into the world, this thought of the mind's animating powers would seem to require that the future use of an expression be somehow *present* in two senses: (1) present to the mind of the speaking subject, and (2) present at the present moment, the life-giving moment, in which the meaning of a word is grasped. Hence, unlike the actual use of a sign which is extended in time (cf. §138), the mental act to which such use owes allegiance would take place, as Derrida observes, circling Husserl's word, "in dem *selben Augenblick*" – in a flash or blink of an eye. "It is as if we could grasp the whole use of a word *in einem Augenblick*," Wittgenstein says; as if "the future development [of a word] must in some way already be present ..."(§197).

62 Kripke, *Wittgenstein on Rules and Private Language*, op. cit., p. 97.

63 Ibid., pp. 70–1.

64 Ibid., pp. 5, 69–70.

65 Like Kripke, Derrida tends to represent matters as if a correct account of meaning requires that one affirm the negation of a suspect metaphysical thesis. Consider again *Limited Inc*, op. cit., p. 151:

> I take into account and believe that it is necessary to account for this stability [of interpretive contexts]. . . . But . . . to account for a certain stability . . . is precisely not to speak of eternity or of absolute solidity. . . . I say that there is no stability that is absolute, eternal, intangible, natural, etc.

To be exact, Derrida feels no hesitation in *speaking* about "absolute solidity," for he goes on to do just that: "I say there is no stability that is absolute. . . ." The implication is not that it would be unfruitful to speak about "absolute solidity," only that it would be wrong to assert that it exists.

66 The third stage of my argument does not attempt to consider the merits of a substitute account of meaning in terms of social agreements, only to place such an account in relation to Wittgenstein. However, it seems relevant to mention one way in which such an account seems lacking in perspicuity. Consider that for a certain decision to be required by a rule consists, on this picture, in nothing more than the community agreeing that it is required. How does this differ from a picture of a community merely pretending to agree that something – anything at all – is *required* by the rule? Essentially, this is to ask: can such a substitute account of correctness in matters of meaning really sustain the sense that there is *meaning* once it is seen that, at the basic level (beneath our normative talk of "accord"), there is nothing but "the brute fact" of convergent behavior? For an inquiry along these lines, see J. McDowell, "Wittgenstein on Following a Rule," *Synthese*, 1984, vol. 58, pp. 325–63. Kripke (*Wittgenstein on Rules and Private Language*, p. 69) attempts to clarify the implications of his denial of "objective facts" about meaning by saying that he merely wishes to deny a philosopher's notion – the notion of a "superlative fact" – not any commitment present in ordinary talk about meaning. But in the context of Kripke's account this contrast itself seems unclear. If the implication is that what is denied lacks any substantive significance (compare the use of "2 + 2 is not 5"), it seems hard to understand how such a denial could be seen as a skeptical threat to our notion of meaning, requiring a substantive solution. But if the denial of the "superlative fact" is taken to be a substantially significant denial of something which would have secured our entitlement to speak of "facts" in the ordinary sense (so that its denial is now felt to make urgent the provision of some alternative account), it ought to be at least questionable whether such a denial doesn't also threaten commitments present in our ordinary talk of meaning. In any case, Kripke's way of formulating Wittgenstein's thought misses the extent to which Wittgenstein's own formulations are motivated by his sense of philosophical difficulty as thriving on this sort of unclarity: "What gives the impression that we want to deny anything?" (§305).

67 I am indebted for this point to Cavell, *A Pitch of Philosophy*, op. cit., p. 68.

68 Cora Diamond's discussion of the use of a "frame" in the *Tractatus* sheds a helpful light on Wittgenstein's later use of such framing devices. See "Ethics, Imagination and the Method of Wittgenstein's *Tractatus*," reprinted in this volume.

69 It looks specifically like one of Derrida's main *targets*: the privileging of "inner speech" over writing. See note 61 above.

70 "Interpretation" begins to look like a mere ghost – "the ghost," to use a phrase of Derrida's, of "the undecidable": "The undecidable remains caught, lodged, at least as a ghost – but an essential ghost – in every decision . . ." "Force of Law," op. cit., p. 24.

71 In one way, it *is* the idea of "interpretation" as linguistic substitution which produces a paradox when interpretation is made into a general requirement. But if one were clear from the beginning that this is what "an interpretation" was supposed to be, interpretivism, and hence the paradox, would never get off the ground. In this sense, the paradox-inducing use of "interpretation" is actually the one framed at the end of §201.

72 Thus it may look as if the instruction given in §201 – "there is a way of grasping a rule which is *not* an *interpretation*" – if it is not a platonistic relapse, must really mean: "which doesn't *appear* to be an interpretation given that the community is unanimous in ratifying a particular way of following the rule."

73 Cf. §§197, 194c, 196, 692.

74 This gloss on "platonism" is indebted to John McDowell's exploration of the philosophical motivation and consequences of such a (restricted) conception of "nature" in *Mind and World*, Cambridge, Massachusetts, Harvard University Press, 1994. Cf. *Investigations*, §108c.

75 The idea that philosophy's "how possible" question may be motivated by materials of thought which carry an unrecognized implication of "impossibility" plays an important role in McDowell, ibid.

76 McDowell ("Meaning and Intentionality," op. cit., p. 47) helpfully suggests that we might trace the origins of the rail imagery to the following thought: "What one wishes to say is: 'Every sign is capable of interpretation; but the meaning mustn't be capable of interpretation. It is the last interpretation',," *The Blue and Brown Books*, p. 34. Following McDowell's diagnostic suggestion, we might thus see such imagery as a philosophical compromise-formation resulting from the attempt to hang onto an (interpretivist) picture of the mind as comprised, like any bit of nature, only of inert items (on the one hand) and the need to stem the skeptical threat to the realm of meaning implicit in this picture (on the other).

77 On the idea of such an account, see Diamond, *Realism and the Realistic Spirit: Wittgenstein, Philosophy and the Mind*, Cambridge, Mass., MIT Press, 1991, pp. 68–9, whose formulation I am adopting here.

78 Cf. §432: "Every sign *by itself* seems dead. *What* gives it life?" If we take this question as a request for an "account" of meaning, we would apparently have to choose between (1) present mental acts that are queer in their powers to fix the whole use of a sign, and (2) the thesis that the fixity of meaning is possible only by way of interpretation, where a paradoxical regress can be avoided only by making the notion of interpretation itself queer. But the point of Wittgenstein's remark lies elsewhere. It seeks to draw our attention to the strangeness of the abstraction – a "sign by itself" – which serves us in raising a difficulty about how a sign can have a fixed meaning while prescinding from the practical setting that is the life of – or better *our life with* – signs. On the notions of seeing signs from the "outside," their lifelessness, and the need for interpretation, see also *Zettel*, §§233, 235–6.

79 Cf. *Remarks on the Foundations of Mathematics*, §VI-28: "Following according to the rule is FUNDAMENTAL to our language game." This invites us to think that any account of psychological processes or social behavior serviceable in *deriving* the possibility of following a rule would not be an account of the patterns of commitment involved in our speaking a language and finding meaning in each other's words. (Which is not to say, of course, that meaning is not contingent upon such processes and behavior or that language could exist in their absence.)

80 Wittgenstein calls this a "crossing of different pictures of determination" (§191) – one involving a normative, the other a causal, relation.

81 Derrida, *Speech and Phenomena*, op. cit., p. 79.

82 These formulations of the deconstructivist's intention have benefited from Cora Diamond's elaboration of Wittgenstein's idea of rejecting an account of what one means "on the ground of its significance." See "Ethics, Imagination and the Method of Wittgenstein's *Tractatus*," in this volume. Consider a remark by one of Derrida's sympathetic commentators concerning the deconstructive use of another relatively everyday term:

> The deconstructive leverage supplied by a term like *writing* depends on its resistance to any kind of settled or definitive meaning. To call it a "concept" is to fall straight away into [a] trap. ... Once the term is fixed within a given explanatory system, it becomes ... usable in ways that deny or suppress its radical insights.
> (C. Norris, *Deconstruction: Theory and Practice*, London, Routledge, 1991, pp. 31–2)

Norris does not, I think, mean to suggest that the *word* writing resists clarification or explanation, much less that one would be falling into error if, by explaining it, one made the word useful in a way that involved no aspiration to philosophical insight. The point is that the deconstructivist would find *his* purpose in using such a word to be thwarted by any such clarification. For a similar point concerning *"differance,"* see J. Caputo, *Deconstruction in a Nutshell,* New York, Fordham University Press, 1997, p. 99 and Derrida, *"Differance,"* op. cit., pp. 132, 134.

83 Cavell helpfully suggests that we might frame the issue between Derrida and Wittgenstein as a question of "the autonomy of metaphysical philosophy, of the direction of the burden of proof of its existence," *A Pitch of Philosophy,* op. cit., p. 119.

84 L. Wittgenstein, *Tractatus Logico-Philosophicus,* D. Pears and B. McGuinness (trans.) §6.53.

85 An appropriate elaboration of this point would need to consider the intellectual motivation of Wittgenstein's "austere" conception of nonsense, and of his related view that there are no limits to sense (e.g., no logically illegitimate propositions). See Diamond, *The Realistic Spirit,* op. cit. chapters 2, 3 and 6, and James Conant's chapter in this volume.

86 F. Nietzsche, *Ecce Homo,* Walter Kaufmann (trans.), New York, Random House, 1967, p. 217 (translation altered slightly).

87 F. Nietzsche, *Twilight of the Idols (or How to Philosophize with a Hammer),* R.J. Hollingdale (trans.) London, Penguin Books, 1968, p. 51.

88 R. Rhees, *Discussions of Wittgenstein,* London, Routledge, 1970, pp. 42–3.

89 Cf. Wittgenstein's remark in the *Tractatus* that the value of his work consists in showing "how little is achieved when [philosophy's problems] are solved."

6

WITTGENSTEIN'S PHILOSOPHY IN RELATION TO POLITICAL THOUGHT

Alice Crary

There is an ongoing debate, within discussions of Wittgenstein's philosophy, about the significance of his work for political thought. The debate in its most familiar form presupposes a widely accepted interpretation on which Wittgenstein advocates a view of meaning that inclines towards ruling out the very possibility of criticism of practices and traditions. Some commentators argue that Wittgenstein's work is deeply conservative and locate its putatively conservative character in a tendency to undermine the critical modes of thought required to make sense of demands for progressive change. Their suggestion is that to the extent that his work teaches that our established practices cannot be criticized it implies that the only way for us to live consistently is to quit aspiring to move beyond them. At the same time, other commentators argue that his thought sheds light on our efforts to bring about social and political change and, moreover, that it does so even in cases in which what is at issue is radical or revolutionary change. Their competing suggestion is that to the extent that Wittgenstein shows that changes in our ways of life are unconstrained by responsibility to our critical concepts he enables us to make sense of social changes which go beyond the realm of possibilities imaginable from within those ways of life.

In what follows, I will not try to arbitrate this debate about the bearing of Wittgenstein's philosophy on political thought. This paper's central line of argument aims to establish that both positions in the debate draw on a misinterpretation of his view of meaning and that both are therefore unable to illuminate ways in which his philosophy can inform political thought. It is, however, no part of my aim in developing this line of argument to suggest that Wittgenstein's philosophy lacks any significant implications for political thought. What I hope to show is that any accurate assessment of the implications it has must fall outside the space in which the ongoing debate takes place and, more specifically, must begin by equipping itself with a more faithful interpretation of his view of meaning. At the close of the paper, after tracing the emergence of the ongoing debate out of a widely accepted interpretation of Wittgenstein's view of meaning, I will revisit the question of the relation between his philosophy and political thought.[1]

1 Right-wing Wittgenstein, lefter-wing Wittgenstein

Our only task is to be just. That is, we must only point out and resolve the injustices of philosophy, and not posit new parties – and creeds.

(Wittgenstein[2])

Throughout his later writings, Wittgenstein insists that when in philosophy we are concerned with questions about the meaning of bits of language, we should attend to ways in which those bits of language are used. His insistence is often understood as suggesting that he rejects a more traditional conception of meaning on which our use of particular expressions is in some sense a consequence of the meanings those expressions already possess in favor of a conception of meaning on which our use of a particular expression somehow constitutes its meaning. He is taken to be claiming that the place a bit of language has in our lives – the public techniques to which it is tied – fixes or determines its meaning.[3] (Such a view of meaning is sometimes called a "use-theory of meaning."[4])

This results in an understanding of Wittgenstein as advancing the following thesis: any time our use of a combination of words changes that combination of words changes in meaning. It follows from this thesis that we are never in a position from which it makes sense to talk about the adequacy or inadequacy of our discourses to the nature of what we are talking about.[5] If we change our use of a combination of words, that combination of words will now simply have a new meaning. So we will not be talking about the same thing in a different and, perhaps, more appropriate way, but will simply be talking about something else. The game we play with a particular bit of language is not distinguishable from and thus not answerable to what we are talking about, and it follows that it can be no more than a mark of confusion that we sometimes want to argue that our discourses are superior or inferior to those of our ancestors or neighbors or that we sometimes agitate for what we think of as reform of our current discourses.[6]

Commentators who attribute to Wittgenstein the view that we cannot ask whether or not our linguistic practices are superior or inferior to others, or whether they are themselves reasonable or justified, do not for the most part, however, take him to be putting forth the implausible claim that we never justify or assess what we say or what we do, that we never weigh what speaks for and against a particular mode of conduct or form of speech. Rather they tend to take him to be claiming that there are permissible forms of criticism (viz., those which we engage in *within* language-games) and also prohibited forms of criticism (viz., those which involve attempts to as it were get outside a language-game in order to provide it with rational foundations).[7]

The idea of a distinction between prohibited external and permissible internal forms of criticism flows naturally from the principles of a use-theory of meaning. The theory can be extended so that it represents the meanings of even our most basic logical concepts as fixed by linguistic conventions and accordingly issues in a thoroughly conventionalist account of logical necessity. If we understand by our "language-game" a set of social conventions governing our linguistic practices – as commentators who develop this basic interpretative line for the most part do – then we can say that the theory, thus extended, represents our language-game as immune

119

to external criticism. What blocks efforts to submit it to criticism is that doing so would require us to undermine whatever critical or normative concepts we want to use in assessing it by bringing into question the practices within which they function and are intelligible. There is, on this extended use-theory of meaning, a logical barrier cutting us off from criticism of our language-game. The theory invites us to resign ourselves to our inability to surpass a limit imposed by the very nature of language which we would need to pass beyond if we were to bring our critical or normative concepts to bear on our language-game itself. At the same time, the theory leaves room for the employment of critical or normative concepts in accordance with practices established within the language-game. There is, on its terms, nothing inherently confused about raising a question about, e.g., whether a given expression is being used consistently as long as, in raising it, we do not challenge the idea that what counts as consistency is determined by linguistic conventions. So internal forms of criticism remain permissible.

Where our language-game is understood, as it is here, as a set of linguistic conventions, Wittgenstein's invocation of the notion of "our shared form of life" is often understood as intended to underline social and conventional aspects of our lives as possessors of a language. Talk of our form of life is taken to be equivalent to talk of social conventions governing our linguistic practices – and hence as equivalent to talk of our language-game. We can thus say that it follows from a use-theory of meaning, extended along the above lines, that our form of life is immune to external criticism. (For the sake of convenience, I will hereafter refer to interpretations of Wittgenstein on which he develops a use-theory of meaning so that it prohibits external criticism of our form of life as "inviolability interpretations.")

Taking inviolability interpretations as their point of departure, many commentators argue that Wittgenstein espouses a species of ethical or cultural relativism. The idea is that he is committed to the possibility of people who have essentially different linguistic conventions and who are therefore properly understood as having logical standards essentially different from ours. When we encounter such people and find ourselves separated from them by, say, certain moral, religious or cultural distances, we should conceive the distances in question, not as disagreements which can be settled through rational conversation, but rather as differences resistant to all efforts at reasoned resolution. The discrepancy between our respective logical standards ensures that we are never in a position to say that our words meet or should be translated to meet theirs and hence that we are never in a position in which we can meaningfully evaluate their linguistic practices either. They are not talking about the same thing we are, so attempts to assess the relative merits of their linguistic practices and ours will be ethically unsound and philosophically suspect. The gulf between us is one which can be spanned, if at all, only with purely rhetorical or persuasive methods.[8]

The rest of this section is devoted to a series of illustrations of how commentators draw on inviolability interpretations (some further developed so that they explicitly support an understanding of Wittgenstein as a relativist) in arguing in favor of different accounts of the political tendency of Wittgenstein's philosophy. But before turning to these illustrations, it will be helpful to mention a troubling feature of the interpretations which figure in them which does not depend on their being invoked in favor of any particular account of the political tendency of his work.

On inviolability interpretations, Wittgenstein is understood as claiming that we are prevented by the structure of language from bringing our critical concepts to bear on our form of life: attempts to bring such concepts to bear on it disintegrate into incoherence because they call for extending the concepts beyond the range of their legitimate application. He thus appears to be endorsing the view that we recognize certain utterances (namely, those we produce in our futile attempts to apply our critical concepts to our form of life) as unintelligible because of what they try (unsuccessfully) to say. He appears to be saying that while these utterances are ultimately *unintelligible*, they are none the less to some extent *intelligible* (in so far as we can discern what they are attempts to say). There are two basic respects in which this feature of inviolability interpretations is troubling. Here Wittgenstein is represented as helping himself to a view of the limits of sense which, as familiar and natural as it may be, can seem problematic in so far as it makes room for a notion of *coherent nonsense*. Further, he is at the same time represented as endorsing a view which, now leaving aside any questions about its adequacy, seems to come directly into conflict with an important strand of his own thought about the relation between nonsensical combinations of words and intelligible bits of language. It is a characteristic gesture of Wittgenstein's, throughout his work, to distance himself from the idea that when we reject a sentence as nonsense, we do so because we grasp what it is an attempt to say and then discern that *that* cannot be said. (On one occasion, he puts it this way: calling a sentence senseless is not a matter of identifying a "senseless sense."[9]) One of my objects in examining a set of inviolability interpretations in the following pages is to record their tendency to present us with portraits of him on which he betrays the spirit of this gesture. This tendency of inviolability interpretations is, I will argue in §2, connected with their tendency to misrepresent another moment in Wittgenstein's thought about meaning – viz., the moment, a source of puzzlement to many readers, at which he suggests that he is not developing anything that could properly be described as a philosophical *explanation* of meaning. Wittgenstein's remarks on the relation between the meaning and use of expressions must, if their significance is to be appreciated, be understood in a way which does justice, simultaneously, to his remarks about the limits of sense and to his remarks about the nature of his own philosophical procedures.

(i) Wittgenstein as a conservative philosopher

Most commentary on Wittgenstein's philosophy which represents it as having a conservative bent draws on versions of inviolability interpretations on which he is explicitly understood as a relativist. Such commentary attempts to show that his brand of relativism resembles dominant forms of conservative political thought and should be understood as supporting a conservative political outlook. The characterization of "conservative thought" taken for granted is typically one which is conceived as broad enough to include within its scope the work of thinkers as diverse in their historical and cultural circumstances and specific preoccupations as (to mention several often named in connection with Wittgenstein) Burke, Spengler, Mannheim and Oakeshott and which represents such thought as marked, above all, by a concern with demonstrating the priority of "Life over Reason,

Practice over Norms and Being over Thought."[10] Interpretations of Wittgenstein as a relativist are invoked to show that he shares the tendency of conservative thinkers to privilege life and practice over reason and rationality. He is understood as claiming that criticism of any form of life "has to be immanent and not transcendent."[11] He thus appears to be disqualifying rational reflection from overseeing and governing either our own practices or those of others and granting our established ways of life authority over the exercise of reason. The transition to a specifically conservative conclusion is then made as follows. Since Wittgenstein maintains that reason cannot provide our ways of life with "external compulsion,"[12] he renders the very concept of social change problematic. Social criticism is impotent to recommend genuine changes in our ways of going on, and so we are forced to concede that "the given form of life cannot be *consciously* transcended."[13] And this is taken as evidence that he thinks we must, on pain of irrationality, adhere to our established practices and, at the same time, refrain from efforts to assess other, divergent ways of life.

This approach to Wittgenstein's philosophy is shared by champions and critics of his alleged conservatism. In this connection, one might, for instance, consider the work of J.C. Nyíri, one of the most outspoken fans of Wittgenstein's alleged conservatism, together with the work of Ernest Gellner, one of the earliest thinkers to attack his alleged conservatism. Both Nyíri and Gellner argue from relativistic interpretations of Wittgenstein to the conclusion that he should be understood as recommending a conservative attitude towards our practices and a tolerant or non-judgmental attitude towards the practices of others.[14] Nyíri lauds Wittgenstein for demonstrating how a conservative social attitude towards our own practices (an attitude he thinks is thrust upon us when we appreciate that "traditions cannot be judged"[15]) can be compulsory in a world which contains many different social practices, a world which is undeniably pluralistic. Wittgenstein's "solution" to this "neo-conservative paradox," according to Nyíri, is "his insight that the possibility of other orders does not in the least weaken the inexorable binding force of our own."[16] Nyíri argues Wittgenstein should be credited with having demonstrated that, although we can recognize different forms of order in the lives of others, we nevertheless "cannot entertain a liberal attitude as regards irregularities in our *own* society."[17] In the same vein, but from a different perspective, Gellner complains that Wittgenstein paints a picture of us as trapped within our own traditions – within "a cozy, self-contained conceptual cocoon"[18] – unable even to scrutinize the traditions of our ancestors and neighbors. This has the disastrous result, he declares, that "a cognitively cumulative culture" is placed "on the same level as stagnant and self-revering ones."[19]

Nyíri's and Gellner's respective accounts of Wittgenstein's putative conservatism are representative of the larger class of such accounts in that they both offer descriptions of him as a relativist which take for granted the at least apparently unstable view of the limits of sense I touched on a moment ago. They take him to be saying that certain of our sentences (namely, those we formulate when we are vainly attempting to criticize forms of life) should be jettisoned as unintelligible because of *what it is* – they are intelligible at least to the degree that we can make this out – they futilely aspire to say.

(ii) Saving Wittgenstein from conservatism (Richard Rorty)

The most influential reading of Wittgenstein which has the characteristic features of an inviolability interpretation and which, moreover, represents his philosophy, not as conservative, but rather as furnishing us with resources for making sense of even radical social change is Richard Rorty's. Rorty's reading of Wittgenstein has been particularly influential within literary-theoretical circles. This is due in part to the fact that one of Rorty's preoccupations is highlighting similarities between the view of language he attributes to Wittgenstein and the views developed within the class of theories which dominate such circles – i.e., the class of *deconstructivist* theories. Given the current standing of deconstructivist theories, the convergence that Rorty (and others[20]) underline between such theories and inviolability interpretations undoubtedly helps to make the interpretations appealing within literary-theoretical discourses. In a moment, I will offer a representative illustration of this convergence by turning to the work of one very prominent contemporary theorist – Stanley Fish.[21]

But before turning to a discussion of Rorty's reading of Wittgenstein and its relation to this literary-theoretical tradition, I want to stress that his work is distinguished from that of most theorists by its sensitivity to pitfalls which stand in the way of the articulation of a consistent inviolability view. One sign of this sensitivity is his effort, most strongly accented in his recent work, to bypass some of the objections his view might otherwise be taken to invite by arguing that it is not the appropriate target of any specifically philosophical criticisms. Rorty claims that he is defending his view of language on pragmatic or political grounds as opposed to philosophical ones and that that view is accordingly open only to pragmatic or political objections. Moreover, he suggests that in abandoning any strictly philosophical defense of his view and relying exclusively on pragmatic or political terms of criticism, he is moving closer to Wittgenstein. He is taking a decisive step away from any engagement with the explanatory projects of traditional metaphysics and is thus entitled to regard himself as doing justice to the moment in Wittgenstein's thought at which Wittgenstein denies that he is in the business of giving a metaphysical explanation of the workings of language. So if we take Rorty on his own (most recent) terms, the sorts of philosophical worries to which other inviolability interpretations are vulnerable can't get a foothold on his supposedly Wittgensteinian view of language. At the end of this section, after describing the view Rorty ascribes to Wittgenstein and discussing how Rorty thinks it is suited for illuminating the nature of social change, I will argue that the view is, after all, held hostage by the metaphysics he claims it allows us to set aside and that it thus fails, even by his own standard of success, to do justice to the spirit of Wittgenstein's philosophy.

Two more preliminary comments are called for here. First, a central concern of Rorty's throughout his writing – and one which guides his discussions of Wittgenstein – is liberating himself from modes of thought which presuppose some form of what he calls "realism." When Rorty speaks of realism, he typically has in mind either the thesis that truth is a correspondence relation between the world and bits of language which represent features of the world – or the further thesis, which he often represents as an expansion or consequence of the first, that (objective) truth is a matter of a bit of language's representing the world in a manner purified of all traces of anything perspectival so that it affords a transparent, metaphysically privileged mode of access to the way things are. Rorty's habit of moving, in his discussions of realism, between versions of these two different theses tends to obscure the possibility that forms of words which figure in the former thesis (e.g., "correspondence between language and the world," "representation of features of the world") might have ordinary, non-metaphysical uses and might not in every context (even, say, when employed with great emphasis) commit the person using them to some version of the latter, unambiguously metaphysical thesis. His talk of realism will accordingly strike the thinker committed to taking this possibility seriously as misleading. It will seem to her that Rorty slides, in his discussions of realism, between targeting a clearly metaphysical position and taking issue with modes of thought and speech which, although they may be taken up and used in elaborating such a position, are in themselves philosophically innocent. Now one of the main aims of this paper is to show that, as we might put it at this point, Wittgenstein takes this possibility seriously. Another slightly more local aim is to show that one of the most important differences between Wittgenstein and Rorty's Wittgenstein has to do with the fact that Rorty's Wittgenstein fails to take this possibility seriously. For these reasons, I do not want unquestioningly to inherit the bit of Rorty's terminology which makes it difficult to see that there might be a genuine possibility here. I will in what follows signal that I am referring to the peculiar position Rorty calls "realism" by placing it in single quotes ('realism').

Rorty represents Wittgenstein as developing one of the deepest and most original attacks on 'realism'.[22] The centerpiece of this supposed attack is a view of language on which a sentence has a meaning and is a truth-value candidate in virtue of being embedded in a coherent set of practices. Rorty argues that the "pure 'language-game' view of language" he attributes to Wittgenstein does not permit "questions about 'ties to the world'" to arise.[23] Here mastery of a sentence consists, not in knowledge of the state of affairs it represents, but rather in the ability to participate in the practices in which it is used. This means that, as Rorty puts it: "to know methods of verification [is] to know *all* there [is] to know about the semantical features of statements. Such knowledge [is not] a matter of semantical *theory*, but simple 'know-how'."[24] So, according to Rorty, the upshot of things Wittgenstein says about the relation between the meaning and use of expressions is that we should no longer conceive of the truth of a bit of language as a matter of its accurately representing how things are in the world.

This brings me to the second of my preliminary comments. Rorty tends to speak of what emerges from Wittgenstein's remarks on meaning, not as a *view* of language, but rather as a *vocabulary* for talking about language. In doing so, he marks what he sees as a fundamentally important distinction. The distinction – it is one which, as I will discuss in just a moment, he draws most clearly in recent work – is between, on the one hand, representing Wittgenstein as championing a vision of language which emerges out of a conversation with traditional philosophical positions and which can therefore at least to some extent be assessed in traditional philosophical terms and, on the other, representing him as advocating a way of talking which is not philosophical and which should therefore be assessed, not in philosophical terms, but in practical or political ones. In reference to this Rortian distinction, I will in what follows speak of Rorty's "allegedly Wittgensteinian vocabulary."

On Rorty's allegedly Wittgensteinian vocabulary, there is no such thing as deter-mining that one discourse provides us with a more accurate representation of the world than another, and, accordingly, no room for the idea that changes in our discourses can be recommended as containing a more accurate account of our needs or our natures. One discourse may *seem* better to us – it may, as Rorty often puts it, help us to "cope better" – but to say this is not to say that there is some stan-dard, common to the discourses at issue, by reference to which one can be seen as doing us more justice than another. In so far as Rorty's allegedly Wittgensteinian vocabulary is characterized by a distinction between talk of the accuracy or inac-curacy of discourses (which he thinks we should relinquish because, as he sees it, it presupposes that we have found "some way of breaking out of language in order to compare it with something else"[25] and thus represents a slide back into 'realism') and talk about one discourse *seeming* superior or inferior to another (which he takes to be happily free from any such 'realist' presupposition), it provides a home for an opposition of the sort characteristic of inviolability interpretations between prohibited external forms of criticism and permissible internal forms of criticism.

A version of this same opposition figures in Stanley Fish's work on the possi-bility of theory. Fish's aim is to dismantle a traditional understanding of theory as a set of principles or procedures which operate as constraints on practice but are completely independent of it in the sense of not being derived from it.[26] There is, he claims, no such thing as theory if theory is "something an agent thinks with" as if from a standpoint outside language, but there is nevertheless nothing wrong with talking about theorizing if we think of theory as "something an agent thinks within":[27] the kind of theory we actually engage in is "no more (or less) than a kind of talk."[28] Here Fish's thought converges with Rorty's in that it is structured by a distinction between prohibited forms of theory which aim to place external constraints on practices and permissible forms of theory(-talk) which lack any such aim and operate only within our practices.

The bits of Rorty's allegedly Wittgensteinian vocabulary touched on thus far give the idea of social change the same problematic status it has within the work of commentators who see Wittgenstein as a conservative thinker. There is no such thing as criticism which gives expression to demands for social change (say, by calling for the development of modes of thought which more accurately reflect the way things are). When we say that some way of thinking and talking is flawed, we are not saying that it fails to do justice to some feature of the world, but rather that it seems to us to hinder our abilities to cope. Similarly, when we say that a way of thinking and talking marks an improvement over an older practice, we are not saying that it does more justice to some feature of the world, but rather that it seems to enable us to cope better. If our political discourses were gradually supplanted by a way of talking characteristic of neo-fascism, it might seem to us either that we "cope better" by brutalizing Jews, communists, foreigners, gypsies and homosexuals; or, alternatively, it might seem to us that we "cope better" by talking about individuals as the possessors of certain inviolable human rights.[29] In neither case could we say that the new discourse we had adopted was strictly speaking more accurate than our old way of talking.

The thought that rational reflection can't give rise to demands for genuine change does not, however, lead Rorty to conclude that we should stop aspiring to improve our ways of life; rather, it leads him to the conclusion that we need to equip ourselves with a radically revised view of change on which it occurs as we come to use expressions in new ways and, as he sees it, thus come to open new realms of meaning. The stage for change is set when a sentence is coined which doesn't have a fixed place in our language-games and is not yet meaningful or truth-valued. Such a sentence would be a sentence which:

> one cannot confirm or disconfirm, argue for or against. One can only savor it or spit it out. But this is not to say that it may not, in time, *become* a truth-value candidate. If it *is* savored rather than spat out, the sentence may be repeated, caught up, bandied about. Then it will gradually acquire a habitual use, a familiar place in the language game.[30]

As Rorty sees it, it is by finding a habitual use for such new sentences that we create new regions of meaning and inaugurate change. Further, although there is, on his view, no room for rationally assessing the new language that emerges in terms of the old or vice versa (since the regions of meaning encompassed by the new are unavailable within the old), it is nevertheless central to his thought to insist that we can experiment with various new forms of words in the hope of producing linguistic practices which offer liberation to those who feel oppressed or marginalized by our established modes of thinking and speaking.[31] Far from taking his allegedly Wittgensteinian vocabulary to speak in favor of conservative political attitudes, he takes it to be capable of helping us to understand what we are doing when we agitate for radical social change.

Fish moves from (what Rorty would call) "a pure 'language-game' view of language" to a similar account of change. He argues that we can make sense of what we are doing when we agitate for change if we understand theory as essentially a "rhetorical and political phenomenon whose effects are purely contingent":[32] there is no such thing as change which is a matter of altering our theoretical definitions, categories, levels, etc., so that they are brought to correspond more closely with the phenomena they are invoked to explain,[33] but change in a practice may result from an agitation which is internal to it.[34] We say that change is needed when our current ways of doing things seem limiting or oppressive to us, and we say that we have made a change for the better when our altered practice seems more liberating to us.

Thus far I have not considered the account Rorty gives of what speaks in favor of the transition from a 'realist' jargon to a pure language-game jargon. It is with regard to the details of this account – or at least with regard to the relative emphasis given to particular details of it – that Rorty's work has changed most dramatically in recent years. Until relatively recently, Rorty seemed to be happy to represent Wittgenstein's discussions of meaning as making a case against 'realism' that showed that 'realism' is *confused* or *incoherent*. Wittgenstein should be understood, Rorty suggested, as arguing that it is impossible to break out of language to compare it with something else and as concluding that we should therefore free ourselves from 'realist' forms of thought and speech. An essentially similar line of argument is developed in Fish's discussions of the bankruptcy of a traditional conception of theory – a line of argument which moves from an attempt to demonstrate that (to put it in Rorty's terms) 'realism' is confused to the conclusion that we should give up 'realist' locutions.

This line of argument is threatened by the same tension that infects other inviolability views. Putting the worry now in the terms I am using to describe Rorty's work, the tension can be traced to a pair of mutually inconsistent depictions of the 'realist' thesis that the line of argument is intended to dislodge. This line of argument endeavors to show both that the thesis is incoherent and also that we should draw certain substantive conclusions from its rejection (in particular, conclusions about our entitlement to certain epistemic ideals). That is, it moves from repudiating the thesis as nonsense to affirming its negation (or something very close to that) and taking its negation to shed light on the nature of discourse. This move is suspicious in so far as it draws conclusions from the negation of an allegedly unintelligible thesis. The difficulty is that if the thesis of 'realism' is incoherent, as this line of argument purports to show, then there is something confused about the idea that we can negate *it* and draw substantive conclusions from its negation. To the extent that this line of argument draws such conclusions, it undermines its own conclusions by treating the thesis which it itself declares to be incoherent as (at least partially) coherent.[35]

In recent writings, however, Rorty distances himself from the line of argument containing this inconsistency and attempts to make a very different case in favor of the transition from a 'realist' terminology to the allegedly Wittgensteinian vocabulary he favors. He claims that his willingness to forsake the jargon of 'realism' is not a function of a failure to make sense of it, but instead of the "relative inutility" of the picture of our lives it encourages us to develop. He describes this "pragmatic" turn in his thinking as follows:

> I should not have spoken of "unreal" or "confused" philosophical distinctions, but rather of distinctions whose employment has proved to lead nowhere, proved to be more trouble than they were worth. For pragmatists like. . . . me, the question should always be "What use is it?" rather than "Is it real?" or "Is it confused?" Criticisms of other philosophers' distinctions and problematics should charge relative inutility, rather than "meaninglessness" or "illusion" or "incoherence."[36]

Rorty consistently represents the shift in his work from reliance on philosophical terms of criticism such as "meaninglessness," "incoherence," etc. to an exclusive reliance on what he calls pragmatic terms of criticism as an important part of his project of setting aside (as opposed to analyzing, puzzling over or endeavoring to answer) traditional metaphysical questions. But there is a perspective from which this claim about what the shift to pragmatic terms allows him to achieve can seem misguided. I just pointed out that some of Rorty's earlier attacks on 'realism' are plagued by inconsistency. The inconsistency results from his tendency to go from declaring the thesis of 'realism' incoherent to affirming its negation and drawing substantive conclusions from it, thus in effect undercutting his own assessment of the thesis as incoherent by treating it as having a meaningful negation. Now the conclusions Rorty draws from the affirmation of the negation of the thesis of 'realism' – conclusions about our entitlement to certain epistemic ideals – are what originally provide the framework within which he develops his allegedly Wittgensteinian vocabulary. This should lead us to suspect that the vocabulary, in spite of the fact that it is supposed to represent a complete change of topic, winds up bearing the imprint of the 'realist' tradition, now in its negative image. The claim I want to defend here is that Rorty's recent insistence on defending the vocabulary exclusively in pragmatic terms, although it rids it of the inconsistency that once ran through it, does not rescue it from its entanglement with this metaphysical tradition.

This objection has a bearing on a moment in Rorty's work at which it clearly stands in a conflicted relation to Wittgenstein's philosophy. I noted earlier that Rorty claims to be following in Wittgenstein's footsteps when he (i.e., Rorty) says that he is not in the business of offering answers to traditional metaphysical questions. Rorty suggests that it is precisely his abandonment of philosophical terms of criticism like "nonsense," "incoherence," etc. which helps him to dissolve any lingering attachment to such questions. This is noteworthy because it is a signature gesture of Wittgenstein's philosophy – and one which, significantly, figures in his thought as part of the project of defusing the power traditional metaphysical questions have over our thinking – to appeal to "nonsense" as a term of philosophical criticism. This means that at the moment in his work at which the above objection is directed, Rorty is both claiming to inherit one of Wittgenstein's philosophical aims while, at the same time, repudiating methods Wittgenstein takes to be suited to achieving it. So, even if Rorty succeeds in developing a consistent pragmatic view along the lines of his recent work – I am arguing that he does not – it's not clear that there is any strong sense in which the view in question should be called a Wittgensteinian one.

Rorty has a rejoinder to the sort of objection to his work I just made (in the last paragraph but one). It is a refrain of his recent writings that such philosophical objections depend for any appearance of plausibility they have on a misrepresentation of what he is doing when he puts forward his allegedly Wittgensteinian vocabulary. Rorty denies that in recommending his vocabulary he is advocating a reform of ordinary language. He has, he says, "urged that we continue to speak with the vulgar while offering a different philosophical gloss on this speech than that offered by the realist tradition."[37] The function of his vocabulary is to get us to regard metaphysical disputes as pointless and to go on to talk about something else. According to Rorty, we miss this point if we insist on saying things (of the sort I want to say here) about how the resources of his vocabulary are drawn from the tradition from which it is supposed to liberate us. As he sees it, any "resources" employed in his vocabulary are only resources for *it* in so far as they promote the independent ends towards which it is employed. This, for him, is what it comes to to say that its success is to be assessed exclusively in pragmatic terms – in terms of its ability, say, to direct us to new topics of conversation – and not in philosophical ones.

There are good reasons not to accept Rorty's characterization of his work at face-value, but, before considering some of those reasons, I want to mention a concern we might have about his work even if we did accept it. Here Rorty describes himself as equipping us simply to turn our backs on traditional metaphysical questions: he is exhorting us, not only to refrain from puzzling over those questions in the hopes of coming up with answers, but also to refrain from investigating the sort of fascination they have for us, the sort of influence they exert on our imaginations. We might worry that in the absence of any such investigations our efforts simply to turn our backs on traditional metaphysical questions will result, not in the development of modes of discourse purged of their every trace, but rather in the development of modes of discourse which remain haunted, in ways which may be very difficult to recognize, by the sense of loss occasioned by their abandonment. (Rorty himself signals that he thinks this worry is an empty one by talking about our tendency to be gripped by it as a sign that we are "nostalgic" for the – imagined – grandeur of metaphysical debates.) My suggestion here is that the worry is a well-founded one in the case of Rorty's work in particular.

If we are to employ Rorty's allegedly Wittgensteinian vocabulary strictly in the way he instructs in passages like the one I just considered, then we must use it, not as a substitute for our ordinary forms of speech, but rather as a tool for persuading the person who has become engrossed in metaphysical discourse of the futility of her language-game. Now one thing which is striking about Rorty's work is the regularity with which he himself seems to depart from this program. He regularly speaks up in favor of revising this or that ordinary stretch of discourse. That is, he frequently objects to the use of expressions such as "objectivity" or "truth" or "representation" in bits of the writings of literary authors and social thinkers who aren't obviously (except, I suppose, to Rorty) doing metaphysics. Rorty's objections seem to be driven by the tacit assumption that the consistent or emphatic employment of these expressions is in itself, without regard to the context in which they are being used, a sign of participation in the 'realist' metaphysical tradition. It is a consequence of this assumption that the person who has freed herself from this tradition – in Rorty's terms, the Wittgensteinian or pragmatist – will express herself, in quite ordinary speech, using different words, and Rorty often seems happy to embrace this consequence. When, for instance, he writes that "[f]or pragmatists, the desire for objectivity is . . . simply the desire for as much intersubjective agreement as possible,"[38] he is suggesting that the pragmatist will tend to employ, not "objectivity," but rather some suitable pragmatic surrogate such as, to mention the term Rorty prefers, "solidarity." And Rorty is similarly suspicious, not just of authors who speak frequently of "objectivity," but also of those who speak frequently of, for instance, "truth" and "knowledge" and who are fond of expressions like "accurate representation of the facts of the matter."

I am arguing that it is difficult to see how Rorty can be entitled to his claim to be abstaining from calling for a rearrangement of everyday discourse, but my point can also be made as follows: we may grant Rorty his claim, but if we do so, we should add that what, for him, counts as the everyday is determined by a mysterious capacity for distinguishing it from the metaphysical simply by attending to the presence of certain quite ordinary words.

At this point, I can begin to sketch a contrast between Rorty's Wittgenstein and Wittgenstein that will emerge more fully in the next section when I discuss Wittgenstein's view of meaning and its implications for an understanding of our practices of criticism. For Wittgenstein, unlike Rorty, questions about whether particular forms of words are metaphysically suspicious or innocent are questions which cannot be answered apart from investigations of how these forms of words are being *used*. We cannot avoid slipping into metaphysics simply by ridding our language of certain words and by developing a new *vocabulary*. We can keep ourselves from slipping – to the extent that we can – only by familiarizing ourselves with routes along which we move from ordinary employments of words to metaphysical employments of them and, in addition, by bringing ourselves to the recognition, in particular cases in which we are inclined to give our words meta-physical employments, that those words don't say anything we can imagine ourselves saying (even though we may once have taken them to express important truths) and should be rejected as not saying anything, as *nonsense*. Wittgenstein describes his aim in philosophy as showing us what is involved in thus recovering words from flights into metaphysical speculation. ("What *we* do," he writes, "is to bring words back from their metaphysical to their everyday use."[39]) Wittgenstein's discussions of meaning, for instance, are intended to enable us to rescue "meaning" from a metaphysically inflated use and, at the same time, also to rescue words – such as "criticism" – whose use is caught up with it. This brings me to my next topic.

2 Bringing back "meaning" and "criticism" to their everyday use

The difficult thing here is not, to dig down to the ground; no, it is to recognize the ground that lies before us as the ground.[40]

The last section contained illustrations of how an understanding of Wittgenstein as excluding the possibility of (external) criticism is sometimes taken to speak in favor of conservative political attitudes and sometimes taken to enable us to make sense of even radical political attitudes. It is a consequence of this understanding that Wittgenstein's work comes under attack from both the left and the right. There is a common theme – one not varying with the political disposition of the critic – which runs through such attacks (as well as through many other attacks which, while they also take for granted inviolability interpretations, are not explicitly concerned with the implications of Wittgenstein's philosophy for political thought). Many are driven by the desire to provide some sort of philosophical backing for our practices of criticism and, in addition, by the thought that genuine criticism can only be possible if meaning is somehow fixed independently of use. Critics have accordingly argued, against what they take to be Wittgenstein's view, that it is confused to elide questions about meaning and use. The meanings of expressions may be fixed in a way which doesn't vary with changes in their use, and the fact that they may be fixed in this way explains how it is that we can submit linguistic practices, either our own or those of others, to rational assessment: we can change our way of speaking and yet still be talking about the same thing. Critics who argue along these lines don't think they are at odds with Wittgenstein in assuming that talk about progressive or regressive social changes presupposes that the meanings of at least certain expressions are determined independently of their use, but they take themselves to be disagreeing with him in so far as they want to assert that meanings are sometimes determined in this way and that they therefore do some-times accompany bits of language across changes in use.

130

This dispute about Wittgenstein's view of meaning takes place in a logical space in which the sole alternative to a use-theory of meaning of the sort he is presumed to favor (a theory which threatens to rule out the possibility of genuine criticism of our lives) is some version of a traditional theory of meaning which stipulates that meanings are at least sometimes fixed independently of use (a theory which therefore seems to enable us to offer a philosophical explanation of the possibility of criticism). My aim in this section is to show that Wittgenstein's view of meaning does not fit into this space of alternatives. Although it is right to read him, as most commentators indeed do, as attacking views which stipulate that meaning is fixed independently of use, he should not therefore be understood as claiming that use fixes meaning.

It may be difficult to see how Wittgenstein's view of meaning can fail to involve *either* the thesis that meaning is fixed by use *or* the thesis that meanings are sometimes fixed independently of use. Resolving the difficulty requires a sense of how different what he is doing in his investigations of meaning is from traditional philosophical discussions of meaning. I mentioned above that Wittgenstein himself highlights peculiar features of his own philosophical procedures, insisting, for instance, that he should not be understood as being in the business of presenting a philosophical explanation of meaning. In one frequently cited remark, he suggests that he is not putting forward philosophical theses and that we misunderstand him if this is what we take him to be doing.[41] In this section, I will examine a set of different passages in his work in which he is concerned with questions about the relation between the meaning and use of expressions. What I hope to show is that once we appreciate how these passages are animated by his conception of philosophy as he practices it, we are in a position to see that they contain the working out of a view of meaning which falls outside the space of alternatives to which the dispute just sketched is limited.

(i) Meaning and methods of checking truth

It may seem that clear support for an understanding of Wittgenstein as advancing some version of a use-theory of meaning can be found in passages in his writings from 1929 to the early thirties – in what is sometimes called his "middle period" – in which he connects the meaning of a proposition with methods we employ in checking its truth.

Here Wittgenstein claims, for instance, that we appreciate the meaning of mathematical propositions by attending to their proofs. "If you want to know what is proved," he writes, "look at the proof."[42] Further, he notes that tying the meaning of a mathematical proposition to its proof has the apparently paradoxical consequence that a mathematical proposition, before there is any proof, does not mean the same – that is, is not the same proposition – once a proof is provided, and hence that there is a sense in which there can be no such thing as solving hard problems in mathematics (for now it appears that any "solutions" we come up with won't make contact with the "problems" we originally took ourselves to want to solve). A sustained treatment of these topics is found in a section of the *Philosophical Grammar* in which he discusses, among other things, Fermat's problem.[43] One of his concerns here is clarifying the notion of a conjecture in mathematics. A conjecture in mathematics, he writes, is like an empirical hypothesis in that we can either confirm or disconfirm it by seeing whether or not it holds in particular cases. In the case of Fermat's conjecture, we have "an empirical structure that we interpret as a *hypothesis*." But once we have a proof, we have a very different sort of technique for checking the truth of a proposition than we did when we only had a conjecture. Wittgenstein concludes that "in a certain sense what the problem asks for is not what the solution gives"[44] and that it may be a sign of confusion to think of conjectures like Fermat's as yet unsolved mathematical problems.[45]

In this period of his work, Wittgenstein also frequently claims that we appreciate the meaning of empirical propositions by attending to methods for verifying them. "How a proposition is verified," he writes, "is what it says."[46] And in thus tying the meaning of empirical propositions to methods for verifying them, he invites us to draw the apparently paradoxical conclusion that an empirical proposition does not mean the same after we have developed new techniques for verifying it.

These two sets of passages from Wittgenstein's middle period, taken together, might be read as expressing the view that there cannot be a change in the method of checking the truth of a sentence without a corresponding change in meaning and that we therefore cannot comment on practices across such changes. It may accordingly seem appropriate to protest, against what is alleged to be his view, that we can comment on practices, both our own and those of others; and, moreover, that we can do so because the meaning of a sentence at least sometimes stays the same across changes in methods for checking its truth. Thus one critic has argued, for instance, that our attempts to solve Fermat's problem are rooted in and structured by an understanding of the problem, an understanding of *what* stands in need of proof. The idea is that we can bring the solution we ultimately accept to meet the problem with which we began if we allow that questions about the meaning of Fermat's theorem and questions about the use we make of it can come apart.[47] Similarly, critics have argued that our attempts to develop new techniques for verifying empirical sentences are guided by an understanding of those sentences. The idea is that we can connect techniques we develop with the sentences with which we began if we allow that questions about the meaning of a sentence and questions about methods we rely on in verifying it sometimes come apart.[48]

Wittgenstein continues to make a connection between the meaning of a proposition and methods for checking its truth in his later writings.[49] So if passages in which he makes such a connection are taken to speak in favor of a use-theory of meaning, it may seem appropriate to read him as advocating such a theory from 1929 more or less until the end of his life.

(ii) Solving problems and making progress

Although in passages in which he ties the meaning of a mathematical proposition to its proof, Wittgenstein is concerned to draw attention to differences between what we do with mathematical propositions before and after a proof has been provided, he insists, even in his writings in the early thirties, that we misunderstand him if we take him to be "wip[ing] out the existence of mathematical problems."[50] He notes that there is *some* similarity between searching for a proof and other problem-solving activities: a conjecture in mathematics doesn't make way for a systematic search for a proof – one whose every step is "prescribed by the calculus"[51] – but it nevertheless "trains your thoughts on a particular object"[52] and thus allows for a search which is more than a random groping. This line of thought is further developed in a later discussion of Fermat's problem where Wittgenstein writes that "mathematicians are not *completely* blank and helpless when they are confronted by [Fermat's theorem]" and that "they try certain methods of proving it" which occur to them because they are "acquainted with criteria of the truth of *similar* propositions."[53] Wittgenstein is not denying – not in the early thirties and not later – that attempts to find a proof are guided by mathematicians' sense of what connections with current mathematical practice need to be maintained for a proof to count as a proof of a given theorem or that, when something is accepted as a proof, it is because they recognize it as a consistent development of their previous practice and thus take the proposition for which a proof has been provided to be in an important sense the same as the proposition with which they began.

There are many other passages in his later writings in which Wittgenstein distances himself from the claim that any difference in the use of an expression must be accompanied by a difference in meaning. Consider, for example, a passage in *Zettel* in which we are invited to imagine a tribe which has two words whose use in some ways resembles our use of the word "pain."[54] One of the words of the members of the strange tribe is applied when there is physical damage (e.g., when the skin has been broken and there is bleeding). The other word is applied when there is no damage visible and is connected with making fun of and shaming a person who complains. Thus when the members of this tribe rush over to someone who has been wounded, they may say (pointing to a part of her body), "It hurts a lot there." If the injured person claims that it does not hurt there, her companions may take her to be too dazed to register her pain. Seeing whether or not someone is in pain is, for them, like seeing whether someone is bruised or bleeding: it is something anyone can do. So there is a clear contrast with our language-game in which an appropriate response to the statement "It hurts a lot there" would be "*I* know where it hurts." In talking about the hurt suffered by a particular person, we defer to that person.

Wittgenstein acknowledges that we may be inclined to assume that the difference between their practice with their words and our practice with "pain" must signal a difference in meaning ("of course it must look like that [i.e., as if their concept does not designate the same as ours] if [their] concept is different"[55]), but he discourages us from simply assuming that the difference between their practice with their words and our practice with ours must amount to a difference in meaning: he suggests that if we are to determine whether or not they mean the same (or part of the same) as we do, we need to investigate differences between our respective practices and figure out whether they are important or essential differences.

How do we figure out whether a given difference or similarity is important? One place Wittgenstein addresses this question is in a set of remarks in the *Investigations* in which someone demands to know how one can "decide what is an essential, and what an inessential, accidental, feature of the notation." This is one of the many points in the book at which he invokes an analogy between language and a game of chess. Determining whether a word has more than one meaning is, he suggests, like determining whether a chess-piece has more than one role. Just as we draw on our sense of the point (*Witz*) of chess in figuring out whether differences between the ways in which a given piece is used are essential features, we draw upon our sense of the point of our practice with a word in figuring out whether differences between the ways in which it is used are essential.[56]

The set of passages from Wittgenstein's middle and later writings discussed here and in §2(i) might well be read as supporting an inviolability interpretation. These passages make up a representative selection of the remarks taken to speak in favor of an understanding of him as claiming – in a way which supports such an interpretation – that whether or not a change in the use of an expression constitutes a change in its meaning is determined by linguistic conventions governing the practice within which we employ it. With reference to these passages, it does not seem unreasonable to claim that Wittgenstein holds the view that when a question arises, for instance, about whether differences between the ways we use a mathematical proposition at different times constitute a change in its meaning, the answer is given by standards fixed by our current mathematical practice. Nor does it seem unreasonable to claim that he holds the view that when a question arises about whether differences between the way we use "pain" and the way members of a strange tribe use certain words constitute a difference in meaning, the answer is given by standards fixed by the language-game into which our talk of "pain" is woven.

However, even though there are many remarks in Wittgenstein's writing which may initially seem to speak in favor of inviolability interpretations, his writings nevertheless do not contain any of the specific theoretical claims about the relation between meaning and use attributed to him on such interpretations. Proponents of inviolability interpretations sometimes try to account for this alleged omission by connecting it with things he says about how he is not offering a philosophical explanation of meaning. The upshot of this interpretative strategy (which is often described as laying bare "Wittgenstein's quietism") is that Wittgenstein's denial that he is developing a philosophical explanation of meaning is regarded as a sign of some sort of intellectual irresponsibility: in issuing this denial, he signals his refusal openly to embrace philosophical claims which his stated views imply or strongly suggest. This apologetic account of remarks in which Wittgenstein distances himself from the project of giving a philosophical explanation of meaning cleanly misses their point. These remarks are internal to the articulation of the view of meaning he favors. (It is part of the same point to say that the peculiar way in which Wittgenstein writes – his *style* – is internal to his thought.) Any accurate account of how they are internal to his view of meaning will be at least implicitly informed by an understanding of his conception of logical necessity. For this reason, I turn now to a set of passages often read – wrongly, I will argue – as showing that he holds a conventionalist view of logical necessity, the view of logical necessity, that is, which inviolability interpretations attribute to him.

(iii) The "contingency" of concepts

Wittgenstein's later writings – and, in particular, the *Remarks on the Foundations of Mathematics* – contain many remarks about people who appear to have fundamentally different ways of inferring, calculating, measuring, etc. It is often assumed that the point of such remarks is to demonstrate that it is no more than a contingent fact about us that we think in the ways that we do – or that our basic logical concepts (such as rationality, consistency, objectivity, etc.) have the shapes that they do – by presenting us with illustrations of other possible ways of thinking. If the point of these remarks is to provide us with depictions of people who calculate, infer and measure essentially differently from the ways in which we do these things – people whose practices of reason therefore cannot legitimately be submitted to terms of criticism derived from our own – then it would be appropriate to follow in the footsteps of commentators who champion inviolability interpretations and read Wittgenstein as holding that our language-games are conventional arrangements to which we may be able to imagine alternatives.

The relevant set of remarks concern people whose activities, while they resemble our activities of measuring, calculating, inferring, etc. in many ways, also diverge from them in fundamental respects. In one of the most basic scenarios, we are presented with people who seem to be calculating in the way we do but who, when they arrive at different results on different occasions, don't take themselves to have made a mistake.[57] In a more elaborate version of this scenario, we are presented with people who seem to be buying and selling goods for money (they hand over what appear to be coins in exchange for various items), but we can discover no regular relation between the number of "coins" given and the number of goods received.[58] And in the most elaborate version, we are presented with people who seem to be buying and selling timber for money, but "they [pile] the timber in heaps of arbitrary, varying height and then [sell] it at a price proportionate to the area covered by the pile" and justify this with the words "of course, if you buy more timber, you must pay more."[59]

A very natural attitude to adopt towards the people in these different scenarios is that they are confused about how to calculate, measure, etc. Suppose we adopt this attitude, for instance, towards the people in the most basic one and think of them as calculating inconsistently. We might now try to show them that adding specific numbers always gives the same result by pointing out an error in one of their sums in cases in which, in adding the same numbers, they have arrived at different results. Wittgenstein imagines that while such efforts "*might* convince them*" (perhaps they are children who, although they have been instructed in how to do basic sums, have not yet arrived at a reflective grasp of what they are doing), they may simply say something along the lines of "yes, now the numbers add up to the same." Our first attempt to convince them of the confusion in their practices need not be the end of the matter. We may be inclined to think that they really are doing something coherent (we may have been inclined to think that they are "following a rule which escapes us"[60]), and we may accordingly try new demonstrations with them. For instance, we may say: "Surely you don't believe that if we wait a little bit numbers which give one sum might come out to more." And perhaps they reply: "But naturally we do." We try yet again: "But isn't it absurd to think that a man could correctly calculate on one day that he needs 10 foot boards for a building project only to determine on the next day, again correctly, that he needs 12 foot boards?" And they respond: "Where's the absurdity? Nothing could be more natural than to think this." Perhaps, at least for the time being, this is the end of the matter. The reasons we can give for thinking our practices correct have been exhausted. Because we have said all we can now say, we mutter something useless about differences in meaning ("they simply do not mean the same by 'calculating sums' as we do"). We may nevertheless continue to assume that we will find our feet with them, possibly by attempting to make sense of their behavior using different concepts.

In so far as we haven't yet said anything coherent about how these mathematical strangers calculate, we haven't yet said anything about what they are doing. It is premature to conclude that they are relying on a confused or erroneous understanding of calculating because we don't yet have a coherent picture of them *as calculating*. (Perhaps one day we will discover that they were engaged in a religious ritual which just happened to bear superficial resemblance to our activities of calculating.) If we assert that they are calculating and doing so badly, we will be implying that their "calculating-activities" have essentially the same place in their lives that calculating has in ours and hence that if we draw their attention to the fact that their methods sometimes lead them to one result and sometimes to another, they will recognize that they made a mistake. But these strangers happily admit that they sometimes come out with different results. Our willingness to say that they were calculating and doing so badly would be a sign that we were overlooking characteristic features of our own practices of calculation – or that we were simply discounting the absence of these features in their practices – and visiting them with empty criticism.[61]

Nor do these remarks about the mathematical strangers amount to pictures of "intelligible alternatives to our ways of thinking, calculating, measuring, etc." The remarks begin by seeming to take seriously an idea of people who think and speak yet do so (by our lights) illogically. They invite us to try to realize such an idea in imagination and then dramatize for us the fact that we inevitably fail to do so. The difficulty is that we want anything that we will count as an acceptable rendering of our idea to satisfy both of two conflicting conditions: we want it to be (i) an account of people whose lives we recognize as resembling ours in fundamental respects and, in particular, in respects which would warrant us in saying that they *are* calculating and, at the same time, we want it to be (ii) an account of people whose lives we can't recognize as bearing any fundamental resemblance to ours in just these respects (so that they can be said to be calculating in a manner which is radically different from that in which we calculate).

It would be a sign of misunderstanding to take these remarks to speak in favor of inviolability interpretations: here Wittgenstein is not advocating a conventionalist view of logical necessity of the sort that inviolability interpretations attribute to him; he is, instead, attacking such a view.

However, although Wittgenstein's remarks about the mathematical strangers bring into question an idea, one which is internal to inviolability interpretations, of the contingency of our concepts, there is nevertheless a sense in which these remarks *are* intended to impress upon us the contingency of our concepts. The sorts of encounters they ask us to imagine are encounters in which we have run out of things to say in favor of the correctness of certain of our practices: all our efforts to show the mathematical strangers what is right about our practices of calculating fail. There is a philosophical picture of what we are doing when we talk about the correctness of our practices which makes it difficult to explain the possibility of this sort of failure (or, rather, which makes it difficult to explain the possibility of this sort of failure when it is not simply the product of, say, an unwillingness to listen or of distraction or some other form of inattention). The picture represents such talk as proceeding from a perspective on language from which it is possible to discern, independently of any contingent responses we possess as language-users, features of reality which determine the correctness of our practices. Given the picture, it appears that we can demonstrate that our practices are "absolutely the correct ones"[62] by pointing to features of reality which underwrite them. And it also appears that the fact that the mathematical strangers are "strange" in the sense that they do not have normal responses to instruction will not keep them from appreciating the correctness of our practices. Wittgenstein's remarks about these strangers are intended to teach us something about (what we might describe as) the contingency of our concepts by showing us that the picture does not shed light on our efforts to demonstrate the correctness of our practices and that when we try to appeal to the picture in a specific case it turns out to be of no use.

It is natural to take Wittgenstein's attack on this philosophical picture as intended to show that there are *no* features of reality which determine the correctness of our practices and that our practices are at best merely the product of, say, convention. And this is in fact, as I have been discussing, the response of a great number of readers of these – and other thematically similar – remarks of Wittgenstein's who take them to show that he is a thorough-going conventionalist. So it is important to stress that these remarks are no less opposed to views which depict our practices as radically contingent than they are to views which, drawing on the picture, suggest the possibility of showing that our practices are absolutely correct. Wittgenstein's concern here is with an idea common to both types of views. He is attacking the idea of a perspective on language as if from outside from which we can discern either that there are features of reality which underlie our practices and determine their correctness or that there are no such features and that something else – such as our linguistic conventions – determines what counts as correct. His remarks about the mathematical strangers are supposed to remind us that our ability to discover that the practices of others are correct or incorrect depends on nothing more and nothing less than our ability to *perceive* regularity or some failure of regularity in those practices. And they are supposed to remind us that our ability to show that our practices are correct depends on nothing more and nothing less than our ability to get others to perceive the regularity in them.

Consider again the passages of §§2(i) and 2(ii) in which Wittgenstein is concerned with the relation between meaning and use of expressions. These remarks from the *Remarks on the Foundations of Mathematics* can help us to see both (a) that Wittgenstein's claims about the significance of attending to use are directed, not towards the development of a new philosophical theory of meaning, but rather towards combating a specific prejudice which leads us to think that no investigation of use of the kind he takes to be required could be pertinent to answering questions about meaning and also (b) that the prejudice in question is an expression of the idea I just discussed – the idea of a perspective on language from which we can assess applications of words independently of any contingent responses or reactions.

When Wittgenstein urges us to attend to use – as he does in the passages touched on in §§2(i) and 2(ii) – his aim is to get us to see that a specific kind of investigation of use is relevant to answering our questions about meaning. The kind of investigation in question can only be undertaken by someone competent in a given region of discourse. It calls for exploring contexts of use in a way which draws on sensitivities acquired in learning the language. Wittgenstein wants us to recognize that it is only in so far as we thus survey the use of a word that we are in a position to say whether a given projection of a word preserves its meaning. Only now can we say whether the projection is a *natural* one, whether the connections with other uses of the word it respects are important. In the context of the idea of an external perspective on language, however, it appears that any investigation of this kind is beside the point. This is not to say that there may not be *other* kinds of investigations of use which seem to be pertinent. If we think that it is possible to survey language from an external perspective and if we also think that such a survey reveals that use fixes meaning, then it will appear to us that certain descriptions of how we use words – in particular, descriptions which could be understood even by someone who wasn't competent in the region of discourse in question – are relevant. But the task of arriving at such descriptions does not involve the kind of investigation of use that Wittgenstein thinks is needed.

One way of summarizing these points is to say that the fundamental tendency of Wittgenstein's discussions of meaning is obscured when his denial that he is concerned with a philosophical explanation of meaning is taken as a sign of – a perhaps unfortunate – reticence. For this denial is in fact an expression of the central insight of his view of meaning. Wittgenstein is attacking the prejudice that keeps us from undertaking the kind of investigation of use he takes to be required on two different levels. He is suggesting both (1) that the prejudice leads us into philosophical confusion in particular cases by encouraging us to look in the wrong place for answers to our questions about meaning and also (2) that it is therefore *mere prejudice*. To say that the prejudice is mere prejudice is to say that the idea of a perspective on language which obviates the need for the relevant kind of investigation of use should in the end be rejected as a bit of metaphysical fantasy. In so far as what is at issue is the idea of a perspective from which it is possible to give *philosophical explanations* of meaning or advance *philosophical theses* about meaning, his denial that he is in the business of giving a philosophical explanation of meaning can be seen as internal to his view of meaning.

So it is wrong to read Wittgenstein as endorsing the assumption which underwrites the ongoing debate about the political tendency of his philosophy – viz., the assumption that there can be no such thing as critically assessing practices if meanings are not at least sometimes fixed independently of use. Wittgenstein hopes to expose as confused the idea that meanings might somehow be "fixed" (whether independently of use or otherwise). There is, he wants us to grasp, no such thing as a metaphysical vantage point which, if we managed to occupy it, would disclose to us that meanings were "fixed" in one way or another and would therefore enable us to bypass the (sometimes enormously difficult) task of trying to *see* whether or not a new employment of a given expression preserves important connections with other employments. His aim is to get us to relinquish the idea of such a vantage point and, at the same time, to relinquish the idea that what we imagine is to be seen from such a vantage point has some bearing on our ability to submit practices to criticism. It is in so far as we do these things that we will have succeeded in leading back "meaning" – and "criticism" – from their metaphysical to their everyday use.

(iv) The limits of sense and the limits of criticism

These points connect directly with Wittgenstein's view of the limits of sense. Use-theories of meaning of the sort attributed to Wittgenstein on inviolability interpretations agree with more traditional theories of meaning, on which the meaning of a word is fixed independently of its use, in taking for granted an idea Wittgenstein is concerned to criticize: the idea of a vantage point on language as if from outside. The members of these two classes of theories of meaning contain analogous views of the limits of sense in virtue of this shared idea. Members of both presuppose that it is possible to identify the logical categories of expressions independently of their use in meaningful discourse and to see that those categories determine a limit to the legitimate use of the expressions. The difference between them on this score is simply that while the members of the one class represent logical categories as fixed by linguistic conventions, the members of the other represent them as fixed by something independent of such conventions. It follows from members of both classes that an utterance may fail to make sense because it combines expressions with incompatible logical categories – that it may fail to make sense because of *what* it is trying to say. The sorts of limits of sense at issue in both cases are thus limits which presuppose that we can make out what lies on the far side of them, what it is we are cut off from making sense of. In this respect, members of both classes of theories run afoul of Wittgenstein's remarks about the limits of sense.

The view of meaning Wittgenstein favors is characterized by the rejection of the idea of a vantage point from which we can identify logical categories outside meaningful bits of language. On this view, a bit of language is rejected as nonsense – not when there is something wrong with (what we are tempted to call) the sense it does have, but – when we have failed to give meaning to it; that is, when we have no notion what (if anything) will count as the fulfillment of it. This is the view Wittgenstein is developing in describing his philosophically unorthodox conception of the limits of sense. The idea of such limits, as he conceives them, doesn't imply that we are cut off from thinking or saying particular things. The limits of sense are (to put it in terms he uses as far back as in the *Tractatus*) limits drawn *in* language.

If we want to read Wittgenstein as holding a view of the limits of criticism, the limits in question should be limits in this sense. He should not be read, as proponents of inviolability interpretations read him, as claiming that there are particular features of our lives or of the lives of others which cannot be submitted to criticism. Rather, he should be read as making room for cases in which, although we take ourselves to be critically assessing some feature of our lives or of the lives of others, we have no notion what (if anything) will count as the fulfillment of the words we are uttering. Wittgenstein does at various points in his work explore "limits of criticism," conceived in this way. He examines forms of words which are put forward as assessments of this or that feature of our lives or of the lives of others but which, as he sees it, have not (yet) been given any meaning. In *Remarks on Frazer's Golden Bough*, for instance, he considers Frazer's criticisms of historical practices involving magic and concludes that the words Frazer comes out with are idle.[63] And in *On Certainty*, he repeatedly accents the idea that when we try to assess our own lives we may come out with forms of words which fail to say anything we want to say.[64] His reminders that our critical endeavors are limited in *these* ways belong to the project of leading us back to our everyday practices of criticism.

3 Conclusion: Wittgenstein's philosophy in relation to political thought

I don't try to make you *believe* something you *don't* believe, but to make you *do* something you won't do.[65]

One way of capturing what distinguishes Wittgenstein's view of meaning from the two classes of theories considered in the last section is in terms of the role it assigns to human agency in language. On his view, the task of understanding and assessing an utterance is one which calls on us to draw on and perhaps seek to further develop sensitivities we acquired as we mastered the language. It calls on us, as we might put it, to use – and perhaps stretch – our *imagination*. The central proposal of this paper is that the contribution Wittgenstein's philosophy can make to political thought is a function of what it teaches us, along these lines, about how the exercise of rational responsibility requires a distinctively human form of activity in language. This proposal provides new terms for capturing what is misguided about the different positions in the debate about Wittgenstein and politics outlined in §1. These positions all agree in attributing to Wittgenstein (what by his lights count as) certain philosophical *theses* about meaning. Where they differ is simply in their views of the implications of the theses for political thought. What is misguided about the positions, putting it now in terms of the proposal, is that philosophical theses invite us to think we can peer at and assess language from an external perspective, and they thus suggest that rational reflection requires no human activity of the sort Wittgenstein wants to show us is needed.

Fans of inviolability interpretations – above all those who claim that Wittgenstein's thought can help us to understand even radical political change – will undoubtedly protest any suggestion that they fail to take note of the role Wittgenstein assigns to human agency in language. They will emphasize that they represent Wittgenstein as claiming that meaning is determined by linguistic conventions and, further, that they also represent him as underlining the fact that such conventions are the product of human agency and subject to change. *Here* Wittgenstein can be seen as making room for agency in language and teaching us what it is to be responsible for what we say and think.[66] What is problematic about this approach to Wittgenstein's thought is that it represents him as allowing human activity, in the form of linguistic conventions, to shape language only by *fixing* meaning and hence only by playing an *external* role with regard to language. It is in this respect that inviolability interpretations misrepresent some of Wittgenstein's deepest philosophical concerns, and it is in this respect that, from the perspective of his philosophy, they appear to be internally inconsistent. But leaving aside for the moment worries about the internal coherence of such interpretations – as well as worries about their relation to Wittgenstein's thought – we might inquire into the *practical* value of the conception of rational responsibility they give us. That is, we might inquire into the practical value of a conception of rational responsibility on which such responsibility floats free of the idea of a world to which we are responsible.

In his recent writings, Rorty has directed attention to this practical question by trying to detach the way of talking about language he favors from the problematic metaphysical arguments which he once used to defend it (and which he once represented as Wittgenstein's). Rorty now insists, as we saw, that his way of talking should be appraised solely in practical or political terms. To the extent that Rorty succeeds in achieving a strictly practical focus, his work invites a strictly practical worry. It is not clear that the state of life he looks forward to – a state in which talk of getting at the *truth* of this or that, where it is not taken as a sign of nostalgic attachment to weary metaphysical debates, is taken as a sort of slogan to be assessed in terms of its practical effects – is one that we ought to wish for. Such a state of life would, I suspect, be bleaker and more sinister than Rorty imagines. But I want to close – not by exploring this issue directly, but – by describing an approach to Rorty's practical question from a somewhat different angle.

The approach I have in mind would involve showing that the lesson about rational responsibility Wittgenstein's writings contain is of practical value and that, practically speaking, it is therefore ill-advised to adopt a vocabulary like Rorty's which, under the rubric of promoting forms of speech exclusively with regard to their political usefulness, blocks its articulation. The lesson has to do with the fact that Wittgenstein rejects as the product of metaphysical confusion the idea that we must choose between, on the one hand, having the world and forfeiting responsibility and, on the other, having responsibility and losing the world.[67] He presents us with a view of the conditions of human knowledge on which there is human activity in the forms of thought and speech we use in attempting to understand the world: here getting at the facts of a situation may require us to try to see it in a different light, to use our imagination in a variety of ways, to seek new experiences which help us to refine our sensitivities and so on. Wittgenstein's writings in this respect teach us something about the kind of challenge we confront when we turn to investigating established modes of thought and speech (such as those that bear directly on political life), sorting out their injustices and developing more rigorously just and consistent ways of thinking and speaking. I suspect (although I cannot further discuss the grounds for my suspicions here) that this lesson is one which we would find reflected in forms of social life that embody the ideals of liberal democracy – in forms of social life, that is, that embody the ideals Rorty himself hopes to foster.[68]

Notes

1 It may be worth underlining that my topic here is not *Wittgenstein's* political inclinations but rather the bearing of Wittgenstein's *philosophy* on political thought. There is a flourishing literature on the former topic, and thinkers who contribute to it differ widely on the question of his political outlook – some representing him as a political conservative, some representing him as a political progressive and some offering more variegated representations of his political orientation. (For Wittgenstein as a conservative, see, e.g., J.C. Nyíri, "Wittgenstein 1929–31: The Turning Back" in S. Shanker (ed.) *Ludwig Wittgenstein: Critical Assessments*, London, Croom Helm, 1986, pp.29–69, "Wittgenstein's Later Work in relation to Conservatism" in B. McGuinness (ed.) *Wittgenstein and his Times*, Oxford, Basil Blackwell, 1982, pp.44–68 and "Wittgenstein's New Traditionalism," *Acta Philosophica Fennica*, 1976, vol.27, pp.503–9; for

Wittgenstein as a progressive, see, e.g., J. Moran, "Wittgenstein and Russia," *New Left Review*, 1972, vol.73, pp.85–98; for a more nuanced picture of Wittgenstein's political and moral convictions, see, e.g., R. Monk, *Ludwig Wittgenstein: The Duty of Genius*, New York, Penguin, 1990.) Many thinkers who take an interest in Wittgenstein's political orientation are in the first instance concerned with the question of the political significance of his philosophical views and appeal to biographical data only in the hope of corroborating their preferred answer to it. (A clear case of this is Nyíri. I touch on his work below, but only in so far as it is concerned with showing that Wittgenstein's philosophy has conservative implications.) One of the premises of this paper is that most discussions about the political significance of Wittgenstein's philosophy – without regard to whether or not they appeal to details of his political life – go astray because they help themselves to a misinterpretation of his view of meaning. The paper tries to arrive at a more adequate account of the bearing of his philosophy on political thought by clarifying his view of meaning. This project of clarification is by itself an involved one, and I am inclined to think that entering into biographical matters simply threatens to complicate matters. I have for this reason chosen to leave to one side the topic of Wittgenstein's political attitudes and to devote my efforts solely to examining relevant areas of his thought.

2 *Philosophical Occasions: 1912–1951*, p.181.

3 Wittgenstein never makes this claim. In the remark most often cited in favor of an interpretation of him as advancing such a claim, he writes: "For a *large* class of cases – though not for all – in which we employ the word 'meaning' it can be defined thus: the meaning of a word is its use in the language" (*Philosophical Investigations*, §43). Below in §2, I argue against taking remarks like this one, which connect the meaning of an expression with its use, as saying that the use of an expression fixes its meaning.

4 The two most influential readings of Wittgenstein as championing a use-theory of meaning are those of Norman Malcolm (see the essays in *Thought and Knowledge*, Ithaca, Cornell University Press, 1977) and Saul Kripke (*Wittgenstein on Rules and Private Language: An Elementary Exposition*, Cambridge, Mass., Harvard University Press, 1982). In *The Later Wittgenstein: The Emergence of a New Philosophical Method*, Oxford, Basil Blackwell, 1987, Stephen Hilmy argues that an examination of various unpublished manuscripts of Wittgenstein's supports an understanding of him as developing a version of a use-theory of meaning.

5 More precisely, it follows from this allegedly Wittgensteinian thesis that we are never in a position from which it makes sense to talk about the adequacy of our discourses to the nature of what we are talking about if Wittgenstein's talk of "meaning" [*Bedeutung*] in passages in which he is concerned with the relation between the meaning and use of expressions marks, at least for the most part, a concern with reference – with *what is being talked about*. Proponents of the interpretation of Wittgenstein I am sketching here are right to suggest that a central strand of his thought connects reference with use, but, as I argue below in §2, they nevertheless misrepresent his thought in other significant respects.

6 Some commentators accordingly present themselves as undertaking a project in the spirit of Wittgenstein's philosophy when they propose to sort out confusions resulting from taking two expressions which are used in different ways to mean the same. For one of the first – and most involved – allegedly Wittgensteinian projects along these lines, see Norman Malcolm's monograph *Dreaming*, London, Routledge and Kegan Paul, 1959.

7 Thus, e.g., Malcolm writes in *Thought and Knowledge*, op. cit., that Wittgenstein holds the view that "*[w]ithin* a language-game there is justification and lack of justification, evidence and proof, mistakes and groundless opinions, good and bad reasoning, correct measurements and incorrect ones. One cannot properly apply these terms to a language-game itself" (p.208).

8 An understanding of Wittgenstein as advocating this sort of relativism is developed in, e.g., H.O. Mounce and D.Z. Phillips' "Wittgensteinian" analysis of moral discourse in *Moral Practices*, New York, Schocken Books, 1970, especially chapters 3, 4 and 9

and Kai Nielsen's "Wittgensteinian" analysis of religious discourse in *An Introduction to the Philosophy of Religion*, New York, St. Martin's Press, 1982, chapters 3, 4 and 5. Peter Winch's *The Idea of a Social Science and its Relation to Philosophy*, 2nd edn, London, Routledge, 1990 has often been read as presenting a Wittgensteinian analysis of intercultural conversations which is similarly relativist. (In this connection, see, e.g., E. Gellner, "A Wittgensteinian Philosophy of (or Against) the Social Sciences" in *Spectacles and Predicaments: Essays in Social Theory*, Cambridge, Cambridge University Press, 1979, pp.65–102. I don't think Winch is best read in this way, but this issue is not one that I can sort out here. But see Winch's own discussion of the sort of misreading he thinks various of his own formulations invite in the preface to the second edition.) Among the most comprehensive discussions of Wittgenstein's alleged relativism are D. Bloor, *Wittgenstein: A Social Theory of Knowledge*, New York, Columbia University Press, 1983 and Hilmy, op. cit.

9 *Philosophical Investigations*, §500. Compare *Philosophical Grammar*, p.130 and *Wittgenstein's Lectures, Cambridge, 1932–35*, pp.63–4.

10 Bloor, op. cit., p.162. It is worth stressing that in this paper I am not taking a stand on whether or not the allegedly Wittgensteinian, conservative line of thought I am sketching does indeed tally with central lines of thought in the work of prominent and self-avowedly conservative thinkers such as Burke, Spengler, Mannheim and Oakeshott.

11 Ibid., p.161.

12 Ibid., p.2.

13 Nyíri, "Wittgenstein's Later Work in Relation to Conservatism," op. cit., p.59.

14 For relevant writings of Nyíri's, see n.1, above. Relevant work of Gellner's can be found in "Concepts and Community," *Relativism and the Social Sciences*, Cambridge, Cambridge University Press, 1985, "The Gospel According to Ludwig," *The American Scholar*, 1984, vol.53, pp.243–63, especially p.254 and "A Wittgensteinian Philosophy of (or Against) the Social Sciences," op. cit. The basic reading of Wittgenstein underwriting Gellner's attack on "Wittgenstein's conservatism" is already worked out in *Words and Things: An Examination of, and an Attack on, Linguistic Philosophy*, London, Routledge and Kegan Paul, 1959. For praise of "Wittgenstein's conservatism" along similar lines to Nyíri's, see Bloor, op. cit., chapter 8. For criticism of "Wittgenstein's conservativism" along similar lines to Gellner's, see T. Eagleton, "Wittgenstein's Friends," *New Left Review*, 1982, vol.135, pp.64–90, especially pp.70 1, "Introduction to Wittgenstein" in *Wittgenstein: The Terry Eagleton Script, The Derek Jarman Film*, London, British Film Institute, 1993, especially pp.8–11 and W.H. Walsh, *Metaphysics*, London, Hutchinson University Library, 1963, §§8.4–8.8.

15 Nyíri, "Wittgenstein's Later Work in Relation to Conservatism," op. cit., p.59.

16 Ibid., p.59.

17 Ibid., p.61.

18 Gellner, "A Wittgensteinian Philosophy of (or Against) the Social Sciences," op. cit., p.71.

19 Gellner, "Concepts and Community," op. cit., p.173.

20 See also, e.g., Henry Staten's *Wittgenstein and Derrida*, Lincoln, University of Nebraska Press, 1984.

21 For Fish's speculations about Wittgensteinian influences on his thought, see "Fish Tales: A Conversation with 'The Contemporary Sophist'," an interview conducted by G.A. Olson, reprinted in *There's No Such Thing As Free Speech*, Oxford, Oxford University Press, 1994, pp.281–307, especially pp.292–4.

22 Rorty's thought is *not* that Wittgenstein champions a metaphysical view which might be regarded as an alternative to 'realism' (say, a view which might merit the label "anti-realism"), but rather that he equips us with forms of thought and speech which disarm the temptation to debate the relative merits of 'realism' and any other metaphysical view which might be put forward as a competitor to it.

23 *Consequences of Pragmatism*, Minneapolis, University of Minnesota Press, 1982, p.114.

24 Ibid.

25 Ibid., p.xix.

26 In *Doing What Comes Naturally*, Durham, Duke University Press, 1989, Fish defines theory as

> a set of principles or rules or procedures that is attached to (in the sense of being derived from) no particular field of activity, but is of sufficient generality to be thought of as a constraint on (and explanation of) all fields of activity.
>
> (p.14)

27 Ibid, p.386.
28 Ibid., p.377.
29 The example is from H. Putnam, *Realism with a Human Face*, Cambridge, Mass., Harvard University Press, 1990, pp.23–4.
30 *Contingency, Irony, and Solidarity*, Cambridge, Cambridge University Press, 1989, p.18.
31 For a clear and well-developed case in which Rorty argues in favor of the importance of such experimentation, see, e.g., his Tanner Lectures, published as "Feminism and Pragmatism," reprinted in *Truth and Progress: Philosophical Papers*, vol.3, Cambridge, Cambridge University Press, 1998, pp.202–27. Here he argues that part of the value of separatism to feminism lies in the fact that it creates a setting in which sentences which lack a place within our current language-game – and which women may find liberating for talking about their lives – can acquire such a habitual use.
32 Fish, *Doing What Comes Naturally*, op. cit., p.380.
33 See, e.g., ibid., p.143.
34 See ibid., p.147.
35 Hilary Putnam develops this basic objection to Rorty in several of the essays in J. Conant (ed.) *Words and Life*, Cambridge, Mass., Harvard University Press, 1994, especially pp.299–300 and 349. In his "Introduction" to this collection of Putnam's papers, pp.xxiv–xxxiii, James Conant further elaborates Putnam's objection.
36 "Putnam and the Relativist Menace," reprinted in *Truth and Progress*, op. cit., pp.43–62, p.45.
37 Ibid., p.44.
38 *Objectivity, Relativism and Truth: Philosophical Papers*, vol.1, Cambridge, Cambridge University Press, 1991, p.23.
39 *Philosophical Investigations*, §116.
40 *Remarks on the Foundations of Mathematics*, VI, §31.
41 *Philosophical Investigations*, §128.
42 *Philosophical Grammar*, p.369. See also p.366 and *Philosophical Remarks*, p.193.
43 Part V, §22, pp.359–65.
44 *Philosophical Grammar*, p.362. Compare *Philosophical Remarks*, pp.183 and 191 and also *The Blue and Brown Books*, pp.28–9 and 41.
45 *Philosophical Remarks*, p.189. It is, of course, helpful to bear in mind that Wittgenstein is writing a good sixty years before anything had been accepted as a proof of Fermat's theorem.
46 *Philosophical Remarks*, p.200. See the remark immediately following this one on p.200 as well as remarks on pp.89 and 174; see also *Wittgenstein and the Vienna Circle: Conversations Recorded by Friedrich Waismann*, pp.47–8.
47 Roger White raises this objection in "Riddles and Anselm's Riddle," *Aristotelian Society*, 1977, suppl. vol.51, pp.169–86, especially pp.171–3.
48 This form of protest is familiar from discussions in the philosophy of science about the implications of the Wittgensteinian view of meaning embraced by Thomas Kuhn.
49 At *Philosophical Investigations*, §353, e.g., he writes: "Asking whether and how a proposition can be verified is only a particular way of asking 'How d'you mean?' The answer is a contribution to the grammar of the proposition."
50 *Philosophical Remarks*, p.170.
51 *Philosophical Grammar*, p.379.
52 *Philosophical Remarks*, p.190.
53 *Remarks on the Foundations of Mathematics*, pp.314–15.

54 §§373–81.
55 Ibid., §381.
56 *Philosophical Investigations*, §§562–4. Hilmy (op. cit.) takes this passage to be an important one for establishing that Wittgenstein is a relativist and, for this reason, he points out that there are several passages in the *Nachlaß* which resemble it in fundamentals.
57 Ibid., I, §155. There is also a case in which we encounter people who seem to be doing multiplications, but who do so only in rhyming verse and who treat each "multiplication" as an original, creative task. See V, §15.
58 Ibid., I, §153.
59 Ibid., I, §149. I am indebted in this section to discussions of Wittgenstein's wood-sellers in S. Cavell, *The Claim of Reason: Wittgenstein, Skepticism, Morality and Tragedy*, Oxford, Oxford University Press, 1979, especially pp.115–25 and B. Stroud, "Wittgenstein and Logical Necessity" in G. Pitcher (ed.) *Wittgenstein: The Philosophical Investigations*, Notre Dame, University of Notre Dame Press, 1966, pp.477–96. See also D. Cerbone's discussion of this passage in his chapter in this volume.
60 Ibid., VI, §45.
61 Wittgenstein describes cases of this sort of empty criticism in *Remarks on Frazer's Golden Bough*, reprinted in *Philosophical Occasions*, pp.118–55. Here he draws our attention to the fact that Frazer, in his study of historical practices involving "magic," conceives many of the traditions and rituals he is examining as rudimentary scientific practices. Because Frazer takes these practices to have the structure of primitive sciences, he thinks it is appropriate to say that many of them involve errors – errors in scientific reasoning. Wittgenstein suggests that Frazer, in thus assimilating spiritual practices of historical peoples to modern scientific practices, ignores characteristic connections which link those practices to other activities in the lives of the people he is studying and, since he thus remains blind to the essential character of the practices he is studying, winds up offering a critique which is no better than empty.
62 *Philosophical Investigations*, p.230.
63 See, above, n.61.
64 This comment about *On Certainty* is at odds with a widely accepted interpretation of it, one which seems to speak in favor of inviolability interpretations. I make the comment here in part to indicate that there is an alternative reading of *On Certainty* – I take it to be the best one – which coheres with the things I've been saying about Wittgenstein's view of meaning. On the prevalent interpretation, Wittgenstein is taken to be arguing that there are aspects of our lives which *cannot* be doubted. The alternative reading I favor claims that, although it is correct to see Wittgenstein as challenging the thought (common to the skeptic and the skeptic's Moorean, dogmatic interlocutor) that *any* aspect of our lives can be submitted to criticism, tested, investigated, doubted, etc., it is wrong to read him as insisting that there are specific things we cannot doubt. Wittgenstein is drawing our attention to cases in which we have no idea what would count as the realization of a sentence or utterance which we nevertheless confusedly think of as expressing a doubt about an aspect of our lives.
65 Wittgenstein, cited in R. Rhees, *Discussions of Wittgenstein*, New York, Schocken Books, 1970, p.43.
66 It is a recurring theme of the writings of deconstructive theorists – many of whom, as I noted in §1(ii), present their ("inviolability") views as Wittgensteinian in spirit – that only deconstructive modes of thought take seriously the role of freedom in rational reflection.
67 The choice is one which Rorty, as I argued, winds up making in spite of his attempts to distance himself from any such metaphysical choices. Rorty might be described, in this connection, as failing to grasp the Kantian character of Wittgenstein's thought.
68 I want to thank James Conant for a couple of conversations a number of years ago from which the original idea for this paper emerged – and for continuing to discuss these topics with me. I am indebted to Cora Diamond, Nathaniel Hupert, Kelly Dean Jolley, Elijah Millgram, Paul Muench, Hilary Putnam, Rupert Read and Sebastian Rödl for helpful comments on previous drafts. I owe a debt to John McDowell for making a number of useful suggestions about Richard Rorty's work.

Part II

THE *TRACTATUS* AS FORERUNNER OF WITTGENSTEIN'S LATER WRITINGS

7

ETHICS, IMAGINATION AND THE METHOD OF WITTGENSTEIN'S *TRACTATUS*

Cora Diamond

1 To read the *Tractatus* with understanding, Wittgenstein tells us, is not to read it as a textbook. His intention is not that the book should teach us things that we did not know; it does not address itself to our ignorance. In what we might call the frame of the book – its Preface and its closing sentences – Wittgenstein combines remarks about the aim of the book and the kind of reading it requires. The problems I shall discuss arise from these framing remarks; and in this section I describe the frame and some of the book's other significant features.

A. Wittgenstein offers us, in the Preface, this summary of the whole sense of the book: "What can be said at all can be said clearly, and about what cannot be spoken of one must be silent."

He goes on immediately:

> Thus the aim of the book is to draw a limit to thought, or rather – not to thought, but to the expression of thoughts: for in order to draw a limit to thought, we should have to be able to think both sides of this limit (we should therefore have to be able to think what cannot be thought).

He then draws the conclusion from those remarks that it will therefore only be in language that the limit can be drawn, and what lies on the other side of the limit will simply be nonsense.

The first remark that I quoted, that what can be said at all can be said clearly, and what cannot be spoken of, one must be silent about, very clearly suggests that there are two categories: things speakable about and things not speakable about, and the suggestion appears to be that Wittgenstein is going to draw the line between them: what words can reach and what they cannot. But the following paragraphs then seem to be meant to get us to question just that picture, to ask ourselves whether such a picture is not confused. He began that next paragraph by first giving the aim of the book as drawing a limit to thought and then withdrawing that account of its aim. You cannot draw a limit to thought because to do so you would have to be specifying what cannot be thought, you would have to grasp it in thought. And so you draw the limit in language instead: you will specify what can be said.

That can be done; his book is going to back up the claim that it can be. But once you draw that limit, what there is besides straightforwardly intelligible sentences will simply be nonsense.

For us as readers, there should then be a question about Wittgenstein's remark that what lies on the other side of the limit will be plain nonsense. Does it make us reject the picture we had of two categories, things we can reach by words and things beyond them? If Wittgenstein had done this:

What can be spoken about	What cannot be spoken about ←	.....
Straightforwardly intelligible sentences	Sentences that are nonsense but that would mean these things if they could count as sense	Mere nonsense

then perhaps our original picture would be all right. But his statement that what is on the other side of the limit is simply nonsense seems to be meant to rule out exactly the idea that some of our sentences count as nonsense but *do* manage to gesture towards those things that cannot be put into plain words.

Here I am not arguing for or against an interpretation of those remarks of Wittgenstein's but rather drawing attention to what is thrown at us in the paragraphs that I have discussed.

I want now to turn to the end of the book, the other part of the frame. Here we have these sentences:

My propositions serve as elucidations in this way: anyone who understands me finally recognizes them as nonsensical, when he has climbed out through them, on them, over them. (He must so to speak throw away the ladder, after he has climbed up it.)

He must overcome these propositions; then he sees the world rightly.

About what cannot be spoken of one must be silent.

I want to draw attention to a slight oddness in phrasing, slight but deliberate. Wittgenstein says: my propositions serve as elucidations in that whoever understands me will recognize them as nonsensical. It is very natural to misremember that sentence, to think that Wittgenstein said that his propositions serve as elucidations in that whoever understands them will recognize them as nonsensical. But the sentence is meant to strike the reader by its not being that. The sentence fails to be what we expect at just that point, and very deliberately. That is, at this significant point in the book, Wittgenstein chooses his words to draw attention to a contrast between understanding a person and understanding what the person says. If you recognize that Wittgenstein's propositions are nonsense, then you may earlier have thought that you understood them, but you did not. In recognizing that they are nonsense, you are giving up the idea that there is such a thing as understanding them. What Wittgenstein means by calling his propositions nonsense is not that they do not fit into some official category of his of intelligible propositions but that there is at most the illusion of understanding them.

The frame of the book contains instructions, as it were, for us as readers of it. Read it in the light of what it says at the beginning about its aim, and what it says at the end about how you are meant to take what it contains. These instructions introduce us to a central difficulty of the book, its use of the notions of what cannot be said and of nonsense.

(B) Before turning to the problems one may confront in trying to connect the *Tractatus* with ethics, I need to describe how it carries out its aim, and to touch on some of its other features.

(i) Most of it is explicitly concerned with the character of language and the relation between language and possibilities of the world. What a proposition is is explained in completely general terms: propositions are truth-functions of so-called elementary propositions. There are two central results of this part of the *Tractatus*: (1) an account of logic as internal to what propositions are, and (2) an account of the comparability of propositions with reality, their being either true or false, also as internal to what they are. Wittgenstein argues that these internal features of all propositions may be presented by a variable: that is, he thinks that there is a way of specifying a variable whose values will be all propositions; what this variable presents then is the general form of a proposition. The importance of this variable is clear if you go back to the frame of the book, and the statement that the aim of the book is to set the limits of the expression of thoughts. That is what Wittgenstein takes himself to have done by giving a variable whose values are all propositions, by giving, that is, a description of all propositional signs of any language whatever. Any such sign can be used with a sense (see Tr. 4.5), used so that it stands in logical relations to other constructions of signs to which sense has been given. If one or more of its constituents has been given no meaning in the particular context, the sentence will be nonsense. This account explains what is meant by "setting limits to the expression of thoughts". Wittgenstein does not try to demarcate such a limit by specifying kinds of sentence which are meaningless because of the kind of sentence they are. There is in the *Tractatus* no "demarcation" of sense in that sense. A sentence that is meaningless is not any special kind of sentence; it is a symbol which has the general form of a proposition, and which fails to have a sense simply because we have not given it any (Tr. 5.4733, also Tr. 4.5).

(ii) The book contains remarks about what it is to ascribe to someone the thought that p or the belief that p or even to say that he or she says that p. When you ascribe to someone the thought that p, this involves you in using a sentence giving the content of the thought, a sentence that you understand, a sentence of some or other language that you understand. You are not ascribing a belief to someone if you say that she believes that piggly wiggle tiggle, if "piggly wiggle tiggle" is nonsense (although it may be that she has been hypnotized and somehow or other made to think that when she says "piggly wiggle tiggle" out loud or to herself she is making sense.) If "piggly wiggle tiggle" is nonsense, then "Mary thinks that piggly wiggle tiggle" or "Mary says that piggly wiggle tiggle" is nonsense.[1]

(iii) The *Tractatus*, as I mentioned, calls its own propositions nonsense, but its own nonsense is intended (I shall discuss this later) to counter the kind of nonsense that it takes to be characteristic of philosophy. This intention is tied to Wittgenstein's description of the book as not a textbook. Philosophical questions, and the answers philosophers have given to them, are for the most part, Wittgenstein says, not false but nonsensical. And the book contains remarks about how it is possible for philosophers not to have realized this, as well as some specific remarks about confusions to which philosophers have been subject. (The most important of these concern necessity.)

2 I turn now to ethics.

A. At the end of the *Tractatus*, there are about two pages of remarks which are explicitly ethical. And there are also, at the end of the notebooks that Wittgenstein wrote before the *Tractatus*, a number of related remarks, also explicitly ethical. But we should put with these explicitly ethical remarks the comments that Wittgenstein made about the book before it was published, when he wrote to Ludwig von Ficker, whom he hoped would publish the book. He told Ficker that he didn't think Ficker would get much out of reading the book, because he wouldn't understand it, "its subject-matter will seem quite foreign to you". He went on:

> It isn't really foreign to you, because the book's point is ethical. I once meant to include in the preface a sentence which is not in fact there now, but which I will write out for you here, because it will perhaps be a key for you. What I meant to write then was this: my work consists of two parts: the one presented here plus all that I have *not* written. And it is precisely this second part that is the important one. For the ethical gets its limit drawn from the inside, as it were, by my book; and I am convinced that this is the ONLY *rigorous* way of drawing that limit. In short, I believe that where *many* others today are just *gassing*, I have managed in my book to put everything firmly into place by being silent about it . . . For now I would recommend you to read the *preface* and the *conclusion*, because they contain the most direct expression of the point."[2]

Here Wittgenstein provides instructions for reading the book, similar to those in the frame of the book itself, but different in emphasizing the ethical point of the book. That ethical aim is to be achieved by what the book does *not* say: the ethical is thereby delimited in the only way it can be, "from the inside". This puts differently what the Preface puts by saying that we set limits to thought only through setting limits to the expression of thoughts. We give the limit from the inside; and that is the only way to make clear what is not there. And this giving of the limits of expression from the inside is what Wittgenstein takes the book to have achieved in its presentation of the general form of a proposition.

The letter to Ficker adds something to the Preface: the result is that the way the book leads us up to the general form of a proposition is a way of delimiting the ethical. Working from the inside of what can be said, we see that in the totality of what can be said, nothing is ethical. And this is indeed put explicitly by Wittgenstein. He says that it is impossible for there to be ethical propositions; ethics cannot be put into words (Tr. 6.42, 6.421). He adds that it is transcendental (6.421), a remark that I shall discuss later. I can now explain the problems I have been leading up to, the problems I have in reading the *Tractatus* and thinking about the remarks on ethics in relation to the rest of the book.

(B) The first problem is this. I believe that the *Tractatus* takes what you might call an austere view of nonsense. Nonsense is nonsense; there is no division of nonsense as in the diagram of §1. So if there are no ethical propositions (intelligible sentences in the lower left part of the diagram), then there are no propositions through which we are able to gesture, however ineptly, at unspeakable truths, and anything we take to be an ethical proposition has no more sense than "piggly wiggle tiggle". This, however, looks like the view of ethics taken by some of the logical positivists, like Carnap and Ayer. And yet I do not believe that Wittgenstein's consigning of ethical talk to the realm of nonsense should be likened to that of the positivists. But that leaves me with the task of explaining how one can distinguish Wittgenstein's view of ethics from that of the logical positivists, without giving up the ascription to him of what I have called an austere view of nonsense. (I should add that my sense of the pinch of the problem has been made acute by reading James Conant's "Must We Show What We Cannot Say?"[3] and by conversation with him.)

(C) The second problem arises differently from my reading of the *Tractatus*. I read in it the austere view of nonsense; yet I then try to articulate what I think Wittgenstein is committed to in ethics, and I find myself using language incompatible with the ascription to him of that austere view. I shall give two examples of the kind of articulation of his ethical views that I find myself inclined to give.

(i) I begin by contrasting two approaches to ethics. The first is characteristic of philosophers in the English-speaking tradition. We think that one way of dividing philosophy into branches is to take there to be, for every kind of thing people talk and think about, philosophy of that subject matter. Thus we may, for example, take psychology to be an area of thought and talk, a branch of inquiry, and so to have, corresponding to it, philosophy of psychology, containing philosophical consideration of that area of discourse. We may then think that there is thought and talk that has as its subject matter what the good life is for human beings, or what principles of action we should accept; and then philosophical ethics will be the philosophy of that area of thought and talk. But you do not have to think that; and Wittgenstein rejects that conception of ethics. I said, however, that I wanted, as part of my articulation of his view, to give a contrast with that conception of ethics, to set something over against it. And I might do that this way: just as logic is not, for Wittgenstein, a particular subject, with its own body of truths, but penetrates all thought, so ethics has no particular subject matter; rather, an ethical spirit, an attitude to the world and life, can penetrate any thought or talk. Wittgenstein, like some other writers, speaks of two different as it were attitudes to the world as a whole; he refers to them as that of the happy and that of the unhappy. The happy and the unhappy as it were inhabit different worlds (Tr. 6.43; cf. also *Notebooks*, pp. 73–86). I find myself inclined to put Wittgenstein with some other writers who have used similar imagery: among others G. K. Chesterton, who characterizes two types of attitude to life in terms of the notion of attachment or loyalty on the one hand and disloyalty on the other, and Wordsworth, who, in his great poem about the growth of his mind, speaks of those who live in a world of life, and of others in a universe of death.[4] So the contrast I want is that between ethics conceived as a sphere of discourse among others in contrast with ethics tied to everything there is or can be, the world as a whole, life. In articulating this second sort of ethical view, I try to show how an attitude to the world as a whole may be seen in the things that people do. An example that has struck me is Nathaniel Hawthorne's story *The Birthmark*, in which the central character, Aylmer, is shown as "unhappy" in Wittgenstein's sense: the world does not meet conditions he lays down. This ethical spirit is first obvious in his response to the birthmark on his beautiful wife; but it is also meant to be seen by us in what he goes on to do, seen to be the spirit in his destructiveness of life, goodness, beauty.

This first sort of attempt to articulate Wittgenstein's view of ethics thus involves me in trying to show how an attitude to the world or to life is connected to the moral character that we may perceive in actions, thoughts, feelings, or things said.

(ii) In another attempt to articulate Wittgenstein's views on ethics, I first formulated an attitude to the world in terms of acceptance of the independence of the world from one's own will. I thought that I could explain what this came to by looking at the tentative remarks Wittgenstein made about suicide, at the very end of the notes that have survived from before the *Tractatus*. "If anything is not allowed, then suicide is not allowed." But, he asks, is even suicide in itself neither good nor evil? (*Notebooks*, 91) – If one says that the ethical spirit is tied to living in acceptance of the fact that what happens, happens, that one's willing this rather than that is merely another thing that happens and that one is in a sense "powerless" (see *Notebooks*, 73), then one may see suicide as a sort of saying to oneself this: "My going on with life I make conditional on things being this way not that: in my heart I reject the powerlessness that belongs to life, by the will to *leave life* if things don't go as I will". The importance of suicide for Wittgenstein I thought could be seen by contrasting his view of it with Hume's, in the essay "Of Suicide". Hume I read as thinking that it is always "superstitious" to refrain from fulfilling a human want through a sense that here, in this particular case, we need to recognize and accept "powerlessness" in Wittgenstein's sense. Such acceptance goes with the possibility of constraints on the will, constraints the justification of which is not any achievable end in the world. The significance of suicide for Hume is exactly what it is for Wittgenstein, only in the opposite direction. If Wittgenstein was inclined to call suicide the elementary sin, for Hume its prohibition might be called the elementary superstition. – I saw Wittgenstein, then, as not going Hume's way, the way that leads to everything's being permissible, and not attempting to throw transcendental roadblocks in that direction: a sort of piety in action, in life, is possible, that looks with clear eyes at the happenings of the world, at the happenings of the world being whatever they are. What I want to emphasize here is the disagreement in the face of the extent of the agreement with Hume. For Hume and Wittgenstein, there is nothing, no facts in the world and no facts beyond it, on which a prohibition on suicide can rest. I shall not now try to say why Wittgenstein thought that perhaps suicide was neither good nor evil, nor to explain further the difference I see with Hume, since my aim is to make clear a particular problem.

(iii) The two examples show how I find myself trying to articulate what Wittgenstein says about ethics. In both, I make heavy use of the idea of differing attitudes to the world. In the first example, I try to make clear to myself the difference between the happy and the unhappy attitude to the world as a whole by taking, as exemplifying the attitude of the "unhappy", a character in a story, for whom a central problem is his lack of control over what happens. In the second example, I make use of the case of suicide to try to do something similar, to try to suggest that what Wittgenstein discerns in suicide is its expressing a certain attitude to life. But my own phrases – "attitude to life", "attitude to the world as a whole" – are curious ones. An attitude is an attitude to something or other: to a person, or something else in the world; or to things being this way rather than that, as I may be disappointed or pleased by something's having turned out as it has. The phrase "attitude to the world as a whole" is not only curious, but from the point of view of the *Tractatus* anyway, mere nonsense. If I am using a phrase which is simply nonsense in sup-posedly articulating Wittgenstein's views, what can I think I am achieving? He uses what he says is nonsense in the book, as part of its leading people out of philosoph-ical confusion. But it would appear to be confused of me to think that I can talk non-sense and be giving the content of a kind of ethical position. For is that not what I keep trying to do? Do I not keep trying to give the content of his ethical views? If we must keep silent about that about which we cannot talk, and if I really take that seriously, what can I be doing making so much noise? James Conant has put this point extremely forcefully in criticizing the attempts people make to say what Wittgenstein's views on ethics are. He notes that commentators on Wittgenstein's "ethical views" characteristically project into the work either something out of their own heads or some combination of thoughts from Schopenhauer, Tolstoy and other writers.[5] Am I not doing just that, and therefore (as he has argued) going back on my own recognition that when Wittgenstein calls something nonsensical he implies that it has really and truly got no articulable content?

3 That ends the part of the paper in which I state my problems. I now turn to solving them. I shall argue that we cannot understand how we are supposed to read the sequence of remarks about ethics in the *Tractatus* except through a better under-standing of how the *Tractatus* views its own philosophical procedure. To get that understanding we need to go back to the second part of the frame of the book. When I described that part of the frame, I emphasized that, just where you might think that Wittgenstein would explain how the propositions of his book elucidate by referring to the intended effect of understanding them, he instead refers to under-standing him. That remark is part of *Tractatus* 6.54. Immediately before 6.54, we have 6.53, where Wittgenstein says that the correct method in philosophy would be to say nothing except propositions belonging to natural science, and then, when-ever someone wanted to say something metaphysical, to show the person that he failed to give a meaning to some or other sign – in other words, you show him that, as far as the meaning goes, "piggly wiggle" would do as well as some word he used. That – the "only strictly correct" method – is plainly not the method of the *Tractatus*. How exactly, then, does Wittgenstein mean to contrast the not-strictly-correct method of the *Tractatus* with the "strictly correct" method that it does not follow? We might say that the *Tractatus* departs from the strictly correct method in that it contains nonsensical propositions. But that, I think, is not the point. It is true; it is important – but it does not get to what is central. To see how Wittgenstein conceives his own method, you have to see 6.53 with 6.54, and with the explicit description there of what Wittgenstein demands of you the reader of the *Tractatus*, the reader of a book of nonsensical propositions. You are to understand not the propositions but the author. Take that directive to you as reader, take it with you

to 6.53, the reference to the method of the *Tractatus*. You are to read his nonsensical propositions and try to understand not them but their author; just so, he takes himself to have to respond to the nonsense uttered by philosophers through understanding not their propositions but them. The *Tractatus* is a book that understands its own departure from the only strictly correct method to lie in its understanding of those who utter nonsense, and that demands exactly that understanding from its own readers.

So my claim now is that we cannot see how we are supposed to read the remarks on ethics in the *Tractatus* without seeing how Wittgenstein thought of its philosophical method, and crucial to that is his conception of what it is to understand a person who utters nonsense. What is it then to understand a person who talks nonsense?

4 In order to see how Wittgenstein conceives "understanding a person who talks nonsense" we need to see how that notion depends on his idea of understanding a person who talks sense, what that is and what it is not. When we understand a person who talks sense, we can say such things as that he says that such-and-such, or that she believes that so-and-so. As I mentioned earlier, the *Tractatus* view is that, when you ascribe to someone the thought that p, you give what that person thinks by using a sentence that you understand. Your understanding of the person who talks sense is an understanding of what he or she says, an understanding that is the same thing as your capacity to use an intelligible sentence of your own language in giving the content of that person's saying or thought. Thus if you cannot make sense of the sentence "God is three persons" then you can say that Smith uttered the words "God is three persons" and you can say that he uttered them with the intonation of asserting something, but you cannot say of him that he said that God is three persons. "Smith said that p" is itself nonsense unless what we put for "p" makes sense. That is a part of the *Tractatus* view of what it is to understand a person whom one takes to be making sense; but just as important a part is what the *Tractatus* is rejecting, the sort of account it would regard as changing the subject. What Wittgenstein rejects, and would treat as a sort of changing of the subject, is the attempt to treat people's sayings and believings and thinkings in the terms provided by empirical psychology. In fact this rejection runs through the whole of his philosophical thinking, from before the *Tractatus* (even before the notebooks for it) to the end of his life.[6]

What empirical psychology can tell us of the person who judges that such-and-such or who says that so-and-so is that he or she puts together signs, has associations of various sorts, has feelings tied to different words or even some feeling of asserting something; possibly also that he or she intends to have some effect on other people; possibly also that he or she comes to have inclinations of this sort after certain kinds of experience in accordance with such-and-such natural laws; and possibly also that he or she will now be inclined, given certain further stimuli, to make mental transitions to other collections of signs, or to actions, in accordance with other natural laws including what you might call the natural laws of inferential behavior.[7] The *Tractatus* has no interest in excluding the possibility of natural laws covering mental processes; it is meant, though, to make clear that what such laws are concerned with is different from what we are concerned with when we ascribe to anyone beliefs, or sayings that so-and-so, in all those cases in which what we ascribe has logical characteristics. In summary, then: when you understand someone who is making sense, you understand what the person says, and that is shown in your putting what he or she says in a sentence of your language, i.e., a sentence with its logical relationships to other sentences of your language and its possibility of being either true or false. That is not to describe what is happening in that person's mind from the point of view of empirical psychology. So far as one can speak of empirical psychology as giving us understanding of a person who talks sense, what would be meant is very different.

We can now turn to what it is to understand a person who utters nonsense. This is something that we often want to do in philosophy. I may say to you that you are under the illusion that such-and-such, and, when I specify the illusion that I take you to be under, I may not mean something that makes sense. The *Tractatus* invites us to understand Wittgenstein, the utterer of nonsense. What is such an understanding supposed to be? When you understand someone who utters nonsense, you are not, on the one hand, remaining as it were outside his thought and describing what goes on from the point of view of empirical psychology. But, on the other hand, you are not inside his thought as you are when he makes sense and you understand what he says, because there is no such internal understanding, there is no thought that such-and-such to understand. You are not inside, because there is as it were no inside; you cannot remain outside, because outside all you can see is someone inclined to put together words, to come out with them in certain circumstances, to associate with them images, feelings and so on: from the outside, there is nothing to be seen that could be called his being in the grip of an illusion that so-and-so, as opposed to his being inclined to come out with certain word-constructions. There is, as I said, no inside. But what it is to understand a person who utters nonsense is to go as far as one can with the idea that there is.

The understanding of a person who talks nonsense uses the type of linguistic construction that we use when we understand someone who talks sense. "You are under the illusion that p" is modelled on "You believe that p". But sentences with that structure, all of them, make sense only when they contain, in the clause giving the content of what is believed or thought or denied or said or whatever, an intelligible sentence. "You are under the illusion that p" does not do that. It is essential, then, to what is going on in the case of understanding a person who talks nonsense that you use a sentence-structure which gives a sentence with a sense only when what it contains in its "that"-clause is a sentence that makes sense; and you want to fill it in with a sentence that makes no sense. You want the type of sentence suitable for internal understanding of sense; and yet it is exactly that sort of sentence that will be nonsensical in the circumstances for which you want it. But, as I said, remaining outside, and just talking about how the person puts together words and associates with them feelings and so on, would not give you what you want. To want to understand the person who talks nonsense is to want to enter imaginatively the taking of that nonsense for sense. My point then is that the *Tractatus*, in its understanding of itself as addressed to those who are in the grip of philosophical nonsense, and in its understanding of the kind of demands it makes on its readers, supposes a kind of imaginative activity, an exercise of the capacity to enter into the taking of nonsense for sense, of the capacity to share imaginatively the inclination to think that one is thinking something in it. If I could not as it were see your nonsense as sense, imaginatively let myself feel its attractiveness, I could not understand you. And that is a very particular use of imagination.

Let me put in another way the position of the person who wants to understand the utterer of nonsense. The would-be understander takes himself to be speaking a language in which the things that the other person says have not been given any determinate sense, although they could be given sense – any sentence-construction can be. Yet he also wants to say to the other person, "You think that p"; he wants a language in which he can give the content of the illusion, in which he can say to the other what he is thinking, and say of that that it is only the illusion of a thought, or even argue that it is the illusion of a thought. He wants to be speaking a language in which the sentences that the other person utters have been given sense, because he wants to mean them himself; yet he also wants to remain in the language in which no meaning has been given to those sentences. We could say that he has not got clear what language he wants to be in. He can have whatever he wants; but he does not have a singleness of purpose in his wants. To be self-conscious about all this is to realize that there is no such thing as having what one wants, not because it cannot be had, but because one has not got some definite "it" that one wants.

5 The *Tractatus*, I said, supposes a particular kind of imaginative activity, the imaginative taking of what is nonsense for sense. I want now to set alongside that use of imagination the role of imagination in the putting forward of metaphysical sentences by someone who believes that he or she is making sense. My aim is to clarify two related ideas about nonsense-sentences and their role in the *Tractatus*. The first idea is that there are no nonsense-sentences that are as it were closer to being true than any others. I am rejecting an idea that was put very clearly by Elizabeth Anscombe: that there are some sentences which are nonsense but which would say something true if what they are an attempt to say could be said. The unsayability of what they attempt to say precludes its being said, but we can nevertheless grasp what they attempt to say. And they can thus, on her view, be contrasted with nonsense-sentences which are attempts to deny such truths-that-cannot-be-said. What the latter sort of sentence intends to say is "not just incorrect but quite incoherent and confused" and she adds that "the demonstration that this is so completely destroys the idea that there is anything at all behind the would-be statement".[8] So she works with the contrast between nonsense-sentences that have something, something true but unsayable, behind them, and those that have nothing but confusion behind them. Applied then to the views of the *Tractatus* itself, her account would imply that, for example, its fundamental distinction between objects and facts cannot be put into a senseful sentence, but, if one were to say "There is a distinction between objects and facts", that sentence intends something that is true, or at any rate taken to be true by the *Tractatus*, although the sentence itself is nonsense. The first idea, then, is the opposite of hers: there is no dividing nonsense-sentences so that, although none *say* anything true or false, some have and some lack a truth behind them. (A consequence of this first idea is that the *Tractatus* does not have as its purpose the conveying to its readers of truths which in Professor Anscombe's sense "stand behind" its own nonsense-sentences.) The second idea is this: There is a distinction

that can be made, not dividing nonsense-sentences into the good and the bad, those pointing to a truth and those not pointing to anything, but between different roles that imagination has in our coming out with nonsense-sentences. Nonsense-sentences are as it were internally all the same; all are *einfach Unsinn*, simply nonsense. Externally, however, they may differ: in a particular case of the utterance of a nonsense-sentence, its utterance may fail to reflect an understanding of oneself or of others; it may depend on this or that type of use of imagination. But there is no way of taking any nonsense-sentence and saying that, by the sentence it is, it is philosophical elucidation not metaphysical nonsense. For a sentence that is nonsense to be an elucidatory sentence is entirely a matter of features external to it.[9]

My aim now is to distinguish between two contexts in which nonsense-sentences are put forward; and I shall do that by looking at the role of imagination in them.

Part of Wittgenstein's inheritance from Frege is the distinction between psychology and logic. Frege had emphasized that, although many words call up ideas in our minds, the connection of those ideas with the thought expressed by our words may be "entirely superficial, arbitrary and conventional".[10] That point of Frege's is very important for Wittgenstein. Two sentences may make use of the same word, but they may give that word quite different logical roles, as for example when I describe an object as green, and speak about a Mr. Green. If, when I refer to Mr. Green, what is going on in my mind, the images I have, the associations, happen to be exactly like what is going on in my mind when I speak about the green tomatoes I am cooking, those images and associations have nothing to do with the role of the word "Green" in the sentence about the man Green. In the case of that example, the sentence with the irrelevant associations may be meaningful. But now consider a sentence "The letter e is green". And suppose that I have a lot of images of green things when I utter that sentence. That collection of images is no more relevant to the meaning of the sentence "The letter e is green" than it is to "Mr. Green teaches geometry". The mental accompaniments of a sentence are irrelevant to its logical characteristics. And yet it is exactly those familiar mental accompaniments of the sentence that may give us the illusion that we mean something by a sentence which contains some familiar word, even though the word is not being used in its familiar logical role, and has not been given a new assignment of meaning. That, then, is one of the ideas in the *Tractatus* about the role of imagination in the producing of metaphysical nonsense. We are attracted by certain sentences, certain forms of words, and imagine that we mean something by them. We are satisfied that we mean something by them because they have the mental accompaniments of meaningful sentences.

But that is only part of the role of imagination in the producing of nonsense. For what one could call false imagination is also important in attracting us to those forms of words in the first place. The attractiveness of the forms of words expressive of philosophical confusion arises out of the imagining of a point of view for philosophical investigation. And it is precisely that illusory point of view that the *Tractatus* self-consciously imagines itself into in an attempt to lead one to see that there was only false imagination in the attractiveness of the words one had been inclined to come out with.

Take the opening sentences of the *Tractatus* after the preface: "The world is all that is the case. The world is the totality of facts, not of things." With those sentences we imagine a point of view from which we can consider the world as a whole. That idea, not recognized as an illusion, characterizes the practice of philosophy as it has gone on.[11] My claim, then, about how we are to read Wittgenstein is that he does not intend us to grasp what can be seen from the point of view of philosophical investigation (where what can be seen from there cannot be put into language, with the result that the propositions of his book are nonsense). On my reading, the book understands the person who is in the grip of the illusion that there is philosophy in the traditional sense. It understands him through entering into that illusion in order to lead him out of it; and the upshot will not be any grasp of what can be seen from the philosophical point of view on the world. Here, then, is a description – an external description – of the difference between the propositions of the *Tractatus* and the propositions of the metaphysician. The former are recognized by their author to be plain nonsense, the latter are not; the former are in the service of an imaginative understanding of persons, the latter are the result of a sort of disease of imagination, and the philosopher who comes out with them lacks that understanding of himself which the *Tractatus* aims to secure for us. This difference between the sentences of the *Tractatus* and those of the philosopher is marked in the book by its frame. If I say "I am inclined to say that the letter e is green", I frame the sentence by putting at the beginning words that may in a particular context indicate that I do not regard the sentence "e is green" as sense. Note how this differs from "I should like to believe that Vitamin C prevents colds". The framing words there are entirely consistent with the sentence "Vitamin C prevents colds" being good sense. But "I am inclined to say that e is green" may be meant to distance the speaker from any commitment to the sensefulness of saying "The letter e is green". The *Tractatus*, I am suggesting, tells us, in part through its framing propositions, that its own propositions belong to the activity of providing a kind of self-understanding to those attracted by philosophy, a self-understanding that would be marked by their no longer being attracted by philosophy, by their no longer coming out with unframed philosophical nonsense.

6 I can now turn back to ethics. From the point of view of the *Tractatus*, there is no class of sentences distinguishable by their subject matter as "ethical sentences". The sentences of the would-be engager in ethics, the would-be speaker about Good and Evil, are like the sentences of philosophers and like the sentences of the *Tractatus* in being plain nonsense. As I said, the *Tractatus* does not recognize any categories of nonsense, good nonsense and bad, illuminating nonsense and dark murky muddle. So there is no question whether Wittgenstein puts sentences purporting to be ethical into one or other of those categories of nonsensical sentences; for they do not exist. But the "ethical" sentences are also like the others in this regard, that the utterer of the sentences can be understood, where the understanding of the utterer of nonsense is peculiar in being modelled on understanding someone who makes sense. There is an understanding of the would-be engager in ethics as someone who has what looks to him as if it is a point of view from which he speaks, an understanding that imaginatively enters into seeing from that point of view (which it nevertheless takes to be illusory) and does not simply restrict

itself to the empirical psychology of ethical nonsense. As seen from that imaginative view, the sentences he utters can be said to be concerned with what has value, with the sense of the world; i.e., it is from such a point of view that they appear to be ethical. From the point of view of empirical psychology, the ethical disappears. There is simply a person who comes out with words, has feelings, tries to get others to behave in certain ways and behaves in certain ways himself. *Nothing ethical there.* (I shall say more about this in § 7 below.) This account can be fitted into the general story I have given of how the *Tractatus* conceives itself. (I should note that, although I have just said that the *Tractatus* allows for understanding the utterer of nonsense, this is itself subject to the qualification that such "understanding" issues in nonsense-sentences: "You are under the illusion that p", "You are inclined to say that p" are nonsense if p is nonsense. The understander of an utterer of nonsense is someone who can be understood only by further imaginative activity.)

I have also argued that the *Tracatatus*, which does not allow us to distinguish kinds of nonsense-sentence through our understanding of them, does allow us to distinguish nonsense-sentences by the external circumstances of their utterance, by the character of the imaginative activity involved in it. And I believe that if we consider the external features of "ethical sentences" we can see them as a third group: they are different in some ways from both the *Tractatus*'s own sentences and from philosophical nonsense-sentences. In § 5, in giving the difference between the sentences of the *Tractatus* and those of the metaphysician, I said that the former were in the service of an imaginative understanding of persons; they were self-conscious uses of nonsense intended to liberate the metaphysician: if they were successful, the spell of such nonsense would be broken. The intention of the would-be engager in ethics is not like that, is not in that way therapeutic. So "ethical sentences" are distinguishable from those of the *Tractatus* by the intention with which they are uttered or written. They are distinguishable from philosophical nonsense-sentences by their relation to the self-understanding towards which the *Tractatus* aims to lead us. Wittgenstein, as I said, aims to understand the utterer of nonsense, where this involves imaginatively entering into the tendency to be attracted by such sentences. There is an important resemblance between ethical sentences and philosophical ones, seen imaginatively as apparently making sense: both ethical and philosophical nonsense reflect the attractiveness of the idea of a point of view on the world as a whole, whatever may happen in it. But I think that if we read the *Tractatus* right, the upshot of the book will be different in regard to the two sorts of utterers of nonsense. The attractiveness of philosophical sentences will disappear through the kind of self-understanding that the book aims to lead to in philosophers; the attractiveness of ethical sentences will not. But if we understand ourselves, ourselves the utterers of ethical nonsense, we shall not come out with ethical sentences under the illusion that we are talking sense. We may show this by framing our sentences; for example, someone might say "I am inclined to say 'The goodness of life does not depend on things going this way or that'". Words like "This is what I am inclined to say", used to frame such sentences, may thus mark both that they are recognized by the utterer as nonsense, and that that recognition does not involve their losing their attractiveness, their capacity to make us feel that they express the sense we want to make.

For an example of exactly this sort of framing of ethical sentences, see Wittgenstein's "Lecture on Ethics",[12] one important feature of which is the explicit discussion of the kind of linguistic intention that characterizes the self-aware user of nonsense. Every account of what he means which would make it out to be sense he would reject "on the ground of its significance"; the nonsensicality of what is said belongs to the essence of the linguistic intention. The same is true of the intentions with which the *Tractatus* is written. But, as Wittgenstein saw traditional philosophical activity, it would not survive recognition that the intentions in it were incompatible with making sense. The differences that I have pointed out between "ethical sentences" and the nonsense of philosophers and that of the *Tractatus* are not meant to enable us to pick out the ethical. The only picking out of the ethical goes by way of imaginative understanding, through which plain nonsense appears to have a subject matter.

7 I can now look again at my problems about ethics in the *Tractatus*. I deal with the first problem in this section and with the second in § 8.

If I see in the *Tractatus* an austere view of nonsense, not one distinguishing any kind of nonsense as deeper or with more truth behind it than any other, and if, according to the *Tractatus*, there are no senseful ethical sentences, how is that different from the view of logical positivists like Ayer and Carnap, and their understanding of ethical sentences as nonsensical?[13]

Wittgenstein's approach forces a choice on us. i. We can imagine ourselves into the point of view from which the sentences we call ethical have something ethical in them; in that case what we are doing is imaginatively understanding an utterer of nonsense (perhaps ourselves), imaginatively engaging in being taken in by the appearance of sense of what is actually plain nonsense. Sentences of ours in which such an understanding is reflected will equally be nonsense. ii. Or we can look at such sentences and the utterers of them from the point of view of empirical psychology and of philosophy that does not engage in what it recognizes to be nonsense. In that case we can come up with an account of particular groups of sentences, constructed by people who want certain things or feel certain things or aim to persuade others to do certain things; this we may call meta-ethics, but it will have nothing to do with what one might be tempted to call the ethical meaning of the sentences in question. What characterizes the meta-ethics of the logical positivists is that they do not see themselves as confronted with that choice. It is important here to note that if you see such a choice as Wittgenstein does, you are rejecting a fundamental part of the way philosophy conceives its relation to ethics; you are rejecting the conception embodied in the very word "meta-ethics". The word "meta-ethics" reflects the idea that sentences which are in some way "ethical" can be recognized and discussed philosophically in sentences that make sense and that do not wholly ignore whatever is ethical in those sentences. But it is just *that* that Wittgenstein's choice does not allow. Grasp the sentences in question as ethical by imaginatively treating nonsense as sense *or* stick to talking and thinking sense yourself and lose touch with anything ethical in the sentences. So part of the answer to the problem how I distinguish Wittgenstein on ethics from the positivists is that the positivists are from Wittgenstein's point of view under an illusion in all they say about ethics, the illusion that anything can be said about it within philosophy as they conceive it.[14]

One way in which the difference between Wittgenstein and the positivists shows up is in the tendency of some of them (and of those influenced by them) to treat evaluation in general as capable of being given some single account, covering the evaluation of good strawberries or sewage effluent and good and evil deeds or good and bad human lives. From Wittgenstein's point of view, evaluation of straw-berries and sewage effluent can be understood without requiring imaginative participation in taking nonsense for sense, and is thus utterly distinct from ethics. The idea of a *general* account of evaluation, within which ethical judgments can be fitted, is from the point of view of the *Tractatus* one striking way in which the total omission of what makes ethics ethics shows itself in philosophy.

The logical positivists intended their accounts of ethics to bear on what we might call ordinary ethical talk. It has been put to me that the *Tractatus*, although it says that it is impossible for there to be propositions of ethics, is not committed to viewing ordinary ethical talk (as opposed to theoretical or philosophical ethics) as nonsense.[15] If that is correct, would it not mark a significant difference between Wittgenstein's approach to ethics and that of the positivists?

There is an objection to my way of putting the question. It shares the logical positivists' view that there are philosophical issues about "ordinary ethical discourse": Are the sentences of which it is composed sense or nonsense? Do they have or lack a truth-value? For Wittgenstein, any sentence can make sense (Tr. 5.4733). If someone is talking nonsense, that is not because the sentence he utters belongs to a category of sentences that are nonsensical, a category of sentences that lack truth-value. We may, though, recognize that the person who utters some sentence speaks with an intention that would (though he himself may not be aware of this) be frustrated by his sentence's making sense. That understanding depends on our own similar impulses and intentions; it involves the imagination in ways I have tried to suggest. I do not think that we can ascribe to Wittgenstein any view about whether the sentences of "ordinary ethical discourse" are, or are for the most part, uttered by people with the intentions and impulses that Wittgenstein aims to have us understand in ourselves. We are left to make shift for ourselves in understanding what others say.

I have just criticized the question "Does Wittgenstein differ from the positivists on whether the remarks we ordinarily take to be ethical are sense or nonsense?", but the answer I have implied is nevertheless Yes. The positivists' view of evalu-ation in general is that it involves the use of sentences to express or to change attitudes or emotions, or to express adherence to some prescriptive principle, or to guide action, and that, because of that function (however specified), evaluative sentences will be logically distinguishable from straightforward statements of fact. For Wittgenstein, a sentence is nonsensical if it contains a word or words to which no meaning has been given; but the use of sentences to express or to change emotions or attitudes, or to express adherence to prescriptive principles or what-ever, does not involve the utterer in refusing to assign meaning to any word or words. It is no part of the linguistic intention of would-be judgers of strawberries or pens that what they say be "about Value that has Value"; what they say will normally make sense. There are no "ethical propositions" on Wittgenstein's view, because what he calls ethics is characterized by the linguistic intention to "reach beyond the world"; any sentence which was not nonsense would not be what one wanted. But that intention is no part of evaluation in general. If one considers ordinary ethical remarks, e.g., about what one must do, or about how someone has behaved, there may be a connection with what Wittgenstein calls the ethical, but it may perfectly well be carried by tone of voice. What I am warning against is any idea that we should take Wittgenstein's remarks about ethics to constitute philosophical analysis of a kind of discourse, rather than as remarks aimed at bringing about a kind of self-understanding through the reader's imaginative activity.

We need to trust Wittgenstein more than we do. There is – if we read the *Tractatus* right – no fact-value distinction in it. There is the distinction between sentences with sense and those of logic and mathematics; there is the distinction between all those and sentences containing one or more symbols without meaning, nonsensical sentences. Ethical sentences are not a subcategory of the latter but a non-category. The book also aims to let us see that sometimes the purposes with which we speak would not be served by sentences that make sense. As part of our imaginative understanding of ourselves or others with such purposes, we may wish to describe what we or they say as "about Value". Any such seeing of what is said draws on the same sources in us as the "ethical" remark itself. Philosophical understanding of this is shown, as in the *Tractatus*, by what it does not attempt; philosophical misunderstanding by what Wittgenstein spoke of as the "chatter about ethics".[16]

I hope in this section to have shown that we are not confronted by the choice: to read Wittgenstein either as a mystic or as a logical positivist. The idea that those are the alternatives[17] is encouraged by a failure to grasp that his philosophical method involves the exhibition of the author of the *Tractatus* as someone who requires an imaginative understanding dependent on the reader's own impulse towards ethics.

8 What about my second problem with the *Tractatus* remarks about ethics? (Note that my references to that sequence of remarks as "about ethics" can now be seen to be problematic. For if I understand Wittgenstein in the way he asks to be understood, then I read the sentences in question twice: first, entering (wittingly or not) into the nonsense that they are about ethics; secondly, entering into the nonsense of the book as argument to a conclusion that those remarks are not "about ethics", for nothing is a "remark about ethics". There are no "ethical propositions", and the sentences in question have no more to do with "ethics" than "piggly wiggle tiggle". If I understand Wittgenstein, I enter the nonsense of reading the sentences as ethics, and of reading the book in such a way that it leads me to self-consciousness about the activity of such reading. The structure of this paper thus duplicates that of the *Tractatus*. When I began to discuss Wittgenstein's remarks about ethics, I called them remarks about ethics, because the idea that there is no such thing as what they present themselves to us as, the idea that we are taken in by them in reading them as about ethics – that idea we cannot start with. So too the *Tractatus* itself. The reading it requires requires that it take us in at first, requires that it should allow itself to be read as sense, read as about logic and so on, despite not being so. What I have just said about the *Tractatus*'s remarks "about ethics" goes then equally for its remarks about logic. It contains no remarks about logic, because the only kind of remarks about logic that there could be that make sense would be remarks like "Such-and-such is a good textbook for teaching children to do these manipulations of symbols", i.e., remarks that do not treat of logic as logic.)

The second problem I had with the *Tractatus*'s remarks about ethics was that I was inclined to explain them, to articulate Wittgenstein's ethical views, first by looking at the role in those views of an attitude to the world as a whole, secondly by trying to show the relation between that attitude and what we might recognize as judgements about good and evil in human life and action, and thirdly by contrasting his view of ethics with that of Hume, treating as central their strikingly different views about suicide. But, if I recognized that the *Tractatus* view was that we must keep silent about that about which we cannot talk, what was all that articulation and explanation of Wittgenstein's views? It looked very much as if I thought I could put those views into words.

Part of the solution to this problem should be clear from what I have already said. There are three quite different questions that can be asked about my articulation of Wittgenstein's views on ethics: i. What is it that I am doing? ii. Should I not be doing it? and iii. If the answer to that is that it is not necessarily something to stop doing, am I doing well or badly whatever it is I am doing? It looks as if it is something that I should not be doing at all, given that it follows from ascribing to Wittgenstein an austere view of nonsense (the view that all nonsense is just nonsense) that there is no articulating of the meaning of a particular bit of nonsense. There is no way of indicating something that lies behind it if nothing does. But what I have tried to argue in this paper is that the situation is more complex than that. Although all nonsense is simply nonsense, there is an imaginative activity of understanding an utterer of nonsense, letting oneself be taken in by the appearance of sense that some nonsense presents to us. One thing the matter with my articulation of Wittgenstein's ethics was lack of awareness of what I was doing, lack of awareness of the kind of imaginative activity I was engaged in. So my answer to the question what I was doing is that I was trying to see from the point of view that takes nonsense for sense, and from which a sentence can be taken to be concerned with ethics. This paper then provides a frame of the sort we may give such an activity when we engage in it with awareness of its character. My answer to the second question is that, although it follows from the austere view of nonsense that there is no articulating or explaining any bit of nonsense, it does not follow that awareness of its nonsensicality leads one to give up the activity of articulating; it rather enables one to see the activity as an imaginative understanding of oneself or others, who may be attracted by the appearance as of sense that some plain nonsense presents. As for the third question, I am not sure how one tells whether such articulating is well or badly done. There is, as I mentioned earlier, the danger pointed out by James Conant, of one's projecting some or other favored ethical view into Wittgenstein's remarks. That danger has to be kept in mind; and I hope I am not ignoring it in what follows. I think I see something that was buried in the two examples I presented earlier, and that it will be helpful to dig out.

9 Recall the important *Tractatus* point that when I ascribe a thought or belief to someone, I must use an intelligible sentence of a language I understand. And if I understand a person who utters nonsense, I enter imaginatively into the seeing of it as sense, I as it were become the person who thinks he thinks it. I treat that person's nonsense in imagination as if I took it to be an intelligible sentence of a language I understand, *something I find in myself the possibility of meaning*.

Bearing those two points in mind, I now want to turn back to good and evil and to the two examples I used, in both of which I found myself specially concerned with describing evil in the heart of a person. I want to ask whether, in my descriptions, I was imaginatively making use of something in myself, imaginatively finding in myself the possibility of meaning something, and whether I was connecting that use of imagination with the suggestion of something evil in a person.

Thus, in the case of the character Aylmer in Hawthorne's story, I felt about him that what was evil in his heart could be glimpsed already in his original response to his beautiful wife's birthmark, and I wanted to connect that sense of his heart as evil with his having (as I put it) a deep dissatisfaction with the world's not meeting conditions he lays down. Now the particular event, if we just look at it on the surface, is that a man does not like a woman's birthmark. That seems a trivial thing. Whence then the sense of evil here? – Let me take another example, to make more conspicuous what I now see as present in the two earlier examples. I have a sense of something terrible when I read *The Fisherman and His Wife*. In the tale the Fisherman spares the life of a Flounder who is really an enchanted prince, and is then sent by his wife to get the Flounder to carry out various wishes of hers: she begins by wishing her way into a decent little hut, and ends by wishing to be God, finding it an offence that the sun and moon should rise whether she wills it or not. The sense that something terrible and sinister is being described may be felt already with her very first wish, but has nothing to do with that wish on the surface. There is nothing terrible or sinister in thinking that it would be nice to live in a cosy little hut instead of a privy, and that if the Flounder can arrange it he should be asked to do so. Wilhelm Grimm puts very clearly the element in the tales that I mean, when he speaks of the evil in them, not as something inconsequential or close to home, not as something very bad which one could get accustomed to, but something terrible, black and wholly alien that you cannot even approach.[18] I am suggesting that the tale of the Fisherman and his Wife has three features: i. the kind of evil Grimm means; ii. its presence, as something of which one may have a sense, already in what is on the surface perfectly matter-of-fact; and iii. its explicit connection ultimately with the wife's resentment that things in the world go as they do independently of her will.[19] These features parallel what I pointed out in the Hawthorne tale.

Wittgenstein himself, writing much later, made plain a continuing interest in this sort of phenomenon, the kind of case that may lead one to ask: whence the sense of something dark and terrible in what at one level may seem entirely innocent? He made notes in the late 1930s about the anthropologist James Frazer's description of the Beltane Festival in 18th century Scotland. In it a cake with knobs on it was baked, divided into pieces and distributed; a sort of ritual was enacted with the person who drew as his portion one particular piece. Why should that not be entirely innocent? If Wittgenstein says he has a sense of something terrible and sinister in these games, whence that sense of the terrible? For on the surface there is nothing terrible; and even if one knows that the ritual had some distant historical connection with human sacrifice, that would not account for one's sense of something terrible still in it, some sense of what lies in the human heart.[20]

Considering now only evil, I can see that in my articulation of Wittgenstein's ethical views the idea was missing that some of the thoughts we are inclined to have about evil seem to be justified by nothing that is as it were available on the surface of events, including here what is available to empirical psychology. We have a sense of something dark and terrible "within", as we might say. Since that was not given any prominence in my articulation, there was also missing from it any discussion of what this sense of evil draws on. That is what I now need to bring in; that is why I brought up the issue of what we are imaginatively drawing on in ourselves in our grasp of ourselves or others as capable of evil. The attempt to articulate Wittgenstein's views on ethics leads one, I want to suggest, to an analogy between his idea of the understanding of someone who utters nonsense and an idea of the understanding of someone – oneself or someone else – to whom one ascribes an evil will. I now want to develop that analogy.

In neither case will one be dealing with what one wants to deal with if one remains with the sort of understanding provided by empirical psychology. Empirical psychology sees the mental processes accompanying the uttering of nonsense-sentences, but from that point of view we cannot see the person as in the grip of an illusion. I argued that the understanding of a person in the grip of an illusion models itself on the understanding of a person who talks sense, in using the grammatical constructions whereby we give the content of someone's thought or belief, but uses those constructions in cases in which there is no content to give; what we draw on is our capacity to be taken in, at least in imagination, by the nonsense in question. – The analogy, in the case of seeing someone as having an evil will, is this. Again, empirical psychology will not do for us what we may want; it gives us only states of mind, mental processes, imagery, feelings, no combination of which is the evil intention or will. In understanding a person whose will is evil, we model our understanding on the understanding of a person who wills some particular thing, the content of whose will can be given in a sentence of our language: the content might be (in the case of the Fisherman's Wife) that she should live in a hut not a privy. That is how we give the content of the will in intelligible sentences. In ascribing evil, we use a sentence modelled on such sentences giving what people want or will, but consider two of them: i. "The Wife's character is revealed when it comes out that she as it were says in her heart 'Let nothing on earth or in the heavens happen independently of my will'"; ii. earlier I said that what characterizes Aylmer, in Hawthorne's story, is his deep dissatisfaction that the world does not meet conditions he lays down. The world is independent of his will; *that* he resents; he would have it not be so.[21] In the group of cases with which I am concerned, there is then a tie between the sense of something evil in a person, in that person's will, and an understanding of the person in which one sees him or her as willing something, but one specifies what is willed in words that have no content. We let ourselves imagine that there is sense there, that we grasp such words as giving what is willed. One central point of the analogy between the two cases (understanding a person in the grip of an illusion, ascribing an evil will to someone) is that unless one engages in this activity of imagination, of giving "content" where there is no content to give, one misses one's aim. One will not be speaking about what one had wanted to speak about. An illusion is not something understandable; and, in a related sense, neither is the evil will in the cases with which I am concerned. This is not a psychological or metaphysical fact, but one which Wittgenstein would later have called grammatical.

Let me now summarize this. The structure of §§ 4–9 of this paper has had three parts. First (§§ 4–5) there was an account of understanding the writer of the *Tractatus* and others who utter nonsense-sentences. Secondly (§§ 6–8) there was an account of understanding those who utter sentences that present themselves as ethical, with a discussion of the problems presented in § 2. And lastly (§ 9) there is a discussion of one kind of ascription of good or evil to the will (though I have spoken only of evil); I have treated such ascriptions as cases of understanding a person as saying in his heart something that makes no sense, but something which we have the imaginative resources to grasp as attractive, where that imaginative capacity is tied to our own capacities as moral agents.

If you have followed my account of Wittgenstein, you may have noticed that there is some similarity and some dissimilarity to Kant. The similarity and the dissimilarity are contained in one word, the word "transcendental". Wittgenstein said that ethics is transcendental; he had earlier in the *Tractatus* said that logic is transcendental.[22] The word "transcendental" does mark a kind of resemblance to Kant; but it has nevertheless a quite different meaning in the *Tractatus* from what it had for Kant. When logic or ethics is said by Wittgenstein to be transcendental, this does not mean that it is concerned with the activities of some transcendental subject. What "transcendental" means in the *Tractatus* is that the "sign" for whatever is called transcendental is the general form of a proposition, not some particular proposition or set of propositions that says something in particular. The only thing that could be said to do any meaning here – in logic or in ethics – is a sign that *says* nothing, but which contains (in a sense) every combination of signs to which we do give sense, every combination of signs that does say something, and no one of which expresses a logical state of affairs or an ethical one. There – in the general form of a proposition – you can see that logic and ethics are not spheres in which we express ourselves by means of signs.[23] What we can thus see is whatever is internal to language. In reading Wittgenstein or Kant, we can take the word "transcendental" as a kind of warning. For Kant, the connection between ethics and the transcendental subject is such that ethics is destroyed, there is no ethics, if you try to move ethical thought into the realm of what we can know, the empirical world. For Wittgenstein, the connection between ethics and the transcendental is not, as it was for Kant, a matter of tying ethics to something other than what we can know, other than the empirical world. But, for him as for Kant, ethics is destroyed, there is no ethics, if we try as it were to push ethics into the empirical world. Not as with Kant, it is equally destroyed if we try to push it into synthetic a priori judgments. The resemblance I want especially to emphasize is in Kant's and Wittgenstein's rejection of an empirical psychology of the will with which we are concerned in our thought about good and evil. That which I take myself to see in myself or another if I think of that person as having an evil will – that thought of mine about a person – has no room in the sphere of thoughts about the world of empirical facts. Put there it is not about what I wanted it to be about.

10 There are two endings to this paper.

(A) In what sense is the aim of the *Tractatus* ethical? The understanding that it is meant to lead to is supposed to be a capacity to "see the world in the right way". That is, it is a matter of not making false demands on the world, nor having false expectations or hopes; our relation to the world should not be determined by the false imagination of philosophy. False imagination is not directly tied to what we say or do, but may be recognized in what we say or do, how we live, by an understanding that draws on another use of imagination. I hope it is clear not only that I am not using the word "false" as it is used when a meaningful sentence is said to be true or false; I hope it is clear also that the words I used just now purporting to give the aim of the book are nonsense. Wittgenstein's description of the book as having an ethical intention moves us to some forms of words which look as if they had, as their sense, something about "our relation to the world as a whole"; and so, if he as writer of the book is understood, words purporting to give the book's ethical intention can be understood only in the make-believe way that we are invited to use in reading the sentences composing the book. The book's ethical intention includes the intention of the book not to be interpreted.

'Wie Wundervoll sind diese Wesen,
Die, was nicht deutbar, dennoch deuten . . .'[24]

(B) The second ending concerns where all this leaves us.

There is a tendency that readers of Wittgenstein may have to think in something like this way. In the *Tractatus*, Wittgenstein got into a position in which ethical propositions were taken to be nonsense, on account of their failure to conform to the conditions that senseful discourse meets. In his later philosophical work, one of the main things that he subjects to criticism is the very idea that there are such general conditions. There is no general form of a proposition, no general form of making sense; and when we recognize that there is no such logical generality to be found in senseful discourse as such, we can see ethical thought and talk without preconception. We shall then be able to see that ethical thought and talk itself has great variety and complex resemblances and differences from thought and talk that enters our lives in other ways. And we shall then not be forced to push ethical talk into some mystical limbo out beyond senseful talk.

The reading I have just given of some main elements of the *Tractatus* may, however, suggest that there is something wrong with that conception. For the *Tractatus* places itself before readers whom it takes to be drawn to the illusion that there is philosophical investigation as traditionally understood, drawn also to the illusion that there is what has come to be called meta-ethics. I have tried to present Wittgenstein as, like Kant, concerned with what you might call a will to evade the character of the ethical, a will that is for both of them tied not just to making ethics empirical but to treating its psychology as empirical.

If Wittgenstein changed his philosophical understanding of many things, it does not follow that on such a matter as the character of philosophy (of the traditional sort) as illusion, and the related matter of the possibility of evading the character of the ethical, he changed his views. But that needs explaining.

Consider the remarks I quoted earlier, of Wilhelm Grimm's, about terrible evil, which we may contrast with evil that could be taken to be part of how things are. That contrast is marked again and again in the tales that he and his brother collected and that he revised. Think of *Rumpelstiltskin*, and the far from admirable character of the miller who brags about his daughter and endangers her life, and the king who sets the girl an impossible task, threatens to kill her if she does not carry it out, and is so avaricious that he is not satisfied by two rooms full of gold. The miller and the king are not nice decent folk. But their badness is not connected by the tale with our capacity to respond to evil as unapproachable and terrible, as Rumpelstiltskin's evil is. Wittgenstein himself, I have suggested, had a sense, expressed in the notes on Frazer, of that sort of difference. Some things in human life arouse in us a sense of the possible terribleness of what may be in our hearts: something sinister and dark, in his words, something black and unapproachable, in Grimm's. We may mark the sense of the terrible as the tales do, for example in the kind of fate that awaits Rumpelstiltskin, or the cosmic storm that accompanies the final wish of the Fisherman's Wife. But it may also be marked in our language by our setting talk about such evil apart from talk about how things go in the world, this way or that. The removal of thought and talk about the evil will from empirical talk is a technique of our language, just as stories about Rumpelstiltskin and the Fisherman's Wife are techniques of our language. These two techniques have in common the maintaining of a contrast between thought and talk about some evils and thought and talk about the "unapproachably evil".

There is a guiding principle in Wittgenstein's philosophical work, all of it: what you are talking about is given in how you talk about it. Change the logical features of how you talk about it and you change the subject, you are talking about something else.

If the dark and sinister in the human heart is the subject, we may mark our talk about it through the logical feature of cutting such talk off from ordinary talk about what goes on, not giving it entry there. That logical feature may be seen, I have argued, in the fairy tales, and, in different ways, in Kant's and Wittgenstein's refusal of an empirical psychology of the evil will. And there is no reason to think that Wittgenstein's later philosophical thinking precludes us from recognizing that kind of contrast. We shall not be inclined to describe the contrast by appealing to notions like the limits of language, or the general form of a proposition; but we can nevertheless describe the ways in which we mark that contrast and the significance it has for us, if it still has significance for us.

But what has tended to happen, and this is exemplified by many interpretations of how Wittgenstein's later thought bears on ethics, is that his thought has been put into the service of the will not to be concerned with the ethical (what Wittgenstein meant by that), the will to turn away from the kind of understanding of human life expressed, I have suggested, in the fairy tales.

Let me put alongside each other three cases.

(i) Consider first one of the aims of John Rawls's work. Rawls sees himself as helping to detach "the force and content of Kant's doctrine . . . from its background in transcendental idealism", to make it available within "the canons of a reasonable empiricism".[25]

(ii) We may see Wittgenstein's later work as enabling us to put back into the world the will that is capable of good and evil, after it had been moved by the *Tractatus* outside of the world, outside of all happening and being the case.

(iii) Those concerned nowadays with *Grimm's Fairy Tales* turn away from the difference that so struck Grimm between evil that thought encompasses and "unapproachable" evil; readings of *Rumpelstiltskin*, for example, in which the king is greedy and unjust, the father a braggart and liar, the girl a promise-breaker and poor Rumpelstiltskin himself the victim of loneliness – i.e., all the characters are morally mediocre, with the king perhaps the worst – are common.[26]

The point to be made in all three cases is the same. The will to move good and evil into the world is a will not to make certain distinctions in one's talk and thought and life, and not to have that in oneself, or not to recognize it, that would make those distinctions. I mean the distinction that for Kant and Wittgenstein was marked by ethics being called transcendental, the distinction that is marked in the fairy tales often by the difference between natural and supernatural evil. That will not to make the distinction may represent itself as mere sensibleness, reasonableness, down-to-earthness, matter-of-factness, rational disdain for mystery and mysticism; in other contexts, as being fair, being liberal-minded and sympathetic (or radical-minded and sympathetic) about poor old Rumpelstiltskin, about the unjustly vilified older woman in *Snow-White*, and the poor old witch in *Rapunzel*.

My suggestion is that we do not read the *Tractatus* well unless we see how its temper is opposed to the spirit of the times, and how it understands that spirit as expressed in connected ways in the idea of natural laws as explanatory of phenomena, in philosophy, and in relation to what Wittgenstein thinks of as ethics. I have also suggested that we should see that spirit as expressed in denying the distinction that Kant and Wittgenstein call on the word "transcendental" to mark. If we understand the temper of the *Tractatus*, we are not likely to read Wittgenstein's later work as enabling us to be more in tune with the times. The reading of that later work as enabling us to put ethics back into the world is at best a partial truth. It does enable us to see the relation between ethics as the *Tractatus* was concerned with it and quite other elements that we may think of as belonging in ethics. The *Tractatus* use of "outside the world" marks – is simply one way of marking – that mode of thought about human life that Wittgenstein meant by ethics; it is as good as *Rumpelstiltskin* or *The Fisherman and His Wife* at marking it.

Fania Pascal recalls an extraordinary conversation with Wittgenstein, in which he picked up a volume of Grimm's tales and read out "with awe in his voice

'Ach, wie gut ist, daß niemand weiß,
daß ich Rumpelstilzchen heiß!'

'Profound, profound', he said." She adds that she liked the tale, and understood that the dwarf's strength lay in his name being unknown to humans, but she was "unable to share Wittgenstein's vision". "To watch him in a state of hushed, silent awe, as though looking far beyond what oneself could see, was an experience next only to hearing him talk."[27]

I have put her description of this episode here, because I think we can see something of the ethical aim of the *Tractatus*, and where it is left after Wittgenstein's later work, when we connect it with his hushed, silent awe that day. The point I am making is simple. If Wittgenstein's understanding of ethics can be tied to his sense of the power and profundity of that tale, then whatever change there may have been in his approach to philosophy and to the treatment of philosophical illusion will not be a change that makes ethics fit our temperament.

Notes

This paper owes much to conversations with James Conant. I am also very grateful for comments and suggestions from B. J. Diggs, J. B. Schneewind, G. E. M. Anscombe, David Sachs, Peter Winch and A. D. Woozley. Discussion of an earlier version of the paper ("Wittgenstein, Ethics and the Psychology of Illusion"), at the Coloquio Wittgenstein in Lima in 1989, was particularly helpful to me. The translations of passages in Wittgenstein, *Tractatus Logico-Philosophicus*, are drawn from the D. F. Pears and B. F. McGuinness translation (London, 1961) or from the London 1992 reissue of the translation by C. K. Ogden and F. P. Ramsey; some translations are mine.

1 See also P. T. Geach, *Mental Acts*, London 1957, pp. 10 and 85.
2 Ludwig Wittgenstein, *Briefe an Ludwig von Ficker*, ed. G. H. von Wright, Salzburg 1969, p. 35. The translation is a slightly modified version of that given by B. F. McGuinness, in Wittgenstein, *Prototractatus*, London 1971, p. 16.
3 In *The Senses of Stanley Cavell*, ed. Richard Fleming and Michael Payne, Lewisburg, Pennsylvania, London and Toronto 1989, pp. 242–283.
4 G. K. Chesterton, *Orthodoxy*, Garden City, N. Y. 1959, chapters II and III; Wordsworth, *The Prelude*, Book Thirteenth (1805 edition), Book Fourteenth (1850 edition). Chesterton's conception of ethics is tied (as is Wittgenstein's) to rejecting as illusion the idea that natural laws explain natural phenomena. For comments on a similar view in Wordsworth, see Raymond Dexter Havens, *The Mind of a Poet*, Baltimore 1941, vol. I, p. 143.
5 Conant, op. cit. p. 274.
6 That claim would take more argument than this paper can contain. It would start with what is in the June 1913 letter to Russell (*Notebooks*, 121); it would include a discussion of Part III of *Philosophical Remarks*; it would show how Wittgenstein's remarks about intention and expectation are related to his discussions of calculation (see, e.g., *Philosophical Grammar* § 111); and it would examine the way related topics are treated in *Philosophical Investigations* and in *Remarks on the Foundations of Mathematics*. The basic point is that the ascription to someone of the judgment that p contains (as he put it in 1913) "p v ~ p", i.e., it contains the internal relation between the judgment-fact and the possibility of p. (In *Tractatus* terms, the internal relation is that of determination by the judgment-fact of a place in logical space.) That is what empirical psychology does not discuss.
7 See, e.g., F. P. Ramsey, "General Propositions and Causality" (in *The Foundations of Mathematics*, Totowa, N. J. 1965, pp. 237–255) on the psychological laws covering those habits which make the meaning of logical connectives like "all"; see also his general views about inference in that paper.
8 G. E. M. Anscombe, *An Introduction to Wittgenstein's Tractatus*, London 1963, p. 162.
9 The connection that I see between Wittgenstein's use of "elucidate" at the end of the *Tractatus* and his uses, elsewhere in the book, of "elucidation" (3.263, 4.112) is that a proposition's being an elucidation is a matter of the context of use, not of the content. I may teach you the meaning of a word by using it in a sentence; that the sentence serves as an elucidation has nothing to do with its internal features. Similarly, if I were to use "propositions of natural science" in the course of trying to free someone from philosophical confusion, those propositions, so used, serve as elucidations. That philosophy consists of elucidations and that it is not a body of doctrine but an activity (4.112) come to the same. It is a consequence of my reading that when a sentence of the *Tractatus* is taken to express some view of its author's the sentence is not serving as an elucidation but exemplifies the confusion from which the book was meant to liberate us. (I am grateful to Edward Minar for raising a question about Wittgenstein's use of "elucidation".) The question whether metaphysical confusion is internal or external to remarks that express it is connected with issues raised by Warren Goldfarb in "I Want You to Give Me a Slab: Remarks on the Opening Sections of Philosophical Investigations", *Synthese* 56 (1983).
10 *The Foundations of Arithmetic*, trans. J. L. Austin, Oxford 1974, p. 71.

11 There is an important characterization of the illusion in the notes that Wittgenstein dictated to G. E. Moore in 1914. The attempt in philosophy to give essential features of the Universe is an attempt to speak in a language that lacks the corresponding logical properties; "and it is impossible that this should be a *proper* language" (*Notebooks*, p. 107). The sentences of the *Tractatus* pretend to be in just such a language.

12 *Philosophical Review* 74 (1965), pp. 3–12.

13 When I refer in what follows to the views of the logical positivists, I have particularly in mind the views of Ayer and Carnap. Some of what I say applies also to the views of Schlick; some of it applies to ethical theories which have certain resemblances to the views of Ayer and Carnap, like those of Charles Stevenson and R. M. Hare.

14 Compare the structure of Stanley Cavell's discussion (in *The Claim of Reason*, Oxford 1979, part 3) of Charles Stevenson's views on ethics, his argument that what distinguishes those views is the absence of the concept of morality.

15 I am grateful to J. B. Schneewind and James Conant for their arguments about this. David Sachs and Elizabeth Anscombe have raised related questions.

16 Friedrich Waismann, "Notes on Talks with Wittgenstein", in *Philosophical Review* 74 (1965), p. 12.

17 On the idea that there are only those two readings, see Conant, "Must We Show What We Cannot Say?".

18 Preface to Volume I of the first edition of *Kinder- und Haus-Märchen*, Berlin 1812, reprinted Göttingen 1986, S. xi; translated by Maria Tatar in *The Hard Facts of the Grimm's Fairy Tales*, Princeton 1987, p. 207.

19 It is interesting that *The Fisherman and His Wife* is one of the two tales which the Grimm brothers got from Philipp Otto Runge and which then served as model texts. See Heinz Rölleke, *Die Märchen der Brüder Grimm*, München 1985, pp. 52–60, Walter Scherf, "A Few Small Corrections to a Commonly Held Image", in *The Brothers Grimm and Folktale*, ed. James M. McGlathery, Urbana, Illinois 1988, pp. 178–191, especially pp. 184–185.

20 "Remarks on Frazer's *Golden Bough*", in *The Human World* 3 (May 1971), pp. 39–40.

21 What he rejects is thus describable as "birthmark" in a further sense; for it is what life on earth has as its distinguishing mark; the end of the story makes the connection plain.

22 This does not, incidentally, mean that he thinks that ethics and logic have identical characteristics, as has been suggested. See Rudolf Haller, "What do Wittgenstein and Weininger have in Common?", in *Questions on Wittgenstein*, Lincoln, Nebraska 1988, pp. 90–99, especially p. 95, and note that Haller writes as if logical propositions and ethical propositions were treated in the same way by the *Tractatus*.

23 Cf. *Tractatus* 6.124.

24 Hugo von Hofmannsthal, in *Der Tor und der Tod*.

25 "The Basic Structures as Subject", *American Philosophical Quarterly* 14 (1977), p. 165.

26 See, e.g., Roger Sale, *Fairy Tales and After*, Cambridge, Massachusetts 1978, p. 44; Maria Tatar, *The Hard Facts of the Grimm's Fairy Tales*, p. 127; Irmela Brender, "Das Rumpelstilzchen hat mir immer leid getan", translated by Jack Zipes, in Zipes, *Breaking the Magic Spell: Radical Theories of Folk and Fairy Tales*, London 1979, pp. 181–182.

27 "Wittgenstein: A Personal Memoir", in *Wittgenstein: Sources and Perspectives*, ed. C. G. Luckhardt, Ithaca, N. Y. 1979, p. 30. Reprinted in *Recollections of Wittgenstein*, ed. Rush Rhees, Oxford and New York 1984.

8

ELUCIDATION AND NONSENSE IN FREGE AND EARLY WITTGENSTEIN

James Conant

This paper is excerpted from a manuscript in which James Conant argues that Wittgenstein's famous closing description of sentences of the Tractatus *as nonsensical draws on a conception of nonsense at odds with the conceptions at play in a couple of standard interpretations. Conant describes these interpretations as (i) positivist interpretations which depict Wittgenstein as furnishing a method for distinguishing meaningful from meaningless discourse and which depict him, further, as using this method to reveal metaphysical claims as inherently nonsensical and (ii) ineffability interpretations which agree with positive interpretations in characterizing Wittgenstein as furnishing a method for distinguishing meaningful from meaningless discourse but disagree with positive interpretations in so far as they suggest that he does so with an eye toward illuminating metaphysical claims which, while they cannot properly be put into words, nevertheless remain accessible to thought. Conant claims that we can arrive at a more faithful account both of how Wittgenstein uses "nonsense" as a term of philosophical appraisal and also of what he means when he says that the nonsensical sentences of the* Tractatus *serve as "elucidations" if we recognize that Wittgenstein's renderings of the notions of* nonsense *and* elucidation *are the product of his efforts to refashion Fregean construals of them. The part of Conant's manuscript included here isolates as far as possible his account of how the* Tractatus *can be understood as Wittgenstein's reshaping of lines of thought inherited from Frege.*

A.C., ed.

This paper aspires to supply two of the pieces of the puzzle which need to be in place before we can make out the point of the famous penultimate section of the *Tractatus*:[1]

> My propositions serve as *elucidations* in the following way: anyone who understands me eventually recognizes them as *nonsensical*, when he has used them – as steps – to climb out through them, on them, over them. (He must, so to speak, throw away the ladder after he has climbed up it.)[2]

This passage tells a reader of the work what he must "eventually recognize" in order to understand its author. No understanding of the *Tractatus* is possible apart from an understanding of what this passage asks of its reader – apart, that is, from an understanding of what the authorial strategy of the work as a whole is. Wittgenstein says of Carnap that he failed to understand this passage and *therefore* failed to understand "the fundamental conception of the whole book."[3] What did Carnap fail to understand, and how did that failure lead him to misunderstand the fundamental conception of the whole book? Two important terms occur in this passage. Not only Carnap, but several subsequent generations of commentators have paid insufficient heed to what the *Tractatus* itself has to say about how these terms (as deployed within the work) are to be understood. The two terms in question are:

(1) to elucidate [*erläutern*]
(2) nonsense [*Unsinn*]

This paper is about how to understand these two words in the *Tractatus*. Only once we understand the specific valence these terms have in this work will we be in a position to understand what the *Tractatus* says (in §6.54) about its method.

In §4.112 of the *Tractatus*, we are told that a work of philosophy "consists essentially of elucidations." "Philosophy" here means: philosophy as practiced by the author of the *Tractatus*. The notion of elucidation is tied in §4.112 to the idea of philosophy being a certain kind of *activity*: "Philosophy is not a theory [*Lehre*] but an activity. A philosophical work consists essentially of elucidations" (§4.112). The word "*Lehre*" – which Ogden translates as "theory" – is rendered as "body of doctrine" by Pears and McGuinness.[4] Wittgenstein claims that the work of philosophy, as he pursues it, does not consist in putting forward a doctrine but rather in offering elucidations.[5] This provides a criterion of adequacy that must be met by any textually faithful account of what Wittgenstein means by "elucidation": it must be able to illuminate how Wittgenstein could intelligibly have thought that the philosophical work accomplished by the *Tractatus* "consists essentially of elucidations" – where "elucidation" is the name of an activity which contrasts with the (conventional philosophical) activity of presenting the reader with a doctrine. When Wittgenstein says (in §4.112) that a philosophical work consists essentially of elucidations, the term "elucidation" is a rendering of the same German word [*Erläuterung*] which occurs in §6.54 and which also, as we shall see in a moment, figures pertinently in Frege's writings.[6]

We are told in §6.54 that the author's propositions serve as elucidations by *our* – that is, the reader – coming to *recognize* them as nonsensical. But how can the recognition that a proposition is *nonsense* ever elucidate – ever shed light on – anything? Evidently we need a better understanding of how this work thinks about nonsense. We need to look closely at those passages in which the work tells us what it takes *Unsinn* to be and, in particular, what it tells us it takes it *not* to be. This is what the *Tractatus* has to say about what is distinctive about its own conception of nonsense:

> Frege says: Every legitimately constructed proposition must have a sense; and I say: Every possible proposition is legitimately constructed, and if it has no sense this can only be because we have given no *meaning* to some of its constituent parts.
>
> (§5.4733)

Wittgenstein here contrasts a formulation of Frege's[7] with one of his own. At first blush, it is hard to see how they differ. The critical difference between Frege's formulation and the one which the *Tractatus* endorses is that the former implicitly distinguishes between those propositions that are legitimately constructed and those that are not, while the latter rejects the idea that there is such a thing as a logically illegitimately constructed proposition: "Every *possible* proposition is legitimately constructed." It is this difference (that Wittgenstein sees between his own view and Frege's) that we need to understand. As this passage suggests – and as the preface of the *Tractatus* makes clear – a good place to seek further understanding is "the great works of Frege."[8]

1 The neglect of Frege?

Wittgenstein's *Tractatus* has captured the interest and excited the admiration of many, yet almost all that has been published about it has been wildly irrelevant. If this has had any one cause, that cause has been the neglect of Frege. ... In the *Tractatus* Wittgenstein assumes, and does not try to stimulate, an interest in the kind of questions that Frege wrote about.

G.E.M. Anscombe[9]

How can the neglect of Frege be the reason why much of the commentary on Wittgenstein's *Tractatus* is wildly irrelevant to a proper understanding of that work? What more widely accepted platitude about the book could there be, than that it develops and responds to ideas put forward by Frege and Russell? But Anscombe's point presumably is not that Frege is seldom mentioned in discussions of Wittgenstein's *Tractatus*. Her point must rather be that we do not know who Frege is for the author of the *Tractatus* – an appreciation of that work presupposes an immersion in a certain philosophical background ("an interest in the kind of questions that Frege wrote about") which most of the commentary on that work has lost sight of. It is not that we are unfamiliar with Frege's or Wittgenstein's texts, but that we have failed to see what it is that is at issue in them. We fail to get hold of the questions which figure most centrally in these texts and of *the kind of questions* these questions are for Frege and for Wittgenstein. One aim of this paper is to draw attention to two aspects of that background (there are others[10]) of which we have lost sight: Frege's thought about the character of philosophical nonsense and Frege's conception of elucidation.

The central claim of this paper can be summarized as follows: Wittgenstein saw a tension in Frege's thought between two different conceptions of nonsense, which I shall call the *substantial conception* and the *austere conception* respectively. The substantial conception distinguishes between two different kinds of nonsense: mere nonsense and substantial nonsense. Mere nonsense is simply unintelligible – it expresses no thought. Substantial nonsense is composed of intelligible ingredients combined in an illegitimate way – it expresses a logically incoherent thought. According to the substantial conception, these two kinds of nonsense are logically distinct: the former is mere gibberish, whereas the latter involves (what commentators on the *Tractatus* are fond of calling) a "violation of logical syntax." The austere conception, on the other hand, holds that mere nonsense is, from a logical point of view, the only kind of nonsense there is. Along with these two different conceptions of nonsense go two different conceptions of elucidation: according to the substantial conception, the task of elucidation is to "show" something which cannot be said;[11] according to the austere conception, it is to show that we are prone to an illusion of meaning something when we mean nothing. The *Tractatus* is standardly read as championing the substantial conception. This is to mistake the bait for the hook – to mistake the target of the work for its doctrine. On the reading of the *Tractatus* I shall try to sketch here, the *Tractatus* is to be seen as resolving the tension in Frege's thought between these two conceptions of nonsense in favor of the austere view.[12] The strategy of the *Tractatus* is to short-circuit Frege's view from within, by bringing these two halves of Frege's thought in immediate proximity with each other.

The substantial conception of nonsense represents the common ground between the positivist and ineffability interpretations of the *Tractatus*. (It is in opting for this conception, according to the *Tractatus,* that the crucial move in the philosophical conjuring trick is made and it is the one that we are apt to think most innocent.) This tiny patch of common ground can seem insignificant in comparison with the vehemence with which the ineffability interpretation laments the obtuseness of the positivist interpretation (epitomized by its failure to allow for the possibility of illuminating nonsense) and the equal vehemence with which the positivist interpretation rejects the mysticism of the ineffability interpretation (epitomized by its hankering after ineffable forms of insight[13]). In seeking to emphasize their differences from one another, proponents of the two interpretations tend to articulate the details of the substantial conception in apparently distinct ways. It will therefore help to distinguish between two (apparently distinct) variants of the substantial conception. I shall term these the *positivist variant* and the *ineffability variant* (after the readings of the *Tractatus* in which they respectively figure).[14] According to the former variant, violations of logical syntax are a kind of *linguistic* phenomenon: identifying a violation of logical syntax is a matter of isolating a certain kind of (logically ill-formed) linguistic string. According to the latter variant, a violation of logical syntax is a kind of phenomenon which can only transpire in the medium of thought and necessarily eludes the medium of language. Though proponents of the ineffability variant hold that language is powerless to express such thoughts, they nonetheless deem language an indispensable tool for "conveying" such thoughts. They hold that language can "hint" at what it cannot say.

Before we turn to how the *Tractatus* seeks to resolve the tension in Frege's thought between the substantial and austere conceptions of nonsense, it will help first to see that Frege can be read as a champion not only of the substantial conception *per se* but specifically of the ineffability variant.[15] To see this requires that we see how what is typically taken to be the central and most original doctrine of the *Tractatus* – the doctrine that there are certain insights which can only be "shown" and cannot be said – can be discerned (by some readers of Frege) to be a central doctrine of Frege's philosophy. That such a doctrine already figures in Frege's thought has been argued particularly forcefully by Peter Geach; and, indeed, Geach attributes the occurrence of such a doctrine in the *Tractatus* to the influence of Frege:

[R]eflection upon 'the great works of Frege' . . . can never be out of place for anybody who seriously wants to understand Wittgenstein. . . . The influence of Frege on Wittgenstein was pervasive and life-long, and it is not of course just confined to places where Frege is mentioned by name or overtly referred to. . . . [F]undamental aspects of the Wittgensteinian saying/showing contrast are already to be discerned in Frege's writings.[16]

I think Geach is right to think that Wittgenstein found in Frege a conception of what cannot be said but only "shown" – and that the *Tractatus* has therefore been credited in putting forward such a conception with an originality to which it cannot justly lay claim. Geach continues:

Paradoxical as is the doctrine of aspects of reality that come out but cannot be propositionally expressed, it is hard to see any viable alternative to it so long as we confine ourselves to philosophy of logic: and in this domain Wittgenstein revised Frege's views without unfaithfulness to Frege's spirit.[17]

Geach here attributes a certain doctrine to both Frege and the *Tractatus*: the doctrine that there are *certain aspects of reality* that cannot be expressed in language but can nonetheless be conveyed through certain sorts of employment of language. I think Geach is mistaken in supposing that the *Tractatus* seeks simply to incorporate this Fregean doctrine into its own teaching. That is to say, I think Geach is right to find this doctrine propounded where most commentators have failed to look for it (namely in Frege), and wrong to find it propounded where most commentators assume they are supposed to look for it (namely in the *Tractatus*). I shall therefore be concerned to argue that the *Tractatus*, in its criticism of Fregean doctrines, seeks to mount a criticism of the very doctrines which are standardly attributed to it.

In order to see this, we first need to refrain from speaking about the distinction between saying and showing in the usual loose fashion. Where most commentators on the *Tractatus* discern only one distinction, we need to see that there are two different distinctions at work. A version of each of these distinctions is already at play in Frege's work. But these distinctions are drawn in Frege's work in such a way as to be deeply entangled in one another, whereas they are refashioned in the *Tractatus* in a manner which allows them to become disentangled. The first distinction is drawn *within* the body of meaningful propositions. (Thus, according to this first sense, only meaningful propositions can *show*.) The second distinction marks off, from various ways of employing language, a particular way of employing (apparently meaningful) sentence-like structures – an employment which "takes as its object" (what Wittgenstein calls in his letter to Ogden) "philosophic matters."[18] (Thus, according to this second sense of "show," nonsense can show.[19]) The first of these distinctions is (at least terminologically) the more familiar and notorious of the two: it is (the one which gets called in the *Tractatus*) the distinction between saying and showing (or more precisely, in Tractarian jargon, the distinction between what *a proposition* says and what it shows).[20] The second distinction is relatively neglected and is the one with which the rest of this paper is concerned. It is a distinction between two different kinds of use of language:[21] constative uses,[22] in which a proposition states what is the case (or, in Tractarian jargon, represents a state of affairs) and elucidatory uses, in which an apparently constative use of language (one which offers an appearance of representing a state of affairs) is revealed as illusory.[23] It is primarily through the manner in which the *Tractatus* reshapes the second of these Fregean distinctions that the criticism of Frege is mounted. Only once we understand how the *Tractatus* seeks to modify Frege's conception of elucidation [*Erläuterung*] will we be in a position to understand what the *Tractatus* means to say about itself when it declares that it is a work which "consists essentially of elucidations."[24]

2 Frege on concept and object

The style of my sentences is extraordinarily strongly influenced by Frege. And if I wanted to, I could establish this influence where at first sight no one would see it.

(Wittgenstein[25])

Here is how Geach summarizes the region of Frege's thought that is "revised without unfaithfulness" in (what he takes to be) the Tractarian distinction between saying and "showing":

Frege ... held ... that there are logical category-distinctions which will clearly show themselves in a well-constructed formalized language, but which cannot properly be asserted in language: the sentences in which we seek to convey them in the vernacular are logically improper and admit of no translation into well-formed formulas of symbolic logic.[26]

Frege's favorite example of a logical-category distinction which clearly shows itself in a well-constructed formalized language (but which "cannot properly be asserted in language") is the distinction between concept and object – and it is an example which continued to exercise Wittgenstein throughout his life.[27] For something to be an object (or a concept), for Frege, is not for it to possess certain metaphysical or psychological characteristics, but rather for it to belong to a particular logical category. Frege takes it to be "a sure sign" of confusion if logic seems to stand in "need of metaphysics or psychology."[28]

Frege's most famous discussion of the distinction between concept and object is his article entitled "On Concept and Object" – an article which is structured around his reply to an objection put forward by Benno Kerry.[29] Kerry objects to Frege's claim that concepts cannot be objects and objects cannot be concepts. Kerry proposes as a counter-example to Frege's claim the statement "the concept *horse* is a concept easily attained." This statement seems to assert that something – the concept *horse* – falls under a concept (namely, that of being a concept easily attained). Now anything which falls under a (first-level) concept must – on Frege's conception of an object – be an object. That is what it is to be an object for Frege – to be the kind of a thing of which concepts can be predicated. So, for Frege, the grammatical subject of Kerry's statement – the concept *horse* – (since it falls under a concept) must be an object. But, if what the statement says is true, then it is a concept easily attained; and if it is a concept easily attained then it is a kind of a concept. The two prongs of Kerry's argument, based on his putative counter-example, can thus be summarized as follows: (a) given Frege's conception of what it is to be an object, we have reason (by virtue of its logical role in the statement) to conclude that "the concept *horse*" is an object; and (b) given the (apparent) truth of what the statement itself asserts, we have reason to conclude that it is a concept. So Kerry concludes that his statement furnishes us with an example of something – the concept *horse* – that is both an object and a concept.

Frege's article responding to Kerry begins with the following remark:

> The word 'concept' is used in various ways; its sense is sometimes psychological, sometimes logical, and perhaps sometimes a confused mixture of both. Since this license exists, it is natural to restrict it by requiring that when once a usage is adopted it shall be maintained. What I decided was to keep to the strictly logical use. . . . It seems to me that Kerry's misunderstanding results from his unintentionally confusing his own usage of the word 'concept' with mine. This readily gives rise to contradictions, for which my usage is not to blame.[30]

Frege insists here that he uses the word "concept" in "a strictly logical sense" and that Kerry's misunderstanding of his view is due to his failure to appreciate this. In particular, Frege will charge that Kerry's apparent counter-example is generated by equivocating between "a strictly logical" and (what Frege will call) a "psychological" sense of the term "concept."[31] But what is it to use the word "concept" in a strictly logical sense? This question is best approached through a consideration of Frege's three principles (which he presents at the beginning of his *Die Grundlagen der Arithmetik*):

> In the enquiry that follows, I have kept to three fundamental principles:
> [1] always to separate sharply the psychological from the logical, the subjective from the objective;
> [2] never to ask for the meaning of a word in isolation, but only in the context of a proposition;
> [3] never to lose sight of the distinction between concept and object.[32]

Each of these principles is reworked and plays a central role in the *Tractatus*. These three principles are closely linked: to deny any one of them is to deny each of the other two. Frege himself immediately goes on to explicate how a denial of the first principle leads to a denial of the second:

> In compliance with the first principle, I have used the word "idea" always in the psychological sense, and have distinguished ideas from concepts and from objects. If the second principle is not observed, one is almost forced to take as the meanings of words mental pictures or acts of the individual mind, and so to offend against the first principle as well.[33]

If we disobey the second principle and ask for the meaning of a word in isolation, we shall look for an answer in the realm of the psychological – we shall explain what it is for a term to have a meaning in terms of mental accompaniments (such as the psychological associations the word carries with it), or in terms of mental acts (such as the linguistic intention with which we utter it); and *that* will constitute a violation of the first principle.

Underlying these principles is a doctrine of the primacy of judgment. Frege writes: "I do not begin with concepts and put them together to form a thought or judgment; I come by the parts of a thought by analyzing the thought."[34] Frege here opposes an extremely intuitive view of how we come by a thought: namely, by taking hold of its independently thinkable components and putting them together so as to form a coherent whole.[35] The sort of "parts"[36] which are at issue here are only to be identified by comparing and contrasting the logical structure of whole propositions and seeing how the respective "parts" resemble and differ from one another in the contributions they make to the respective wholes.[37] Here is one of Frege's many exhortations to the reader not to lose sight of the primacy of the propositional whole over its parts:

> [W]e ought always to keep before our eyes a complete proposition. Only in a proposition have the words really a meaning. It may be that mental pictures float before us all the while, but these need not correspond to the logical elements in the judgement. It is enough if the proposition taken as a whole has a sense; it is this that confers on the parts also their content.[38]

In order to determine the meaning of a word, according to Frege, we need to discover what contribution it makes to the sense of a proposition in which it figures. We need to know what logical role it plays in the context of a judgment.[39] What we want to discover is thus not to be seen at all, if we look at the mere isolated word rather than at the working parts of the proposition in action.[40] Thus, for example, the mere fact that the words at the beginning of Kerry's sentence purport to refer to (something called) "the concept *horse*" hardly suffices, by Frege's lights, to ensure that they indeed successfully refer to a concept. When Frege insists that he is going to keep to a strictly logical use of the word "concept," he is declaring his interest in how a certain kind of working part of a judgment – what he calls the unsaturated or predicative part – contributes to the sense of a judgment as a whole.[41]

There are no symbols for terms such as "function," "concept" and "object" in Frege's *Begriffsschrift*. Nevertheless, these terms play an ineliminable role in his explanations of his symbolism. He thinks that an understanding of these terms is required if one is to master the notation of the symbolism and properly understand its significance. Yet he also insists that what he thus wishes to draw our attention to – when he employs, for example, the word "concept" in its strictly logical sense – is not something which can be properly defined. It can only be exhibited through (what Frege calls) an elucidation.[42] Such elucidations, in turn, play only a transitional role: once they have successfully conveyed the logical distinctions which form the basis of Frege's *Begriffsschrift*, we are to see that there is no way to express the thoughts which they (appear to be attempting to) convey in a *Begriffsschrift*.[43] Yet if we appreciate the logically fundamental character of the distinctions upon which Frege's *Begriffsschrift* is based then we will see that anything which can be thought can be expressed in *Begriffsschrift*. In grasping the distinction between that which can and that which cannot be expressed in a *Begriffsschrift*, we furnish ourselves with a logically precise articulation of the distinction between that which ("in a strictly logical sense") is, and that which is not, a *thought*. Thus Frege's elucidations are meant to play the role of a ladder which we are to climb up and then throw away.[44] Frege might have said about his own elucidatory remarks, echoing §6.54 of the *Tractatus*: "My propositions serve as elucidations in the following way: he who understands me recognizes that my propositions cannot be expressed in my *Begriffsschrift*, once he has used them – as steps – to climb up beyond them. He must, so to speak, throw away the ladder after he has used it to climb up to my *Begriffsschrift*."

3 Fregean elucidation

God can do everything, it is true, but there is one thing He cannot do, and that is speak nonsense.

(Leo Tolstoy[45])

The distinction between elucidation and definition in Frege rests upon a prior distinction between what is primitive and what is defined in a theory. Any theoretical term which is not susceptible of a formal definition requires elucidation. Every science must employ some primitive terms whose meanings must be presupposed from the outset. Even in a logically perfect language there will be some terms which are not (and cannot) be introduced by definition and which must remain undefinable. The purpose of elucidations is to convey the meanings of such terms:

Definitions proper must be distinguished from elucidations. In the first stages of any discipline we cannot avoid the use of ordinary words. But these words are, for the most part, not really appropriate for scientific purposes, because they are not precise enough and fluctuate in their use. Science needs technical terms that have precise and fixed meanings, and in order to come to an understanding about these meanings and exclude possible misunderstanding, we give elucidations [*Erläuterungen*] of their use.[46]

In "On Concept and Object," Frege is concerned with only one species of the genus elucidation, namely the activity of elucidating what is *logically* primitive.[47] When one is engaged in this particular species of elucidation Frege thinks one is compelled to come out with sentences which cannot be translated into a proper *Begriffsschrift*.

One might ask: doesn't Frege furnish us with examples of statements which define what a concept or an object is? Frege will answer that nothing his own sentences (appear to) assert about the nature of concepts or objects can ever, without entering into a confusion, be taken as (a contribution to) a definition of what kind of a thing a concept or an object is.[48] For something to count as a definition, for Frege, it must be possible to invoke it in proofs. Wherever the *definiendum* occurs in a sentence, it must be possible to replace it with the *definiens*. Nothing of the sort is possible, Frege maintains, for those terms occurring in his elucidatory remarks which refer to logically primitive categories.[49] Their meaning must be presupposed from the outset. The most one can do is to lead the reader to what is meant by such terms – what it is one's words are trying to gesture at – by means of a series of *hints*.[50] Early on in his reply to Kerry, Frege insists upon the ineliminable role of hints in offering an elucidation of that which is logically fundamental and hence indefinable:

> Kerry contests what he calls my definition of 'concept'. I would remark, in the first place, that my explanation is not meant as a proper definition. One cannot require that everything shall be defined, any more than one can require that a chemist shall decompose every substance. What is simple cannot be decomposed, and what is logically simple cannot have a proper definition. Now something logically simple is no more given to us at the outset than most of the chemical elements are; it is reached only by means of scientific work. If something has been discovered that is simple, or at least must count as simple for the time being, we shall have to coin a term for it, since language will not originally contain an expression that exactly answers. On the introduction of a name for what is logically simple, a definition is not possible; there is nothing for it but to lead the reader or hearer, by means of hints, to understand the word as it is intended.[51]

Yet only a few lines further on, Frege offers something which has the appearance of offering a specification of the meaning of the term "concept": "A concept (as I understand the word) is predicative. On the other hand, a name of an object, a proper name, is quite incapable of being used as a grammatical predicate."[52] Frege immediately goes on to say: "This admittedly needs elucidation, otherwise it might appear false." The term "elucidation" here stands for the activity of leading the reader by means of hints to what is intended by a term which denotes something logically primitive. This requires not only that we count on the patience and goodwill of our audience while we encourage them to guess at our intended meaning, but also that – here in the antechamber to that most precise of all sciences: the science of logic – we resort to figurative modes of expression (for example, to talk about objects being "saturated" and concepts being "unsaturated"[53]). Worse still, Frege thinks that in the elucidation of logically primitive notions (such as that of *concept* or *object*) there is an ineliminable role to be played by (the artful employment of) nonsense.[54] According to Frege, in elucidating the meaning of terms such as "object" and "concept," we attempt to help our audience to latch on to the intended meaning of a term for something logically fundamental by coming out with forms of expression that misfire, and then helping our audience to see how and why they misfire.

It is of crucial importance when offering such an elucidation, Frege goes on to say, that the originator of the elucidation himself understand the transitional character of the talk that he engages in, and that he know at every point what he means by a particular term and remain throughout in agreement with himself:

> Since definitions are not possible for primitive elements, something else must enter in. I call it elucidation [*Erläuterung*]. ... Someone who pursued research only by himself would not need it. The purpose of elucidations [*Erläuterungen*] is a pragmatic one; and once it is achieved, we must

be satisfied with them. And here we must be able to count on a little goodwill and cooperative understanding, even guessing; for frequently we cannot do without a figurative mode of expression. But for all that, we can demand from the originator of an elucidation [*Erläuterung*] that he himself know for certain what he means; that he remain in agreement with himself; and that he be ready to complete and emend his elucidation [*Erläuterung*] whenever, given even the best of intentions, the possibility of a misunderstanding arises.[55]

Frege frankly concedes that such a process of offering hints and relying on guesswork might, in principle, never culminate in the desired meeting of minds between the elucidator and the audience of an elucidation. He hastens to reassure us, however, that it turns out that, in practice, we are quite good at guessing what another person means even when all we are offered is a series of such hints:

Theoretically, one might never achieve one's goal this way. In practice, however, we do manage to come to an understanding about the meanings of words. Of course we have to be able to count on a meeting of minds, on others guessing what we have in mind. But all this precedes the construction of a system and does not belong within a system.[56]

This last sentence alludes to a point touched on earlier: once the elucidation is successful the recourse to figurative modes of speech and bits of nonsense can be dispensed with; the elucidations will have served their transitional pragmatic purpose and are to be thrown away. The activity of elucidation "has no place in the system of a science." Its role is entirely that of a propaedeutic.[57]

Frege's procedure in "On Concept and Object" relies on an understanding of the logical structure of language implicit in his reader's everyday command of ordinary language. Frege's purpose – when he introduces terms such as "concept" and "object" – is to isolate and coin terms for the logically discrete functioning parts of a judgment: parts that can be seen to play logically distinct roles in the antecedently understood content of the sentences of everyday language. In aiming to communicate the meaning of these terms he has coined, Frege (since he cannot resort to definition) appeals to "the general feeling" for our common language (our shared sense of the contribution which the parts of a proposition of ordinary language make to the sense of the whole).[58] It is through our general feeling for our common language that we achieve agreement on what is a proper logical segmentation of a sentence of our language and hence what is (and what is not) a concept or an object.

The elucidatory strategy of the essay "On Concept and Object" can (according to this reading of Frege in the spirit of Geach) be seen as proceeding in five steps: (1) to make explicit a logical distinction implicit in our everyday linguistic practices, (2) to demonstrate that Kerry's employment of the terminology of "object" and "concept" fails to track the distinction in question, (3) to furnish statements (employing the terminology of "object" and "concept") that aim to track the distinction in question, (4) to elicit an appreciation of what is defective about such statements, and (5) to indicate how a recognition of the defective character of such statements enables one to attain an insight (into, e.g., what a concept is) which could not have been communicated in any other way. Thus Frege might have said: he who *recognizes* my elucidatory remarks in "On Concept and Object" *as nonsense* understands me. Such a reading of Frege (in the spirit of Geach) – according to which Fregean elucidation is to be understood as a strategy for conveying insights into ineffable features of reality – as we shall see, closely parallels the reading of the *Tractatus* favored by proponents of the ineffability interpretation.

4 Elucidatory nonsense

Don't, for heaven's sake, be afraid of talking nonsense! But you must pay attention to your nonsense.

(Wittgenstein[59])

By way of further response to Kerry's counter-example, Frege goes on in "On Concept and Object" to make a remark which is likely to cause even an inattentive reader to pause. He says: "The concept *horse* is not a concept." This remark is evidently intended to be paradoxical. The self-defeating character of Frege's counter-thesis, which he opposes to Kerry's thesis, is meant to draw attention to what is already self-defeating (though less self-evidently so) in the form of words that Kerry calls upon to express his claim. If one is partial to a reading of Frege that aligns him with the standard reading of the *Tractatus* (as Geach is), then one will think that part of Frege's point here is to draw our attention to how Kerry's words represent an attempt to say something that cannot be said. Such a reading of Frege attributes to Frege a commitment to the ineffability variant of the substantial conception of nonsense. In a passage such as the following, Frege can be heard as pressing a claim (concerning how a primitive feature of the logical structure of language can never itself figure as the subject of a logically well-formed judgment) of a sort that many have taken to be a Tractarian claim:

> [W]hat is . . . asserted about a concept can never be asserted about an object. . . . I do not want to say it is false to assert about an object what is here asserted about a concept; I want to say it is impossible, senseless, to do so.[60]

The idea that what such an attempt (to assert of a concept what can only be asserted of an object) ends up saying is not merely false, but senseless, is one which runs throughout Frege's writings.[61] But what are we to make of such an admission? In claiming that what Kerry says is nonsensical, Frege commits himself to the conclusion that what he himself wants to say about concepts (both in response to Kerry and elsewhere) is also nonsensical.[62] Indeed, Frege seems at various junctures to be disarmingly ready to embrace such a conclusion about the status of many of his own remarks:

> In the case of a concept we can also call the unsaturatedness its predicative nature. But in this connection it is necessary to point out an imprecision forced on us by language, which, if we are not conscious of it, will prevent

us from recognizing the heart of the matter: i.e. we can scarcely avoid using such expressions as 'the concept *prime*'. Here there is not a trace left of unsaturatedness, of the predicative nature. Rather, the expression is constructed in a way which precisely parallels 'the poet Schiller'. So language brands a concept as an object, since the only way it can fit the designation for a concept into its grammatical structure is as a proper name. But in so doing, strictly speaking, it falsifies matters. In the same way, the word 'concept' itself is, taken strictly, already defective, since the phrase 'is a concept' requires a proper name as grammatical subject; and so, strictly speaking, it requires something contradictory, since no proper name can designate a concept; or perhaps better still [would be to say that], it requires something nonsensical.[63]

Frege's discussion here turns on the idea that we know *what* it is that we are trying to say (when we employ an expression such as "the concept *prime*"), but when we try to say "it," we realize that what we are trying to say requires that what we actually say be something nonsensical. We have in passages such as this the idea that we can discern what a piece of nonsense is *trying* (but failing) to say. When we use such expressions as "the concept *X*" we are trying to refer to a concept, but in the mode of expression with which we end up – when we try to express our thought – there is not a trace of unsaturatedness left.[64] We are left with something that does not have a predicative nature and, Frege therefore concludes, we have failed to refer to a concept. An attempt to treat a concept as an object is an attempt to do something *impossible*, an attempt to do something we *cannot* do:

If I want to speak of a concept, language, with an almost irresistible force, compels me to use an inappropriate expression which obscures – I might almost say falsifies – the thought. One would assume, on the basis of its analogy with other expressions, that if I say 'the concept *equilateral triangle*' I am designating a concept, just as I am of course naming a planet if I say 'the planet Neptune'. But this is not the case; for we do not have anything with a predicative nature. Hence the meaning of the expression 'the concept *equilateral triangle*' (if there is one in this case) is an object. We cannot avoid words like 'the concept', but where we use them we must always bear their inappropriateness in mind. From what we have said it follows that objects and concepts are fundamentally different and cannot stand in for one another. And the same goes for the corresponding words or signs. Proper names cannot really be used as predicates. Where they might seem to, we find on looking more closely that the sense is such that they only form part of the predicate: *concepts cannot stand in the same relations as objects*. It would not be false, but impossible to think of them as doing so.[65]

This passage (and many others, in Frege's work, like it) make reference to there being a *thought* underlying the nonsense we come out with (when we attempt to assert of a concept what can only be asserted of an object). Language itself obstructs us from expressing the thought we are after: "language, with an almost irresistible force, compels me to use an inappropriate expression which obscures – I might almost say falsifies – *the thought*." The nonsense we come out with represents an unsuccessful attempt to put that (unsayable) thought into words. Thus, for example, in responding to Kerry, Frege says certain things that by his own lights are nonsense, and what we (his readers) are to do is attend not simply to what he says (since it is, after all, nonsense) but to "the thought" which his words fail to express but attempt to gesture at.[66]

One such example of Fregean elucidation occurs in a letter to Russell:

> In the proposition 'Something is an object', the word 'something' . . . stands for a proper name. Thus whatever we put in place of 'something', we always get a true proposition; for a function name cannot take the place of 'something'. Here we find ourselves in a situation where the nature of language forces us to make use of imprecise expressions. The proposition 'A is a function' is such an expression: it is always imprecise; for A stands for a proper name. . . . While I am writing this, I am well aware of having again expressed myself imprecisely. Sometimes this is just unavoidable. *All that matters is that we know we are doing it and how it happens.*[67]

The proposition "A is a function" is here invoked as an example of the paradoxical character inevitably attaching to the sort of utterances one comes out with when one attempts to elucidate what a function is. Consider the following four propositions:

(1) "A is an object."
(2) "Everything is an object."
(3) "A is a function."
(4) "Nothing is a function"

In (1), the word "A" stands for a proper name; and so, by Frege's lights, whatever we plug in for "A" will occupy the argument place for an object, and thus (according to Frege's second principle) will be an object. Thus it would appear that no matter what we plug in for "A," (1) will be true. But if (1) is true no matter what we plug in for "A," it would seem to follow that (2) is true! Similarly, in (3), as in (1), the word "A" stands for a proper name; and so, once again, whatever occupies this argument place will be an object. Thus it would appear in this case that no matter what we plug in for "A," (3) will be false. But if (3) is false no matter what we plug in for "A," it would seem to follow that (4) is true! The point of this elucidation is not to secure the truth of the paradoxical claim that "Nothing is a function" (or "There are no functions"). On the contrary: it is to offer a *reductio ad absurdum* of the idea that the proposition "A is a function" can just straightforwardly *say* what Russell (for the sake of his argument with Frege) wants it to. The point is to show that sentences in which the expression "function" occurs misfire, and to show that – as long as we know what we are doing with such sentences – such self-defeating sentences can none the less be put to use to communicate an insight into what a function is. What matters when we employ such sentences, as Frege's final sentence (in the passage quoted above) indicates, is that we know what we are doing (i.e., uttering nonsense) when we come out with them, and that we know how it has come to pass that we find ourselves doing it.

The point of the paradoxical assertions that comprise the preceding elucidation is to show us (i) that we end up speaking nonsense when we try to say what a function is, (ii) that we here "find ourselves in a situation where the nature of language itself" makes it impossible for us to say that which we want to say and (iii) that to grasp how it is that the nature of language itself thus stands in the way of saying what we want to say (when we want to say what a function is) is to grasp what a function is. The point is thus not *merely* to expose what we end up saying when we employ such a term as nonsense (in order to debar us from engaging in such ways of speaking) but, rather, to teach us how *self-consciously* to cultivate such ways of speaking (in order to allow us to attain insight into the nature of functions). The point of cultivating such ways of speaking is to enable us to recognize *why* it is that we end up with nonsense when we try to say such things. The attainment of such a recognition constitutes the sign that we have grasped an elucidation of the meaning of a term (such as "function") which denotes something logically primitive.[68]

Frege repeatedly says, when offering such elucidatory examples, that he is *forced* or *compelled* to express himself in an infelicitous manner: he is attempting to struggle against "an imprecision forced on us by the nature of language," one which "compels" him "to use an inappropriate expression which obscures – falsifies – the thought." Now, as I've already indicated, what is significant about such remarks for our purposes is that they reveal a parallel between a possible reading of Frege and a standard reading of the *Tractatus*. On this reading, Frege (1) takes himself in such cases to be trying to say something which, properly speaking, *cannot* be said, and (2) speaks in such cases of there being a *thought* which his words struggle but fail adequately to express. In a famous passage in "On Concept and Object" he writes:

> I admit that there is a quite peculiar obstacle in the way of an understanding with the reader. By a kind of necessity of language, my expressions, taken literally, sometimes miss my *thought*; I mention an object when what I *intend* is a concept. I fully realize that in such cases I was relying upon a reader who would be ready to meet me half-way – who does not begrudge a pinch of salt. [my emphases][69]

His words miss his thought (and end up being nonsense); so there is a thought they are aiming at: an understanding of what his words intend to say depends upon his reader latching onto the thought his words fail properly to express. This failure is due, according to Frege, to "a kind of necessity of language." If he is to convey the thought he here seeks to convey he has no alternative but to have recourse to (elucidatory) nonsense.

A reading of Frege (on the impossibility of asserting of a concept what can only be asserted of an object) such as the one sketched above involves attributing to Frege a commitment to the substantial conception of nonsense; that is, it involves attributing to Frege the very conception of philosophically illuminating nonsense which is standardly thought to be the innovation of the *Tractatus*. Once one sees how this conception is at odds with other aspects of Frege's philosophy – those aspects of his philosophy that the *Tractatus* is most concerned to inherit – one is in a better position to see where the philosophical innovation of the *Tractatus* truly lies.[70]

5 The Tractarian critique of the substantial conception

The great difficulty here is not to represent the matter as if there were something one couldn't do.

(Wittgenstein[71])

Is it possible to identify an expression as being of a particular logical category if it occurs in the wrong place? It is here, in its response to this question, that the *Tractatus* sees a tension in Frege's view. A number of Frege's doctrines and a great deal of his own methodological practice suggest that the answer to this question should be: No! It is reflection on these aspects of Frege's thought and practice that leads Wittgenstein to embrace the austere conception of nonsense. If one takes Frege's three principles to heart – as the author of the *Tractatus* does – then one will say: if you want to know whether a particular word in a proposition is an object-expression or a concept-expression, you cannot just rely on your previous commerce with that word; you have to analyze the logical structure of the judgment and see what logical role is played by that segment of the proposition – how it contributes to the sense of the whole.

Frege warns in "On Concept and Object" (and elsewhere) that the same word in ordinary language can be used in some contexts as a proper name and in others as a concept word. Frege's favorite example of such a word is "moon."[72] It can also happen in ordinary language that an object-expression which has *never* been previously used to express a concept can suddenly be used, for the first time, as a concept-expression; and that we can understand what is meant by such an unprecedented usage. A famous example of a proper name suddenly being used as a concept expression is Lloyd Bentsen (in the 1988 vice-presidential debate) saying to Dan Quayle: "You're no Jack Kennedy." Bentsen's point was not that two individuals (Quayle and Kennedy) are not identical, but rather that there is a concept (of, say, exemplary statesmanship) which Quayle does not fall under. Frege offers as an example of this sort of creative use of language the lovely sentence "Trieste is no Vienna":

> We must not let ourselves be deceived because language often uses the same word now as a proper name, now as a concept word; in our example ["There is only one Vienna"], the numeral indicates that we have the latter; 'Vienna' is here a concept-word, like 'metropolis'. Using it in this sense, we may say: "Trieste is no Vienna".[73]

In this example, Frege says, we encounter a word which usually functions as a proper name playing the role of a concept-expression. Frege's reading of this sentence is arrived at through reflection upon what possible use this combination of words might have; that is, by asking himself: in what context would one utter such words and what thought would one then be expressing? If we reflect on when we would utter such a sentence and what we might mean by it, Frege suggests, we will see that "Vienna" here could mean something like "metropolis" (or perhaps even beautiful or majestic metropolis) – and thus the sign "Vienna" used in this way should be expressed in a proper logical symbolism by a completely different kind of symbol than that which we would use to express the occurrence of the word "Vienna" in the sentence "Vienna is the capital of Austria."[74] Notice that Frege does not conclude that what we have here in his lovely sentence about Trieste is a piece of nonsense – one which results from trying to put a proper name where a concept-expression should go. He concludes instead that what fills the argument place for a concept-expression here *is* a concept-expression – and then makes a suggestion about what the sentence as a whole might mean (and hence about *which* concept might be meant). Thus Frege's methodology here is to begin with our *understanding* of the proposition as a whole and to use that as a basis for segmenting it into its logically discrete components.[75] One can see Frege's methodological practice here as illustrating the close relationship between his three principles. If we disobey the second principle in our approach to this example, we end up violating the third: when we consider the word in isolation we take "Vienna" for an object-expression, yet in this context it does not denote an individual; so if we fail to attend to the logical role of the word in this context, we mistake a concept for an object. What fuels such a mistake is one's tendency to think that one already knows what "Vienna" means taken all by itself outside the context of that proposition – it means one presumes roughly what it means in a sentence like "Vienna is the capital of Austria." Although we do not realize it, Frege thinks that what is really going on when we think in this way is that we succumb to the all but irresistible urge to transgress against his first principle. When we ask for the meaning of the word in isolation, we unwittingly end up looking for the meaning in what Frege wants to teach us to recognize as the realm of the psychological. It may well be true that when I utter the word "Vienna" in saying the sentence "Trieste is no Vienna" I intend to mean the same thing as when I utter the word "Vienna" in saying "The capital of Austria is Vienna" – the same mental image of the spires of the *Stefansdom* rising up over the skyline of the city of Vienna may float before my mind's eye – but that, Frege thinks, does not bear on whether the word has the same meaning in these two sentences.

The methodological import of Frege's three principles is developed in the *Tractatus* through the claim that in ordinary language it is often the case that the same sign symbolizes in different ways. The distinction between sign [*Zeichen*] and symbol [*Symbol*] which this claim presupposes can be summarized as follows:

* sign   an orthographic unit, that which the perceptible expressions for propositions have in common (a sign design, inscription, icon, grapheme, etc.)[76]
* symbol   a logical unit, that which meaningful propositions have in common (i.e., an item belonging to a given logical category: proper name, first-level function, etc.)

Armed with the Tractarian distinction between sign and symbol, we can formulate the contrast between the two conceptions of nonsense (which Wittgenstein sees Frege as torn between) in a more precise manner. To recall, the two conceptions of nonsense were:

* the substantial conception which holds that there are two logically distinct kinds of nonsense: *substantial nonsense* and *mere nonsense*
* the austere conception which holds that there is, from a logical point of view, only one kind of nonsense: *mere nonsense*

The italicized terms in the above formulations can now be defined as follows:

* substantial nonsense a proposition composed of signs which symbolize, but which has a logically flawed syntax due to a clash in the logical category of its symbols
* mere nonsense a string composed of signs in which no symbol can be perceived, and which hence has no discernible logical syntax

I have earlier pretended to be able to distinguish between the positivist and ineffability variants of the substantial conception. But, armed with the distinction between symbol and sign, we can start to see why the distinction between these two variants is an inherently unstable one.[77] Any attempt to clearly articulate the positivist variant will lead to its collapse either into the ineffability variant or into the austere conception. Either the proponent of the positivist variant holds that a violation of logical syntax involves an impermissible combination of symbols or he holds that it involves an impermissible combination of signs. If he holds the former, then the positivist variant collapses into the ineffability variant; if the latter, then he abandons the substantial conception altogether.[78]

In order to begin to see why this is so, it will help to look more closely at the distinction between sign and symbol as it is drawn in the *Tractatus*. It is introduced as part of the commentary on §3.3 which is the *Tractatus*'s reformulation of Frege's second principle.[79] §3.3 runs as follows: "Only the proposition has sense; only in the context of a proposition has a name meaning." Then, beginning immediately thereafter (with §3.31), comes the following commentary:

> Every part of a proposition which characterizes its sense I call an expression (a symbol).
> (The proposition itself is an expression.)
> Everything essential to their sense that propositions can have in common with one another is an expression.
> An expression is the mark of a form and a content.
> An expression presupposes the forms of all propositions in which it can occur. It is the common characteristic mark of a class of propositions . . .
> (§§3.31–3.311)

An expression has meaning only in a proposition ...

(§3.314)

I conceive the proposition – like Frege and Russell – as a function of the expressions contained in it ...

(§3.318)

The sign is that in the symbol which is perceptible by the senses.

(§3.32)

Two different symbols can therefore have the sign (the written sign or the sound sign) in common – they then signify in different ways.

(§3.321)

It can never indicate the common characteristic of two objects that we symbolize them with the same signs but by different *methods of symbolizing*. For the sign is arbitrary.

We could therefore equally well choose two different signs [to symbolize the two different objects] and where then would remain that which the signs shared in common?

(§3.322)

The point of the commentary is in part to clarify the notion of "proposition" which figures in the context principle (only the *proposition* has sense; only in the context of a *proposition* has a name meaning[80]). The relevant notion is one of a certain kind of a symbol – not a certain kind of a sign – something which only has life in language.[81] The sign, Wittgenstein says, "is that in the symbol which is perceptible by the senses" (what is now sometimes called the sign design). The symbol is a logical unit, it expresses something which propositions – as opposed to propositional signs – have in common.[82] Thus the sentences "Trieste is no Vienna" and "Vienna is the capital of Austria" have the sign "Vienna" in common. These two sentences taken together offer an instance of what Wittgenstein means when he says (in §3.321) "two different symbols can have the sign (the written sign or the sound sign) in common – they then signify in different ways." The sentences "Trieste is no Vienna" and "Vienna is the capital of Austria" have no symbol in common – all they have in common are the signs "Vienna" and "is." In (what Wittgenstein calls) a proper logical grammar, each sign would wear its mode of symbolizing on its sleeve. We can, somewhat anachronistically, use modern logical notation to illustrate this point:

(a) Vienna is the capital of Austria $\quad$ $v = c$
(b) Trieste is not the capital of Austria $\quad$ $t \neq c$
(c) Trieste is not (identical to) Vienna $\quad$ $t \neq v$

(a′) Trieste is no Vienna $\quad$ $\neg\, Vt$
(b′) Trieste is no metropolis $\quad$ $\neg\, Mt$
(c′) Trieste is a Vienna $\quad$ Vt

When written in ordinary language, sentences (a) and (a') have two signs ("Vienna," "is") in common; when expressed in a proper logical notation, they are inscribed in such a way that their lack of a common symbol is reflected in the absence of a common sign. When written in ordinary language, sentences (c) and (a') have three signs ("Trieste," "Vienna," "is") in common; when expressed in a proper logical notation, it is rendered perspicuous that they have only a single symbol in common. Wittgenstein comments on this feature of ordinary language:

> In the language of everyday life it very often happens that the same word signifies in two different ways – and therefore belongs to two different symbols – or that two words, which signify in different ways, are apparently applied in the same way in the proposition.
>
> Thus the word "is" appears as the copula, as the sign of equality, and as the expression of existence; "to exist" as an intransitive verb like "to go"; "identical" as an adjective; we speak of *something* but also of the fact of *something* happening.
>
> (In the proposition "Green is green" – where the first word is a proper name and the last an adjective – these words have not merely different meanings but they are *different symbols*.)
>
> (§3.323)

It is perhaps worth elaborating how Wittgenstein's example in the last paragraph illustrates the point of the first paragraph of §3.323. The propositional sign "Green is green" can be naturally taken as symbolizing in any of three different ways[83] – and hence can be understood as an expression for any one of three different thoughts:

(a) Mr. Green is green   Gg
(b) Mr. Green is Mr. Green $g = g$
(c) The color green is the color green $(\forall x)\,(Gx \equiv Gx)$

One way of noticing how the same sign symbolizes differently in each of these three cases is to focus on the word "is." In each of the propositions expressing each of these three different thoughts, the sign "is" symbolizes a different logical relation. In (a), the sign "is" symbolizes the copula (a relation between a concept and an object); in (b) we have the "is" of identity (a relation between objects); in (c) we have the "is" of co-extensionality (a relation between concepts).[84] In the ordinary language version of (a) – "where the first word is a proper name and the last an adjective" – "green" can be seen to be not merely ambiguous with respect to its meaning (the way "bank" is in "The bank is on the left bank"), but ambiguous with respect to its logical type: "these words have not merely different meanings but they are *different symbols*." The point of the example is to show us that we cannot gather from the notation of ordinary language how a given sign (e.g. "green," or "is") symbolizes in a given instance. Wittgenstein suddenly follows this example with the observation: "Thus there easily arise the most fundamental confusions (of which the whole of philosophy is full)" (§3.324). In a proper *Begriffsschrift*, a different sign would express each of these "different methods of symbolizing," thus enabling us to identify the sources of certain confusions. In §3.325, Wittgenstein immediately goes on to say that in order "to avoid such errors" we require a symbolism which obeys the rules of *logical* grammar. How can such a *Begriffsschrift* enable us to avoid "the most fundamental confusions (of which the whole of philosophy is full)"? In order to answer this question, we need first to explore: (i) what sorts of "confusions" are these? (ii) what role in their elucidation does a *Begriffsschrift* play?

In the *Tractatus*, Wittgenstein argues that once we appreciate how Frege's three principles work in conjunction with one another we will see that there will always be room for a question as to whether a given sign, when it occurs in two different sentences of ordinary language, is symbolizing the same way in each of those occurrences. And this question cannot be settled simply by appealing to the fact that the same word (sign) ordinarily occurs (symbolizes) as a name[85] (for example, as a name of the capital of Austria); nor by appealing to the fact that if I were asked what I meant when I uttered one of those sentences I would reply that I meant the word in the same sense as I have on other occasions; nor by appealing to the fact that I, on this occasion of utterance, exert a special effort to mean the word in the same way as before. How can this question be settled? Wittgenstein says: "In order to recognize the symbol in the sign we must consider the context of significant use" (§3.326). We must ask ourselves on what occasion we would utter this sentence and what, in that context of use, we would then mean by it.[86] (This is what we saw Frege do in his handling of the example "Trieste is no Vienna.") In asking ourselves this, we still rely upon our familiarity with the way words (signs) ordinarily occur (symbolize) in propositions to fashion a segmentation of the propositional sign in question.[87]

In §3.326, "the context of significant use" translates *sinnvollen Gebrauch* and "recognize" translates *erkennen*. The latter is the same word that occurs in §6.54: "My propositions serve as elucidations in the following way: anyone who understands me eventually *recognizes* them as nonsensical."[88] It is a condition of being able to recognize the symbol in the sign that the string in which the sign occurs be *sinnvoll*. To recognize a *Satz* as nonsensical [*Unsinn*] is to be unable to recognize the symbol in the sign. For the *Tractatus*, these two forms of recognition eclipse one another.[89] To recognize a *Satz* as nonsensical [*Unsinn*], for the *Tractatus,* is not a matter of recognizing that it is attempting to say something that cannot be said, but rather a matter of recognizing that it fails to say anything at all. Building on Frege's own methodological practice, the *Tractatus* argues that in the case of a piece of nonsense – that is, in the absence of the provision of a context of *sinnvollen Gebrauch*: a possible logical segmentation of the *Satz* – we have no basis upon which to isolate the logical roles played by the working parts of a proposition; for, *ex hypothesi*, there are no working parts of the proposition. One can identify the contribution the senses of the parts of a proposition make to the sense of the whole only if the whole has a sense[90] – if it stands in some identifiable location with respect to the other occupants of logical space. According to the *Tractatus*, there are [no examples of putting a proper name where a concept word belongs], for if one can properly make out that what belongs in that place is a concept word, then that is a sufficient condition for treating whatever is in that place as a concept word. There isn't anything, on the conception of *Unsinn* which the *Tractatus* advances, which corresponds to a proposition's failing to make sense because of the meaning which the parts already have taken in isolation. On the Tractarian conception, there is only one way a sentence can be *Unsinn*: by its failing to symbolize. This conception does not rule out the possibility of *Sätze* (such as tautologies and contradictions) which have logical structure and yet are devoid of *Sinn*. (To think that it did would be to lose sight of the distinction between that which is *Unsinn* and that which is *sinnlos*.[91]) It only rules out a sentence's having an "impossible sense" – a sense that it *cannot* have because of the senses that its parts already have.

6 The method of the *Tractatus*

There is nothing which requires such gentle handling as an illusion – that is, if one wishes to dispel it. If anything prompts the captive of the illusion to set his will in opposition, then all is lost. . . . So one must approach him from behind. . . . [T]his requires . . . a kind of deception in which one deceives a person for the truth's sake. . . . 'To deceive' in such a case means to begin by accepting the other man's illusion as good money.

(Søren Kierkegaard[92])

Recall how Fregean elucidation is supposed to work. The aim of Fregean elucidation is to help us to understand the principles of construction which underlie his *Begriffsschrift*. The mark of our having grasped his elucidations is that we have mastered his symbolism and are able properly to use it to express thoughts. Frege's elucidatory "propositions" cannot be expressed in *Begriffsschrift*, but the logical distinctions which they attempt to convey – such as the distinction between concept and object – show themselves through the difference in the signs of *Begriffsschrift* whose employment we have mastered. Frege, in offering his elucidations, self-consciously employs a kind of nonsense in order to bring out the confusions of people like Kerry.[93] But – according to the interpretation of Frege which Geach favors – for Frege, that is only part of the purpose of the activity of elucidation. Frege takes his elucidations also to convey insights into necessities founded "deep in the nature of things."[94] Though his expressions, through a kind of necessity of language, misfire, the insights they seek to impart can be latched onto by the reader who meets him halfway and does not begrudge him a pinch of salt. This additional positive role (of imparting a kind of inexpressible insight) which Geach ascribes to Fregean elucidation corresponds to the central purpose ascribed to Tractarian elucidation by proponents of the ineffability interpretation of the *Tractatus*.[95] The ascription of such a conception of elucidation (to either Frege or Wittgenstein) presupposes the prior ascription of the substantive conception of nonsense.

But, as we have seen, it is possible to find in certain of Frege's doctrines a ground for hostility towards the substantive conception and for hospitality towards the austere conception of nonsense. Moreover, as we have also seen, there is ample textual evidence that the *Tractatus* seeks to erect its teachings on just those doctrines of Frege's. But if one attempts to credit this textual evidence, and thus ascribe to the *Tractatus* the austere conception, what then should one take the aim of Tractarian elucidation to be? How, according to such a reading, are we to make sense of the fact that the *Tractatus* takes itself to be engaged in an activity which is properly termed one of "elucidation" – an activity, that is, which is able to achieve or confer some form of clarity, enlightenment or insight? To understand how the *Tractatus*'s own *Unsinn* is supposed to elucidate (when that of other philosophers mostly only misleads), some distinction between misleading nonsense and illuminating nonsense is evidently required; but, on the austere reading, illuminating nonsense is no longer a vehicle for a special kind of thought. If the aim of elucidation, according to the ineffability interpretation, is to reveal (through the employment of substantial nonsense) that which cannot be said, then, according to the austere reading, the aim of Tractarian elucidation is to reveal (through the employment of mere nonsense) that what appears to be substantial nonsense is mere nonsense. While the aim of the former sort of elucidation was supposed to be the conferral of insight into inexpressible features of reality, the aim of the latter is not insight into metaphysical features of reality, but rather insight into the sources of metaphysics. The premise underlying the procedure of the *Tractatus* (and this is connected to why the point of the work is an ethical one) is that our most profound confusions of soul show themselves in – and can be revealed to us through an attention to – our confusions concerning what we mean (and, in particular, what we fail to mean) by our words.

The *Tractatus* aims to show that (as Wittgenstein later puts it) "I cannot use language to get outside language."[96] It accomplishes this aim by first encouraging me to suppose that I can use language in such a way, and then enabling me to work through the (apparent) consequences of this (pseudo-)supposition, until I reach the point at which my impression of there being a determinate supposition (whose consequences I have throughout been exploring) dissolves on me. So on the reading of the *Tractatus* suggested here, what is to happen, if the book succeeds in its aim, is *not* that I (1) succeed in conceiving of an extraordinary possibility (illogical thought), (2) judge "it" to be impossible, (3) conclude that the truth of this judgment cannot be accommodated within (the logical structure of) language because it is about (the logical structure of) language and (4) go on to communicate (under the guise of only "showing" and not "saying" "it") what it is that cannot be said. Rather, what is to happen is that I am lured up all four of these rungs of the ladder and then: (5) throw the *entire* ladder (all four of the previous rungs) away. On this reading, first I grasp that there is something which *must* be; then I see that it cannot be said; then I grasp that if it can't be said it can't be thought (that the limits of language are the limits of thought); and then, finally, when I reach the top of the ladder, I grasp that there has been no "it" in my grasp all along (that that which I cannot think I cannot "grasp" either). In order for a reader to pass through the first four stages of ascent up this Tractarian ladder he must take himself to be participating in the traditional philosophical activity of argument – to be inferring conclusions from premises (as, e.g., Frege appears to be doing when he reasons from a pair of premises concerning (a) the nature of *Begriffe* and (b) the logical structure of certain propositions – such as "The concept *horse* is not a concept" – to the conclusion that his words "miss his thought"). A reader of the *Tractatus* only ascends to the final rung of the ladder when he is able to look back upon his progress upwards and "recognize" that he has only been going through the motions of "inferring" (apparent) "conclusions" from (apparent) "premises." Thus the elucidatory strategy of the *Tractatus* depends on the reader's provisionally taking himself to be participating in the traditional philosophical activity of establishing theses through a procedure of reasoned argument; but it only succeeds if the reader fully comes to understand what the work means to say about itself when it says that philosophy, as this work seeks to practice it, results not in doctrine but in elucidations, not in *Philosophische Sätze* but in *das Klarwerden von Sätzen*. And the attainment of this recognition depends upon the reader's actually undergoing a certain *experience* – the attainment of which is identified in §6.54 as the sign that the reader has understood the author of the work: the reader's experience of having his illusion of sense (in the "premises" and "conclusions" of the "argument") dissipate through its becoming clear to him that (what he took to be) the *philosophische Sätze* of the work are *Unsinn*.

Thus what happens to us as readers of the *Tractatus* – assuming the work succeeds in its aim – is that we are drawn into an illusion of occupying a certain sort of a perspective. From this perspective, we take ourselves to be able to survey the possibilities which undergird how we must represent things as being, fixing what is "logically" necessary and what is merely contingent. From this perspective, we contemplate the logical structure of thought as it is and imagine that we are also able to contemplate the possibility of its being otherwise. We take ourselves to be occupying a perspective from which we can view the logical structure of language "from sideways on."[97] This illusion of perspective is engendered by the perception of a flawed sense in certain nonsensical propositions; we take these substantially nonsensical propositions to be attempting to express a state of affairs that *cannot* be – and thereby to be disclosing the limits of possibility. Tractarian elucidation aims to show us that these sentences that apparently express substantially nonsensical thoughts actually express no thoughts. The "problems of philosophy" that the *Tractatus* sets itself the task of "solving" are all of a single sort: they are all occasioned by reflection on possibilities (of running up against the limits of thought, language or reality) which appear to come into view when we imagine ourselves able to frame in thought violations of the logical structure of language. The "solution" to these problems (as §6.52 says) lies in their disappearance – in the dissolution of the appearance that we are so much as able to frame such thoughts. The "propositions" we come out with when we attempt to formulate these problems are to be recognized as *Unsinn*. The only "insight" that a Tractarian elucidation imparts, in the end, is one about the reader himself: that he is prone to such illusions of thought.

The assumption underlying Tractarian elucidation is that the only way to free oneself from such illusions is to fully enter into them and explore them from the inside. This assumption – one which underlies both Wittgenstein's early and later work[98] – is nicely summarized in the following remark (from a 1931 manuscript of Wittgenstein's): "In philosophy we are deceived by an illusion. But this – an illusion – is also something, and I must at some time place it completely and clearly before my eyes, before I can say it is only an illusion."[99] The illusion that the *Tractatus* seeks to explode, above all, is that we can run up against the limits of language. The book starts with a warning about a certain kind of enterprise – one of attempting to draw a limit to thought. In the body of the text, we are offered (what appears to be) a doctrine about "the limits of thought." With the aid of this doctrine, we imagine ourselves to be able both to draw these limits and to see beyond them. We imagine ourselves able to do what the Preface warns we will fall into imagining ourselves able to do (once we imagine ourselves able to draw a limit to thought): we imagine ourselves able "to think both sides of the limit" (and hence "able to think what cannot be thought").[100] The aim of the work is to show us that beyond "the limits of language" lies – not ineffable truth, but rather – (as the preface of the *Tractatus* warns) *einfach Unsinn*, simply nonsense.[101] At the conclusion of the book, we are told that the author's elucidations have succeeded only if we recognize what we find in the body of the text to be nonsense. In §6.54, Wittgenstein does not ask his reader here to "grasp" the "thoughts" which his nonsensical propositions seek to convey. He does not call upon the reader to understand his sentences, but rather to understand *him*, namely the author and the kind of activity in which he is engaged – one of elucidation. He tells us in §6.54 how these sentences serve as elucidations: by enabling us to recognize them *as* nonsense.[102] One does not reach the end by arriving at the last page, but by arriving at a certain point in an activity – the point when the elucidation has served its purpose: when the illusion of sense is exploded from within. The sign that we have understood the author of the work is that we can throw the ladder we have climbed up away. That is to say, we have finished the work, and the work is finished with us, when we are able to *throw* the sentences in the body of the work – sentences about "the limits of language" and the unsayable things which lie beyond them – *away*.[103]

Notes

1 This paper is drawn from a longer manuscript of mine, "The Method of the *Tractatus*" which is forthcoming in *From Frege to Wittgenstein: Perspectives on Early Analytic Philosophy*, Erich Reck (ed.) Oxford, Oxford University Press.

2 *Tractatus Logico-Philosophicus*, §6.54; my emphases. All subsequent unspecified references to a section number are to the *Tractatus*. Quotations from the *Tractatus* will be drawn from either the Pears and McGuinness translation or the Ogden translation, or some emendation or (as in this case) combination thereof.

3 "I cannot imagine that Carnap should have so completely and utterly misunderstood the last sentences of the book – and therefore the fundamental conception of the whole book" (Wittgenstein, Letter to Moritz Schlick, August 8, 1932; quoted in *Ludwig Wittgenstein, Sein Leben in Bildern und Texten*, M. Nedo and M. Ranchetti (eds) Frankfurt am Main, Suhrkamp, 1983, p. 255. For further discussion of this remark, see my "On Putting Two and Two Together: Kierkegaard, Wittgenstein and the Point of View for Their Work as Authors" in *The Grammar of Religious Belief*, D.Z. Phillips (ed.) New York, St. Martins Press, 1995.

4 Each of these translations has something to recommend it.

5 On most interpretations, the aim of the *Tractatus* is taken to be precisely one of advancing a doctrine.

6 That the notion of *Erläuterung* figures centrally in both Frege and the *Tractatus* is also the topic of Joan Weiner's paper "Theory and Elucidation: The End of the Age of Innocence" in *Future Pasts: Reflections on the History of Analytic Philosophy*, J. Floyd and S. Shieh (eds) Cambridge, Mass., Harvard University Press, 1999.

7 For Frege's own formulation, see *The Basic Laws of Arithmetic*, Montgomery Furth (trans.) Berkeley, University of California Press, 1967, §32.

8 It is, Wittgenstein acknowledges in his Preface to the *Tractatus*, "to the great works of Frege and the writings of my friend Bertrand Russell that I owe in large measure the stimulation of my thoughts."

9 *An Introduction to Wittgenstein's Tractatus*, Philadelphia, Pa., University of Pennsylvania Press, 1971, p. 12.

10 See my "The Search for Logically Alien Thought: Descartes, Kant, Frege and the *Tractatus*," *Philosophical Topics*, 1991, vol. 20, pp. 115–180.

11 I am using the word "show" here *not* in the sense which the *Tractatus* itself reserves for this term (which, as we shall see, is not applicable to nonsense), but rather (as it is often used by proponents of the ineffability interpretation) to refer to the activity of "hinting" or "gesturing" at ineffable truths by means of nonsense. Whenever I employ the word in this latter sense I will place it in scare-quotes. I am here adopting the idiom of many of the commentators with whose work I wish to take issue. But I hereby invite confusion in two ways; so let me just say for now: (1) that, in adopting this idiom, I do not take myself to be making any contact with the (actual) Tractarian notion of *zeigen*, and (2) that any commentator who holds that the sentences of the *Tractatus* aspire to hint or gesture at ineffable truths counts, by my lights, as a proponent of the ineffability interpretation, even if they (unlike most proponents of the ineffability interpretation) are textually scrupulous enough carefully to refrain from ever employing the term "showing" to designate the activity of so hinting or gesturing.

12 In claiming that the *Tractatus* is to be seen as resolving a tension in Frege's thought (between these two different conceptions of nonsense), I raise interpretative questions about how Frege is to be read – questions which I do not hope to resolve in this paper. I mean to take sides on this question only in so far as it bears on the claim that Wittgenstein can be fruitfully read as having read Frege in certain ways. I do not wish to deny that Frege can be fruitfully read as adhering to either one of these two conceptions of nonsense, and as having faced up to the implications of such a commitment. (Peter Geach reads Frege as an adherent of the position that there are certain truths which can be "shown" but cannot be said. Cora Diamond, in chapters 2 and 4 of *The Realistic Spirit* (Cambridge, Mass., MIT Press, 1991), reads Frege as having already anticipated the conception of nonsense which I attribute in this paper to the *Tractatus*.) I am inclined to think that each of these readings of Frege has its exegetical advantages, each has moments where it stumbles over the text, and both are able to account for most of the texts (which, depending on the angle from which they are viewed, can assume the gestalt of either a substantial rabbit or an austere duck). My concern here will not be to referee such a dispute about Frege, but rather only to advance a claim about Wittgenstein and how he read Frege: namely, in a way which assigns to each of these readings half of the truth about Frege.

13 The positivist interpretation is all for showing that some sentences are nonsensical, but it wants no truck with the idea of philosophically illuminating nonsense. It wants to hold onto the substantial conception of nonsense (the idea that metaphysical nonsense arises through violations of logical syntax), while eschewing the idea that there are things which can be "shown" but not said.

14 I distinguish between these two variants because proponents of the substantial conception tend to present themselves as prima facie distinct in this respect. As we shall see, however, these variants cannot in the end be clearly distinguished from one another in the manner that I am here pretending that they can be.

15 In fact, the range of interpretative options available in connection with this dimension of Frege's thought perfectly parallel those available in connection with the *Tractatus*. Some commentators have ascribed to Frege the positivist variant of the substantial conception (e.g., Dummett), others (as mentioned in the previous note but two) the ineffability variant (e.g., Geach) or the austere conception (e.g., Diamond). I repeat: this paper is agnostic as to which of these readings represents the true Frege.

16 "Saying and Showing in Frege and Wittgenstein" in *Essays in Honor of G. H. von Wright*, J. Hintikka (ed.) *Acta Philosophica Fennica*, 1976, vol. 28, p. 55.

17 *Ibid*, p. 68.

18 *Ludwig Wittgenstein: Letters to C.K. Ogden*, p. 51.

19 Contrary to the assumption implicit in most of the secondary literature on it, the *Tractatus* itself scrupulously marks this distinction (between what I misleadingly refer to here as two senses of "show") by reserving *zeigen* to refer only to the first notion and using *erläutern* to refer to the second. Both of these notions are, in turn, to be

distinguished from the notion of "showing" which figures in the ineffability interpretation (see note 11).

20 The widespread assumption in the scholarly literature that this distinction (between saying *[sagen]* and showing *[zeigen]*) is crucial for understanding §6.54 arises from the conflation of the two distinctions I am trying to disentangle here. The distinction between *sagen* and *zeigen* has no application to *Unsinn*. A proposition which is *sinnvoll* says what is the case and shows its sense (§§4.021–4.022). A proposition which is *sinnlos* shows that it says nothing (§4.461). A "proposition" which is *unsinnig* (contrary to the ineffability interpretation) neither says nor shows anything (which is not to say that it cannot elucidate). §6.54 is concerned with those sentences of the work which are (to be recognized as) *unsinnig*.

21 I speak here of different "*kinds* of use of language" – instead merely of different "uses of language" – in order to note a distinction which must be respected if we are to avoid confusion later when we turn to the topic of what §3.326 of the *Tractatus* calls "significant use." To distinguish (what I here call) "kinds of use" is to distinguish the different sorts of things one can *do* with language over and above putting it to the use of *saying* something. Later on in this paper, when I turn to the point of §3.326, I will employ the expression "uses of language" to discriminate *within* the (primary) field of the assertoric employment of language different ways to use language to say things. Whenever the *Tractatus* itself speaks of the "use" *[Gebrauch]* of a sign it is always in this latter sense.

22 I borrow this useful term from J. L. Austin's *How to Do Things with Words*, Cambridge, Mass., Harvard University Press, 1962.

23 The early Wittgenstein did not think these two kinds of use of language (the constative and the elucidatory) comprised an exhaustive classification – he thought there was also a distinct *ethical* employment of language. (What comprises an ethical use of language needs to be understood before one can approach the question of what Wittgenstein means when he says that "the point of the *Tractatus* is ethical"; see Diamond, *The Realistic Spirit*, op. cit., chapter 8 and "Ethics, Imagination and the Method of Wittgenstein's *Tractatus*," reprinted in this volume.) There is therefore good reason to be wary of an oft-repeated textbook platitude concerning the fundamental difference between the thought of the early and the later Wittgenstein: that early Wittgenstein thought that language can only be put to *one* kind of use, whereas later Wittgenstein demolished his earlier doctrine by pointing out that language has a multiplicity of kinds of use. A way to put what is sound in the textbook platitude would be to say: for early Wittgenstein, non-constative kinds of use of language (1) come in only two flavors (elucidatory and ethical), and (2) are not, properly speaking, employments of *language per se* (see §§4–4.001) but rather employments of *language-like* structures; whereas for later Wittgenstein, the category of non-constative kinds of use (1) subtends many more kinds of use than ever dreamed of in the philosophy of early Wittgenstein (expressive uses of language, performative uses of language, etc.) and (2) represents not a mutually exclusive alternative to the constative employment of language but rather a pervasive dimension of all language use.

Since, as a matter of terminology, elucidation does not count as a kind of *Gebrauch* for early Wittgenstein (see the previous note but one) the gulf between early and later Wittgenstein can appear greater than it is. When I allow myself to describe (what for the *Tractatus* count as) elucidations as uses of *language*, I am describing a feature of Wittgenstein's early philosophy in the idiom of his later philosophy (with its correspondingly broader conception of language). Later on in this paper, we will be in a position to express this distinction in (what I have been calling) kinds of use of language in the idiom of Wittgenstein's early philosophy by distinguishing kinds of employment of linguistic *signs* (as opposed to symbols).

24 That what is at issue when Wittgenstein speaks of his sentences serving as elucidations is an implicit distinction in kinds of uses of linguistic signs is critical for answering a number of questions which typically arise in connection with §6.54 – e.g., isn't the passage self-refuting? (The last note but one of this paper addresses some of these questions.)

25 *Zettel*, §712.

26 "Saying and Showing in Frege and Wittgenstein," op. cit., p. 55. The kind of *showing* which is at issue in the first half of this passage (one according to which logical category-distinctions show themselves in a well-constructed formalized language) is a kind of showing that the Tractarian notion of *zeigen* aims to accommodate (though in this sense of "show," according to the *Tractatus*, logical category-distinctions only show themselves in *sinnvolle* sentences). Geach speaks of the nonsensical "sentences" which form the subject of the latter half of this passage (sentences in the vernacular which "are logically improper and admit of no translation into well-formed formulas of symbolic logic") as seeking to "convey" these same distinctions of logical category. Such sentences, according to Geach, seek to convey something which cannot be said. The idea that the latter sort of "sentences" intend to *convey* what the former sort *show* might invite the idea that it ought to be possible to formulate a more inclusive notion of "showing" – one which construes as a single sort of activity something which logically proper sentences (of either a natural language or a well-constructed formalized language) and certain logically improper sentences (of a natural language which admit of no translation into a well-constructed formalized language) are both able to engage in. Some commentators on the *Tractatus* employ the term "showing" in this (by my lights, hybrid) way to encompass both these sorts of cases. Most commentators on the *Tractatus*, however, seem to have only the latter sort of case in view when they employ the term. Geach himself, however, is careful to employ the term to refer only to the former sort of case. In order to avoid confusion, I remind the reader (see note 11) that when I employ the term "show" in scare-quotes I am using it in a way that Geach does not. I shall continue to do so even when expounding Geach's views (concerning how nonsense can convey something which cannot be said).

27 See, for example, *Remarks on the Philosophy of Psychology*, §42.

28 *The Basic Laws of Arithmetic*, op. cit., p. 18. For further discussion of why logic, for Frege, does not stand in need of psychology, see Thomas Ricketts's article "Objectivity and Objecthood: Frege's Metaphysics of Judgment" in *Frege Synthesized*, L. Haaparanta and J. Hintikka (eds) Dordrecht, Reidel, 1986, and chapter 2 of Joan Weiner's *Frege in Perspective*, Ithaca, NY, Cornell University Press, 1990. For further discussion of why logic, for Frege, does not stand in need of metaphysics, see Ricketts's "Truth, Thoughts and Objectivity in Frege" (forthcoming), and Weiner's "Realism *bei* Frege," *Synthese*, 1995, vol. 102 and her "Burge's Literal Interpretation of Frege," *Mind*, 1995, vol. 104.

29 What Frege has done for Kerry (not to mention Schubart, Thomae and others) brings to mind Heinrich Heine's remark (from Part Two of *Religion and Philosophy in Germany*) à propos Lessing's polemics against Götze, Reimarus and others: "He has snatched many a name from a well-deserved oblivion . . . and preserved it for posterity like an insect trapped in amber."

30 *Collected Papers on Mathematics, Logic, and Philosophy*, Brian McGuinness (ed.) London, Blackwell, 1984, p. 182.

31 This charge is expressed more emphatically in the unpublished version of "On Concept and Object." See *Posthumous Writings*, H. Hermes, F. Kambartel, and F. Kaulbach (eds) Chicago, University of Chicago Press, 1979), pp. 104–5. Frege and early Wittgenstein both use the expression "concept" in the same ("strictly logical," non-surface-grammatical) way. What Frege calls a concept ("in the strictly logical sense") is what Wittgenstein in *The Blue Book* calls a non-grammatical kind (p. 19). Frege and Wittgenstein differ, however, about which kinds are non-grammatical kinds – e.g. "number" is for Frege a non-grammatical kind, for (both early and later) Wittgenstein it is merely a grammatical kind.

32 *The Foundations of Arithmetic*, J. L. Austin (trans.) Evanston, Ill., Northwestern University Press, 1980, p. x.

33 Ibid., p. x.

34 *Posthumous Writings*, op. cit., p. 253.

35 In conformity with this doctrine of the primacy of judgment, Frege's concept-script forbids the isolated occurrence of designations for the various possible components of a judgment. See ibid., pp. 15–17.

36 Frege worries that the all but unavoidable (and in itself potentially innocent) locution of a thought's having "parts" or "components" will mislead one into attributing a false independence to the parts of a thought – so that we imagine that the parts could retain their identity apart from their participation in a whole thought:

> But the words 'made up of', 'consist of', 'component', 'part' may lead to our looking at it the wrong way. If we choose to speak of parts in this connection, all the same these parts are not mutually independent in the way that we are else-where used to find when we have parts of a whole.
>
> (*Collected Papers*, op. cit., p. 386)

Frege's context principle – and the correlative doctrine of the primacy of judgment (which refuses to allow that the parts of the whole are "mutually independent in the way that we are elsewhere used to find when we have parts of a whole") – in no way denies the compositionality of either thought or language. It insists only upon the mutual interdependence of compositionality and contextuality. (Diego Marconi nicely summarizes the position in the slogan: "Understanding without contextuality is blind; understanding without compositionality is empty.") Frege's view of natural language – upon which the *Tractatus* builds its "understanding of the logic of language" – affirms both (1) that it is in virtue of their contributions to the senses of the whole that we identify the logical "parts" of propositions, and (2) that it is in virtue of an identification of each "part" as that which occurs in other propositional wholes that we segment the whole into its constituent parts (see note 39).

37 Gilbert Ryle attempted to summarize this "difficult but crucial point" of Frege's by saying that the meanings of words "are not proposition components but propositional differences":

> Frege's difficult but crucial point . . . [is] that the unitary something that is *said* in a sentence or the unitary sense that it expresses is not an assemblage of detach-able sense atoms, of, that is, parts enjoying separate existence and separate thinkability, and yet that one truth or falsehood may have discernible, countable, and classifiable similarities to and dissimilarities from other truths and falsehoods. Word meanings or concepts are not proposition components but propositional differ-ences. They are distinguishables, not detachables; abstractables, not extractables.
>
> (*Collected Papers*, vol. 1, London, Hutchinson, 1971, p. 58)

As this paper goes on, it will prove to be a matter of some interest that Gilbert Ryle – the man who made the notion of a category-mistake famous as a term of philo-sophical criticism – should have (at least occasionally) had such a firm grip on "Frege's difficult but crucial point."

38 *Foundations of Arithmetic*, op. cit., p. 71.
39 How do we find this out? What determines the logical segmentation of a sentence, for Frege, are the inferential relations which obtain between the judgment the sentence expresses and other judgments. Identifying an expression as a logical unit and deter-mining its logical role consequently turn on appreciating the inferential relations which obtain between the judgment in which the expression occurs and other judgments.
40 It has been thought by some commentators that Frege's claim that objects – unlike concepts – are "self-subsistent" should be interpreted to mean that the context prin-ciple does not apply to object-expressions: that object-expressions mean – or name – objects prior to and apart from any contribution they make to the sense of (whole) propositions. Frege explicitly repudiates such an interpretation:

> The self-subsistence which I am claiming for number is not to be taken to mean that a number word signifies something when removed from the context of a propo-sition, but only to preclude the use of such words as predicates or attributes.
>
> (*Foundations of Arithmetic*, op. cit., p. 72)

41 The only way to refer to a concept, for Frege, is to *use* a concept expression: i.e., to employ it predicatively within the context of a judgment. Thus his argument against Kerry can be rephrased as a substitutional argument. Two expressions mean the same thing (have the same *Bedeutung*) only if the new expression can be substituted for the original expression without changing the truth-value of any judgment in which the original expression occurred. Whenever we attempt, however, to substitute an object expression (such as "the concept horse") for a concept expression (such as "_____ is a horse") not only do we not get a new sentence with the same truth-value, we get nonsense. See Weiner, *Frege in Perspective*, op. cit., pp. 251ff for an excellent discussion of this point.

42 The sign that such a Fregean elucidation has been successful – that the desired "meeting of minds" between the elucidator and his audience has been achieved – is that the other person is able to go on as a user of *Begriffsschrift* on his or her own in the right way. Frege therefore has an answer to an obvious objection (voiced by some commentators on the *Tractatus*) to the doctrine that there are fundamental logical distinctions which underlie but cannot be expressed in language. The objection goes as follows: there is no way to adjudicate the success of an attempt to communicate such distinctions – for there is no way for someone who has grasped such a distinction to exhibit his mastery of the distinction. But Frege furnishes a touchstone of success: the sign that we have grasped his elucidations is that we emerge masters of his symbolism. A reader can be said to have grasped one of Frege's elucidations (for example, his elucidation of the distinction between concept and object) if he is able to employ the appropriate elements of the symbolism (the symbol for an object only if an object is denoted, etc.) when segmenting judgments and translating them from ordinary language into *Begriffsschrift*. His segmentation of the judgment can, in turn, be checked by making sure that the translation of the judgment into *Begriffsschrift* preserves the appropriate inference and substitution licenses between the judgment in question and other judgments.

43 This and related aspects of Frege's conception of elucidation are discussed in illuminating detail in the final chapter of Weiner's *Frege in Perspective*, op. cit.

44 Geach is one of the few commentators who sees a connection between this moment in Frege's work and the concerns of both the *Tractatus* and Wittgenstein's later work. (See "Philosophical Autobiography" in *Peter Geach: Philosophical Encounters*, Harry A. Lewis (ed.) Dordrecht, Kluwer, 1991, pp. 13–14, 16.) It is remarkable, with a few notable exceptions (Anscombe, Diamond, Geach, Ricketts and Weiner) how little of the secondary literature on the *Tractatus* has interested itself in this moment in Frege's thought. For a contrast between Frege (who has no use for the idea that nonsense can be illuminating) and Wittgenstein (who does have a use for the idea) which is typical of the sort of contrast between them one finds throughout the secondary literature on the *Tractatus*, see Max Black, *A Companion to Wittgenstein's Tractatus*, Ithaca, NY, Cornell University Press, pp. 378–9.

45 *The Gospel According to Tolstoy*, David Patterson (trans.) Tuscaloosa, University of Alabama Press, 1992, p. 11.

46 *Posthumous Writings*, op. cit., p. 207 (I have emended the translation).

47 Henceforth, whenever it is employed in connection with Frege, the term "elucidation" will be used only to refer to the species of elucidation at issue in "On Concept and Object." (In their original context, some of the passages from Frege's work I cite below are concerned in the first instance with the broader genus, but pertain *a fortiori* to the species, and are adduced below solely to illuminate the nature of the species.)

48 Contrary to what some commentators have claimed, this is an oft-repeated refrain in Frege's work. A list of representative passages would include: *Collected Papers*, op. cit., pp. 147, 281–2, 292 and 381, *Posthumous Writings*, op. cit., p. 235 and *Mathematical Correspondence*, G. Gabriel, H. Hermes, F. Kambontel, C. Thiel and A. Veraart (eds), H. Kaal (trans.), Chicago, Chicago University Press, 1980, pp. 37 and 141–2.

49 The word "categories" won't really do here. But, as we shall see, there is, according to Frege, no word that will do. I shall continue, throughout the rest of this paper, to

finesse this problem by pretending that talk of "logical categories" is able to possess greater referential powers than Frege thinks it can.

50 Here, again, is a list of some representative passages: *Collected Papers*, op. cit., pp. 147 and 292, *Correspondence*, op. cit., p. 37 and *Posthumous Writings*, op. cit., p. 235.

51 *Collected Papers*, op. cit., pp. 182–3.

52 Ibid., p. 183.

53 "I am well aware that expressions like 'saturated' and 'unsaturated' are metaphorical and only serve to indicate what is meant – whereby one must always count on the co-operative understanding of the reader" (ibid., pp. 281–2).

54 It is only this species of elucidation that Frege thinks compels us to traffic in nonsense. Within the broader genus of elucidation, elucidations will generally take the form of perfectly meaningful propositions (such as, for example, elucidations of *geometrically* primitive terms). It is worth noting, however, that a parallel distinction between a generic and a specific notion of elucidation must also be drawn if one seeks to understand the different occurrences of the term *Erläuterung* in the *Tractatus*. In §3.263 what is at issue is a generic notion (which I will not explore further here, other than to remark that perfectly meaningful propositions can serve as elucidations of this sort), whereas an understanding of §6.54 is unattainable apart from an understanding of what is peculiar to that species of the genus which aims to elucidate "philosophic matters" (and which proceeds through the employment of *Sätze* that the reader is to recognize as *Unsinn*). For further discussion of this issue, see "The Method of the *Tractatus*," op. cit., note 67.

55 *Collected Papers*, op. cit., pp. 300–1 (I have emended the translation).

56 *Posthumous Writings*, op. cit., p. 207 (I have emended the translation).

57 For two representative passages, see: *Collected Papers*, op. cit., pp. 300–1 and *Correspondence*, op. cit., p. 37.

58

> [W]e cannot come to an understanding with one another apart from language, and so in the end we must always rely on other people's understanding words, inflexions, and sentence-construction in essentially the same way as ourselves. As I said before, I was not trying to give a definition, but only hints; and to this end I appealed to the general feeling for the German language.
>
> (*Collected Papers*, op. cit., pp. 184–5)

59 *Culture and Value*, op. cit., p. 56.

60 *Collected Papers*, op. cit., p. 189. The final hedge here – first he says "impossible" and then "senseless" – occurs frequently in Frege's discussion of this topic and can be taken to be indicative of a profound ambivalence on his part. The ambivalence is tied to the tension the *Tractatus* discerns in Frege's thought: a tension between (a) wanting to say that there are inexpressible *thoughts* which certain forms of words attempt to express, and (b) wanting to say that the distinction between what can and what cannot be rendered in *Begriffsschrift* provides a precise logical demarcation of what is and what is not a thought (and hence that there is *no* thought expressed by forms of words which cannot be so rendered).

61 In order to avoid a possible confusion, I should remark that although I have followed the practice of translating Frege's term *sinnlos* as "senseless," I think it could equally well be rendered as "nonsense." In similar contexts, Frege sometimes employs the term *unsinnig* instead in order to make the same sort of point. Unlike Wittgenstein in the *Tractatus*, in his alternating between these terms, Frege does not have any systematic distinction in view.

62 Throughout Frege's corpus we find numerous remarks that appear to be defective in just the way he takes Kerry's remark to be – remarks in which Frege employs expressions of the form "the concept *X*" and in which he wants to put forward this or that claim either about the nature of concepts *überhaupt* or about some particular concept (most famously, for example, the concept of number). Frege seems to be committed to the claim that these remarks (in which expressions of the form "the

concept *X*" figure) have the status of elucidations. I only mean here to be pointing out a consequence of Frege's doctrines. (I am not committed to defending the claim that Frege himself faced up to this implication of his views.) See Weiner, *Frege in Perspective*, op. cit., chapter 6 for a spirited defense of the claim that Frege's doctrines do indeed have this consequence (though Weiner herself is careful to insist that the views that she thus attributes to Frege – on the grounds that they are the only views that she thinks can make sense of the relevant portions of Frege's writings – may well be views that "Frege-the-historical-person" would have disavowed).

63 *Posthumous Writings*, op. cit., pp. 177–8 (I have emended the translation). There's that hedge again: "it requires something contradictory . . . or perhaps better still . . . something nonsensical."

64 Frege actually goes so far as to argue that the terms "function" and "concept" *even when they occur predicatively* are defective (because they function in ordinary language as names of first-level functions rather than themselves ranging over first-level functions) and thus "should properly speaking be rejected":

> [T]he words "function" and "concept" should properly speaking be rejected. Logically, they should be names of second-level functions; but they present themselves linguistically as names of first-level functions. It is therefore not surprising that we run into difficulties in using them.
>
> (*Correspondence*, op. cit., pp. 141–2)

65 *Posthumous Writings*, op. cit., pp. 119–20. The claim that "concepts cannot stand in the same relations as objects" might strike one as false. What about the relation of identity, can't both concepts and objects stand in that relation? Frege thinks not:

> [T]he relation of equality between objects cannot be conceived as holding between concepts too, but . . . there is a corresponding relation for concepts. It follows that the word "the same" that is used to designate the former relation between objects cannot properly be used to designate the latter relation as well. If we try to use it to do this, the only recourse we really have is to say "the concept φ is the same as the concept X" and in saying this we have of course named a relation between objects, where what is intended is a relation between concepts.
>
> (pp. 121–2)

If by "the relation of identity" we mean a relation in which objects can stand to one another, then it is not a relation in which concepts can stand to one another. We can of course say that this object is "the same" as that one; and we can also say that this concept is "the same" as that one. But Frege thinks there is no univocal notion of "sameness" here. We are misled by the fact that in ordinary language we use the same sign to express two logically distinct kinds of relation into thinking that there is some overarching mode of relation into which both concepts and objects can enter. The difference between these two cases is rendered manifest in a proper *Begriffsschrift*: a different arrangement of signs expresses each of these distinct kinds of logical relation – in modern logical notation: $x = y$ and $(\forall x) (Fx \equiv Gx)$. There is no way in a proper *Begriffsschrift* to express the (by Frege's lights, philosophically confused) thought that these two logically distinct kinds of relation are both species of a single genus (say, the genus *ways of being the same*). An attempt to express such a (pseudo-)thought in a proper *Begriffsschrift* can help to make manifest the confusion that (its apparent expressibility in) ordinary language disguises. This is a nice example of the feature of a proper *Begriffsschrift* that interests early Wittgenstein most: its potential as a tool for making latent nonsense patent.

66 The *Tractatus* will seek to press the question: to what extent is Frege, by his own lights, entitled to look upon that which his words here intend (but fail) to express as a *thought*?

67 My emphasis; *Correspondence*, op. cit., p. 136.

68 "Something" is, again, a weasel word here. *Tractatus*, §§4.126–4.1272 rework the same sort of example which figures in Frege's correspondence with Russell:

> [W]e can speak of formal concepts. . . . I introduce the expression in order to make clear the confusion of formal concepts with proper concepts. . . . That anything falls under a formal concept as an object belonging to it, cannot be expressed by a proposition. But it is shown in the symbol for the object itself. (The name shows that it signifies an object, the numerical sign that it signifies a number, etc.)
> (§4.126)
> So the variable name "x" is the proper sign of the pseudo-concept *object*.
>   Wherever the word "object" ("thing", "entity", etc.) is rightly used, it is expressed in logical symbolism by the variable name.
>   For example in the proposition "there are two objects which . . .", by "(x,y,) . . . ."
>   Wherever it is used otherwise, i.e. as a proper concept word, there arise nonsensical pseudo-propositions.
>   So one cannot, e.g. say "There are objects" as one says "There are books". . . .
>   The same holds of the words "Complex", "Fact", "Function", "Number", etc.
>   They all signify formal concepts and are presented in logical symbolism by variables. . . .
> (§4.1272)

Wittgenstein's way of putting the point in this passage (about "X is an object") appears at first blush to parallel Frege's discussion of "X is a function": what an object is can only be "shown in the symbol for the object itself," and if we try to say what an object is by employing the word "object" as a proper concept word, then "there arise nonsensical pseudo-propositions." Thus Peter Hacker, for example, summarizes the point of the passage in a way that parallels Geach's reading of Frege: "An attempt to describe the essence of things will unavoidably violate the bounds of sense . . . and produce nonsense. . . . Thus, for example, that A is or is not an *object* cannot be said because 'object' is a formal concept" (*Insight and Illusion*, revised edn, Oxford, Oxford University Press, 1986, p. 21). On Hacker's view, "A is an object" is nonsense, but we know *what* it is trying to say and we know that "it" cannot be said.

There is this much of a disanalogy between Geach's reading of Frege and Hacker's reading of Wittgenstein: Hacker talks as if the invocation of "formal concepts" allowed for the introduction of a device for *saying* why the sentences in question are nonsense (as opposed to one which simply enables the production of more nonsense). On Geach's reading, to grasp the teaching of the *Tractatus* as a whole is to grasp why a passage such as §4.126 is nonsense. (Geach's view is nicely summarized by Anscombe's remark in her book on the *Tractatus*: "Sentences ... cannot represent, and nothing in them can stand for, 'the logic of the facts': they can only reproduce it. An attempt to say what they so reproduce leads to stammering"; *An Introduction to Wittgenstein's Tractatus*, Bristol, Thaemmes Press, 1971, p. 164.) On Hacker's reading, on the other hand, §4.126 seems to succeed in *saying* why certain subsequent passages in the book are nonsense by specifying the "it" which cannot be spoken about. But this (by Geach's lights) is to miss the point of §4.1272. If it were possible thus to refer to that which allegedly cannot be spoken about then there would be no problem about putting "it" into words. Hacker's reading threatens to leave Wittgenstein in the position of a fool – one who first says that there are these things that can't be spoken about and who then proceeds to *tell* what they are.

Hacker is untroubled by the lack of difficulty he encounters in telling us *what* it is that cannot be said, and he apparently takes Wittgenstein's introduction of the notion of formal concept to be a device designed to facilitate the telling of such things. Hacker tries to make clear what a formal concept is by saying things like "in a logically perspicuous notation it will be evident that formal concepts are expressed by variables" (op. cit., pp. 21–2). This appears to present us with a way of saying what a formal concept is: "A formal concept is what is expressed by a variable . . ." – and we can then apparently go on and add: ". . . and *that* is something which can only be shown but not said." But the question is whether the preceding sentence can, by the lights of the *Tractatus*, be informative? (But one might object: "How can what Hacker says be mistaken if he is just paraphrasing what the *Tractatus* itself says about formal concepts?" For my response to this objection, see note 99.) In order for what Hacker says to be informative, it must say something; and in order for it to say something, the expression "formal concept" must refer. Hacker evidently takes himself to refer to something when he so employs it. Similarly, when Hacker tells us that "A is or is not an *object*," we are apparently not to understand the term "object" in his employment of it to be failing to signify altogether. In so far as Hacker takes himself to be able thus to employ the terms "object" and "concept" in his explanations of the point of §§4.126 and 4.1272, he misses the point of these sections altogether.

Hacker wants to say that "object," when he employs the expression, does not signify a kind of thing; but he wants to be able to use the expression so that it can occur in propositions of a recognizable logical form – the form "X is an object." But the whole (Fregean) point of §4.1272 is that for an expression to occur in a proposition of this form is for it to refer to a kind of thing. According to the *Tractatus*, the only way for an expression to so much as try to mirror the logical feature of reality that Hacker wants the expression "object" to try (but fail) to mirror is for it to occur in the context of a proposition as (what the *Tractatus* calls) a *name*. (If Hacker were to name his cat "object" and to announce that his cat is hungry by saying "Object is hungry now" then "object" would occur, in his employment of it, as a name; but in such an employment, it would no longer even appear to furnish a device for rounding on the logical structure of language and viewing it from sideways on.) Similarly, if the term "formal concept" occurred significantly when one said "The concept *object* is a formal concept" it would be playing the logical role of a concept. Hacker may well, of course, deny he *intends* to designate a concept by "formal concept." That is, after all, not what Hacker *says* "formal concept" refers to. Hacker might try the following formulation of his point: "X is a formal concept if X refers to that which in a logically perspicuous notation is expressed by variables." But this is still to employ the term "formal concept" predicatively. Hacker may still protest: "Just forget about the logical role that the term appears to have in my use of it, damn it all! What I mean to refer to is just *that* which is represented by a variable and don't begrudge me the requisite pinch of salt!" But what is the reference of "that" here? Can a sufficiently emphatic use of the word "that" reach all the way to the "_____ which is expressed by a variable"? To think one can thus circumvent the point of §4.1272 – by accompanying one's employment of the word "that" (or "formal concept") with the requisite intention or with a sufficiently emphatic emphasis – is to play Benno Kerry to §4.1272's Frege. Hacker does, at one point, say that "formal concepts must be employed as if they were genuine concepts" (op. cit., p. 21). But this falls short of locating the true depth of the problem for the *Tractatus*: it makes it sound as if there could be something to an expression's signifying a genuine concept over and above its being "employed as if it were a genuine concept." How, in Hacker's employment of the term "formal concept," does the term play the logical role of a concept and yet manage to signify a (formal) "_____" of different logical type? Hacker's answer seems to be that it manages this by his (engaging in a psychological act of) meaning it in a certain way. (We, too, are then apparently supposed to fix its referent for ourselves by each of us going on to "mean" it in the same way for ourselves.) But to think that meaning can thus be conferred on an expression through a psychological act is precisely to refuse to credit the Fregean problematic about what it is to refer to a *Begriff* (which the *Tractatus* takes even more seriously than Frege himself did) and which forms the point of the very passages Hacker purports (on pp. 21–2 of his book) to expound. (See note 80 below for a discussion of the putative textual support for the attribution to the *Tractatus* of the view that meaning is conferred on signs via a psychological act.)

The point of the opening sentences of §4.1272 is that when the word "object" is "rightly used" (i.e., according to its *üblicher sinnvolle Gebrauch*) in ordinary language – in sentences such as, e.g., "Smith saw an object on the windowsill, about three inches high" – its use is properly "expressed in logical symbolism by the variable name" (and not, say, by a first-level concept with an enormous extension). The philosophical "use" of the word, nicely exemplified by Hacker's discussion, hovers between (1) wanting it to have the kind of logical significance it has when it is thus ("rightly") used (and symbolizes a variable), and, at the same time, (2) wanting it to have the logical significance of a concept-expression (which symbolizes a *Begriff*). Such wavering gives rise to (what Wittgenstein calls) a *Scheinbegriff* – an expression employed predicatively to mean something other than a *Begriff* (thereby failing to mean anything at all.) Wittgenstein says he introduces his pseudo-notion of a formal concept in order "to make clear the confusion" involved in thinking that one can employ a term such as "object" as if it were a "genuine concept" [*eigentlicher Begriff*] (§4.126). The point of Wittgenstein's introduction of the notion of a formal concept would then be "to make clear the confusion" involved in thinking that a so-called "formal concept" is a special kind of "genuine concept" [*eigentlicher Begriff*]. The term "formal concept" in Wittgenstein's employment of it – like the term "object" in Hacker's employment of it – is an example of a term that only apparently refers to an *eigentlicher Begriff*. This is not to say that it refers to an *uneigentlicher Begriff*. It is to say that it does not refer. What the *Tractatus* calls an *uneigentlicher Begriff* or a *Scheinbegriff* is not a special (unsayable) kind of concept – "a non-genuine one." It is a sign masquerading as a symbol for a concept. It is not a kind of concept at all, any more (to borrow an analogy of Frege's from *Posthumous Writings*, op. cit., p. 130) than stage-thunder is a kind of thunder. The same holds equally for what the *Tractatus* calls *Scheinsätze*: they are not a species of the genus *proposition* (e.g., ones that "violate the bounds of sense") – but rather strings of signs which we are prone to mistake for propositions. The goal of the *Tractatus* is to enable us to recognize such signs for what they are.

Returning to the parallel between Geach's and Hacker's readings – the focal question for the remainder of this paper will be the following: is it the *Tractatus*'s view that "*unsinnige* pseudo-propositions" arise (when, e.g., we attempt to employ the word "object" as a concept word) because we "violate the bounds of sense" and try to say what "cannot be said"? It depends on what the *Tractatus*'s conception of *Unsinn* is; and whether it squares with the one which readers such as Geach find in Frege. If the *Tractatus* holds to an austere conception of nonsense, then the ultimate aim of elucidation (of, e.g., sentences in which so-called "formal concepts" figure) will be to lead us one step past the point where an elucidation of the sort which Geach finds in Frege leaves us (at which we imagine we glimpse the unsayable thing our words attempt to mean) to the point where our conviction that we understand what a sentence such as "A is an object" is even attempting to say completely dissolves on us (and all we are left with is a string of words in which we are no longer able to discern even an abortive attempt to mean something).

69 *Collected Papers*, op. cit., p. 193.
70 I hear a reader grumbling: "What about *Russell*? Isn't the *Tractatus* as much a response to Russell as to Frege?" Of course. But the relation to Frege is more instructive for seeing how the *Tractatus* is (and especially for seeing how it is *not*) to be read – for seeing, that is, what the *method* of the *Tractatus* is. I have thus confined myself in this paper to showing how the problematic of the *Tractatus* develops out of Frege's work. See, however, note 83 of "The Method of the *Tractatus*," op. cit., for a discussion of a line of filiation between Russell's work and the *Tractatus* parallel to the one sketched in this paper which runs from Frege to the *Tractatus*.
71 *Philosophical Investigations*, §374.
72 As, for example, in §51 of *The Foundations of Arithmetic*, op. cit.:

> With a concept the question is always whether anything, and if so what, falls under it. With a proper name such questions make no sense. We should not be deceived by the fact that language makes use of proper names, for instance Moon, as concept words, and vice versa; this does not affect the distinction between the two.
>
> (p. 64)

73 *Collected Papers*, op. cit., p. 189.

74 It is worth noting that on this point Frege's views, contrary to standard accounts, do not conflict with those of later Wittgenstein on ordinary language. Indeed, they importantly anticipate a recurring theme in later Wittgenstein: namely, that in ordinary language we are constantly extending the uses of our words and thereby creating new possibilities of meaning for them. Frege and Wittgenstein are in agreement that the expressions of ordinary language can be – and indeed constantly are – used in logically (later Wittgenstein prefers to say: grammatically) unprecedented yet perfectly intelligible ways; and that for all sorts of bizarre forms of words for which there is at present no language-game, we can dream up a context (in Wittgenstein's later idiom: find a language-game) in which we would be drawn without loss of intelligibility to call upon that particular form of words.

75 This is not to say that, in general, any proposal which yields a possible segmentation of a string is equally tenable. In real life cases of interpretation, we are obliged, on the one hand, to make sense of the way a sentence occurs within a larger stretch of discourse. ("Understanding without contextuality is blind.") To commit oneself to a segmentation of the string, on the other hand, is to commit oneself to patterns of inference which are a function of how these words (of which the string is composed) occur in other propositions. ("Understanding without compositionality is empty.") The attribution of the endorsement of inferences of certain patterns to a speaker is governed by those considerations of charity and relevance which govern all aspects of interpretation. These considerations generally uniquely determine a segmentation (and, if not, at least severely constrain the range of reasonable proposals).

76 For purposes of simplifying the exposition, I have restricted my definition to (what the *Tractatus* calls) "written signs" – the *Tractatus* explicitly allows for "sound signs" (see §3.321) and implicitly for other sorts.

77 My self-defeating exposition of the alleged distinction between the two variants of the substantial conception mirrors, albeit in a highly summary fashion, the first half of the elucidatory strategy of the *Tractatus*. Half of the central point of the *Tractatus,* on my reading, is to show that once one has bought into the substantial conception one has implicitly committed oneself to a conception on which there are ineffable thoughts – thoughts which we can gesture at (with the aid of nonsensical language) but cannot express in language. (A central part of the interest of Frege's work for Wittgenstein, as he reads him, is that Frege recognized and drew this consequence.) The second half of the point of the work is to show that the way to escape this consequence is to abandon the substantial conception of nonsense altogether (not, according to Wittgenstein, an easy thing to do). As will become clear, my exposition of the alleged distinction between the substantial and austere conceptions of nonsense aims to mirror, in equally summary fashion, this second (and largely unnoticed) half of the elucidatory strategy of the *Tractatus*.

78 To anticipate: the *Tractatus* is not concerned to argue that there are *no* ways to distinguish between kinds of nonsense – or even that there is no distinction to be drawn in the neighborhood of the distinction sought by the proponent of the substantial conception (i.e., one which marks off cases of "philosophical" nonsense from (other) cases of mere nonsense) – but only that there are no *logically* distinct kinds of nonsense (or more precisely: that talk of "logically distinct kinds of nonsense" is itself to be recognized as (mere) nonsense). The coherence of the entire procedure of the work, indeed, rests upon the assumption that there *is* a distinction to be drawn in the neighborhood of the distinction sought by the proponent of the substantial conception; but, as we shall see, the *Tractatus* takes it to turn on *psychologically* distinct kinds of nonsense.

79 I say "reformulation of Frege's second principle" (rather than restatement of it) because the *Tractatus* is concerned to refashion Frege's distinction between *Sinn* and *Bedeutung*. §3.3 is worded as it is precisely in order to mark a departure from Frege in this regard. Just what sort of departure from Frege is here being marked, however, is far less clear (at least to me). In Friedrich Waismann's *Thesen* (which is his attempt to furnish the members of the Vienna Circle with an overview of the main ideas of the *Tractatus*,

based on detailed conversations with Wittgenstein), we find the following: "A proposition has *Sinn*, a word has *Bedeutung*" (*Wittgenstein and the Vienna Circle*). Enigmatic as that may seem, it is straightforward compared to anything to be found anywhere in the *Tractatus* itself on the subject. §3.3 (along with §3.144) does appear to seek to exclude the applicability of *Sinn* to any kind of symbol other than a *Satz*. When read in the light of §3.3, a number of earlier passages (§§3.142, 3.144, 3.203, 3.22) also appear to be worded in a manner suggesting that the overall doctrine of the work indeed is that (at least) *names* – i.e., the constituent parts of a fully analyzed sentence – do not have *Sinn*. The corresponding principle in regard to *Bedeutung* does not obviously hold, however: the application of *Bedeutung* in the *Tractatus* does not appear to be restricted (as the passage from Waismann's *Thesen* might seem to imply) to the sub-judgmental components of propositions. Throughout the *Tractatus*, the term "*Bedeutung*" is employed in a (relatively non-technical) manner so as to suggest that any sign (including a *Satz*, i.e., a propositional sign) with a determinate linguistic function can be said to have a *Bedeutung* (see, e.g., §5.451 for the claim that the negation sign has a *Bedeutung*), and, as such, are to be contrasted only with signs which have no *Bedeutung* or (as the *Tractatus* prefers to say) with signs to which no *Bedeutung* has been given (see, e.g., §§5.4733, 6.53). What *Tractatus*, §3.3 is concerned to withhold endorsement from is – not the bare idea that *Sätze* can be said to have *Bedeutungen*, but rather – "Frege's theory of the *Bedeutung* of *Sätze* and *Funktionen*" (§5.02), i.e., Frege's assimilation of sentences and functions to the category of proper names (and especially his doctrine that the *truth value* of a sentence is its *Bedeutung*). For useful discussion touching on this extraordinarily obscure region of the *Tractatus*, see Cora Diamond's "Inheriting from Frege" (forthcoming in *The Cambridge Companion to Frege*, T. Ricketts (ed.) Cambridge, Cambridge University Press) and Peter Hylton's "Functions, Operations and Sense in Wittgenstein's *Tractatus*" in *Early Analytic Philosophy*, W.W. Tait (ed.) Chicago, Open Court, 1997).

80 A number of commentators have attributed to the *Tractatus* the view that a special mental act (of intending to mean a particular object by a particular word) is what endows a name with meaning (see, e.g., Hacker, *Insight and Illusion*, op. cit., pp. 73–80; Black, *A Companion to Wittgenstein's Tractatus*, op. cit., pp. 114–22; Norman Malcolm, *Wittgenstein: Nothing is Hidden*, Oxford, Basil Blackwell, 1986, pp. 63–82). If textual support for this attribution is adduced at all, it is usually through appeal to texts outside of the *Tractatus* – usually passages from *Notebooks: 1914–16*; e.g., pp. 33–4, 99, 129–30, or corresponding passages from Wittgenstein's correspondence with Russell. (When a passage from the *Tractatus* is adduced it has to be supplemented by a song and dance which purports to explain how it is supposed to support the attribution.) According to these commentators, the *Tractatus* holds that the connection between a name and its meaning can only be fixed by such a mental act: it is this act which confers upon the word the power to signify the object one has in mind. To think that one can fix the meanings of names by means of such an act just is to think that one can fix their meanings prior to and independently of their use in propositions; and it is just this psychologistic conception of meaning that Frege's and early Wittgenstein's respective versions of a context principle are concerned to repudiate.

There is no reference anywhere in the *Tractatus* to a distinct *act* of meaning (through which a *Bedeutung* is conferred on a sign). The passage from the *Tractatus* most commonly adduced to provide a semblance of textual support for this psychologistic attribution is §3.11 which Pears and McGuinness translate as follows: "The method of projection is to think of the sense of the proposition." So translated, this remark can be taken to refer to an act of thinking and to ascribe an explanatory role to such an act. The Ogden translation is more faithful: "The method of projection is the thinking of the sense of the proposition." Rush Rhees glosses this (quite properly, I think) as: "The method of projection is what we *mean* by 'thinking' or 'understanding' the sense of the proposition." Rhees comments: "Pears and McGuinness read it [i.e., §3.11] . . . as though the remark were to explain the expression 'method of projection'. . . .

[On the contrary], 'projection', which is a logical operation, is ... to explain '*das Denken des Satz-Sinnes*'. The '*ist*' after '*Projecktionsmethode*' might have been italicized" (*Discussions of Wittgenstein*, London, Routledge and Kegan Paul, 1970, p. 39). Rhees's point here is that the last sentence of §3.11 has the same structure as, e.g., the last sentence of §3.316: the *explanans* is on the left and the *explanandum* on the right – not the other way around as the psychologistic interpretation supposes. I believe – but I cannot go into detail at this point – that the subsequent passages of the *Tractatus* (as well as *Notebooks*, pp. 20, 41) clearly bear this reading out. (Acknowledging the justice of Rhees's criticism, and finding it more natural in English to place the *explanandum* on the left, McGuinness later recanted his and Pears's original translation of §3.11 and proposed the following translation instead: "Thinking the sense of the proposition is the method of projection." McGuinness goes on to offer the following lucid summary of the actual point of the passage: "Thinking the sense into the proposition is nothing other than so using the words of the sentence that their logical behaviour *is* that of the desired proposition" ("On the So-called Realism of the *Tractatus*" in *Perspectives on the Philosophy of Wittgenstein*, I. Block (ed.) Cambridge, Mass., MIT Press, 1981, pp. 69–70).) The point being made at this point in the work about "thinking" is an illustration of a general feature of Wittgenstein's method. What the *Tractatus* does throughout is explicate putatively psychological *explananda* in terms of logical *explanantes*. The Malcolm/Black/Hacker reading of §3.11 takes Wittgenstein to be explaining one of the central logical notions of the book in terms of a psychological notion, thus utterly missing the way Wittgenstein here takes himself to be elaborating and building upon Frege's first two principles.

For further discussion of this point, see note 115 of "The Method of the *Tractatus*," op. cit.

81 Although the notion of *Satz* which figures in the context principle (only the *Satz* has sense; only in the context of a *Satz* has a name meaning) is of a certain kind of a symbol, the term "*Satz*" in the *Tractatus* floats between meaning (1) a propositional symbol (as, e.g., in §§3.3ff and §§4ff) and (2) a propositional sign (as, e.g., in §§5.473 and §6.54). It is important to the method of the *Tractatus* that the recognition that certain apparent cases of (1) are merely cases of (2) be a recognition that the reader achieve on his own. Consequently, at certain junctures, the method of the *Tractatus* requires that the reference of *Satz* remain provisionally neutral as between (1) and (2). At the corresponding junctures in my own discussion, I leave *Satz* untranslated.

82 A version of this distinction (between sign [*Zeichen*] and symbol [*Symbol*]) is implicit in Frege's work; for example, in his "Introduction to Logic," Frege writes:

> The same thought cannot be true at one time, false at another. ... [T]he reason ... [people] believe the thought to be the same is that in such cases what is the same is the form of words; the form of words [which is said to be both true and false] will then be a counterfeit (non-genuine) proposition [*wird dann ein uneigentlicher Satz sein*]. We do not always adequately distinguish the sign [*Zeichen*] from what it expresses.
>
> (*Posthumous Writings*, op. cit., p. 186 – I have emended the translation)

Wittgenstein's notion of an expression or symbol (that which is common to a set of propositions) – as opposed to a sign (that which is common to, what Frege here calls, forms of words) – builds on Frege's idea that what determine the logical segmentation of a sentence are the inferential relations which obtain between the judgment that sentence expresses and other judgments. *Language* [*Sprache*] is Wittgenstein's term for the totality of such propositional symbols; and *logical space* is his term for the resulting overall network of inferential relations within which each proposition has its life. §§4–4.001 build on the notion of *Satz* developed in §§3.31ff ("The thought is the *sinnvolle* proposition. The totality of propositions is the language"). *Language* [*Sprache*] in the *Tractatus* refers to the totality of *possible* propositional symbols. One might think of this as Wittgenstein's attempting to follow Frege's example (in his exchange with Kerry about concepts) by "keeping to the strictly logical use" of the word "language." It is trivially true, if one applies this idiom, that *there is only one language* – though there are, of course, countless alternative systems of signs which may differ widely in their respective expressive powers.

83 The ensuing exposition of this example only really works if we assume all the letters of the sentence to be capitalized so that we have no orthographic clues as to when the expression "GREEN" is being used as the proper name of a person and when as a concept-expression.

84 The sequence of (a), (b) and (c) nicely brings out a further asymmetry between sign and symbol. In the rendition of (b) into logical notation, we might think of the sign "=" as corresponding to the sign "is" in the ordinary language version of (b); that is, we might think of these two signs ("=," "is") as symbolizing the same relation (the relation of identity). But in the rendition of (a) into logical notation, there is no candidate for a sign that corresponds to "is" – there is here nothing which is *the* sign which symbolizes the copula. The *Tractatus* draws five morals from this: (M1) a method of symbolizing is not simply a matter of a sign *naming* an item of a particular logical category, (M2) a symbol is expressed not simply through a sign but through *a mode of arrangement* of signs, (M3) not every logically significant aspect of a mode of arrangement of signs corresponds to an argument place (into which a different sign can be substituted), (M4) it is not the case that each method of symbolizing requires the employment of a distinct sign to express the method of symbolizing (a method of symbolizing can be expressed through a mode of arrangement of signs, such as the method of symbolizing the copula in modern logical notation), (M5) for certain methods of symbolizing the employment of a distinct sign is required.

(M4) is of great importance. The *Tractatus* distinguishes between kinds of symbol by distinguishing degrees of "dispensibility" of signs for different kinds of symbol. The degree of the "dispensibility" of a sign depends on how easy it is to express the symbolic function of the sign while making the sign itself (as the *Tractatus* puts it) "disappear." (My appreciation of the importance of this point for the *Tractatus* is indebted to discussion with Michael Kremer.) (M4) sets up two further doctrines which play a central role in the *Tractatus*: (i) that any sign which symbolizes a *relation* can in principle be dispensed with and expressed instead through a mode of arrangement of signs (§§3.1431–3.1432), (ii) that this shows us something about such symbols: they are not (in the Tractarian sense) *names* (§§3.1432–3.22). For further discussion of these issues, see "The Method of the *Tractatus*," op. cit., note 119.

85 This is not to claim that it is possible to understand a sentence, if *none* of its constituent signs symbolize in the same manner in which they symbolize in other sentences. (Hence *Tractatus*, §4.03: "A proposition must use old expressions to communicate new senses.") It is only to claim that not *all* of the constituent signs must symbolize in a precedented fashion. But an unprecedented usage of a sign will only be intelligible if the constituent signs which symbolize in the "old" manner determine a possible segmentation of the propositional sign – where such a segmentation specifies both (i) the logical role of the sign which symbolizes in an unprecedented manner and (ii) the position of the resulting propositional symbol in logical space.

86 One standard way of contrasting early and later Wittgenstein is to say that later Wittgenstein rejected his earlier (allegedly truth-conditional) account of meaning – on which considerations of use have no role to play in fixing the meaning of an expression – in favor of (what gets called) "a use-theory of meaning." Our brief examination of §3.326 should already make one wary of such a story. The popularity of this story rests largely on an additional piece of potted history, according to which the *Tractatus* advances the doctrine that it is possible (and indeed, according to most readings, semantically necessary) to fix the meanings of names prior to and independently of their use in propositions (either through ostensive definition or through some special mental act which endows a name with meaning; see note 80). This putative teaching of the *Tractatus* is standardly taken to be the primary target of the opening sections of *Philosophical Investigations*. But the whole point of §§3.3–3.344 of the *Tractatus* is that

the identity of the object referred to by a name is only fixed by the use of the name in a set of significant [*sinnvolle*] propositions. An appeal to use thus already plays a critical role in Wittgenstein's early account of what determines both the meaning of a proposition as a whole and the meanings of each of its "parts." With respect to this topic, the opening sections of *Philosophical Investigations* is properly seen as recasting and extending a critique of Russellian doctrines already begun in the *Tractatus*.

87 In the absence of any familiarity with the way words (signs) ordinarily occur (symbolize) in propositions, we would have no basis upon which to fashion possible segmentations of propositional signs, and hence no way to *recognize* (rather than simply fantasize) the symbol in the sign. (This is the situation we find ourselves in when faced with a sentence of a language which we do not know and which does not in the least resemble any which we do know.)

88 *Erkennen* can also be translated "perceive." I will occasionally favor this translation.

89 Both the positivist and ineffability readings of the *Tractatus* require that these two forms of recognition be mutually compatible: that we be able to recognize the symbol in the sign *and* that we recognize his propositions as nonsensical (because the symbols clash with one another).

90 We can now begin to see how misleading the standard attribution to early Wittgenstein of (what gets called) a "logical atomist theory of meaning" is. It is just such a theory that is under indictment in passages such as §§3.3, 3.314, 3.341, 3.344. Gilbert Ryle noticed that already early Wittgenstein (building on Frege) had been concerned to attack Russell's atomism; and he offered a rather eloquent summary of Wittgenstein's criticisms of an atomistic theory of meaning:

> It was ... Wittgenstein who, developing arguments of Frege, showed that the sense of a sentence is not, what had hitherto been tacitly assumed, a whole of which the meanings of the words in it are independently thinkable parts but, on the contrary, that the meanings of the parts of a sentence are abstractible differences and similarities between the unitary sense of that sentence and the unitary senses of other sentences which have something but not everything in common with that given sentence. To put it in epistemological terms, we do not begin with the possession of concepts and then go on to coagulate them into thoughts. We begin and end with thoughts, and by comparative analysis we can discriminate ways in which something is constant *vis à vis* what else is varied between different unitary things we think. ... [A]n assertion is not a molecule of which the meanings of the words in which it is worded are the atoms. . . . Concepts are not things that are there crystallized in splendid isolation; they are discriminable features, but not detachable atoms, of what is integrally said or integrally thought. They are not detachable parts of, but distinguishable contributions to, the unitary senses of completed sentences. To examine them is to examine the live force of things we actually say. It is to examine them not in retirement, but doing their co-operative work.
>
> (*Collected Papers*, vol. 1, op. cit., pp. 184–5)

Aside from a few notable exceptions (such as Cora Diamond, Hidé Ishiguro and Anthony Palmer), no one writing on the *Tractatus* over the subsequent several decades seems to have either noticed early Wittgenstein's repudiation of an atomist theory of meaning or noticed that Ryle noticed it. Some commentators have, however, noticed something which is intimately related to what Ryle noticed: namely, that the notion of an "object" is developed in the *Tractatus* with the aim of undercutting the *ontological* doctrines of logical atomism. See `Brian McGuinness's "On the So-called Realism of the *Tractatus*," op. cit.; Tom Ricketts's "Pictures, Logic, and the Limits of Sense in the *Tractatus*' in *The Cambridge Companion to Wittgenstein*, Hans Sluga and David Stern (eds) Cambridge, Cambridge University Press, 1996 and Warren Goldfarb's "Objects, Names and Realism in the *Tractatus*" (unpublished).

91 In order to count as *sinnvoll* a *Satz* has to be able to serve as a vehicle of *communication*: it has to make a *statement* about how things are – it has to *assert* what is the

case [*der sinnvolle Satz sagt etwas aus*] (§6.1264). Such a *Satz* is characterized by both a form [*Form*] and a content [*Inhalt*] (§3.31). A *Satz* which is *sinnlos* possesses a (logical) form but no content. *Unsinn*, on the other hand, possesses neither a form nor a content.

For a *Satz* to be contentful [*gehaltvoll*] – to bear on how things are – there has to be room for a distinction between what would make it true and what would make it false. Its truth is determined by (consulting) whether things are in accordance with what it asserts. A *Satz* which is *sinnlos* does not make a claim on reality; it has no bearing on how things are. There is no need to consult how things stand in order to determine its truth value – mere "inspection of the sign" is sufficient to determine its truth value. The *Tractatus* therefore distinguishes between the broader genus of *Sätze* (*sinnlos* or *sinnvoll*) characterized by a logical form (i.e., in which we can recognize the symbol in the sign) and the narrower genus of (genuine [*eigentliche*]) *Sätze*. The latter sort of *Satz* asserts "This is how things stand" ["*Es verhält sich so und so*"] and thus is characterized by "the general form of a proposition" (cf. §4.5) – where this latter phrase should be understood to mean: "the general form of a *genuine* proposition." In saying that a "proposition" of logic is *sinnlos*, the *Tractatus* is identifying it as belonging to a degenerate species (or "limiting case," cf. §4.466) of the genus proposition – it has the logical form of a proposition without its being *gehaltvoll* (§6.111): "the representational relations it subtends cancel one another out, so that it does not stand in any representational relation to reality" (§4.462).

To say of a *Satz* (a propositional sign) that it is *Unsinn* is to say that it is a mere sign: no determinate method of symbolizing has yet been conferred on it. Whereas to say of it that it is *sinnlos* is to affirm that a method of symbolizing has been conferred on it, but that the method of symbolizing in question fails to yield a proper proposition. A *Satz* which is *sinnlos* is unlike a genuine proposition (and like *Unsinn*), in that it fails to express a thought (it does not restrict reality to a yes or no and hence does not represent a state of affairs): it says *nothing*. Yet it is like a genuine proposition (and unlike *Unsinn*), in that we are able to recognize the symbol in the sign and hence are able to express it in a *Begriffsschrift* – it forms, as the *Tractatus* puts it, "part of the symbolism" (§4.4611). Thus what logic is, for the *Tractatus*, is internal *to* what it is to say something; and hence which *Sätze* are logical *Sätze* (and thus form part of the symbolism) only shows itself [*zeigt sich*] *in* language – that is, in the meaningful employment we already make of (what the *Tractatus* calls) "our everyday language" [*unsere Umgangssprache*].

According to a widely accepted reading of the *Tractatus*, the so-called "propositions" of logic represent a set of *a priori* "conditions on the possibility of thought" – a set of *requirements* laid down in advance on what can and cannot be said. Yet it is, in fact, just such a Fregean/Russellian conception of the "substantiality" of logic which is under indictment in the *Tractatus* on the grounds that (i) the so-called "truths of logic" are not only not *prior* to, but rather parasitic on ordinary garden-variety truths, (ii) logic therefore cannot be abstracted from language so as to form a body of *independently* thinkable or assertable truths, (iii) the "propositions" of logic (because they are void of content [*inhaltsleer*]) cannot be construed as forming a body of *truths* at all (let alone, as Frege and early Russell would have it, a body of maximally general truths), and (iv) (because they say nothing) they cannot *require* anything and hence cannot be construed as "laws of thought," so (v) there is no (Fregean/Russellian) *science* of logic. For more on (iii)–(v), see my "The Search for Logically Alien Thought," op. cit.

92 *The Point of View for My Work as an Author* (my translation), Part Two, chapter 1.
93 Note: everything I have said so far in this paragraph – understood in the appropriate way – is perfectly consistent with an "austere" reading of Frege (such as that offered by Cora Diamond).
94 *Collected Papers*, op. cit., p. 156.
95 Except that proponents of the ineffability interpretation of the *Tractatus* pretend, unlike Geach, to be able to see how to go on and adapt the guiding idea of this interpretation – i.e., that attempts to formulate propositions which violate the logical structure

of language are able to convey insights into *logical* features of reality – so that it extends to the possibility of conveying additional insights into other apparently quite different, yet equally ineffable (usually ethical, aesthetic and/or religious) features of reality.

96 *Philosophical Remarks*, §6. Or to put the same point differently: it aims to show us that we cannot use language as proponents of the ineffability interpretation assume Wittgenstein supposes we can. For example, Peter Hacker, as we saw in note 68, takes §§4.126 and 4.1272 of the *Tractatus* to be concerned with showing how a certain sort of attempt to "violate the bounds of sense" – in the case in question, the violation (allegedly) incurred by a certain employment of the expression "object" – enables us to hint at something which cannot be said. Hacker and I agree that these sections of the *Tractatus* do not succeed in *saying* anything. But Hacker takes these passages of the book to be *trying* to say what can not be said but only "shown." He implicitly attributes to the *Tractatus* the doctrines (a) that there is something which is a piece of nonsense's trying but failing to say something, and (b) that there is something which can count as one's knowing what the nonsense in question would be saying if it were something which could be said. Thus, on Hacker's interpretation, the whole point of the book is to show us how to employ language (or at least language-like structures) to get outside language (to what cannot be said but only "shown"). On my interpretation, the whole point of the *Tractatus* is – not to get us to see the truth of (a) and (b), but rather – to get us to see that (a) and (b) rest upon the (only apparently intelligible) notion that nonsense can so much as try to say something.

97 I am here borrowing a phrase of John McDowell's; see his *Mind and World*, Cambridge, Mass., Harvard University Press, 1994 and "Non-cognitivism and Rule-following," reprinted in this volume.

98 See, for example, *Philosophical Investigations*, §464.

99 *Manuscript 110* of Wittgenstein's *Handschriftlicher Nachlass*, p. 239 (quoted by David Stern in *Wittgenstein on Mind and Language*, Oxford, Oxford University Press, 1995, p. 194). When the aim of a work is "to place an illusion before one's eyes," the task of offering an exegesis of the work becomes a delicate one. Much of what proponents of the ineffability interpretation write often amounts to little more than a paraphrase of things Wittgenstein himself (apparently) says in the *Tractatus*. How can a commentator who furnishes us with a seemingly faithful paraphrase of Wittgenstein's own words be leading himself or his readers astray as to the point of the passage in question? Well, it depends on the sort of use to which one wants to put such a paraphrase. It depends on whether the paraphrase is adduced as a transitional remark (whose sense is subsequently to be queried) or as an *explanation* of the meaning of the passage. What is it to exemplify an understanding of the point of those passages from the *Tractatus* which the reader is to recognize as *Unsinn*? Here are two possible answers: (i) one exemplifies one's understanding of the passages in question through a faithful paraphrase of them, where what one says makes explicit what these passages (are at least trying to) say; (ii) one exemplifies one's understanding of the passages in question by bringing out how they are to serve as expressions of philosophical temptations which are eventually to be recognized as *Unsinn* and to be thrown away. (i) is quite properly presupposed in most expositions of most philosophical works; but to presuppose (i) in an exposition of the point of the relevant passages from the *Tractatus* is inevitably to fall into the very confusions which the passages in question seek to expose. An undue confidence on the part of a commentator in the reliability of paraphrase as a method of explicating the point of a passage will lead to a complete missing of its point if the point is to carry the reader along a movement of thought which culminates in an undermining of its credentials as thought (if it is latent nonsense which is to be recognized as patent nonsense). To think that one can faithfully exhibit an understanding of those passages of the *Tractatus* which are to be recognized by the reader as *Unsinn* by offering (what one takes to be) a faithful paraphrase of them is to fail (to do what §6.54 calls upon the reader to do: namely) to understand the author of the book and the character of the project of elucidation in which he is engaged.

100

> The book will, therefore, draw a limit . . . not to thinking, but to the expression of thoughts; for, in order to draw a limit to thinking we should have to be able to think both sides of this limit (we should therefore have to be able to think what cannot be thought).
>
> (*Tractatus*, Preface)

101 "The limit can, therefore, only be drawn in language and what lies on the other side of the limit will be *simply nonsense*" (my emphasis) (ibid.).

102 In §6.54, Wittgenstein draws the reader's attention to a kind of employment of linguistic signs which occurs within the body of the work. Commentators fail to notice that what Wittgenstein says in §6.54 is not: "*all* of my sentences are nonsensical" (thus giving rise to the self-defeating problematic Geach has nicely dubbed *Ludwig's Self-mate*). §6.54 characterizes the way in which those of his propositions which serve as elucidations elucidate. He says: "my sentences serve as elucidations in the following way: he who understands me recognizes them as nonsensical"; or better still – to quote from the English translation of §6.54 that Wittgenstein himself proposed to Ogden: "my propositions elucidate – *whatever they do elucidate* – in this way, he who understands me recognizes them as nonsensical" (*Letters to C.K. Ogden*, op. cit., p. 51). The aim of the passage is (*not* to propose a single all-encompassing category into which the diverse sorts of propositions which comprise the work are all to be shoehorned, but rather) to explicate how those passages of the work which succeed in bearing its elucidatory burden are meant to work their medicine on the reader.

Question: *which* sentences are (to be recognized as) nonsensical? Answer: those that elucidate. §4.112 does not say: "A philosophical work consists *entirely* of elucidations." It says: "A philosophical work consists *essentially* of elucidations." Not every sentence of the work is (to be recognized as) nonsense. For not every sentence serves as an elucidation. Some sentences subserve the elucidatory aim of the work by providing the framework within which the activity of elucidation takes place. Some of them do this by saying things about the work as a whole (and offering instructions for how the work is be read); others by saying things with the aim of helping us to see what is going on in some part of the work (i.e., within a particular stretch of elucidation). Many of the sections of the *Tractatus* to which this paper has devoted most attention – e.g., the Preface, §§3.32–3.326, 4–4.003, 4.111–4.112, 6.53–6.54 – belong to the frame of the work and are only able to impart their instructions concerning the nature of the elucidatory aim and method of the work if recognized as *sinnvoll*. (Indeed, what I have just done in this endnote is offer a partial explanation of what §4.112 and §6.54 *say*.)

Question: what determines whether a remark belongs to the *frame* of the work (preparing the way for those remarks which do serve as elucidations) or to the (elucidatory) *body* of the work? Answer: its role within the work. The distinction between what is part of the frame and what is part of the body of the work is not, as some commentators have thought, simply a function of *where* in the work a remark occurs (say, near the beginning or the end of the book). Rather, it is a function of *how* it occurs.

Question: how are we to tell *this*? What criteria govern whether a given remark is *Unsinn* or not? This question presupposes that certain strings of signs are intrinsically either cases of *Unsinn* or cases of *Sinn*. But the *Tractatus* teaches that this depends on us: on our managing (or failing) to perceive [*erkennen*] a symbol in the sign. There can be no fixed answer to the question what kind of work a given remark within the text accomplishes. It will depend on the kind of sense a reader of the text will (be tempted to) make of it. Many of the remarks are carefully designed to tempt a reader to find a (substantially) "nonsensical sense" in them. In order to ascend the ladder a reader must yield to (at least some of) these temptations.

Certain remarks in the *Tractatus* can be seen to have a triple-aspect structure: liable to flip-flop between (1) (apparently) substantial nonsense, (2) mere *Sinn*, and (3) (what the *Tractatus* calls) *Unsinn* – i.e., between (1) a remark in which the reader (imagines she) is able to perceive a symbol in each sign but is unable to attach *Sinn* to the resulting combination, (2) a remark in which the reader is able to perceive a logically unproblematic proposition in the propositional sign, and (3) a remark in which the reader perceives [*erkennt*] a mere string of signs upon which no determinate method of symbolizing has been conferred. Some remarks – including the final remark (read, e.g., as the tautology: "We must be silent [i.e., say nothing] where there is nothing to say" – can present yet a fourth aspect: that of *Sinnlosigkeit*. What sort of foothold(s) a given remark provide(s) a given reader in her progress up the ladder thus depend(s) upon the sort(s) of aspect it presents to her, and that will depend on *her* – on the use(s) to which she is drawn to put it in the course of her ascent.

103 This paper has been gestating for so long that it has become difficult to keep track of everyone who has helped to shape it. It is indebted to conversations with Stanley Cavell, Piergiorgio Donatelli, David Finkelstein, John Haugeland, Michael Kremer, John McDowell, Hilary Putnam and Ed Witherspoon; to work on Frege by Bob Brandom, Peter Geach, Tom Ricketts and Joan Weiner; to Peter Hylton's work on Russell, and to Lynette Reid's work on Wittgenstein; to a Pitt graduate seminar I co-taught with Jamie Tappenden; to a session in which a portion of this paper was discussed at the University of Pittsburgh Department of Philosophy Faculty Colloquium; and to comments on earlier drafts by Alice Crary, Peter Hacker, Kelly Dean Jolley, Diego Marconi, Stephen Mulhall, Martin Stone, Michael Thompson, Lisa Van Alstyne and Peter Winch. My most pervasive debt is to Cora Diamond with whom – at some point or other over the past thirteen years – I have discussed every aspect of it. This paper is dedicated to the memory of Peter Winch at whose request it was originally written, at whose instigation it was revised, and to whom, now that it is done, it cannot be sent.

9

RETHINKING MATHEMATICAL NECESSITY

Hilary Putnam

We had been trying to make sense of the role of convention in *a priori* knowledge. Now the very distinction between *a priori* and empirical begins to waver and dissolve, at least as a distinction between sentences. (It could of course still hold as a distinction between factors in one's adoption of a sentence, but both factors might be operative everywhere.)[1]

A consequence of Quine's celebrated critique of the analytic-synthetic distinction – a consequence drawn by Quine himself – is that the existence of mathematical entities is to be justified in the way in which one justifies the postulation of theoretical entities in physics. As Quine himself once put it,[2]

> Certain things we want to say in science may compel us to admit into the range of variables of quantification not only physical objects but also classes and relations of them; also numbers, functions, and other objects of pure mathematics. For mathematics – not uninterpreted mathematics, but genuine set theory, logic, number theory, algebra of real and complex numbers, and so on – is best looked upon as an integral part of science, on a par with the physics, economics, etc. in which mathematics is said to receive its applications.

As I read this and similar passages in Quine's writings, the message seems to be that in the last analysis it is the utility of statements about mathematical entities for the prediction of sensory stimuli that justifies belief in their existence. The existence of numbers or sets becomes a hypothesis on Quine's view, one not dissimilar in kind from the existence of electrons, even if far, far better entrenched.

It follows from this view that certain questions that can be raised about the existence of physical entities can also be raised about the existence of mathematical entities – questions of indispensability and questions of parsimony, in particular. These views of Quine's are views that I shared ever since I was a student (for a year) at Harvard in 1948–49, but, I must confess, they are views that I now want to criticize. First, however, I want to present a very different line of thinking – one which goes back to Kant and to Frege. This line is one that, I believe, Carnap hoped to detranscendentalize; and in Carnap's hands it turned into linguistic conventionalism. My strategy in this essay will be to suggest that there is a different way of stripping away the transcendental baggage while retaining what (I hope) is the insight in Kant's (and perhaps Frege's)[3] view; a way which has features in common with the philosophy of the later Wittgenstein rather than with that of Carnap.

Kant and Frege

What led me to think again about the Kantian conception of logic was a desire to understand an intuition of Wittgenstein's that I had never shared. For the early Wittgenstein it was somehow clear that logical truths do not really say anything, that they are empty of sense (which is not the same thing as being nonsense), *sinnlos* if not *unsinnig*. (There are places in the *Investigations* in which Wittgenstein, as I read him, confesses that he still feels this inclination, although he does not surrender to it.) *Obviously*, sentences of pure logic are statements with content, I thought; if proved, they are moreover *true* statements, and their negations are *false* statements. But I felt dissatisfaction; dissatisfaction with my own inability to put myself in Wittgenstein's shoes (or his skin) and to even imagine the state of mind in which one would hold that truths of logic are "tautologies," that they are *sinnlos*. It was then that I thought of Kant.

Kant's lectures on logic[4] contain one of his earliest – perhaps the earliest – polemic against what we now call "psychologism." But that is not what interests me here, although it is closely related to it. What interests me here is to be found in *The Critique of Pure Reason* itself, as well as in the lectures on logic, and that is the repeated insistence that illogical thought is not, properly speaking, thought at all. Not only does Kant insist on this, both in the lectures on logic and in the *Critique*, but his philosophical arguments in the *Critique* employ this doctrine in different ways. One employment has to do with the issue of thought about noumena. Kant allows that noumena are not in space and time. They are not related as "causes" and "effects." They may not be "things" as we creatures with a rational nature and a sensible nature are forced to conceive "things." But we are not allowed to suppose that they violate laws of logic; not because we have some *positive* knowledge about noumena, but because we know something about thought, and the "thought" that the noumena might not obey the laws of logic is no thought at all, but rather an incoherent play of representations.

This is in striking contrast to Descartes's view that God could have created a world which violated the laws of logic.

But Kant's view goes further than this. A metaphysician who thinks of "logical space" as a Platonic realm of some sort might agree with Kant: logical laws hold not only in "the actual world" but in all the other "possible worlds" as well. On such a view, logical laws are still descriptive; it is just that they describe *all* possible worlds, whereas empirical laws describe only some possible worlds (including the actual one). This opens the possibility of turning Kant's flank, as it were, by claiming that while indeed the laws of logic hold in all possible worlds, *God could have created an altogether different system of possible worlds.*

On my reading of the first *Critique*, there are points in that work at which Kant at least entertains the idea that talk of "noumena" is empty, that the notion of a noumenon has only a kind of formal meaning. But even when he entertains this possibility, Kant never wavers from the view that even *formal* meaning must conform to the laws of logic. It is this that brought home to me the deep difference between an *ontological* conception of logic, a conception of logic as descriptive of some domain of actual and possible entities, and Kant's (and, I believe, Frege's) conception. Logic is not a description of what holds true in "metaphysically possible worlds," to use Kripke's phrase. It is a doctrine of *the form of coherent thought*. Even if I think of what turns out to be a "metaphysically impossible world," my thought would not be a thought at all unless it conforms to logic.

Indeed, logic has no metaphysical presuppositions at all. For to say that thought, in the normative sense of *judgment which is capable of truth*, necessarily conforms to logic is not to say something which a metaphysics has to *explain*. To explain anything *presupposes* logic; for Kant, logic is simply prior to all rational activity.

While I would not claim that Frege endorses this view of Kant, it seems to me that his writing reflects a tension between the pull of the Kantian view and the pull of the view that the laws of logic are simply the most general and most justified views we have. If I am right in this, then the frequently heard statement that for Frege the laws of logic are like "most general laws of nature" is not the whole story. It is true that as *statements* laws of logic are simply quantifications over "all objects" – and all concepts as well – in *Begriffsschrift*. There is in Frege no "meta-language" in which we could say that the laws of logic are "logically true"; one can only assert them in the one language, *the* language. But at times it seems that their *status*, for Frege as for Kant, is very different from the status of empirical laws. (It was, I think, his dissatisfaction with Frege's waffling on this issue that led the early Wittgenstein to his own version of the Kantian view.)

It was this line of thinking that helped me to understand how one might think that logical laws are *sinnlos* without being a Carnapian conventionalist. Laws of logic are without content, in the Kant-and-possibly-Frege view, in so far as they do not *describe* the way things are or even the way they (metaphysically) *could* be. The ground of their truth is that they are the formal presuppositions of thought (or better, *judgment*). Carnap's conventionalism, as interpreted by Quine in "Truth by Convention" (in *From a Logical Point of View*), was an *explanation* of the origin of logical necessity in human stipulation; but the whole point of the Kantian line is that logical necessity neither requires nor can intelligibly possess any "explanation."

Quine on analyticity

In a certain sense, Quine's attack on analyticity in "Two Dogmas of Empiricism" (in *From a Logical Point of View*) does not touch the truths of pure logic. These form a special class, a class characterized by the fact that in them only the logical words occur essentially.[5] If we define an "analytic" truth as one which is either (a) a logical truth in the sense just specified, or (b) a truth which comes from a logical truth by substituting synonyms for synonyms, then the resulting notion of analyticity will inherit the unclarity of the notion of *synonymy*; and this unclarity, Quine argued, is fatal to the pretensions of the philosophical notion in question. But if we choose to retain the term "analytic" for the truths of pure logic, this problem with the notion of synonymy will not stop us.

But what would the point be? The definition of a logical truth as one in which only logical words occur essentially does not imply that logical truths are *necessary*.

And Quine's doctrine that "no statement is immune from revision" implies that (in whatever sense of "can" it is true that we can revise any statement) it is also true that we "can" revise the statements we call "logical laws" if there results some substantial improvement in our ability to predict, or in the simplicity and elegance of our system of science.[6]

This doctrine of the *revisability of logic* would of course be anathema to Kant and to Frege (who says that the discovery that someone rejects a logical law would be the discovery of a hitherto unknown form of madness).

The idea that logic is just an empirical science is so implausible that Quine himself seems hesitant to claim precisely this. There are two respects in which Quine seems to recognize that there is something correct in a more traditional view of logic. In the first place, he suggests that the old distinction between the analytic and the synthetic might point to a sort of continuum, a continuum of unrevisability ("There are statements which we choose to surrender last, if at all"),[7] or of bare behavioristic reluctance to give up, or of "centrality." We were wrong, the suggestion is, in thinking that any statement is absolutely immune from revision, but there are some we would certainly be enormously reluctant to give up, and these include the laws of traditional logic. And in the second place, Quine sometimes suggests that it is part of translation practice to translate others so that they come out believing the same logical laws that we do.[8] Thus revising the laws of logic might come to no more – by our present lights – than *changing the meanings* of the logical particles. It is on the first of these respects that I wish to focus now.

It seems right to me that giving up the analytic-synthetic dichotomy does not mean – that is, *should not mean* – thinking of all our beliefs as empirical. (To think that way is not really to give up the dichotomy, but rather to say that one of the two categories – the analytic – has null extension.) "There are no analytic sentences, only synthetic ones" would be a claim very different from "There is no epistemologically useful analytic-synthetic *distinction* to be drawn." Saying that there is an analytic-synthetic *continuum* (or rather, an *a priori–a posteriori* continuum – since Quine identifies the rejection of the analytic with the rejection of the *a priori* in his writing)[9] rather than an analytic-synthetic *dichotomy* is a promising direction to go if one wishes to reject the dichotomy as opposed to rejecting the analytic (or the *a priori*). But does the idea of "reluctance to give up" capture what is at stake, what is *right* about the idea that logical truths are quite unlike empirical hypotheses?

Consider the following three sentences:

(1) It is not the case that the Eiffel Tower vanished mysteriously last night and in its place there has appeared a log cabin.
(2) It is not the case that the entire interior of the moon consists of Roquefort cheese.
(3) For all statements p, $\ulcorner -(p \blacksquare -p)\urcorner$ is true.

It is true that I am much more reluctant to give up (3) than I am to give up (1) or (2). But it is also the case that I find a fundamental difference, a difference in kind, not just a difference in degree,[10] between (3) and (2), and it is this that Quine's "account 2" may not have succeeded in capturing. As a first stab, let me express the difference this way: I can imagine finding out that (1) is false, that is, finding out

221

that the Eiffel Tower vanished overnight and that a log cabin now appears where it was. I can even imagine finding out that (2) is false, although the reluctance to trust our senses, or our instruments, would certainly be even greater in the case of (2) than in the case of (1). But I cannot imagine *finding out* that (3) is false.[11]

It ain't necessarily so

But is talk about "imagining" so and so not gross psychologism? In some cases it is. Perhaps I could be convinced that certain describable observations would establish to the satisfaction of all reasonable persons that the interior of the moon consists entirely of Roquefort cheese. Perhaps I could be convinced that my feeling that it is "harder to imagine" the falsity of (2) than to imagine the falsity of (1) is just a "psychological fact," a fact about *me*, and not something of methodological significance. But to convince me that it is possible to imagine the falsity of (3) you would have to put an alternative logic in the field;[12] and *that* seems a fact of methodological significance, if there is such a thing as methodological significance at all.

To explain this remark, I would like to review some observations I made many years ago in an essay titled "It Ain't Necessarily So."[13]

In that essay, I argued against the idea that the principles of Euclidean geometry originally represented an empirical hypothesis. To be sure, they were not necessary truths. They were *false*;[14] false considered as a description of the space in which bodies exist and move, "physical space," and one way of showing that a body of statements is not necessary is to show that the statements are not even true (in effect, by using the modal principle $-p \supset -\Box p$). But, I argued, this only shows that the statements of Euclidean geometry are synthetic; I suggested that to identify "empirical" and "synthetic" is to lose a useful distinction. The way in which I proposed to draw that distinction is as follows: call a statement *empirical relative to a body of knowledge B* if possible observations (including observations of the results of experiments people with that body of knowledge could perform) would be *known* to disconfirm the statement (without drawing on anything outside of that body of knowledge). It seemed to me that this captures pretty well the traditional notion of an empirical statement. Statements which belong to a body of knowledge but which are not empirical relative to that body of knowledge I called "necessary relative to the body of knowledge." The putative truths of Euclidean geometry were, prior to their overthrow, simultaneously synthetic and necessary (in this relativized sense). The point of this new distinction was, as I explained, to emphasize that there are at any given time some accepted statements which cannot be overthrown merely by *observations*, but can only be overthrown by thinking of a whole body of alternative theory as well. And I insisted (and still insist) that this is a distinction of methodological significance.

If I were writing "It Ain't Necessarily So" today, I would alter the terminology somewhat. Since it seems odd to call statements which are false "necessary" (even if one adds "relative to the body of knowledge B"), I would say "*quasi*-necessary relative to body of knowledge B." Since a "body of knowledge", in the sense in which I used the term, can contain (what turn out later to be) false statements, I would replace "body of knowledge" with "conceptual scheme." And I would further emphasize the nonpsychological character of the distinction by pointing out that the question is not a *mere* question of what some people can imagine or not imagine; it is a question of what, given a conceptual scheme, one *knows* how to falsify or at least disconfirm. Prior to Lobachevski, Riemann, and others, no one knew how to disconfirm Euclidean geometry, or even knew if anything *could* disconfirm it. Similarly, I would argue, we do not today know how to falsify or disconfirm (3), and we do not know if anything could (or would) disconfirm (3). But we do know, at least in a rough way, what would disconfirm (1), and probably we know what would disconfirm (2). In this sense, there is a qualitative difference between (1), and probably (2), on the one hand, and (3) on the other. I do not urge that this difference be identified with analyticity; Quine is surely right that the old notion of analyticity has collapsed, and I see no point in reviving it. But I do believe that this distinction, the distinction between what is necessary and what is empirical relative to a conceptual scheme, is worth studying even if (or especially if) it is not a species of analytic-synthetic distinction. Here I shall confine myself to its possible significance for the philosophy of mathematics. First, however, I shall use it to try to clarify, and possibly to supplement,[15] some insights in Wittgenstein's *On Certainty*.

Some thought experiments in *On Certainty*

There are a number of places in *On Certainty* at which Wittgenstein challenges the very conceivability of what look at first blush like empirical possibilities. I will consider just two of these. The statement that water has boiled in the past, that is, that it has on many occasions boiled, or even more weakly that it has boiled on at least *one* occasion, looks like a paradigmatic "empirical statement." The conventional wisdom is that its degree of confirmation should, therefore, be less than one; its falsity should be conceivable, even given our experience so far. But is it? Can we, that is to say, so much as make sense of the possibility that we are deceived about *this*; conceive that our entire recollection of the past is somehow mistaken, or (alternatively) that we have all along been subject to a collective hallucination?[16]

A different kind of case: Can I be mistaken in thinking that my name is Hilary Putnam,[17] in thinking, that is, that that is the name by which I am called and have been called for years?

To take the second case first: Certainly I can imagine experiences as of waking up and discovering that what I call my life (as Hilary Putnam, as husband, father, friend, teacher, philosopher) was "all a dream." One might "make a movie" in which just that happened. And Wittgenstein (who, of course, wrote "Ludwig Wittgenstein" and not "Hilary Putnam") admits[18] that such experiences might *convince* one. (Of course, they might not convince one; one might break down mentally, or one might commit suicide – there are many ways of telling such a story.) But, Wittgenstein points out, saying that such experiences might convince one is one thing; saying that they *justify* the conclusion that it was all a hallucination, that I am not Hilary Putnam, is something else. Why should I not say that *those* experiences are the hallucination (if I come to have them)? If experiences call into question *everything* that I take for granted – including the evidence for every single scientific theory I accept, by the way – then what is left of notions like "justification" and "confirmation"?

The question Wittgenstein raises here has a significance that reaches far beyond these examples. There is a sense in which they challenge not just the truth but the very intelligibility of the famous Quinian slogan that no statement is immune from revision. *Can* "Water has sometimes boiled" be revised? Can I (rationally) revise my belief that my name is Hilary Putnam?

In one sense, of course, we can revise the *sentences*. We could change the very meaning of the words. In that sense it is trivial that any *sentence* can be revised. And, since Quine rejects talk of "meaning" and "synonymy" at least when fundamental metaphysical issues are at stake, it might seem that the very question Wittgenstein is raising cannot even make sense for Quine (when Quine is doing metaphysics), depending, as that question does, on speaking of "beliefs" rather than "sentences." But things are not so simple.

Quine's philosophy of logic

The reason they are not so simple is that Quine himself has at times suggested[19] that it is difficult to make sense of the notion of revising the laws of classical logic. The problem is that – at least in the case of truth-functions – the fact that a translation manual requires us to impute violations of these laws to speakers calls into question the very adequacy of the translation manual. By so much as raising this question, Quine has opened the door to the sort of question I saw Wittgenstein as raising two paragraphs back. Can we now conceive of a community of speakers (1) whose language we could make sense of, "translate," in Quine's sense, who (2) assent to a sentence *which we would translate as* "Water has never boiled"? Can we now conceive of a community of speakers whom (1) we could interpret and understand, and who (2) assent to a sentence *which we would translate as* "7 + 5 = 13"?

Well, suppose we cannot. What significance does it have if we admit that we cannot do this? Here I would like to recall again what I wrote in "It Ain't Necessarily So." In my view, if we cannot *describe* circumstances under which a belief would be falsified, circumstances under which we would be prepared to say that –B had been confirmed, then we are not presently able to attach a clear *sense* to "B can be revised."[20] In such a case we cannot, I grant, say that B is "unrevisable," but neither can we intelligibly say "B can be revised." Since this point is essential to my argument, I shall spend a little more time on it.

Consider a riddle. A court lady once fell into disfavor with the king. (One easily imagines how.) The king, intending to give her a command impossible of fulfillment, told her to come to the Royal Ball "neither naked nor dressed." What did she do? (Solution: she came wearing a fishnet.)

Concerning such riddles, Wittgenstein says[21] that we are able to give the words a sense only after we know the solution; the solution bestows a sense on the riddle-question. This seems right. It is true that I could translate the sentence "She came to the Royal Ball neither naked nor dressed" into languages which are related to English, languages in which the key English words "naked" and "dressed" have long-established equivalents. But if I didn't know the solution, could I *paraphrase* the question "How could she come to the ball neither naked nor dressed?" *even in English itself*? I would be afraid to make *any* change in the key words, for fear of losing exactly what the riddle might turn on. Similarly, I would be afraid to translate the riddle into a foreign language which was not "similar" to English in the sense of having obvious "equivalents" to "naked" and "dressed." And if someone asked me, "In what sense, exactly, was she neither naked nor dressed?" I could not answer if I did not know the solution.

But are we not in the same position with respect to a sentence like "In the year 2010 scientists discovered that 7 electrons and 5 electrons sometimes make 13 electrons"? Or with respect to "In the year 2010 scientists discovered that there are exceptions to $5 + 7 = 12$ in quantum mechanics"? If this is right, and I think it is, then perhaps we can see how to save something that is right in the Kant-Frege-early Wittgenstein line that I described earlier.

Kant-Frege-Wittgenstein (again)

Before trying to say what might be saved of the position I attributed to Kant, possibly Frege, and the early Wittgenstein at the beginning of this essay, it is important to specify what is metaphysical excess baggage that should be jettisoned. According to these thinkers, logical (and mathematical) truths are true by virtue of the nature of thought (or judgment) as such. This is a highly metaphysical idea, and it receives a somewhat different inflection in the writings of each of them.

In Kant's case, the metaphysics is complicated by the need to distinguish the truths of logic not only from empirical truths, but also from synthetic *a priori* truths. In the case of a synthetic *a priori* judgment, say, "Every event has a cause," Kant tells us that what makes the judgment true is not the way the world is – that is, not the way the world is "in itself" – but the way our reason functions; but this talk of the function and constitution of human reason has to be distinguished (by Kant) from talk of the nature of thought, and of the (normative) laws of thought, alluded to above. There is, according to Kant, such a thought as the thought that there is an event with no cause; but I can know *a priori* that that thought is false, because the very constitution of my reason ensures that the data of the senses, as those data are represented to my mind, will fit into a certain structure of objects in space and time related by causality. There is a sense in which the negations of synthetic *a priori* truths are no more descriptions of a way the world could be than are the negations of logical truths. Yet there is an enormous difference (for Kant) between the negation of a synthetic *a priori* truth and a logical contradiction. The negation of a synthetic *a priori* truth is thinkable; and the reason such a statement could never turn out to be a truth is explainable – to provide the explanation is precisely the task of the *Critique of Pure Reason*. The negation of a logical truth is, in a sense, unthinkable; and it is unthinkable precisely *because* it is the negation of a logical truth. Explanation goes no further. "Logical truth" is, as it were, itself an ultimate metaphysical category.[22]

Frege's views are less clear, although he too seems to have retained the notion of synthetic *a priori* truth.[23] At the same time, Frege prepares the way for Wittgenstein by identifying the Kantian idea of the nature of thought with the structure of an ideal language. The early Wittgenstein, however, tried (if my reading is correct) to marry a basically Kantian conception of logic with an empiricist rejection of the synthetic *a priori*. For the Wittgenstein of the *Tractatus*, the opposition is between logical truths and empirical truths, not between logical truths and synthetic truths in the Kantian sense. The problem of distinguishing the way in which the structure of thought (which, as just remarked, becomes the structure of the ideal language) guarantees the unrevisability of logic from the way in which the structure of reason guarantees the unrevisability of the synthetic *a priori* no longer arises, because either a judgment is about the world, in which case its negation is not only thinkable but, in certain possible circumstances, confirmable, or it is not about the world, in which case it is *sinnlos*.

My suggestion is not, of course, that we retain this idea of a nature of thought (or judgment, or the ideal language) which metaphysically guarantees the unrevisability of logic. But what I *am* inclined to keep from this story is the idea that logical truths do not have negations that we (presently) understand. It is not, on this less metaphysically inflated story, that we can say that the theorems of classical logic are "unrevisable"; it is that the question "Are they revisable?" is one which we have not yet succeeded in giving a sense. I suggest that the "cans" in the following sentences are not intelligible "cans": "Any statement can be held true come what may, if we make drastic enough adjustments elsewhere in the system. Even a statement very close to the periphery can be held true in the face of recalcitrant experience by pleading hallucination or by amending certain statements of the kind called logical laws. Conversely, by the same token, no statement is immune from revision."

A few clarifications

Let me spend a few moments in explaining how I am using some key terms, to prevent misunderstandings. I have already illustrated the idea that a question may not have a sense (or, at any rate, a sense we can grasp), until an "answer" gives it a sense, with the example of the riddle. And I want to suggest that, in the same way, saying that logic or arithmetic may be "revised" does not have a sense, and will never have a sense, unless some concrete piece of theory building and applying *gives* it a sense. But saying this leaves me open to a misunderstanding; it is easy to confuse talk of "senses" with talk of meanings in the sense in which translation manuals are supposed to be recursive specifications of meanings. But the word "sense" (in "In what sense do you mean *p*?") is much broader and much less specific than the term "meaning." When I learned the sense of "She came to the ball neither naked nor dressed" I did not learn anything that would require me to revise my dictionary entries for either the world *naked* or the word *dressed*.[24] Knowing the "sense" of a statement (or a question) is knowing how the words are used in a particular context; this may turn out to be knowing that the words had a "different meaning," but this is relatively rare. (Yet knowing the sense of the question or statement is connected with our ability to paraphrase discourses intelligently.) I may know the meaning of words, in the sense of knowing their "literal meaning," and not understand what is said on a particular occasion of the use of those words.

It follows that "giving words a sense" is not always a matter of giving them a new literal meaning (although it can be). "Momentum is not the product of mass and velocity" once had no sense; but it is part of Einstein's achievement that the sense he gave those words seems now *inevitable*. We "translate" (or read) old physics texts homophonically, for the most part; certainly we "translate" *momentum* homophonically.[25] We do not say that the word "momentum" used not to refer, or used to refer to a quantity that was not conserved; rather we say that the old theory was wrong in thinking that momentum was exactly *mv*. And we believe that wise proponents of the old theory *would* have accepted our correction had they known what we know. So this is not a case of giving a word a new meaning, but, as Cavell put it (using a phrase of Wittgenstein's), "knowing how to go on."[26] But that does not alter the fact that the sense we have given those words (or the use we have put them to) was not available before Einstein.

A different point of clarification. There is an old (and, I think futile) debate about whether contradictions are "meaningless." When I suggested that Frege was attracted to (and the Wittgenstein of the *Tractatus* held) the position that the negation of a theorem of logic violates the conditions for being a thinkable thought or judgment, I do not mean to exclude contradictions from "meaning" in the sense of well-formedness in the language, or in an ideal language. (For Kant, of course, it would be anachronistic to raise this issue.) The point is rather that a contradiction cannot be used to express a judgment by itself. Frege would perhaps say that it has a degenerate *Sinn*, that a contradiction functions as a mode of presentation of the truth value $\perp$ (falsity). (This would explain how it can contribute to the meaning of a complex judgment, say, $q \supset (p \cdot -p)$, which is just a way of saying $-q$.) But for Frege, as for Kant, the notion of *thinking that* $(p \cdot -p)$ makes no sense (except as "a hitherto unknown form of madness").

In any case, it is well to remember that part of the price we pay for talking as if science were done in a formalized language is that we make it harder to see that in every language that human beings *actually* use, however "scientific" its vocabulary and its construction, there is the possibility of forming questions and declarative sentences to which we are not presently able to attach the slightest sense. If we formalize English, then in the resulting formal idiom, "John discovered last Tuesday that $7 + 5 = 13$," or the formula that corresponds to that sentence in regimented notation, may be "well formed," but it does not follow that one could *understand* that sentence if one encountered it.

Arithmetic

One last point of clarification: it may seem that, given any *p* of the kind I have been discussing, any *p* that has the status of being "quasi-necessary relative to our present conceptual scheme," there must be a fact of the matter as to whether *p* is *merely* quasi-necessary or truly "necessary." But a review of the considerations I have employed should dispel this impression. Whether a given statement, say, the parallels postulate of Euclidean geometry, or some formulation of determinism, or an ordinary arithmetic truth "could be revised" depends on whether an "alternative theory" could really be constructed and confirmed (and on whether or not we would translate *p* homophonically into our present language, were such an alternative theory described to us); and all of the crucial terms – "theory," "confirmation," "acceptable translation manual" – have far too much indeterminacy to make application of the principle of bivalence convincing. The illusion that there is in all cases a fact of the matter as to whether a statement is "necessary or only quasi-necessary" is the illusion that there is a God's-Eye View from which all possible epistemic situations can be surveyed and judged; and that is indeed an illusion.

We can now, perhaps, see how the position I have been suggesting differs from the position of Rudolf Carnap. On Carnap's position, an arithmetic truth, say $5 + 7 = 12$, or a set-theoretic truth for that matter, is *guaranteed* to be unrevisable – guaranteed by a recursive linguistic stipulation.[27] We *know* that the truths of mathematics are unrevisable (that any revision would be a change of meaning), and we know this because we have *stipulated* that they are unrevisable (and changing the stipulations just *is* changing the meaning of the terms). As Quine has pointed out,[28] Carnap wanted a notion of analyticity that would have epistemological clout! By contrast, what I have suggested is simply that, as a matter of descriptive fact about our present cognitive situation, we *do not know* of any possible situation in which the truths of mathematics (as we take them to be) would be disconfirmed, save for situations in which the meanings of terms are (by our present lights) altered. To insist that these statements *must* be falsifiable, or that *all* statements must be falsifiable – is to make falsifiability a third (or is it a fourth by now?) dogma of empiricism.

It might be argued,[29] however, that there must be more to the truth of the theorems of mathematics than my story allows, for the following reason: even if the theorems of mathematics are consequences of principles whose negations could not, as far as we now know, intelligibly be true – principles such that the idea of *finding out that they are false* has not been given a sense – still there are statements of mathematics whose truth value no human being may ever be able to decide even if more axioms become accepted by us on grounds of "intuitive evidence" or whatever. Certainly there are (by Gödel's theorem) sentences whose truth value cannot be decided on the basis of the axioms we presently accept. Yet, given that we accept the principle of bivalence, many of these sentences are true (as many as are false, in fact). And nothing *epistemic* can explain the truth of such undecidable statements, precisely because they *are* undecidable. To this objection, I can only answer that I am not able to attach metaphysical weight to the principle of bivalence; but a discussion of *that* issue would take another essay at least as long as this one.

The existence of mathematical objects

It is time to consider the effect of the position I am considering (and tentatively advocating) on the issues with which this essay began. Some of Quine's doctrines are obviously unaffected if this line of thinking is right. What I have called the metaphysical analytic-synthetic distinction, that is, the idea of a notion of "analyticity" which will do foundational work in epistemology, is still jettisoned. Indeed, I have made no use of the idea of "truth by virtue of meaning," and the only use made of the notion of sense is the claim that there are some "statements" to which we are presently unable to attach any sense – something which I take to be a description of our lives with our language, rather than a piece of metaphysics. The principal effect of this line of thinking is on the idea, described at the beginning of this essay, that the existence of mathematical entities needs to be justified.

To begin with, let me say that, even apart from the issues I have been discussing here, talk of the "existence" of mathematical entities makes me uncomfortable. It is true that when we formalize mathematics, we at once get (as well-formed formulas, and as theorems) such sentences as "Numbers exist," in addition to sentences which might really occur in a mathematics text or class, sentences like "There exist prime numbers greater than a million." For Quine, this shows that arithmetic commits us to the existence of numbers; I am inclined to think that the notion of "ontological commitment" is an unfortunate one. But I will not discuss that issue here. What is clear, even if we accept "Numbers exist" as a reasonable mathematical assertion, is that if it makes no sense to say or think that we have discovered that arithmetic is *wrong*, then it also makes no sense to offer a reason for thinking it is not wrong. A reason for thinking mathematics is not wrong is a reason which excludes nothing. Trying to justify mathematics is like trying to say that whereof one cannot speak one must be silent; in both cases, it only looks as if something is being ruled out or avoided.

If this is right, then the role of applied mathematics, its utility in prediction and explanation, is not at all like the role of a physical theory. I can imagine a "possible world" in which mathematics – even number theory, beyond the elementary counting that a nominalist can account for without difficulty – serves no useful purpose. (Think of a world with only a few thousand objects, and no discernible regularities that require higher mathematics to formulate.) Yet imagining such a world is not imagining a world in which number theory, or set theory, or calculus, or whatever is *false*; it is only imagining a world in which number theory, or set theory, or calculus, or whatever, is not *useful*. It is true that if we had not ever found any use for applied mathematics, then we might not have developed pure mathematics either. The addition of mathematical concepts to our language enlarges the expressive power of that language; whether that enlarged expressive power will prove useful in empirical science is an empirical question. But that does not show that the truth of mathematics is an empirical question.

The philosophy of logic and mathematics is the area in which the notion of "naturalizing epistemology" seems most obscure. The suggestion of this essay is that the problem may lie both with "naturalize" and with "epistemology." The trouble with talk of "naturalizing" epistemology is that many of our key notions – the notion of understanding something, the notion of something's making sense, the notion of something's being capable of being confirmed, or infirmed, or discovered to be true, or discovered to be false, or even the notion of something's being capable of being stated – are normative notions, and it has never been clear what it means to naturalize a normative or partly normative notion. And the trouble with talk of epistemology in the case of mathematics is that this talk depends on the idea that there is a problem of *justification* in this area. But perhaps mathematics does not require justification; it only requires theorems.

Notes

I am indebted to Warren Goldfarb and Charles Parsons for valuable discussions of previous drafts of this paper.

1 W. V. Quine, "Carnap on Logical Truth" *Synthese* (1960), p. 364.
2 "The Scope and Language of Science," *British Journal of the Philosophy of Science*, 8 (1957), 16.
3 I am aware that many people (for instance, Michael Dummett) read Frege as a Platonist rather than as a Kantian. However, two of my colleagues at Harvard, Burton Dreben

and Warren Goldfarb, convinced me long ago that this is a mistake. For a reading of Frege which is close to the views of Dreben and Goldfarb, see Joan Weiner's *Frege in Perspective* (Ithaca: Cornell University Press, 1991).

4 Immanuel Kant, *Logic*, trans. R. Hartman and W. Schwarz (Mineola, N. Y.: Dover, 1974).

5 A term F is defined to "occur essentially" in a sentence (after that sentence has been "regimented" in the style of quantification theory) if there is a term G of the same syntactic class (e.g., a monadic predicate if F is a monadic predicate, a dyadic predicate if F is a dyadic predicate. . .) such that replacement of every occurrence of F in the sentence by an occurrence of G results in a sentence with a different truth-value. Notice that this Quinian definition of "occurs essentially" uses no *modal* notions.

6 Quine himself draws this conclusion, for example on p. 40 of "Two Dogmas of Empiricism" in *From a Logical Point of View* (Cambridge: Harvard University Press, 1953): "Any statement can be held true come what may, if we make drastic enough adjustment elsewhere in the system. Even a statement very close to the periphery can be held true in the face of recalcitrant experience by pleading hallucination or by amending certain statements of the kind called logical laws. Conversely, by the same token, no statement is immune to revision. Revision even of the logical law of the excluded middle has been proposed as a means of simplifying quantum mechanics; and what difference is there between such a shift and a shift whereby Kepler superseded Ptolemy, or Einstein Newton, or Darwin Aristotle?"

7 "Truth by Convention," pp. 350–351, in *Philosophy of Mathematics: Selected Readings*, 2nd ed., eds Hilary Benacerraf and Hilary Putnam (Cambridge: Cambridge University Press, 1984).

8 For example, in "Carnap on Logical Truth" Quine writes (p. 354), "Deductively irresoluble disagreement as to logical truth is evidence of deviation in usage (or meanings) of words" (emphasis in the original). In *Word and Object* (Cambridge: MIT Press, 1960), it is part of translation practice to translate others so that the verdict-tables for their truth functions come out the same as ours (otherwise, one simply does not attribute truth functions to them) and so that "stimulus analytic" sentences have stimulus analytic translations. Indeed, in *Philosophy of Logic*, 2nd ed. (Cambridge: Harvard University Press, 1986), Quine seems to hold that one *cannot* revise propositional calculus without losing simplicity; but he has later rejected this view.

9 On this, see my "Two Dogmas Revisited," in *Realism and Reason*, vol. 3 of my *Philosophical Papers* (New York: Cambridge University Press, 1983).

10 I recall that Herbert Feigl asked me once, shortly after the appearance of "Two Dogmas," "Is the difference between a difference in kind and a difference in degree a difference in kind or a difference in degree?" This essay is, in a way, a return to this issue.

11 I do not claim, by the way, that *no* revisions in classical logic are conceivable. I myself have expressed sympathy for both quantum logic (which gives up the distributive law) and intuitionist logic. But the principle of contradiction seems to me to have quite a different status. On this see "There Is at Least One A Priori Truth" in my *Realism and Reason*.

12 I am aware that some people think such a logic – paraconsistent logic – has already *been* put in the field. But the lack of any convincing application of that logic makes it, at least at present, a *mere* formal system, in my view.

13 Reprinted in *Mathematics, Matter, and Method*, vol. 1 of my *Philosophical Papers* (New York: Cambridge University Press, 1975).

14 One way to see that they were false, regarded as descriptions of the space in which bodies are situated, is that they imply that space is infinite, whereas, according to our present physics, space is finite. See the discussion in "It Ain't Necessarily So."

15 In my view, the propositions Wittgenstein calls "grammatical" are often better conceived of as necessary relative to our present conceptual scheme. The use of the term "grammatical," with its strong linguistic connotations, inevitably suggests to many readers something like the notion of analyticity.

16 *On Certainty*, ed. G. E. M. Anscombe and G. H. von Wright (Oxford: Basil Blackwell, 1969), §§338–341.

17 *Ibid.*, §515.
18 See ibid., §517.
19 See n. 8 above for references.
20 The way I expressed this in "It Ain't Necessarily So" (in *Mathematics, Matter, and Method*), using the example of Euclidean geometry, was to say that prior to the construction of an alternative geometry plus physics, the statement "There are only finitely many places to get to, travel as you will" did not express anything we could conceive.
21 In an unpublished manuscript cited by Cora Diamond in *The Realistic Spirit* (Cambridge: MIT Press, 1991), p. 267. Readers of that book will see how much my thinking has been influenced by Diamond's brilliant essays on Frege and Wittgenstein.
22 I do not, of course, use the word "category" here in the sense of the Kantian table of categories.
23 For example, Frege never doubted that the truths of *geometry* are synthetic *a priori*.
24 But see Donald Davidson on "passing theories" in "A Nice Derangement of Epitaphs," in *Truth and Interpretation: Perspectives on the Philosophy of Donald Davidson*, ed. Ernest Lepore (Oxford: Basil Blackwell, 1984), p. 446.
25 Likewise, we treat "place" (in "There are only finitely many places to get to, travel as you will" homophonically, when we are relating the Euclidean view of the world — infinite space – with the Einsteinian. Cf. "It Ain't Necessarily So," p. 242. That is why I wrote, "Something that was literally inconceivable has turned out to be true."
26 See Cavell, *The Claim of Reason* (Oxford: Oxford University Press, 1979), pp. 121–122.
27 See Quine's "Truth by Convention."
28 See Quine's "Reply to Geoffrey Hellman," in *The Philosophy of W. V. Quine*, ed. L. E. Hahn and P. A . Schilpp (La Salle, Ill.: Open Court, 1986).
29 I argued this way myself in "What Is Mathematical Truth?" in *Mathematics, Matter, and Method*.

10

WITTGENSTEIN, MATHEMATICS AND PHILOSOPHY[1]

Juliet Floyd

That a sentence is a logical picturing of its meaning is obvious to the uncaptive eye.

(L. Wittgenstein, 20.9.14[2])

A *picture* held us captive. And we could not get outside it, for it lay in our language and language seemed to repeat it to us inexorably.

(L. Wittgenstein[3])

It is ancient custom for philosophers to draw on mathematics to exemplify certain philosophical difficulties about the nature of belief, especially philosophical belief. In Wittgenstein, as in Plato, such philosophical practice is complex and dialectical. Wittgenstein writes to refashion our conception of the aims and limits of philosophy, and part of his technique is to attempt to recast our philosophical preconceptions about certain features of mathematics and logic: their precision and clarity, their universal applicability, their necessity and their certainty. He presents mathematics and logic as no more, and no less, than motley parts of the "MOTLEY" which is our ordinary language.[4] In so doing, he treats traditional ideas about the privileged epistemic status of mathematics and logic as if they present a special danger to the achievement of genuine precision and clarity in philosophy, as if the philosopher's appeal to logic and mathematics in the name of clarity risks promoting, in our time, the most powerful superstitions of all, illusions of clarity.[5] Thus, it has seemed to me, Wittgenstein's discussions of mathematics epitomize much of what is most valuable in his philosophy, marking him out as a philosopher grappling in extraordinarily novel ways with central threads of a tradition stretching from Plato through Turing. And thus, I would add, is his work urgently relevant to contemporary philosophy of mind, language and logic.

But for over forty years the majority of Wittgenstein's readers, pro and con, have treated his discussions of mathematics as a sideline to his main philosophical work. Appropriators of his thought who stressed the importance of "ordinary language" felt his writings on logic and mathematics to be philosophically marginal, while most philosophers of mathematics took Wittgenstein's skeptical attitude toward the use of mathematical logic in philosophy as a sign of his technical incompetence.

In this chapter I shall question such received wisdom by indicating how seamlessly Wittgenstein's discussions of mathematics are woven into his life's work. Indeed, his investigations of mathematics ought often to be seen to epitomize, for him and for us, the overall spirit of his philosophy. Not because Wittgenstein advocated any particular "philosophy of mathematics" – an essential hallmark of his thought is that philosophy does not divide itself up into specialized subject matters.[6] Instead, his discussions of mathematics and logic are part and parcel of his investigations of philosophy. Wittgenstein's remarks on mathematics are best taken – as I think Wittgenstein took them – to allude to the whole of his attitude, to be illustrations of what philosophy, as he practices it, aims to accomplish. As I see it, Dummett erred in claiming that for Wittgenstein,

> philosophy and mathematics have nothing to say to one another; no mathematical discovery can have any bearing on the philosophy of mathematics. ... Wittgenstein's segregation of philosophy from mathematics ... springs only from a general tendency of his to regard discourse as split up into a number of distinct islands with no communication between them (statements of natural science, of philosophy, of mathematics, of religion).[7]

Unlike the positivists, and unlike certain ordinary language philosophers, Wittgenstein had no interest in principled compartmentalization. His aim was to overcome false barriers. In his work – as in Plato's – the interplay between mathematics and philosophy is extraordinarily subtle and open-ended, a crucial part of his larger investigation of human claims to "self-evidence," "clarity" and "necessity."[8]

Focusing on Wittgenstein's thought in this way helps us to see that a distinction between "ordinary" and "mathematical" (or "scientific") language is utterly alien to his philosophy, early, middle and late. This should help to demonstrate how false is the notion that in his youth Wittgenstein was an "ideal language philosopher," in his early middle age a "verificationist," and in his old age an "ordinary language philosopher." Wittgenstein's philosophy developed through his tenacity in pursuing a set of relatively continuous themes over several decades, not through his repeatedly shifting his philosophical stance. In what follows I shall indicate such continuities in numerous citations from every period of Wittgenstein's life. I especially delight in juxtaposing passages from *The Notebooks 1914–16* and the *Tractatus* with related ones from *On Certainty*,[9] a technique of midrash I learned from Burton Dreben.

1 Wittgenstein continually struggled to find a way to discuss mathematics philosophically. His remarks on mathematics in the *Notebooks 1914–16* and in the *Tractatus* are, though notoriously cryptic, plentiful. In his writings of the late 1920s and early 1930s examples from arithmetic and set theory constantly recur, and constantly vex him.[10] Wittgenstein stopped working on the typescripts of material posthumously published as *Remarks on the Foundations of Mathematics* toward the end of the Second World War, and though this cessation of work is probably best read as evincing his dissatisfaction with what he had written,[11] there can be no doubt that by 1913, if not earlier, he found himself determined to resist the claims of Frege and Russell to have presented the nature of mathematics in a single,

overarching "logical" system. Wittgenstein rejected their proposed account of the nature of mathematics by rejecting their philosophical conceptions of logic, questioning whether their function/argument analysis of the proposition even applied to the merely "apparent propositions" (*Scheinsätze*) of mathematics.[12] As early as 1914 Wittgenstein labeled the Frege–Russell (new) logic "the old logic," pejoratively lumping his teachers in with what he saw as 2,500 years of flawed philosophizing about logic and mathematics.[13] His difficulty with the so-called "reduction" of mathematics to logic was not that it consists of false mathematics, but, rather, of a false philosophy, false in misleading us about mathematics *and* about philosophy. The claimed "reduction" was, he wrote, analogous to "the claim that cabinet-making consists in gluing";[14] that is, it is not so much incorrect as it is an intellectual swindle: it overlooks the aims, the purposes and the techniques of our mathematical practices, their history, their artistry (Wittgenstein did not dismiss the importance of cabinet-making). The Frege–Russell use of logic misteaches, he held, by presenting diverse mathematical techniques in the guise of just one sort of technique:

> The Russellian signs veil the important forms of proof as it were to the point of unrecognizability, as when a human form is wrapped up in a lot of cloth.[15]

> "By means of suitable definitions, we can prove '25 × 25 = 625' in Russell's logic." – And can I define the ordinary technique of proof [*gewöhnliche Beweistechnik*] by means of Russell's? But how can one technique of proof be *defined* by means of another? How can one explain the *essence* of another? For if the one is an 'abbreviation' of the other, it must surely be a *systematic* abbreviation. Proof is surely required that I can systematically shorten the long [formalized] proofs and thus once more get a system of proofs.
>
> Long proofs at first always go along with the short ones and as it were tutor them. But in the end they can no longer follow the short ones and these show their independence.
>
> [My] consideration of *long* unsurveyable [*unübersehbaren*] logical proofs is only a means of showing how this technique – which is based on the geometry of proving – may collapse, and new techniques become necessary.
>
> I should like to say: mathematics is a MOTLEY of techniques of proof. – And upon this is based its manifold applicability and its importance . . .
>
> I should like to say: Russell's foundation of mathematics postpones the introduction of new techniques – until finally you believe that this is no longer necessary at all.[16]

Wittgenstein owed a great debt to the work of Frege and Russell. He never retracted his early remark that "the great work of the modern mathematical logicians . . . has brought about an advance in Logic comparable only to that which made Astronomy out of Astrology, and Chemistry out of Alchemy."[17] But the philosophical temptation to use this new tool as an organon for the development of theories of language, mind and knowledge was, he felt, riddled with confusion and bound to obfuscate both the genuine contribution of the new logic and the nature of philosophy. Wittgenstein took Frege's, Russell's, Hilbert's and Gödel's philosophical work to evince new forms of philosophical confusion, deeper and more difficult to expose than the excesses of traditional metaphysics. For in their hands genuine scientific work masquerades as metaphysics, rather than the other way around. Many of Wittgenstein's writings on mathematics criticize what he took to be "the disastrous invasion of mathematics by logic"[18] – that is, what he took to be the claims of Frege, Russell and others to have mathematically analyzed our notion of mathematics.

It is as cardinal a point as any in his philosophy that Wittgenstein never equates "proof" with "formal derivation." The true form of a proof includes the ways in which it is used. And for Wittgenstein a proof is something connected to a characteristic sort of use, to the production of *conviction*. Thus by 1918 did he label so-called "proof" *within* logic mere "calculation"[19] and thus in 1950–1 did he deny the status of "proof" to Moore's attempt to refute external world skepticism.[20]

A central question Wittgenstein explored throughout his writings is, What is it for a sequence of sentences – for example, a formalized derivation – to carry conviction, to express cogent, forceful reasoning? What, in other words, is a *forcible ground* (*triftiger Grund*[21])? Mathematics is one place where forcible grounds – proof, necessity and conviction – play a central role in the practice. But for Wittgenstein, our concept of a forcible ground is not itself a wholly mathematical notion; Frege, Russell, Hilbert, Gödel and others did not fully analyze our notion of proof. Wittgenstein would not deny that formalization might play, in certain contexts, a genuine (perhaps even a mathematical) role, a check on our understanding of a particular proof. And he would readily admit that if someone claimed to exhibit deductive reasoning whose logic could in principle not be formally represented in any familiar way, we would have every right to raise questions about that claim. His objection was to the idea that logic is the sole criterion of mathematical understanding or the sole source of conviction. He is attacking Frege's conception of a *Begriffsschrift*.[22] Conviction is essential to a proof's use, but no proof convinces solely in virtue of its capacity to be formalized in a logical structure taken to express a universally applicable set of logical laws. Mathematical models alone cannot resolve the deepest philosophical questions.[23]

Wittgenstein's insistence on the autonomy of mathematical techniques and structures from their presentation in formal derivations (i.e., in series of sentences fulfilling certain formal, grammatical and deductive requirements) is not separable from his insistence on the autonomy of linguistic techniques from such presentations elsewhere. That insistence he does sometimes express in battling the notion that "everyday" or "ordinary" forms of life require improvement or perfection in a philosophical theory.[24] But what he calls throughout the *Investigations* our "ordinary" uses of language and forms of life include, and do not contrast with, mathematics.[25] In particular, mathematics is for Wittgenstein as prone to philosophical distortion as any other region of our language. And so he requires his philosophical investigations of what is specific to mathematics to confront as multifarious and detailed a dose of examples as any other philosophical investigation in which he engages. That some mathematical examples are more complex than others, and that only some aspects of mathematics are especially prone to mislead us when we discuss them in philosophy does not distinguish mathematics from the rest of our language.[26]

It is clear to Wittgenstein that his philosophical investigations do not, as do mathematical ones, issue into *proofs*. He has no wish to emulate in philosophy the very same certainty, clarity, unrevisability and necessity we seem to be able to find in much mathematics. Here, he rightly believed, lay a sharp difference between him and, for example, Russell.[27] The sort of conviction and insight his philosophical investigations aim to produce is not to be generated mathematically or by means of what might be exhibited in a formally deductive argument.

It is thus more than a little striking that in the heart of *Philosophical Investigations* Wittgenstein avails himself of his notions of *perspicuousness* and *surveyability* (*Übersichtlichkeit, Übersehbarkeit*) – notions he had developed and frequently used in his discussions of mathematical proof – to characterize his conception of the sources and aims of philosophy (Cavell discusses the aesthetic ramifications of this surprising turn in "The *Investigations'* Everyday Aesthetics of Itself"[28]):

> A main source of our misunderstanding is that we do not *perspicuously overview* [*übersehen*] the use of our words. – Our grammar is lacking in this sort of perspicuity [*Übersichtlichkeit*]. A perspicuous presentation [*Übersichtliche Darstellung*] produces just that understanding which consists in 'seeing connections'. Hence the importance of finding and inventing *intermediate* cases.[29]

These uses of "perspicuous" to characterize his philosophical aims and methods directly parallel several features of Wittgenstein's treatment of mathematical proof. During the 1930s and 1940s he used the notion of "perspicuousness" (*Übersichtlichkeit*) as a shorthand device for summarizing some of his (motley) insights into the "MOTLEY" character of mathematics. He never took the notion of the perspicuous to provide an analysis of our concept of mathematics or of proof; the concept of the perspicuous is not sharply bounded. Nor is it a mathematical or mathematizeable notion: the perspicuous is not itself perspicuous.[30] But throughout *Remarks on the Foundations of Mathematics* Wittgenstein repeatedly remarked – and repeatedly meditated upon his remarking – that "proof must be perspicuous." Many different yet interconnected features of mathematical proofs fall within the compass of this notion of "perspicuousness." Among the most important are that in being "perspicuous," a proof: (i) *convinces* us, and so possesses a kind of organic quality which perfectly suits it to completely answering a precise mathematical question in such a way that a particular mathematical problem (or conjecture) *vanishes* as a problem (or a conjecture), and nothing hypothetical seems to remain or be required in the answer;[31] (ii) shows us something independent of any particular empirical or causal process or event;[32] (iii) is surveyable, readable, reproducible – it can be taken in and then communicated;[33] (iv) provides us with a model or standard for guiding empirical and mathematical judgments;[34] (v) yields conviction independently of any prior theory of proofs, it generates conviction self-sufficiently, playing the role of its own foundation;[35] (vi) (re)forms our concepts, leading us to a shift in our way of seeing things, to a new picture, a shift in what we do;[36] (vii) strikes us as a transparent and exact picture of a procedure which is necessary and certain, inherently unsurprising, even if we are surprised at its existence or outcome;[37] (viii) shows us *how* to reach a resolution of a mathematical problem, and not simply *that* it has a particular solution;[38] (ix) does not generate conviction in a way we can adequately construe as conviction in the truth of this or that proposition or series of propositions;[39] and (x) is open-ended in its applications, that is, it offers only a partial insight into mathematical techniques, a glimpse which is always subject to being recontextualized, shifted into a new and *differently* perspicuous series of connections.[40] – These are of course all metaphors, only several among many characteristics of mathematical proof.[41] But Wittgenstein's investigations of (what to say about) mathematics, always partial, proceed by exploring and exploiting the power of such metaphors, and then using them to question traditional philosophical ideas – for example, the idea that the sort of conviction generated by proof is best viewed as the result of a process of step-by-step reasoning from proposition to proposition according to a universally applicable, explicitly specifiable set of logical laws.

In *Philosophical Investigations* §122, when Wittgenstein writes that "the concept of a perspicuous presentation is of fundamental significance for us," he is explicitly remarking that in the notion of "perspicuousness" he sees a symbolic or figurative presentation of his aims and achievements in philosophy. That is, the metaphors he associates with *Übersichtlichkeit* in discussing mathematics have come to be applied, by means of a philosophical turn of the notion, to his own philosophical enterprise. We may briefly list the features characteristic of a Wittgensteinian philosophical investigation relevant to this turn. Undoubtedly most readers of Wittgenstein are fully aware of them.[42] But what I wish to underscore is how tightly Wittgenstein draws the parallel between those features of the *Übersichtlichkeit* of mathematical proof just cited and features of "perspicuous presentations," "*Übersichtliche Darstellungen*," in philosophical investigations – for this indicates one way in which Wittgenstein's discussions of mathematics come to epitomize all his philosophy, how it is that for him philosophy too is a "MOTLEY." A Wittgensteinian "perspicuous presentation" of our grammar resolves a philosophical problem, then, in so far as it: (i) resolves a particular problem by making it disappear with complete clarity, convincing us in such a way that we feel the need of no further hypothesis or conjecture;[43] (ii) shows us something about aspects of things independent of any empirical or causal phenomena;[44] (iii) is a readable and reproducible presentation of a route to a specific form of conviction; (iv) provides us with a synoptic overview of our grammar, i.e., a model or standard which guides future judgments;[45] (v) persuades us of its being a solution without appeal to a prior general principle or philosophical theory;[46] (vi) shows us the dawning of a new aspect of things;[47] (vii) strikes us as transparently clear and precise, as inherently unsurprising, even if difficult to see;[48] (viii) affords us a demonstration of *how* the philosophical solution is a solution;[49] (ix) convinces us in a way not fully expressed by the firmness of our assent to a particular proposition or thesis;[50] (x) is open-ended in its applications, always partial, never exempt from being shifted and seen anew in the context of a new and different philosophical investigation.

Section 122 of the *Investigations* ends with a parenthetical question, namely, "(Is this a '*Weltanschauung*'?)," to which Wittgenstein's implicit answer is, I take it, Yes and No. No, because the traditional philosopher's quest for an intuitive sense of the world as a whole, *sub specie aeterni*, will not be satisfied by the kind of all-too-human "perspicuousness" Wittgenstein's investigations offer.[51] But equally Yes, because Wittgenstein's philosophical spirit is nevertheless expressed in something more partial and limited than the traditional philosopher's goal: in *"Überblicken"* which are limited, "perspicuous" presentations within the world. And the perspicuousness of these presentations cannot be articulated in terms of the assertion or denial of propositions.[52]

To sound the significance of Wittgenstein's willingness to apply the notion of "perspicuousness" in both mathematics and in philosophy we need to attend to specific ways in which his procedures seem to show how philosophical discussions of mathematics and philosophical discussions of philosophy may usefully inform one another. My focus in what follows shall be Wittgenstein's recurrent discussions of classical impossibility proofs in mathematics. We shall see that his treatments of such proofs inform (and are informed by) what he writes about philosophical insight into philosophical illusion: mathematical proofs of impossibility illustrate how it is that we may succeed or fail to extricate ourselves from a deeply felt but wrongly articulated sense of conviction and obviousness. A "perspicuous" showing of an impossibility, be it in a mathematical context or in the course of a philosophical investigation, can produce a certain very special sort of understanding, the sort of understanding characteristic of philosophy as Wittgenstein practices it.

2 In one of two essays written about Wittgenstein's 1930s Cambridge lectures, Moore reports that

> Wittgenstein's answer to the ... question ['How can we look for a method of trisecting an angle by rule and compasses, if there is no such thing?'] was that by proving that it is impossible to trisect an angle by rule and compasses 'we change a man's idea of trisection of an angle' but that we should not say that what has been proved impossible is the very thing which he had been trying to do, because 'we are willingly led in this case to identify two different things'. He compared this case to the case of calling what he was doing 'philosophy', saying that it was not the same kind of thing as Plato or Berkeley had done, but that we may feel that what he was doing "takes the place" of what Plato and Berkeley did, though it is really a different thing. He illustrated the same point in the case of the 'construction' of a regular pentagon, by saying that if it were proved to a man who had been trying to find such a construction that there isn't any such thing, he would say 'That's what I was trying to do' because 'his idea has shifted on a rail on which he is ready to shift it'. And he insisted here again that (a) to have an idea of a regular pentagon and (b) to know what is meant by constructing by rule and compasses, e.g. a square, do not in combination enable you to know what is meant by constructing, by rule and compasses, a regular pentagon.[53]

Moore's report is a description, in Moore's characteristically blunt way, of Wittgenstein's dialectical maneuvers in his lectures. We are not in a position to verify its historical accuracy.[54] Nevertheless, I think we may reasonably conjecture that Wittgenstein's (reported) remark on whether what he is doing is or is not continuous with what Plato or Berkeley would have called "philosophy" was itself an extraordinarily interesting instance of his *doing* of philosophy. Moore says Wittgenstein drew an analogy between, on the one hand, a search for a trisected angle culminating in a proof that it is impossible to trisect the angle and, on the other hand, a search for an answer to a traditional philosophical question culminating in a Wittgensteinian treatment of, that is, rejection of, that question. Each case is said to "shift" a person's "idea" of something. It seems that Wittgenstein is suggesting that we try to see his philosophical achievement as consisting in a changing of the subject, something which "takes the place" of what Plato and Berkeley were doing precisely in appearing, without being, the same sort of thing that they were trying to do.

The proof that it is impossible to trisect an angle with straightedge and compass alone is a striking, yet readily accessible achievement of nineteenth-century algebra.[55] It was one of Wittgenstein's most often discussed mathematical examples: he referred to it in every course of lectures for which we have records, and repeatedly in his post-Tractarian writing.[56] Almost always Wittgenstein discussed this and other classical impossibility proofs in connection with the question, what is it to search for, to try to produce, a mathematical proof? This is a philosophical, not just a mathematical question, similar (and related) to the questions, what is a proof? and what makes a proof a proof of *this* particular conjecture? These questions form an essential part of Wittgenstein's inquiry into phenomena of intentionality and their expression in language – thought, understanding, meaning, expectation, desire, conviction, belief and so on.

Section 334 is the first passage in the *Investigations* which explicitly mentions trisection:

> "So you really wanted to say. . . ." [*"Du wolltest also eigentlich sagen. . . ."*]
> – We use this phrase in order to lead someone from one form of expression to another. One is tempted to use the following picture: what he really 'wanted to say', what he 'meant' was already *present somewhere* in his mind even before we gave it expression. Various kinds of thing may persuade us to give up one expression and to adopt another in its place. To understand this, it is useful to consider the relation in which the solutions of mathematical problems stand to the context and origin of their formulation [*zum Anlass und Ursprung ihrer Fragestellung*]. The concept 'trisection of the angle with ruler and compass', when people are trying to do it, and, on the other hand, when it has been proved that there is no such thing.
>
> (*Investigations* §334)

The context of this remark is an exploration of apparently competing conceptions of the relation between thought and its expression in language. The interlocutor asks in *Investigations* §327, "Can one think without speaking?", and *Investigations* §329 examines the temptation of asserting that "When I think in language, there aren't 'meanings' ('*Bedeutungen*') going through my mind in addition to the verbal expressions: the language is itself the vehicle of thought." Section 331 asks us, reminding us of Wittgenstein's builders in §2, to (try to) "Imagine people who could only think aloud. (As there are people who can only read aloud.)" We are being tempted to suppose that the capacity for unexpressed thought is an essential feature of human thought – and also to react against such a supposition by insisting that the possibility of public linguistic expression is an essential requirement for genuine thought. Neither the supposition nor the insistence seems adequate on its own to decide the question. And thus in §334 Wittgenstein mentions the proof of the impossibility of trisecting the angle in order to grant that some sense may be given to the idea that language is the "vehicle" of thought. But he is simultaneously using the example to suggest that this idea can also mislead us.[57] The phrase "So you really wanted to say . . ." is a mark both of the fluency of linguistic communication *and* of its rupture in misunderstanding. Wittgenstein notes the naturalness, in some contexts, of supposing that "what is intended or meant" is present in the mind of the speaker. Examples are numerous: you make a transparent slip of the tongue, and I say "So you really wanted to say . . ." in order to indicate or verify that you meant something other than what you actually uttered. Or again, in listening to a mathematics lecture, I might say "So you really wanted to say..." in order to make sure that I understand precisely what it is that is being proved or claimed. We may hold before ourselves in such cases the picture of a precise thought or content, clearly grasped by the speaker, but more or less precisely expressed or communicated. The listener tries to express the thought in his or her own words, different ones, to settle communication. But the point – that is, the irony – of Wittgenstein's suggestion is that "So you really wanted to say . . ." is also often applied in just those contexts in which we believe that a speaker is not yet thinking what he or she ought to think. Here it is not that we picture a thought clearly grasped by the speaker, but merely unclearly or misleadingly expressed; rather, we take the unclarity of the utterance to indicate that the speaker has not yet thought as precise a thought as he or she might. And so we propose another expression, and urge its adoption as an alternative, not to clarify our thinking, but to clarify the other's. Teachers, editing their students' words (or computations, as in the case of the wayward pupil of *Investigations* §§143 and 185), are apt to use this sort of linguistic strategy to invite, or to argue, their students into behaving, from their point of view, "correctly." "So you really wanted to say . . ." can be used to secure the application of logic: in the course of presenting an argument, when one traces out the implications of a thought, one may be led from one step to the next by use of such a phrase. This is clearly exemplified when proofs are presented in mathematics, and especially vividly in impossibility proofs, where, *via a reductio* argument, one is brought to see that a thought once entertainable as mathematically true cannot really be entertained. It is also an expression much used in philosophy as we try to shift one another's manner of speaking, and so, manner of thinking:

> One of the most important tasks [in philosophy] is to express all false thought processes so characteristically that the reader says, "Yes, that's exactly the way I meant it". To make a tracing of the physiognomy of every error.
> Indeed we can only convict someone else of a mistake if he acknowledges that this really is the expression of his feeling. // . .if he (r e a l l y) acknowledges this expression as the correct expression of his feeling.//

For only if he acknowledges it as such, *is* it the correct expression. (Psychoanalysis.)

What the other person acknowledges is the analogy I am proposing to him as the source of his thought.

("'Philosophy'" §87, p. 7; the slashes and underlines in Wittgenstein's manuscripts express tentativeness and/or suggested revisions)

Wittgenstein's reference to the formulation and the resolution of the problem of trisecting the angle in *Investigations* §334 suggests that the "picture" of something clearly present to the mind ahead of (or apart from) its expression is both a useful picture, and at the same time one whose application is limited, appropriate only in context. Language is a vehicle of communication and thought; but it can also get in the way, duping us into illusions of understanding, illusions of clarity. What, presumably, could be clearer, or more coherent – as a proposition, or an expression of a thought – than the conjecture that "There exists a general method of Euclidean trisection?" For over two thousand years people tried and failed to trisect the angle. We say that they had something definite "in mind" that they wanted, or were trying, to do. In fact, the (later discovered) impossibility proof can only function *as* such because we accept that it rules out the *very* construction trisectors were seeking! And yet, in accepting the proof as a proof, we see that what they were trying to do was not only not done, but could not possibly, mathematically, be done. So that once the proof has been accepted, there can seem to be a conflict between wanting to grant full and determinate sense to the (former, mistaken) conjecture that "A trisection construction exists" and yet wanting, as a result of the proof, to deny that this claim *really* makes any sense at all, to insist that no one *really*, ultimately, wants – or ever wanted – to say such a thing. For is not such insistence essential to accepting, to grasping, to applying, the proof? But then are we forced to say that for over 2,000 years trisectors engaged in an inquiry which made no sense, an inquiry which they didn't *really* want to engage in?

Wittgenstein's discussion of the evolution of the question and its resolution in the proof of the impossibility of trisecting the angle grows from roots in his earlier writings. In the *Tractatus* logical "falsehoods" are treated as "contradictions," limiting cases of genuine propositions which, like "logical propositions," "tautologies," are seen to be lacking in sense, lacking the capacity for truth or falsity altogether (*sinnlos*) (*Tractatus* 4.46). Mathematical "truths" and "falsehoods" are by contrast merely apparent propositions (*Scheinsätze*), not even limiting cases of propositions, but a mere superstructure of equations marking the intersubstitutivity and non-intersubstitutivity of mathematical expressions in genuine propositions (for example, in ascriptions of number). They do not express thoughts (*Tractatus* 6.21); they are understandable from our method of working with the intersubstitutivity of symbols alone (*Tractatus* 6.2341). And it is nonsensical, *unsinnig*, to assert that a person knows that $2 + 2$ is indeed equal to 4 and not equal to 5, or that war is war (*Tractatus* 5.1362). By 1929 Wittgenstein is prepared to speak of the "sense" of a mathematical "proposition." But he continues to bring into question the notion that a general philosophical category, grammar or *Begriffsschrift* is available to explicitly distinguish that which has sense from that which is nonsense.[58] And so he continues to question philosophical (pre)conceptions which are the source of apparent "debates" about sense and senselessness. We might say, with justice, that one cannot really think or entertain or believe a contradiction (see *Tractatus* 3ff, 4.462, 4.466, 5.143), but we may with equal justice maintain that one *can* – as the long history of the trisection question illustrates. We can apparently inquire into something which is "contradictory": nonsense isn't always easy to see, and certain nonsense is perfectly grammatical in the ordinary sense. This point is raised in *Remarks on the Foundations of Mathematics*:

> The difficulty which is felt in connection with *reductio ad absurdum* in mathematics is this: what goes on in this proof? Something mathematically absurd, and hence unmathematical? How – one would like to ask – can one so much as assume the mathematically absurd at all? That I can assume what is physically false and reduce it *ad absurdum* gives me no difficulty. But how to think the – so to speak – unthinkable?
>
> (*Remarks on the Foundations of Mathematics* V §28)

The suggestion here is that the possibility of entertaining something mathematically false or contradictory is somehow more difficult to make sense of than the possibility of entertaining something physically absurd. But elsewhere, Wittgenstein blurs this distinction (see, e.g., *Investigations* §§462–3, discussed below). Wittgenstein responds to his interlocutor:

"What an indirect proof says, however, is: 'If you want *this* then you cannot assume *that*: for only the opposite of what you do not want to abandon would be combinable with *that*'" (*Remarks on the Foundations of Mathematics* V §28). The italics on Wittgenstein's demonstratives here are essential, for with them he wishes to wean us away from certain tempting idealizations of the basis and nature of mathematical conviction (compare *Remarks on the Foundations of Mathematics* V §24). Only someone attached to a conception of proof, and of logic, according to which appreciation of the ultimate logical basis of a judgment is essential to (fully) understanding it would worry that indirect argument in mathematics poses a special problem of coherence.[59] Wittgenstein warns us repeatedly not to forget that the firmness of our subscription to (what we, but not he, call) the "laws" of contradiction and excluded middle is a function of how we apply them in particular cases. We may express respect for certain practices in calling them "inexorable" and "certainly true"; but the "inexorability," the "necessity" – as with any human law – finds its place at least in part in *our* inexorability in applying our statutes, in the practices within which their statement finds its place (*Remarks on the Foundations of Mathematics* I §118).[60]

We may then grant that those who were searching for a trisection construction did not fully understand what they were asking for, what it was they "really wanted" to say. However, in so granting we do not place their contemporaries who were skeptical about the possibility of trisecting the angle on firmer ground. For neither those who attempted to trisect, nor those who conjectured the impossibility of trisection, were in possession of a *proof*, i.e., a mathematical technique for generating conviction in a solution. This is, of course, characteristic of a situation in which conjecturing takes place in mathematics: like an expectation or an intention, it is, as Wittgenstein elsewhere writes, "embedded in its situation, in human customs and institutions" (*Investigations* §337). Conjecturing falsely is analogous to playing a game of chess thinking that it is always possible to force a checkmate with only a king and a knight. One suffers from a misunderstanding in not yet seeing what the rules of chess preclude, though in another sense, one may rightly be said to "understand" the rules of chess – indeed, it must be so, if one is ever to grasp the explanation of why such a checkmate is not always possible (*Remarks on the Foundations of Mathematics* V §28). Whatever shift in understanding takes place as a result of the proof that it is impossible to trisect an angle with ruler and compass, we do *not* move from a situation in which there is no concept of trisecting – that is, a situation in which no meaningful statements may be made concerning trisection – to a situation in which we now have such a concept, can intelligibly talk. This point is illustrated by the only other occurrence of the trisection case in the *Investigations*, where it appears as a *counterexample* to such a view:

> I can look for him when he is not there, but not hang him when he is not there.
> One might want to say: "But he must be somewhere there if I am looking for him." – Then he must be somewhere there too if I don't find him and even if he doesn't exist at all.
>
> "You were looking for *him*? You can't even have known if he was there!" – But this problem really does arise when one looks for something in mathematics. One can ask, for example, how was it possible so much as to *look for* the trisection of the angle?
>
> (*Investigations* §§462–3)

This is a *reductio* of a misguided conception of the object of an intention or search: the trisection example shows that it makes sense to (systematically) "search for" something which not only does not exist, but could not exist: we are not mathematically omniscient. Wittgenstein both compares, and at the same time distinguishes, the empirical and the mathematical cases. This particular mathematical example drives home in a vivid way the absurdity of the idea that the object of an intention or search must in some sense exist (if only "in mind") for there to *be* any intention, desire or sense to the search at all. Wittgenstein is not suggesting that there really is a "problem" which arises in cases like the quest for a trisected angle. Only on an unimaginatively restricted conception of the mind, of intention, is there the illusion of a problem. But that is precisely what allows the proof of the impossibility of trisecting the angle to provide philosophical material for Wittgenstein's investigations.

In the *Investigations* Wittgenstein uses the trisection example to try to complicate our idea of what it is to "really" understand, to fully mean or express, to "really" want to utter, a particular sentence. At stake is what he elsewhere calls the "very vague" quality of our (philosophical) concept of understanding a (mathematical) proposition; and, hence, the complexity of what it is to *really* understand a sentence or a language (*Remarks on the Foundations of Mathematics* V §46). The expression "So you really wanted to say..." has a multitude of legitimate and important applications in our language. It is a crucial term of criticism in Wittgenstein's own practice of philosophy. Clearly Wittgenstein is skeptical that there is any systematic theoretical account which will informatively distinguish, in particular cases, between uttering or thinking a sentence with "real" meaning (that is, clearly and fully or completely expressing a thought, belief, desire or intention) and uttering or thinking a sentence which does not fully, clearly or completely express a thought, belief, desire or intention. The trisection example serves this skepticism concerning a general theoretical account of rational (logical) language use – at least if it is inattentive to our applications of logic in particular circumstances. The skepticism emerges in §334 of the *Investigations* through Wittgenstein's construing such a theory as a (purported) general account of our use of clarifying phrases such as "So you really wanted to say. . . ." That there is no general account of that phrase's proper use implies that there can be no general account of how to practice philosophy, or how to keep one's uses of language within the bounds of sense.

3 Despite what some readers claim[61] – some on account of what they deem to be Wittgenstein's notion of an "internal" or "grammatical" relation; and some on account of the (erroneous) conviction that he must have been a verificationist – Wittgenstein is not insisting that conjectures in mathematics are meaningless, or that we do not understand a mathematical proposition until we possess its proof, or that a new proof, as a new method of verification, always issues into a brand new mathematical proposition. I do not deny that Wittgenstein seems to have been attracted to verificationism, especially in the 1930s. Yet even in the 1930s, he repeatedly stressed that it is a characteristic feature of mathematical proof that we will insist, of any proof, that it "proves the very same thing that was in question before [we had the proof]" (cf. Moore's *Philosophical Papers*, pp. 304–5, quoted above). In this regard there is no fundamental change in Wittgenstein's views through the 1920s and 1930s or even afterward.[62] By 1939–41 Wittgenstein writes that "of course it would be nonsense [*Unsinn*] to say that *one* proposition cannot have two proofs – for we do say just that" (*Remarks on the Foundations of Mathematics* III §58), and that "the proof of a proposition shows me what I am prepared to stake on its truth. And different proofs can perfectly well cause me to stake the same thing" (*Remarks on the Foundations of Mathematics* VII §43 – see also III §54, VII §10). What he resists is the idea that there being just "*one* proposition" is part of the justification for our accepting the proof as a proof. For Wittgenstein, it is the other way around: our acceptance of something as a proof of *this* shows what it is that we *really* take *this* to be.

The following passage of the "middle Wittgenstein," from *Philosophical Grammar*, pp. 387–8, was penned some fifteen years earlier than the sections we have already examined in the *Investigations*:

The trisection of an angle, etc.

We might say: in Euclidean plane geometry we can't look for the trisection of an angle, because there is no such thing, and we can't look for the bisection of an angle, because there is such a thing.

In the world of Euclid's Elements I can no more ask for the trisection of an angle than I can search for it. It just isn't mentioned.

(I can locate the problem of the trisection of an angle within a larger system but can't ask within the system of Euclidean geometry whether it's soluble. In what *language* should I ask this? In the Euclidean? – But neither can I ask in Euclidean language about the possibility of bisecting an angle within the Euclidean system. For in that language that would boil down to a question about absolute possibility, which is always nonsense.)

. . . A question makes sense only in a calculus which gives us a method for its solution; and a calculus may well give us a method for answering the one question without giving us a method for answering the other. For instance, Euclid doesn't show us how to look for the solutions to his problems; he gives them to us and then proves that they are solutions. And this isn't a psychological or pedagogical matter, but a mathematical one. That is, the *calculus* (the one he gives us) doesn't enable us to look for the construction. A calculus which does enable us to do that is a *different* one. (Compare methods of integration with methods of differentiation, etc.)

This discussion has an odd sound, but there are some genuine mathematical points which Wittgenstein is exploiting. We need to look at some details of the proof of the impossibility of trisecting an angle in order to grasp what Wittgenstein is doing here. And for this we must go back to basics, that is, to Euclid himself.

Consider Proposition 9 and its proof in Euclid's *Elements*: to bisect a given rectilineal angle:

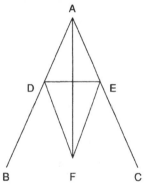

Proposition 9

To bisect a given rectilineal angle.

Let the angle BAC be the given rectilineal angle.
Thus it is required to bisect it.
Let a point D be taken at random on AB;
    let AE be cut off from AC equal to AD; [I,3]
    let DE be joined, and on DE let the equilateral triangle DEF be constructed;
    let AF be joined.
I say that the angle BAC has been bisected by the straight line AF.
For, since AD is equal to AE,
    and AF is common,
The two sides DA, AF are equal to the two sides
    EA, AF respectively.
And the base DF is equal to the base EF;
    therefore the angle DAF is equal to the angle EAF. [I,8]

Therefore the given rectilineal angle BAC has been bisected
    by the straight line AF.[63]

Euclid thus *exhibits, presents* the construction, without any further preliminary remarks or summary. But what is it to formulate a Euclidean problem: to trisect a given rectilineal angle? Wittgenstein's concern is that the answer to this question is not as simple as it may at first appear to be; for to formulate the problem it does not suffice – or, suffices in only a very special sense – to simply form the sentence (in, e.g., English, or Greek) "Is it possible to divide an angle into thirds in the same way?" Evidently, it is not enough to simply refuse to attempt to trisect the angle, or to assert *that* it is or is not so possible. (Behaviorist accounts of proof, of understanding, founder here.) In asking a question, or in making a conjecture about trisection, one places constraints on possible answers or solutions in so far as one asks a mathematical question or makes a mathematical claim at all. Let us see why.

The problem of giving a trisection construction is very ancient – older, certainly, than Euclid.[64] The idea that the problem ought to be determined or resolved in Euclidean terms represents a crucial step in its evolution.[65] For in any case Euclidean methods never exhausted the notion of a geometrical construction. For example, Archimedes offered a "trisection" of the following form:

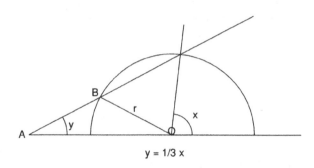

$$y = 1/3\ x$$

Let an arbitrary angle x be given, as above. Extend the base of the angle to the left, and swing a semicircle with O as center and arbitrary radius r. Mark two points A and B on the edge of the ruler such that $AB = r$. Keeping the point B on the semicircle, slide the ruler into the position where A lies on the extended base of the angle x, while the edge of the ruler passes through the intersection of the terminal side of the angle x with the semicircle about O. With the ruler in this position draw a straight line, making an angle y with the extended base of the original angle x.[66]

This construction is not Euclidean, in that it calls for the use of a ruler not merely as a straightedge for drawing straight lines between given points, but also as a measure of distance (that is, in the course of the proof, you must slide the ruler, with a length marked on it, from one position to the other). Within Euclid's scheme, such uses are not discussed, much less permitted. Archimedes gives us a perfectly good geometrical construction; he does trisect the angle. Only not in what we *now* call "the relevant sense."

Furthermore, we must be able to distinguish *practical* from *theoretical* aspects of Archimedes' or Euclid's constructions. The thousands of people who occupy themselves with trying to trisect angles (or square circles, or double the volume of cubes) are often guilty of such confusion – creating a practice of giving what might be called "pseudo-constructions."[67] After all, it is extremely easy to trisect the angle – practically and theoretically – with straightedge and pencil. Just draw a picture:

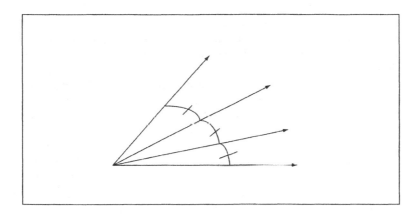

Yet, despite what one might be tempted to insist, the above picture is no picture of a "trisected angle" in the relevant sense. Why not? – Because there *can be* no such construction. Hence there can be no picture which leads, step by step, by Euclidean means, *to* such a construction. Does this observation show that it is impossible to *imagine* trisecting the angle in the relevant sense? – Yes and No. (Recall the discussion of *Investigations* §334 and §463 above in section 2.)

Hobbes not only boasted that he had trisected the angle,[68] but also that he had squared the circle and doubled the cube: three equally impossible feats. What Hobbes really did was to give a method of construction approximating a solution for any particular degree of angle we may choose. In fact it is possible to trisect in Euclid any arbitrary angle within as close approximation as we wish. But this sort of "solution," however ingenious, was not (as we say) "what was wanted." We demanded (or wished to know about the possibility of) an exact solution. Again: it is possible to precisely trisect certain particular angles in Euclid (e.g., 90, 180 degrees). But the trisection question eventually shown to be unsolvable is the general one: to give a single, Euclidean method of construction which can be used to precisely trisect any arbitrary given angle.

Part of Wittgenstein's purpose in focusing on the formulation and the resolution of the trisection problem is to emphasize that there is no absolute requirement – mathematical or otherwise – that we restrict the conditions of a question in the way we do. In the trisection case, it is the *decision* to require that solutions be given within a particular setting, and that solutions take a particular form and be generally applicable which generates the unsolvable – hence, provably resolvable – problem. Of course, this in no way renders the unsolvability of the task a matter of arbitrary human convention: God himself could not "trisect" an angle. But we can always, in Lakatos's words, bar – or create – what we call "monsters."[69]

Mathematically speaking, before headway could be made on a proof of the impossibility of trisecting the angle, an investigation was required into the abstract question, *How is it possible to prove that certain problems of construction can or cannot be solved?*[70] (Note that this general characterization of the notion of a solution is only required because of the need for the proof of a negative impossibility result; it would not have been needed if someone had indeed been able to trisect the angle.) The answer to this problem is to give a complete and rigorous algebraic characterization of all possible Euclidean constructions. Once one sees how to interpret in algebraic terms each legitimate Euclidean step, one has a setting within which to mathematically reinterpret the original notion of "constructible in Euclid." One may use an equation to express the relation between a given set of line segments and the set of line segments needed as the solution to a particular construction problem. Then, using the algebraic notion of a "rational field," a class of so-called "constructible numbers" may be characterized which corresponds to the possible Euclidean steps with ruler and straightedge from a given point in the construction. To prove that it is impossible to give a general Euclidean procedure for trisecting any arbitrary angle, all one needs to do is to present an equation expressing a particular trisection problem which has no solution in certain "extension fields" of the rational numbers. Take an angle of 60 degrees. The appropriate equation for this problem has no rational roots – and it is surprisingly simple in appearance:

$$8z^3 - 6z - 1 = 0^{71}$$

The problem of trisection is thus solved in mathematics by mathematically characterizing the constraints we place on any solution to a construction problem.

In his discussion we have examined from *Philosophical Grammar* Wittgenstein emphasizes the mathematical fact that elementary geometry alone does not hold, i.e., cannot express, a solution to the question about trisection. (In higher algebra, we can clarify what is a possible Euclidean move; but, as we've just seen, in so clarifying, as Wittgenstein insisted, we shift our original question, i.e., we set ourselves *another* problem, we extend the use of our prior concepts.) Within the axiomatic system of Euclid, solutions are exhibited. This is the feel, the structure of Euclid. Questions about the possibility of asking and answering questions, or techniques of searching for solutions, aren't part of Euclid's system, in its original context. Indeed, as Wittgenstein emphasizes in his discussion of trisection in *Philosophical Grammar*, the absence of these possibilities is part of the *mathematical* – not merely the pedagogical or psychological – characterization of Euclid's system. Indeed, Euclid's "system" of displaying solutions to problems contrasts with mathematical contexts in which we have an algorithm or method for finding solutions, e.g., the computation of elementary sums, for mathematically competent adults, or the "calculus" of differentiating functions, for those who have been trained in its use (cf. *Wittgenstein's Lectures, Cambridge 1932–35*, p. 116). Wittgenstein's uses of the words "calculus"[72] and "system" in *Philosophical Grammar* are loose. It would be an overstatement to hold that for Wittgenstein all mathematics is, as such, algorithmic or that only conjectures for which a method of resolution is in hand count as mathematical propositions.[73] Although algorithms and calculations are central to mathematics – they are for Wittgenstein part of the logical character of proof in mathematics – they do not exhaust mathematical activity. Mathematics is not a purely mechanical enterprise. By "calculus" or "system," I suggest, Wittgenstein means a practice of characteristic linguistic action involving (more or less) specific techniques. And by a "conjecture" or a "mathematical question," he means, one for which we make a ("*systematic*") "search" (in the above-named sense) *within* mathematics – in contrast, for example, to prophesying the trisection of the angle, or uttering the words "I wonder whether it's possible to trisect an angle" while doing nothing, or laying down a bet as to the theorem's outcome, or making an empirical prediction about future human behavior.

In this sense of "question" and "conjecture," in the above-quoted passage from *Philosophical Grammar* Wittgenstein refuses to treat either "Is it possible to *bisect* an angle in Euclid?" or "Is it possible to *trisect* an angle in Euclid?" as questions within Euclid's system – though each refusal is for a different reason. I can't ask about the possibility of bisection, because there is a proof already exhibiting the possibility in Euclid's *Elements*. That is: I cannot in any sense systematically search for, wonder about or hypothesize something which I am already aware that I possess. If I accept the proof as a proof, I cannot conjecture its outcome, for if I accept the proof I am convinced, and then I cannot at the same time doubt it (compare *On Certainty* §§24, 39, 46, 650). By contrast, my asking, before I understand and accept the proof, whether it is possible to *trisect* an angle in Euclid is really, as we've seen, a demand for further clarification or definition of the notion of "possible construction in Euclid" (in *Philosophical Grammar*, pp. 389–90 Wittgenstein investigates a trisection problem for a geometry in which the angle of the compass must remain fixed in all "constructions"). No techniques or methods given by Euclid help me to systematically search for this. I can play around with straightedge and compasses and tricks of construction I've already learned from Euclid, but this will take me only so far. What I require is a new way of interpreting the question. In several places Wittgenstein likens a mathematical search for the solution to a difficult question to groping about; to trying to wiggle one's ears, without hands, if one doesn't yet know how to; or trying to will an object to move across the room (*Wittgenstein and the Vienna Circle*, pp. 34, 136, 144; *Philosophical Remarks* XIII; *Philosophical Grammar*, p. 393). Before one succeeds or fails, one has no clear understanding of what it would be like to succeed or fail. All the same, one may search for an answer; one "gropes around," one tries to do something in the face of one's puzzlement which will generate ("perspicuous") conviction. Like a philosophical problem, such searches, the contexts of conjecturing in mathematics, have the form, "I don't know my way about," "I'm stumped," "I'm at a loss" (see *Investigations* §123, "Philosophy" §89, p. 13, *Remarks on the Foundations of Mathematics* III §80, *Remarks on the Philosophy of Psychology*[74] I §§296–301, 548–50, II §§605–6, *Zettel* §393, *Culture and Value*, p. 72). This is not merely a question of one's state of mind, but, rather, of one's mathematical situation: "When I say 'I don't know my way about in the calculus' I do not mean a mental state, but an inability to *do* something" (*Remarks on the Foundations of Mathematics* III §81). Like philosophical investigations, mathematical investigations require reflection on the very notions used to frame the original question. And mathematical solutions can relieve us of torment, bring us peace, by changing the context in which we pursue mathematics. As Diamond has emphasized, trying to prove something that is difficult in mathematics is more like searching for a solution to a riddle than it is like searching for an object which already falls under a concept.[75] Conjectures about trisection in Euclid, even if they can be dressed up to look like hypothetical assertions of propositions with truth-values, operate in contexts where there are outstanding demands for perspicuousness. What will satisfy those demands is *doing* something, i.e., exhibiting or producing a proof. And that requires coming to understand how something could possibly satisfy the conditions placed on a solution to the question. As Wittgenstein theatrically presented the point in his 1934–5 Cambridge lectures:

> What one calls mathematical problems may be utterly different. There are the problems one gives a child, e.g., for which it gets an answer according to the rules it has been taught. But there are also those to which the mathematician tries to find an answer which are stated without a method of solution. They are like the problem set by the king in the fairy tale who told the princess to come neither naked nor dressed, and she came wearing fish net. That might have been called not naked and yet not dressed either. He did not really know what he wanted her to do, but when she came thus he was forced to accept it. The problem was of the form, Do something which I shall be inclined to call neither naked nor dressed. It is the same with a mathematical problem. Do something which I shall be inclined to accept as a solution, though I do not know now what it will be like.
>
> (*Wittgenstein's Lectures, Cambridge 1932–35*,
> pp. 185–6)

Or again,

> Is it a genuine question if we ask whether it's possible to trisect an angle? And of what sort is the proposition and its proof that it's impossible with ruler and compasses alone?
>
> We might say, since it's impossible, people could never even have tried to look for a construction.
>
> Until I can *see* the larger system encompassing them both, I can't try to solve the higher problem.
>
> I can't ask whether an angle can be trisected with ruler and compasses, until I can see the system "Ruler and Compasses" as embedded in a larger one, where the problem is soluble; or better, where the problem is a problem, where this question has a sense.
>
> This is also shown by the fact that you *must* step outside the Euclidean system for a proof of the impossibility.
>
> A system is, so to speak, a world.
>
> Therefore we can't search for a system: What we *can* search for is the expression for a system that is given me in unwritten symbols.
>
> (*Philosophical Remarks*, pp. 177–8)

A "system given me in unwritten symbols" corresponds to the possibility of devising a proof technique, that is, something which will convince me (and enable me to convince others) of the proof's cogency as a solution to a problem – i.e., the cogency of the problem to mathematics. In difficult cases, when one is "at a loss," the search for such perspicuousness is unlike an empirical search, say, for a friend at the theater, or, to use another of Wittgenstein's favored figures, a polar expedition (*Philosophical Grammar*, p. 359): our approach to the perspicuousness has no particular direction or distance we can gauge. The search for perspicuousness in mathematics and in philosophy is like the search for humor in a joke one has not yet made up, or not yet told (cf. *Investigations* §111). A particular, grammatically well-formed sentence which we are trying to prove may be there before our eyes, but exhibit no perspicuousness of use to us (cf. "Cause and Effect: Intuitive Awareness," *Philosophical Occasions*, pp. 368–426, especially p. 403).

So does Wittgenstein therefore hold that the meaning of a problem is given wholly by its method of solution, and that a mathematical statement has sense or meaning (*Sinn*) only once it is proved? No. He always denied that he held (unproved) mathematical conjectures to be meaningless (*Philosophical Remarks*, p. 170, *Philosophical Grammar*, pp. 377–80, *Remarks on the Foundations of Mathematics* VI §13, VII §10; *Wittgenstein's Lectures, Cambridge 1932–35*, pp. 221–2). Even in the early 1930s he wrote:

> My explanation mustn't wipe out the existence of mathematical problems. That is to say, it isn't as if it were only certain that a mathematical proposition made sense when it (or its opposite) had been proved. (This would mean that its opposite would never have a sense (Weyl).) On the other hand, it could be that certain apparent problems lose their character as problems – the question as to Yes or No.
>
> (*Philosophical Remarks*, p. 170)

Sometimes, as we've seen, Wittgenstein will hold that he is simply distinguishing on mathematical grounds among different kinds of (mathematical) "questions":

> Wouldn't all this lead to the paradox that there are no difficult problems in mathematics, since if anything is difficult it isn't a problem? What follows is, that the "difficult mathematical problems", i.e., the problems for mathematical research, aren't in the same relationship to the problem "$25 \times 25 = ?$" as a feat of acrobatics is to a simple somersault. They aren't related, that is, just as very easy to very difficult; they are 'problems' in different meanings of the word.
>
> "You say 'where there is a question, there is also a way to answer it', but in mathematics there are questions that we do not see any way to answer." Quite right, and all that follows from that is that in this case we are not using the word 'question' in the same sense as above. And perhaps I should have said "here there are two different forms and I want to use the word 'question' only for the first". But this latter point is a side-issue. What is important is that we are here concerned with two different forms. (And if you want to say they are just two different *kinds* of question you

251

do not know your way about the grammar of the word "kind".)
 This amounts to asking: Does a mathematical proposition tie something down to a Yes or No answer? (i.e. precisely a sense.)
      (*Philosophical Grammar*, p. 380; cf. *Wittgenstein's Lectures,*
              Cambridge 1932–35, p. 221)

And lecturing in 1932–3, Wittgenstein says explicitly that "the question has as much [mathematical] meaning as the messing about has" (*Wittgenstein's Lectures, Cambridge 1932–35*, p. 221).

4 Commenting on Wittgenstein's early views on ethics and religion, G.E.M. Anscombe writes:

> The most important remark he makes here is: 'The facts all belong to the task set, and not to the solution' ([*Tractatus*] 6.4321). '*Aufgabe*,' which I translate 'task set', is the German for a child's school exercise, or piece of homework. Life is like a boy doing sums. (At the end of his life he used the analogy still.)[76]

Life itself is a task, an *Aufgabe*, like a child learning to do elementary mathematics. What is that like? As so many passages in the *Investigations* show, it is not something wholly mechanical, not something everywhere governed by rules or systems, not an activity in which guarantees or necessities or intuitions can make clear in advance what success will look like. In life, in philosophy, as soon as we have mastered one sort of task we are set another that we haven't a clear notion how to solve.
 Wittgenstein's investigations of mathematical and philosophical answers coalesce in the point that there is nothing within the ordinary grammar of a sentence – or a deductive pattern of (grammatical) sentences – that can produce or express the sense of satisfaction proofs yield. Understanding is itself a vague concept, not wholly specifiable by grammar or by any set of explicitly formulated rules (*Remarks on the Foundations of Mathematics* VI §13). What counts as "nonsense" (*Unsinn*) for Wittgenstein is not any form of words as such, is not a violation of any prior grammatical order in our language. Rather, what is "nonsense" for Wittgenstein are particular uses of sentences, for example, attempts to express mathematical (or philosophical) conviction or understanding by firmly asserting that a sentence such as "There is/is not a Euclidean procedure for trisecting the angle" is true or is false (compare *On Certainty* §35, *Investigations* §§252, 303, *Remarks on the Foundations of Mathematics* VII §§10, 43 and III §58, quoted above). Any such purported use is unperspicuous, even nonsensical, but not in violating any general grammatical rules applying to the linguistic forms appearing in it. Rather, it is unperspicuous in misleading us about the very nature of what we take ourselves to express in its use. The "perspicuousness" of proof in mathematics, and of a grammatical investigation in philosophy, is not in the dimension of assertion, it does not modify a proposition or a belief, as do the notions of "self-evident" or "obviously true" (cf. *Remarks on the Foundations of Mathematics* I §§110ff). "Seeing" a proof's perspicuousness is not the same as believing in the truth of its conclusion; at best we may think of ourselves believing in the proof itself:

The proof convinces us of something – though what interests us is, not the mental state of conviction, but the applications attaching to this conviction.

For this reason the assertion that the proof convinces us of the truth of this proposition leaves us cold, since this expression is capable of the most various interpretations.

(Remarks on the Foundations of Mathematics III §25)*

Even more, as Dreben has emphasized,[77] Wittgenstein's use of the term "*Unsinn*" is in most cases (all cases in *Remarks on the Foundations of Mathematics*) parasitic upon the ordinary grammatical *sense* of the linguistic form whose purported use is the object of criticism – that is, is parasitic upon that combination of words satisfying the ordinary rules of, say, English grammar and semantics. One of Dreben's favorite proof texts for this reading is *Last Writings on the Philosophy of Psychology*[78] I §44, where Wittgenstein apparently grants the rightness of a "compositional" treatment of sense for certain purposes:

Does the sentence "Napoleon was crowned in the year 1804" really have a different meaning [*Sinn*] depending on whether I say it to somebody as a piece of information, or in a history test to show what I know, or etc., etc.? In order to understand it, the meanings [*Bedeutungen*] of its words must be explained to me in the same way for each of these purposes. And if the meaning [*Bedeutung*] of the words and the way they're put together constitute the meaning [*Sinn*] of the sentence, then – – –.

To support this reading of Wittgenstein's use of the term "nonsense," we might equally well point to the *Tractatus* itself, in which tautologies and contradictions, though not violating any rules of "logical syntax," are nevertheless senseless (*sinnlos*).[79] Dreben has often made this suggestion in order to contrast Wittgenstein's attitude toward the notion of a "misuse of language" with that, for example, of J.L. Austin, who seems to have held that ordinary English (say, our verb "to know") really has a grammar which can be explicitly and correctly laid out in a series of assertions.[80]

My point has been that Wittgenstein's use of the concept of perspicuousness – whether in mathematics or in philosophy – is misarticulated if we attempt to express it by means of the assertion or denial of a given sentence or series of sentences (including sentences of the form "But p is a perfectly grammatical statement and so must be true or false," and those of the form "But p violates grammar, it is nonsense"). One way in which one's attempts to express conviction can issue into *Unsinn* is in the appeal to (mere) grammar to defend one's understanding.[81]

Nevertheless, the sort of perspicuousness we have been considering – whether it is exhibited in a mathematical proof of impossibility or in the offering of a perspicuous presentation in philosophy – has a specific sort of application: it is used to stop someone who is under the illusion of making sense from speaking emptily, to wean one away from certain specific lines of thought, to part one from particular ways one might think that conviction can be expressed or produced. It is characteristic of the acceptance of a proof of impossibility that one will be able to use it against a specific illusion, to use it to stop others from trying to do that which they do not *really* want to do. Proof is central to mathematics, and our acceptance of proofs partly makes them what they are. "It must be so" is a characteristic expression – and mode of behavior – of one who accepts a proof. An impossibility proof in mathematics, if it is a *proof*,

> contains an element of prediction, a physical element. For in consequence of such a proof we say to a man: "Don't exert yourself to find a construction (of the trisection of an angle, say) – it can be proved that it can't be done". That is to say: it is essential that the proof of unprovability should be capable of being applied [*anwenden*] in this way. It must – we might say – be a *forcible reason* [*triftiger Grund*] for giving up the search for a proof (i.e. for a construction of such-and-such a kind).
>
> (*Remarks on the Foundations of Mathematics* I Appendix III §14)

Although Wittgenstein sees proofs as contributing to our understanding of the notions at work in them, I have argued that he does not take acceptance of a proof to be a matter of discerning a set of grammatical rules which govern those notions before the proof is given. Though Wittgenstein takes systematic techniques and algorithms to be central to much mathematics, he does not take them to provide us with the whole story about mathematics, to exhaust what we mean by "proof." And this is not because he believes that at each step it is wholly up to us to decide what we find convincing: for Wittgenstein, our absorption in the compulsion of a proof, our sense of the necessity of each of its steps, is part and parcel of the proof's being a proof. We do not choose what will convince us.

In philosophy, by contrast, there are no proofs and there are no algorithms. In philosophy, it is up to us to choose what we examine, and we should examine what does and what does not convince us. For this, we require a certain detachment from what is taken to be obvious or perspicuous, a detachment not characteristic of mathematical practice (even if an unresolved, very demanding problem in mathematics might lead us, on reflection, *to* such detachment). Philosophy's task is to investigate phenomena of necessity and obviousness, the "mustness," what is "certain" or "obviously correct." A mathematical proof proves in so far as we accept it as a forcible ground for mathematical action. But in philosophy, when we ask ourselves to put the forcefulness of that ground into a proposition, or a set of propositions, we falsify it. No one label ("follows by logic," "is intuitively obvious," "is perspicuous," "is necessarily true") will do to explicate it. Wittgenstein philosophizes, like Plato, by a dialectical way of thinking, by reflecting upon his own sense of what is obvious, rounding over and over again on different ways of giving voice to certainty. This is not meant to undermine the practice of proof, but to place it into philosophical perspective. That perspective is up to us to choose.

For in philosophy, a perspicuous overview of grammar does not compel all or most of us to say one or another particular thing. There is nothing in particular that we *really* want to say in philosophy, which is why the phrase "So you really wanted to say . . ." has an endless application in philosophy, as it does not in mathematics. A perspicuous overview of grammar shows me what I do and do not take to make sense; it gives me the feeling that I know my way about my own grammar. I may question that feeling, or I may not. Questioning the feeling of being at home in one's language is difficult; its point and its outcome not always obvious in advance.[82] Philosophy cannot hope to issue into convincing assertions which rest upon the appeal to grammar:

> What is it that is repulsive in the idea that we study the use of a word, point to mistakes in the description of this use and so on? First and foremost one asks oneself: How could *that* be so important to us? It depends on whether what one calls a 'wrong description' is a description that does not accord with established usage – or one which does not accord with the practice of the person giving the description. Only in the second case does a philosophical conflict arise.
>
> *(Remarks on the Philosophy of Psychology* I §548)

It is characteristic both of mathematics and of philosophy that in practice one is frequently faced with the task of trying to understand a person – often oneself – whom one takes to be under the illusion of expressing sense. One moral to draw from Wittgenstein's discussions of mathematics is that his sort of philosophy calls for one to go a very great distance in trying to understand what moves a person attempting to do something which, by that person's own lights, is *not* perspicuous. Wittgenstein's philosophy is devoted, in large measure, to inculcating in his readers, through a dialectical form of writing, an appreciation of the reality, the centrality and the difficulty of bringing about such understanding in philosophy. What is most difficult to voice clearly is what is taken to be most convincing: the eye captivated by its own sense of obviousness is still a captive one. Only the uncaptive eye has learned to see how very complicated, how very unobvious, are phenomena of obviousness in philosophy.

Notes

1 Sections 2 and 3 below rework pp. 381–95 of my "On Saying What You Really Want to Say: Wittgenstein, Gödel, and the Trisection of the Angle," in Jaakko Hintikka (ed.) *From Dedekind to Gödel: The Foundations of Mathematics in the Early Twentieth Century,* © 1995 Kluwer Academic Publishers, Dordrecht, pp. 373–426; passages from that paper are reprinted by permission of the publisher. My primary debt is to Burton Dreben for his teaching and philosophical inspiration. I am also indebted to Arthur Collins, Cora Diamond, Warren Goldfarb, Charles Landesman, Richard Mendelsohn, Rohit Parikh, Hilary Putnam and Mark Steiner for their writings and conversation, and to exchanges with students in my seminars on Wittgenstein from 1991 to 1995 at the City College of New York, The Graduate Center of CUNY and Boston University. Ulrich Ernst, Andrew Lugg, Hilary Putnam and Mark Steiner gave me most helpful comments on drafts of the paper, as did the editors.
2 Ludwig Wittgenstein, *Notebooks 1914–16,* p. 5.
3 *Philosophical Investigations* §115.
4 Compare Ludwig Wittgenstein, *Remarks on the Foundations of Mathematics* III §46, quoted and discussed below.
5 Compare Ludwig Wittgenstein, *Tractatus Logico-Philosophicus,* C.K. Ogden (trans.) 5.1361, 6.371–2.
6 Compare Cora Diamond, *The Realistic Spirit: Wittgenstein, Philosophy and the Mind,* Cambridge, Mass., MIT Press, 1991, chapters 6–7, and "Wittgenstein, Mathematics, and Ethics: Resisting the Attractions of Realism," in Hans Sluga (ed.) *The Cambridge Companion to Wittgenstein,* Cambridge, Cambridge University Press, 1996, pp. 226–60.

7 Michael Dummett, "Wittgenstein's Philosophy of Mathematics," in his *Truth and Other Enigmas*, Cambridge, Mass., Harvard University Press, 1978, pp. 166–85; quotes from pp. 167–8.

8 Compare my "Wittgenstein on 2, 2, 2 . . .: On the Opening of *Remarks on the Foundations of Mathematics*," *Synthese*, 1991, vol. 87, pp. 143–80.

9 Ludwig Wittgenstein, *On Certainty*.

10 See *Wiener Ausgabe*, especially vol. 1, and also *Philosophical Remarks*.

11 See G.H. von Wright, "The Origin and Composition of the *Philosophical Investigations*," in his *Wittgenstein*, Minneapolis, University of Minnesota Press, 1983. I discuss von Wright's work and the provenance of Wittgenstein's discussions of mathematics in my "Wittgenstein on 2, 2, 2 . . .", op. cit.

12 *Tractatus* 6.2ff.

13 See *Notebooks 1914–16*, pp. 89, 109, *Tractatus* 6. 125.

14 *Remarks on the Foundations of Mathematics* V §40.

15 *Remarks on the Foundations of Mathematics* III §25; compare *Tractatus* 4.002, and *Culture and Value*, p. 25.

16 *Remarks on the Foundations of Mathematics* III §§45–6.

17 Wittgenstein, "On Logic and How Not to Do It: Review of P. Coffey, *The Science of Logic*," in *The Cambridge Review*, 1913, vol. 34, p. 351; reprinted in Ludwig Wittgenstein, *Philosophical Occasions 1912–1951*, pp. 1–3. Quote is from p. 3. For a discussion of this review's significance, see B. Dreben and J. Floyd, "Tautology: How Not to Use A Word," *Synthese*, 1991, vol. 87, pp. 23–50.

18 *Remarks on the Foundations of Mathematics* V §24; see also V §46.

19 *Tractatus* 6.126ff.

20 *On Certainty* §§1ff.

21 For "triftiger Grund" see *Remarks on the Foundations of Mathematics* I App. III §§14–15, III §86, and *On Certainty* §271.

22 Even, I believe, in the *Tractatus* – though I admit this is a controversial claim. See my "The Uncaptive Eye: Solipsism in Wittgenstein's *Tractatus*," in L. Rouner (ed.) *Loneliness*, Boston University Studies in Philosophy and Religion vol. 19, South Bend, Ind., University of Notre Dame Press, 1998, pp. 79–108.

23 Compare my "Goedel et les mathématiques selon Wittgenstein", in E. Riga (ed.) *Wittgenstein et les fondements des mathématiques*, Paris, TER, forthcoming.

24 *Philosophical Investigations* §§108, 130–3,156, 235, 402, 494, 600.

25 I have profited from Cavell's recent essay connecting Wittgenstein's conception of philosophy with his discussions of mathematical proof, "The Investigations' Everyday Aesthetics of Itself," in S. Mulhall (ed.) *The Cavell Reader*, Cambridge, Mass., Blackwell, 1996, pp. 368–89. But I do not follow Cavell in using the term "formal proof" to characterize mathematical proof for Wittgenstein, especially when "formal" is being contrasted with the "ordinary" or the "everyday" (compare "The Investigations' Everyday Aesthetics of Itself," op. cit., pp. 377–8, 384). This is not, of course, to deny that there remain important differences between procedures of proof and philosophical procedures for Wittgenstein.

26 This raises the intriguing question of whether we might describe Wittgenstein's treatment of mathematics, and indeed of philosophy, as, from the very beginning, "phenomenological." Compare Paul Bernays, "Comments on Ludwig Wittgenstein's *Remarks on the Foundations of Mathematics*," *Ratio*, 1959, vol. 2 , pp. 1–22; Dagfinn Føllesdal, "Husserl on Evidence and Justification," in R. Sokolowski (ed.) *Edmund Husserl and the Phenomenological Tradition: Essays in Phenomenology*, Studies in Philosophy and the History of Philosophy vol. 18, Washington, DC, Catholic University of America Press, 1988, pp. 107–29, and "Gödel and Husserl," in J. Hintikka (ed.) *From Dedekind to Gödel*, op. cit., pp. 427–46; Jaakko Hintikka and Merrill Hintikka, *Investigating Wittgenstein*, Oxford, Blackwell, 1986; Jaakko Hintikka, "The Idea of Phenomenology in Wittgenstein and Husserl," forthcoming.

27 Cf., e.g., *Notebooks 1914–16*, pp. 2–4 and Ludwig Wittgenstein, *Zettel* §382.

28 I join Cavell in departing from the longstanding tradition of translating *"Darstellung"* by "representation," substituting for it "presentation." One reason for so interpreting the

German is to emphasize connotations of the English word "presentation" which more readily involve the idea of an action, a performance, an exhibition, a happening, as opposed to a static picture or image. These are all crucial aspects of Wittgenstein's conception of proof as something used, applied – say, within mathematics – and not something with a wholly formal or syntactic criterion. These are connotations no less appropriate to his use of the notion of an *"Übersicht"* in philosophy.

29 *Philosophical Investigations* §122; compare Wittgenstein, "'Philosophy'" §89, p. 11.

30 I take this to be the point of Wittgenstein's later remarks on Gödel, in *Remarks on the Foundations of Mathematics* VII §§18–21.

31 *Remarks on the Foundations of Mathematics* III §41.

32 *Remarks on the Foundations of Mathematics* I §36, IV §4.

33 *Remarks on the Foundations of Mathematics* III §§1ff, IV §41.

34 *Remarks on the Foundations of Mathematics* III §§22, 41.

35 *Remarks on the Foundations of Mathematics* III §§42, 55, IV §45. This may seem to be questioned at various points by Wittgenstein, e.g., in *Remarks on the Foundations of Mathematics* VII §10, where he is critiquing the idea that proof alone can settle the sense or *Sinn* of a mathematical proposition. But in remarks such as this one he is not putting forward a general theory of proof, but, rather, he is attacking the notion that there is a unique *Sinn* attached to a particular sentence to *be* settled (by a proof or by any other means). He similarly rejects the notion that we have any unique criterion of our notions of proof and of mathematical proposition (cf. *Remarks on the Foundations of Mathematics* IV §45, V §25). This is a major theme in his neighboring remarks on Gödel (see *Remarks on the Foundations of Mathematics* VII §§11–22). I discuss the context-relativity of Wittgenstein's distinction between a sentence functioning as "prose" *versus* one functioning as part of mathematics in my "Gödel et les mathematiques selon Wittgenstein".

36 *Remarks on the Foundations of Mathematics* I, I Appendix II, III §46, IV §§29ff.

37 *Remarks on the Foundations of Mathematics* I, Appendix II.

38 *Remarks on the Foundations of Mathematics* I §§82ff, 154 (cf. *Tractatus* 6.1261), III §§9, 22, 39, IV §40. This does not rule out non-constructive proofs; see note 41 below.
   The importance of seeing not only *that*, but *why* a theorem holds was stressed by Schopenhauer, who criticized Euclid for having given especially strong impetus to what Schopenhauer took to be "the analytic method" in mathematics, "the prejudice that demonstrated truth has [an] advantage over truth known through perception or intuition, or that logical truth, resting on the principle of contradiction, has [an] advantage over metaphysical truth, which is immediately evident" (Schopenhauer, *The World as Will and Representation*, E.F.J. Payne (trans.) New York, Dover Publications, 1966, vol. 1 §15). Such hostility to the axiomatic, deductive method in mathematics may have influenced Wittgenstein, who read Schopenhauer as a teenager, though there is no indication that Wittgenstein embraced Schopenhauer's account of mathematics. Occasionally Wittgenstein does speak, loosely, of intuitive aspects of mathematical proof (see, e.g., *Remarks on the Foundations of Mathematics* III §§12, 42, IV §§30, 44, V §21, VI §35, *Philosophical Investigations* §144). But I do not see him proposing a general account of proof as resting upon physical or empirical intuition, as Mark Steiner has recently suggested ("Mathematical Intuition and Physical Intuition in Wittgenstein's Later Philosophy," address to the World Congress of Philosophy, Boston, Massachusetts, August 11, 1998). Compare the attack on intuition as a general explanatory notion at *Remarks on the Foundations of Mathematics* I §3 and *Philosophical Investigations* §§213–14, and my discussion of these latter passages in "Wittgenstein on 2, 2, 2 . . .," op. cit.

39 *Remarks on the Foundations of Mathematics* I §§110ff, III §25.

40 *Remarks on the Foundations of Mathematics* VII §§10, 20.

41 It has been objected that Wittgenstein's remarks oversimplify mathematics, applying only to simple or pictorial proofs that are easy to take in, or perhaps only to constructive proofs. It is true that elementary mathematical examples feature prominently – though not exclusively – in Wittgenstein's discussions. That is because the temptation

to idealize necessary truth is most deeply rooted in what most of us take to be most obvious. Wittgenstein never precludes an investigation of features of more complex cases; indeed, he engaged in such investigations himself. Nor does he insist that, for example, a complex or lengthy formalized proof is not a proof. His critical remarks about long proofs are primarily directed at Frege's and Russell's claims to have grounded all of mathematics in logic.

As for constructivism about mathematics, Wittgenstein explicitly denies that he is a finitist or intuitionist (*Remarks on the Foundations of Mathematics* II §61, *Wittgenstein's 1939 Lectures on the Foundations of Mathematics*, C. Diamond (ed.) Chicago, University of Chicago Press, 1989, p. 111). And he never equates truth and provability (compare the whole of section 3 below, especially note 60).

42 See, for example, Garth Hallett, *A Companion to Wittgenstein's "Philosophical Investigations*," Ithaca, NY, Cornell University Press, 1977, chapters 7, 41; P.M.S. Hacker, *Insight and Illusion: Themes in the Philosophy of Wittgenstein*, revised edn, New York, Oxford University Press, 1986, chapters I, VI; Gordon Baker and P.M.S. Hacker, *Wittgenstein: Meaning and Understanding, Essays on the Philosophical Investigations, Volume I*, Chicago, University of Chicago Press, 1983, chapter XIV and *Wittgenstein: Rules, Grammar and Necessity*, Oxford, Oxford University Press, 1985, chapter 1.

43 *Philosophical Investigations* §§109, 133, cf. "'Philosophy'" §89, p. 13.

44 *Philosophical Investigations* §§108–9, II p. 230.

45 *Philosophical Investigations* §122.

46 *Philosophical Investigations* §§111, 124, 126.

47 *Philosophical Investigations* §144.

48 *Philosophical Investigations* §§127–8, 599.

49 *Remarks on the Foundations of Mathematics* I Appendix I §2.

50 *Philosophical Investigations* §§128, 599, p. 178.

51 See *Tractatus* 6.43ff, 6.45ff, *Culture and Value*, p. 9.

52 *Philosophical Remarks*, foreword; *On Certainty* §§93–5, 162–7, 233, 262.

53 G.E. Moore, *Philosophical Papers*, London, Allen and Unwin, 1959, pp. 304–5.

54 Apparently when he was more than 80 years old, Moore went back through the six volumes of detailed notes he had taken at Wittgentein's lectures in 1930–3 and wrote this seventy-one page essay, originally published as two articles in *Mind* 1954–5 (reprinted in his *Philosophical Papers*, op. cit., pp. 252–324). This is Moore's final and perhaps greatest tribute to Wittgenstein. It is, however, a tribute of extraordinary ambivalence. No one who reads Moore's essay can fail to be struck by the irony both of Moore's constant charges that Wittgenstein was misusing ordinary language and of Moore's constant claims that he fails to understand what Wittgenstein said. Indeed, as he records his reactions to Wittgenstein Moore is grappling with Wittgenstein's philosophy as seriously as he ever did. In so doing he mounts what is a very brilliant, thoroughgoing and instructive attack on the fundamentals of Wittgenstein's philosophy, precisely because again and again Moore insists on interpreting what Wittgenstein said according to his own philosophical conception, as if Wittgenstein is giving arguments and explanations about ordinary language in ordinary declarative sentences. See my essay "The Continuing Significance of Moore's Objection to Wittgenstein's Discussions of Mathematics, 1930–33 and Its Bearing on *On Certainty*," in J. Hintikka and K. Puhl (eds) *The British Tradition in 20th Century Philosophy: Papers of the 17th International Wittgenstein Symposium*, Kirchberg am Wechsel, The Austrian Ludwig Wittgenstein Society, 1994.

55 First laid out by Pierre Wanzel in his "Recherches sur les moyens de reconnaître si un Problème de géométrie peut se résoudre avec la règle et le compas," *Journal de Mathématiques Pures et Appliquées*, 1837, vol. 2, pp. 366–72.

56 See, e.g., *Wittgenstein and the Vienna Circle*, pp. 36f, 143f, 204ff; *Philosophical Remarks* XIII, pp. 170–92; *Philosophical Grammar*, pp. 387ff; *Remarks on the Foundations of Mathematics* I Appendix III §14, III §87; IV §§30, 36; VII §15; *Wittgenstein's Lectures, Cambridge 1930–32, from the notes of John King and Desmond Lee*, p. 100;

Wittgenstein's Lectures, Cambridge 1932–35, pp. 8–9, 185–6, 192–3; *Wittgenstein's Lectures on the Foundations of Mathematics: Cambridge, 1939*, pp. 56ff, 86–9; *The Blue and Brown Books*, p. 41; *Philosophical Investigations* §§334, 463; Moore, *Philosophical Papers*, op. cit., pp. 304ff.

57 Compare Warren Goldfarb, "I Want You to Bring Me a Slab: Remarks on the Opening Sections of the *Philosophical Investigations*," *Synthese*, 1983, vol. 56, pp. 265–82, and "Wittgenstein On Understanding," in *Midwest Studies in Philosophy Volume XVII: The Wittgenstein Legacy*, South Bend, Ind., University of Notre Dame Press, 1992, pp. 109–22.

58 This is a controversial reading of the *Tractatus* which I cannot establish here. See my "The Uncaptive Eye: Solipsism in Wittgenstein's *Tractatus*", op. cit.

59 There is precedent in the history of philosophy. For example, in two articles concerning the history and philosophy of mathematics in the seventeenth century, Paolo Mancosu sets out the historical effects, within the pre- and post-Galilean period, of what was called the "Quaestio de Certitudine Mathematicarum," a debate over the question of whether mathematics counted as a true science in Aristotle's sense. Mathematicians came to focus on, and avoid, proofs by contradiction in the wake of this debate. See Mancosu's "Aristotelian Logic and Euclidean Mathematics: Seventeenth-Century Developments of the *Quaestio de Certitudine Mathematicarum*," *Studies in the History and Philosophy of Science*, 1992, vol. 23, pp. 241–65; and his "On the Status of Proofs by Contradiction in the Seventeenth Century," *Synthese*, 1991, vol. 88, pp. 15–41. Compare Frege's and Russell's claims that independence proofs cannot be made in logic as they are in geometry, because the denial of a logical truth vitiates the possibility of reasoning (Russell, *Principles of Mathematics*, 2nd edn, New York, W.W. Norton Co., 1938, p. 15; Russell and Whitehead *Principia Mathematica*, 2nd edn, 3 vols, Cambridge, Cambridge University Press, 1927, I.A.*1 (p. 91); Frege, *On the Foundations of Geometry and Formal Theories of Arithmetic*, E.W. Kluge (trans.) New Haven, Yale University Press, 1971, pp. 6–49. For a discussion of Frege's remarks on geometry, see Thomas Ricketts, "Frege's 1906 Foray into Metalogic," *Philosophical Topics*, vol. 25, no. 2, pp. 169–188.

60 Wittgenstein's concern with the status of Frege's and Russell's general conceptions of logic and understanding, rather than his subscribing to an intuitionistic critique of the application of the law of the excluded middle, governs his discussions of indirect argument. I cannot treat the complex question of Wittgenstein's relation to intuitionism here; but most discussions of his alleged (finitist) "worries" about the law of the excluded middle tend to gloss over the centrality of his concern with Russell and Frege, i.e., his never having granted their idea that logic consists of generally applicable laws. Mathieu Marion's *Wittgenstein, Finitism and the Foundations of Mathematics*, New York, Oxford University Press, 1998, usefully contrasts Wittgenstein's discussions of mathematics in the early 1930s with those of Weyl, Brouwer, Heyting and others – though Marion still wishes to label Wittgenstein a "constructivist," as I do not. Hao Wang had earlier suggested that Wittgenstein subscribes to what Wang calls "variable-free finitism," in his "To and From Philosophy – Discussions with Gödel and Wittgenstein," *Synthese*, 1991, vol. 88, pp. 229–77, section 5.

61 See, e.g., S.G. Shanker, *Wittgenstein and the Turning Point in the Philosophy of Mathematics*, New York, SUNY Press, 1987, chapter 3. In "Wittgenstein's Remarks on the Significance of Gödel's Theorem" (in S.G. Shanker (ed.) *Gödel's Theorem in Focus*, London, Croom Helm, 1988, pp. 155–256) Shanker reiterates his general view that for Wittgenstein there is (p. 185) "the distinction between *mathematical questions* – whose meaning is determined by the rules of the system in which they reside – and *mathematical conjectures*, which by definition inhabit no system." On this view, a mathematical conjecture is a "meaningless expression albeit one which may exercise a heuristic influence on the construction of some new proof-system" (p. 230).

62 For further textual evidence beyond that scrutinized below, see *Notebooks 1914–16*, p. 42, *Tractatus* 6.1261, *Philosophical Remarks*, pp. 143ff, *Philosophical Grammar*, pp. 366ff, *Remarks on the Foundations of Mathematics* III §§53ff.

63 Euclid, *The Elements*, Thomas L. Heath (trans.) New York, Dover, 1957, vol. I, Book I, proposition 9, p. 264.

64 Carl B. Boyer traces, according to legend, the formulation of the three "classical" problems of antiquity (the squaring of the circle, the doubling of the cube, and the trisection of the angle) to the time of the Athenian Plague and the death of Pericles (428 BCE) in his *A History of Mathematics*, Princeton, Princeton University Press, 1968, p. 71. Euclid wrote around 300 BCE, presumably under the patronage of Ptolemy I at Alexandria.

65 Cf. Hobson, *Squaring the Circle: A History of the Problem*, Boston, Chelsea Publishing Co., 1953, p. 16:

> From the time of Plato (429–348 B.C.), who emphasized the distinction between Geometry which deals with incorporeal things or images of pure thought and Mechanics which is concerned with things in the external world, the idea became prevalent that [such] problems . . . should be solved by Euclidean determination only, equivalent on the practical side to the use of two instruments only, the ruler and the compass.

66 Based on the presentation of the construction in Courant and Robbins, *What is Mathematics?*, Oxford, Oxford University Press, 1969.

67 See Underwood Dudley's intriguing presentation of purported "trisections" in his *A Budget of Trisections*, New York, Springer Verlag, 1987.

68 In his *Rosetum Geometricum* (1671) – see Dudley, *A Budget of Trisections*, op. cit., pp. 95–6.

69 See Lakatos, *Proofs and Refutations, the Logic of Mathematical Discovery*, J. Worrall and E. Zahar (eds) New York, Cambridge University Press, 1977, chapter 1.

70 Cf. Richard Courant and Herbert Robbins, *What is Mathematics?*, p. 118.

71 Cf. Courant and Robbins, *What is Mathematics?*, p. 137, where the equation is derived from the trigonometric fact that $\cos\Theta = 4\cos^3(\Theta/3)-3\cos(\Theta/3)$. Compare I.N. Herstein's *Topics In Algebra*, 2nd edn, Lexington, Mass., Xerox, 1975, pp. 230–1.

72 Wittgenstein relies on the notion of a "calculus" primarily during his so-called middle period. Gerrard and Hilmy have stressed that "calculus" comes to be supplanted by the notion of a "language-game" in Wittgenstein's later work. See Steve Gerrard, "Wittgenstein's Philosophies of Mathematics," *Synthese*, 1991, vol. 87, pp. 125–42, and S. Stephen Hilmy, *The Later Wittgenstein*, Oxford, Basil Blackwell, 1987.

73 The former is suggested by Mathieu Marion in his "Wittgenstein and the Dark Cellar of Platonism," address to the XVth International Wittgenstein Symposium, Kirchberg am Wechsel, Austria, 1992; the latter by Shanker in his *Wittgenstein and the Turning Point in the Philosophy of Mathematics*, op. cit., and in his "Wittgenstein's Remarks on the Significance of Gödel's Theorem," in *Gödel's Theorem in Focus*, op. cit., pp. 155–256.

74 Ludwig Wittgenstein, *Remarks on the Philosophy of Psychology*.

75 *The Realistic Spirit*, op. cit., chapter 10.

76 G.E.M. Anscombe, *An Introduction to Wittgenstein's Tractatus*, Philadelphia, University of Pennsylvania Press, 1971, p. 171. The recent publication of Wittgenstein's *Geheime Tagebücher* (Wilhelm Baum (ed.) 3rd edn, Vienna, Turia and Kant, 1992) has reinforced my sense that Wittgenstein's investigations of ethics and of philosophy, logic and mathematics are seamlessly interwoven with one another. A better picture of Wittgenstein's philosophy will emerge when we can see his wartime notebooks in their original unity and entirety (that is, when the *Geheime Tagebücher* and the *Notebooks 1914–16* are published in one volume). It is the same philosopher on the same day in the same terrifying circumstances who wrote about religion, death, life and logical form.

77 Burton Dreben, "Quine and Wittgenstein: The Odd Couple," in *Wittgenstein and Quine*, Robert Arrington and Hans Glock (eds) London and New York, Routledge, 1996, pp. 39–61.

78 Ludwig Wittgenstein, *Last Writings on the Philosophy of Psychology, Volume I*, G.H. von Wright and H. Nyman (eds) C.G. Luckhardt and M. A.E. Aue (trans.) Chicago, University of Chicago Press, 1982.

79 Compare Dreben and Floyd, "Tautology: How Not to Use a Word," op. cit.

80 See J.L. Austin, "Other Minds" and "Ifs and Cans," especially pp. 231–32, both in his *Philosophical Papers*, 3rd edn, Oxford, Oxford University Press, 1979.

81 For further (sometimes contrasting) discussion of Wittgenstein's notion of nonsense see Hacker, *Insight and Illusion*, op. cit., especially chapter 1, James Conant, "Must We Show What We Cannot Say?', in Richard Fleming and Michael Payne (eds) *The Senses of Stanley Cavell*, Lewisburg, Pa., Bucknell University Press, 1989, pp. 242–83, C. Diamond, "Ethics, Imagination and the Method of Wittgenstein's *Tractatus*," in *Bilder der Philosophie: Reflexionen über das Bildliche und die Phantasie*, Richard Heinrich and Helmuth Vetter (eds) Vienna and Munich, Oldenbourg, 1991, pp. 55–90, reprinted in this volume, Douglas G. Winblad, "What Might not be Nonsense," *Philosophy*, 1993, vol. 68, pp. 549–57, Jacques Bouveresse, *Dire et ne rien dire: L'illogisme, l'impossibilité et le non-sens*, Nîmes, Éditions Jacqueline Chambon, 1997, and my "The Uncaptive Eye: Solipsism in Wittgenstein's *Tractatus*," op. cit.

82 Compare Edward H. Minar, "Feeling at Home in Language (What Makes Reading *Philosophical Investigations* Possible?)," *Synthese*, 1995, vol. 102, pp. 413–52.

11

DOES BISMARCK HAVE A BEETLE IN HIS BOX?

The private language argument in the *Tractatus*

Cora Diamond

In fact the private object is one about which neither he who has it nor he who hasn't got it can say anything to others or to himself.[1]

Wittgenstein's "private language argument" we think of as something in the *Philosophical Investigations*, although we may disagree about where exactly in that work the argument is found, and also about what sort of argument it is. We can find earlier adumbrations of the argument, or something like it, in Wittgenstein's writings of the 1930s, and in his notes for lectures during those years. We see the topic of privacy, of our capacity to speak or think about our own private sensations, as a topic of Wittgenstein's *later* philosophy. And we take the appearance of the topic as indicative of a shift in Wittgenstein's philosophical interests to topics within the philosophy of mind, not of interest to him in the *Tractatus*; further, we may take his treatment of the topic as an illustration of the fundamental shifts in his overall philosophical position. Michael Dummett, for example, takes Wittgenstein's private language argument to be deeply anti-realist, and thus at a great distance from Wittgenstein's realism in the *Tractatus*. I shall argue that there is a private language argument in the *Tractatus*, closely related to the argument in the *Investigations*, although also different from it in important respects.

Here are the parts of my argument. I first explain what I mean by something being "in" the *Tractatus*. Next I go over some ideas of Russell's which were important for Wittgenstein when he was writing the *Tractatus*, and for the rest of his philosophical life as well. I go on to explain Wittgenstein's response in the *Tractatus* to those ideas of Russell's; and I shall try to show how those early responses resemble what we now usually refer to as "the private language argument." I also explain the important differences. I need then to consider the question: if Wittgenstein provides, in the *Tractatus*, a criticism of Russell's views, what alternatives to those views are open to him? Finally I discuss briefly why all this about the *Tractatus* might still matter to us, as readers of Wittgenstein and as philosophers concerned with contemporary debates about realism and anti-realism.

1 When I argue that something is "in" the *Tractatus* I do not mean that it is explicitly said there. (Being explicitly said is sufficient but not necessary for something to be in the *Tractatus* in my sense.) Nor do I mean that it follows from what is explicitly said there. (Being inferable from what is said there is not sufficient for something to be in the book in my sense.) My way of talking about what is *in* the book is meant to reflect Wittgenstein's ideas about his own authorship: there are lines of thought which he wanted a reader of his book to pursue for himself. In the case of the *Tractatus*, one can add that there are lines of thought which he wanted *Russell*, as reader – Russell in particular – to pursue. In 1948, he said "Whatever the reader *can* do, leave to the reader."[2] Don't, that is, do it *for* him. While that remark comes from 1948, it reflects a view of writing that was always Wittgenstein's: the reader should not expect to have things done *for* him.[3] When we read any work of Wittgenstein's we need to be aware of what he sees the work as doing for us, what he sees it as leaving it to us to do. And, as I have suggested, in the case of the *Tractatus*, he had Russell specifically in mind as a reader: that work was going to do some things for Russell, but not everything. So, as I use the expression "in the *Tractatus*," I mean it to embrace the conclusions Wittgenstein wants his readers to draw for themselves, the lines of thought he wants his readers to work through for themselves. And, to know what *we* as readers should do or try to do, we need to bear in mind the question what Wittgenstein meant *Russell* to do.[4]

(My way of speaking of what is "in" the *Tractatus* corresponds to Wittgenstein's in a letter to Schlick in 1932, in which, on the basis of Carnap's discussion of physicalism in *Die physikalische Sprache als Universalsprache der Wissenschaften*,[5] he accused Carnap of having plagiarized from the *Tractatus*. He recognized that Schlick would not find in the *Tractatus* itself any explicit presentation of the ideas which he was accusing Carnap of having lifted from it; he describes what Carnap has taken as present in the book in the brevity with which the entire *Tractatus* was written ("*in der Kürze, in der die ganze 'Abhandlung' geschrieben ist*"). In fact the *Tractatus* ideas about "physicalism" which Carnap allegedly used without attribution and the critique of Russell which I shall be discussing are closely related.)

There are obvious difficulties in any argument that something is in the *Tractatus* in my sense. My claim is essentially that I am doing what Wittgenstein wanted Russell to do as a reader of the *Tractatus* (or, rather, part of what he wanted him to do). My argument as a whole rests on a variety of considerations, including the extreme unlikelihood that Wittgenstein was unaware of the critical power of the ideas in the *Tractatus* in relation to Russell's treatment of other minds and closely related topics. The points I shall make about the implications of the text for Russell's theory are, once seen, very obvious; they depend only on ideas which are given considerable prominence in the text of the *Tractatus*; they are therefore of a sort which Wittgenstein might well (so I am suggesting) have thought it reasonable to leave a reader like Russell to work out.

2 I now turn to Russell's views. Before explaining them, I need to mention a problem running through this essay, namely the use of the words "proposition" and "sentence." I use "proposition" when I am expounding Russell; he sometimes uses the word "proposition" to mean something non-linguistic which may be judged or supposed or entertained (and so on), and sometimes to mean the linguistic expression of a proposition in that first sense.[6] I use the word "sentence" to translate Wittgenstein's "*Satz*," which has as its primary meaning in the *Tractatus* a combination of signs in use to mean that something is the case; this does not correspond exactly to either Russellian use of "proposition." The use of two different terms creates some awkwardness; the alternative, which would be to use "proposition" for Wittgenstein's "*Satz*," might create the false impression that the term meant the same for Wittgenstein as for Russell.

The works of Russell's with which I shall be concerned are his essays "On Denoting" and "Knowledge by Acquaintance and Knowledge by Description," the book *Problems of Philosophy*, and his manuscript on theory of knowledge.[7] (It is not known how much of the manuscript Russell actually showed Wittgenstein; but we do know that Russell discussed his work on the book with Wittgenstein.[8]) These writings come from 1905 to 1913; and a fundamental principle of Russell's during that period was that all cognitive relations depend on acquaintance.[9] Acquaintance is *direct* awareness, *direct* cognitive contact; and the objects of acquaintance, according to Russell, include not only sensations and other mental items, but also non-mental items, such as universals and abstract logical facts.[10] Russell's idea that all cognitive relations depend on acquaintance is tied closely to another fundamental principle of his, that every proposition which we can understand must be composed entirely of constituents with which we are acquainted (*Problems of Philosophy*, p.32; cf. "On Denoting," p.56). During the period with which I am concerned those two principles help to shape Russell's epistemology and metaphysics, via the theory of descriptions, used by Russell to explain how propositions about things with which we are not acquainted can have, as their constituents, only things with which we are acquainted.

Here are two important examples of how all this works. Consider first the metaphysical question whether our present experience is all-embracing, or whether instead something can lie outside it. Russell wants to reject the argument that, if something could lie outside our experience, we could not know that there is such a thing. He is perfectly happy to admit that one cannot now give an *actual instance* of a thing not now within one's experience. One can, however, *mention* such a thing by using a descriptive phrase. Here is Russell's argument.

> An object may be *described* by means of terms which lie within our experience, and the proposition that there is an object answering to this description is then one composed wholly of experienced constituents. It is therefore possible to know the truth of this proposition without passing outside of experience. If it appears on examination that no *experienced* object answers to this description, the conclusion follows that there are objects not experienced. [Russell gives as an example that we may know Jones and know that there is the father of Jones, although the father of Jones is not within our experience.][11]

The second example concerns our knowledge of what other people are directly acquainted with, what is present in *their* experience. You and I might possibly experience the same object, but only you experience your experiencing of it: I cannot experience your experiencing of it. Or again, let us suppose that each of us is acquainted with his or her own self. Russell treats that as a serious possibility, during at least part of the period which I am discussing. Now consider a statement about Bismarck. Since we are supposing that Bismarck himself has direct acquaintance with himself, he will be able to use the name "Bismarck" (or "I") so that it directly designates himself. If he makes the statement "Bismarck is an astute diplomatist" or "I am an astute diplomatist," he himself, an object with which he is acquainted, is a constituent of his judgment. But you or I or anyone else can think about Bismarck only via some description; we are not directly acquainted with the object which he denotes by "I." If we say "Bismarck was an astute diplomatist," an analysis of our proposition would show that we are not directly designating Bismarck. We designate him via some description. In the analyzed proposition, the name "Bismarck" is replaced by a description, and we can see from the analysis that Bismarck himself is not a constituent of the proposition. Because the object Bismarck is known to Bismarck by acquaintance, but known to us only by description, our judgment about Bismarck is not the same as Bismarck's judgment about Bismarck. Bismarck has available to him a proposition which he can understand and which we cannot. We can, however, know by description the proposition which Bismarck understands.

It is important that, as Russell sees the situation, there is something which we should like to do but cannot do:

> ... when we say anything about Bismarck, we should like, if we could, to make the judgment which Bismarck alone can make, namely the judgment of which he himself is the constituent. In this we are necessarily defeated, since the actual Bismarck is unknown to us.
> ("Knowledge by Acquaintance and Knowledge by Description," p.218)

In that quotation, Russell uses a descriptive phrase to speak about a judgment which we cannot make or understand. We know that there is such a judgment, but there is a barrier cutting it off from us. There is an ideal position for thinking about Bismarck, a position which no one but Bismarck can be in.

(We can note that Russell's argument applies to itself. Bismarck can say to himself: "When I say anything about Bismarck, I can make a judgment which Russell cannot make; and the judgment which I just made is an example, since I am a constituent of it. Because Russell does not know me, he is necessarily defeated in his attempt to make the judgment which I can make about his being necessarily defeated in his attempt to make judgments about me." But Bismarck is himself necessarily defeated, on this view, in making about Russell the judgments he would like to make (including the judgment that Russell is necessarily defeated in attempting to make the judgment that he is necessarily defeated in attempting to make judgments about Bismarck himself), since no one unacquainted with Russell can make judgments of which Russell is a constituent. Only someone who was acquainted with both Russell and Bismarck could make the judgment which both of them would like to make about Russell's necessary defeat in judgment-making about Bismarck; that judgment is one which both of them, and all of us, can speak about only via a description. And only someone acquainted with both Russell and Bismarck could make the judgment which my last statement was a necessarily defeated attempt to make, and only someone acquainted with both Russell and Bismarck could make the judgment which *that* statement was an attempt to make, and . . .)

Russell's example concerns thought about Bismarck, about Bismarck's self, but the point he is making is more general. Whatever elements there are in one person's experience which another person can know only by description cannot genuinely be constituents of propositions understood by anyone else. The propositions which the person himself can make about that object and the propositions which other people can make about the same object will always have different constituents; the actual experienced object will be a constituent only of the propositions made by the possessor of the experience. Since we do not have acquaintance with any minds other than our own, all our knowledge of other minds is via description. We are cut off from the kind of knowledge of other people's minds which we really want, just as we are cut off from knowing of Bismarck the propositions which Bismarck himself knows, which have as a constituent an object with which only he is acquainted. I want to emphasize that, although Russell's example is the self, his discussion of it is meant to apply to everything with which other people are directly acquainted, and with which we ourselves cannot be acquainted. Russell himself certainly thought that, even if the self is not an object of acquaintance, there are objects of acquaintance to which his argument *would* apply: a person can make judgments about things with which he is acquainted, judgments which other people cannot make or understand. It is reasonable here to use the phrase "private object" in connection with Russell's ideas about objects with which only a single person can be acquainted. (In writings a little later than those which I am using, Russell explicitly refers to toothaches as private sensations: he speaks of toothaches as essentially private. There is no reason to think that that talk of toothaches marks any significant change in his views about objects knowable only to one person. He speaks, in *Problems of Philosophy* (p.27), of "my desiring food" as an object with which I am acquainted. In *Theory of Knowledge* (pp.7–8) he says that we can denote objects with which we are acquainted by a proper name. In the case, then, of those objects with which only I can be acquainted, the proper names which I use for these objects are names which only I can understand. If I speak about these private objects to myself, using such names, I cannot be in error. In this essay I sometimes use the example of Bismarck's *toothache*, instead of Bismarck's *self*, as an example in discussing Russell's views.[12])

Although my aim is to show how Wittgenstein responds to these ideas in the *Tractatus*, I want to note first how clearly it is these ideas which he also has in mind in *Philosophical Investigations*. When, in §243, he introduces the question whether there could be a private language, he explains it as a language in which the words "refer to what can only be known to the person speaking"; "another person cannot understand the language."[13] Again, in §289 of the *Investigations*, he takes the idea of a private language to include the idea that, in using it, one is directly aware of the justification for one's use of the words of the language; and this connects directly to Russell's description of the use of proper names for objects of acquaintance: one cannot be in error in one's application of these names, because they name objects directly available for naming (*Theory of Knowledge*, p.7; cf. *Problems of Philosophy*, p.63).

One further point should be mentioned concerning Russell's views, and that is the seriousness of the threat of solipsism as he saw it. Russell takes himself to have good arguments against any form of idealism or solipsism. Indeed he writes "the chief importance of knowledge by description is that it enables us to pass beyond the limits of our private experience. In spite of the fact that we can only know truths which are wholly composed of terms which we have experienced in acquaintance, we can yet have knowledge by description of things which we have never experienced" (*Problems of Philosophy*, p.32; cf. *Theory of Knowledge*, p.10, for the image of present experience as apparently a "prison" from which, however, knowledge by description can liberate us).

The theory of descriptions is important, then, within the theory of knowledge, in explaining how we can avoid solipsism.[14] Russell's idea that knowledge by description enables us to pass beyond the limits of our private experience could also be expressed this way: the limits of *the* world, about which I can have knowledge, and the objects in which I can denote (whether directly or in some cases only indirectly), lie outside the limits of the realm of my own experience. There are implicit in Russell's statement about the significance of knowledge by description *two limits which do not coincide*. (Russell's realism, we could say, is a two-limits realism.) When we read in the *Tractatus* that the world is *my* world, we should at least raise the question whether we are reading a criticism of Russell's ideas about how knowledge by description enables one to pass beyond the limits of one's own experience.[15] I shall return to this question in section 10.

What lies outside the realm of things with which I am directly acquainted includes not only the experiences of others but also physical objects; and Russell's view of physical objects was changing during the period with which I am concerned.[16] He arrived at an account of physics involving the notion of "private worlds," where a private world may be somebody's but need not actually be anybody's.[17] I agree with Thomas Ricketts that Wittgenstein is, in the *Tractatus*, "as concerned to reject Russell's view of sensibilia as he is to reject Russell's view of Bismarck's toothache," but I shall not here trace how the concern with these two related topics works out.[18] Much of what I describe as being the *Tractatus* view about Russell on private objects will, however, be applicable to Russell on our knowledge of the physical world.

3 Much of Wittgenstein's philosophy, throughout his life, is constituted by responses to central elements of Russell's approach.[19] Before turning, in section 4, to the principles forming the basis for the *Tractatus* response to Russell, I shall here note two passages, one from the *Investigations* and one from around 1930, illustrating Wittgenstein's interest in what we might call *Russellian indirection*.

Earlier I quoted Russell's remark that whenever we say anything about Bismarck, we are, in a sense, necessarily defeated: we cannot make the judgment we should really like to make, the judgment Bismarck himself can make. We can ourselves, with our words, reach only indirectly, by description, what Bismarck can talk about directly. Section 426 of *Philosophical Investigations* applies to just this sort of view. Wittgenstein says there that we may think of an expression as having an ideal kind of use, which is unfortunately permanently unavailable to us. We cannot use the straight road, and have to use detours, side-roads. Wittgenstein's metaphor applies to what Russell says about Bismarck: Bismarck, using words that he alone can understand, can reach by the straight road of acquaintance what we can get to only by side-roads, by descriptions. The road that we can see to be available to Bismarck is permanently closed to us.[20]

There is an earlier, explicit, reference to Russellian indirection in the *Philosophical Remarks*:

> ... Russell has really already shown by his theory of descriptions, that you can't get a knowledge of things by sneaking up on them from behind and it can only *look* as if we knew more about things than they have shown us openly and honestly. But he has obscured everything again by using the phrase "indirect knowledge."[21]

Wittgenstein implies there that Russellian indirection (as I have called it) goes against what Russell's theory of descriptions had in fact accomplished, although Russell himself was not aware of its significance.

4 In order to see how the *Tractatus* responds to Russell, we should look at three things: the metaphor of logical space, Wittgenstein's ideas about what is accomplished by logical analysis and his treatment of quantifiers.

Why are quantifiers important? Russell sees the theory of descriptions as explaining how we can, by using descriptions, reach indirectly the things with which Bismarck is directly acquainted; the theory supposedly explains how, by the use of quantification, we can indirectly speak about Bismarck's private objects. So Russell's idea of how we avoid solipsism, how we get to something outside our own experience, is based on what he thinks quantifiers enable us to encompass in our use of words.

Let me spell out further how the use of quantifiers will be important for my overall argument. The *Tractatus* shows, I shall hold, that *no* role in language is played by the things with which Bismarck is acquainted and which he can name in his language, but to which, according to Russell, we cannot refer by the proper names of our language. These things are not "denoted indirectly": the supposition that we mean them is empty. In the *Investigations*, Wittgenstein uses the metaphor of the beetle in the box in criticizing the idea one may have of things in one's own mind, things to which one can give proper names, and which no one else can know. If sensations are conceived in accordance with that model they would be, he argues, irrelevant to the language game: it would not make any difference to the language game if the box in which each of us kept our beetle were empty (§293). We are going to see him in the *Tractatus* provide an argument which in effect shows that any beetles in other people's boxes drop out of the language game. This *Tractatus* approach may indeed leave us with our own beetles; the beetle population does not disappear until Wittgenstein develops powerful new coleoptericides in the 1930s. But other people's beetles are getting attacked already in the *Tractatus*. The idea that we can reach indirectly, by our use of quantifiers, the beetles in Bismarck's box, his private objects, depends on Russell's conception of quantifiers, and that is why the difference between Wittgenstein and Russell about quantifiers will turn out to be important for us.

Let us start here with the famous example Russell used in explaining the theory of descriptions.

"The present King of France is bald"
"(∃x){[(x is king of France).(y)(y is king of France ⊃ y = x)].(x is bald)}"

As Wittgenstein understands Russell's accomplishment, the analysis enables us to see the original sentence as a construction using quantifiers and sentential connectives. When we understand it as constructed in this way, we see how it represents a possible situation whether or not there is a king of France. And, at the same time, the Russellian rewriting of the sentence makes clearer how the inferential relations of the sentence depend on how it is constructed.

Wittgenstein thought that the process of logical analysis could continue, and the ultimate result would be that we should see all sentences as constructed logically from what he called elementary sentences. In the process of analysis we make clear both *what possible situation* is represented by any sentence, and *what inferential relations* the sentence has. The idea here is expressed in the metaphor of "logical space." Analysis makes it possible for us to see how each sentence represents a situation in a space of possible situations: this is "logical space." Just as a spatial description or a map, say a topographical map of Scotland, represents something in 3-dimensional space, each of our sentences, by its construction, represents a possible situation in logical space: it represents a reality as *so*; and the reality will actually *be* so, will be as represented, or not.[22] The relation of logical consequence between sentences, as Wittgenstein understands it, is meant to be illuminated by the same metaphor. The space of possible situations is logically structured. If you take any sentence, it is so constructed that it represents a situation in logical space; at the same time, the sentence so constructed has fully determinate logical relations to all other sentences, all other constructions of signs used to represent situations in logical space. Although any sentence itself determines only a *single* place, a *single* possible situation, in logical space, "nevertheless the *whole* of logical space," Wittgenstein says, "must already be given by it" (*Tractatus* 3.42, my italics). He says that the sentence *reaches right through* logical space; this means that inferential relations between sentences are relations within this "space." The sentence's "reaching through" logical space, touching every location in it, is the determinacy of the logical relations between that sentence and every other. What the metaphor brings out is the tie between, on the one hand, two sentences each representing something as being so, and, on the other, their standing in logical relations to each other. (Compare two topographical maps of anywhere. By virtue of being topographical maps, they represent parts of the globe that do or do not overlap. In the latter case, they are logically compatible. If the two maps represent overlapping parts of the surface of the earth, they will either be compatible or not; they cannot represent how things stand topographically somewhere and not stand in determinate logical relations to each other.)

We can now move on to two profoundly connected things: how Wittgenstein's ideas involve a criticism of Russell's, and how he thinks *quantifiers* fit into the general picture. (The rest of this section is about the difference between Wittgenstein and Russell; the next section concerns the effect of that difference on Bismarck and his beetles.)

Wittgenstein's metaphor of logical space is tied, I claimed, to his idea that in the construction of sentences you can see how they have their logical relations to other sentences: this comes out in the metaphor of logical space as not just a space of possible situations, but also a space within which sentences have their logical relations to other sentences, the space of inference. What then is the connection with Wittgenstein's account of the quantifiers? The basic logical feature of quantifiers is the logical relation between sentences with quantifiers and singular sentences (or sentences with fewer quantifiers). Two of the most familiar such logical relations are the inferability of "Some x is f" from any such sentence as "fa" and the inferability of sentences like "fa" from "All x is f." If these logical relations can be seen in the construction of our sentences, then we shall need to see the quantified sentences as themselves constructions out of singular sentences. I shall give a brief explanation of how this is supposed to work in the *Tractatus*, but what is important is not the details of how it works but the overall contrast between the *Tractatus* view and that of Russell; and what matters in Russell's view is that the logical notions of *all* and *some* are, for him, primitive ideas.[23] So sentences with quantifiers are not seen by Russell as they are by Wittgenstein, as constructions from sentences which do not contain quantifiers.

Here is the brief explanation of Wittgenstein's view. To see how a quantified sentence is a construction from singular sentences, we need two things. We need rules which will generate, from a common feature of sentences, a set of sentences sharing that feature; for example, a rule that would generate, from the predicate "is red," all allowable combinations of that predicate with the name of an object. Also, we need operations that work this way: given as bases any number of sentences (specified as the values of a sentence-variable), the operations will form a single new sentence out of them by making a truth-table using all of the input sentences, and systematically setting out all truth-value combinations for those sentences. (Any such operation is a general rule for sentence-construction from base sentences.) One such operation works by putting the truth-value T in the "result" column in all the rows of the truth-table, except the row in which all the input sentences are false. Here is that operation applied to three sentences.

p	q	r	O(p, q, r)
T	T	T	T
F	T	T	T
T	F	T	T
F	F	T	T
T	T	F	T
F	T	F	T
T	F	F	T
F	F	F	F

That construction shows you that the resulting sentence follows from p, follows from q and follows from r. Given that that is how the O operation works, let us now have *this* construction: the O operation applied to *all* the sentences which are values of the sentence-variable (*Satzvariable*) "fx," i.e, all the sentences formed by

270

replacing "x" with an appropriate name: "O[f(a), f(b), f(c), f(d) . . .]." A sentence constructed in that way follows from each of the singular sentences "fa" etc. If we now treat "Some x is f" as a sentence constructed in that way, we can see how, by its construction, it follows from the singular sentences "fa" etc. The quantified sentence and each of the singular sentences from which it follows all lie in logical space; all reach to each other in that space.[24]

This is a big departure from Russell's approach to the quantifiers. Russell gives somewhat different explanations of the quantifiers at different times, but they all fit into a basic picture different from Wittgenstein's. His idea is that, since we understand logical words like "some" and "all," we are acquainted with the logical objects "involved" in those logical notions. (See *Theory of Knowledge*, p.99; cf. also p.97.) And that idea – that the understanding of logical words goes *via* our acquaintance with logical objects – is exactly what Wittgenstein rejected in the *Tractatus*. He explicitly denies (twice) that there are "logical objects" (*Tractatus* 5.4, also 4.441); and he gives as his "fundamental idea" the idea that logical words do not work by standing for something (*Tractatus* 4.0312). There are no logical objects for which they stand, no logical objects with which we have to be acquainted in order to understand logical words or signs. (The fact that a logical word occurs in a sentence is not an indication of any element of meaning shared with other sentences containing the logical word. What it is for a logical word to be used consistently is for it to mark, in a consistent way, differences between sentences. Thus, for example, the occurrence of "not" in a sentence marks the difference in truth-conditions between that sentence and the sentence with "not" removed; and the word would work in exactly the same way if by "not-p" we meant what we mean by "p," and vice versa.[25] Hence the importance for Wittgenstein of the fact that a logical word like "not" can be cancelled out entirely by a second use of "not." This possibility of cancellation shows that the occurrence of "not" indicates no common feature of the meaning of the sentences in which it occurs. The idea that logical words mark differences between sentences is connected with Wittgenstein's fundamental conception of logic: logical relations are relations between ordinary sentences of our language.)

Getting back to Russell: what his view comes to, then, is that we can understand the words "some" and "all," or the quantifier notation, if we have a *general* grasp of what it is for a property or relation to be instantiated in *some* or *all* cases. (And in *Principia Mathematica*, the explanation of the quantifiers goes via precisely those two primitive ideas, tied in with the *Principia Mathematica* account of propositional functions.) In 1913, Russell's view was that our understanding of a proposition like "For all x, x is red," depends on our acquaintance with *red* together with our general logical grasp of the notion *all* (together with our acquaintance with a logical form). He does not see the sentence "For all x, x is red" as a construction from singular sentences, in the way Wittgenstein does. And similarly with "Something is red." This too is not, on Russell's view, a construction from sentences about named or nameable individuals. So here too there is a big difference from Wittgenstein's idea that whenever sentences stand in logical relations to each other, those relations can be seen in the sentences themselves, in how they are constructed. Russell and Wittgenstein *agree* that *There is some x such that fx* follows from *fa*; for Wittgenstein but not for Russell, if you make clear what sort of construction the quantified sentence is, you can see how its logical relations to sentences about individuals simply fall out of the construction.

(There is some discussion of the relation between Wittgenstein's view and Russell's in G.E.M. Anscombe, *Introduction to Wittgenstein's Tractatus*;[26] she quotes F.P. Ramsey's discussion of the same subject. (Or, rather, of what she takes to be the same subject. What Ramsey discusses is the relation between Wittgenstein's view and the "alternative" view. Presumably he does mean Russell, but he does not mention Russell or anyone else by name; and, taken as an account of Russell's view, his discussion has some puzzling features.[27]) What Anscombe and Ramsey emphasize, as the crucial difference between Wittgenstein's view and the alternative view of the quantifiers, is that Wittgenstein's account does, and the alternative view does not, provide an "intelligible connection between *a* being red and red having application." Their objection itself needs more elaboration before it can be judged how far it does apply to Russell or to Frege; it seems to me possible to argue instead that Russell and Frege do each provide a connection, but that the *Tractatus* rejects the sort of account they can provide.)

5 How then does the difference between Wittgenstein and Russell form the basis of a *Tractatus* attack on the Russellian view of Bismarck's private language for his private objects?

The basic Russellian picture involves the relation between Bismarck's judgment about his own private object and Russell's judgment about that very same object:

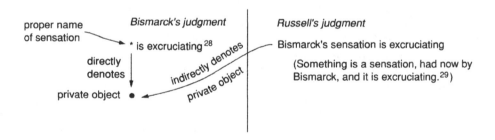

(The vertical line represents the limitation of judgments on either side. On the left, the constituents of judgment are items with which Bismarck is acquainted; on the right, the constituents of judgment are items with which Russell is acquainted.)

The *Tractatus* attacks this picture by attacking the conception of quantification on which it depends, as well as the underlying conception of logic. Russell's account requires that there be a logical relation between the proposition on the left, which only Bismarck can understand (and which everyone other than Bismarck can speak about only by description), and the quantified proposition on the right, which Russell uses. The quantified proposition *follows from* Bismarck's private proposition. And, on the *Tractatus* view, that is a crucial clue to the incoherence of the Russell conception. For Russell, there has to be that logical relation; but, on the *Tractatus* view, Russell has available no satisfactory account of what it is for there to be such a relation. The *Tractatus* view is that, if one sentence follows from another, then they are both *within* the space of constructible sentences of my language; they are both *in logical space.* Any grasp which I have of their logical relations is inseparable from my grasp of the sentences themselves, of each as a sentence saying that such-and-such is the case. Russell has told us that there is a proposition which only Bismarck can affirm. Well, if there *were* a sentence which Bismarck could utter to himself with understanding, and which I could not understand, it could not be taken to stand in logical relations to any sentence which I can understand. *If I can take a sentence to stand in logical relations to other sentences, then I can understand that sentence.* Logic is precisely what joins together the sentences of *the* language which I do understand. This *Tractatus* conception of logic rules out the idea of quantifying over objects for which I cannot have names. Here is another way of getting at the same point: the Bismarckian private proposition has to stand in logical relation to the quantified proposition which I do understand: a quantified proposition has to stand in logical relation to propositions about the objects quantified over. But, although there has to be a logical relation between the two propositions, Russell's views preclude my making an inference from one proposition to the other; I cannot grasp the two propositions *with* their supposed inferential relation.[30] Wittgenstein's conception of logic as joining together the sentences of the language which I do understand involves a denial that a sentence of my language can stand in logical relations to a sentence which cannot figure in any inference which I can make. A logical relation going outside *the* space of possible inference is an incoherent idea, and that is what is wrong with Russell's account.[31]

(Thomas Ricketts has argued that my references in this section and elsewhere to "understanding" are potentially misleading, since they suggest that the notion of understanding could be used to set out the issues, while a Russellian conception of understanding is itself at issue.[32] I entirely agree with that. When I speak of logic as joining the sentences of "the language which I understand," I am picking up the use of "understand" from *Tractatus* 5.62, where indeed Russell's ideas are at issue. Here, and elsewhere in the *Tractatus*, references to understanding can be explicated in terms of Wittgenstein's account of the use of language. Thus, e.g., if we understand "not" (see *Tractatus* 5.451), this is not because we are acquainted with something, a logical object or anything else, but because a negation sign has been introduced via a rule covering its use in *all* propositional combinations.)

At *Tractatus* 5.54, Wittgenstein says that in the general sentence-form, sentences occur in other sentences only as bases of "truth-operations." A full explanation of that remark would take us too far out of the way, but it does have an important consequence for the issue between Wittgenstein and Russell. *Tractatus* 5.54 does not rule out quantifying over sentences, or referring to them by descriptive phrases or abbreviations; what it does rule out is cases in which a sentence spoken about or quantified over is in a language which we cannot understand. Russell does, in stating his theory, explicitly use descriptive phrases in referring to sentences which we cannot understand; but what is important is that his position cannot be stated without such quantification. It is an essential part of his explanation of how we can understand propositions which indirectly denote Bismarck's private objects. The logical structure by which our use of quantification enables us to denote Bismarck's private objects requires there to be a propositional function which has among its values propositions which we can denote only indirectly. My argument is that there is an inseparable connection between the Russellian view that we can quantify over objects which we cannot name and his view that we can quantify over propositions which we cannot understand, and hence that Wittgenstein's rejection of the latter constitutes part of the structure of argument against the former. The issue here is not separable from what I discussed in the last-but-one paragraph. Logical relations are relations between the sentences of the language which I understand; there is no coherent notion of a logical relation between a quantified sentence of my language and a sentence outside that language. If one claimed that there were such logical relations, one would have to gesture at the supposed incomprehensible sentence or sentences by a description or by quantification. And here one would be fooling oneself. What you can't think you can't think, and you can't sneak up on it by quantifiers. That, at any rate, is the *Tractatus* view.

In the *Tractatus*, Wittgenstein is also rejecting the Russell picture of the mind's relation to the objects which it thinks about: the idea that the mind directly connects up with some objects, and reaches others via descriptions. Some of those can be reached, supposedly, only by descriptions. On Wittgenstein's view, what objects we are thinking about is something that is shown in the language we use. If, in logical analysis, we come to see the full structure of inferential relations *within* our language, then *that is* for it to be made clear what objects we are thinking about, what objects our quantified sentences quantify over.[33]

Let me summarize this: the disagreement between Russell and Wittgenstein over "some" and "all" underlies the disagreement about private objects in the minds of other people. The importance of the disagreement about quantification, which itself depends on the disagreement about how logical words function, is one reason why Wittgenstein says that it is his fundamental idea that logical words and signs do not have meaning by standing for something. They do not stand for or connect up with logical objects. Russell's logical-object story about "some" and "all" provides essential support for his idea that there can be a logical relationship between Bismarck's proposition, which we cannot understand or mean, and propositions of ours about *there being* such-and-such private objects. Russell's basic picture allows for our quantified sentences to be true in virtue of the properties and relations of things to which we cannot refer directly; and that basic picture depends on the logical-object story about the notions of *some* and *all*.

The alternative *Tractatus* conception is that logical relations are relations between sentences in logical space, i.e., between sentences which we understand. This is tied to the "construction" story about the quantifiers, and also to a general "construction" story about *all* sentences, and, as I have suggested, also to what Wittgenstein regards as his fundamental insight in the *Tractatus* about how logical words contribute to the sentences in which they occur. There is here no appeal to an independent notion of understanding.

What I have done so far is present the two opposing views, and tried to show that a clear understanding of Wittgenstein's view would enable us to see how it not only involves a *general* criticism of Russell on "some" and "all," but also undercuts, quite specifically, Russell's idea that quantified sentences enable us to talk about things which we cannot directly mean, including other people's private objects. But showing that there is in the *Tractatus* an attack on Russell on private objects and private language does not itself show that the *Tractatus* argument actually resembles anything in the *later* discussion of private language.

So that is the next question: in what ways does the argument against Russell resemble the private-language argument in the *Investigations*?

6 A central insight in the *Investigations* is that, if we take our capacity to talk about and think about our own sensations as a matter of our having, each of us, a private object, then the object thus understood plays no role in our actual language games. Wittgenstein's conclusion is not that there are no sensations, but that our words for sensations do not have their meaning by connecting up with private objects. To think that they do is to have a confused picture of their grammar.

What now about the *Tractatus*, and Russell's idea that, when we speak of *other people's* mental life, we want to be able to refer to objects which are private to *them*, objects which only *they* can name and refer to *directly*? The issue here is, in two ways, importantly different from that in the *Investigations*. First, we are not concerned with my language for *my own* sensations, as in the *Investigations*, but only with my language for the sensations of *other people*, conceived as private objects which only *they* can mean directly. Further, in the *Tractatus*, there is no idea of things which have or lack a role "in the language game." What there is instead is the idea of what plays a role in the representational capacities and inferential relations running through language.

Keeping those two differences in view, we can see how Wittgenstein's conception of logic in the *Tractatus* underpins an argument with some close analogies to the later private language argument. A basic idea in the earlier private language argument is that a private object nameable only by Bismarck plays no role in my language or my thought. The idea that other people's private objects do have a role in our thought dissolves into incoherence. Since the ordinary language which I speak and understand has meaningful sentences about Bismarck's sensations, those sentences do not involve the indirect denoting of Bismarck's private objects. Objects known only to Bismarck play no role in the language which I use in everyday life in talking about Bismarck and things in his mental life. (An important premise in the *Tractatus* private language argument is that our ordinary everyday language is not in any way logically inadequate. Without that premise it might be thought that the absence of reference in our language to other people's private objects makes that language incapable of achieving its aims.[34]) In terms of the *Investigations* image of the beetle in the box, what the *Tractatus* shows us is that any beetle which there might be in Bismarck's box drops out of consideration as *irrelevant* – irrelevant, that is, to all the logical relations reaching through language (including the representational relations). The fact that Russell is inclined to treat this private object of Bismarck's as the essential thing which we are trying to mean when we speak about Bismarck's mental life shows only how we can be misled in philosophy, misled by similarities between sentences which have different logical structure. There is then a real irony in the idea that *Russell* is being misled by such similarities, because Russell's theory of descriptions showed so clearly how such similarities can mislead. But what then happened was that Russell himself was taken in by superficial similarities: he knows that he speaks about but is not acquainted with either Bismarck's head or Bismarck's headache; and then he takes it that the headache, like the head, not being an object of acquaintance, must be an object known by description. And here one can see the *Tractatus* response as prefiguring that of the *Investigations*

(§304): we need to make a break with the idea that our language always functions in the same way, whether to convey thoughts about Bismarck's head or his headache.

In the *Investigations* discussion of private language, Wittgenstein uses a group of related metaphors: there is the mechanism of language (the language which we use in talk about sensations), which has some wheels and knobs which do genuinely connect up with the working of the mechanism, which do switch things on or off; and there are also, in contrast, knobs which look as if they do some work, but which are mere decoration – there are wheels which are not part of the mechanism at all, wheels which turn nothing. The idea that, when one speaks about one's own sensations, one needs to identify one's own private objects: this is one of the knobs which looks like part of the mechanism, but which connects with nothing (§§270–1). If we use that metaphor in explaining the *Tractatus* view, what corresponds to genuine connections of the "mechanism" is inferential and representational relations belonging to the language which one speaks and understands. A complete view of the mechanism would show no connections with objects nameable only in some other language. The indirect denoting of private objects we may take for an essential working switch, but it connects with nothing.[35]

7 There are two important elements of the *Tractatus* critique of Russell on privacy which I have not yet discussed: the *Tractatus* conception of what it is for an expression to be used with a constant meaning in different contexts, and the *Tractatus* rejection of Russell's idea of acquaintance as a relation between a self or subject (for Russell the word "subject" carries no implication of persistence through time) and an object.

Consider a Russellian account of a statement which I might make about a mental image of Bismarck's: the statement that the image is red. On Russell's view, I can indirectly denote some private mental object of Bismarck's, his image; and my acquaintance with *redness* is also involved in my understanding the statement that the image is red. Acquaintance with redness is involved not only when I judge, of something with which I am acquainted, that it is red, but also when I judge of things known only by description that they are red, even things with which I cannot be acquainted, as in the case of Bismarck's images.

We need to trace some implications of that Russellian account. When I make a judgment about Bismarck's private objects, I need, in addition to descriptions which indirectly denote the objects, things to say about those private objects; I need words for predicates and relations. In speaking about the objects with which I am not acquainted I use words the meaning of which is secured by my acquaintance with things like the universal *redness*. My acquaintance with redness arises from acquaintance with complexes; since I am not acquainted with the complex *Bismarck's having a red image*, my acquaintance with redness does not come from acquaintance with that complex. So, when I use the word "red" in speaking about Bismarck's image, I must understand the meaning of that word from other complexes involving redness, complexes with which I am acquainted, and I must be able to carry that meaning into the context of application to Bismarck's image, with which I cannot be acquainted. We saw that one possible focus for criticism of Russell's views about other minds is his conception of quantification (essential to his idea of how we indirectly denote other people's private objects); we can now see another possible focus for such criticism. This second focus of criticism is the idea that we can *go on* from uses of words about things with which we are acquainted to uses of those same words, in the same meanings, but applied to other people's private objects, with which we cannot be acquainted. (You could put this second issue as that of the projection of predicates and relations into the private realm of another person.)

These two possible central focuses for a critique of Russell on privacy, available within the *Tractatus*, correspond to two of the central focuses in the *Investigations* discussions of private language. The first focus is on the idea of sensations, wishes and so on as hidden objects accessible only to the person who has them, and the criticism is that such objects play no role in the language game; the second focus is on the idea of using a word in speaking about a private object while keeping it to a fixed meaning, and the criticism is that we have no coherent idea of fixity of meaning in such cases. In both the *Investigations* and the *Tractatus*, Wittgenstein is concerned with what it is for an expression to be used in a single consistent way, what it is for a word to be kept to the meaning it has been given. In the two books, he has quite different ideas of what is involved in consistent use of an expression. In the *Investigations* the discussion of consistency of meaning is intertwined with the criticism of the idea of a language for one's own private objects; in the *Tractatus* the treatment of consistency of meaning can be seen to form the basis of an argument against Russell's views about how our thought reaches other people's private objects.

I am not going to spell out these arguments against Russell (because to do so would require a detailed account of how the *Tractatus* explains consistency of meaning in terms of the notion of the presentation of an expression or symbol[36]). What I shall simply assert is that the *Tractatus* provides us with an argument against Russell on privacy, an argument which is to some degree analogous to the *Investigations* arguments which focus on what it is to use a term *in the same way*, and which have as their conclusion that words supposedly descriptive of private objects have no genuinely fixed use (see especially §§350–1, 261, 294). As with the arguments I considered earlier (the first-focus arguments), the existence of close analogies between *Tractatus* and *Investigations* critiques of privacy goes with some very significant differences. The most important difference in connection with the second-focus arguments is that the *Tractatus* view of what it is for an expression to be kept to a fixed use depends on a conception of rules which is criticized and rejected in the *Investigations*.

The *Tractatus* bears as it does on questions about privacy and other minds because (like the *Investigations*) it rejects the idea of some sort of *general* logical grasp of instantiation, supposedly running ahead of and underpinning inferential practice. But a "general logical grasp of instantiation" is built into Russell's idea of a propositional function; and a central difference between Russell's views and those of the *Tractatus* is the replacement of Russell's idea of a propositional function by the idea of a "sentence-variable." What I have referred to as two focuses for criticism of Russell are not two independent issues: both issues involve the Russellian conception of a propositional function. A propositional function, in Russell's sense, has values, propositions, which we ourselves may be able only to *describe*. The two elements of Russell's account – quantification over Bismarck's private objects, and projection of predicates and relations into Bismarck's supposed private realm

– depend on the idea of there being propositions, values of a propositional function, which people other than Bismarck can describe but not understand. The *Tractatus* notion of a sentence-variable replaces that of a propositional function. A sentence-variable is given *with all* of its values; there is no such thing as its having a value which can be described but not understood. (This *Tractatus* idea depends on the *Tractatus* conception of rules.) The values of a sentence-variable "fx" are the bases for construction of the quantified sentence "There is an x such that fx"; those values also fix the total range of sentences within which the predicate "f" has its consistent use. The Russellian propositional function can include among its values propositions which are understandable only by those who are acquainted with objects beyond *my* experience; the values of a *Tractatus* sentence-variable are sentences of my language. The *Tractatus* idea of the sentence-variable, with its values, is essential in the way the *Tractatus* rules out both the coherent use of a predicate to say something about someone else's private object, and quantification over such an object. There is available no *general conception of instantiation of a predicate or relation* (or satisfaction of a propositional function) running beyond sentences constructed from the elements of my language (and these elements do not include any signs standing for logical objects). The idea of inaccessible-to-me private objects (objects which I cannot name) being cases of *sensations* or *mental images* or whatever, being cases of *anything*, proves to be a non-idea. That, at any rate, is what the *Tractatus* invites us to recognize.

The conclusion – to put it again – is that, since our ordinary sentences do make sense as they stand, and since we do speak about Bismarck's sensations, etc., our ordinary language and thought about other minds is not to be construed as Russell does, as a means by which we indirectly reach things beyond the direct reach of language. Our language shows what we are talking about. We are not talking about, reaching by indirection with our words, Bismarck's private objects. If one identifies that insight (the rejection of Russell's conception of access to what lies "beyond" experience) as what solipsism really means to say, then we can say, as Wittgenstein does, that what solipsism means to say is correct. (This is not to say that solipsism is correct.[37])

Russell conceived acquaintance as a relation the domain of which is *subjects* and the converse domain of which is *objects* (*Theory of Knowledge*, p.35). He was uncertain (at any rate until towards the end of the period about which I am writing) whether one's self is an object with which one is acquainted. But he held that, if it is not an object of acquaintance it is nevertheless known by description, perhaps as "the subject of *this* present experience." The *Tractatus* arguments which I have discussed support a further criticism of Russell on experience, a criticism of Russell's conception of objects of acquaintance as *belonging to subjects*. The philosophical idea of "experience" as a sort of realm defined by acquaintance is undercut: it is not a realm with neighboring realms; it has no "possessor" (compare *Investigations* §398); and there is nothing "outside" it (compare *Investigations* §399). The Russellian question whether, and if so how, one can get beyond its limits is confused. Our ordinary language is about how things are in the world. It is possible to translate sentences in our ordinary language into what one might call "experience-sentences." We can, as it were, rewrite all that we believe to be the case: we can transform ordinary sentences about how things are in the world into sentences of an experience-book "The World *as I found it*." The possibility of experience-language – its possibility alongside that of ordinary everyday language – is misunderstood when I think of experience-language as a language in which I can speak to myself about what belongs peculiarly to me, while other people have their own experience-languages, in which they can speak to themselves about things beyond the limits of my private experience. I have argued that what Wittgenstein means when he says that solipsism is after something correct is that the conception (Russell's conception, but not just Russell's) of a multiplicity of subjects, each with its own realm, is confused. But when we are free of that confusion, we should also see that the "realm of experience" has no owner outside it, and none inside it. We are left with the translatability into each other of experience-language and ordinary physical-world language: they are not about different objects. It was Carnap's picking up *that* point from the *Tractatus*, and making it central in his 1931 physicalism, that underlay Wittgenstein's accusation of plagiarism. Wittgenstein's criticism of the construing of experience as a relation between a subject and objects-within-the-subject's-experiential-realm is one of the more obvious points of connection between the treatment of privacy in the *Tractatus* and that in the *Investigations*.

8 What does it mean, according to the *Tractatus*, to say that Bismarck's toothache is getting worse? If Russell's account is wrong, what alternative is there?

The *Tractatus* holds that what philosophy does is to make our thoughts, which otherwise would be as it were cloudy and indistinct, clear and sharply bounded (4.112). Philosophy clarifies what our thoughts are, what our sentences mean. In this work of clarification we rely on inferential relations: in logical analysis, we arrive at clarity about the truth-conditions of our sentences (clarity about how the sentences are logically constructed, and hence clarity about what we mean) by following through on logical relations. What a sentence says is the case comes out in how that sentence is used. In its use, it represents a possible situation in logical space, and we see how it does that as we see its logical relations to other sentences.

Take the sentence "Bismarck's toothache is getting worse." We might say that its truth-condition is that Bismarck's toothache is getting worse; but that way of putting the truth-condition shows that philosophy has not yet helped us to make our meaning clear. We may begin our philosophical clarification by noting that our sentence will not be true if Bismarck has a toothache but it is not getting worse, and also will not be true if Bismarck has no toothache. Wittgenstein, following Russell, takes those logical relations to imply that "Bismarck's toothache is getting worse" is not an elementary sentence: *it can be analyzed*. Here we can see the importance Wittgenstein attached to the theory of descriptions. Russell looks at the inferential relations between existential propositions and propositions containing what look like expressions referring directly to individuals. And on the basis of those inferential relations he gives a theory of how the propositions with the apparent denoting expressions can be analyzed, and those apparent denoting expressions will disappear. The logical structure of what we say and think is thus made clear by attention to inferential relations. (The *Tractatus* version of this can be seen in the passage going from 3.2 to 3.262, together with 5.557 and the remarks in the 5.55s leading up to it.)

In terms of the metaphor of logical space, the *Tractatus* view can be put this way: we become clear what our sentences mean by becoming clear what place within logical space they determine. We get the layout (as it were) of logical space through our grasp of logical relations. Only in that way can we find out what elementary propositions there are; only in that way can we thus actually get clear what the exact truth-conditions of our sentences are.

We have seen that Russellian analysis of propositions about Bismarck's self (or any other objects with which only Bismarck is acquainted) involves quantifying over objects which we ourselves cannot name, and that the *Tractatus* does not allow such analysis. What shows us how to analyze the sentence will be pursuing further the sentence's inferential relations. What does the sentence's truth follow from? What does its falsity follow from? The sentence is not an elementary sentence; if it were, the only sentences from which its truth followed would be the sentence itself and conjunctions containing the sentence itself, and its falsity would not follow from any sentence other than its own negation, and conjunctions including its negation; there could then be no spelling out of its truth-conditions.[38] But, since it is not an elementary sentence, there will be some combination or combinations of sentences, other than conjunctions including the sentence itself, from which it follows, or some combination or combinations of sentences other than conjunctions including its negation, from which its negation follows; the former will constitute grounds for accepting the sentence as true, and the latter, grounds for taking it to be false; clarity about these will lead us towards clarity about what the sentence means. Only by considering what the grounds are for accepting the sentence as true and for taking it to be false will we find the logical route leading back to a full understanding of the sentence's truth-conditions.

Suppose we think that Bismarck's behavior gives us grounds, but merely inductive grounds, for inferring that his toothache is getting worse. Probably, on the basis of his behavior, the toothache is getting worse. Well, what is it that the behavior gives us inductive evidence for? What would show us that *THAT* is the case? There has to be an answer to that question within logical space; there has to be an informative answer, not just that what the behavior is evidence for is Bismarck's toothache's getting worse. If such-and-such behavior is mere inductive evidence, then *something else* has to be what it is evidence *for*: there has to be something else that would, if it were established, constitute grounds for inferring that the toothache is getting worse. The argument here starts from the fact that "Bismarck's toothache is getting worse" is not an elementary sentence; it therefore must be entailed by some truth-functional combination or combinations of other sentences. There cannot be merely *symptoms* of Bismarck's toothache's getting worse; there has to be something which would, if established, count as non-inductive grounds for holding that it is getting worse.

I have been arguing that, in the case of any meaningful non-elementary sentence, the *Tractatus* requires that there be grounds for inferring truth and falsity which are not merely inductive, not mere symptoms but criteria, in the sense of criteria which we find in the early 1930s (as in the *Blue Book* example (p.25): the "defining criterion of angina" may be that such-and-such a bacillus is present in the blood). Making clear what the non-inductive grounds are for the truth of our sentence about Bismarck's toothache will show us what it means, will make clear what its truth-conditions are.[39] There is a continuity of development between the *Tractatus* conception of how the meaning of our sentences can be clarified, and Wittgenstein's later ideas about criteria (as seen, for example, in §§353–6 of *Philosophical Investigations*), including the argument that, if experience can teach us that such-and-such usually is associated with some phenomenon, there must be something that establishes that we have the phenomenon in question: there cannot be *just* symptoms. The *Investigations* tells us that, if experience can mislead us about whether it is raining, the possibility of the false appearance depends on the definition of rain; the *Tractatus*, I am suggesting, is committed to the idea that, if we can be misled about whether Bismarck has a toothache, the possibility of the false appearance depends on the definition of Bismarck having toothache.

The upshot of this discussion is that the *Tractatus* view of analysis involves agreement with Russell that sentences about Bismarck's toothache are analyzable, but disagreement with Russell about what that analysis can be.[40] Russellian analysis of statements about other minds involves quantifying over objects which we cannot speak about without quantifiers. The alternative analysis available within the *Tractatus*, once Russellian realism is rejected, involves an early version of the later insistence that where there are symptoms (inductively based justifications for a kind of statement) there must also be criteria (something which would count, non-inductively, as justification). In the *Investigations*, Wittgenstein says that an "inner process" stands in need of outward criteria. I have been arguing that the rejection of quantification over objects about which we cannot speak without quantifiers leads, in the *Tractatus*, to the view that a process *in someone else's mind* stands in need of outward criteria. (To say, as I should, that the germ of the *Investigations* idea can be seen in the *Tractatus* is not to deny that there are important differences. One such difference lies in Wittgenstein's later abandonment of the *Tractatus* account of quantification. A further, connected, point is that, while the *Tractatus* account of analysis involves our moving from the original non-elementary sentence to a truth-functional combination of sentences from which the original sentence follows, and from the negation of which its negation follows, the result of the analysis need not be the specification of grounds for the original sentence which have any connection with what, in our actual practice, we really do count as grounds for accepting that sentence as true. *Tractatus* analysis works with what you might call a logically purified picture of the application of language, a picture subjected to criticism later. Hence, if one introduces the word "criterion" in giving the earlier view, the word is being used in a sense which is deeply colored by the surrounding *Tractatus* structure of ideas.)

Here is a summary of this section. (1) Logical relationships enable us to spot *which* sentences are elementary. There is no problem about what an elementary sentence says is so: it simply shows us what it says is so, and this cannot be spelled out more fully by analysis. (2) Sentences about the contents of other people's minds are not elementary. Analysis will spell out what such sentences say is the case. (3) The alternatives for logical analysis of sentences about Bismarck's supposed private objects are: (a) Russellian analysis, quantifying over objects which no one but Bismarck can name; (b) non-Russellian analysis, which does not quantify over other people's private objects. As far as I can see, such analysis would involve the principle that, if there is inductive inference for Bismarck's having violent headache, it must be specifiable what would count as non-inductive grounds for inferring that Bismarck has a violent headache. Otherwise it is not fixed what it means to say that Bismarck has a violent headache, what the supposed inductive evidence is evidence for. In the *Tractatus*, the stage is set for the kind of view discussed in *Philosophical Remarks* part VI, pp.88–95, the view on which what is expressed by "Bismarck has toothache" is expressible in another and logically more revealing notation this way: "Bismarck is behaving as Wittgenstein behaves when there is toothache."

(There is available within the *Tractatus* material which could be the basis of an alternative treatment of sentences about Bismarck's sensations and so on. Wittgenstein sketches an account of natural laws like the laws of mechanics: these give us a form for sentences describing the world, but are not themselves such sentences. In the early 1930s he developed that conception of natural laws into the account of "hypotheses": an hypothesis is a law or rule by which we can construct sentences. An account of sentences about other minds as "hypotheses" is entirely consistent with the fundamental *Tractatus* view, which requires that the difference between sentences about my experience and sentences about the experience of others is a difference in the logical rules applying to the sentences, not (as we might try to put it) a difference in "realm." See the logically parallel discussion of realism and idealism, *Wittgenstein's Lectures, Cambridge 1930–32*, pp.80–1.)

9 How does finding a private language argument in the *Tractatus* matter? This section is about its relevance to our understanding of Wittgenstein, and the next section is about connections with the realism–anti-realism debate.

Wittgenstein's remarks about the limits of language and the world, in the *Tractatus* starting at 5.6, are concerned with the difference between a Russellian two-limits view (see section 2 above) and a one-limit view. When Wittgenstein speaks about the limits of language, he means the limits of what can be said in sentences which are truth-functional constructions from elementary sentences. None of these sentences is about anything which I cannot name; the world is *my* world in the sense that there is nothing (no private object of Bismarck's or anyone else's) which is in *the* world and which *I* cannot name. The idea that the use of quantifiers enables me to reach beyond the limits of my experience to objects "outside" experience is incoherent. The rejection of the two-limit view does not, though, leave us with one of a sort of thing, namely a limit, of which the Russell view had had two. It is the mistake of solipsism to treat the rejection of a two-limit view as leaving us confined within the limit which Russellian realism had sought to get beyond. That is, solipsism rejects the Russellian idea that we can get beyond the "limit of private experience" but keeps its conception of that limit: it precisely does give us one of what Russell had given us two of. The solipsist does not rigorously follow out his solipsism; if he did, it would lead him to a non-Russellian realism. A one-limit view self-destructs; we are not left, at the end of the *Tractatus*, with a philosophical view about a "far side" of the "limit," but merely with there being the sentences of our language (sentences which we do understand), and also sentences which we could use to make sense if we chose to assign a meaning to expressions in them to which no meaning has been given. The Russell notion of the "limit" of experience is meant to be the notion of something about which we can ask: "Can we get beyond it, and if so how?" The *Tractatus* technique first makes available a criticism of the Russellian answer to that question; we are then meant to see that the Russell question has been shown to be not a question at all. The criticism of Russell on private objects in the minds of other people is an essential part of Wittgenstein's overall philosophical project in the *Tractatus*.[41]

I have argued that concern with private objects is not something new for Wittgenstein in the *Philosophical Investigations* or in the work leading up to it in the 1930s. What *is* new in his later treatment of privacy can be summarized in terms of what we have seen.

The first difference is that the *Tractatus* private language argument is directed against what is only an element of a deeply attractive view of how our words reach to things in the world, whereas the private-language argument in the *Investigations* is part of an attempt to bring that larger view to awareness, and to enable us to resist its attractiveness. The *Tractatus* provides us with arguments against the Russellian idea of someone else's private object, the beetle in Bismarck's box. It lets us see that any such beetle would have no role in language or thought, but it left unmolested the beetle in one's own box. Russell's conception of how we can think about things in the minds of others was subjected to a critique, but the *Tractatus* left unexamined a questionable conception of what it is for our words to be about things in our own minds. The move beyond the *Tractatus* is plain in the "neither . . . nor" in the quotation which I have used as an epigraph (from Wittgenstein's notes for the "Philosophical Lecture," written in the middle 1930s): "the private object is one about which neither he who has it nor he who hasn't got it can say anything to others or to himself." What is the matter with the idea of the private object cannot be explained until the examination takes in not just our thought about the minds of others, but also our awareness of our own.

Secondly, the *Tractatus* argument takes for granted a notion of *rules* determining all their instances in advance. What is new in Wittgenstein's later discussions of privacy results in large part from the questioning of that conception of rules, and the related questioning of the *Tractatus* view of language and the self.

Thirdly, the great shift in Wittgenstein's conception of philosophical method and in how he understands logic affects all the continuities in Wittgenstein's thought which I have discussed. (The shift is the subject of the sections of *Philosophical Investigations* beginning at §89, on the treatment of logic as "sublime" and on the need to return to the perspective afforded by our ordinary understanding; for earlier discussion of the "change in perspective," see *Philosophical Remarks* §§18 and 24.[42])

In the *Investigations*, p.222, Wittgenstein describes what he does as the condensing of a whole cloud of philosophy into a drop of grammar. Something like that is Wittgenstein's aim in the *Tractatus* too. The particular *cloud of philosophy* with which we have been concerned is Russell's theory of our knowledge by description of the private objects in the minds of others. As we saw, Russell has a whole metaphysics and epistemology concerned with what lies beyond our own experience. The *Tractatus* is meant to show us what sorts of rules we are applying when we use a word in different contexts in the same meaning, and when we use logical words like "if," "or," "not," "some" and "all." We can certainly recognize, from the point of view of the *Tractatus*, the great difference between ascriptions of sensations (or thoughts or mental images or whatever) to other people and awareness of our own sensations, thoughts, images and so on. But that difference is conceived by the *Tractatus* as a difference in location within a network of logical relations, not, as Russell does, as the difference between directly accessible objects and objects out beyond direct accessibility. The cloud of Russellian philosophy is meant to be condensed to a drop of difference in logical relations.

10 A reading of the *Tractatus* as containing a private language argument matters not just to our understanding of Wittgenstein. It also bears on the contemporary discussion of realism and anti-realism, especially as that discussion has been shaped by Michael Dummett. Dummett holds that what is crucial in the debate between realists and anti-realists concerning some subject matter is the determinacy of truth-value of all the understandable sentences about that subject matter, all the sentences on which a fully specific sense has been conferred. A realist in his sense holds that all such sentences have determinate truth-value irrespective of our actual capacity to decide what that truth-value is; an anti-realist denies that they do. Realists will then accept classical logic, including the principle of bivalence: the principle that sentences with determinate sense all have one or other of the two truth-values. Anti-realists will, or at any rate in consistency should, give up the principle of bivalence, and thus also classical logic.[43]

Dummett reads Wittgenstein as having put forward global realism in the *Tractatus* and global anti-realism in his later writings, a reading which rests on taking Wittgenstein to have gone from an account of meaning in terms of truth-conditions in the *Tractatus* to a later account of meaning in terms of assertion-conditions.[44] The issues here are complex, and I can merely suggest briefly how my reading of the *Tractatus* can put them in a different light.

I start from a very simple point. The metaphysical and epistemological views of Russell with which we have been concerned make him a realist in a familiar philosophical sense; he is also a realist in Dummett's sense. He is a realist about other people's private objects; and Wittgenstein, in the *Tractatus*, is *anti*-Russell's realism. In a straightforward sense which is accepted by Dummett, the *Tractatus* is therefore anti-realist, at any rate about other people's private objects.[45] An anti-realist about some subject is, according to Dummett, someone who criticizes and rejects realism about that subject. (See *Logical Basis of Metaphysics*, p.4: ". . . the colourless term 'anti-realism' . . . denotes not a specific philosophical doctrine but the rejection of a doctrine"; cf. also *Seas of Language*, p.464.)

We should note how very well Russell's view fits Dummett's picture of realism. Here is a brief redescription of Russell's view, the structure of which is taken almost verbatim from Dummett on what a realistic theory of meaning involves.[46]

> Russell gives us a model of what it would be to recognize the truth of a proposition about Bismarck's private objects by the most direct means. These means are available only to Bismarck. *We*, however, can recognize the truth of Bismarck's propositions only indirectly, by inductive inference, because his propositions contain expressions whose sense is given in terms of mental operations which lie beyond our capacities; but our conception of these operations is derived by analogy from those which we can perform.

Further, there is a conception of generality which Dummett spells out in connection with Frege's realism (*Frege: Philosophy of Language*, pp.517–18), which is also present in other forms of realism, including Russell's. Russell's realism about Bismarck's private objects is tied to his idea of a domain over which he can quantify, containing objects which he can designate by descriptions; and Russell also has the idea that he can attach a quantifier to a predicate if he knows in general terms what it is for the predicate to be true or false of any arbitrary element of the domain. And that way of thinking about generality is the logical side of the notion of *analogy* used by Dummett in explaining what realism is.

The situation then is that Dummett thinks that the *Tractatus* is not just a realist work but a particularly good example of a realist approach to meaning. On the other hand, if I am correct about the *Tractatus*, it is not merely opposed to Russell's realism, but implies a powerful and generalizable critique of realist views. So there is a certain tension here. Dummett, I think, misreads the *Tractatus*. If we can see why he misreads it, that may help us to see better what is at stake in the realism/anti-realism debate. I shall first look very briefly at Dummett's misreading of the *Tractatus*, and then draw some lessons for the issue of realism vs. anti-realism.

Dummett treats the *Tractatus* as a very good example of realism because it accepts classical logic (and, in particular, it holds that every meaningful sentence is either true or false) and also because it holds that the meaning of our sentences is fixed in terms of truth-conditions, entirely independently of our capacity to establish whether the sentences are true or false. Thus Dummett says that the notion of truth in the *Tractatus* has no connection with the means available to us for judging a sentence to be true. He takes the *Tractatus* view to be open to serious objection precisely because it thus (supposedly) sunders the connection between what it is for a sentence to be true and the means by which we can recognize it as true. The most serious objection to this sort of realism, he thinks, is that our supposed grasp of the truth-conditions of sentences going beyond what we can establish cannot itself be manifested in our behavior.

Dummett misses a kind of critique of realism which runs through all of Wittgenstein's philosophy, and which is more important than the criticisms of realism to which he does attend, including his own criticism concerning the behavioral manifestation of understanding. The critique of realism in the *Tractatus* is invisible to him in large part because he does not see clearly Wittgenstein's conception of logic, and of logical analysis.

As Wittgenstein understands logic, it does not serve the purposes to which a realist like Russell tries to put it. The point at which the *Tractatus* view of logic interferes with Russell's realism is the point at which Russell tries to quantify over Bismarck's private objects. But there are more fundamental issues underlying the disagreement about quantification. Russell believes that, although we cannot understand sentences directly denoting Bismarck's private objects, we can grasp the semantics of such sentences well enough to see that they are instances of a propositional function which we do understand, and thus to see that those sentences stand in logical relations to sentences of our language quantifying over Bismarck's private objects. The *Tractatus* rejects the Russellian conception of how semantics and logic hang together; that is, it rejects not just the Russellian idea of how we can quantify over things with which we cannot be acquainted, but also any substantive conception of semantic theory which would allow a theory to explain the legitimacy of inferences independently of whether we ourselves could be in a position to make those inferences. For the *Tractatus*, inferential relations cannot be explained by such a theory, since such relations are internal to *what* our sentences *are*: what construction from what other sentences. A sentence has no *semantic identity* (as we might put it) which could be taken to form part of an explanation of its logical relations to other sentences, since it is only in the sentence's use *as* standing in these and those logical relations that it is such-and-such meaningful combination of signs at all.[47] The very idea of there being legitimate inferences beyond what we can understand is undercut; logic can only be internal to the language we speak and understand. (The intimate connection between rejection of a Russellian realism about logic and rejection of Russellian realism about objects in the minds of others is underscored in the *Tractatus* remarks about limits, starting at 5.6.)

Dummett also does not see how the *Tractatus* conception of logical analysis involves a tie between what our non-elementary sentences say is so, and sentences capable of serving as grounds for taking those sentences to be true or false. The *Tractatus* combination – its commitment to analysis *and* its ruling out of Russellian analysis – leads to an idea of analysis as showing what our sentences mean by tracing what would be non-inductive justification for accepting or rejecting them, and thus spelling out their truth-conditions. The methodology of the *Tractatus* does preclude attention to actual inferential practice, and one could describe this as involving a kind of philosophical realism about the structure of logical relations within language. The picture one gets of the relation between a sentence and its truth-grounds is "mythologized," to use a term of criticism coming from Wittgenstein's later thought.[48] Dummett is aware that a weakness of the *Tractatus* account is precisely this failure to connect truth-conditions with the ways in which we actually establish truth; that is, he sees the kind of realism that does indeed remain in the *Tractatus* despite its critique of Russellian realism. What he does not see, though, is the critique of Russellian realism, and the presence within that critique of the germ of some of Wittgenstein's later thoughts about the intertwined topics of privacy and language. I believe that this is because he does not see the importance, for the critique of realism, of the idea of logic as the logic of *unserer Umgangsprache* (our everyday language, *Tractatus* 5.5563).

Both Dummett and Wittgenstein are concerned with philosophical realism as involving the idea of our thought reaching, by a kind of indirection, beyond the cases from which we grasp what it is for such-and-such kind of thing to be the case. For Wittgenstein, from the beginning, that element of indirectness in the realist conception is a clue to why it is confused. In the *Tractatus* we see him attaching great significance to the idea that there are no logical objects: consistency of meaning in the use of logical words is not a matter of there being *something* they mean, the grasp of which would allow us to do what Russell tries to do, namely, to get by indirection beyond the space of our own understandable sentences. There are no logical objects: in the *Tractatus* this is meant to let us see that logic is the logic of everyday sentences in their everyday relations to each other; that is all it is. The logical words have nothing to them but their role in those sentences and their relations. If one were to elucidate those sentences, in their ordinary logical relations, that would show us all that they mean, all that they say is so. – This is meant to stop philosophical realism from starting, and to stop responses to it that, in their denials, share the confusions underlying realism.[49]

Notes

1 Wittgenstein, "Notes for the 'Philosophical Lecture'," in *Philosophical Occasions*, p.451.
2 *Culture and Value*, p.77; my translation.
3 See discussion of Wittgenstein's conception of authorship in James Conant, "Putting Two and Two Together: Kierkegaard, Wittgenstein and the Point of View for their Work as Authors," in *The Grammar of Religious Belief*, T. Tessin and M. von der Ruhr (eds) New York, St. Martin's Press, 1995, pp.248–331. In the case of the *Tractatus*, it is important also to note Wittgenstein's responses to questions from Russell about both the *Tractatus* and the earlier material. (See *Letters to Russell, Keynes and Moore*, pp.33–42, 71–3.) There is extreme impatience with Russell's questions in the letters of late 1913 – for example: "It distresses me that you did not understand the rule dealing with signs in my last letter because it bores me BEYOND WORDS to explain it. If you thought about it for a bit you could discover it for yourself!" In 1919, Wittgenstein explains the shortness of the *Tractatus* and its consequent obscurity in terms of the great difficulty he has giving lengthy explanations of logical matters. He is still impatient (although less sharp with Russell than in 1913); there is still the insistence that Russell will find the answers to his questions if he will only try to understand the book. "Trying to understand," as Wittgenstein uses that expression, means working out for oneself everything he did not put explicitly into the book.
4 I do not mean that the only reader whom Wittgenstein had specifically in mind was Russell; he certainly also had Frege in mind as a reader, and others as well.
5 Carnap, *Erkenntnis*, 1931, vol.2, pp.432–65; a revised edition, translated by Max Black, was published under the title *The Unity of Science*, London, Kegan Paul, 1934. For the accusation of plagiarism, see *Ludwig Wittgenstein: Sein Leben in Bildern und Texten*, M. Nedo and M. Ranchetti (eds) Frankfurt, Suhrkamp, 1983, pp.254–5.
6 For the sake of ease of exposition I move back and forth between the linguistic and non-linguistic uses. In all cases it would be possible to rephrase the argument, often at considerably greater length, in a way that avoided these shifts. See Peter Hylton, *Russell, Idealism and the Emergence of Analytic Philosophy*, Oxford, Clarendon Press, 1990, pp.342 and 366, on Russell's use of "proposition"; see pp.334–6 on the changes in Russell's views about propositions in the non-linguistic sense.
7 Russell, "On Denoting," *Mind*, 1905, vol.14, pp.479–93; page references are to the reprinted essay in Russell, *Logic and Knowledge*, London, Allen and Unwin, 1956, pp.41–56; "Knowledge by Acquaintance and Knowledge by Description," *Proceedings of the Aristotelian Society*, 1910–11, vol.11, pp.108–28, reprinted in *Mysticism and Logic*, London, Allen and Unwin, 1917; page references in the text are to the 1932 reprint in which the essay appears on pp.209–32); *Problems of Philosophy*, London, Williams and Norgate, 1912; page references are to the 1967 London, Oxford University Press, reprint of the 1946 edition); *Theory of Knowledge: The 1913 Manuscript*, E. R. Eames (ed.) London, George Allen and Unwin, 1984. The first six chapters of the manuscript were published in *The Monist* in 1914 and 1915.
8 See E. R. Eames, Introduction to Russell, *Theory of Knowledge*, op. cit., pp.xxv–xxviii. Wittgenstein was, it seems, predisposed to believe that a further treatment by Russell of problems in epistemology before he had reached a correct theory of propositions was a recipe for disaster. See pp.xxvii–xxviii.
9 My formulation of the principle comes from *Theory of Knowledge*, op. cit., p.5; cf. also *Problems of Philosophy*, p.26. For a discussion of the role of the principle in Russell's thought, see Hylton, *Russell, Idealism and the Emergence of Analytic Philosophy*, op. cit., chap.8 (especially p.364), and part II.
10 *Theory of Knowledge*, op. cit., p.5; cf. also *Problems of Philosophy*, op. cit., p.26, p.79 and chap.10.

11 *Theory of Knowledge*, p.34; see also pp.10–11 for Russell's statement of the problem of knowledge of things not within our personal experience. The argument can also be found in *Problems of Philosophy*, pp.23–4; cf. also p.62.

12 For Russell on toothaches as essentially private, see "On Propositions: What They Are and How They Mean," *Proceedings of the Aristotelian Society*, 1919, vol.2, pp.1–43; reprinted in *Logic and Knowledge*, pp.285–320. James Conant has pointed out to me that Moore uses toothache as an example in the 1910–11 lectures (delivered in London) which became *Some Main Problems of Philosophy*, London, Allen and Unwin, 1953. For the contrast between private and public objects, see *Problems of Philosophy*, p.9.

13 Russell actually took the impossibility of acquaintance with another person's experiencing of something to be empirical; see *Theory of Knowledge*, pp.34–5. I cannot experience your desiring of something; but that impossibility is not a "theoretical impossibility." Wittgenstein's later writings suggest that he took such a view to reflect confusion; see, e.g., *The Blue and Brown Books*, p.55. See also John McDowell on "quasi-memory" in "Reductionism and the First Person," in *Reading Parfit*, J. Dancy (ed.) Oxford, Blackwell, 1997, pp.230–50. What Russell has in mind could be called "quasi-experience," on the model of "quasi-memory'; and McDowell's criticisms of Parfit on "quasi-memory" apply to Russell's view.

14 Russell's idea of our predicament, of our need for some route to what lies beyond the realm of our own experience, resembles that of Thomas Nagel, in his introductory book on philosophy, *What Does It All Mean?*, New York, Oxford University Press, 1987. Nagel's first sentence (after the Introduction) is: "If you think about it, the inside of your own mind is the only thing you can be sure of" – that is all you have to go on, directly. Can we get beyond what is thus directly available? That, for Nagel as for Russell 75 years earlier, is the starting point for much of philosophy. Compare also Nagel's discussion (p.20) of the impossibility of experiencing the other person's experiencing: Nagel's language echoes Russell's.

15 The idea of the two non-coinciding limits forms an important part of the background to Russell's discussion of the value of philosophy, in chap. 15 of *Problems of Philosophy*. Thus any difference between Wittgenstein and Russell on the matter of coinciding versus non-coinciding limits may be taken to be connected with their differences about the aims of philosophy.

16 See Hylton, *Russell, Idealism and the Emergence of Analytic Philosophy*, op. cit., pp.375–88.

17 'The Relation of Sense Data to Physics," *Scientia*, 1914, no.4, reprinted in *Mysticism and Logic*, op. cit., pp.145–79; see pp.159–60. Cf. the slightly different use of "private world" in *Our Knowledge of the External World as a Field for Scientific Method in Philosophy*, London, Allen and Unwin, 1914, Lecture III. Wittgenstein asked Keynes in early 1915 to send him a copy of the latter; somewhat later in 1915 a reference by Wittgenstein to Russell's "Scientific Method in Philosophy" suggests that a packet from Keynes with at least some 1914 publications by Russell got through to Wittgenstein.

18 Thomas Ricketts, "Comment on Cora Diamond, 'Does Bismarck Have a Beetle in His Box?'" (unpublished), p.4. Ricketts adds that Wittgenstein treats the two topics, of Russell on sensibilia and Russell on the private objects of others, together in the *Tractatus*.

19 I am not suggesting that what I call here elements of Russell's approach are not also found in the thought of other philosophers. See, for example, Frege ("Thoughts," in *Collected Papers*, Oxford, Blackwell, 1984, pp.351–72) on the idea that each of us has a primitive way in which he is presented to himself, and thus has thoughts about himself which he cannot communicate to others.

20 Another very important example of the straight road which is permanently closed is the road which we may think of as available to a god, giving direct access to mathematical truths. This is the road which it may seem to us we should really want to take in our use of mathematical propositions, but, because we cannot see mathematical reality directly, we are forced to go the roundabout way of constructing proofs.

21 *Philosophical Remarks*, pp.200–1. James Conant has drawn my attention to the related discussion in *Zettel*, beginning at §250. See especially §262 for the idea of sneaking round from behind.

22 Here I follow G.E.M. Anscombe's practice (in "Ludwig Wittgenstein," *Philosophy*, 1995, vol.70, pp.395–407) in the translation of *"die Wirklichkeit."* The reality represented by a topographical map of Scotland, e.g., is the topography of Scotland.

23 See A.N. Whitehead and B. Russell, *Principia Mathematica*, Cambridge, Cambridge University Press, 1910, §9; see also Russell's preliminary explanation of his symbolism in chap.1.

24 The explanation is very abbreviated. It does not deal with multiple quantification. It ignores differences between elementary and non-elementary sentences, and supposes a notation in which there is no more than one name for any object. I have also not explained the idea of a "sentence-variable." My explanation emphasizes the double role of general rules in the construction of quantified sentences (the rule for generating all the values of the sentence-variable, and the rule for constructing a single sentence from them). This is intended to mark a point at which Wittgenstein's later discussion of rules bears on the fundamental ideas of the *Tractatus* about the construction of sentences.

25 See P.T. Geach, "Truth and God," *Proceedings of the Aristotelian Society*, 1982, supp. vol.56, pp.83–97, at p.89; see also Peter Hylton's account of Wittgenstein's notion of an *operation*, in his "Functions, Operations, and Sense in Wittgenstein's *Tractatus*," in *Early Analytic Philosophy*, W. W. Tait (ed.) Chicago, Open Court, 1997, pp.91–105.

26 G.E.M. Anscombe, *Introduction to Wittgenstein's Tractatus*, London, Hutchinson, 1959, chap. 11.

27 *Foundations of Mathematics*, London, Routledge and Kegan Paul, 1954, pp.153–4. Ramsey says, for example, that, on the alternative view, "There is an x such that fx" should be regarded as an atomic proposition of the form "$F(f)$" (f has application). "Atomic proposition" is a term Russell uses but, in *Principia* at any rate, he certainly does not treat quantified propositions as atomic propositions. Atomic propositions, as explained in *Principia*, are about particulars, not about propositional functions (which is what general and existential propositions are about on Russell's view). If Ramsey means his discussion to apply to Russell in *Principia*, then he means that Russell's account makes quantified propositions into atomic propositions in some non-Russellian sense, or that, despite Russell's own separation of quantified from atomic propositions, quantified propositions should count as atomic even in Russell's sense.

28 Bismarck's judgment may involve a universal; and Bismarck might be wrong about what the word in public language is for that universal. But he can make judgments, in his own thought, of which the universal is a constituent, without committing himself on the issue of the word for that universal in public language. My representation of Bismarck's judgment, using the word "excruciating," thus involves an element subject to error, not present, according to Russell, in Bismarck's judgment itself. Russell has a clear account of this in a considerably later paper, "The Limits of Empiricism," *Proceedings of the Aristotelian Society*, 1936, vol.36, pp.131–50, which clarifies some ideas about private judgment which are present much earlier in Russell's thinking.

29 This representation of Russell's judgment ignores Russell's view that Bismarck's self may be a private object.

30 We should note the contrast with the objection raised by Ramsey and Anscombe, mentioned at the end of section 4. Their objection was essentially that, on the "alternative" account of the quantifiers, identified by Anscombe as that of Frege and Russell, there are inferential relations between quantified sentences of our language and singular sentences of our language, but the "alternative" account of the quantifiers does not explain these relations. Our grasp of the sentences is supposed to enable us to see that there is an inferential relation (and we can ourselves make the relevant inferences), but the sentences themselves are not conceived in a way which explains inferability. The objection which I am here ascribing to Wittgenstein is that Russell's view requires there to be inferential relations between sentences which I understand and sentences which I cannot understand, supporting inferences which I cannot make. The Russell view involves

an implicit appeal to a position inaccessible to me, from which the supposed inferential relation between the sentences could be grasped through understanding of the sentences, rather than indirectly through knowledge about the sentences, only one of which I can be in a position to affirm.

31 There are important connections here with issues concerning realism about logic. Russell's account commits him to there being one "space of possible inference" associated with the language which I understand and thus with inferences which I can make, and another "space of possible inference" associated with a position which I should really like to be in, a position in which I should be able to understand not only propositions quantifying over Bismarck's private objects, but also propositions containing genuine proper names for those objects. The *Tractatus* remarks about limits are directed against that conception of logic.

32 Ricketts, "Comment on Cora Diamond, 'Does Bismarck Have a Beetle in His Box?'" op. cit.

33 My argument connects here with Warren Goldfarb's criticisms of interpretations of the *Tractatus* which ascribe to Wittgenstein the idea that simple objects are given names by us in mental acts; see Goldfarb, "Objects, Names, and Realism in the *Tractatus*" (unpublished). There is a question how far Wittgenstein's view resembles an earlier view of Russell's. In Peter Hylton's description of the development of Russell's thought, an important difference between *Principles of Mathematics* and the next Russell period, 1906–13, is that Russell earlier took the view that what we are acquainted with is whatever the best logical theory implies that we are acquainted with, and in the later period held that an independent investigation (independent of logical theory) into the nature of acquaintance and into what we are acquainted with is necessary (Hylton, *Russell, Idealism and the Emergence of Analytic Philosophy*, pp.328–30). While Wittgenstein certainly rejects the later view, his account is also, I think, different from the earlier Russell view, but I shall not here discuss those differences.

34 See *Tractatus* 5.5563. I have spoken of a premise of the argument, but that is really an abbreviation for a more complex story. The *Tractatus* does not hold that we have a genuine conception of what it would be for a language to be "adequate" and of what it would be for a language to be "inadequate," and that language *is* the former, not the latter. The idea of language being "inadequate," for example by there being simple objects which our linguistic resources do not enable us to reach, itself is incoherent. A good example of what the *Tractatus* would take to be an incoherent account is that of Wilfrid Sellars, "Realism and the New Way of Words," in H. Feigl and W. Sellars (eds) *Readings in Philosophical Analysis*, New York, Appleton-Century-Crofts, 1949, pp.424–56. See especially pp.428–9, and Sellars's idea of what an adequate language would be. Our language, he thinks, claims such adequacy, but it does not have it; "we use [general propositions] as though we spoke a complete language proper to which they belonged."

35 See also Russell's account of how we who are not Bismarck are able to communicate with each other about an object with which only Bismarck can be acquainted ("Knowledge by Acquaintance and Knowledge by Description," op. cit., p.218). Communication between us about such an object is supposedly possible only because there is a single proposition which we are all interested in and which each of us can describe, using various different descriptions, although none of us can actually affirm or understand that proposition. Here again the *Tractatus* has available the criticism that the "unknowable proposition," far from being essential to communication, has no role in our everyday language; it does not gear in to the "mechanism."

36 See *Tractatus* 3.3–3.317, 5.501; cf. also B.F. McGuinness (ed.) *Wittgenstein and the Vienna Circle*, pp.237–8.

37 See also section 9 below.

38 By "conjunctions containing the sentence itself" I mean sentences which are actually written as such conjunctions, or sentences which are logically equivalent to such sentences. See *Tractatus* 5.141 for Wittgenstein's sense of "the same sentence." Thus, for example, "p and not-p" is the same sentence as "(p and not-p) and q"; for any sentence, any contradiction is a conjunction "containing" that sentence.

39 G.E.M. Anscombe has argued that the *Tractatus* does not share the logical positivist's idea that we can test a proposition for significance by seeing if we can state the sense-observations which would verify it (*Introduction to Wittgenstein's Tractatus*, op. cit., p.150). I am not ascribing to Wittgenstein the view which she says that he does not hold. I am ascribing to him the view that our everyday sentences, including those about other minds, are analyzable, that their analysis shows what they say is so, and that recognition of the incoherence of Russellian realism about the logical relations of our sentences leads (in the context of the *Tractatus*) to a conception of analysis in which the tracing of logical relations leads us back to sentences which do not even appear to denote or to quantify over objects which we cannot name. This tracing of logical relations goes by way of moving back to the non-inductive grounds for the truth of sentences which look as if they "want" a realist treatment. There is no appeal, in this conception of analysis, to any idea of "sense-observations," only to the idea of sentences either having or not having the *logical* characteristics of elementary sentences. See *Tractatus* 6.3751.

40 Here, and elsewhere in this essay, I am rejecting a view of G.E.M. Anscombe's, namely, that Wittgenstein accepted Russell's theory of descriptions as giving the correct account of the statement of truth-conditions for sentences containing definite descriptions. On my view, he accepted Russell's theory for sentences in which the resulting quantification would be quantification over nameable objects, as in the "King of France" example, but rejected it for sentences of the "Bismarck's toothache" type. See *Introduction to Wittgenstein's Tractatus*, op. cit., p.46.

41 For further discussion of the overall project, see Cora Diamond, *The Realistic Spirit*, Cambridge, Mass., MIT Press, 1991, chaps 3 and 6, and my "Ethics, Imagination and the Method of Wittgenstein's *Tractatus*," in *Bilder der Philosophie*, R. Heinrich and H. Vetter (eds) Vienna, Oldenbourg, 1991, pp.55–90, reprinted in this volume; also the essays in this volume by James Conant and Peter Hacker, and Conant's "Must We Show What We Cannot Say?," in *The Senses of Stanley Cavell*, R. Fleming and M. Payne (eds) Lewisburg, Pennsylvania, Bucknell University Press, 1989, pp.242–83, "Throwing Away the Top of the Ladder," *Yale Review* 1991, vol.79, pp.328–64, and "Kierkegaard, Wittgenstein and Nonsense," in *Pursuits of Reason*, T. Cohen, P. Guyer and H. Putnam (eds) Lubbock, Texas, Texas Tech Press, 1993, pp.195–224. See also Thomas Ricketts, "Pictures, Logic and the Limits of Sense in Wittgenstein's *Tractatus*," in *Cambridge Companion to Wittgenstein*, H. Sluga and D.G. Stern (eds) Cambridge, Cambridge University Press, 1996, pp.59–99, and his "Comment on Cora Diamond's 'Does Bismarck Have a Beetle in His Box?'" op. cit.; Warren Goldfarb, "Metaphysics and Nonsense: on Cora Diamond's *The Realistic Spirit*," *Journal of Philosophical Research*, 1997, vol.22, pp.57–73; Michael Kremer, "Contextualism and Holism in the early Wittgenstein: from *Prototractatus* to *Tractatus*," *Philosophical Topics*, 1977, vol. 25, pp. 87–120; Juliet Floyd, "The Uncaptive Eye: Solipsism in Wittgenstein's *Tractatus*," in *Loneliness*, L. S. Rouner (ed.) Notre Dame, Indiana, University of Notre Dame Press, 1998, pp.79–114, and "Wittgenstein, Nonsense and the Limits of Analysis in the *Tractatus*," unpublished; John Lippitt and Daniel Hutto, "Making Sense of Nonsense: Kierkegaard and Wittgenstein," *Proceedings of the Aristotelian Society*, 1998, vol.98, pp.263–86; Lynette Reid, "Wittgenstein's Ladder: The *Tractatus* and Nonsense," *Philosophical Investigations*, 1998, vol.21, pp.97–151.

42 See also Diamond, *Realistic Spirit*, op. cit., pp.4–6 and chap. 1.

43 For a full discussion of the complex issues here, see Dummett, "Realism and Anti-realism," in *The Seas of Language*, Oxford, Clarendon Press, 1993, pp.462–78.

44 For a short statement of Dummett's view of Wittgenstein on realism and anti-realism, see *The Logical Basis of Metaphysics*, Cambridge, Mass., Harvard University Press, 1991, pp.303–7.

45 The situation with regard to Russell's views about physical objects is more complex; what I say in this section could not be applied in any simple way to Russell on physical objects and the implicit response to his views in the *Tractatus*.

46 *Frege: Philosophy of Language*, London, Duckworth, 1973, p.465; cf. also *Logical Basis of Metaphysics*, op. cit., pp.345–6.

47 It may be thought that, on my reading of the *Tractatus*, it is open to the objection formulated by A.N. Prior in "The Meaning of Logical Connectives," *Analysis*, 1960, vol.21, pp.38–9. Prior's argument depends on an assumption rejected by the *Tractatus*, the assumption that if we lay down inference rules for some new logical word, say "tonk," we can somehow will it to be the case that we shall have defined only one logical constant, i.e, that there can be no problem arising from our unwittingly having introduced two (or more) logical homonyms. If we introduce two rules of inference, the rule that from any statement P we can infer the statement formed by joining P to Q by "tonk" and the rule that from any statement joining P and Q by "tonk" we can infer Q, the *Tractatus* conclusion will be that we have (partially) determined two different logical operation-signs confusingly using the same word. Here truth-functional logic does not fix which inferences we can make; it sets constraints on what we can be understood as saying if we infer in certain ways. This is part of what is involved in Wittgenstein's idea (*Tractatus* 5.473, cf. Wittgenstein, *Notebooks* 1914–16, p.2) that logic must look after itself. The point applies also to the use of "T" and "F" in truth-tables. Whether those letters mean *true* or *false* (and whether they are being used in some consistent way) is not settled independently of the use of sentence-constructions containing the letters; i.e., it is something that shows itself. For some further discussion of these and related issues, see my "Truth Before Tarski: After Sluga, After Ricketts, After Geach, After Goldfarb, Hylton, Van Heijenoort and Floyd," in *From Frege to Wittgenstein: Perspectives on Early Analytic Philosophy*, E. Reck (ed.) Oxford, Oxford University Press, 2000.

48 For a wonderful example of what is getting left out of the *Tractatus* view, see Dummett's discussion of the use of place-names, in *Origins of Analytical Philosophy*, Cambridge, Mass., Harvard University Press, 1994, p.145. Dummett mentions, for example, that "the institution of maps and atlases, but also that of transport systems and their agencies are part of the entire social practice that gives place-names their use." The *Tractatus* conception of the use of language and of philosophical method makes it impossible to see the significance of that kind of attention to the ways words really do work in our life.

49 I am greatly indebted to Thomas Ricketts for his commentary at a meeting of the American Philosophical Association in 1996 at which this paper was discussed, and for his helpful account of the connections between elements of the critique of Russell in the *Tractatus*. An early version of the argument in this chapter was included in my Whitehead Lectures at Harvard University in 1993, and I am grateful to those present for their questions and comments, and to the Philosophy Department for honoring me with the invitation to give the lectures. I want also to thank, for their helpful comments and criticisms, Juliet Floyd, Mike Dunn, James Conant, Alice Crary and Joan Weiner.

12

HOW TO DO THINGS WITH WOOD

Wittgenstein, Frege and the problem of illogical thought

David R. Cerbone

1 Introduction

In the Preface to the *Tractatus*, Wittgenstein writes that

> the aim of the book is to draw a limit to thought, or rather – not to thought, but to the expression of thought: for in order to be able to draw a limit to thought, we should have to find both sides of the limit thinkable (i.e. we should have to be able to think what cannot be thought).[1]

Wittgenstein's point here, and throughout the *Tractatus*, is that the idea of a limit to thought is self-undermining in the sense that there is no *intelligible* way in which one can be drawn. Doing so, Wittgenstein is saying here in the Preface, would require having some grasp of what lies beyond such a limit; indeed, the very suggestion of a *limit* implies that there is *something* which is being excluded, which lies outside of the range of thought and so cannot be reached.

One way of characterizing the aim of the *Tractatus* is to put the reader in a position to see that even Wittgenstein's prefatory remark is misleading, since his talk of "what cannot be thought" as something that we are not "able to think" still gives the impression of a limit's having been imposed, with our being trapped on the near side of it. Call what lies on our side, on the side consisting in what we "can" think, the "logical," then the far side, what lies beyond the limit, might be called the "illogical." Given this way of labeling the terrain, the idea of a limit to thought becomes the idea that we cannot think illogically. *Illogical thought*, then, appears to be that which lies beyond the limit, to be the something upon which we cannot get a grasp. One thing to be learned by working from the Preface to the conclusion of the *Tractatus* is that there is no something answering to the combination of words "illogical thought." That is, before reading the *Tractatus* I may have thought that the statement "I cannot think illogically" is on a par with "I cannot jump over the Empire State Building." Both statements appear to express a particular inability on my part. What Wittgenstein wants to show in the *Tractatus* is that despite their surface similarities, these two statements are not on a par at all: in the second case, where I say that I cannot jump over the Empire State Building, I have a clear idea (or at least a fairly clear idea) of what would be involved in doing what I have claimed to be unable to do; I understand what it is to jump over the Empire State Building, even though I am confident of my inability to do so. My understanding could perhaps be illustrated by my drawing a picture or making a cartoon depicting my jumping over the Empire State Building and then saying, not without a tinge of regret, that I cannot do *that*.

In the first case, however, what I lack is precisely a clear idea of what it is that I cannot do: I do not understand what it would be like (or even look like) to think illogically, and not just for me but for anyone of whom I would be willing to say that he or she was *thinking* at all. The relation between logic and thought is, one might say, an *internal* one in the sense that there is nothing that could be at one time thinking (or a thought) and illogical. I take this to be what Wittgenstein is driving at in the opening of the 3s of the *Tractatus*, when he writes that "a logical picture of facts is a thought," namely that there is no extra-logical notion of a thought. This remark is followed by several which expand upon the idea of illogical thought's being impossible; this idea is especially prominent in the following remarks, where Wittgenstein writes:

> 3.03 Thought can never be of anything illogical, since, if it were, we should have to think illogically.

> 3.031 It used to be said that God could create anything except what would be contrary to the laws of logic. – The truth is that we could not *say* what an 'illogical' world would look like.

> 3.032 It is as impossible to represent in language anything that 'contradicts logic' as it is in geometry to represent by its coordinates a figure that contradicts the laws of space or to give the coordinates of a point that does not exist.[2]

As the numbering of these remarks shows, they are all ultimately explications of remark number three; they are all, loosely speaking, consequences of the remark that a logical picture of facts is a thought. Again, however, it should be emphasized how misleading Wittgenstein's talk of impossibility is here, since ultimately he wants to show that there is no thing, no real possibility, which is being excluded. All of his remarks pertaining to impossibilities and inabilities are rungs on the ladder which must ultimately be kicked away as itself consisting only in nonsense. Once kicked away, the confused idea of thought as somehow being limited likewise disappears.

In this chapter, I do not want to discuss the intricacies and difficulties of Wittgenstein's methodology in the *Tractatus*.[3] My concern instead lies on either side of that work, with, before it, Frege's conception of logic and, in particular, his attempt to articulate the distinction between logic and psychology and, after it, with Wittgenstein's critical examination of that attempt in his later writings, most notably in Part I of the *Remarks on the Foundations of Mathematics*. My aim is to show how Wittgenstein in his post-Tractarian philosophy preserves the appreciation he had in his early period of the confusions one lands in when trying to characterize the laws of logic as imposing a kind of limit to thought. I will show that it is precisely Frege's attempt to defend logic from the intrusion of psychologism (the intrusion of empirical, psychological concerns with human thinking) that most clearly illustrates this kind of confusion. Appreciating the nature of Wittgenstein's criticisms of Frege in turn provides a way of understanding the kind of philosophical quietism Wittgenstein encourages in his later work.

I will proceed in the following manner. In the next section, I lay out the salient features of Frege's polemical attack on psychologism in order to illustrate the deep tensions in his conception of logic that are revealed in that attack: what appears to be a fairly straightforward defense of an almost platitudinous distinction between the logical and the psychological results in an inherently unstable conception of logic. The instability, I argue, can be seen as stemming from an attempt to think both sides of a limit to thought. In the third section, I turn to Wittgenstein's examination of Frege's polemic against psychologism and focus primarily on a curious scene depicting an encounter with a strange group of people with a strange method for collecting and distributing wood. The principal interpretive difficulty this scene poses resides in determining just how it constitutes a criticism of Frege. In the final section, I consider Wittgenstein's more general conception of philosophy in his later period and show how his treatment of Frege serves to illustrate that conception.

2 Frege's polemic against psychologism

In the Preface to his *Basic Laws of Arithmetic*, Frege engages in his most sustained polemic against what he considers to be the "prevailing logic," namely *psychologism*. What passes for logic among his contemporaries "seems," Frege declares, "to be infected through and through with psychology," and it is the "corrupting incursion of psychology into logic" that "stands in the way" of the reception of his work among logicians.[4] For this reason, Frege finds it necessary to devote attention to what he regards as a hopelessly flawed view.[5]

On the view Frege is opposing, logic is simply a branch of psychology: logical laws, the laws of thought, are empirical, psychological laws governing how human beings in fact think in the same way as the laws of motion govern the movements of celestial bodies. Frege's initial complaint against such a conception of the laws of thought is that it neglects another sense in which one may speak of a law. That is, the locution "laws of thought" is ambiguous between two senses of "law." In one sense, a law describes or asserts how things are. It is in this sense of "law" that one speaks of the laws of nature as describing the (necessary) regularities of natural phenomena. In a second sense, however, a law prescribes how things ought to be, and here we might think of ethical or moral laws, since these do not describe how human beings in fact behave, but how they ought to behave in order to be morally or ethically good. It is in this second sense of "law" that Frege wants to speak of logical laws as laws of thought, since they prescribe how human beings ought to think rather than describe how they in fact think.[6]

The psychologistic logician's willingness to identify logical laws with descriptive, empirical laws betrays, according to Frege, a further, and far deeper, confusion, and this concerns the distinction between something's being true and its being taken to be true. Frege argues that his opponent runs these two distinct notions together by identifying logical laws with the realm of psychology, since the psychologistic logician's laws of thought are ultimately only laws of human beings' taking things to be true; they are, that is, laws concerning only the psychological states of believing something to be the case and the relations that obtain between and among such states, but they do not say anything with respect to what is in fact the case. Frege, quite rightly, takes it as simply obvious that there is such a distinction between something's being true and its being taken to be true:

> All I have to say is this: being true is different from being taken to be true, whether by one or many or everybody, and in no case is to be reduced to it. There is no contradiction in something's being true which everybody takes to be false.[7]

The independence Frege notes here between something's being true and its being taken to be true underwrites his conception of logic: "If being true is thus independent of being acknowledged by somebody or other, then the laws of truth are not psychological laws."[8]

In order to bring out further the limitations upon a psychological conception of logical laws, Frege engages in a bit of imaginative speculation. Since his opponent considers the laws of logic to be laws governing the actual thought processes of human beings, he must be open to the possibility of discovering human beings or other creatures who display different patterns of thought: "Accordingly the possibility remains open of men or other beings being discovered who were capable of bringing off judgments contradicting our laws of logic."[9] Frege's point in raising this possibility is to show the absurdity of his opponent's position: when confronted with such a possibility, the psychologistic logician could only acknowledge it as indicating a need to restrict or in some way modify the current formulation of his psychological laws. As Frege puts it, his opponent could only say "here we see that these principles do not hold generally," to which Frege responds: "Certainly! – if these are psychological laws, their verbal expression must single out the family of beings whose thought is empirically governed by them."[10] The problem with his opponent's response to the imagined discovery is that it leaves no room for describing these "variations" in patterns of thought as constituting any kind of *error* on the part of these beings.

Frege pushes on this problem by envisaging a discovery of a more radically different kind of beings whom I shall call "logical aliens." He asks: "But what if beings were even found whose laws of thought flatly contradicted ours and therefore led to contrary results even in practice?"[11] He again notes that "the psychologistic logician could only acknowledge the fact and say simply: those laws hold for them, these laws hold for us," whereas Frege would say: "we have here a hitherto unknown kind of madness."[12] In supplying this verdict upon these imagined beings, Frege's point is to underscore the idea that when faced with contradictory ways of thinking, the question arises as to which way is correct, ours or theirs. He writes:

> Anyone who understands laws of logic to be laws that prescribe the way in which one ought to think – to be laws of truth, and not natural laws of human beings' taking a thing to be true – will ask, who is right? Whose laws of taking-to-be-true are in accord with the laws of truth?[13]

These questions are posed in order to bring out the restrictions upon the psycho-logical account Frege is opposing, since "the psychologistic logician cannot ask these questions; if he did he would be recognizing laws of truth that were not laws of psychology."[14]

Frege introduces the idea of logical aliens, then, in order to demonstrate more vividly the limitations upon a psychological conception of logic. The question I now want to raise concerns just what kind of possibility Frege has here introduced. Do logical aliens constitute any kind of genuine possibility? Can we, that is, really imag-ine creatures who think, who make judgments, inferences and arguments and yet con-tradict the laws of logic? If we look further into Frege's attack on psychologism, it becomes apparent that Frege himself is divided on how to answer such questions.[15]

In the paragraph following his introduction of logical aliens, Frege raises the issue of the basis upon which one acknowledges a logical law to be true: "The question why and with what right we acknowledge a law of logic to be true, logic can answer only by reducing it to another law of logic. Where that is not possible, logic can give no answer."[16] Following this admission that one will ultimately reach a point where a logical justification for a logical principle can no longer be provided, Frege engages in some psychological speculation:

> If we step away from logic, we may say: we are compelled to make judg-ments by our own nature and by external circumstances; and if we do so, we cannot reject this law – of Identity, for example; we must acknowledge it unless we wish to reduce our thoughts to confusion and finally renounce all judgment whatever.[17]

About this piece of speculation, Frege goes on to say that he is, from a logical point of view, entirely agnostic as to whether we are so compelled to acknowledge certain logical laws: whether we are or not is a psychological question and cannot be taken as a reason for concluding that such laws are true. Furthermore, even if we assume that we are psychologically constrained in terms of what laws we may reject and acknowledge, this does not affect our ability to imagine other kinds of beings who are capable of rejecting a logical law:

> [T]his impossibility of our rejecting the law in question hinders us not at all in supposing beings who do reject it; where it hinders us is in supposing that these beings are right in doing so, it hinders us in having doubts as to whether we or they are right.[18]

Now, given Frege's conception of the laws of thought as normative, as, that is, prescribing how we ought to think, this is precisely what he should say, and so it would seem that logical aliens are, in some straightforward sense, a genuine possi-bility: such unfortunate creatures would forever be wrong in their judgments, but, as Frege states, nothing hinders us in imagining such beings. Call this one strand of Frege's thought the "normative strand."

A second strand of Frege's thought, however, can be discerned as one examines his final piece of argumentation against psychologism: the deepest problem with the psychologistic logician's view is that it blurs the distinction between the objective and the subjective, and indeed does so in such a way as to obliterate the very possibility of communication. This is so because Frege's opponent ultimately identifies concepts with ideas (understood here as discrete mental items). The possibility of communication is removed because our discourse no longer concerns any common objects over which we can agree and disagree: "If every man designated something different by the name 'moon', namely one of his own ideas, much as he expresses his own pain by the cry 'Ouch', then ... an argument about the properties of the moon would be pointless."[19] In such a case, Frege continues, "there would be no logic to be appointed arbiter in the conflict of opinions" since the "conflict" depicted here would not be contradiction, but instead mere difference.[20] I assert one thing of "my" moon, you assert the contrary of "your" moon, and so we do not so much disagree as have different ideas. We are not engaging in a meaningful dispute about a common object, but instead are giving expression to our inner states, as when we say "Ouch."

What this last piece of argumentation against psychologism suggests is a very different role for logic than the normative conception outlined above would provide. That is, Frege's talk of logic as an "arbiter" of opinions suggests a conception of logic as providing a kind of framework or background within which the relations of agreement and disagreement can be discerned.[21] In other words, the availability of *logical* notions such as contradiction and entailment serves as a condition on the possibility of judging (as opposed to merely venting one's inner states). But if this is so, then logic cannot be seen as bearing a normative relation to our judgments: it does not prescribe how we *ought* to proceed in our making of judgments; it instead forms a background for our making judgments at all.

On this second strand, call it the "constitutive strand," the idea of logical aliens, the idea, that is, of beings whose laws of thought flatly contradict our own, receives a very different treatment than it had on the normative strand. If the laws of logic, as the second strand suggests, provide a framework or background for the very possibility of agreement and disagreement, then there is no room for the possibility of beings who *disagree* with this framework itself. The idea of a logical alien, on this second strand, simply dissolves: when thought through, one realizes that there is no sense to be made of beings who *make judgments* and yet disagree with the laws of logic.

Frege's strategy of appealing to the possibility of logical aliens, then, has the effect of bringing to light tensions in his own conception of logic between the notion that logic provides laws in accordance with which one *ought* to think and the notion that logical laws are internal to thinking. That is, on first blush, logical aliens appear to present a kind of possibility, namely the possibility of illogical thought, to which Frege appeals in order to show the deficiencies of the psychological conception of logic. As one tries, however, to take seriously this kind of possibility, one begins to lose sight of its being a possibility at all. We are told by Frege that these beings are "capable of bringing off judgments contradicting our own laws of logic," but the problem that emerges is one of understanding just what kind of capability these beings supposedly possess. What does it mean to be able to "bring off" judgments contradicting logic, if the idea of one judgment's contradicting another presupposes precisely the laws of logic?[22]

All Frege says on this matter is that whatever kind of remarkable psychological capability these beings possess, it is a capability beyond the limits of our powers of judgment. For me (or any of us) to try to judge in accordance with *their* laws would be tantamount to my trying to "jump out of my own skin."[23] Frege's appeal to such a feat, and his urgent warning that one should not try to accomplish it, leaves the impression that there is *something* beyond my skin to which I cannot approach; it still leaves the impression that there is some *way of thinking* in which I cannot participate.

Logical aliens, I want to say, serve to personify the limits of thought, by appearing to provide a kind of contrast to the way in which we think: they appear to represent the possibility of beings with capabilities or capacities which I or any of us lack. My point, though, in teasing out the second strand of Frege's conception of logic has been to show just how problematic this attempt at personification really is, since the possibility these beings supposedly embody turns out to be self-destructive: if I imagine beings who make judgments and assertions, who infer and argue, then I cannot imagine them to be residing outside of the realm of logic. There is no realm beyond logic in which one can say that judging, asserting, inferring and arguing take place, but if this is so, then the idea of logical aliens cannot be maintained. And if the idea of logical aliens cannot ultimately be cashed out as constituting some kind of possibility, then the idea of our thought's being limited in some way must also be abandoned.

3 Wittgenstein's examination of Frege's polemics

I now want to turn to Wittgenstein's later remarks and, in particular, to his own imaginary scenario of the wood sellers, in order to show how he approaches the question of logical aliens which Frege's polemic had raised.[24]

The wood sellers are introduced following a number of remarks that point out, innocuously enough, the variety of methods by which one can set the price for a quantity of wood: wood can be sold by the cubic measure, by weight or, more creatively, by taking into account the age and strength of the persons who cut the wood; one could also, Wittgenstein points out, allow people to take what they want for some fixed price, or simply give the wood away. None of these methods is especially unfamiliar or provocative, and it is clear that Wittgenstein does not wish to have raised any issues of particular importance prior to his introduction of the wood sellers. His succinct "Very well" which begins the remark introducing the wood sellers registers his expectation that the reader has acquiesced to what has been said thus far; what follows, however, is intended to prompt more of a reaction:

> Very well; but what if they piled timber in heaps of arbitrary, varying height and then sold it at a price proportionate to the area covered by the piles?
> And what if they even justified this with the words: "Of course, if you buy more timber, you must pay more"?[25]

In the methods of determining the cost of any given pile of wood listed prior to this case, each of them fixes a means for justifying the determined cost: the difference in price between two piles of wood sold by the cubic measure, for example, can be justified by showing that the respective piles have different volumes; given a fixed price per unit volume, one can justify one pile's costing more than another, and one does indeed get more wood by paying more. If the price were fixed according to the age and strength of the woodcutter, a smaller pile might cost as much as a larger pile if the former is cut by an older, weaker cutter, and the justification for the sameness in price would appeal to those facts about the respective cutters. One might be unwilling to accept those facts as the best means for determining the cost of a pile (such a method certainly doesn't favor the buyer in many cases), but, given the method, the justification is more or less straightforward and is one that we can understand. In the prior cases in general, one might say that a given method determines an avenue of justification, and so the notion of a *correct* price for a pile only becomes viable once a method has been specified. Different methods will fix different prices for piles of wood, and these different prices will be differently justified by referring to those methods.

The lately introduced wood sellers, however, disrupt this last line of reasoning concerning the relation between standards and methods. Although they certainly seem to have a determinate method for fixing prices (given some price per unit surface area, one simply multiplies this by the surface area covered by the base of any particular pile), the difficulty here appears to be that we cannot accept their avenue of justification: a pile with a larger base area is not always a larger pile of wood, and so to say, "If you buy more timber, you must pay more" does not *really* justify a given price. In the second of the wood sellers remarks, Wittgenstein imagines an attempt to point this problem out to them:

> How could I show them that – as I should say – you don't really buy more wood if you buy a pile covering a bigger area? – I should, for instance, take a pile which was small by their ideas and, by laying the logs around, change it into a 'big' one.[26]

Wittgenstein continues by noting that "this *might* convince them," and if this were so, then the case would merely be one in which they were missing something, as though they were a group of children corrected by a well-meaning adult: they just hadn't noticed that a pile with a small base might contain more wood than one with a larger base.[27] Wittgenstein, however, notes that his demonstration might provoke a different response: "but perhaps they would say: 'Yes, now it's a *lot* of wood and costs more'," and he darkly concludes "and that would be the end of the matter."[28] With this second imagined response, the wood sellers now no longer appear simply naive, as they would if they were convinced by the demonstration; it is "the end of the matter" in so far as their response signals a failure of communication. We now feel that we are talking past them (and they past us). Wittgenstein closes the remark by concluding: "We should presumably say in this case: they simply do not mean the same by 'a lot of wood' and 'a little wood' as we do; and they have a quite different system of payment from us."[29] This conclusion registers the idea that, given the failure of the proposed demonstration, communication with these wood sellers has broken down.

When first presented with the wood sellers, the overwhelming temptation is to say that we've been presented with a group whose practices contain an error: the wood sellers are doing things which we do, namely measuring, calculating and fixing prices on the basis of those measurements and calculations, but they are doing so incorrectly. They are, it might be said, *trying* to do what we do, only their efforts are falling short. Wittgenstein's conclusion to the second of the remarks on the wood sellers, however, forces us to reconsider our initial appraisal: they are not, perhaps, mistakenly calling piles of wood with a larger base more wood, but are saying something entirely different; indeed, we do not know what they mean when they use words such as "a lot of wood" and "a little wood" and we do not know what their exchanges are really about.

The initial appearance of error, when pressed, reveals instead a lack of understanding on our part. The problem we confront in thinking about this community is not a problem *in* their practices, but rather a problem *for us* in interpreting just what it is they are doing. Wittgenstein alludes to this sort of problem of interpretation and its relation to determining whether someone is, for example, calculating incorrectly or not calculating at all, in the following passage, which appears elsewhere in the *Remarks on the Foundations of Mathematics*, but is pertinent to our considerations here:

> We come to an alien tribe whose language we do not understand. Under what circumstances shall we say that they have a chief? What will occasion us to say that this man is the chief even if he is more poorly clad than others? The one whom the others obey – is he without question the chief?

> What is the difference between inferring wrong and not inferring? between adding wrong and not adding? Consider this.[30]

The wood sellers, I want to claim, are such a tribe "whose language we do not understand." Suppose, for example, that not all of the wood sellers' words were homophonic with our own. The scenario might then run something like this: we encounter a group of people who arrange piles of wood in various ways. We notice that members of their group take away (purchase?) piles in exchange for, let us assume, pieces of silver. If a pile has a larger base area than some other one, the would-be taker hands over more pieces for the former, regardless of the heights of the respective piles. Now, we further notice that in comparing piles, they say that the one with a larger base area is "plonk wood." They apply the locution "plonk wood," however, not just when comparing *two* piles, but also when one pile has been rearranged so as to have a larger base area: about the pile that has been thus rearranged they say that it is "now plonk wood." Imagine further that upon rearrangement, a member of the group is willing to hand over more pieces of silver than before.

Telling the story in this way forces more clearly the question of just what the wood sellers mean by their words, since what, for example, "plonk" means is something that must be determined, rather than assumed. Telling the story in this way, in other words, deflects the temptation to conclude that "plonk wood" simply means "more wood." Isn't the fact that a pile that has only been rearranged so as to have a larger base area becomes "plonk wood" sufficient to show that "plonk" doesn't simply mean "more"? Of course, we might discover (or imagine) that "plonk" means *something* like "more" or "a lot," since our imagined wood sellers might say things like "plonk silver" when requesting or handing over larger numbers of silver pieces. Conjoining this piece of information with what the wood sellers say about piles of wood, we might conclude that "plonk" means something like "more valuable," and then draw the further conclusion that piles with larger base areas are, for some reason or other (perhaps for aesthetic reasons, perhaps because of some rather odd animistic beliefs), more valuable to these people. On this interpretation, when, following Wittgenstein's imagined intrusion, the wood sellers say "Yes, now it's a lot of (plonk) wood and so costs more (plonk)," what they mean is, "Yes, now the wood is more valuable and so one must part with more valuable things [a greater number of silver pieces] to get it."

Wittgenstein prepares us for the wood sellers by pointing to a variety of familiar practices of measuring and calculating and by showing further the connections among these practices to other activities such as fixing prices and building things such as houses. The concepts of measuring and calculating have, one might say, a home within this nexus of activities. To have the concept of measuring *is* to engage in a practice that has these sorts of connections; divorced from these connections, removed from such circumstances, the actions we perform when *we* measure or calculate may now, despite any superficial resemblance, have nothing at all to do with measuring or calculating.[31] Consider how little we know about the wood sellers, how little we are told about them: what they do with wood, why they are distributing wood, how they distribute other products, these and other questions regarding their lives cannot be answered, and as long as they cannot, whether or not they are measuring and calculating (let alone correctly or incorrectly) must remain undecided. Saying that the wood sellers are measuring and calculating quantity *incorrectly* presupposes that we are first licensed in saying that they are measuring and calculating, and Wittgenstein's point here is that we are unjustified in identifying their practices in this way.

The wood sellers scenario, by calling forth the idea of a home for a concept, contributes toward the dissolution of a particular picture of concepts and our relation to them, wherein a concept is something (some *thing*) specifiable and available apart from the practices in which that concept is applied.[32] Someone in the grip of this picture would, when confronted with the wood sellers, succumb to the temptation I described earlier, namely to see the situation as one where the concept of measuring (or quantity) is there, only it is being misapplied; the wood sellers display a faulty or deviant grasp of *it*. Wittgenstein's move against such a picture is to point out that a practice that looks like *that* (where, for example, attention is paid only to the base of the piles) and that lacks *these* surroundings (namely, the familiar ones into which our practices of measuring and calculating fit) is not one in which we would say that measuring (of quantity) is taking place. The concept is not being misapplied; it is conspicuous instead by its absence.

Wittgenstein's attack on this picture of the relation between a concept and its application is of a piece with his more general insistence on thinking of the meanings of words in terms of their use. Along with this insistence comes the insight that the use of a word is something *complicated* and cannot be understood in isolation. Consider the following remark: "The sign (the sentence) gets its significance from the system of signs, from the language to which it belongs. Roughly: understanding a sentence means understanding a language."[33] Similarly, in the *Investigations*, we find remarks such as "to imagine a language means to imagine a form of life";[34] "To understand a sentence means to understand a language";[35] and "What is happening now has significance – in these surroundings. The surroundings give it its importance."[36]

The case of the wood sellers instantiates these general remarks by demonstrating the difficulties involved in identifying their practices by means of our concepts. Without knowing anything more about the surroundings of their activities, of their uttering phrases such as "more wood," "a lot of wood" and the like, we are unable to determine just what it is that they mean by them. As I tried to show by replacing "more" and "a lot" with "plonk," our initial inclination to take their words to have the meanings they have for us when we say them, because they sound just like our own, is undermined by Wittgenstein's (our) failure to communicate with them using such words.[37]

Reflection on the import of the surroundings of the use of a word to the determination of its meaning shows the futility of simply insisting that the wood sellers do mean *more* by "more" and *a lot* by "a lot" and are just plain wrong a lot of the time. That is, someone might insist that what they mean is simply *stipulated* in the very describing of the scenario. But what does this "stipulation" amount to? What, that is, does it mean to mean *more* by "more"? Isn't it the use of the word that shows what is meant? That the wood sellers do not use "more" the way we do suggests that although homophonic to our word, they mean something else by it. Any attempt at simply stipulating what they mean must be evaluated relative to what is then described, and given what we are told about the wood sellers' practices (including their uses of words) the stipulation that they mean what we mean with their words carries little force.

Two remarks subsequent to those which present the wood sellers, Wittgenstein writes: "Frege says in the Preface to the *Grundgesetze der Arithmetik* '. here we have a hitherto unknown kind of insanity' – but he never said what this 'insanity' would really be like."[38] With this remark, it becomes clear that Wittgenstein intends the wood sellers scenario to prompt a reconsideration of Frege's prior scenario of logical aliens.[39] In Frege's scenario, what we were to imagine were beings who *infer*, but to results that contradict the results of our inferences, who *think* but according to laws of thought different from, and indeed contradictory to, our own. Wittgenstein's remark about Frege's charge of insanity is that "he never said what this 'insanity' would really be like" and I take him here to be challenging the notion that we have a clear idea of the phenomenon being so labeled by Frege. That is, Wittgenstein is questioning Frege's verdict by challenging the sense of the descriptions "inferring, but to results always contradictory to our own" and "thinking, but according to different laws of thought." The cogency of Frege's description presupposes the availability of a notion of inference apart from our actual practices of inferring. The wood sellers scenario, via examination of the concept of measuring, undermines the intelligibility of this notion. Any practice which appeared consistently to yield such contrary results is not one, Wittgenstein is reminding us, that we would call inferring at all.

Shortly before introducing the wood sellers, Wittgenstein writes:

The propositions of logic are 'laws of thought', 'because they bring out the essence of human thinking' – to put it more correctly; because they bring out, or show, the essence, the technique, of thinking. They show what thinking is and also show kinds of thinking.

Logic, it may be said, shows us what we understand by "proposition" and by 'language'.[40]

Wittgenstein uses the wood sellers scenario as a way of illustrating these remarks, as a way, that is, of illustrating how "logic shows us what we understand by 'proposition' and by 'language'." Frege's logical aliens were meant to provide a case of beings who think and speak and yet contradict the laws of thought; they were meant, that is, to be beings who are "capable" of illogical thought. What I take Wittgenstein to be doing with the wood sellers is showing how any attempt to get beyond the mouthing of the words "beings who think according to laws of thought contradicting our own," any attempt really to imagine such creatures, breaks down, because no beings we imagine of whom we would be willing to say that they are thinking would answer to this initial description.

It might be helpful to flesh out Wittgenstein's point here by recourse to Quine. As I read him, the view Wittgenstein takes toward the possibility of illogical thought accords well with much of what Quine says regarding the idea of deviance in logic. What accounts for the similarity is, I think, a deeper similarity as regards their respective views on meaning: Wittgenstein's insistence that in thinking about the meaning of an expression, one looks at how it is used resonates with Quine's idea that there is nothing more to the idea of meaning than what can be exhibited in behavior.[41]

Quine's discussion in *Philosophy of Logic*[42] begins with the suspicion that little sense is to be made of the idea of deviance in logic: "It would seem that such an idea of deviation in logic is absurd on the face of it. If sheer logic is not conclusive, what is? What higher tribunal could abrogate the logic of truth functions or of quantification?"[43] Quine's talk of a "higher tribunal" here suggests that nothing, no piece of evidence, could serve to dislodge or make us question the status of logic. But this is not really what's at issue in the case of logical aliens, since, on the face of it, it's perfectly consistent that one could acknowledge the possibility of such beings while maintaining that nothing could lead *us* to doubt the propositions of logic.

Quine's subsequent discussion reveals, however, that the absurdity of the idea of deviance in logic consists not only in the notion that nothing could make us doubt the propositions of logic, but, and more importantly for our considerations, nothing could persuade us to think that we had found beings who do doubt these propositions or affirm propositions contrary to them:

Suppose someone were to propound a heterodox logic in which all the laws which have up to now been taken to govern alternation were made to govern conjunction instead, and vice versa. Clearly we would regard his deviation merely as notational or phonetic. For obscure reasons, if any, he has taken to writing 'and' in place of 'or' and vice versa. We impute our orthodox logic to him, or impose it upon him, by translating his deviant dialect.[44]

Quine's point is this: let us assume that the "laws governing" alternation (disjunction) and conjunction are given by a truth-table, such that

p	q	p and q	p or q
T	T	T	T
T	F	F	T
F	T	F	T
F	F	F	F

On the "heterodox logic" Quine initially considers, the supposed evidence of heterodoxy consists perhaps in the fact that the would-be deviant writes "T T T F" under "p and q" and writes "T F F F" under "p or q." Quine's claim is that when confronted by such a person, rather than having met someone who is *logically* deviant, we have instead found someone who means by the locution "and" what we mean by "or," and by the locution "or" what we mean by "and"; such a person is perhaps phonetically or inscriptionally deviant, but this hardly counts as a deviation in logic. The aura of logical deviance is removed, according to Quine, simply by imputing or imposing our orthodox logic upon the person by translating his idiolect into ours, i.e., we translate his uses of "or" with our "and," and his uses of "and" with our "or."

However, one might object here that we are overstepping our bounds with such an imputation or imposition: what right have we to impose our orthodox logic upon this person? Couldn't he still mean by "and" what we mean by "and" and disagree with us as to the truth-functional properties of conjunction?[45] Quine wastes little time in dismissing this objection, since it only begs the question of what there is to conjunction *besides* its truth-functional properties: there is no sense to an inscription or utterance being an instance of conjunction beyond what is given in a truth table. Quine writes:

> Could we be wrong in so doing? Could he really be meaning and thinking genuine conjunction in his use of 'and' after all, just as we do, and genuine alternation in his use of 'or', and merely disagreeing with us on points of logical doctrine respecting the laws of conjunction and alternation? *Clearly this is nonsense.* There is no residual essence to conjunction and alternation in addition to the sounds and notations and the laws in conformity with which a man uses those sounds and notations.[46]

According to Quine, the idea of a deviant logic is undermined by reflection upon the task of translation. That is, in order to conclude that someone is committed to a deviant logic, we must have first succeeded in translating that person's language into our own. That is, we must first have determined which among that person's words are to be translated by our words "or," "and," "not," etc. This requirement tells against the idea of discovering that such a person is committed to a deviant logic, since any linguistic behavior which might appear to suggest a deviant grasp of, say, disjunction would count as evidence against translating the connective in question by "or." In translating, Quine notes that:

> We impute our orthodox logic to him, or impose it on him, by translating
> his language to suit. We build the logic into our manual of translation. Nor
> is there cause here for apology. We have to base translation on some kind
> of evidence, and what better?[47]

I claimed previously that the wood sellers scenario raises a problem of translation: before imputing to these imagined beings a deviant form of measuring, we
first have to ascertain what they mean by their words, in particular by locutions
such as "a lot of wood" and "a little wood." Given the circumstances under which
they apply such locutions, it becomes questionable, to say the least, that we are
entitled to take what they mean by such locutions as what we mean when *we* say
"a lot of wood" and so forth. These considerations were meant, in turn, to cast
doubt upon the imaginability of a phenomenon of the kind Frege had called "a
hitherto unknown kind of insanity." Quine has likewise detected the impact of
considerations regarding translation upon the idea of illogical thought with the
result being that the former undermines the cogency of the latter. This is especially
evident in his "Carnap and Logical Truth," where Quine attacks what he calls a
"caricature" of the idea of pre-logical mentality promulgated in the writings of the
anthropologist Lévy-Bruhl. Quine writes:

> Oversimplifying, no doubt, let us suppose it claimed that these natives
> accept as true a certain sentence of the form 'p and not p'. Or – not to
> oversimplify too much – that they accept as true a certain heathen sentence
> of the form 'q ka bu q' the English translation of which has the form 'p
> and not p'. But now just how good a translation is this, and what may the
> lexicographer's method have been? If any evidence can count against a
> lexicographer's adoption of 'and' and 'not' as translations of 'ka' and 'bu',
> certainly the natives' acceptance of 'q ka bu q' as true counts over-
> whelmingly.

Quine concludes from this that "we are left with the meaninglessness of the doctrine
of there being pre-logical peoples; pre-logicality is a trait injected by bad translators."[48]

From what we have seen, it should be apparent that Wittgenstein has seized upon
and articulated more explicitly what I called the "constitutive strand" of Frege's
conception of logic. Moreover, Wittgenstein is willing to accept the consequences
of a commitment to that strand of Frege's thought, in that he is willing to give up
the idea that the laws of thought, the propositions of logic, themselves consist in
truths. This is something Frege would have been unwilling to acknowledge, since
for him logic is the maximally general science, whose laws are thus the maximally
general truths. Understanding logic as a science is wedded to what I called previously the normative strand in Frege's conception: to return to the Preface of *Basic
Laws*, there Frege writes that "any law asserting what is, can be conceived as
prescribing that one ought to think in conformity with it, and is thus in that sense
a law of thought."[49] He adds that "this holds for laws of geometry and physics no
less than for laws of logic."[50] What distinguishes logical laws from those of the
special sciences is the former's generality, but all such laws are on a par as regards

their expressing substantive truths, and thereby laying down requirements as to how we ought to think.

If one develops the constitutive strand, as I take Wittgenstein to be doing, one result of doing so is an abandonment of the idea that logic is the maximally general science. In other words, if logic provides the framework or background for the possibility of thought, then logic itself does not consist in thoughts. This is so because a thought, for Frege, is the kind of thing that can be entertained as true or false. However, if, as the ultimately futile attempt to imagine logical aliens shows, there is no standpoint from which one could entertain the falsity of a proposition of logic, then, by symmetry, there is also no standpoint from which such propositions can be entertained as true.[51] Wittgenstein himself spells out this consequence of taking logic to be constitutive of, rather than normative for, thought in the following passage, which appears shortly after the wood sellers scenario and the allusion to Frege:

> Isn't it like this: so long as one thinks it can't be otherwise, one draws logical conclusions. This presumably means: so long as *such and such is not brought into question at all.*

> The steps which are not brought into question are logical inferences. But the reason why they are not brought into question is not that they 'certainly correspond to the truth' – or something of the sort, – no, it is just this that is called 'thinking', 'speaking', 'inferring', 'arguing'. There is not any question at all here of some correspondence between what is said and reality; rather is logic *antecedent* to any such correspondence; in the same sense, that is, as that in which the establishment of a method of measurement is *antecedent* to the correctness or incorrectness of a statement of length.[52]

Wittgenstein's talk of *antecedence* here is another way of saying that logic provides a kind of framework or background to what we call thinking, speaking, inferring and arguing, but if logic does provide such a framework, then there is no sense to be made of thinking, speaking, inferring and arguing in ways that "contradict logic." There is no sense, in other words, to be made of the idea of "illogical thought."[53]

I claimed previously that Frege's logical aliens could be seen as a personification of the limits of thought, by appearing to provide a point of contrast to our way of thinking. They appear, that is, to present a kind of possibility, which we would have to jump out of our skins to realize. The wood sellers challenge this attempt at personification by showing that there is nothing beyond our skins, so to speak, which we are prevented from grasping. What we come to realize by reflecting upon the wood sellers is that the idea of logical aliens does not present any possibility at all. Indeed, such an idea is of a piece with the confused idea that there is a limit to be drawn to thought. Recall Wittgenstein's prefatory remark to the *Tractatus*: drawing a limit to thought requires our being able to think both sides of the limit, and one way of understanding this requirement is to say that it requires us to acknowledge the possibility of logical aliens as beings who reside on "the other side." But if logical aliens constitute, as I take Wittgenstein to be showing in *both* his early and later work, only the illusion of an idea and not a genuine possibility at all, then the idea of drawing a limit and placing us on one side of it must itself only be an illusion.

In this way, Wittgenstein's treatment of the (ultimately confused) notion of logical aliens provides a kind of antidote for our thinking that our logical or conceptual skin *confines* us in some way and that there is something "out there" beyond our skin, only we cannot, due to the constraining effect of our skin, get to it. Indeed, I would suggest that the real point of Wittgenstein's treatment is to get us to give up the idea of our having a conceptual *skin* at all and with it the notions of *inside* and *outside* that accompany such an idea.

4 Wittgenstein's quietism[54]

At the outset of this paper, I stated that Wittgenstein's treatment of Frege and the idea of a limit to thought serves as a basis for understanding the kind of quietism Wittgenstein encourages in his later work. I now want by way of conclusion to sketch out what I mean by this.

At one point in the *Philosophical Investigations*, Wittgenstein writes:

> The results of philosophy are the uncovering of one or another piece of plain nonsense and of bumps that the understanding has got by running its head up against the limits of language. These bumps make us see the value of the discovery.[55]

The wood sellers scenario, I want to suggest, provides one such opportunity for the understanding to bump its head on the limits of language. Note here that Wittgenstein does *not* speak of the limits of *thought*, but of language: what goes wrong in our thinking about the wood sellers or about logical aliens is not that we are, in some mysterious sense, thinking the unthinkable (or even saying the unsayable); rather, what happens is that we have reached a point where there is only the illusion of a possibility, where our words have seduced us into thinking that there is a possibility beyond our reach. Our words fail us, and not because there is *something* which we cannot say: the failure instead consists in our not saying anything at all. We "bump our heads" because we feel ourselves to have reached a kind of limit, but this is a limit only to the sense that we make with our words, with our language, and not to what we can or cannot think. Saying that we have arrived at something unthinkable implies that we are, in mouthing words about logical aliens and the like, still making a kind of sense. Wittgenstein's aim, as I read him, is to reveal that we have indeed lapsed into nonsense and so to show that there is no such implication here at all. As he writes at another juncture of the *Investigations*: "When a sentence is called senseless, it is not as it were its sense that is senseless. But a combination of words is being excluded from the language, withdrawn from circulation."[56]

The kind of quietism I associate with Wittgenstein's later work is contained in the idea that philosophy "leaves everything as it is."[57] One way in which someone might resist this idea is in thinking that there is a kind of perspective to which we might attain (call it a transcendental perspective), and that from such a vantage-point we can survey the form of our thinking from the outside and so see it as having borders or limits. The *imposition* of a limit is one way of not leaving every-thing as it is, as it consists in an attempt to *explain* our thinking as containing some possibilities but not others. On the other hand, *denying* that such a limit can be imposed itself amounts to a kind of resistance to "leaving everything as it is," because issuing such a denial still takes the question of whether or not there is a limit to thought seriously, as a form of words that raises a question in need of an answer. Leaving everything as it is means giving up or letting go of certain combi-nations of words, of finally admitting or confessing that they are only senseless.

I want to close with one final remark, from *On Certainty*, which was written in the last year and a half of Wittgenstein's life. At § 501 of *On Certainty*, he writes: "Am I not getting closer and closer to saying that in the end logic cannot be described? You must look at the practice of language, then you will see it."[58] There is a certain irony in this remark, since Wittgenstein describes himself as "getting closer and closer" to a view, or perhaps an attitude, that is markedly similar to one he held nearly forty years previously. The very first entry of his *Notebooks 1914–16*, which contain preliminary formulations of the remarks which make up the *Tractatus*, is the sentence "Logic must take care of itself"[59] and this too suggests an attitude that in the end logic cannot be described, and that it must instead be seen *in* the practice of language. Both remarks, that "logic cannot be described" and that "logic must take care of itself," present the kind of quietism that I take Wittgenstein to be recommending, a kind of quietism that simply leaves us where we are, with our thinking and our language, and with all confused and misleading talk of limits "withdrawn from circulation."[60]

Notes

1 Wittgenstein, *Tractatus Logico-Philosophicus*, D. Pears and B. McGuinness (trans.), p. 3.
2 Ibid., p. 19. See also Wittgenstein's remarks about an "illogical language," in "Notes Dictated to G. E. Moore in Norway" in *Notebooks 1914–16*, pp. 108–19; see especially p. 108.
3 For a discussion of the intricacies and difficulties which attend interpreting the *Tractatus*, see C. Diamond, "Throwing Away the Ladder: How to Read the *Tractatus*" in her *The Realistic Spirit*, Cambridge, Mass., MIT Press, 1991, pp. 179–204. Diamond is espe-cially concerned to understand Wittgenstein's claim at the end of the *Tractatus* that those who understand him will see that his remarks are nonsensical. Taking this claim seriously requires that one not, in Diamond's words, "chicken out." To chicken out means to hang on to the idea that there are features of reality (the ontology of simples, facts, etc.) toward which one can gesture but about which one can say nothing. My discussion of illogical thought is of a piece with Diamond's more general interpreta-tion: to chicken out about illogical thought would be to maintain that there was *something* one cannot do, that there was, in other words, a kind of thought which is excluded given our psychological make-up or linguistic capacities. Throwing away the ladder with regard to illogical thought means acknowledging that there is no *it*, no kind of thought, about which one can say (or show) that *it* is impossible.
4 Frege, *The Basic Laws of Arithmetic: An Exposition of the System*, M. Furth (ed. and trans.) Berkeley, University of California Press, 1969, p. 12.
5 Frege's attack on psychologism is not restricted to the Preface of *Basic Laws*. See, in particular, the two fragments entitled "Logic" in *Posthumous Writings*, H. Hermes, F. Kambartel and F. Kaulbach (eds) P. Long and R. White (trans.) Chicago, University of Chicago Press, 1979, pp. 1–8 and pp. 126–51.

6 In "Thoughts," Part I of his "Logical Investigations" (in *Collected Papers on Mathematics, Logic, and Philosophy*, B. McGuinness (ed.) London, Blackwell, 1984, pp. 351–406), Frege offers a somewhat different account of the idea that the laws of logic are the laws of thought. Rather than emphasizing the normative notion of law, as he does in *Basic Laws*, here Frege takes as basic the idea that the laws of logic are the laws of *truth*, and so logical laws, like other natural laws, are descriptive. What might be called their normativity arises from considering their application to human thinking. Frege writes:

> Laws of nature are general features of what happens in nature, and occurrences in nature are always in accordance with them. It is rather in this sense that I speak of laws of truth. Here of course it is not a matter of what happens but of what is. From the laws of truth there follow prescriptions about asserting, thinking, judging, inferring. And we may very well speak of laws of thought in this way too.
>
> (p. 351)

Understood as laws of *thought*, logical laws bear a normative relation to thinking; understood as laws of truth, logical laws are descriptive, and differ from other laws of nature only by dint of their generality. I return to this distinction in section 3.
7 Frege, *Basic Laws*, op. cit., p. 13.
8 Ibid.
9 Ibid., p. 14.
10 Ibid.
11 Ibid.
12 Ibid.
13 Ibid.
14 Ibid.
15 It should be emphasized that I do not raise these questions in order to defend psychologism against Frege's attack. Nor should Wittgenstein, when he examines Frege's polemics, be taken to be doing so. Indeed, Wittgenstein's aim is to undermine *both* the Fregean and the psychologistic conceptions of logic. Consider the following passage from *Wittgenstein's Lectures on the Foundations of Mathematics: Cambridge, 1939*, where Frege's *Basic Laws* polemic figures prominently:

> Next time I hope to start with the statement: "The laws of logic are laws of thought." The question is whether we should say we cannot think except according to them, that is, whether they are psychological laws – or, as Frege thought, laws of nature. He compared them with laws of natural science (physics), which we must obey in order to think correctly. I want to say they are neither.
>
> (p. 230)

16 Frege, *Basic Laws*, op. cit., p. 15.
17 Ibid.
18 Ibid.
19 Ibid., p. 17.
20 Ibid.
21 For a fuller discussion of how, on Frege's conception, logic provides a framework or background for agreement and disagreement, and how, moreover, this conception emerges out of his attack on psychologism, see T. Ricketts, "Objectivity and Objecthood: Frege's Metaphysics of Judgment" in L. Haaparanta and J. Hintikka (eds) *Frege Synthesized*, Boston, D. Reidel, 1986, pp. 65–95.
22 My reading of Frege's use of logical aliens differs from the one offered in J. Conant, "The Search for Logically Alien Thought: Descartes, Kant, Frege, and the *Tractatus*," *Philosophical Topics*, 1992, vol. 20, pp. 115–80. Conant maintains that Frege's polemic as a whole is to be read as offering an "argument *against the possibility* of such logical aliens," and this argument, "read in its strongest form amounts to an argument against the very intelligibility of this scenario" (p. 142). Conant thus calls Frege's polemic a

"peculiar form of philosophical criticism," since Frege only appears to be putting forward a possibility, over the significance of which he and his opponent disagree. Conant suggests that Frege's initial commitment to the possibility of logical aliens is an opening move in a complex, dialectical argument, the structure of which Conant likens to an onion: the argument consists in several layers, and as one moves inward toward the central and more "peculiar" criticisms, one abandons the outer layers as having served the purpose of leading one on to the center but as being no longer relevant. Conant is certainly right that there *is* a strand of Frege's polemic which dictates a rejection of the possibility of logical aliens, but I want to maintain that it is only one strand. On what I have called the normative strand of Frege's conception of logic, Frege acknowledges logical aliens as constituting a genuine possibility, and he does not ever explicitly retract this acknowledgment. Thus, although he offers a fascinating reading of Frege's polemic, I don't think the text can support Conant's imposition of such an elaborate argumentative structure. Moreover, as Conant himself acknowledges, there *are* tensions in Frege's views, between the idea of logic as a science and a more Kantian conception of logic as constitutive of the possibility of thought. What I am suggesting here is that this latter tension and Frege's ambivalent stance toward the possibility of logical aliens are one and the same. Despite this disagreement, I have learned much from Conant's paper, in part because it helped me to focus my reading of the *Basic Laws* polemic and because of its more general treatment of the relations among Kant, Frege and Wittgenstein concerning the nature of logic.

23 Frege, *Basic Laws*, op. cit., p. 15.
24 A shorter version of the following discussion of the wood sellers can be found in my "Don't Look But Think: Imaginary Scenarios in Wittgenstein's Later Philosophy," *Inquiry*, 1994, vol. 37, pp. 159–83. There, my discussion of the wood sellers is in the service of developing an argument against those readers of Wittgenstein who see in his use of imaginary scenarios a kind of ersatz sociology or anthropology.
25 Wittgenstein, *Remarks on the Foundations of Mathematics*, I, § 149.
26 Ibid., I, § 150.
27 Of course, children are not always so easily corrected. As Piaget's experiments suggest, a child's understanding of such concepts as quantity, distance and number develops over time, and over the course of that development the child will make numerous mistakes in applying these concepts (some of which suggest that the concept has not yet been grasped at all). Stanley Cavell, in his reading of the wood sellers (in *The Claim of Reason*, Oxford, Oxford University Press, 1979; see Part I, Chapter 5, pp. 86–125), has explored the suggestion that we read this scenario (and others like it in Wittgenstein's writing) as though the characters described were children. As Cavell recognizes, a difficulty with this approach is that with children we expect them to acquire, eventually, the concepts of quantity, distance, number, etc. which we employ every day, and we explain their difficulties with these concepts by reference to their *immaturity*. With the wood sellers scenario, however, Wittgenstein's description, such as it is, suggests our coming upon an autonomous community, and this poses a problem of interpretation not found in the case of children. With children, the starting point of interpretation is that they are at least trying to speak our language and so we correct their attempts in an effort to shape their use of language to conform with ours, whereas with the wood sellers, this very starting point needs to be called into question.
28 *Remarks on the Foundations of Mathematics*, I, § 150.
29 Ibid.
30 Ibid., VI, § 48.
31 For an illuminating discussion of this point, see C. Diamond, "Rules: Looking in the Right Place" in D. Z. Phillips and P. Winch (eds) *Wittgenstein: Attention to Particulars*, London, Macmillan and Company, 1989, pp. 12–34.
32 Wittgenstein can be seen to be attacking this picture in the following remark, from Lecture XX of *Wittgenstein's Lectures on the Foundations of Mathematics: Cambridge, 1939*, p. 191 (one lecture prior to presenting a version of the wood sellers scenario), here using the example of negation:

What use of a word characterizes that word as being a negation? Isn't it the *use* that makes it negation?

It is not a question of our first *having* negation, and then asking what logical laws must hold of it in order for us to be able to use it in a certain way. The point is that using it in a certain way is what we mean by negating with it.

See also Peter Winch's discussion of Wittgenstein on iterated negation in his "Persuasion" in P. French, T. Uehling, Jr and H. Wettstein (eds) *Midwest Studies in Philosophy*, vol. XVII ("The Wittgenstein Legacy"), Notre Dame, University of Notre Dame Press, 1992, pp. 123–37; see especially pp. 125–6.

33 Wittgenstein, *The Blue and Brown Books*, p. 5.

34 Wittgenstein, *Philosophical Investigations*, § 19.

35 Ibid., § 199.

36 Ibid., § 583. Consider also the following remarks from Wittgenstein's *Remarks on the Philosophy of Psychology*: "I should like to say: conversation, the application and further interpretation of words flows on and only in this current does a word have its meaning" (Vol. 1, § 240). And similarly: "Only in the stream of thought and life do words have meaning" (Vol. 2, § 504).

37 On this point, my reading diverges from B. Stroud, "Wittgenstein and Logical Necessity" in G. Pitcher (ed.) *Wittgenstein: The Philosophical Investigations*, Notre Dame, University of Notre Dame Press, 1966, pp. 477–96. At one place in his discussion, Stroud spells out the alien character of the wood sellers as arising in part from their meaning what we mean, and as a result having strange beliefs:

> And what would the relation between quantity and weight possibly be for such people? A man could buy as much wood as he could possibly lift, only to find, upon dropping it, that he had just lifted more wood than he could possibly lift. Or is there more wood, but the same weight? Or perhaps these people do not understand the expressions "more" and "less" at all. They must, if they can say, "Now it's a lot of wood, and costs more."
>
> (p. 488)

I find the last sentence of this passage to be problematic: while the wood sellers may mouth the words, "Now it's a lot of wood, and costs more," the circumstances under which they consistently use those words tell against the idea that what they *mean* with those words is what we mean when we say them. I agree with Stroud that the wood sellers do present a problem of intelligibility, but I want to spell out that problem in a different way. I should emphasize that, in taking issue with some of the details of Stroud's reading, I do not intend thereby to take issue with his broader attack on conventionalist readings of Wittgenstein.

38 *Remarks on the Foundations of Mathematics*, I, § 152.

39 It should be emphasized here that the wood sellers are *not* to be understood as logical aliens, or even an attempt at a sketch of such creatures. Rather, as I read Wittgenstein, his treatment of the wood sellers suggests a treatment which can be applied to the idea of logical aliens. The wood sellers scenario is a sketch of what prima facie look to be, say, measuring aliens, but as we reflect upon the scenario we lose our grip on the idea that what these people are doing is (best described as) measuring at all, and so the claim that they are measuring aliens loses its force. This scenario suggests a treatment of logical aliens in that one can raise analogous questions with respect to attempts to describe, say, inference aliens or negation aliens. Why call what's described in these cases inference or negation?

40 *Remarks on the Foundations of Mathematics*, I, §§ 133–4.

41 I do not mean to suggest here that Wittgenstein is a behaviorist. Behavior, for Wittgenstein, is not the austere production of noises and bodily movements that some of Quine's writings suggest it is.

42 W.V.O. Quine, *Philosophy of Logic*, Cambridge, Mass., Harvard University Press, 1986. See also his *Word and Object*, Cambridge, Mass., MIT Press, 1960; see especially § 13,

pp. 57–61. It should be noted that there is a difficulty in evaluating Quine's remarks about the intelligibility of deviance in logic in light of the pragmatic view of logic he offers in "Two Dogmas of Empiricism" in his *From a Logical Point of View*, Cambridge, Mass., Harvard University Press, 1980, pp. 20–46. In "Two Dogmas," Quine argues that in the ongoing process of squaring our total theory with experience, nothing is in principle immune from revision, including the laws of logic. That revisions are made elsewhere than logic in order to accommodate new experience is explained by Quine as simply the operation of pragmatic considerations. This implies that changes to logic *could* be made. In *Word and Object* and in the discussion I cite, both of which come after "Two Dogmas," the possibility of revising logic is more difficult to understand, since Quine is intent on dismissing the very intelligibility of having a deviant logic. Quine appears to be contradicting the position adopted in "Two Dogmas," which suggests an abandonment of the thoroughgoing pragmatism offered in that paper. These changes (or tensions if one reads him uncharitably) in Quine's views about logic are discussed in M. Dummett, "Is Logic Empirical?" in his *Truth and Other Enigmas*, Cambridge, Harvard University Press, 1978, pp. 269–89 and in S. Haack, *Deviant Logic: Some Philosophical Issues*, Cambridge, Cambridge University Press, 1974. The difficulties (if any) this change poses for Quine need not concern us here.

43 Quine, *Philosophy of Logic*, op. cit., p. 81.

44 Ibid.

45 Note the parallel between this question (and Quine's response) and the discussion above concerning what the wood sellers mean by "more" and the futility of simply stipulating (or insisting) that they mean what we mean.

46 Ibid., my emphasis.

47 Ibid., p. 82. For Quine, this is not simply a point about logic, but about any sentence whose truth or falsity is obvious given the circumstances in which assent or dissent is elicited from the natives by the translator. Logical truth is the limiting case of this constraint, since the truths of logic, at least ones which are simple in form, are obvious under any such circumstances.

> . . . logical truth is guaranteed under translation. The canon 'Save the obvious' bans any manual of translation that would represent the foreigners as contradicting our logic (apart perhaps from corrigible confusions in complex sentences).
>
> (p. 83)

This assimilation of logic to obvious truths more generally marks a point of divergence from Wittgenstein. As I discuss below, Wittgenstein, in continuing what I have called the constitutive strand of Frege's conception of logic, rejects the idea that logic consists in truths at all; their role in language is, as he puts it, "antecedent" to the articulation of truths and falsities. Some of Wittgenstein's last writings do suggest that this antecedence is not a hard and fast matter, that the role of various propositions within the language can change. I have in mind here especially §§ 95–9 of *On Certainty*. Even in these remarks, however, he rejects the idea that logic is an empirical science.

48 Quine, "Carnap and Logical Truth" in his *The Ways of Paradox and Other Essays*, Cambridge, Harvard University Press, 1980, pp. 107–32; citation from p. 109.

49 Frege, *Basic Laws*, op. cit., p. 12.

50 Ibid.

51 For a discussion of how this consequence is played out in the context of Wittgenstein's *early* philosophy, see T. Ricketts, "Frege, the *Tractatus*, and the Logocentric Predicament," *Nous*, 1985, vol. XIX, pp. 3–15. It should be noted that this consequence of the constitutive strand is one which Frege himself never recognizes; indeed, one might say that the normative strand represents Frege's official conception of logic. That this is so can be seen in the following passage from "Compound Thoughts," Part III of his "Logical Investigations" (in *Collected Papers on Mathematics, Logic, and Philosophy*, op. cit.) wherein Frege comes close to rejecting as nonsensical the possibility of entertaining the negation of a logical law, but does not do so:

Let 'O' be a sentence which expresses a particular instance of a logical law, but which is not presented as true. Then it is easy for 'not O' to seem nonsensical, but only because it is thought of as uttered assertorically. The assertion which contradicts a logical law can indeed appear, if not nonsensical, then at least absurd; for the truth of a logical law is immediately evident of itself, from the sense of its expression. But a thought which contradicts a logical law may be expressed, since it may be negated. 'O' itself, however, seems almost to lack content.

(p. 405)

52 *Remarks on the Foundations of Mathematics*, I, §156.
53 More accurately, no sense *has been* made of the words, "illogical thought." As I explain in the next section, Wittgenstein is concerned to reject the idea that problematic expressions like "illogical thought" have a kind of nonsensical sense, as though such words gestured at something lying beyond our powers of speech. Such an attitude toward nonsense can already be found in the *Tractatus*; consider, for example, Wittgenstein's remark that "any possible proposition is legitimately constructed, and, if it has no sense that can only be because we have failed to give a *meaning* to some of its constituents." Wittgenstein continues by adding parenthetically: "Even if we think we have done so" (see *Tractatus Logico-Philosophicus*, 5.4733). Such is the case with Frege's appeal to the "possibility" of logical aliens: Wittgenstein uses the wood sellers scenario to show that no sense has yet been made with such a combination of words.
54 The term "quietism" as applied to Wittgenstein's later philosophy has been discussed recently in J. McDowell, *Mind and World*, Cambridge, Harvard University Press, 1994. My usage agrees with McDowell's in so far as he urges that this term not be taken as an acknowledgment of *defeat* in the face of genuine philosophical problems. As I suggest below, my use of the label is consonant with his (and Wittgenstein's) insistence that philosophy "leaves everything as it is," where a proper understanding of this remark consists in giving up the idea that there are limits upon our thinking which *cannot* be transcended. For McDowell's discussion, see his "Postscript to Lecture V" in *Mind and World*, op. cit., pp. 175–80. I have also profited greatly (on this point and more generally) from E. Minar, "Feeling at Home in Language (What Makes Reading *Philosophical Investigations* Possible?)," *Synthese*, 1995, vol. 102, pp. 413–52. In Section 1.1 of this paper (pp. 417–22), Minar is also concerned to remove a misunderstanding of Wittgenstein's attitude toward philosophical theorizing as amounting to a kind of "defeatism."
55 *Philosophical Investigations*, § 119.
56 Ibid., § 500.
57 Ibid., § 124.
58 *On Certainty*, § 501.
59 *Notebooks 1914–16*, p. 2. The entry is dated August 22, 1914. See also *Tractatus Logico-Philosophicus*, 5.473.
60 A version of this paper was presented to the Philosophy Department at the University of California, Berkeley. I am grateful to the audience there for their comments and criticism. I would especially like to thank Hubert Dreyfus, Hans Sluga, David Stern and Barry Stroud. Thanks also to Steven Affeldt, James Conant, Alice Crary and Rupert Read for their encouragement and many helpful suggestions. I would also like to acknowledge a long-standing debt to two discussions of the wood sellers, those of Stroud and of Stanley Cavell, which have influenced my thinking on these matters well beyond my brief references to them in this paper might suggest.

13

CONCEPTIONS OF NONSENSE IN CARNAP AND WITTGENSTEIN

Edward Witherspoon

Introduction

In the *Tractatus*, Wittgenstein expressed the following assessment of the philosophical tradition: "Most statements and questions that have been written about
philosophical matters are not false, but nonsensical. We cannot therefore answer
questions of this sort at all, but only establish their nonsensicality" (*Tractatus*,
4.003).[1] This dismissal of philosophy became a rallying point for the members of
the Vienna Circle in their attacks on "metaphysics." The logical positivists had
independent reasons for wanting to do away with metaphysics, but Wittgenstein's
blanket rejection of traditional philosophy and his use of logical analysis influenced
the direction of their critique. Carnap in particular acknowledged a significant debt
to the *Tractatus*. He was impressed not only by the sweep of Wittgenstein's charge,
but also by his diagnosis of what goes wrong in philosophy. In the continuation of
the *Tractatus* passage quoted above, Wittgenstein wrote: "Most questions and statements of philosophers result from the fact that we do not understand the logic of
our language" (*Tractatus*, 4.003). Under the impression that he was supplying the
theoretical foundation for Wittgenstein's critique of metaphysics, Carnap developed
a theory of meaningfulness around the idea that nonsense arises from violations
of logical syntax. He provided an account of logical syntax that was supposed
to expose and rectify philosophers' misunderstandings concerning the logic of our
language.

Wittgenstein's influence on Carnap gradually waned, yet the two philosophers'
subsequent critiques of philosophy followed seemingly parallel courses. In the
Philosophical Investigations, Wittgenstein's discussions of the logical structure of
sentences gave way to discussions of language-games. His new view seemed to be
that philosophical confusion arises from the use of expressions outside the language-
games to which they belong. Carnap had meanwhile put forward a theory of meaningfulness according to which meaningful sentences are those that have a place within
what he calls a "linguistic framework"; philosophers lapse into nonsense by using
words and sentences outside any such framework.[2] It can be tempting to regard
Wittgenstein's and Carnap's later views as variants of the same basic conception of
nonsense, according to which a sentence makes sense if it lies within the limits
of the relevant linguistic system and doesn't make sense if it lies outside them.

315

The apparent similarities between Carnap and Wittgenstein, early and late, suggest the following narrative. Early in their careers, Wittgenstein and Carnap both thought that philosophical nonsense results from violations of the logic that governs the meaningful use of language; the task of the critic of philosophy is to lay out the system of logic so that violations are clearly identifiable. Each of them came to reject his early view, and to replace it with a version of a quite different conception of nonsense. On this conception, nonsense results from the use of language outside the limits of a language-game or linguistic framework; the task of the critic of philosophy is to point out when and how philosophers have transgressed the limits of their linguistic system.

This narrative has such apparent plausibility that it is perhaps surprising that commentators on Wittgenstein have not done more to link his thought with Carnap's. I suspect that this omission stems from a lack of appreciation for Carnap's subtlety. Many philosophers regard Carnap as a verificationist, and so not worth troubling about. Although Carnap did embrace verificationism for a time, his more characteristic reflections on meaningfulness have little in common with it. There are other philosophers who know that the *Tractatus* inspired much of Carnap's work, but they tend to regard Carnap as a thinker who never caught up with what they regard as the radical advances in Wittgenstein's later work. Whether for these or other reasons, commentators tend to think that Carnap's work does not illuminate Wittgenstein's.

There is an irony here. For despite the absence of explicit references to Carnap, commentators often develop critiques of traditional philosophy that follow the lines Carnap laid down – and then attribute these critiques to Wittgenstein. I will consider in detail two such readings of later Wittgenstein: one offered by G. Baker and P.M.S. Hacker and another offered by Marie McGinn. On Baker and Hacker's reading, Wittgenstein determines whether a piece of philosophical discourse is meaningful by testing it against "rules of grammar." I will argue that, despite Baker and Hacker's insistence on the distance between later Wittgenstein and logical positivism, their reading of Wittgenstein exhibits the characteristic features of Carnap's logical syntax theory of meaningfulness. Marie McGinn is concerned in the first instance with Wittgenstein's response to skepticism. She takes the key to this response to lie in the notion of a "framework of inquiry"; according to her reading, a framework of inquiry makes questions and statements possible. I will argue that McGinn's reading has the characteristic earmarks of Carnap's linguistic framework theory of meaningfulness.

The rough equivalences between Carnap's views and the views these commentators attribute to Wittgenstein would be unproblematic if the narrative of the parallel development of Carnap and Wittgenstein were correct. But I will argue that this narrative is misleading or mistaken at every point. First, I will suggest that it is misleading to assert that Carnap's early conception of nonsense is fundamentally different from his later one; when Carnap's conception of nonsense is articulated at an appropriate level of generality, then we can see both his logical syntax position and his linguistic framework position as versions of one underlying conception of nonsense. Second, this narrative is mistaken in asserting that there is a rupture in Wittgenstein's thinking about nonsense between the *Tractatus* and the *Philosophical Investigations*; in fact, Wittgenstein advances one conception of nonsense throughout his work. Most importantly, this narrative is mistaken in aligning Wittgenstein's and Carnap's conceptions of nonsense. Wittgenstein's conception of nonsense is fundamentally opposed to Carnap's. As we will see, even in the *Tractatus*, the work that Carnap looked to for inspiration, Wittgenstein's position is wholly incompatible with Carnap's. If I am right that the apparent parallels between Wittgenstein and Carnap mask a fundamental opposition, then commentators on Wittgenstein who unwittingly attribute Carnap's position to him have profoundly misunderstood Wittgenstein's reflections on nonsense and the critiques of philosophy that spring from them.

Because the conception of nonsense Carnap propounded can be found in writers who don't have Carnap in mind at all, we need a special term for it. I will call it "Carnapianism." In using this term, I mean to suggest that Carnap's work contains an exemplary statement of this conception of nonsense; I don't mean to imply that he invented it or was primarily responsible for disseminating it. Carnap figures in my account as someone who takes up an extremely natural view of nonsense, states it clearly, and tries to work out theories of meaningfulness that embody it. I am not primarily concerned with Carnap's historical influence; rather, I use Carnap's formulations of this natural conception of nonsense to bring out important commonalities among superficially disparate readings of Wittgenstein.

It is no accident that commentators end up ascribing the Carnapian conception of nonsense to Wittgenstein. As we will see, Carnapianism holds that taking words that are in themselves perfectly meaningful and using them in illegitimate ways yields nonsense. This idea can seem so uncontroversial as to be scarcely worth stating. Yet, as we will see, Wittgenstein rejects this principle and the Carnapianism that embodies it; indeed, he thinks that Carnapianism is incoherent. In other words, Wittgenstein rejects as incoherent the very conception of nonsense that is now standardly attributed to him.

1 Carnap and Carnapianism

When Carnap criticizes traditional philosophy, he takes himself to be elaborating Wittgenstein's claim that "[m]ost statements and questions that have been written about philosophical matters are not false, but nonsensical" (*Tractatus*, 4.003). Carnap sets himself the task of providing a theoretical apparatus – a theory of meaningfulness – to underwrite Wittgenstein's dismissal of traditional philosophy. Carnap conceives this project as a matter of providing a general principle for distinguishing disputes in which rational discussion and disagreement is possible (i.e., disputes that have rational content) from disputes in which there is no basis for rational disagreement (i.e., disputes that are devoid of rational content, or are "non-cognitive"). A rational dispute, for Carnap, is one in which conflicting claims are *adjudicable*, that is, one in which there are agreed-upon standards for deciding for or against competing claims. A particular claim is meaningful if and only if there is some rational basis for deciding for or against it. The paradigms of rational dispute for Carnap are the natural sciences. Scientific disputes are always in principle resolvable, he thinks, by means of standards inherent in science. His various theories of meaningfulness are attempts to articulate those features of science that make scientific disputes resolvable, so as to provide a test for determining whether other disciplines have rational content. He thinks that applying this test to traditional metaphysics reveals that it lacks rational content; metaphysics belongs in the intellectual dustbin along with pseudo-sciences like astrology. Disputants in these putative disciplines talk past each other because they have not established the meanings of their terms or agreed on the considerations that would weigh for or against what purport to be different claims. In the absence of these common standards, the differences between devotees of a pseudo-discipline are in principle irresoluble, so we may not even say that they are *disputes* in the full-blooded sense. The devotees of pseudo-disciplines generate sound and fury, but no rational content.

Carnap's views about exactly what makes a dispute adjudicable evolve throughout his career. We may distinguish three phases: a verificationist phase, a logical syntax phase, and a linguistic frameworks phase.[3]

According to Carnap's verificationism, the link between adjudicability of disputes and meaningfulness is assured by the principle that a sentence is meaningful if and only if it is possible to specify what experiences would confirm or disconfirm it. Carnap soon came to think that verificationism encounters intractable philosophical difficulties. On account of them, and under the impression that he was elaborating Wittgenstein's *Tractatus* views, Carnap developed a theory of meaningfulness in terms of logical syntax. He presented an initial version of this theory in an essay entitled "The Elimination of Metaphysics through the Logical Analysis of Language."[4] According to this logical syntax theory, a sentence must satisfy two criteria in order to be meaningful. It must consist of meaningful words, and it must combine those words in accordance with the rules of logical syntax.[5] Metaphysical disputes, Carnap thinks, violate one or the other of these criteria. He cites the metaphysical dispute about "substance" as an example of nonsense generated by the use of meaningless words; he cites Heidegger's use of the term "the Nothing" as an example of nonsense generated by a violation of logical syntax.

Carnap is surely right to say that a sentence-like linguistic formation that contains a meaningless word is nonsense. (I do not, however, want to endorse his account of what it is for a word to be meaningful. We can separate the issue of how one establishes that the words of a sentence are meaningful from the rest of his theory.) The part of his theory that does the heavy lifting in his critique of metaphysics – the part I will focus on – is his claim that some nonsense arises from violations of logical syntax.

The concept of logical syntax is modeled on that of ordinary grammatical syntax. According to Carnap, ordinary syntax governs the way words may be put together into sentences; it comprises rules for what kind of word (what part of speech) may go into what position in the sentence. A violation of the rules of ordinary syntax (for example, "Number prime Caesar is a") yields nonsense. For a critic of metaphysics, ordinary syntax (though it forbids some nonsensical strings) is insufficient, because its rules allow the formation of sentences that are nonsensical. Carnap writes: "The fact that natural languages allow the formation of meaningless sequences of words without violating the rules of grammar, indicates that grammatical syntax is, from a logical point of view, inadequate" ("The Elimination of Metaphysics," p. 68). To rule out *all* meaningless sequences of words (for example, "Caesar is a prime number" – a sequence which Carnap thinks is well-formed according to the rules of English grammar), we need a system of rules of *logical*

318

syntax. Such a system will assign words to logical categories and provide rules governing the combination of these logical parts of speech. For example, a system of logical syntax will specify the logical categories of the predicate "is a prime number" and of the noun "Caesar," and its rules will forbid the combination of words from those categories. By appeal to these rules, the grammatical sentence "Caesar is a prime number" can be shown to be logically forbidden. Carnap's position is that when words are combined in violation of a rule of logical syntax, the result is nonsense.

In "The Elimination of Metaphysics," Carnap characterizes the notion of logical syntax by reference to a "correctly constructed language," or a "logically correct language." This would be a language whose rules for the combination of words (its "grammatical syntax") "corresponded exactly to logical syntax" (p. 68). In this language, it would be impossible to formulate sentences that are grammatically correct (and so appear to express a proposition) but that violate logical syntax – sentences like "Caesar is a prime number." In a logically correct language, the sentence "Caesar is a prime number" could not even be formulated, because the syntax of such a language would forbid it, just as the syntax of English forbids, e.g., "Number prime Caesar is a." Since natural languages are not logically correct, we have to do some work to determine whether a given utterance adheres to the rules of logical syntax. Carnap thinks that we have to translate the natural language utterance into a logically correct language; it will then be easy to see whether this counterpart formula is well-formed according to the rules of logical syntax.

To understand the relations between Carnap's early logical syntax position, his later theories of meaningfulness, and Carnapian readings of Wittgenstein, it will be useful to highlight the following tenets of Carnap's position in "The Elimination of Metaphysics" position:

LS1. Putting meaningful words together in violation of certain rules yields nonsense.[6]

LS2. The rules that determine whether a combination of meaningful words makes sense or not are rules of logical syntax.[7]

In "The Elimination of Metaphysics," Carnap writes as if there is just one body of rules of logical syntax, although he does not explicitly claim this. But Carnap is impressed by the possibility of alternative formulations of physics and of different systems of logic; furthermore, he recognizes that no one system of language will be sufficient for inquiry in every field of knowledge. In *The Logical Syntax of Language*, these ideas lead him to propound what he calls the "principle of tolerance":

In logic, there are no morals. Everyone is at liberty to build up his own logic, i.e. his own form of language, as he wishes. All that is required of him is that, if he wishes to discuss it, he must state his methods clearly, and give syntactical rules instead of philosophical arguments.[8]

There can be any number of different sets of syntactical rules: this will not impair the adjudicability of conflicting claims so long as the parties to a given dispute have agreed to abide by one set or another. Carnap's change of position suggests a distinction between two kinds of logical syntax theory: what we might call a monistic logical syntax theory, which holds that there is a unique system of logical syntax, and what we might call a pluralistic one, which allows for a multiplicity of systems of syntactic rules.

Carnap's tolerant stance towards different types of language belongs to a line of thought that issues in the idea that different languages are appropriate to talking about different kinds of things. This idea is the centerpiece of the third phase of his thinking about meaningfulness, which I will call his "linguistic framework theory of meaningfulness."[9] According to this theory, a sentence is meaningful if and only if it is internal to a linguistic framework. Linguistic frameworks are modeled on formalizations of physics. There can be different formalizations of physics, each with its own primitive concepts and laws and with its own rules for the formation of sentences. Yet each formalization provides an effective means for deciding for or against sentences formed according to its rules; all the formalizations provide rational content. A linguistic framework provides terms for talking about a certain kind of entity (names for the entities and expressions for the properties they can have and the relations they can stand in) and rules for combining these terms into meaningful sentences; it also tells how to decide for or against sentences built according to its rules. By fixing the standards for the construction and adjudication of sentences about a certain kind of entity, a framework insures that those sentences have rational content.[10]

The concept of a linguistic framework allows Carnap to distinguish two kinds of questions. (An exactly parallel distinction holds for statements.) He distinguishes internal questions, which are those asked within the framework, from external questions, which are those asked about the framework as a whole.[11] An internal question is answered according to the standards which the framework articulates; those standards guarantee that the question is adjudicable, so such a question has rational content. The status of external questions, by contrast, is problematic. Some external questions are what Carnap calls "pragmatic": these are questions as to whether it is advisable to adopt a given framework or not. Such questions are legitimate, although they are not subject to purely rational adjudication. The metaphysician asks a question that looks like a pragmatic question but that actually has a quite different status. He asks whether the framework as a whole is *justified*, or *real* or *true*. But questions of the justification or truth of claims, or of the reality of entities, are adjudicable only *within* a framework. The metaphysician takes a concept, such as *justification*, that is only meaningful within a framework and applies it to the framework as a whole. In applying the concept of, say, justification to the framework as a whole, the metaphysician violates the limits on the meaningful use of the concept and so produces nonsense.

Having surveyed the major phases of Carnap's thinking about meaningfulness, we are now in a position to characterize Carnapianism. Carnap's criticisms of metaphysics apply to sentences composed of meaningful words. Rules of logical syntax apply to words in so far as they belong to logical categories, and for a word to belong to a given logical category is for it to have a certain kind of meaning (e.g., to be a word for a property of numbers). The evaluation of a sentence in terms of its position *vis-à-vis* a linguistic framework requires that we determine what framework all of its component words belong to; this is to determine what each word means. Carnap thinks that philosophers employ words that belong to determinate logical categories or that play definite roles in determinate frameworks, but they employ these words *illegitimately* – either in violation of logical syntax or outside the relevant framework. The crucial task of a theory of meaningfulness is to articulate the conditions that a sentence has to satisfy in order to be meaningful, so as to allow us to distinguish legitimate from illegitimate uses of meaningful words, or, in other words, to distinguish meaningful sentences from nonsense.

We may summarize the common core of Carnap's views about meaningfulness in the following theses:

C1. Words that are themselves meaningful can be used either legitimately or illegitimately.

C2. The illegitimate use of individually meaningful words yields nonsense.

C3. The critic of nonsense is to articulate substantive principles by appeal to which it is possible to determine whether a given employment of meaningful words is legitimate or illegitimate.

These three theses articulate what I will call "Carnapianism."

The conception of nonsense that Carnap's writings articulate comes naturally to most of us. When we consider examples like "Caesar is a prime number," it seems obvious that the words themselves are perfectly ordinary words of our everyday language, and so, it seems, whatever problem there is with the sentence must lie in the way those meaningful words are assembled or in the way the resulting sentence is used. Moreover, it can seem that Wittgenstein in particular is committed to some version of Carnapianism. For the philosophical utterances he singles out as pieces of nonsense appear to consist entirely of meaningful words; it can appear that for Wittgenstein, the philosopher's characteristic error is using these meaningful words in illegitimate ways. But despite the naturalness of the Carnapian conception of nonsense, and despite many readers' sense that Wittgenstein must be committed to it, Wittgenstein in fact rejects all versions of Carnapianism. His criticisms of philosophical utterances as nonsensical employ a radically different conception of nonsense – a conception that remains essentially constant throughout his work.

2 Wittgenstein on nonsense

My claim that Carnapianism is incompatible with Wittgenstein's conception of nonsense, as it is expressed both in the *Tractatus* and in the later work, goes against the grain of two assumptions about Wittgenstein that are deeply entrenched in the secondary literature. The first is that the *Tractatus* embodies a theory of meaningfulness based on logical syntax, or, in other words, that Carnap was basically right in his reading of the *Tractatus*. The second assumption is that there is a radical rupture in Wittgenstein's thinking about the character of nonsense between the

Tractatus and his later work. The notion of logical syntax does figure prominently in the *Tractatus*. For Wittgenstein as for Carnap, if there were a language whose grammatical syntax perfectly mirrored logical syntax, then expressions in that language would clearly display the logical character of every propositional compo-nent[12] and the use of that language would prevent "the most fundamental confusions (of which the whole of philosophy is full)" (*Tractatus*, 3.324). But Wittgenstein differs from Carnap in how he conceives of the nature of these confusions, and so also in how he uses the notion of logical syntax. Carnap thinks that philosophers construct sentences that accord with the formation-rules of natural language but that violate the rules of logical syntax; he thinks, that is, that there are sentences which are illegitimately constructed.

Wittgenstein's attitude toward the idea of an illegitimately constructed sentence emerges in the following passage:

> Frege says that any legitimately constructed sentence [*Satz*] must have a sense. I say: Every possible sentence is legitimately constructed, and if it has no sense this can only be because we have given no *meaning* to some of its constituent parts.
>
> (Even if we think that we have done so.)
>
> (*Tractatus*, 5.4733)[13]

The view that Wittgenstein here attributes to Frege is a version of Carnapianism. In saying that a legitimately constructed sentence must have a sense, Frege is committing himself to the possibility of sentences that are *illegitimately* constructed and that therefore presumably lack sense. Such a sentence would be an expression that conforms to the ordinary syntax of a natural language (so that it can be described as a *sentence* rather than a word salad or a string of gibberish) but that is somehow logically illegitimate. Commitment to such a possibility is, I have argued, the essence of the Carnapian conception of nonsense. In this passage, Wittgenstein rejects the defining tenet of Carnapianism: he says there is no such thing as a sentence that is illegitimately constructed. No sentence is inherently defective (that is, unusable for expressing a thought), for any sentence can be given a sense.

As against the Carnapian's diagnosis of the nonsensicality of the sentences that he says are illegitimately constructed, Wittgenstein says that the *only* problem with a sentence that is nonsense is that "we have given no *meaning* to some of its constituent parts."[14] For Wittgenstein, all nonsense results from the use of mean-ingless expressions. Carnap distinguishes nonsense that arises from the use of meaningless words from nonsense that results from the illegitimate use of mean-ingful words. These are logically distinct kinds of nonsense. The one kind has logical structure, which is determined by the logical categories or linguistic frame-works to which the component expressions belong; the other kind contains expressions that belong to no logical category or linguistic framework. Wittgenstein, in the *Tractatus*, asserts that there is not the distinction the Carnapian purports to draw. There is only one kind of nonsense.

In the *Tractatus*, therefore, logical syntax is not a tool for identifying violations of the laws of logic. It is instead a tool for displaying the meaning of expressions. It allows us to see that an expression that functions in one way in one sentence is functioning in a quite different way in another sentence. It exposes cases in which we mistakenly think we are using a meaningful symbol, when in fact we are simply using a sign (a sensible mark) which in other instances is meaningful but which isn't meaningful in the utterance at issue.

Wittgenstein's conception of nonsense can be seen as a consequence of one of the fundamental insights he draws from Frege's work. This is the "context principle," which Frege enunciates as follows: "never ... ask for the meaning of a word in isolation, but only in the context of a proposition."[15] Frege thinks it leads to confusion to try to determine the meaning that words have in a sentence without knowing the sense of the sentence as a whole. For Frege, the meaning of a given word is the logical contribution it makes to the sense of the sentences in which it appears. Thus, if a sentence as a whole lacks sense, we cannot determine the meanings of its component words. A Carnapian cannot accept this principle, because, in order to determine that a particular sentence is illegitimately constructed, he needs to determine what its component words mean, and he must do this without reference to the sense of the sentence as a whole, since the sentence as a whole doesn't make sense.

The *Tractatus* restates the context principle as follows:

> Only the proposition has sense; only in the context of a proposition has a name meaning (*Tractatus*, 3.3).

> An expression has a meaning only in a proposition (*Tractatus*, 3.314).

So an expression in a *Scheinsatz* – a form of words that looks like the statement of a proposition but that is really nonsense – does not have a meaning at all. Both Wittgenstein's rejection of what I call Carnapianism and his embrace of the idea that all nonsense arises from the use of meaningless expressions can be seen to follow quite directly from this commitment.

Thus far I have tried to sketch Wittgenstein's conception of nonsense in the *Tractatus* and to bring out how it differs from Carnapianism. When we turn to the later work, we can see that, far from overthrowing his earlier conception of nonsense, Wittgenstein only deepens and clarifies his commitment to it. Again, a fundamental tenet of this conception is the context principle, which Wittgenstein frames as follows:

> We may say: *nothing* has so far been done, when a thing has been named. It has not even *got* a name except in the language-game. This was what Frege meant too, when he said that a word had meaning only as part of a sentence [*nur im Satzzusammenhang*].[16]

This is essentially the context principle stated in the *Tractatus*, though modified in a way that makes it more demanding and further removed from Carnapianism. Like Frege, Wittgenstein in the *Tractatus* thinks that the sentence is the minimal unit of sense, in that an isolated sentence can express a sense, but no smaller unit can. In his later work Wittgenstein revises this. He comes to think that sentences in isolation do not have senses: sentences have senses in their context of use, in their relations to other sentences, in language-games. An expression (a name, for instance) has a meaning only as it contributes to the sense of the sentence in which it appears, which sense in turn depends on the sentence's belonging to a language-game.

At several points in his Cambridge lectures Wittgenstein emphasizes a feature about his conception of nonsense that follows from his adherence to the context principle. He says, for example:

> Most of us think that there is nonsense which makes sense and nonsense which does not – that it is nonsense in a different way to say "This is green and yellow at the same time" from saying "Ab sur ah." But these are nonsense in the same sense, the only difference being in the jingle of the words.[17]

The sentence "This is green and yellow at the same time" contains words that certainly seem meaningful; indeed, the problem, if any, with the sentence would seem to be a function of what it says. If it is nonsensical, that must be because it expresses a logical impossibility, and the rules of logical syntax or the rules governing the linguistic framework for talking about colors are so constructed as to ban such expressions. On the other hand, the phrase "Ab sur ah" is a transcription of a bit of gibberish; it contains no meaningful words, so *a fortiori* its nonsensicality does not result from the illegitimate use of meaningful words. But Wittgenstein says that both expressions are nonsense in the same. This means that, according to Wittgenstein, the Carnapian diagnosis of the nonsensicality of "This is green and yellow at the same time" is mistaken. Our sense that its words are meaningful is illusory. For both utterances, Wittgenstein's diagnosis of their nonsensicality is the same: the words are meaningless.[18] Logically, both utterances are on a par.

Wittgenstein does not deny that there is a difference between "This is now both green and yellow" and "Ab sur ah." But he thinks that this difference is merely a matter of how the two utterances strike us – their jingle. About a similar pair of utterances Wittgenstein says, "We are inclined to say the one, and be puzzled by it, but not the other."[19] But this is a psychological rather than a logical difference.

In his lecture remark, Wittgenstein says that "[m]ost of us think that there is nonsense which makes sense and nonsense which does not." This is a puzzling characterization of the common view of nonsense; for presumably no one would *say* that there is nonsense that makes sense. But Wittgenstein thinks that the common view of nonsense – the view that gets fully articulated in the theses of Carnapianism – is nevertheless committed to there being nonsense that makes sense. We will not be in a position to evaluate the justness of Wittgenstein's charge until the final section of this chapter. At this point let me simply note that Wittgenstein's characterization of what I call Carnapianism is connected with central themes in both the *Tractatus* and the *Investigations*. A leitmotif of the *Tractatus* is the problematic nature of attempts to specify what lies beyond the bounds of logic, beyond the limits of the thinkable: "We cannot think anything illogical"; "we could not *say* of an 'illogical' world how it would look."[20] It will turn out, I will argue in section 5 below, that the view that Wittgenstein says is held by "most of us" *is* committed to talking about what is illogical; it is committed to describing illogical thought in ways that turn out to be highly problematic. Wittgenstein's recognition of these problems inherent in the common view of nonsense (the view which is articulated in Carnapianism) leads him to reject it.

We may capture Wittgenstein's conception of nonsense both early and late in the following statements.

W1. An expression has meaning only as used in a meaningful sentence.

W2. When a sentence is nonsense, it is because one or more of its component expressions lacks a meaning.

W3. There is no logical distinction to be drawn between different kinds of nonsense.

The conception of nonsense that these claims articulate shapes Wittgenstein's whole approach to the criticism of traditional metaphysics. If we fail to recognize his adherence to this conception of nonsense, we run the risk of misconstruing or missing altogether Wittgenstein's distinctive philosophical contribution. As we will see, this is exactly what happens in many readings of Wittgenstein.[21]

3 Baker and Hacker: nonsense as a violation of rules of grammar

Baker and Hacker, in *Wittgenstein: Rules, Grammar and Necessity*, argue that the core of later Wittgenstein's thought is the delimitation of the bounds of sense. As they read Wittgenstein, "philosophy is not concerned with what is true or false, but rather with what makes sense and what traverses the bounds of sense."[22] On their reading, the bounds of sense are set by grammar. The task of the Wittgensteinian philosopher is to articulate the rules of grammar and then to scrutinize utterances (especially metaphysical utterances) for violations of those rules. They think that if you violate the rules of grammar, then you lapse into nonsense. As they put it:

> Grammar, as Wittgenstein understood the term, is the account book of language (PG 87). Its rules determine the limits of sense, and by carefully scrutinizing them the philosopher may determine at what point he has drawn an overdraft on Reason, violated the rules for the use of an expression and so, in subtle and not readily identifiable ways, traversed the bounds of sense.[23]

There is at least a superficial similarity between Baker and Hacker's conception of the later Wittgenstein's aim and method in philosophy and the aim and method we have seen in Carnap's work. Carnap too, in his logical syntax phase, wants to articulate the rules for the use of expressions (or to have the proponents of an expression articulate such rules) and then to apply those rules to metaphysical utterances. When an utterance violates those rules, Carnap, like Baker and Hacker's Wittgenstein, declares it to be nonsense.

This similarity in fact runs quite deep. The conception of meaningfulness that Baker and Hacker attribute to Wittgenstein has the essential structure of Carnap's logical syntax theory of meaningfulness. The parallel is obscured by the fact that Baker and Hacker explicitly deny that they attribute a logical syntax theory to Wittgenstein. Thus one of my essential tasks is to show that the differences between their interpretation of Wittgenstein and logical syntax theories do not suffice to distinguish their interpretation from Carnapianism.

Baker and Hacker say at several points that later Wittgenstein made a great advance by giving up the view that nonsense arises from violations of logical syntax in favor of the view that nonsense results from violations of "rules of grammar." For example, they write:

> This conception of rules of logical syntax which Wittgenstein had when he wrote the *Tractatus* and even 'Some Remarks on Logical Form' is a far cry from the conception of rules of grammar which dominates his later work. . . . Many of the central theses of the *Tractatus* concerning logical syntax and its relation to reality now seemed muddles flagging treacherous terrain.[24]

As I have indicated, I think it is a mistake to regard the *Tractatus* as espousing the idea that nonsense arises from violations of rules of logical syntax. But I will not be concerned to contest the details of Baker and Hacker's reading of the *Tractatus*, since their purpose is to interpret the *Investigations* and my purpose is to show how even astute readers of the later work can be led to ascribe Carnapianism to Wittgenstein.

To clarify the nature of the rules of grammar that are central to Baker and Hacker's reading, and to bring out how little they differ from what Carnap called rules of logical syntax, we may consider the following specific differences Baker and Hacker cite between rules of grammar and what they call rules of logical syntax. (1) Logical syntax governs the combinatorial possibilities of logically proper names, where "logically proper names" are the basic building blocks of language, out of which "elementary propositions" are constructed. It is not yet known what the "logically proper names" or the "elementary propositions" of our language are: determining what they are awaits a final analysis of our ordinary forms of speech. Hence logical syntax cannot be applied to our actual language. Rules of grammar, on the other hand, govern the combinatorial possibilities of the words of our language as it stands. (2) Logical syntax is supposed to mirror the logical form of reality, whereas grammar is "autonomous," i.e., "grammar is a free-floating structure" that is not "answerable to the nature of reality, to the structure of the mind or to 'the laws of thought'."[25] (3) A consequence of the second difference is that there is only one logical syntax, whereas there are many grammars – one grammar for each language. (4) Rules of logical syntax apply to sentences by virtue of their syntax alone, whereas rules of grammar apply to sentences both by virtue of their syntax and by virtue of the meanings of the sentence's words.[26]

These four contrasts do distinguish the rules of logical syntax that Baker and Hacker claim to find in the *Tractatus* from the rules of grammar that they claim to find in Wittgenstein's later work. But they do not distinguish a *Carnapian* conception of logical syntax from the conception of grammar that Baker and Hacker attribute to later Wittgenstein. Let us take up each contrast in turn.

Concerning (1): Carnap thinks that rules of logical syntax are made explicit, and perhaps ought to be formulated, in an artificial, logically correct language. And a perfect, logically correct language has yet to be constructed; perhaps this construction awaits a complete analysis of ordinary language. But Carnap thinks that we needn't wait on the complete construction of a logically perfect language before we can use the apparatus of logical syntax. He thinks that we already have a sufficient grasp of what a logically perfect language would be to allow us to formulate and apply rules of logical syntax to philosophical utterances. Furthermore, the rules of logical syntax, though they are framed in a logically correct language, apply also to natural languages, via the translations of natural language words into the symbolism of a logically correct language. Indeed, in "The Elimination of Metaphysics," Carnap applies rules of logical syntax directly to natural language utterances. Thus it seems fair to say that Carnap's rules of logical syntax apply to the words of a natural language just as it stands.[27]

Concerning (2): in "The Elimination of Metaphysics," Carnap writes as if there is just one logical syntax. (This is what we have called his "monistic logical syntax phase.") At this stage of his career, Carnap may have believed that there is just one logically correct language, to which every meaningful piece of natural language has to conform. One might therefore attribute to him the idea that this logically correct language has some metaphysical underpinnings, or "mirrors the logical form of reality." But even if this were Carnap's view during his monistic logical syntax phase, it could not be his view during his subsequent pluralistic logical syntax phase. In *The Logical Syntax of Language*, he embraces the possibility of different logical syntaxes. It follows that a logical syntax does not have to answer to anything that we could plausibly call "the logical form of reality." This characteristic of Carnap's pluralistic position is sufficient to make logical syntax "autonomous" in Baker and Hacker's sense.

Concerning (3): even a pluralistic Carnap might not say that there is a different logical syntax for every natural language. But Baker and Hacker themselves think that "many languages which share a massive core of common concepts will have a large array of isomorphic rules."[28] Carnap would have focused on the large array of isomorphic rules that are common to what Baker and Hacker call "developed" languages. If the "grammar" of a language were to differ from other "grammars" in a way that is not subsumed by these isomorphic rules, Carnap could deal with it by extending the relevant logical syntax. So every natural language has (at least one) logical syntax, but some languages might have identical (or isomorphic) logical syntaxes. This does not seem to mark a significant difference between Carnap's view and the view Baker and Hacker attribute to Wittgenstein.

Concerning (4): Carnap calls the rules that determine meaningfulness "rules of logical *syntax*." This might suggest that he is thinking of the rules as purely syntactic rules governing the permissible combinations of symbols in a formal system. Carnap does think that in a logically correct language the logical category (and so the allowable combinations) of each symbol will be manifest in the symbol's form, just as in Russell's notation the difference between predicate-expressions and names is manifest in their form. But Carnap also thinks that you cannot apply the rules of logical syntax (you cannot take advantage of the logically correct language's perspicuous notation) unless you pay attention to the meaning of the sentence you are testing. To apply the rules of logical syntax, you have to first translate the sentence in question into the logically correct language. This entails that you have to identify the meanings of the natural language words. Moreover, Carnap hypothesizes that in a logically correct language the logical category of a word will depend on what it means; he assumes, for example, that nouns will be divided into different logical categories "according as they designated properties of physical objects, of numbers etc."[29] Carnap's rules of logical syntax are in fact rules governing words considered as bearers of meaning. In his logical syntax phase, Carnap does not isolate syntactic considerations from semantic ones. This fits nicely with what Baker and Hacker say of later Wittgenstein in the following passage: "Wittgenstein clearly thought . . . that there was no essential dividing line in the patterns of use of words between so-called 'syntax' and 'semantics'."[30]

We may conclude that Baker and Hacker's attempt to distinguish the position they attribute to Wittgenstein from logical syntax theories of meaningfulness does not succeed. The differences they cite between rules of grammar and rules of logical syntax do not mark a substantive divergence between the conception of meaningfulness they attribute to Wittgenstein and Carnap's logical syntax theory. But in order to say that Baker and Hacker's position is Carnapian, we need more evidence than just their failure to explicitly distinguish their view from Carnapianism; we need to see that they are in fact committed to a Carnapian conception of meaningfulness. We can see this commitment in their method of criticism. When we see how Baker and Hacker wield their grammatical apparatus to criticize philosophical utterances as nonsense, we will see Carnapianism at work. (Here and in the rest of my exposition, I refer to the view that Baker and Hacker attribute to Wittgenstein as "Baker and Hacker's view," for the conception of meaningfulness they find in the later Wittgenstein is one that they endorse but that Wittgenstein – I will argue – does not.)

Here is a representative instance of Baker and Hacker's method of criticism:

> If someone (whether philosopher or scientist) claims that colours are sensations in the mind or in the brain, the philosopher must point out that this person is misusing the words 'sensation' and 'colour'. Sensations in the brain, he should remind his interlocutor, are called 'headaches', and colours are not headaches; one can have (i.e. it makes sense to speak of) sensations in the knee or in the back, but not in the mind. It is, he must stress, extended things that are coloured. But *this* is not a factual claim about the world (an *opinion* which the scientist might intelligibly gainsay). It is a grammatical observation, viz. that the grammar of colour licenses predicating 'is coloured' (primarily) of things of which one may also predicate 'is extended'. And minds and sensations are not extended, i.e. it makes no *sense* to say 'This pain is 5 cm long' or 'This itch is 2 cm shorter than that.'[31]

Here Baker and Hacker imagine someone (I'll call him "the scientist") who says, "Colors are sensations in the mind." Perhaps we can agree that there is something odd about this imagined utterance; upon further inquiry we might end up concluding that it is nonsense. My purpose in considering this example is not to dispute such a conclusion, but only to show that Baker and Hacker's argument for their conclusion commits them to Carnapianism.

It will take some rational reconstruction to use the materials that Baker and Hacker provide in the above passage to build a cogent argument that the scientist's utterance is nonsense, since Baker and Hacker consider several different utterances and give extremely condensed arguments; I'll focus on what I think is their strongest argument. Baker and Hacker think that to show that an utterance is nonsense is to show that it violates one or more rules of grammar. We may thus begin our reconstruction of their argument by extracting a clear statement of the rules at issue. Baker and Hacker seem to base their argument on two "grammatical observations," which I reformulate as follows:

(a) If you may say "x is colored," then you may say "x is extended."[32]

(b) You may not say "x is a sensation and x is extended."[33]

They seem also to employ the following general principle:

(c) It is a violation of a rule of grammar to say anything that *entails* a sentence that violates a rule of grammar.[34]

Baker and Hacker assert that it makes no sense to speak of sensations in the mind, but the only support they provide for this claim is their reference to some such rules as (a) and (b) above. The sentence "Colors are sensations in the mind" does not involve the predicates "is colored" or "is extended." Since the scientist's sentence does not violate the rules Baker and Hacker cite, it is hard to see why they declare it to be nonsense. In order to find a connection between the scientist's utterance and Baker and Hacker's argument, we must assume that Baker and Hacker think that the scientist is committed to a claim about colored things. All he has said is that *colors* are sensations in the mind; but Baker and Hacker seem to take him to be saying that *colored things* are sensations in the mind.[35]

Let us follow Baker and Hacker in imagining that the scientist has said, "If something is colored, then it is a sensation in the mind." At this stage of their argument, Baker and Hacker take it for granted that they know what rules apply to this utterance. On the assumption that rules (a) through (c) are among the rules applying to the scientist's utterance, we may construct the following argument to show that it violates those rules. Suppose I may say about a child's marble, "This marble is colored." Then by rule (a), I may say "This marble is extended." And the scientist's conditional implies "This marble is a sensation in the mind." So in this case the scientist's sentence, along with rules of grammar, implies "This marble is extended and is a sensation in the mind." This violates rule (b). Therefore, by principle (c), the scientist's claim itself is a violation of a rule of grammar. Since anything that violates a rule of grammar is nonsense, the scientist's utterance is nonsense.

This elaboration of Baker and Hacker's critical practice shows that on their view certain combinations of words are forbidden because of the categories to which they belong. They argue, for example, that sensation-phrases (like "pain") may not be combined with extension-phrases (like "is 5 cm long"). According to Baker and Hacker, the relevant categories are *grammatical*; but their notion of a grammatical category is merely a slight variant of Carnap's notion of a "syntactical category."[36] Despite their apparent differences concerning the character of the relevant rules of language, Baker and Hacker agree with Carnap (in his logical syntax phase) that nonsense arises when you combine words in violation of rules that govern how words from different categories may be combined.

We are now in a position to locate Baker and Hacker's conception of nonsense in relation to Carnapianism and Wittgenstein's own conception. According to Baker and Hacker's diagnosis, the scientist's words are themselves perfectly meaningful. He is using the word "sensations" to mean sensations, for example; it is only because the word has its usual meaning that their rule (b) gets any grip on the scientist's utterances. If the scientist were using one or more meaningless words, Baker and Hacker could not make an argument based on rules of grammar, which determine how concepts may and may not be combined. Because the scientist's utterance violates those rules, it is nonsense. The philosopher's proper task, as Baker and Hacker see it, is to identify such violations and, in general, to assemble the rules of grammar into a perspicuous array, so that violations of the rules will be readily identifiable. The theses that Baker and Hacker thus turn out to be committed to are precisely the theses characteristic of Carnapianism (C1, C2 and C3).

Baker and Hacker are not just committed to Carnapianism in the generic sense. Their position has the two further features that are essential to the logical syntax version of Carnapianism. First, they insist that putting words together in violation of grammatical rules yields nonsense, and we have seen that they must think of these words as bearers of meaning. Thus they are committed to tenet LS1. As to LS2, the tenet that the relevant rules are rules of logical syntax, the situation is more complicated. Baker and Hacker say that their rules of grammar are not rules of logical syntax. But, as we saw, their attempt to draw this distinction fails; there is no significant difference between what Baker and Hacker call "rules of grammar" and what Carnap calls "rules of logical syntax." Since they insist on the multiplicity of systems of rules of grammar, we may classify their position as a pluralistic logical syntax theory.

By virtue of their Carnapian commitments, Baker and Hacker diverge from Wittgenstein's conception of nonsense. But they obscure this divergence in the way they interpret passages that are central expressions of Wittgenstein's conception. Consider the context principle (articulated as W1 above). Baker and Hacker are aware of the importance of this principle, but they misunderstand what it implies. The following passage is revealing:

> A word, he [Wittgenstein] stressed, has a meaning only in the context of a sentence – a dictum which should be understood as saying that something is a symbol only in so far as it actually fulfils a role in a system of symbols.[37]

Here we have an admirable paraphrase of the context principle, followed by a gloss that eviscerates it. Wittgenstein thinks that a sentence's having sense (being meaningful) and its component words' having meanings (in that use) are inseparable. But in Baker and Hacker's gloss, there is no mention of *sentences*: the role that the (meaningful) *sentence* occupies in Wittgenstein's context principle is occupied in their version by the *system of symbols*. This change turns the context principle into something that does not threaten Baker and Hacker's method of criticism. On their construal of the principle, if words belong to a system of symbols, then they are meaningful symbols. This leaves open the possibility that meaningful symbols might be combined into a sentence-like formation that is not itself meaningful. Their method of criticism is committed to the possibility of such a combination. But this is exactly the possibility that the context principle (as stated in the first part of the above passage) rules out.

A similar failure to think through the implications of a remark mars Baker and Hacker's interpretation of another important passage. They refer to the lecture remark in which Wittgenstein uses the example "Ab sur ah" when they write:

> Grammarians are prone to distinguish grammatical nonsense 'The was it blues no' from gibberish 'Ab sur ah' and from 'sensible nonsense' e.g. 'Green ideas sleep furiously', the latter being a 'well-formed' sentence of English. Wittgenstein disagreed: nonsense is nonsense; the only difference lies in the jingle, the *Satzklang*.[38]

But when Baker and Hacker go on to explain the nonsensicality of "north-east of the South Pole," they say that the expression "north-east of" must be followed by a noun or pronoun designating a place, an object or a person at a place, or an event occurring at a place, and that further "North Pole" and "South Pole" are not acceptable place-designators in that context.[39] But this kind of diagnosis cannot even get started with "Ab sur ah." We can't say that it violates a particular rule about (for example) the object-designations a given preposition may take; we can't even identify nouns and prepositions in the utterance. There is no way to see "Ab sur ah" as the violation of a rule of grammar; its nonsensicality is due simply to the lack of meaning of its "words." So Baker and Hacker are committed to a distinction between two logically distinct types of nonsense: nonsense resulting from the use of words that lack a meaning, and nonsense resulting from a violation of grammar. Their interpretation does not accord with principle W3.

Up to this point I have not actually criticized Carnapianism in general or Baker and Hacker's view in particular, except to say that Baker and Hacker are mistaken in thinking that their view captures Wittgenstein's conception of nonsense. Now that we have laid out Baker and Hacker's Carnapianism in some detail, we can begin to see that it suffers from both polemical and philosophical defects.

The polemical defects emerge particularly clearly if we try to imagine how Baker and Hacker would carry on a dialogue with the scientist in their example. After Baker and Hacker have brought forward their rules of grammar and pointed out that "Colors are sensations in the mind" violates them, how is the scientist supposed to respond? Is he to say, "Oh dear! I forgot how we use the words 'color', 'sensation' and 'mind'. Sorry to have troubled you with my pseudo-theory"? Or perhaps, "Yes, I never noticed it before, but you are right: there *is* a rule against my utterance"? If the scientist is willing to withdraw his words or to express his idea in words that conform to the rules of grammar, then the dialogue can end happily; a bit of dubious language will have been eliminated or cleaned up to everyone's satisfaction.

But surely the interesting cases, the cases that have motivated philosophers to try to delimit sense from nonsense, are those in which the person who makes a problematic utterance insists on it. The metaphysicians that Carnap attacks and the scientist-philosophers that Baker and Hacker attack make the utterances they do because they take themselves to have reasons for them. Metaphysicians feel compelled by their arguments to make their (apparent) claims, and they present these arguments to support conclusions that they themselves admit to be strange.

Against someone who takes himself to have compelling reasons for his utterance, Baker and Hacker have little to offer. Their practice suggests that they think their rules of grammar are obvious and that everyone will recognize that they are binding.[40] They proceed as though all who look will immediately recognize that "it makes no *sense* to say 'This pain is 5 cm long'," for example. But in the problematic cases the appeal to the obviousness of the rule will not move the metaphysician: he or she knows already that the utterance is problematic by the lights of ordinary usage.

If a speaker like the scientist in Baker and Hacker's example chooses to flout the supposedly obvious rule of grammar, Baker and Hacker rely on a fall-back criticism. They say that, if you are not following their rules of grammar, then you are using words with different meanings; you are using a different grammar, and there is no interesting point of contact between what you say about "colors" in your sense and what we call "colors." In their continuation of the discussion of their imagined scientist, Baker and Hacker write:

> The wayward interlocutor may insist that he is using 'colour' and 'sensation' in a special new sense, a sense more useful perhaps for scientific purposes. . . . But now we should elicit from him the new rules according to which he is proceeding, pointing out where they differ from our rules. We should now stress why the concepts *differ*, and how it is that what seemed a startling discovery (that colours are in the mind or are really dispositions to cause sensations) is either no more than a recommendation to adopt a new form of representation (for which he has yet to make a case) or a confusion of different rules for the use of homonyms.[41]

This passage initially promises to open up a productive line of criticism. Baker and Hacker are surely right to be puzzled by the utterance "Colors are sensations in the mind"; and surely the responsible critic of such an utterance ought to begin by finding out what it is supposed to mean. Baker and Hacker begin looking for a meaning in the scientist's words when they say, "we should elicit from him the new rules according to which he is proceeding." But they spoil this line of criticism by assuming that the scientist can be doing only one of two things. Either he is making "a recommendation to adopt a new form of representation" (for example, using the term "color" as a name for sensations of a certain type), or he has mixed up two words that happen to sound the same but that have very different meanings. Baker and Hacker rule out from the start the possibility that the scientist might actually have made a claim (albeit a claim that we do not immediately understand). That is exactly the possibility we ought to leave open if we want to try to understand him; yet leaving open that possibility is incompatible with declaring the scientist to have violated a rule of grammar. Baker and Hacker's invitation to the scientist to specify what he means can only be pro forma: they already know what he is trying to say and that it cannot be said without violating the rules of grammar.

Wittgenstein realizes that the criticism of an utterance as violating a rule of grammar requires the critic to pretend to a knowledge of what the speaker means by her words, while it precludes any genuine interpretative engagement with the speaker. This realization lies behind his rejection of Carnapianism. But the appeal of Carnapianism is not confined to discussions of grammar and nonsense. Carnapian assumptions sometimes distort readings of Wittgenstein that initially seem to have little concern with issues of meaningfulness. We will see just such a distortion in Marie McGinn's interpretation of Wittgenstein's response to skepticism, which she offers in her book *Sense and Certainty*.[42]

3 Marie McGinn: Wittgenstein as a framework theorist

Although McGinn does not explicitly consider Wittgenstein's conception of meaningfulness, her interpretation makes the meaningfulness of skepticism a central concern. And her discussion of the meaningfulness of skepticism in many ways echoes Carnap's treatment of metaphysical problems in his linguistic framework phase. According to McGinn, the skeptic observes (i) that "our practice of making and accepting knowledge claims" takes place within a framework, and (ii) that this framework consists of "judgements that [one] accepts without doubt."[43] The skeptic's reflections reveal, McGinn thinks, that there is a distinction between two types of propositions or judgments: those that are part of the framework (which McGinn calls "framework propositions" or "Moore-type propositions") and those that are made within the framework ("non-framework," or "ordinary," propositions). According to McGinn, Wittgenstein's insight is to see that the distinction that the skeptic's reflections reveal (i.e., the distinction between framework and ordinary propositions) can be used to undermine the viability of the skeptic's doubts.

This position could appear to be a simple variant on Carnap's linguistic framework position, and so as unworthy of the praise that McGinn heaps on Wittgenstein's brilliantly innovative response to skepticism. But, even though McGinn doesn't mention Carnap, her reading would entitle her to say that the framework theory she attributes to Wittgenstein is superior to Carnap's framework theory because of how Wittgenstein (on her reading) conceives of the components of the framework. We may give the following initial characterization of the relevant difference between Carnap and McGinn's Wittgenstein: for Carnap, all the propositions that belong to the framework are *analytic*, whereas for McGinn's Wittgenstein the propositions that belong to the framework include both analytic propositions and propositions like those that Moore advanced (for example, "I have two hands").

We may understand the position of McGinn's Wittgenstein as a revamping of Carnap's distinction between analytic and synthetic sentences (or propositions, or judgments). According to Carnap, this is a distinction between two ways that sentences can be adjudicated (that is, two ways one can decide for or against a sentence). Some sentences are adjudicable solely by reference to the sentence-formation rules of the framework, without any input from experience, evidence, or whatever other kinds of grounding the framework describes; these are *analytic* sentences. Analytic sentences are those to which you are committed simply by virtue of accepting a framework: once you decide to talk about, say, physical things, you have to accept the consequences of the rules for talking about them, for example, "No more than one object can occupy a given space-time point." Other sentences are adjudicable by experience, evidence, etc.; these are *synthetic* sentences. Synthetic sentences are by their nature open to dispute (albeit dispute that is in principle resolvable according to the standards articulated as part of the framework).

McGinn could argue that the framework theory she attributes to Wittgenstein is an improvement on Carnap's framework theory by pointing to Wittgenstein's reflections on Moore's propositions (of which the most famous is "I have two hands"). According to McGinn, Wittgenstein thinks that these propositions, in ordinary contexts, are not subject to confirmation or disconfirmation. On McGinn's reading, these propositions are instead the fixed points around which inquiry revolves; they constitute the framework without which inquiry is impossible. Since "I have two hands" is not a consequence of the sentence-formation rules of the framework (i.e., it is not analytic), Carnap would have regarded it as subject to confirmation or disconfirmation; for Carnap, this proposition is a massively well-confirmed synthetic proposition. McGinn's Wittgenstein believes that accepting Moore's propositions is a pre-condition for confirmation or disconfirmation, just as for Carnap accepting analytic truths precedes confirmation or disconfirmation. Therefore, for McGinn's Wittgenstein, it is wrong to say with Carnap that Moore's propositions are merely synthetic propositions that are well-confirmed by our methods of inquiry. Carnap takes the notion *proposition acceptance of which is constitutive of inquiry* to be equivalent to the notion *analytic proposition*. According to McGinn's Wittgenstein, Carnap does not have any place for Moore's propositions, since Moore's propositions are constitutive of inquiry but are also (in Carnap's terms) synthetic. McGinn's Wittgenstein has no use for the analytic–synthetic distinction in his account of the structure of inquiry; he replaces it with the distinction between ordinary propositions and framework propositions (where these include both the propositions Carnap would have regarded as analytic and Moore-type propositions that Carnap would have regarded as synthetic).

On McGinn's reading of Wittgenstein, the distinction between framework propositions and ordinary ones is based on the structure of inquiry: whatever propositions are presupposed by our practices of inquiry belong to the framework, whatever propositions come up as topics of inquiry are ordinary propositions. Correlative to this distinction between kinds of propositions is a distinction between the kinds of relation we can sustain to these two kinds of propositions; McGinn uses the labels "non-epistemic" and "epistemic" for these two kinds of relations. We stand in non-epistemic relations to framework propositions, and in epistemic relations to ordinary propositions. Examples of epistemic relations to a proposition p are: knowing p, believing p, wondering whether p, being certain that p, suspending judgment about p. By contrast, according to McGinn's Wittgenstein, we stand in *non-epistemic* relations to framework propositions: we hold them fast, we do not question them, we take them for granted in giving justifications, etc. Standing in non-epistemic relations to framework propositions is "prior to knowledge,"[44] in that inquiry presupposes framework propositions: we must accept framework propositions in order to be in a position to know anything at all.

What propositions exactly belong to this special class of propositions that we have to accept in order to be able to conduct any inquiry at all? McGinn provides some examples gleaned from *On Certainty*:

> 'The world existed a long time before my birth', 'Everyone has parents',
> . . . 'I have two hands', 'That's a tree', 'I am in England', 'I have never
> been on the Moon', . . . 'Water boils at 100 degrees C', . . . 'I am a human
> being', . . . 'I am sitting writing at the table'.[45]

According to McGinn, some of the indications that these propositions belong to the framework are that they are obvious, they may be spoken with authority, they may be taken for granted. (Here and in what follows I will frequently refer to McGinn's interpretation of Wittgenstein as McGinn's view. McGinn, like Baker and Hacker, attributes to Wittgenstein a position which she endorses, but which I will argue is untenable as a reading of Wittgenstein.)

McGinn bases her critique of skepticism on the distinction between framework and ordinary propositions. What differentiates framework from ordinary propositions? According to McGinn, the defining feature of framework propositions and judgments is that accepting them *constitutes* our technique for using ordinary propositions and making ordinary judgments. McGinn writes that framework propositions are a "system of judgements which together constitute our techniques for describing [or inquiring about] the world."[46] Unless we non-epistemically accept framework propositions and judgments, we cannot ask a question, conduct an investigation, offer a description or indeed say anything.

McGinn thus shares the Carnapian concern with meaningfulness. The idea that the acceptance of framework propositions constitutes inquiry prompts the question, "What if you don't accept framework propositions?" McGinn thinks that if you do not accept the framework propositions, if you do not accept the techniques of description, then what you say will be nonsense. One way of not accepting framework propositions is to try to question them; this is to attempt to adopt an epistemic relation towards propositions to which we can only properly adopt a non-epistemic relation. McGinn says that if you try to deny or question a Moore-type proposition, then you have violated "a condition of the meaningful employment of the expressions of our language,"[47] and so your utterance is meaningless. According to McGinn, the propositions that belong to the framework set limits on what can be meaningfully said or asked. She writes: "[S]peaking meaningfully . . . means speaking within the framework of judgements that constitute the techniques of description, or customary way of employing expressions."[48] Nonsense arises when you violate these limits, and you violate them when you either question or claim to know a framework proposition.

McGinn's argument that the skeptic's utterance is meaningless commits her to the Carnapian conception of nonsense. McGinn's diagnosis of the skeptic's error is a version of thesis C1: although the skeptic's words are themselves meaningful, he uses those words illegitimately when he questions a framework judgment. This illegitimate use of meaningful words results in nonsense; this is thesis C2. Furthermore, McGinn thinks that the novel framework epistemology she attributes to Wittgenstein satisfies the requirement that the critic provide principles for demarcating legitimate from illegitimate employments of words. The framework epistemology provides a way of recognizing framework propositions; this criterion, together with a straightforward acquaintance with epistemic operators like "I know _____," allows for the necessary demarcation. This is a version of thesis C3.

Since McGinn's view is an instance of Carnapianism, it is incompatible with Wittgenstein's conception of nonsense, as we can now readily see. Since McGinn has to be able to identify the framework proposition embedded in the skeptic's ostensibly meaningless utterance, she must deny the context principle. Her diagnosis of the nonsensicality of the skeptic's utterance is *not* that he is using a meaningless expression; she is thereby committed to a distinction between logically distinct kinds of nonsense (the kind of nonsense that the skeptic traffics in versus the kind of nonsense that results from, e.g., coming out with a bit of gibberish). Broadly Carnapian ideas have led McGinn to an interpretation of Wittgenstein that is incompatible with his actual conception of nonsense. As we are about to see, her position encounters other problems.

McGinn's conception of meaningfulness exhibits a fundamental instability when we reflect on the supposed nonsensicality of the skeptic's utterances. McGinn argues that when a skeptic tries to deny (or even tries to question) a framework proposition, for example "I have two hands," he thereby ceases to non-epistemically accept the techniques of description that make assertion, denial and questioning possible. The form of words he produces is, according to McGinn, not false but nonsense. It makes no sense to say "I don't have two hands." But if it makes no sense to say "I don't have two hands," then what sense does it make to say "I *do* have two hands"? Wittgenstein thinks that the sense of a proposition is intimately tied to the sense of its negation. If it is meaningless to (attempt to) deny a proposition, then it is meaningless to (attempt to) assert it. Consequently, McGinn's conception of the meaninglessness of the skeptic's utterances seems to imply that the framework propositions themselves cannot be meaningfully asserted. And if they cannot ever be asserted, then it is hard to see how they can be meaningful.

But McGinn's remarks about framework propositions do not sit well with this conclusion that framework propositions lack meaning. She regards framework propositions as expressions of especially obvious judgments, as propositions that may be taken for granted. These characterizations of framework propositions make sense only if framework propositions are meaningful. Indeed, to say that they are framework *propositions* is to imply that they are meaningful. But the theory of meaningfulness that she constructs from the notion of framework propositions implies that they are not meaningful.

McGinn manifests the tension in her view by oscillating. Sometimes she treats framework propositions as proper, meaningful, truth-valued propositions. Other times she regards these "propositions" as doing a different kind of work: as defining techniques, determining how words are to be used, etc. (At this moment of the oscillation, she writes as though framework "propositions" lack truth-values.[49]) As one would expect, this oscillation about the status of framework propositions has a counterpart in McGinn's oscillation with respect to the status of the skeptic's expressions of doubts concerning framework propositions. If the framework consists of meaningful propositions, then it ought to be possible to doubt one of those propositions. When McGinn is thinking of the framework in this way, she says that the skeptic does raise a doubt – though she hastens to add that it is a doubt that is "odd" or "misplaced."[50] But, since she also thinks that framework propositions constitute our practices of inquiry, she sometimes says that the skeptic's attempt to doubt a framework proposition is "incoherent," or, as one might say, that the skeptic only appears to raise a doubt.[51]

McGinn is unaware of the tensions which these twin oscillations produce. When she says that the skeptic's doubts are *misplaced*, she commits herself to their being intelligible. The following passage illustrates this commitment:

> The skeptic's doubts are misplaced for precisely the same reason that Moore's knowledge claims are: *His doubts misrepresent our relationship to propositions that are, in the context, technique-constituting propositions and treat it as an epistemic relation to empirical judgements.*
>
> (p. 159, her emphasis)

If the skeptic's doubts *misrepresent* our relationship to framework propositions, then it follows that the expressions of the skeptic's doubts are meaningful, for only a meaningful expression is capable of representing or misrepresenting (i.e., representing falsely) a state of affairs (such as our relationship to a certain body of propositions). But in the same breath McGinn writes: "Wittgenstein's account of the role of Moore-type propositions reveals the skeptic's attempt to question them as incoherent."[52] But if the attempt to doubt is incoherent, then the skeptic cannot have produced a meaningful utterance when he asks, for example, "Do you know that you have two hands?"

McGinn exhibits the tension in her views in particularly pungent form when she writes: "Wittgenstein's account of our relationship to Moore-type propositions now allows us to see why the skeptic's doubts are, on the one hand, misplaced, and on the other, incoherent."[53]

One might be tempted to dismiss this oscillation, in which McGinn finds herself sometimes committed to saying that the skeptic's doubts are meaningful and sometimes committed to saying that they are nonsensical, as carelessness on McGinn's part. But in fact the oscillation is inherent in the structure of the framework theory of meaningfulness. Indeed, as we will see in section 5, the oscillation is inherent in Carnapianism itself.

The inherent instability of McGinn's position emerges in her argument that the skeptic's attempt to doubt is incoherent. According to McGinn, the skeptic's attempt to doubt is incoherent because he replaces "an attitude of commitment to Moore-type propositions" with "an attitude of questioning."[54] Now I am not sure what exactly McGinn means by "an attitude of questioning," but surely it is revealed by the skeptic's attempt to question. McGinn would say that the skeptic utters some words (e.g., "How do you *know* that you have two hands?") which express the skeptic's attitude of questioning. With these words the skeptic attempts to question a framework proposition; because unquestioning acceptance of all framework propositions is a necessary condition for the possibility of inquiry, the skeptic thereby "destroys the meaning" of his words. McGinn concludes that the skeptic's attempt to doubt is incoherent.

There is a parallel moment in Carnap's linguistic framework phase. Carnap's criticism of the skeptic's questions is that he takes a concept (for example, "real") that is meaningful only within a framework and tries to apply it to the framework itself.[55] For both Carnap and McGinn, the criticism that the skeptic lapses into nonsense depends on understanding what he is trying to ask. According to McGinn, the skeptic is trying to question (or adopt an epistemic relation towards) a framework proposition; according to Carnap, he is trying to apply concepts that are available only inside the framework to the framework as a whole. Giving this specification of what is going on in the skeptic's utterance requires at least a partial understanding of what the skeptic *says*. McGinn has to be able to recognize the embedded framework proposition in the skeptic's words. She has to determine that "I have two hands" in the skeptic's "How do I know that I have two hands?" expresses a determinate, meaningful framework proposition. (If McGinn does not determine what proposition, if any, is embedded in the skeptic's words, then she has no basis for accusing the skeptic of trying to doubt a component of the framework.) Carnap has to determine that the skeptic is trying to apply the concept *real* – the same concept that figures in claims such as "Unicorns are not real" – to the system of physical things.

We are now in a position to see why McGinn oscillates between regarding the skeptic as expressing doubts that are meaningful but misplaced and regarding him as speaking nonsense. In the moment of the oscillation we have been concerned with, when McGinn argues that the skeptic's utterance is meaningless, she relies on the logical structure of the utterance. She takes it to be clear both that the skeptic's move has to do with a framework proposition which is embedded in his question and that he is attempting to doubt that proposition. If we stop with this characterization of the utterance, before continuing with McGinn's argument that such an attempt to doubt renders the utterance meaningless, then we have a characterization of the utterance that ought to let us make sense of it. We have a particular proposition and an expression of an attitude (viz. doubt) towards it. Given this characterization of the skeptic's utterance, one ought to conclude that the skeptic *has* expressed a doubt. McGinn's own argument for why the skeptic's utterance is meaningless forces her to the other moment of her oscillation, the moment in which she says that the skeptic expresses genuine, though perhaps "odd," doubts.

McGinn cannot simply stop at one or the other moment of her oscillation. As we have just seen, the moment in which she claims that the skeptic's expressions of doubt are meaningless impels her to the moment in which she says that they are merely misplaced. If she tried to rest at the second moment of the oscillation, that is, if she tried to say only that the skeptic's doubt is *odd*, then she would not provide a satisfactory response to skepticism. A doubt is a doubt, regardless of whether it's the kind of doubt one ordinarily worries about, and if a doubt about a proposition cannot be answered, it renders all the knowledge that is built on that proposition doubtful too. McGinn is therefore deeply committed to both moments of the oscillation. But it is an unhappy position to be forced to say both that the skeptic expresses meaningful doubts and that he is speaking nonsense. This unhappy position is, I will argue, characteristic of Carnapianism generally.

5 The Incoherence of Carnapianism

The cornerstone of Carnapianism is the claim that there is a kind of nonsense that results from the illegitimate use of concepts. In theories of meaningfulness built around the ideas of logical syntax or of grammar, a use of concepts is illegitimate when it violates rules for the combination of concepts. In theories of meaningfulness built around the idea of a framework, the illegitimate use is the application of concepts (e.g., the concepts of *justification* or *knowledge*) outside the limits within which they are meaningful.

To evaluate these theories, let's work through their application to an ideal case. Consider an example that would seem to be a flagrant case of the illegitimate use of concepts: suppose a speaker says, "My telephone has a batting average of 0.328." A Carnapian of the logical syntax stripe would say that this speaker is trying to apply the concept of having a batting average, which makes sense only when applied to players of baseball or some similar game, to something that is not and cannot be a ballplayer; the concepts *is a telephone* and *has a batting average* are incompatible. The speaker utters nonsense when she tries to combine them. A Carnapian of the linguistic frameworks stripe would say that the speaker is using the concept *has a batting average* outside the domain in which it can be meaningfully applied: this concept can be meaningfully applied only in the framework of baseball (or another context involving batting), not in the linguistic framework in which we talk about telephones.[56]

What confidence should we have in the Carnapian diagnosis of this imagined utterance? Before we declare that the speaker has lapsed into nonsense, it would be advisable to ask her what she means. And she might give an answer that makes perfect sense of her utterance; for example, she might say, "It means that, out of all the attempted calls I make on that phone, I reach the person I want 32.8% of the time." If she makes sense of her utterance in some such way, no one will contend that she is using concepts illegitimately. A Carnapian could agree that if the example is fleshed out in such a way, then it is perfectly meaningful. But, he would explain, that only shows that it is not an example of the sort he is concerned with. He could say that in this example a word is being given a new meaning or a concept is being extended in a new way.

The Carnapian's criticism applies to cases in which concepts have been illegitimately combined or used beyond their limits. To identify such cases, the Carnapian critic has to determine which concepts are in play in the utterance under consideration. He needs to establish that the speaker is using the word "telephone" for the concept *telephone*, and the words "has a batting average" for the concept *has a batting average*. This requires interpreting her utterance. It is natural to think that interpreting an utterance is the process by which one comes to understand, or make sense of, an utterance that is initially baffling; it would seem that you don't even have a candidate interpretation of an utterance unless you have *made sense* of it. By contrast, the Carnapian needs an interpretation that precisely does *not* make sense of the utterance he is criticizing. We can mark this difference between what the Carnapian seeks and a normal interpretation by saying that the Carnapian needs a "quasi-interpretation." Just as a normal interpretation provides an understanding of a baffling utterance, the Carnapian's quasi-interpretation provides a sort of "understanding" of the utterance he is criticizing. This sort of "understanding" cannot be understanding properly so-called: the whole point of the Carnapian's criticism is to show that the sentence is nonsense, and there is no understanding a piece of nonsense. Let's say that the Carnapian achieves a "quasi-understanding" of the utterance in question. The quasi-understanding resembles a genuine understanding, in that both enable their possessor to see what concepts are in play in an utterance. The Carnapian would agree that you can't *understand* the utterance he criticizes; indeed, he would maintain that his quasi-understanding allows you to see exactly why you can't understand it, for his quasi-understanding allows you to recognize its illegitimate use of concepts.

Let us assume that the Carnapian critic has achieved a quasi-understanding of the utterance ("My telephone has a batting average of 0.328") that is his target. Now, what does the Carnapian's quasi-understanding yield exactly? A quasi-understanding does not yield an understanding of what the utterance *says*, since there is no such thing. But it does yield knowledge of which concepts are combined in the utterance. Indeed, the Carnapian's quasi-understanding has to yield more, for the Carnapian critic needs to know, not only which concepts are combined in the utterance, but also *how* those concepts are combined. To know only that the concepts *telephone* and *having a batting average of 0.328* have been combined in an utterance provides no grounds for saying that it is nonsensical, since these concepts may be combined in any number of perfectly sensible ways, as for example in the sentence "I'm on the telephone with a prospect who's batting 0.328." The Carnapian critic finds fault, not with *any* combination of the relevant concepts, but with a *particular* combination of concepts that are playing determinate logical roles in the utterance. In our example, the Carnapian finds fault with the utterance because (he wants to say) it uses the concept *telephone* as its logical subject and the concept *has a batting average of 0.328* as its logical predicate. But to say, for example, that a form of words has the logical subject *telephone* and the logical predicate *has a loud ringer* is a way of saying that it is (for example) a sentence that predicates the latter concept of an instance of the former one. To describe a form of words in terms of its logical subject and logical predicate is to describe it as expressing a predication, and to describe a form of words as expressing a predication is to describe it as making sense. But of course the Carnapian does not want his analysis of the utterance in question to describe it as making sense. Thus Carnapianism requires a third distinction, parallel to those between interpretation and quasi-interpretation and between understanding and quasi-understanding. This is a distinction between predications (which are expressed by meaningful sentences) and quasi-predications (which are expressed by sentences that are nonsense but that possess a logical structure of concepts analogous to the logical structure that meaningful sentences possess).

This distinction enables us to characterize the Carnapian diagnosis of our sample utterance as follows: the utterance quasi-predicates the concept *has a batting average* of *my telephone*, and this is an illegitimate use of concepts. (Depending on which flavor of Carnapianism he advocates, the Carnapian will say either that the quasi-predication violates the rules of logical syntax or that it applies a concept outside the framework, or frameworks, in which alone it is meaningful.) We have supplied the Carnapian with a form of words for his diagnosis. But what is it really to quasi-predicate one concept of another? The Carnapian needs to say that both predications and quasi-predications are assemblages of concepts into a logical structure; a quasi-predication differs from a predication in that the quasi-predication's logical arrangement of concepts is illegitimate, while the predication's is legitimate. This account of quasi-predication presupposes the notion of a logical structure of concepts. And this notion is surely to be explicated by analysis of predications, not by a sort of quasi-analysis of quasi-predications. Surely what it is to be, for example, the logical subject of a sentence is shown by comparing the structures of various genuine predications; the role of logical subject in a quasi-predication is an extrapolation from the role of logical subject in genuine predications. To bring out the way the quasi-analysis of quasi-predications is related to the analysis of predications, we may express the Carnapian's description of our ideal case as follows: it is a quasi-predication in which the concepts *telephone* and *has a batting average* are combined in just the way the concepts *telephone* and *has a loud ringer* are combined in the sentence "My telephone has a loud ringer." But this isn't exactly right. It isn't that our example utterance combines its concepts in *just* the way concepts are combined in "My telephone has a loud ringer." The latter combination is meaningful – it expresses a predication – whereas the corresponding combination of *telephone* and *has a batting average* is (the Carnapian wants to argue) nonsensical.

The Carnapian needs to mark the difference between genuine predications and quasi-predications. They both have logical structure. Because the notion of logical structure has its home in genuine predications, the Carnapian wants to explicate the logical structure of a quasi-predication using notions such as *logical subject* and *logical predicate*. Thus he wants to say that a quasi-predication is a combination of logical subject and logical predicate, or that a quasi-predication combines concepts in just the same way that a genuine predication does. But the Carnapian isn't entitled to this description of quasi-predication: to be a logical subject is to be the subject of a genuine predication, and to be a logical predicate is to be that which is predicated of a subject in a genuine predication. Because the Carnapian is attempting to describe quasi-predications, not genuine predications, he needs to introduce another set of analogues. For every logical role that can contribute to the meaning of a meaningful sentence, the Carnapian needs an analogue that is just like that role, except that it doesn't contribute to the meaning of the sentence. Rather, these "quasi-logical roles" contribute to the *meaninglessness* of the sentence. Thus, for example, a quasi-subject plays a role in quasi-predications like the role that subjects play in predications. That is, the *quasi-subject* of a sentence makes a contribution to the sentence's *meaninglessness* that is analogous to the contribution that the *subject* of a sentence makes to the *meaning* of its sentence. And so on with all the other logical roles.

In order to give an account of the structure of nonsensical sentences like our example, the Carnapian has had to stipulate a realm of meaninglessness with a tremendously rich structure. It is a realm in which quasi-subjects are linked with quasi-predicates to effect quasi-predications. The Carnapian critic quasi-understands these quasi-predications, which he quasi-analyzes so as to reveal that they possess a structure of concepts playing various quasi-logical roles. Carnapianism holds that the meaning of a sentence is a function of the sentence's logical structure and its concepts (the meanings of its words). (This thesis underlies the central

Carnapian idea that logical analysis – in terms of logical syntax or of frameworks – can provide criteria for demarcating meaningful sentences from meaningless ones.) But Carnapianism is also committed to the thesis that a sentence like our example has a particular form of meaninglessness, and that this particular form of meaninglessness is a function of the sentence's quasi-logical structure and its concepts. We might as well call the particular form of meaninglessness of a sentence of this sort a "quasi-meaning."

It is becoming difficult to resist the conclusion that quasi-meaning has all the hallmarks of genuine meaning. Quasi-meaningful sentences have structure (quasi-logical instead of logical), meaningful components, quasi-logical relations to other sentences. The Carnapian wants to say that there are certain rules or conditions that these sentences do not conform to, and that they are therefore nonsense. But the sentences that possess quasi-meaning do accord with *some* formation rules, namely, all those rules that determine the structure of quasi-logical roles which the sentences possess. Indeed, in this realm of quasi-meaning, sentences conform to rules governing the use of concepts that sentences in the realm of meaning violate. For example, in the realm of quasi-meaning, there is a rule that says "Don't combine a quasi-subject from the category of number-nouns with a quasi-predicate from the category of number-concepts." (Alternatively, we can think of the realm of quasi-meaning as the realm in which concepts are always used outside their framework – or inside their "quasi-framework.")

In short, the Carnapian, in fleshing out his characteristic criticism, has had to describe a realm of meaninglessness that is the mirror image of the realm of meaning. The Carnapian, in order to criticize an utterance as an illegitimate use of concepts, has had to quasi-analyze the utterance so as to show that it consists of meaningful concepts combined into a determinate quasi-logical form. To quasi-analyze sentences is to quasi-understand them as items in a structure governed by standards that are parallel to the standards governing logical structure. The realm of quasi-meaning has, it seems, all of the features that (by the Carnapian's own lights) contribute to the meaningfulness of sentences in the realm of meaning. If this is right, then the Carnapian is committed to the claim that sentences in the realm of quasi-meaning have senses. The most the Carnapian is entitled to say against quasi-meaningful sentences is that they have the wrong *kind* of senses – senses governed by the wrong set of standards. The Carnapian is in an unhappy position: he claims that certain sentences are nonsense because of the kind of sense they have.

There remains a way for the Carnapian to attempt to evade this conclusion. The argument I have given in this section starts from the idea that the Carnapian must achieve a sort of understanding (a "quasi-understanding") of how concepts are combined in the utterance that he wants to criticize as nonsense. Having a quasi-understanding, I have argued, amounts to making sense of the utterance in question. But the Carnapian can reject my argument's starting place. He can say that he doesn't need to (quasi) understand how concepts are actually combined into an utterance. (Since the utterance is nonsense, the Carnapian might say, it doesn't actually combine any concepts at all.) All he needs to know is what the speaker is *trying* to do with her concepts. The Carnapian's criticism requires, not that he determine that the speaker *succeeds* in combining the concepts, but only that he determine that she *attempts* to combine them. The Carnapian can claim that this allows him to describe the speaker in a way that does not commit him to making sense of her utterance. "The speaker is *trying* to combine the concepts *telephone* and *has a batting average*," the Carnapian might want to say. "This description of what she is trying to do gets its content from ordinary ideas about how people use concepts. We all know what the concepts *telephone* and *has a batting average* are, and we all know what it is to combine two concepts into a predication. Well, that lets me say what the speaker is trying to do: she's trying to put those concepts together. She can't succeed, of course, because they don't fit together (either because there's a grammatical rule that bars that combination or because she is using one of the concepts beyond the limits of its legitimate use)."

But we may question whether this description of what the speaker is trying to do is in fact free from an implicit commitment to making sense of what the speaker is saying with her (supposedly) nonsensical utterance. The Carnapian says that the speaker is trying to combine such-and-such concepts. But, as we have seen, this description of what the speaker is trying to do is not sufficient to let us see the problem with the combination. There are many innocuous combinations of the concepts in question that make perfect sense. The problem is not in trying to combine those concepts *per se*, but in trying to combine them in a particular logical arrangement, namely, as subject and predicate. So the Carnapian's fleshed-out description of what the speaker is doing has to have the following shape: "she is trying to predicate *having a batting average* of her *telephone*."

The intelligibility of the Carnapian's description rests on the intelligibility of his talk about predication. In particular, the intelligibility of the Carnapian's diagnosis has come down to the intelligibility of this description of the *attempt* to predicate *having a batting average* of *my telephone*. How are we to evaluate whether this description of an attempt is meaningful? If we specify a goal, then to say that someone is trying to reach that goal makes sense. The speaker's "goal" in our example is making the predication expressed by "My telephone has a batting average." But of course the conclusion the Carnapian wants to reach is that there is no such goal; there is nothing that is making such a predication. To be consistent with his own desired conclusion, the Carnapian cannot specify the goal which the speaker is supposedly trying to reach.

But if we do not specify a goal, then it does not mean anything to say "She's trying to reach that goal": we have so far not picked out a "that goal" for the description of the trying to refer to. We may consider another example to bring out how this affects the Carnapian's recourse to the language of "trying." By the Carnapian's own lights, it does not make sense to say, for example, "She is dividing Julius Caesar by 7." Because the name *Julius Caesar* and the concept *division by 7* are incompatible, there can be no action such as the sentence purports to describe. Now suppose the Carnapian were faced with the example, "She is *trying* to divide Julius Caesar by 7." Logical analysis would reveal, surely, that this sentence contains "dividing Julius Caesar by 7" as a proper part; since according to Carnapianism this part is meaningless, the whole sentence must be meaningless too.

A similar account applies to our main example. By the Carnapian's lights, "She is predicating *to have a batting average* of a *telephone*" does not make sense. Because the concepts *to have a batting average* and *telephone* are incompatible, there is no such predication; therefore we cannot say that someone is effecting such a predication. But if it doesn't make sense to say that someone is actually predicating a certain concept of another, it doesn't make sense to say that she is *trying* to predicate a certain concept of another. The expression of the predication is embedded in the Carnapian's own description of the speaker as trying to effect the predication.

We may conclude that the Carnapian's own diagnosis of the utterance "My telephone has a batting average of 0.328" makes sense if and only if the utterance itself does. For the Carnapian to maintain that his own diagnosis of the speaker's confusion is intelligible, he must grant that her utterance has a kind of sense. The Carnapian conception of nonsense thus comes down to the claim that certain utterances are nonsense because of the kind of sense they have. The Carnapian is committed to saying that some senses are nonsensical.

Wittgenstein had such accounts of nonsense in mind when he wrote: "When a sentence is called senseless, it is not as it were its sense that is senseless. But a combination of words is being excluded from the language, withdrawn from circulation" (*Philosophical Investigations*, §500). It can be hard to see why Wittgenstein makes this remark or others related to it.[57] In particular, it can be hard to see why Wittgenstein bothers to say that when a sentence is nonsense, it is not "its sense that is senseless." But our examination of Carnapianism permits us to recognize that Wittgenstein's remark is directed against a pervasive conception of nonsense. In this passage, Wittgenstein differentiates his conception of what it is to criticize a sentence as nonsense from the Carnapian conception of such criticism, and he rejects the latter as incoherent.

The commentators I have discussed do not realize that the conception of nonsense they attribute to Wittgenstein is precisely a conception according to which some sentences have a sense that is senseless. Our articulation of Carnap's theories of nonsense has allowed us to recognize the Carnapianism that is a common thread in these widely accepted readings of Wittgenstein. Moreover, by drawing out the consequences of the Carnapian conception, we have seen both that it is incoherent and that Wittgenstein definitively rejects it. Wittgenstein, it turns out, rejects the conception of nonsense that is standardly attributed to him.

The incoherence of Carnapianism is an instance of a general problem with which Wittgenstein was explicitly concerned in the *Tractatus* and which informs all his writings. This is the problem of drawing a substantive limit to thought. As Wittgenstein puts it in the preface to the *Tractatus*: "[I]n order to draw a limit to thinking we should have to be able to think both sides of this limit (we should therefore have to be able to think what cannot be thought)." The Carnapian wants to draw a substantive limit to thinking, via his distinction between sense and nonsense. The sentences that are meaningful express all the contents one can think; the sentences that are nonsense have no content, so they cannot be thought. The Carnapian wants to mark off what can be said by contrasting it with what cannot be said. He therefore describes what lies on the other side of the limit in a way that makes it seem like a *something*: on the far side of the limit are illegal combinations of meaningful sub-sentential parts or uses of concepts beyond their proper domains. Then he says that what lies on the inside of the limit are *legal* combinations of meaningful sub-sentential parts or uses of concepts *within* their proper domains. This gives the impression that he has drawn a boundary separating thinkable senses from non-thinkable combinations of meanings. But, as we have seen, this way of demarcating thoughts from non-thoughts requires that the Carnapian be able to think (to quasi-understand) the illegal combinations on the far side of the limit. And so the Carnapian fails, after all, to draw a substantive limit to thinking, in just the way anticipated by Wittgenstein in the *Tractatus*.

The unraveling of Carnapianism provides an opportunity for a few remarks about how Wittgenstein criticizes a philosophical utterance as nonsense. He says that calling a sentence senseless is a way of excluding it from the language. The sentence is not excluded because it has the wrong sort of meaning or because it has a disallowed sense. In fact, the exclusion is not an absolute prohibition: nothing can stop someone from assigning a sense to the form of words in question, and so long as everyone is clear about this assignment, the words can be meaningfully used without confusion. But the expressions that are philosophers' stock-in-trade continually invite confusion. For various reasons, we are inclined to think that we have determined a meaning for them, when really we haven't. They are forms of words that have been dissociated from a language-game.

To accuse a philosopher of using one of these expressions without determining a meaning for it requires a kind of criticism quite different from that practiced by Carnapians. A Carnapian thinks she can identify the components of the philosopher's utterance and specify their meaning. She needs to engage with the target of her criticism only in so far as the meanings of the components may be unclear from the words' immediate context. By contrast, when Wittgenstein is confronted with an utterance that has no clearly discernible place in a language-game, he does not assume that he can parse the utterance; rather, he invites the speaker to explain how she is using her words, to connect them with other elements of the language-game in a way that displays their meaningfulness. Only if the speaker is unable to do this in a coherent way does Wittgenstein conclude that her utterance is nonsense; ideally, the speaker will reach the same conclusion in the same way and will retract or modify her words accordingly. Applying Wittgenstein's conception of nonsense therefore requires an intense engagement with the target of criticism; an examination of the words alone is not enough. When Wittgenstein criticizes an utterance as nonsensical, he aims to expose, not a defect in the words themselves, but a confusion in the speaker's relation to her words – a confusion that is manifested in the speaker's failure to specify a meaning for them.[58]

Notes

1 Ludwig Wittgenstein, *Tractatus Logico-Philosophicus*, C.K. Ogden (trans.). I have departed from the Ogden translation here and in subsequent quotations.

2 This view is expressed in "Empiricism, Semantics, and Ontology," reprinted in Rudolf Carnap, *Meaning and Necessity*, 2nd edn, Chicago, University of Chicago, 1956, pp. 205–21.

3 For economy of exposition, I am oversimplifying the development of Carnap's thought. A full account of Carnap's development would start with *Der Logische Aufbau der Welt*

(*The Logical Structure of the World*, Rolf George (trans.) Berkeley, CA, University of California Press, 1967), which can be seen as containing the seeds of his later theories. The *Aufbau* view resembles verificationism, in that it is an attempt to express the empirical content of sentences in phenomenalistic (so experiential) terms. But Carnap in the *Aufbau* is also clear that you don't have to adopt his phenomenalistic construction; there are other possible frameworks that would equally well express empirical content. Then, under the influence of the Vienna Circle, Carnap comes to think that the empirical content of a sentence is captured *only* by connecting it to possible experience; Carnap's verificationist phase thus involves giving up an aspect of his *Aufbau* view (viz., the importance of alternative schemes). Later, when he develops his logical syntax theory of meaningfulness, Carnap abandons a feature common to both (one part of) the *Aufbau* and verificationism, namely, the idea that the meaningfulness of a sentence is determined by its connection to possible experience: instead, according to the logical syntax theory, meaningfulness is determined by an ostensibly formal criterion, namely, whether the sentence is well-formed. But in allowing for a plurality of logical-syntactic systems, he returns to the pluralism of his *Aufbau* view; and when he comes to what I am calling his linguistic framework phase, he recovers yet another feature of the *Aufbau*, namely, the notion that a test for meaningfulness requires more than purely formal criteria.

4 Arthur Pap (trans.) in A.J. Ayer (ed.) *Logical Positivism*, Glencoe, IL, Free Press, 1959, pp. 60–82.

5 It is perhaps worth emphasizing that verificationism all but disappears from Carnap's later theories of meaningfulness. The requirement that meaningful sentences be logically well-formed, which he employs in his logical syntax phase, does not have any obvious connection to the requirement that meaningful sentences be confirmable by experience. But Carnap is not entirely clear that he is articulating a new criterion. He continues to employ verificationist slogans, as when he writes that "the meaning of a statement lies in the method of its verification" ("The Elimination of Metaphysics," op. cit., p. 76).

6 As we have seen, this thesis shouldn't be taken to be an account of the origin of *all* philosophical nonsense, since Carnap states that some philosophical nonsense arises from the use of meaningless words.

7 There is a danger of reading too much into the word "syntax" here. Nowadays we are inclined to think of "syntax" as sharply distinguished from "semantics." Carnap himself in later works insisted on this distinction between "purely formal, uninterpreted calculi" and "interpreted language systems" (*Introduction to Semantics*, Cambridge, MA, Harvard University Press, 1948, p. vii). But at the time he articulated his logical syntax theory of meaningfulness he had not made the distinction so sharply. His test for the meaningfulness of natural language sentences is not a test involving only syntax in the sense of "purely formal, uninterpreted calculi"; it relies on considerations concerning the meanings of the words. I elaborate this point in the discussion of Baker and Hacker below.

8 Rudolf Carnap, *The Logical Syntax of Language*, Amethe Smeaton (trans.) New York, Harcourt, Brace and Co., 1937, p. 52.

9 The term "linguistic framework" risks being ambiguous. In the context of Carnap's logical syntax writings, the term "linguistic framework" would refer to a system of syntactical rules – rules such as those Carnap mentions in his formulation of the principle of tolerance. In "Empiricism, Semantics, and Ontology," op. cit., the source for the view I am now discussing, Carnap takes a "linguistic framework" to include not only rules of syntax, but also explicitly semantical elements. In this paper, I use "linguistic framework" exclusively in this latter sense.

10 Carnap's linguistic framework view is quite different from his verificationism, despite a superficial resemblance between them. According to the linguistic framework view, a sentence is meaningful if and only if it belongs to a framework that establishes what evidence would count for or against it. This criterion echoes the verificationist principle that a (non-logical) statement is meaningful if and only if it is possible to specify what evidence would count for or against it. The crucial difference lies in what can count as "evidence." According to verificationism, the only evidence that counts is experience,

or observation. By contrast, the linguistic framework theory imposes no restrictions on the sort of evidence that a framework may use to decide for or against statements within it.

11 "Empiricism, Semantics, and Ontology," op. cit, p. 206.

12 *Tractatus*, 3.325.

13 The German *"Satz"* is rendered better sometimes by "proposition," sometimes by "sentence." Both C.K. Ogden and David Pears and Brian McGuinness use "proposition" in their translations of this passage; they thereby make it more difficult to understand than it needs to be. In translating the *Tractatus*, we do well to reserve the term "proposition" for contexts in which Wittgenstein uses *"Satz"* to mean a sentence which has a significant use – i.e., a sentence that expresses a thought, a sentence functioning as what he calls a *symbol* (*Tractatus*, 3.326); otherwise we are forced to bend our minds around the notion of a nonsensical proposition. In this passage, Wittgenstein is drawing a contrast between *Sätze* that make sense and *Sätze* that don't, so we ought to understand him to be talking about sentences. I have emended Ogden's translation accordingly.

14 This is confirmed by Wittgenstein's account of how the "right method of philosophy" would curb the urge to do metaphysics: that method is "always, when someone else wished to say something metaphysical, to demonstrate to him that he had given no meaning to certain signs in his propositions" (*Tractatus*, 6.53). Wittgenstein doesn't entertain the method of philosophy envisioned by Carnapianism, which would require sometimes demonstrating that, in saying something metaphysical, the philosopher has used signs illegitimately. (Incidentally, for complex dialectical reasons explored in the papers by James Conant cited below, the actual method of the *Tractatus* is not what Wittgenstein here labels the "right method of philosophy.")

15 Gottlob Frege, *The Foundations of Arithmetic*, 2nd edn, J.L. Austin (trans.) Evanston, IL, Northwestern University Press, 1980, p. x.

16 Ludwig Wittgenstein, *Philosophical Investigations*, §49.

17 *Wittgenstein's Lectures, Cambridge 1932–35*, p. 64.

18 Wittgenstein's position in this passage seems to be that *none* of the words of "This is green and yellow at the same time" are meaningful. But according to the formulation from the *Tractatus* quoted above (*Tractatus*, 5.4733), the problem with a nonsensical utterance is that we have given no meaning to some of its component parts, which suggests that a nonsensical sentence might contain some meaningful words and some meaningless ones. (This impression is further strengthened by Wittgenstein's discussion of the phrase 'Socrates is identical'.) I take it that the position suggested by the lecture remark is the view best attributed to Wittgenstein; it expresses the consequence of a rigorous adherence to the context principle. In the *Tractatus*, Wittgenstein is giving expression to a psychologically important feature of the jingle of the words: there is a natural route (or several natural routes) to giving a sense to them; but, strictly speaking, none of the words can be said to be meaningful until that further specification has been made.

19 Unpublished lecture notes taken by Margaret Macdonald. Quoted in Cora Diamond, *The Realistic Spirit*, Cambridge, MA, MIT Press, 1991, pp. 106–7.

20 *Tractatus*, 3.03 and 3.031. There are difficulties inherent in these statements of Wittgenstein's, in that our grasp of their sense depends on our having some grasp of what is said to be unthinkable. The peculiar structure of the *Tractatus* – especially Wittgenstein's request that we come to regard the sentences it contains as nonsense – reflects his attempt to come to grips with these difficulties. For my purposes, I can ignore the difficulties; I will be content with a preliminary turn or two of the dialectical crank that is ultimately to reveal Carnapianism to be but the illusion of a position.

21 Cora Diamond has drawn the distinction between Wittgenstein's conception of nonsense and what I call Carnapianism (what she calls "the natural view") in "What Nonsense Might Be," in her *The Realistic Spirit*, op. cit. James Conant, in "The Method of the *Tractatus*" (an extract from which appears in this collection), further clarifies Wittgenstein's conception of nonsense; he develops a reading of the *Tractatus* akin to the one I have just sketched and provides it with more textual support than I am able to give here. For highlighting the centrality of ideas about nonsense in Wittgenstein's

thought, and for exploring the way the structure of the *Tractatus* relates to those ideas, I am indebted to Diamond's "Throwing Away the Ladder" in *The Realistic Spirit*, op. cit. and "Ethics, Imagination, and the Method of Wittgenstein's *Tractatus*," reprinted in this volume, and to James Conant, "The Search for Logically Alien Thought," *Philosophical Topics*, 1991, vol. 20, pp. 115–80.

22 G.P. Baker and P.M.S. Hacker, *Wittgenstein: Rules, Grammar and Necessity*, Oxford, Blackwell, 1985, p. 39.

23 Ibid., p. 55. It will turn out that Baker and Hacker do not in fact think that the philosopher's lapse into nonsense is "subtle and not readily identifiable." These words are a bit of Wittgensteinian rhetoric to which they are not entitled.

24 Ibid., p. 36.

25 Ibid., pp. 37, 40.

26 Items (1)–(3) on this list are drawn from a section entitled "From Logical Syntax to Philosophical Grammar" (ibid., pp. 37–41); item (4) is implicit at ibid., p. 56.

27 This does not imply that Carnap thinks that all the rules of logical syntax are already known. On the contrary, he says that logicians have a great deal of work to do to get a complete inventory of rules of logical syntax. But Baker and Hacker also think that there is still work for philosophers to do in uncovering the non-obvious rules of grammar.

28 Ibid., p. 40.

29 "The Elimination of Metaphysics," op. cit., p. 68.

30 Ibid., p. 56.

31 Ibid., p. 53.

32 This is my gloss on the so-called "observation" that "the grammar of colour licenses predicating 'is coloured' (primarily) of things of which one may also predicate 'is extended'." Baker and Hacker's formulation leaves open the possibility of exceptions to the rule. In my gloss, I close this possibility in order to construct a cogent argument on Baker and Hacker's behalf. For if we allow that it is grammatically acceptable to predicate "is colored" of some things that are *not* extended, then we have to confront the possibility that the scientist is taking advantage of this exception. And in the face of this possibility, Baker and Hacker provide nothing to say against the scientist's utterance. Baker and Hacker's argument works only if we drop the exception from the statement of the rule. (Of course, without the exception the rule is no longer obviously right.)

33 This is my gloss of part of what Baker and Hacker mean by "minds and sensations are not extended."

34 This principle turns out to be highly problematic. The principle is implicit in the last sentence of the quoted passage. Consider the question of *why* it makes no sense to say "This pain is 5 cm long." According to Baker and Hacker, this question is equivalent to the following one: what rule of grammar does "This pain is 5 cm long" violate? Baker and Hacker's answer seems to lie in the grammatical observation that sensations are not extended. But to get from the illegality of "This pain is extended" to the illegality of "This pain is 5 cm long," we have to recognize that the latter entails the former; there is no relation at the level of the words themselves.

The alternative to rule (c) would be a myriad of special rules, (e.g., if you may say "x is a sensation," then you may not say "x is 5 cm long" nor "x is 6 cm long" nor "x is the size of a nickel" nor "x is the shape of California," etc., etc.). To cite one of these special rules against someone who says, for example, "My pain is the size of a nickel" is going to seem hopelessly *ad hoc* unless Baker and Hacker can relate the special rule to a general rule like (b). And the relation of the special rules to the general rule will involve, it seems, a principle like (c).

If I am right that Baker and Hacker are committed to some such principle involving entailment, then they are committed to there being sentences that violate rules of grammar and yet have a sense. For entailment is a relation between sentences only in so far as they are meaningful. If Baker and Hacker consider the entailments of a sentence-like form of words in order to determine that it violates rules of grammar, they must impute a sense to the sentence-like form of words; at the same time, they want to say that, because the sentence violates a rule of grammar, it is nonsense. This is a preview of the paradox of Carnapianism in general.

35 This bizarre claim is a most uncharitable reading of the scientist's sentence. But only if Baker and Hacker construe the scientist in some such way can they get any use out of their rules (a) and (b).

36 Compare ibid., p. 55 with "The Elimination of Metaphysics," op. cit., p. 68.

37 Baker and Hacker, *Wittgenstein: Rules, Grammar and Necessity*, op. cit., p. 47.

38 Ibid., p. 57.

39 Ibid., p. 59.

40 Baker and Hacker write, "Rules must be more or less transparent to participants in a rule-governed practice" (ibid., p. 63).

41 Ibid., p. 53.

42 Marie McGinn, *Sense and Certainty: A Dissolution of Scepticism*, New York, Blackwell, 1989.

43 Ibid., p. 3.

44 Ibid., p. 116.

45 Ibid., p. 103.

46 Ibid., p. 142.

47 Ibid., p. 160.

48 Ibid., p. 159–60.

49 Ibid., pp. 128, 161.

50 Ibid., pp. 108, 159.

51 Ibid., pp. 159–60.

52 Ibid., p. 159.

53 Ibid., p. 159.

54 Ibid., p. 160.

55 Carnap, "Empiricism, Semantics, and Ontology," op. cit., p. 207.

56 The linguistic framework diagnosis that applies to this example has a very general form: it holds that the utterance is nonsense because a concept is being used outside the framework in which it can be meaningfully applied. The linguistic framework version of Carnapianism offers a more specific diagnosis of some philosophical nonsense: some philosophical nonsense results from the application of a concept from within a framework to the framework as a whole. This more specific diagnosis does not apply to my example; an example to which it would seem to apply is "The game of baseball has a batting average of 0.328." I use an example susceptible to the general diagnosis in order to make my argument against Carnapianism more general.

57 These include Ludwig Wittgenstein, *Philosophical Grammar*, p. 130, and unpublished lecture notes taken by Margaret Macdonald (quoted in Cora Diamond, *The Realistic Spirit*, op. cit., pp. 106–7).

58 I am indebted to many friends for help on this paper. Logi Gunnarsson, Stephen Engstrom, Hibi Pendleton, Rupert Read, Lisa Van Alstyne and Mary Witherspoon read versions of the paper and helped me fix problems both philosophical and literary. Alice Crary shepherded the manuscript through several crucial revisions. David Finkelstein helped me to frame the structure of the paper, to focus my arguments and to clarify my writing. John McDowell provided an unfailing stream of invaluable comments. Most of all, I would like to thank Jim Conant, without whose guidance I could never have written this paper.

A DISSENTING VOICE

14

WAS HE TRYING TO
WHISTLE IT?[1]

P.M.S. Hacker

1 'A baffling doctrine, bafflingly presented'

That there are things that cannot be put into words, but which *make themselves manifest* (*Tractatus* 6.522) is a leitmotif running through the whole of the *Tractatus*. It is heralded in the preface, in which the author summarizes the whole sense of the book in the sentence 'What can be said at all can be said clearly, and what we cannot talk about we must pass over in silence', and it is repeated by the famous concluding remark 'What we cannot speak about we must pass over in silence'. Wittgenstein's claim is, or at least seems to be, *that by the very nature of language*, or indeed of any system of representation whatsoever, there are things which cannot be stated or described, things of which one cannot speak, but which are in some sense *shown* by language. The numerous truths that seemingly cannot be stated, but which are nevertheless apparently asserted in the course of the *Tractatus*, can be sorted into the following groups:

(i) The harmony between thought, language and reality: There is (or seems to be) a harmony (or as Wittgenstein later put it, with deliberate Leibnizean allusion, a 'pre-established harmony' ('Big Typescript' 189)) between representation and what is represented. This harmony does not consist in the agreement of a true proposition with reality, since there are also false propositions. Rather it consists in the agreement of form between any proposition whatever and the reality it depicts either truly or falsely. This shared form, however, cannot itself be depicted. A picture can depict any reality whose form it has, but it cannot depict its pictorial form –it displays it (*Tractatus* 2.171). Propositions *show* the logical form of reality (*Tractatus* 4.12–4.121).

(ii) Semantics: One cannot say what the meaning of a symbol is. It is impossible to *assert* the identity of meaning of two expressions (*Tractatus* 6.2322). One cannot say what the sense of a proposition is; rather, a proposition *shows* its sense. A proposition *shows* how things stand if it is true, and it *says* that they do so stand (*Tractatus* 4.022).

(iii) Logical relations between propositions: One cannot say that one proposition follows from another, or that one proposition contradicts another. But that the propositions '$p \supset q$', 'p' and 'q', combined with one another in the form '$(p \supset q).(p): \supset :(q)$', yield a tautology shows that 'q' follows from 'p' and '$p \supset q$' (*Tractatus* 6.1201). A tautology shows the internal relations between its constituent propositions.

(iv) Internal properties and relations of things and situations: Internal properties and relations of a thing are properties and relations which are such that it is unthinkable that the thing should not possess them (*Tractatus* 4.123). But it is impossible to say that a thing possesses an internal property or stands in an internal relation to some other thing, for example, that light blue is lighter than dark blue. Rather, internal properties and relations make themselves manifest in the propositions that represent the relevant states of affairs and are concerned with the relevant objects (*Tractatus* 4.122). Similarly, one cannot say that a proposition is a tautology, since that is an internal property of the proposition. But every tautology itself shows that it is a tautology (*Tractatus* 6.127).

(v) Categorial features of things and type classifications: One cannot say that a thing belongs to a given category, e.g. that red is a colour or that *a* is an object (*Tractatus* 4.122–4.125). For the ontological category of a thing is given by its logical form, which consists in its combinatorial possibilities with other objects. But the logical form of an object cannot be named, since it is not itself an object – it is rather the common features of a whole class of objects, in particular the combinatorial possibilities in reality of the objects of the common category. And that is represented in a perspicuous notation by a variable. Apparent categorial or formal concepts, such as space, time, colour, or fact, object, relation, number, or proposition, name, function, are in effect variable names, not real names. They cannot occur in a fully analysed, well-formed proposition with a sense.

(vi) The limits of thought: One cannot circumscribe what can be thought in language by saying what cannot be thought, for in order to say it one would have to be able to think what is not thinkable (Preface). Nor can one justify excluding a certain form of words as nonsensical by reference to reality (as Russell had tried to do in his theory of types).

(vii) The limits of reality and the logical structure of the world: Empirical reality is limited by the totality of objects, and that limit makes itself manifest in the totality of elementary propositions (*Tractatus* 5.5561). The limits of the world are also the limits of logic, i.e. the limits of all possible worlds are the limits of logical possibility. So we cannot say in logic that the world contains such-and-such possibilities but not such-and-such other possibilities. For that would appear to presuppose that we were excluding certain possibilities (*Tractatus* 5.61). But a logical impossibility is not a possibility that is impossible. Nevertheless, that the propositions of logic are tautologies *shows* the formal – logical – properties of language and the world (*Tractatus* 6.12).

(viii) Metaphysical principles of natural science: The fundamental principles of natural science, such as the laws of causality, of least action, of continuity, etc. are not descriptions of nature, but forms of description. The so-called law of causality amounts to no more than that there are laws of nature. But it cannot be said that there are laws of nature – it makes itself manifest (*Tractatus* 6.36). It is shown by the possibility of giving a complete description of the world by means of laws of the causal form.

(ix) Metaphysics of experience: What the solipsist *means* is quite correct, only it cannot be *said*, but makes itself manifest in the limits of my language being the limits of my world (*Tractatus* 5.62). That there is no soul, no Cartesian soul-substance 'as it is conceived in the superficial psychology of the present day', cannot

be said, but it is shown by the logical form of propositions such as 'A believes that p' (*Tractatus* 5.542–5.5421).

(x) Ethics, aesthetics and religion: It is impossible for there to be propositions of ethics. Propositions can express nothing that is higher. Ethics is transcendental. Ethics and aesthetics are one and the same (*Tractatus* 6.42–6.421). It is impossible to speak about the will in so far as it is the subject of ethical attributes (*Tractatus* 6.423).

The doctrine of what cannot be said but only shown is, as David Pears has observed, a baffling doctrine bafflingly presented.[2] Bafflement is further increased when the author of the *Tractatus*, in the penultimate remark of the book, draws the inevitable corollary of his arguments:

> My propositions serve as elucidations in the following way: anyone who understands me eventually recognizes them as nonsensical, when he has used them – as steps – to climb up beyond them. (He must, so to speak, throw away the ladder after he has climbed up it.)
>
> He must transcend these propositions, and then he will see the world aright.
> (*Tractatus* 6.54)

So the propositions of the *Tractatus* are themselves nonsense. They fail to comply with the rules of logical grammar – logical syntax (*Tractatus* 3.325). For they either employ formal concept-words as proper concept-words, and nonsensical pseudo-propositions are the result (*Tractatus* 4.1272) or they ascribe internal properties and relations to something, which cannot be done by a well-formed proposition with a sense. For a proposition with a sense must restrict reality to, and allow reality, two alternatives: yes or no – it must be bipolar (*Tractatus* 4.023). But any attempted ascription of an internal property would *not* allow reality two alternatives, since it is inconceivable that something might lack its internal properties.

It is not surprising that the early, well-informed readers of the *Tractatus* greeted this conclusion with incredulity. In his introduction to the *Tractatus*, Russell wrote, 'after all, Mr Wittgenstein manages to say a good deal about what cannot be said, thus suggesting to the sceptical reader that possibly there may be some loophole through the hierarchy of languages, or by some other exit' (Introduction, p. xxi). He clearly felt that it was incredible that so many profound insights into the nature of logic should be intelligibly stated and yet be held to be nonsensical. Wittgenstein's restriction on what can be said, he confessed, 'leaves me with a certain sense of intellectual discomfort'. Neurath famously remarked of the closing sentence: 'one should indeed be silent, but not *about* anything'.[3] If, as Wittgenstein wrote in the preface, what lies on the other side of the limit of language is simply nonsense, then metaphysics is simply nonsense and there is nothing to be silent about. Ramsey remonstrated that if the chief proposition of philosophy is that philosophy is nonsense, then 'we must take seriously that it is nonsense, and not pretend, as Wittgenstein does, that it is important nonsense'.[4] Elsewhere he observed that 'But what we can't say, we can't say, and we can't whistle it either'.[5] Indeed, it is not as if one can even think what one cannot say – for as the young Wittgenstein himself (wrongly) insisted, 'thinking is a kind of language' and a thought 'just is a kind of proposition' (*Notebooks 1914–16* 82). So can one whistle what one cannot think, i.e. can one apprehend truths which one cannot even think?

The predicament is serious. It is not merely that Wittgenstein's explanation of what apprehension of the ineffable consists in itself perforce invokes the use of formal concepts. Nor is it merely that Wittgenstein deliberately saws off the branch upon which he is sitting, since if the account of the conditions of representation given in the book is correct, then the sentences of the book are mere pseudo-propositions. But rather, if that is so, then the account of the conditions of representation is itself nonsense. And that seems a *reductio ad absurdum* of the very argument that led to the claim that the sentences of the book are one and all pseudo-propositions.

2 A post-modernist defence

One may well share Russell's qualms. Surely, one is inclined to think, there is much that can be learnt from the book. Even if there is, as the later Wittgenstein laboured to show, much that is wrong with it, there is also much that it has taught us. Few, today, would defend the claim that the logical connectives are names of logical entities (unary and binary functions), or that sentences are names of truth-values or of complexes. Few would claim, as Frege and Russell did, that logical propositions are (what we would call) generalizations of tautologies, or that they are descriptions of relations between abstract entities (Frege) or of the most general facts in the universe (Russell). And there can be no doubt that Wittgenstein's explanation of the tautologousness of the propositions of logic has had a profound effect upon the general understanding of logic.

One response to Wittgenstein's paradoxical conclusion is to try to erect a line of defence which will salvage the insights of the book from self-destructive condemnation. Max Black, author of the only detailed commentary on the *Tractatus*, tried to do just that.[6] He conceded that if communication is equated exclusively with 'saying', then the *Tractatus* communicates nothing. But, since the book itself insists that there is much that can be shown but cannot be said, should we not insist that it shows a great deal, and that what it thus shows can be salvaged? Wittgenstein's propositions about the essences of things consist, Black suggested, in a priori statements belonging to logical syntax. These are formal statements which show things that can be shown, and they are no worse than logical propositions, which do not transgress the rules of logical syntax. But this is mistaken. The propositions of logic are senseless, not nonsense. Wittgenstein's own propositions, which Black called 'formal statements', are, by the lights of the *Tractatus*, nonsensical pseudo-propositions. They show nothing at all. The propositions that *are* held to show the ineffable truths which the *Tractatus* seems to be trying to say are not the pseudo-propositions of the book but well-formed propositions (including the senseless propositions of logic).

Black's suggestion is in effect that Wittgenstein was, as Ramsey had suggested, trying to whistle what he held one could not say. In recent years a quite different defence of Wittgenstein's *Tractatus* has gained popularity, particularly in the United States. On this view, Wittgenstein was *not* trying to whistle it. (Neurath was right to claim that there is nothing to be silent about, and only wrong in imputing to Wittgenstein the contrary view.) It has been propounded by Cora Diamond, further elaborated by James Conant, Juliet Floyd, Warren Goldfarb and Thomas Ricketts. On their side, enthusiastically urging them on, stands the puckish figure of Burton

Dreben, a benevolent and humorous *Geist der stets verneint*. It has won warm approval from Peter Winch.[7] According to them, the *Tractatus* does not self-consciously try, by deliberately flouting the rules of logical syntax, to state deep, ineffable truths, which actually cannot be said but are shown by well-formed sentences of a language. Rather, it engages our temptations to utter nonsense, in particular philosophical nonsense of the kind exhibited in the *Tractatus*, and it demonstrates that such putatively philosophical sentences are indeed plain nonsense, different from mere gibberish only in as much as we are under the *illusion* that such sentences, though nonsensical, are deep nonsense – trying to say what can only be shown. There are significant differences between some of these interpreters. In the compass of a single article, it is impossible to deal in detail with those differences. Hence I shall focus primarily on Diamond's account, mentioning others only *en passant*, and attempt to isolate the various theses they agree upon, all of which seem to me to be mistaken.

Diamond's interpretation depends upon giving maximal weight to the preface and the penultimate remark. This she refers to as 'the frame' of the book, which instructs us how to read it. In the preface, Wittgenstein identified the aim of his book as being to set a limit to the expression of thoughts. This, he declared, can be done only by setting the limit in language, 'and what lies on the other side of the limit will simply be nonsense (*wird einfach Unsinn sein*)'.[8] The penultimate remark declares that 'anyone who understands me eventually recognizes [my propositions] as nonsensical, when he has used them – as steps – to climb up beyond them. (He must, so to speak, throw away the ladder after he has climbed up it.)' The question Diamond poses is: how seriously we are meant to take the latter remark? In particular, does it apply to the leitmotif of the book? After we have thrown away the ladder, she queries, 'Are we going to keep the idea that there is something or other in reality that we gesture at, however badly, when we speak of "the logical form of reality," so that *it*, *what we were gesturing* at, is there but cannot be expressed in words?'[9] This would, she responds, be 'chickening out',[10] i.e. pretending to throw away the ladder while standing as firmly as possible on it. But to throw away the ladder is, among other things,

> to throw away in the end the attempt to take seriously the language of "features of reality". To read Wittgenstein himself as not chickening out is to say that it is not, not really, his view that there are features of reality that cannot be put into words but show themselves. What is his view is that that way of talking may be useful or even for a time essential, but it is in the end to be let go of and honestly be taken to be real nonsense, plain nonsense, which we are not in the end to think of as corresponding to an ineffable truth.[11]

Diamond contrasts two ways of taking the idea that there are, according to the *Tractatus*, no philosophical doctrines. One is to take the book as containing numerous doctrines which *stricto sensu* cannot be put into words – so that they do not, by the lights of the *Tractatus* count as doctrines. On that view (shared by Russell, Ramsey, Neurath, and later also by Anscombe, Geach and myself[12]), one is left holding on to some ineffable truths about reality after one has thrown away the ladder. The other is to hold that the notion of ineffable truths about reality is 'to be used only with the awareness that it itself belongs with what has to be thrown away'. The latter, she claims, is the correct way to interpret the book.

Diamond extracts from these considerations three salient theses. First, all the propositions of the book are nonsense, except for the frame. Secondly, they are plain nonsense, no different from 'A is a frabble', with one proviso. Some of them are 'transitional ways of talking' in a 'dialectic' that culminates in their whole-hearted rejection. They are the (nonsensical) rungs of the ladder up which we must climb before we reject them *in toto*. Hence, thirdly, the distinction between what can be said and what can only be shown but not said is itself part of the nonsense that is to be discarded. These three theses are common ground to most of the proponents of this interpretation of the *Tractatus*.[13] What is the argument for it?

Diamond's argument involves three steps:

(a) If we take a metaphysical sentence such as 'A is an object', then, Diamond contends, in so far as we take ourselves to understand it, we take its truth and falsehood *both* to be graspable.

> Even in thinking of it as true in all possible worlds, in thinking of it as something whose truth underlies ordinary being so and not being so, we think of it as itself *the case*; our thought contrasts it with as it were a different set of necessities. Our ordinary possibilities have the character of possibility, given that these underlying necessities are as they are, not some other way ... possibility and necessity [are being viewed] as fixed some particular way rather than some other; they are still conceived *in* a space. What is possible in the contingent world, what is thinkable, what is sayable, is so because of the way ontological categories are fixed.[14]

Wittgenstein's aim is to show that this philosophical perspective is but an illusion.

(b) It is an illusion that there is any such thing 'as violating the principles of logical syntax by using a term in what, given its syntax, goes against what can be said with it'.[15] It is because of this illusion that one may think that we violate the rules of logical syntax when we form such expressions as 'A is an object' and conceive of them as trying to state necessary features of reality that properly speaking show themselves in language. But the notion here of there being something one cannot do dissolves into incoherence if pressed slightly.[16]

(c) In fact, she argues, Wittgenstein's claim is not that the sentence 'A is an object' is a special kind of nonsense, a kind of nonsense that transgresses the bounds of sense in the attempt to say something that cannot be said. *Pace* Ramsey, Wittgenstein was not committed to the existence of two kinds of nonsense, (i) important nonsense that tries to say what can only be shown, and (ii) plain nonsense.[17] What Wittgenstein says is that *any* possible sentence is, as far as its construction goes, legitimately put together, and if it has no sense, that can only be because we have failed to give a meaning to one of its constituents (*Tractatus* 5.4733). The reason why 'Socrates is identical' is nonsense is that we have given no meaning to 'identical' as an adjective. 'A is an object' is nonsensical in exactly the same way. We have given no meaning to 'object' as a predicate noun, but only as a variable. But, unlike 'Socrates is identical', we are misled by the former kind of sentence, and think of ourselves as meaning something by it that lies beyond what Wittgenstein allows to be sayable. When he insists that we cannot say 'There are objects', he does not mean 'There are, all right, only *that there are* has to be expressed in another way'.[18] Rather, he simply means that this sentence is plain nonsense, not essentially different from 'There are frabbles'. There is nothing to be shown that cannot be said. Indeed, she argues (correctly) that

> It is an immediate consequence of this account of philosophy that the sentences of the *Tractatus* itself are nonsensical, since they treat formal properties and relations as non-formal properties and relations. In their use in the sentences of the *Tractatus*, the words 'world', 'fact', 'number', 'object', 'proposition' (and so on) have been given no meaning.[19]

When we are told to 'throw away the ladder', it seems, we are meant, on pain of 'chickening out' as she puts it, to throw *everything* away, including the bogus distinction between things that can be said and things that cannot be said but only shown.

This is a radical interpretation of the *Tractatus*, according to which the whole book is a dialectic in which one proceeds from one nonsensical rung of a ladder to another. Unlike Hegelian dialectic, however, there is no final synthesis which incorporates what was right about the antecedent theses and antitheses – for it culminates not in a final synthesis of all that precedes it, but in its total repudiation. It is a 'dialectic' only in the sense that the reader is supposed to interrogate the book while reading it, and to realize, as each transitional stage is transcended, each rung ascended, that it was actually nonsense, and indeed to realize in the end, that the whole book is nonsense. James Conant has developed her interpretation in 'Kierkegaard, Wittgenstein and Nonsense' and attempted to draw parallels between Wittgenstein and Kierkegaard. In particular, he compares the author of the *Tractatus* to the pseudonymous Kierkegaardian 'humourist' Johannes Climacus, who wrote his book in order to revoke it. Conant represents the book as an exercise in Kierkegaardian irony. Following Diamond, he writes, 'I would urge that the propositions of the *entire* work are to be thrown away as nonsense'.[20] The aim of the book, he claims,

> is to undo our attraction to various grammatically well-formed strings of words that resonate with an aura of sense. The silence that . . . the *Tractatus* wish[es] to leave us with in the end is one in which nothing has been said and there is nothing to say (of the sort that we imagined there to be). . . . [It] is not the pregnant silence that comes with the censorious posture of guarding the sanctity of the ineffable.[21]

This 'deconstructive' interpretation[22] seems to me to be a most curious way of reading a great book and of dismissing the philosophical insights that it contains, even though many of them are, as Wittgenstein himself later realized, 'seen through a glass darkly', and many of the claims are, as he later laboured to make clear, erroneous. The *Tractatus*, as he remarked to Elizabeth Anscombe, is not *all* wrong: it is not like a bag of junk professing to be a clock, but like a clock that does not tell the right time.[23] On Diamond's interpretation, it was never meant to be a working clock, but a self-destructive one designed to explode as soon as wound up. But it is perhaps not surprising that this interpretation should appeal to the post-modernist predilection for paradox characteristic of our times. I shall argue that it is mistaken.

3 Criticism of the post-modernist interpretation: the *Tractatus* – internal evidence

The following critical assessment of this interpretation involves a pincer movement. On the one hand, we must examine internal evidence of the *Tractatus* text and the manner in which the proponents of the interpretation handle it. On the other hand, we must examine what Wittgenstein wrote and said to others about his work both before, during and after the composition of the book. Both are equally important, and present the proponents with a large array of difficulties which they have not confronted. In this section I shall be concerned only with internal evidence.

One cannot but be struck by the hermeneutic method that informs the interpretation of the *Tractatus* given by Diamond, Conant, Goldfarb and Ricketts, and by the sparseness of the evidence they muster. First, they rightly take seriously the preface to the book and the notorious concluding remarks. But they surprisingly disregard the fact that in the preface Wittgenstein speaks of *the thoughts* expressed in the book, asserts that their *truth* is 'unassailable and definitive', and expresses the belief that he has found, 'on all essential points, the final solution of the problems'. This is problematic, since 'the frame' was supposed to be taken literally and not 'dialectically' or 'ironically'. But it seems evident that, on their interpretation, the frame too is written 'tongue in cheek' – since, in their view, no thoughts are expressed in the book and there are no unassailable and definitive truths, effable or ineffable, in it.

Secondly, they are methodologically inconsistent. (a) Apart from the 'frame', Diamond and Conant implicitly exempt *Tractatus* 4.126–4.1272, 5.473 and 5.4733 from condemnation as nonsense, since these are the passages upon which their argument depends, which distinguish formal concepts from concepts proper, equate formal concepts with variables in order to show that one cannot say that, e.g. 'There are objects', and which explain that 'Socrates is identical' is a possible proposition. I shall return to this point below. (b) When it is convenient for their purposes, proponents of the post-modernist interpretation have no qualms in quoting and referring to further points Wittgenstein makes in the *Tractatus*, which they take to be correct rather than plain nonsense. Thus, for example, Goldfarb argues that Wittgenstein's discussion of objective *possibilia* in *Tractatus* 2ff involves intentional inconsistency. It is merely discourse 'in the transitional mode'. If we press these passages, we shall see the inconsistency.

> Then, in 5.525 Wittgenstein says, "The ... possibility of a situation is not expressed by a proposition, but by an expression's ... being a proposition with sense." So we see what the transitional vocabulary was meant to lead us to: an appreciation that our understanding of possibility is not ontologically based in some realm of the possible, but arises simply from our understanding of ... the sensical sentences of our language.[24]

So this passage is, apparently, not nonsense (even though it employs formal concepts). Diamond discusses approvingly *Tractatus* 3.323, which says that in the proposition 'Green is green' – where the first word is a proper name and the last an adjective – these words do not merely have different meanings, they are different symbols.[25] Yet here too, formal concepts are being used (e.g. name, proposition, symbol). Similarly, she holds that Wittgenstein really did think that the signs '*p*' and '~*p*' *can* say the same thing (*Tractatus* 4.0621), that his criticisms of Frege in 4.063 are not 'plain nonsense' but genuine, powerful criticisms, as are his criticisms of Russell's theory of judgement.[26] With this one must agree, but wonder whether this is not a case of trying to have one's cake and eat it.

Thirdly, they pay no attention to the other numerous passages in the *Tractatus* in which it is claimed that there are things that cannot be said but are shown by features of the symbolism. But it is surely necessary, if their interpretation is sound, to examine these too, in order to show the adequacy of their interpretation. They cannot be brushed aside as ironic or transitional, but must be argued to be so on the basis of evidence from the text and from Wittgenstein's own remarks on the book.

Finally, those among them who contend that some of the propositions of the *Tractatus* are 'transitional ways of talking' in a 'dialectic' in effect distinguish between two kinds of nonsense: plain nonsense and transitional nonsense. Assuming that it is important that we come to realize that apparent sentences that we think make sense are actually nonsense, then transitional nonsense is important nonsense, unlike plain nonsense. So Diamond reinstates the distinction she deplores, not in order to hold on to ineffable truths about reality, but rather to hold on to effable truths about what does and what does not make sense. Moreover, if some bits of (transitional) nonsense enable us to understand that other bits of nonsense are indeed plain nonsense, how do they do this? Not, presumably, by *saying* that they are – for then the 'transitional nonsense' would not be nonsense at all. Nor by *showing* that the other bits of nonsense are nonsense – for the distinction between what can be said and what cannot be said but only shown is itself, according to Diamond, plain nonsense.[27] Can Diamond and her followers, without themselves 'chickening out', explain how this is effected?

I shall now turn to details of this interpretation of the *Tractatus* and demonstrate its inadequacies:

(i) Sawing off the branch

Diamond argues that Wittgenstein did not *really* think that there is anything which cannot be said by well-formed propositions but which can nevertheless be shown. *All* features of the world can be described by well-formed propositions with a sense, and there is nothing that can be shown but not said. So he did not *really* think that there are objects (properties, relations, states of affairs, facts) or that such-and-such propositions are tautologies or contradictions, or that such-and-such a proposition entails such-and-such another proposition, or that red is a colour, 1 is a number, being-greater-than a relation. He did not think that these combinations of words, which employ formal concept-words as if they were genuine concept-words or which predicate internal properties of propositions, are, despite being ill-formed, attempts to say what can only be shown. He thought that they are plain nonsense, and that there is really nothing at all to be shown – neither tautologousness nor contradiction, and not entailment either. But why, in her view, are they nonsense, or rather, why, in her view, did the author of the *Tractatus* think they are? After all, it is natural enough to reply, red *is* a colour, 1 *is* a number, the proposition that *p* v ~ *p is* a tautology, and the proposition that *p* & ~ *p is* a contradiction. If it is misguided to say such things, some argument is necessary. Diamond rightly claims that Wittgenstein thought these combinations of words lack sense because they employ formal concept-words as if they were proper concept-words, and formal concepts are expressed by propositional variables. And a well-formed proposition with a sense cannot contain an unbound variable; hence a formal concept-word cannot occur in a fully analysed well-formed proposition (*Tractatus* 4.126–4.1272). But *these claims themselves* involve the use of formal concepts (proposition, variable, concept, formal concept, formal property, function). They too are nonsense. Wittgenstein did not say, in *Tractatus* 6.54, 'My propositions elucidate in the following way: anyone who understands me eventually recognizes them as nonsensical – *except for propositions 4.126–4.1272*'! So, on Diamond's interpretation, the argument in support of the claim that the sentences of the *Tractatus* are plain nonsense is itself, by the standards of the *Tractatus*, plain nonsense. So too is her claim that, according to what Wittgenstein *really* thought, all features of *the world* (a word which, she has told us (see the first quotation on p. 359 above), has been given no meaning in the *Tractatus*) are describable. Similar considerations apply to Diamond's reliance upon *Tractatus* 5.473 and 5.4733 in order to sustain the claim that the propositions of the *Tractatus* are mere nonsense in as much as we have given no meaning to words, otherwise used as formal concept-words, when they occur as predicates. These claims likewise employ formal concepts (e.g. proposition, property, symbol). And they are surely not bipolar propositions with a sense, contingent truths that could be otherwise. Nor are they senseless but well-formed tautologies. So they too are nonsense, and cannot legitimately be invoked to support Diamond's thesis.

The merit of Diamond's interpretation was supposed to be that it saves Wittgenstein from the embarrassment of sawing off the branch upon which he is sitting. But it now turns out that Diamond's interpretation involves exactly the same embarrassment.

(ii) The rationale for the showing/saying distinction

Diamond rightly emphasizes the fact that the rationale for the claim that one cannot say that A is an object, or that there are objects is that 'object' is a formal concept-word. But it is not the only kind of rationale for claims concerning what cannot be said. One similarly cannot attribute internal properties to an object or to a fact (*Tractatus* 4.122–4.125). It is impossible to assert by means of propositions that such internal properties and relations exist: rather they make themselves manifest in the propositions that represent the relevant states of affairs and are concerned with the relevant objects (*Tractatus* 4.122). Hence one cannot say that Cambridge blue is lighter than Oxford blue (cf. *Tractatus* 4.123) or even that a light blue object is lighter than a dark blue one, even though no formal concepts are involved here.

But it is shown by the pair of propositions 'The Cambridge flag is light blue' and 'The Oxford flag is dark blue'.[28] Similarly, one cannot say that a proposition is a tautology or contradiction, or that one proposition follows from another. For such assertions ascribe formal properties and relations to propositions (which are facts[29]). So they both contain a formal concept, viz. 'proposition', *and* ascribe internal properties and relations. But whatever plausibility attaches to the claim that 'there are objects' is, according to Wittgenstein, plain nonsense (and he certainly thought it was nonsense), very little attaches to Diamond's suggestion that there is never, *stricto sensu* anything to be shown. For on her interpretation, such propositions as 'The Cambridge flag is lighter than the Oxford flag', ' "$p \lor \sim p$" is a tautology' and ' "q" follows from "$(p \supset q).(p)$" ' are also, according to the *Tractatus*, *plain* nonsense which does *not* try to say something that is otherwise shown. But here there evidently *is* something that is manifest – in the first case by the above pair of propositions (which also show that light blue is lighter than dark blue), in the second by the TF notation which visibly *shows* a tautology to be a tautology, and in the third case by the tautologousness of the formula '$(p \supset q).(p): \supset : (q)$'.

(iii) Diamond on the Tractatus

(a) Diamond suggests, as we have seen, that if we take ourselves to have understood a metaphysical sentence such as 'A is an object' ('1 is a number', 'Light blue is lighter than dark blue', '12 o'clock (here, today) is a time') we take *both* its truth and its falsehood to be graspable. Even in thinking of it as true in all possible worlds, 'we think of it as itself *the case*', and think of possibilities and necessities as fixed some particular way rather than some other. To interpret Wittgenstein as holding that there are ineffable truths which he tried to indicate by means of the illegitimate sentences of the *Tractatus* is to view possibility and necessity as fixed some particular way rather than some other way – to conceive of them as being *in* a space.

But this is not so. These sentences purport to ascribe either formal or internal properties and relations (or both) to things. An internal property, as we have noted, is one which it is *unthinkable* that its object should not possess. We do indeed think that we apprehend that 1 is a number, but we would not know what to make of the claim that 1 might not be a number. We see that Cambridge blue is lighter than Oxford blue, but we rightly find it *inconceivable* that this 'necessity' be otherwise, that *these* very colours might *not* stand in the relation of one being lighter than the other. So we manifestly do *not* take the falsehood of these metaphysical assertions to be graspable – we take it to be inconceivable. We do not take A's being an object to be something that is the case and might not be the case, we take it to be something that could not be otherwise. And, of course, that is *one* reason why Wittgenstein does not think that these sentences express genuine propositions: they do not satisfy the essential requirement on a proposition with a sense, namely bipolarity. They attempt to say something that cannot be said.

(b) Diamond rightly claims that 'A is an object' is nonsense in exactly the same sense as 'Socrates is identical' or 'A is a frabble'. But, more contentiously, she claims that the *only* difference between them is that the first is likely to mislead us, for it may lead us to think that we mean something by it, something that lies beyond what Wittgenstein allows to be sayable. But if Diamond allows herself to invoke the nonsensical sentences of *Tractatus* 5.473–5.4733, then we should surely turn to other pertinent passages too which stand on exactly the same level. In particular we should note *Tractatus* 4.1272, which holds that 'Whenever the word "object" ("thing", etc.) is *correctly* used, it is expressed in conceptual notation by a variable name. ... Wherever it is used in a different way, that is as a proper concept-word, nonsensical pseudo-propositions are the result' [emphasis added]. What are these 'nonsensical pseudo-propositions'? Wittgenstein's examples are not mere possible sentences to one of the constituents of which we have patently failed to give a meaning, like 'A is a frabble'. Nor are they such gibberish as 'Good has is'. Rather, they are (nonsensical) putatively metaphysical sentences such as 'There are objects' or 'A is an object', '1 is a number', Russell's axiom of infinity, viz. 'There are $\aleph_0$ objects' (*Tractatus* 4.1272), identity statements (*Tractatus* 5.534) and the propositions of mathematics (*Tractatus* 6.2). And, of course, the sentences of the *Tractatus* itself. These are rungs on the ladder up which we must climb to attain a correct logical point of view from which we shall see that what they try to say cannot be said but is shown by features of our means of representation.

Diamond, to be sure, can try to explain this while denying the conclusion. These strings of words tempt us to think that they make sense, and we need to be disabused of this illusion. Not only are they nonsense in her view, but they are *not* attempts to say what cannot be said – for it is a further illusion to think that there is any such thing. One cannot but sympathize with Diamond and Ramsey: nonsense is nonsense. But the question is whether Ramsey is right in thinking that Wittgenstein was trying to whistle it, or whether Diamond is right that he was not. To be sure, the later Wittgenstein would deny that 'A is an object' is nonsense at all – it is a grammatical proposition, a *rule* (in a misleading guise) licensing, for example, the inference from 'A is on the table' to 'There is an object on the table' (although other examples would be handled differently). But that is not what he thought when he wrote the *Tractatus*, for he did not then think (as he later did) that the concept of a proposition is a family resemblance concept, admitting grammatical propositions, as well as many others excluded by the *Tractatus*, into the family. Did he then think that such pseudo-propositions, as he then conceived of them, are attempts to say something that is, or, *if correct*, would be, shown by features of our symbolism? Yes: 'What the axiom of infinity is intended to say would express itself in language through the existence of infinitely many names with different meanings' (*Tractatus* 5.535). And by parity of reasoning, the denial of the axiom of infinity is nonsense too, but what *it* intends to say would be shown through the existence of finitely many names with different meanings. What Wittgenstein is saying to Russell when he denies that one can say that there are $\aleph_0$ objects is precisely, *pace* Diamond (see above p. 357–8): *if* there are, all right, only *that there are* has to be expressed – has to be *shown* – in another way, namely by features of our symbolism.

How do these pseudo-propositions differ from 'A is a frabble'? In four ways. First, in that they involve the use of expressions which do indeed have a use in our language. For 'object', 'number', etc., unlike 'frabble', do have a use – as variables. The fact that they will not occur in fully analysed propositions does not mean that they are not legitimate signs when used as bound variables. Furthermore, 'The propositional variable signifies the formal concept, and its values signify the objects that fall under the concept' (*Tractatus* 4.127) – so: a name *shows* that it signifies an object, a numeral *shows* that it signifies a number and so on (*Tractatus* 4.126).

Secondly, in that they involve *misuses* of these expressions, *incorrect* uses – uses which do not accord with the rules of logical syntax or grammar. For pseudo-propositions such as 'A is an object' employ formal concept-words as if they were genuine concept-words rather than variables. Consequently 'A is an object' is not a proposition, since the rules for the use of 'object' preclude its occurrence as a predicate name and we have given no meaning to any homonym which can occur as a predicate.

Thirdly, with the exception of the axiom of infinity, they are, unlike 'A is a frabble', attempts to state necessary truths that are not tautologies – truths the denial of which is traditionally taken to be inconceivable.

Finally, and this is the nub of the dispute, unlike 'A is a frabble' *and* 'Socrates is identical', they are attempts to say what can only be shown. Forms, *pace* Russell, are not logical constants, logical objects of which we must have logical experience.[30] Expressions for forms are not names but variables. So one cannot say what the form of an object is; but it is shown by features of the name of the relevant object, namely those features which it has in common with all other names of objects of the same general form, i.e. the combinatorial possibilities in logical syntax of the relevant name. These are represented by the variable of which the name, and all other names of the same logico-syntactical category, are substitution instances. 'A is an object', 'R_n is a colour', etc. are nonsense, in the same *sense* in which 'A is a frabble' is nonsense, for there are no different *senses* of the word 'nonsense'. Nor are there different *kinds* of nonsense – nonsense no more comes in kinds than it comes in degrees. But the nonsense of the pseudo-propositions of philosophy, in particular of the philosophy of the *Tractatus*, differs from the nonsense of 'A is a frabble', for it is held to be *an attempt to say what cannot be said but only shown*. In this sense it can be said to be 'illuminating nonsense'. It is the motive behind it and the means chosen for the objective (e.g. the illegitimate use of formal concepts) that earmarks the nonsense of the *Tractatus*. Unlike such gibberish as 'A is a frabble', the propositions of the *Tractatus* are rungs on the ladder whereby to climb to a correct logical point of view, from which one will apprehend what cannot be said but which manifests itself in what can be said – the essence of the world, the transcendence of good and evil, what the solipsist means, etc.[31]

(c) Diamond and Conant make much of the fact that Wittgenstein never uses the phrase 'in violation of the rules of logical syntax'. Indeed, on the authority of *Tractatus* 5.473, they suggest that according to Wittgenstein there is no such thing as violating the rules of logical syntax. As they conceive matters, it seems, a rule can be violated only if its violation results in doing something that is prohibited, as when we violate the rule against murder. But violating the rules of logical syntax does not result in doing something, e.g. describing something, the doing of which is illicit. So there is no such thing as violating the rules of logical syntax.

But this is at best misleading. For not all rules prohibit something that can be done but should not be done. And one can follow or fail to follow rules even when they do not prohibit something that can be done – as when one follows the rules for making contracts. Failure to follow such rules does not result in illegal contracts, rather it results in invalid contracts. And an invalid contract is not a kind of contract. The pertinent passage in the *Tractatus* runs as follows:

> Logic must look after itself.
>
> If a sign is *possible*, then it is also capable of signifying. Whatever is possible in logic is also permitted. (The reason why "Socrates is identical" means nothing is that there is no property called "identical". The proposition is nonsensical because we have failed to make an arbitrary determination, and not because the symbol, in itself, would be illegitimate.)
>
> In a certain sense, we cannot make mistakes in logic.
>
> (*Tractatus* 5.473)

It seems to me that in taking this to mean that rules of logical syntax cannot be transgressed they have misinterpreted the import of this passage.[32]

There is no such thing as a linguistic rule which cannot (in principle) be followed, and by the same token, no such thing as a linguistic rule that cannot be transgressed (i.e. not complied with, not followed or not observed). Syntax consists of the grammatical rules governing a sign-language (*Tractatus* 3.334, 3.325). *Logical* syntax consists of *logical grammar*. A sign-language governed by logical grammar *obeys* (*gehorcht*) the rules of logical syntax (*Tractatus* 3.325). These rules *exclude logical mistakes*. (The conceptual notation of Frege and Russell is such a language, though an imperfect one since *it fails to exclude all mistakes* (*Tractatus* 3.325, emphasis added).)[33] Logical syntax allows us, for example, to substitute certain symbols for certain other symbols (*Tractatus* 3.344). By the same token, it does not permit substituting certain signs for others, in particular, it prohibits using the same sign for different symbols or using in a superficially similar way signs that have different modes of signification (*Tractatus* 3.325). To use the term 'object' as a variable name (formal concept) is *correct* (for this is the use we have assigned to it), but to use it as a proper concept-word is *incorrect* – for no meaning has been assigned to it as a concept-word (and to do so would generate undesirable ambiguity). To fail to follow or observe, to transgress, go against or *disobey* (to use the negation of Wittgenstein's '*gehorcht*') the rules of logical syntax is to string together words in a manner that is excluded, not permitted, by logical syntax.[34] Once we have assigned a use to the sign 'object' as a variable, it will be incorrect to go on to use it in a form of words such as 'A is an object' (or 'A is not an object'), for there it does not occur as a variable but as a genuine name – and no such use has been assigned to the term 'object', nor should it be, since the term already has a use. However, the rules of logical syntax are constitutive rules. Failure to follow them does not result in a form of words that describes a logical impossibility, for logical impossibilities are expressed by logical contradictions – which *describe* nothing since they are senseless (limiting cases of propositions with a sense). Nor does it result in the description of a metaphysical impossibility, for there is no such thing. To repeat, a logical or metaphysical 'impossibility' is not a possibility that is impossible. A fortiori, there is no such thing as describing one. Hence too, failure to comply with the rules of logical syntax does not result in a form of words that describes a logical or metaphysical necessity either – for the only expressible necessities are logical necessities, which are expressed by tautologies that describe nothing since they are senseless. And internal, formal and structural properties and relations, which metaphysics aspires to articulate cannot, by the very nature of a symbolism, be stated or described. But 'they make themselves manifest in the propositions that represent the relevant states of affairs and are concerned with the relevant objects' (*Tractatus* 4.122).

Failure to comply with the rules of logical syntax results in nonsense. Consequently, like other constitutive rules such as contract law, they do not need a sanction. Their 'sanction' is nonsense, just as the 'sanction' of contract law is invalidity – and, to be sure, these are not properly speaking sanctions. It is in this sense that logic, like contract law, 'looks after itself'.[35] *In a certain sense*, we cannot make mistakes in logic – although that is precious little consolation for Frege and Russell whose notation does not exclude certain *mistakes*. The point is that if we fail to comply with the rules of logical syntax the result is not the expression of a *thought* that is illogical (since there is no such thing), but a nonsense. So it is nonsense to do as Russell did in prefixing the symbol '$p \supset p$' (intended to mean 'p is a proposition' – which is, anyway, a nonsense) to certain propositions in order to exclude from their argument-places everything but propositions. For arguments which are not propositions render the sentence nonsensical anyway, without the assistance of the prefix (*Tractatus* 5.5351). So one *can*, contrary to Diamond and Conant, fail to follow the rules of logical syntax.

To this it might be replied that to make an invalid contract is not to *violate* the law. There is no law against making invalid contracts, only against intentionally passing them off as valid ones. Hence too, there is nothing illicit in combining words in ways that make no sense – only something dishonest in trying to pass them off as good sense. This is correct. But it does not follow that there is no such thing as failing to comply with, or to follow, the laws of contract formation, and no more does it follow that there is no such thing as failing to comply with, or to follow, the rules of logical syntax. So, one may concede that it is misleading to speak of 'violating' the rules of contract formation and equally misleading to speak of 'violating' the rules of logical syntax. One should confine oneself to speaking of *failing to comply with them, of failing to follow or observe* them. But this concession does nothing to salvage Diamond's case. If one fails to comply with, observe or follow the rules of logical syntax one transgresses the bounds of sense, which are given by logical syntax, and to transgress the bounds of sense *is* to talk nonsense. The result of failing to comply with the laws of contract formation is an invalid contract and the result of failure to comply with the rules of logical syntax is nonsense, a *mistaken* form of words, i.e. a form of words that is *excluded* from the language as a nonsensical pseudo-proposition. But one may, so the author of the *Tractatus* thought, deliberately and self-consciously flout the rules of logical syntax with the intention of bringing one's readers to apprehend something that cannot be said but is shown.

It is, incidentally, noteworthy that Wittgenstein did not share Diamond's and Conant's qualms about speaking of *transgressing* rules of grammar or logical syntax. In *Manuscript* 110, 83 ('Big Typescript' 425), he wrote: 'Just as laws only become interesting when there is an inclination to transgress them (*sie übertreten*) // when they are transgressed // certain grammatical rules are only interesting when philosophers want to transgress them'.

(iv) The Tractatus – *trying to say what can only be shown*

Diamond and Conant, like Ramsey, argue (rightly) that if you can't say it, you can't say it, and you can't whistle it either. Unlike Ramsey, they think that Wittgenstein was not trying to whistle it. On their interpretation, there is nothing that the nonsensical pseudo-propositions of the *Tractatus* are *trying* to say, for one cannot *mean* something that cannot be said. But is this what Wittgenstein thought? Since Diamond and Conant allow reference to the 'nonsensical' remarks of *Tractatus* 4.126–4.1272, 5.473 and 5.4733, it is presumably equally legitimate to refer to related passages in the attempt to fathom Wittgenstein's intentions. If we do so, it is immediately evident that he did think that one can *mean* something that cannot be said, but rather expresses itself in a different way, viz. is *shown* by features of our language. Moreover, he insisted, we *can* apprehend, indeed, can see some things which are thus meant but cannot be said.

As noted, he asserted that what Russell's axiom of infinity *was meant to say*, would (if true) be shown by the existence of infinitely many names with different meanings (*Tractatus* 5.535). Similarly, what the solipsist *means* is quite correct; only it cannot be said, but makes itself manifest (*Tractatus* 5.62). We cannot say that 'q' follows from 'p' and '$p \supset q$', for this is an internal relation between propositions. But it is *shown* by the tautology '$(p \supset q) . (p): \supset :(q)$' (*Tractatus* 6.1201). We can recognize that a proposition of logic is true from the symbol alone – indeed, that is a *characteristic mark* (hence an internal property) of a proposition of logic (*Tractatus* 6.113). We can *see* that the truth of one proposition follows from the truth of another, although that is an internal relation that cannot be described (*Tractatus* 6.1221). In complicated cases it is difficult to see these internal relations, hence we need a mechanical expedient to facilitate their recognition – viz. a proof (*Tractatus* 6.1262), which enables us to *recognize* something that cannot be said. In the T/F notation of the *Tractatus*, we can recognize such formal properties of propositions as being tautologous *by mere inspection of the propositions themselves* (*Tractatus* 6.122). So there are, according to the author of the *Tractatus,* ineffable truths that can be apprehended. Indeed, in some cases, they can literally be perceived – for one can *see* that dark blue is darker than light blue, even though, being an internal relation between colours, this cannot be said.

(v) The Tractatus *criticisms of Frege and Russell*

In the preface, Wittgenstein wrote that the truth of the thoughts set forth in the book 'seems to me unassailable and definitive'. Among the thoughts set forth are numerous profound criticisms of Frege and Russell on the nature of logic. There are no 'logical objects' or 'logical constants' (in Frege's and Russell's sense), i.e. the logical connectives are not names of concepts or relations as Frege and Russell thought (*Tractatus* 5.4–5.42). In a different sense of 'logical constants', the 'logical constants' are not representatives – this, Wittgenstein declared, is his *Grundgedanke*. By this he meant that, *pace* Russell, 'object', 'property', 'relation', etc. are not names of indefinable logical entities (pure forms), which are the most general constituents of the universe, obtainable through abstraction, with which we must be acquainted through logical experience. There can be no representatives of the *logic* of facts (*Tractatus* 4.0312). The two truth-values are not objects (*Tractatus*

4.431). A proposition is not a composite name (*Tractatus* 3.143). Frege's and Russell's 'primitive signs of logic' (the truth-functional connectives) are not primitive signs at all (*Tractatus* 5.43) and can be dispensed with in the T/F notation. The propositions of logic, contrary to Frege and Russell, say nothing – are senseless (*Tractatus* 5.43). Frege's and Russell's axiomatization of logic is misleading and redundant, since all the propositions of logic are of equal status, none being more primitive than others (*Tractatus* 6.127), and the appeal to self-evidence to vindicate their axioms is misguided (*Tractatus* 6.1271). There are also many positive claims about the nature of logic made in the wake of his criticisms of Frege and Russell, e.g. that the propositions of logic say nothing, are senseless tautologies (*Tractatus* 4.461, 6.1ff), that logic must look after itself (*Tractatus* 5.473), or, anticipating (and perhaps influencing) Ramsey, a deflationary account of truth: 'A proposition is true if we use it to say that things stand in a certain way, and they do' (*Tractatus* 4.062).[36] These claims, and many more too, are backed with solid argument. And they are all claims about which Wittgenstein never changed his mind, even after the abandonment of his early philosophy (and of the *Tractatus* distinction between what can be said and what cannot be said but only shown). But none of these important claims is a bipolar proposition with a sense. All of them involve the use of formal concepts, and by the lights of the *Tractatus* they are illegitimate in as much as they try to say something that can only be shown. Is it really credible that the author of the *Tractatus* regarded these hard-won insights into the nature of logic as 'plain nonsense'?

Diamond and Conant would presumably reply that points (iv) and (v) too are part of the 'ladder' that is to be thrown away. But whatever prima facie plausibility this may have with regard to Wittgenstein's observation on solipsism (and that is a contested matter) or perhaps on his remark on the axiom of infinity, it has none at all with respect to his observations on logical propositions, to his criticisms of Frege and Russell, and to his deflationary account of truth. Throwing away the ladder is one thing, throwing away the baby together with the bathwater is another.

(vi) The Tractatus *conception of philosophy*

Diamond claims that her paper 'Throwing Away the Ladder: How to Read the *Tractatus*' is an attempt to show what is involved in taking seriously what the *Tractatus* says about the remarks of which it is composed and about philosophy and its possibility.[37] In her view, the metaphysical remarks in the main body of the book are only apparently metaphysical 'in a way that is disposed of by the sentences which frame the book, in the Preface and the final remarks'. According to Diamond, these remarks do not indicate that there *are* things which one cannot talk about, things which can be shown but not said. On the contrary, that there are any such things is an illusion which the book is intended to dispel. Surprisingly, Diamond does not attend to 4.11–4.116 – the methodological remarks on philosophy. Here too Wittgenstein reiterates points made in the Preface: 4.116 says, analogously to the Preface, that everything that can be thought at all can be thought clearly; everything that can be put into words can be put clearly. Section 4.114, like the Preface, says that the task of philosophy is to set limits to what can be thought, and also to what cannot be thought – by working outwards through what can be thought. Section 4.112

says that philosophy aims at the logical clarification of thoughts, and 6.53 correspondingly explains that when someone tries to say something metaphysical, one must demonstrate to him that he had failed to give a meaning to certain signs in his propositions. In this sense, philosophy does not result in 'philosophical propositions', but rather in the clarification of propositions (4.112). So it seems that the methodological remarks on philosophy in 4.11–4.116 are neither 'transitional' (as Diamond would have it) nor ironical (as Conant intimates). Unlike much of the book, they are to be taken seriously. This makes it puzzling that tucked in between the serious claim that philosophy must set limits to what can and what cannot be thought and the claim that everything that can be put into words can be put clearly, Wittgenstein wrote: 'It will signify what cannot be said (*das Unsagbare*), by presenting clearly what can be said' (4.115). It seems implausible to suppose that this is a sudden intrusion of irony into an otherwise serious sequence of remarks, and equally implausible to think that *das Unsagbare* intimates that there isn't anything that cannot be said. It seems to me similarly implausible to suppose ironic or 'transitional' the fourth remark from the end of the book (6.522), which Diamond excludes from what she calls 'the frame', namely 'There are, indeed, things that cannot be put into words ("*das Unaussprechliches*"). They *make themselves manifest* ("Dies *zeigt* sich")'. If we are to take seriously what the *Tractatus* says about philosophy and its possibility, then, I suggest, we should, above all things, take this seriously. Wittgenstein's crucial observation at the end of the book says that anyone who understands *him* will eventually recognize his propositions as nonsensical and transcend them (*Tractatus* 6.54). Diamond and Conant take 'understanding *him*' to signify understanding his temptation to engage in philosophical nonsense. The clarifications or elucidating propositions of the *Tractatus* (which are not to be confused with the 'elucidations' referred to in *Tractatus* 3.263 or 4.112),[38] on their account, are not meant to indicate, by an attempt to say what can only be shown, an array of ineffable truths about the logical structure of the world and about any possible form of representation. They are meant to indicate that the temptation to think that there are any such truths is no more than an illusion, that beyond the limits of language lie not ineffable truths, but plain nonsense. But this is curious, since no philosopher other than Wittgenstein had ever been tempted to think that necessary truths, or synthetic a priori truths, are *ineffable*. This is not a disease of which anyone had ever needed to be cured. For philosophers throughout the ages have thought that such truths could readily be stated in language – in the form of what have traditionally been conceived to be necessarily true propositions. The innovation of the *Tractatus* was to argue that the necessary truths of logic are *senseless*, and that all other putatively necessary truths cannot be said but can only be shown. And there is every reason to think, with Ramsey and Russell, Anscombe and Geach, that this was precisely what Wittgenstein meant. Of course, it does not follow that what he meant makes sense. It is a mistake of Diamond to suppose that the *Tractatus* is a self-consistent work. It is a mistake to suppose that it is a work consisting of transitional nonsenses culminating in wholesale repudiation, or a work of Kierkegaardian irony or of a Zen-like dialectic. The exegetical task is to make sense of his thinking what he thought, not to make sense of what he thought, since we have it on his own (later) authority that what he thought was confused. And he later elaborated, in great detail, precisely what was confused about his earlier thought.[39]

4 The post-modernist interpretation: external criticism

Were the *Tractatus* the sole surviving text, there would be no option but to focus upon it and to construct the most coherent explanation of its argument possible. In fact we are fortunate enough to possess a wealth of source material prior to the *Tractatus*, documents contemporaneous with the *Tractatus*, and a vast quantity of post-1929 writings and lecture notes in which Wittgenstein often discusses the *Tractatus*. If Wittgenstein did not really believe that there are ineffable truths that can be shown but cannot be said, if he intended the ladder metaphor to indicate that the whole of the *Tractatus* was nothing but plain, though misleading, nonsense, then one should expect there to be some trace of this in his numerous later references to the book. If this expectation is disappointed, one would nevertheless *not* expect his later explanations of and allusions to what he thought in his early work to be flatly *inconsistent* with an adequate interpretation of his early views. Diamond and her followers make no attempt to demonstrate either the consistency of these discussions with their interpretation of the book or to explain any inconsistency. This is hermeneutically unsound. I shall therefore go through a selection of this material, each item of which by itself constitutes weighty evidence against their interpretation. It should be stressed that it is no less crucial for the post-modernists to confront this part of the pincer movement than it is for them to block the whole of the argument thus far. For either by itself suffices to undermine their position.

(i) Pre-Tractatus writings

A detailed examination of the early emergence of the showing/saying distinction and of its subsequent elaboration would be a very lengthy task which I shall not undertake here. I believe that it would not even suggest that Wittgenstein thought that the distinction and its consequences were themselves to be 'thrown away'. But it would always be open to Diamond *et al.* to claim that the *Tractatus* doctrine – according to their interpretation of it – only occurred to him later. Nevertheless, a few observations are in order. It is evident that the distinction emerged in the final section of the 'Notes on Logic' of September 1913 (Appendix I to *Notebooks 1914–16*). It resulted from reflecting on Russell's theory of types, and not, as Diamond and Conant assert without textual support, from reflecting upon Frege's puzzlement about the assertion that the concept horse is (or is not) a concept.[40] The 'Notes Dictated to Moore in Norway' (April 1914) are largely concerned with the distinction between what can be said and what cannot be said but is shown. There Wittgenstein insisted that logical propositions *show* the logical properties of language and therefore of the Universe, but say nothing. This means that merely by looking at them, you can *see* these properties. But it is impossible to *say* what these properties are, because in order to do so, you would need a language which hadn't got those properties, and it is impossible that this should be a proper language. A language which *can* express everything *mirrors* certain properties of the world by the properties it must have; and logical propositions show those properties in a systematic way. Indeed, every real (non-logical) proposition shows something, besides what it says, about the Universe (*Notebooks 1914–16* 107). And so on. Nowhere is there an intimation that all this is mere illusion. Nowhere, either here, or in the subsequent *Notebooks 1914–16*, is there any suggestion that what he is trying to do is to explode the *illusion* (whose illusion?) that there are things that cannot be said but are shown. On the contrary, he presents this idea as a profound insight:

> Logical propositions *show* something, *because* the language in which they are expressed can *say* everything that can be *said*.
>
> This same distinction between what can be *shown* by the language but not *said*, explains the difficulty that is felt about types – e.g., as to [the] difference between things, facts, properties, relations. That M is a *thing* can't be *said*; it is nonsense: but *something* is *shown* by the symbol "M". . . .
>
> Therefore a THEORY *of types* is impossible. . . .
>
> . . . Even if there *were* propositions of [the] form "M is a thing" they would be superfluous (tautologous) because what this tries to say is something that is already *seen* when you see "M".
>
> (*Notebooks 1914–16* 108f)

(ii) Letters at the time of the Tractatus

If we turn to Wittgenstein's correspondence at the time of the composition of the *Tractatus* and immediately after its completion, two letters bear on our concerns. According to Diamond and her followers, Wittgenstein did not *really* think that there were ineffable things that could not be said but which manifest themselves. This makes his letter to Engelmann of 9 April 1917 either unintelligible, or a bizarre form of irony. Apropos Uhland's poem 'Graf Eberhards Weissdorn', Wittgenstein wrote: 'The poem by Uhland is really magnificent. And this is how it is: if only you do not try to utter what is unutterable then *nothing* gets lost. But the unutterable will be – unutterably – *contained* in what has been uttered'.[41] This suggests that he took very seriously indeed the idea that there were things that are inexpressible. This was certainly what it suggested to Engelmann, who wrote apropos this letter,

> I attach immense significance to the way in which he formulated his impression [of the poem]. It seems to me indeed that his discovery of what a proposition cannot make explicit because it is manifest in it – in my view the essential core of the *Tractatus* although only adumbrated in the book – has found a lasting expression in this letter.[42]

Though not a 'professional philosopher', indeed *because* not a 'professional philosopher', Paul Englemann is not an insignificant witness. Wittgenstein enjoyed numerous conversations with Englemann, both in Olmütz in 1916, when he was still writing the *Tractatus*, and in later years. He not only gave Engelmann one of the original typescripts of the book, but also discussed his work in detail with Engelmann.[43] As Engelmann understood the *Tractatus* and what Wittgenstein explained about it, Wittgenstein and the logical positivists shared a common endeavour in trying to draw 'the line between what we can speak about and what we must be silent about'. 'The difference is only that they have nothing to be silent about. ... *Whereas Wittgenstein passionately believes that all that really matters in human life is precisely what, in his view, we must be silent about'*. Among Wittgenstein's 'mystical conclusions', Engelmann thought, are, e.g. that the sense of the world must lie outside the world (*Tractatus* 6.41) – yet, he observed, 'he [Wittgenstein] does not doubt that there is such a sense'; that no value exists *in* the world, yet 'that which endows things with the value they have, which they show, is therefore simply not *in* the world ... but that cannot be said'; that 'There is indeed that which is unutterable. This makes itself *manifest*, it is the mystical' (cf. *Tractatus* 6.522) – '(but not a "bluish haze surrounding things" and giving them an interesting appearance [as Wittgenstein once said in conversation])'.[44] There can be no doubt at all that the idea that the *punctum saliens* of the *Tractatus* is that it is plain nonsense to suppose that there are things that cannot be said but show themselves would have horrified Engelmann and been inimical to everything that Wittgenstein had imparted to him – as far as he understood it.

The second letter is that written to Russell on 19 April 1919, shortly after completing the book. Wittgenstein wrote that his main contention in the book

> is the theory of what can be expressed (*gesagt*) by prop[osition]s – i.e. by language – (and, which comes to the same, what can be *thought*) and what can not be expressed by prop[osition]s, but only shown (*gezeigt*); which I believe is the cardinal problem of philosophy.

In the same letter he explained that one cannot say in a proposition that there are two things, but it is *shown* by there being two names with different meanings. A proposition such as 'φ (a, b)' does not say that there are two things, '*but whether it is true or false, it* SHOWS what you want to *express* by saying: "there are two things".' Similarly, he insists that one cannot say that all elementary propositions are given, but this is shown by there being none having an elementary sense which is not given (*Cambridge Letters* 68). It is implausible to suppose that he was pulling Russell's leg, and that the *real* point of the book is that there is nothing at all to be shown.

(iii) Discussions with friends

On the assumption that Diamond's interpretation of the *Tractatus* is correct, it is surprising that Wittgenstein failed to convey what she takes to be his fundamental insight to either Russell or Ramsey. He spent a week with Russell in the Hague going over the book line by line in 1919. Deeply impressed though Russell was by it, he came away with the idea that what Wittgenstein had earlier told him (*Cambridge Letters* 68) was the main point of the book (namely 'the theory of what can be expressed by propositions and what cannot be expressed by propositions, but only shown') was indeed its main point. 'I had felt in his book a flavour of mysticism', he wrote to Lady Ottoline Morrell, alluding no doubt both to *Tractatus* 6.44–6.45 and to the final assertion of the doctrine: 'There are indeed, things that cannot be put into words. They *make themselves manifest*. They are what is mystical'

(*Tractatus* 6.522). But he was astonished, he continued, 'when I found he has become a complete mystic'.[45] It is characteristic of mystics to claim that there are ineffable truths, not to indulge in elaborate existentialist wit. Russell's doubts about the validity of the idea of logico-metaphysical *ineffabilia* are expressed in his introduction to the *Tractatus*, which partly explains Wittgenstein's vehement repudiation of the introduction. It seemed clear to Russell that this idea was 'the part [of the book] upon which he [Wittgenstein] himself would wish to lay most stress' (Introduction p. xxii).

It is equally surprising, if Diamond's interpretation is correct, that Wittgenstein failed to convey it to Ramsey. For Ramsey spent two weeks with Wittgenstein in Puchberg in 1923, during which time Wittgenstein devoted five hours a day to going over the text of the *Tractatus* line by line with him. Nevertheless, Ramsey retained the impression that Wittgenstein was 'trying to whistle it'. And despite the extensive, almost daily, conversations the two had in Cambridge in 1929, Ramsey still thought that Wittgenstein was 'pretending that philosophy is important nonsense' and that he failed to take seriously his own argument that it is just nonsense.[46]

(iv) The Aristotelian Society paper

'Some Remarks on Logical Form' was written no later than the summer of 1929. Here he turned, for the first and only time, to elaborate what he had called 'the application of logic'. The *Tractatus*, as its German title '*Logisch-philosophische Abhandlung*' indicates, was intended to be a treatise on logic. He had argued that one cannot say a priori what the possible forms of elementary propositions are (Tractatus 5.55). For if a question can be decided by logic at all, it must be possible to decide it without more ado, without looking to the world for an answer to the problem (*Tractatus* 5.551). The 'experience' that we need in order to understand logic is not that something or other is the state of affairs, but that something *is*, and that is not an experience. Logic is prior to every experience that something is *so* (*Tractatus* 5.552).[47] It is the *application* of logic that decides what elementary propositions there are. But logic cannot anticipate what belongs to its application. It cannot clash with its application, but it must be in contact with its application. Therefore logic and its application must not overlap (*Tractatus* 5.557). Accordingly, any investigation into the application of logic was excluded from the *Tractatus*. In 'Some Remarks on Logical Form', he turned to this task. He spelt it out clearly: if analysis is carried out far enough, it will reach atomic propositions which represent the ultimate connection of terms which cannot be broken without destroying the propositional form as such. The task is to disclose the inner structure of atomic propositions.

> Now we can only substitute a clear symbolism for the unprecise one [of ordinary language] by inspecting the phenomena we want to describe, thus trying to understand their logical multiplicity. That is to say, we can only arrive at a correct analysis by, what might be called, the logical investigation of the phenomena themselves, i.e. in a certain sense a posteriori, and not by conjecturing about a priori possibilities. . . . An atomic form cannot be foreseen. And it would be surprising if the actual phenomena had nothing more to teach us about their structure.[48]

The programme coheres perfectly with the *Tractatus*.

In the course of the paper, Wittgenstein repeats without more ado numerous central doctrines of the *Tractatus*. Some are metaphysical. For example: space and time are forms of spatial and temporal objects ('Some Remarks on Logical Form' 165; *Tractatus* 2.0251). Colours and sounds are objects ('Some Remarks on Logical Form' 165; *Tractatus* 2.0131). Other doctrines are logico-syntactical. For example: all propositions are truth-functions of elementary propositions ('Some Remarks on Logical Form' 162; *Tractatus* 5). Yet others are logico-metaphysical. For example: internal relations in reality are represented by an internal relation between the statements describing the items that stand in such internal relations ('Some Remarks on Logical Form' 168; *Tractatus* 4.125). The forms of entities described by a proposition are contained in the form of the proposition which is about those entities ('Some Remarks on Logical Form' 169; cf. *Tractatus* 3.13). A proposition must have the same logical multiplicity as what it represents ('Some Remarks on Logical Form' 169f; *Tractatus* 4.04). Some are general remarks about language. For example: that ordinary language disguises logical structure [form], allows the formation of pseudo-propositions, uses one term in an infinity of meanings ('Some Remarks on Logical Form' 163, 165; *Tractatus* 3.323, 4.002).

Apart from these numerous and striking reaffirmations of *Tractatus* claims, there are also points of disagreement. 'I *used to think*', Wittgenstein writes, 'that statements of degree were analyzable' ('Some Remarks on Logical Form' 168, emphasis added), referring to *Tractatus* 6.3751. 'One might think – *and I thought so not long ago* – that a statement expressing the degree of a quality could be analysed into a logical product of single statements of quantity and a completing supplementary statement' ('Some Remarks on Logical Form' 167, emphasis added). 'The mutual exclusion of unanalysable statements of degree *contradicts an opinion of mine which was published by me several years ago* and which necessitated that atomic propositions could not exclude one another' ('Some Remarks on Logical Form' 168, emphasis added).

It is obvious, and well known, that 'Some Remarks on Logical Form' represents the last phase of Wittgenstein's adherence to the overall philosophy of the *Tractatus*. Indeed, it was, in part, his realization in this paper that elementary propositions are not independent, that not all logical relations are consequences of truth-functional composition (since determinate-exclusion is not), which led to the collapse of the philosophy of the *Tractatus*. But if Diamond's interpretation were correct, it would be unintelligible that Wittgenstein should repeat in this paper central metaphysical, logico-syntactical and logico-metaphysical claims made in the book which had been demonstrated by him to be plain nonsense. It would be equally unintelligible that he should refer to sentences in the book as expressions of his opinions and as statements of what he used to think.

It might be argued that 'Some Remarks on Logical Form' was a temporary aberration. After all, Wittgenstein never delivered it at the Joint Session of the Aristotelian Society and the Mind Association in 1929, and later described it to Elizabeth Anscombe as 'quite worthless'. To block this move, we can turn to reports of Wittgenstein's lectures and discussions in 1929–32.

(v) Lectures and discussions

In Desmond Lee's notes of Wittgenstein's lectures 1930–2, we find – in the early lectures (prior to Wittgenstein's rapid shift away from his first philosophy) – that he reaffirms numerous *Tractatus* doctrines. Some of these are points upon which he never changed his mind. For example: words have no meaning save in propositions; they function only in propositions, like levers in a machine (*Wittgenstein's Lectures, Cambridge 1930–32* 2; *Tractatus* 3.3); such words as 'and', 'not', 'or', etc. obviously do not stand for anything (*Wittgenstein's Lectures, Cambridge 1930–32* 45; *Tractatus* 5.4–5.44); all grammar is a theory of logical types; and logical types do not talk about the application of language (*Wittgenstein's Lectures, Cambridge 1930–32* 13; *Tractatus* 3.33–3.333). Others are cardinal doctrines of the *Tractatus*, which he was subsequently to repudiate or drastically to reinterpret. For example: the proposition is a picture of reality (*Wittgenstein's Lectures, Cambridge 1930–32* 4; *Tractatus* 4.01); mathematical propositions so called are not propositions at all (*Wittgenstein's Lectures, Cambridge 1930–32* 13; *Tractatus* 6.2–6.21); the relation of proposition to fact . . . is an internal relation (*Wittgenstein's Lectures, Cambridge 1930–32* 9; *Tractatus* 4.014); in order that propositions may be able to represent at all, something further is needed which is the same both in language and in reality . . . thought must have the logical form of reality if it is to be thought at all (*Wittgenstein's Lectures, Cambridge 1930–32* 10; *Tractatus* 2.16–2.171, 2.18–2.2); there are no logical concepts, such, for example, as 'thing', 'complex', 'number' – such terms are expressions for logical forms, not concepts – they are properly expressed by a variable (*Wittgenstein's Lectures, Cambridge 1930–32* 10; *Tractatus* 4.126–4.1272). And yet others concern the *Tractatus* doctrine of what cannot be said but only shown by language. What can be expressed about the world by grammar being what it is cannot be expressed in a proposition (*Wittgenstein's Lectures, Cambridge 1930–32* 9). Language cannot express what cannot be otherwise. We never arrive at fundamental propositions in the course of our investigations; we get to the boundary of language which stops us from asking further questions. We don't get to the bottom of things, but reach a point where we can go no further, where we cannot ask further questions. What is essential to the world cannot be *said about* the world; for then it could be otherwise, as any proposition can be negated (*Wittgenstein's Lectures, Cambridge 1930–32* 34). What expression [of expectation] and fulfilment have in common is *shown* by the use of the same expression to describe both what we expect and its fulfilment . . . this common element in expectation and fulfilment cannot be described or expressed in any proposition (*Wittgenstein's Lectures, Cambridge 1930–32* 35f).

All these assertions immediately become baffling if, as Diamond claims, the ladder metaphor of the *Tractatus* (and the preface) show that Wittgenstein threw away all the claims apparently made in the book, including the idea that there are ineffable truths concerning the logical form of the world, the essential nature of representation, etc., etc. If *that* was the lesson which the *Tractatus* was trying to convey by Kierkegaardian means, as Conant holds, how could Wittgenstein reaffirm them in his lectures in 1930/1?

If we turn to Wittgenstein's discussions with Schlick and Waismann in Vienna in 1929–31, the same picture emerges. He explicitly refers to things he said in the

Tractatus in order to reaffirm them. For example, that we cannot foresee the form of elementary propositions; only when we analyse phenomena logically shall we know what form elementary propositions have (*Wittgenstein and the Vienna Circle* 42; *Tractatus* 5.55–5.557). Logic is prior to the question 'How?', not prior to the question 'What?' (*Wittgenstein and the Vienna Circle* 77; *Tractatus* 5.552). It is the essential feature of the proposition that it is a *picture* and has compositeness (*Wittgenstein and the Vienna Circle* 90; *Tractatus* 4.01, 4.032). A proposition reaches through the whole of logical space; otherwise negation would be unintelligible (*Wittgenstein and the Vienna Circle* 91; *Tractatus* 3.42). To understand a proposition is to know what is the case if it is true and what is the case if it is false (*Wittgenstein and the Vienna Circle* 86; *Tractatus* 2.223, 4.024; *Notebooks 1914–16* 93f). He reaffirms the correctness of his T/F notation: the multiplicity of this notation is correct from the beginning, which is why he does not need Russell's syntactical rules (*Wittgenstein and the Vienna Circle* 80). He reaffirms his claim that there are things that cannot be said, but that are shown by other well-formed propositions. For example, that $2 > 1.5$, which makes itself manifest by the statement that a (which is 2 m long) is 0.5 m longer than b (which is 1.5 m long) (*Wittgenstein and the Vienna Circle* 54). Similarly, that one colour is darker than another, cannot be said, 'for this is of the essence of colour; without it, after all, a colour cannot be thought'. But this makes itself manifest in the proposition that this (dark blue) suit is darker than that (light blue) one[49] (*Wittgenstein and the Vienna Circle* 55; *Tractatus* 4.123–4.124). He refers to other things he wrote in the *Tractatus* in order to repudiate or qualify them. These, he said, are things *he used to believe*. He once wrote, he remarks, 'A proposition is laid against reality like ruler. Only the end points of the graduating lines actually *touch* the object that is to be measured' (*Tractatus* 2.1512–2.15121). He now prefers to say that 'a *system of propositions* is laid against reality like a ruler'. When he was writing the *Tractatus*, he did not know this:

> At that time I thought that all inference is based on tautological form. At that time I had not seen that an inference can also have the form: This man is 2m tall, therefore he is not 3m tall. This is connected with the fact that I believed that elementary propositions must be independent of one another, that you could not infer the non-existence of one state of affairs from the existence of another.
>
> (Wittgenstein and the Vienna Circle 63;
Tractatus 2.062, 4.211, 5.1314–5.135)

In the same vein he refers to *Tractatus* 2.0131: viz. that a visual object is surrounded by colour-space, an audible object by sound-space, etc. 'When I wrote this', he continues, 'I had not yet seen that the number of positions in this space form the graduating marks of a yardstick as it were and that we always lay the entire system of propositions against reality like a yardstick' (*Wittgenstein and the Vienna Circle* 89). He explained to Waismann his views on elementary propositions.

> First I want to say what I used to believe and what part of that seems right to me now.

I used to have two conceptions of an elementary proposition, one of which seems correct to me, while I was completely wrong in holding the other. My first assumption was this: that in analysing propositions we must eventually reach propositions that are immediate connections of objects without any help from the logical constants, for 'not', 'and', 'or', and 'if' do not connect objects. And I still adhere to that. Secondly, I had the idea that elementary propositions must be independent of one another. A complete description of the world would be a product of elementary propositions. . . . In holding this I was wrong, and the following is what was wrong with it.

I laid down rules for the syntactical use of the logical constants, for example '$p.q$', and did not think that these rules might have something to do with the inner structure of propositions. What was wrong about my conception was that I believed that the syntax of logical constants could be laid down without paying attention to the inner connection of propositions. That is not how things actually are. . . . The rules for the logical constants form only part of a more comprehensive syntax about which I did not know at the time. . . . Thus I can, for example, construct the logical product $p.q$ only if p and q do not determine the same coordinate twice.

But in cases where propositions are independent everything remains valid – the whole theory of inference and so forth.

(Wittgenstein and the Vienna Circle 73f, 76)

In the final recorded discussion in July 1932, by which time his views had changed dramatically, he remarked, alluding *inter alia* to *Tractatus* 2.1511, 'At that time [when he wrote the *Tractatus*] I thought that there was "a connection between language and reality"' (*Wittgenstein and the Vienna Circle* 210). Nowhere is there any suggestion that, of course, he did not *really* believe these things, that he knew at the time that all these assertions were 'plain nonsense', written in a spirit of Kierkegaardian irony or in the manner of a Zen master. On the contrary, what he explicitly accused himself of was *dogmatism* (*Wittgenstein and the Vienna Circle* 182ff).

In response it might be held that these reports of discussions and lectures are unreliable, that we can rely only upon what Wittgenstein himself wrote. So I now turn to that.

(vi) The post-1929 manuscript volumes and typescripts

The early manuscript volumes from 1929–30 convey exactly the same picture. It is evident, even from brief scrutiny, that Wittgenstein continued (for a while) to adhere to his distinction between what can be said and what cannot be said but only shown. He wrote: 'Remember that "the length a is divisible" is not a proposition, but nonsense; that it is divisible is shown by the form of its symbol' (manuscript 106, 205, my translation). Again, 'What belongs to the essence of the world cannot be expressed by language. For this reason, it cannot *say* that everything flows. Language can only say those things that we can also imagine otherwise' (manuscript 108, 1 = *Philosophical Remarks* 84).

But the essence of language is a picture of the essence of the world; and philosophy as custodian of grammar can in fact grasp the essence of the world, only not in the propositions of language, but in the rules for this language which exclude nonsensical combinations of signs.

(manuscript 108, 2 = *Philosophical Remarks* 85)[50]

Similarly, he continued to hold that the harmony between language, thought and reality cannot be described in language, but only shown. He wrote:

The agreement of thought as such with reality cannot be expressed. If one takes the word agreement in the sense in which a true proposition agrees with reality, then it is wrong, because there are also false propositions. But another sense cannot be reproduced by means of language. Like everything metaphysical the (pre-established) harmony between *this* thought and *that* reality is given us by the limits of language.

(manuscript 109, 31, my translation)

More generally, he remarks,

What is common to thought and reality which is expressed in language by common components of the expression / shows itself through something common in the expression / in the expressions / can for that very reason not be represented (described) in language. Here we are again at the *limits of language*. One cannot describe in language the essence of language.

(manuscript 109, 53, my translation)

According to Diamond and her colleagues, Wittgenstein never cleaved to an ontology of facts constituted of objects, and of objects as sempiternal simples.[51] The ontological statements of the *Tractatus*, according to their interpretation, are plain nonsense – not anything Wittgenstein ever believed, and believed to be shown by well-formed analysed propositions of language. In manuscript 110, 250 (= *Philosophical Grammar* 200), written in July 1931, he examined in detail the use and abuse of the terms 'object' and 'complex'. 'To say that a red circle is *composed* of redness and circularity, or is a complex with these component parts, is a misuse of these words and is misleading. (Frege was aware of this and told me.)' And he proceeds to anatomize the confusions of the *Tractatus* ontology of facts, complexes and objects. Is he criticizing himself? Or merely making clear the plain nonsense of which he had already been aware when he wrote the *Tractatus*? He resumed the discussion in the following manuscript volume the same year. He noted that one *can* speak intelligibly of combinations of colours and shapes, e.g. of combinations of the colours red and blue and the shapes square and circle. (I suppose that one might describe a Matisse cut-out thus.) *This*, Wittgenstein observes, is the root of the confusing expression: a fact is a complex of objects (manuscript 111, 19). Is this a criticism of the *Tractatus* or merely an amplification of what he then knew was plain nonsense? It is still unclear. The topic was resumed in 1937/8 when he composed manuscript 142 – the first draft of the early version of the *Investigations*, which was then made into a polished typescript (*Typescript* 220). Section 108 of this 'Proto-*Philosophical Investigations*' was evidently derived from manuscript 111, 19 since the same remark is repeated. But now he writes:

> This is the root of my erroneous expression: a fact is a complex of objects.[52] To say: a red circle *'consists of'* redness and circularity, is a complex [consisting] of these constituents is a misuse of these words, and misleading. . . . The fact that this circle is red does not *consist* of anything. (Frege objected to my expression, in that he said: 'the part is smaller than the whole'.)

This looks fairly clearly as if it is a recantation. And this impression can be strengthened by tracing Frege's remark. For now that we have Frege's letters to Wittgenstein, we know that this was a criticism Frege directed against the *Tractatus* ontology *after* completion of the book. In his letter of 28 June 1919, he observed:

> You write "It is essential to things that they should be possible constituents of states of affairs."[53] Can a thing also be a constituent of a fact? The part of a part is part of the whole. If a thing is a constituent of a fact and every fact is part of the world, then the thing is also part of the world.

It is patently to this criticism that Wittgenstein is referring (probably from memory), and it is a criticism to which he had paid no attention whatsoever at the time. It was only in 1929 and later that he realized the nature of his misleading and erroneous expression, came to recognize that he had misused the expressions 'object', 'complex', 'fact', 'constituent' and 'to be constituted of', and that Frege's criticism, though not exactly on target, was correct. Interestingly, as late as 1 March 1944, Wittgenstein was preoccupied with the same error. On that day, in manuscript 127, he copied out *Tractatus* 4.22, 3.21, 3.22, 3.14, 2.03, 2.0272 and 2.01. He then wrote:

> the ungrammatical use of the words 'object' and 'configuration'! A configuration may consist of five balls in certain spatial relations; but not of the balls *and* their spatial relations. And if I say 'I see here three objects', I don't mean: two balls and their respective position.

He then repeats the passage from manuscript 111, 19, and remarks yet again: 'Here is the root of my mistaken expression'. There can be no serious doubt that this is self-criticism. Moreover, it should be noted that the criticism is not that 'object' and 'fact' are formal concepts which may not occur in a well-formed elementary proposition. It is rather that it is a grammatical mistake to call spatial positions or relations 'objects' and to speak of facts as having 'constituents' or as 'being composed' of anything.

It might be replied that all Wittgenstein is doing is noting that he had not found the very best way of articulating the nonsenses of the *Tractatus*, that he knew that it was all nonsense, but that Frege pointed out to him that the nonsense should be more persuasively put. This is wildly implausible, and there is not a shred of evidence to support any such hypothesis.

A few further points to confirm his later critical stance. In typescript 220, the Proto-*Philosophical Investigations* §92, in a passage that was meant as a sequel of *Investigations* §102, he wrote:

> The ideal, strict construction seemed to me like something concrete. I used a simile; but due to the grammatical illusion that a concept-word corresponds to *one thing*, that which is common to all its objects, it did not seem like a simile.

A different version of this, discussing the illusion of strict clear rules of the logical structure of propositions, is to be found in manuscript 157b, 10f (also written in 1937): 'I used a simile (of a method of projection, etc.) But through a grammatical illusion of the actual concepts it did not seem like a simile'. In manuscript 142, 114, commenting on the general propositional form, he wrote: 'Every proposition says: "Things are thus and so." Here is a form that can mislead us. (And did mislead me.)' And in typescript 220, §95b, in a passage that is actually repeated in the *Philosophical Investigations* §108, he remarked: 'We see that what we call "sentence" and "language" has not the formal unity that I imagined, but is a family of structures more or less united'. But if the *Tractatus*, preface and conclusion apart, is nothing but plain nonsense and was intended by its author as such, it cannot be true that he imagined any such thing, or that he was misled by the propositional variable 'things are thus and so', or that he succumbed to illusions of determinacy of sense.

It is striking that defenders of Diamond's (*et al.*) interpretation have produced no evidence at all from the post-1929 documents to support their view. If Wittgenstein was, as they argue, practising a subtle form of 'dialectic', or Kierkegaardian irony or Zen pedagogy, it would be little short of miraculous that among the 20,000 pages of *Nachlass* and the further thousands of pages of students' lecture notes and records of conversations, *there is not a single trace* of any such strategy. It would be extraordinary that in all his conversations with and dictations to his friends and pupils, with Engelmann, Russell, Ramsey, Waismann, Schlick, Lee, Drury, Rhees, Malcolm, von Wright, Anscombe, etc., of which we have records, he *never*, even once, mentioned or explained what he was up to. If the internal and external evidence mustered in this paper against the post-modernist interpretation does not suffice to undermine it, it would be instructive of Diamond and her followers to inform us what *would* count as sufficient or telling evidence against their account.

I suggest that all the evidence points to the conclusion that when he wrote the *Tractatus*, Wittgenstein did indeed embrace the very view Diamond and her colleagues reject. 'There are, indeed, things that cannot be put into words. They *make themselves manifest*. They are what is mystical' (*Tractatus* 6.522). They cannot be said or indeed thought (for thought too 'is a kind of language') – a conception to which any doctrine of the ineffability of mystical insight into the essence of the world or the transcendence of all that is higher must cleave. But they can be apprehended, *inter alia* by a grasp of the *forms* of what can be expressed. He did indeed think that when one has thrown away the ladder, one is left with a correct logical point of view and that this point of view includes an understanding of *why* the essence of the world and the nature of the sublime – of absolute value – are inexpressible. Any attempt to state such insights inevitably runs up against the limits of language. What one *means* when one tries to state these insights is perfectly correct, but the endeavour must unavoidably fail. For the ineffable manifests itself, and cannot be said. He was indeed, as Ramsey claimed, trying to whistle it. Moreover, it seems that when he did finally realize the untenability of this position, his reaction was to jettison the ladder metaphor, rather than to jettison the philosophical insights of the *Tractatus* that he wished to preserve and sometimes to reinterpret.

> I might say: if the place I want to get to could only be reached by a ladder, I would give up trying to get there. For the place I really have to get to is a place I must already be at now. Anything that I might reach by climbing a ladder does not interest me.
>
> (manuscript 109, 207; *Culture and Value* 7)

Notes

1 A shortened version of this paper was presented at the Boston Colloquium on the History and Philosophy of Science on 23 and 24 April 1998. Professors Diamond, Dreben, Floyd, Goldfarb and Ricketts laboured generously to make their views clearer, even if they did not succeed in making them any the more plausible, to me.
   I thank Dr G.P. Baker, Dr H. Ben-Yami, Dr A. Crary, Dr H.-J. Glock, Dr J. Hyman, Sir Anthony Kenny, Dr S. Mulhall and Professor W. Waxman for their comments on an earlier draft of this paper. I am indebted to Professor J. Conant for an illuminating correspondence about a forthcoming paper of his entitled 'The Method of the *Tractatus*', an extract from which is published in this volume.
2 D. Pears, *The False Prison: A Study of the Development of Wittgenstein's Philosophy*, vol. 1, Oxford, Clarendon Press, 1987, p. 143.
3 O. Neurath, 'Sociology and Physicalism', *Erkenntnis*, 1931–2, vol. 2, pp. 393–431, reprinted in translation in A.J. Ayer (ed.) *Logical Positivism*, Glencoe, Ill., Free Press, 1959, p. 284.
4 F.P. Ramsey, 'Philosophy', in R.B. Braithwaite (ed.) *The Foundations of Mathematics*, London, Kegan Paul, Trench, Trubner and Co, 1931, p. 263.
5 Ramsey, 'General Propositions and Causality', in R.B. Braithwaite (ed.) *F.P. Ramsey: The Foundations of Mathematics*, London, Routledge and Kegan Paul, 1931, p. 238. (The joke alludes to Wittgenstein's famous expertise at whistling.) I am indebted to Professor D.H. Mellor for locating the quotation for me.
6 M. Black, *A Companion to Wittgenstein's Tractatus*, Cambridge, Cambridge University Press, 1964, pp. 378ff.
7 C. Diamond, 'Throwing Away the Ladder: How to Read the *Tractatus*', reprinted in *The Realistic Spirit*, Cambridge, Mass., MIT Press, 1991, pp. 179–204, 'Ethics, Imagination and the Method of Wittgenstein's *Tractatus*', in R. Heinrich and H. Vetter (eds) *Wiener Reihe: Themen der Philosophie*, Band V, Vienna, R. Oldenbourg Verlag, 1991, pp. 55–90, reprinted in this volume and 'Wittgenstein', in J. Kim and E. Sosa (eds) *Companion to Metaphysics*, Oxford, Blackwell, 1995, pp. 513–17; James Conant, 'Must We Show What We Cannot Say?', in R. Fleming and M. Payne (eds) *The Senses of Stanley Cavell*, Lewisburg, Pa., Bucknell University Press, 1989, pp. 242–83

and 'Kierkegaard, Wittgenstein and Nonsense', in T. Cohen, P. Guyer and H. Putnam (eds) *Pursuits of Reason*, Lubbock, Texas, Texas Tech University Press, 1993, pp. 195–224; Juliet Floyd, 'The Uncaptive Eye: Solipsism in Wittgenstein's *Tractatus*', in Leroy S. Rouner (ed.) *Boston Studies in the Philosophy of Religion*, vol. 19, *Loneliness*, Notre Dame, Ind., University of Notre Dame Press, 1998, pp. 79–108; Warren Goldfarb, 'Metaphysics and Nonsense: on Cora Diamond's *The Realistic Spirit*', *Journal of Philosophical Research*, 1997, vol. 22, pp. 57–73; Thomas Ricketts, 'Pictures, Logic and the Limits of Sense in Wittgenstein's *Tractatus*', in H. Sluga and D.G. Stern (eds) *The Cambridge Companion to Wittgenstein*, Cambridge, Cambridge University Press, 1996, pp. 59–99; P. Winch, 'Persuasion', in P.A. French, T.E. Uehling and H.K. Wettstein (eds) *Midwest Studies in Philosophy*, vol. 16, *The Wittgenstein Legacy*, Notre Dame, Ind., University of Notre Dame Press, 1992, pp. 123–37.

8 '*wird einfach Unsinn sein*', contrary to Diamond's original suggestion in her 'Ethics, Imagination and the Method of Wittgenstein's *Tractatus*', op. cit., p. 70, does not mean 'is plain nonsense' but 'is simply nonsense'.

9 C. Diamond, 'Throwing Away the Ladder', op. cit., p. 181.

10 The term is, as Goldfarb points out ('Metaphysics and Nonsense', op. cit., p. 64), picturesque but highly tendentious. He prefers to distinguish 'resolute' interpretations of the *Tractatus*, which resolutely apply the penultimate remark to the text, from 'irresolute' ones which claim that its application is qualified by the distinction between showing and saying. According to him, the *Tractatus*, understood irresolutely 'avoids outright inconsistency only by undercutting any genuine commitment to its basic doctrines' (ibid.). This is mistaken. The author of the *Tractatus* was explicitly committed to a host of claims about logic, language, thought and the logical structure of the world, which cannot be stated in well-formed sentences of language, but are shown by them. That this doctrine is inconsistent, that this position cannot be upheld, is undeniable – as its author later realized. It is, as he remarked, like a clock that does not work (see below, p. 359).

11 Diamond, 'Throwing Away the Ladder', op. cit., p. 181.

12 See G.E.M. Anscombe, *An Introduction to Wittgenstein's Tractatus*, London, Hutchinson University Library, 1959, pp. 161–73; P.T. Geach, 'Saying and Showing in Frege and Wittgenstein', in J. Hintikka (ed.) *Essays on Wittgenstein in Honour of G.H. von Wright*, *Acta Philosophica Fennica* 28, Amsterdam, North Holland, 1976, pp. 54–70; and P.M.S. Hacker, *Insight and Illusion*, Oxford, Clarendon Press, 1972, pp. 17–32, which Diamond criticizes.

13 Professor Dreben would not agree with all these theses, or with Diamond's way of putting matters. I am grateful to him for pointing this out to me in conversation. Professor Floyd, unlike Conant and Diamond, considers the preface too to be 'ironic' ('The Uncaptive Eye', op. cit., p. 87).

14 Diamond, 'Throwing Away the Ladder', op. cit., pp. 195f.

15 Ibid., p. 195.

16 Ibid., p. 195.

17 Juliet Floyd, by contrast, argues that there is a difference between 'deep nonsense' and 'plain nonsense' ('The Uncaptive Eye', op. cit., p. 85). Deep nonsense, in her view, is the nonsense that interests Wittgenstein, for it does have sense 'in the ordinary grammatical sense; it is not *just* gibberish', although like plain nonsense, it 'yields' no ineffable insight. She does not, however, explain what 'having sense in the ordinary grammatical sense' means or give any evidence to show that Wittgenstein drew any such distinction.

18 Diamond, 'Throwing Away the Ladder', op. cit., pp. 197f.

19 C. Diamond, 'Wittgenstein', op. cit., p. 514.

20 J. Conant, 'Must We Show What We Cannot Say?', op. cit., p. 274, n. 16. In 'Kierkegaard, Wittgenstein and Nonsense', he makes the same point: 'when Wittgenstein says "nonsense" he means *plain nonsense*, and when he says "throw the ladder away", he means *throw it away*' (op. cit., p. 198).

21 Conant, 'Kierkegaard, Wittgenstein and Nonsense', p. 216.

22 In so far as 'deconstruction' subscribes to the hermeneutic principle that an author never says what he means or means what he says, this epithet seems eminently suitable to characterize many of the tactical moves of the proponents of this interpretation in disregarding what Wittgenstein actually wrote and said about what he had written.

23 G.E.M. Anscombe, *An Introduction to Wittgenstein's Tractatus*, London, Hutchinson, 1971, p. 78.

24 Goldfarb, 'Metaphysics and Nonsense', op. cit., p. 66. Goldfarb's argument is derived from Ricketts, who argues as follows (using the Ogden translation). The discussion of *Tractatus* 2ff. is intentionally misleading, and intended to be seen as such. (i) It suggests that the determination of the range of possibilities by the forms of objects is itself some sort of fact. (ii) Talk of atomic facts as obtaining or not obtaining (*Tractatus* 2, 2.04–2.06, 4.21) reifies possibilities and treats actualization as a property that some possibilities possess. But this is inconsistent with claiming that an object's form is not any sort of fact about it. It is also inconsistent with identifying atomic facts with combinations of objects (*Tractatus* 2.01, 2.031). Objects being configured thus and so constitute the obtaining of the atomic fact. The obtaining is not a property that the combination of objects has or lacks. So, if an atomic fact does not obtain, there is nothing, no entity that fails to obtain. Finally, the reification of possible atomic facts would make them independent of what is the case. They would then play the role that the 2.02s assign to objects.

This is a mistaken interpretation. First, the determination of the range of possibilities by the forms of objects is not suggested to be a form of fact. For a fact is precisely what is contingently the case. But possibilities of occurrence in states of affairs are *essential* to, and part of the *nature* of, objects. Every possibility is necessarily possible (*Tractatus* 2.012f.), hence not 'some sort of fact'. Secondly, *Tractatus* 2, 2.04–2.06, and 4.21 do not speak of atomic facts as obtaining or not obtaining. It is states of affairs that obtain or fail to obtain. By the lights of the *Tractatus* there is no such thing as a fact that does not obtain (for which Wittgenstein criticized himself later – cf. *Philosophical Grammar* 199). Thirdly, it is true that if, as Ricketts puts it, an atomic fact (i.e. a state of affairs) fails to obtain, there is no *entity* that fails to obtain. But a state of affairs is not an entity of any kind – any more than is a fact. Fourth, states of affairs are not 'possible facts' (a phrase Wittgenstein studiously avoids). Positive facts are the existence or obtaining of states of affairs; negative facts are the non-existence or non-obtaining of states of affairs (*Tractatus* 2.06). But unactualized states of affairs are possibilia. And they are indeed independent of what is the case, of the facts. They do not play the role of objects, which constitute the substance of the world. It is the objects that determine the range of all possible states of affairs in virtue of their combinatorial possibilities (*Tractatus* 2.0124). When he wrote the *Tractatus*, Wittgenstein would have denied that actualization is a property that some possibilities possess: it is no more a *property* of states of affairs than existence is a property of an object or a complex (which is not to be confused with a fact). But it is important to note that Ricketts's penetrating point was precisely one of the criticisms Wittgenstein directed against himself in his later writings (*Philosophical Grammar* 136–8). It is also noteworthy that *Tractatus* 2.01 'A *Sachverhalt* is a combination of objects' is a comment on *Tractatus* 2 – hence obviously a comment on existing or obtaining *Sachverhalten*. A *Sachverhalt* that does not obtain is a possible combination of objects (*Tractatus* 2.0121–2.0123). An obtaining *Sachverhalt* is an actual combination of objects – a positive fact. There is no intentional incoherence here.

25 Diamond, 'Ethics, Imagination and the Method of Wittgenstein's *Tractatus*', op. cit., pp. 70f.

26 These remarks are taken from Diamond's paper 'Truth before Tarski: After Sluga, After Ricketts, After Anscombe, After Geach, Goldfarb, Hylton and Van Heijenoort', presented at the Boston Colloquium on the History and Philosophy of Science on 23 April 1998.

27 I owe this point to John Hyman.

28 Cf. *Wittgenstein and the Vienna Circle* 55 where he introduces for the first time a distinction between a complete and an incomplete description, thus licensing the incomplete

description that the Cambridge flag is lighter than the Oxford flag but excluding the pseudo-proposition that the light blue Cambridge flag is lighter than the dark blue Oxford one. See below, p. 377 and note 49.

29 It has been objected by Professor R.J. Fogelin that Wittgenstein does not hold that propositions are facts (R.J. Fogelin, 'Feature Review Article', *International Philosophical Quarterly*, 1998, vol. 38, p. 77) since what he wrote is that 'A propositional sign is a fact' (*Tractatus* 3.14). But since a proposition is a propositional sign in its projective relation to reality (*Tractatus* 3.12), if a propositional sign is a fact, so too is a proposition.

30 B. Russell, *Theory of Knowledge, the 1913 Manuscript*, vol. 7, *The Collected Papers of Bertrand Russell*, London, Allen and Unwin, 1984, pp. 97ff.

31 Goldfarb holds that 'irresolute' interpretations of the *Tractatus* cannot adequately answer Ramsey's question of how the nonsensical sentences of the book can be helpful. To say that the sentences of the text gesture at the 'what' that is shown, i.e. the 'unutterable' features of reality, is not a good answer. For no account of gesturing has or can be given ('Metaphysics and Nonsense', op. cit., p. 71). The expression 'gesturing at' unutterable features of reality is Diamond's phrase (see above, p. 357), not mine. The well-formed sentences of language do not 'gesture at' categorial truths and truths concerning internal properties and relations, they *show* them by their form and their formal relations (*Tractatus* 4.126–4.1272, 6.1201). The sentences of the *Tractatus* 'gesture' at the truths that they futilely try to state only in the sense that they try to say what cannot be said, but is shown by other sentences. They do so by studiously employing the relevant formal concepts in illicit ways, since these formal concepts represent the forms exhibited by the appropriate well-formed sentences and constituent names (*Tractatus* 4.1271) that *do* show what the *Tractatus* tries to say.

It is, however, noteworthy that the self-styled 'resolute' interpretation of the *Tractatus* does not make it clear how 'plain nonsense' can be 'transitional', let alone how some bits of 'transitional nonsense' can make it evident that other bits of nonsense *are* nonsense – since they can neither *say* this nor *show* it.

32 Goldfarb takes it to mean that there is no such thing as a theory of language ('Metaphysics and Nonsense', op. cit., p. 71).

33 It is surprising to see Floyd assert that in the *Tractatus* no appeal is ever made to definite rules, and claim that according to Wittgenstein there is no such thing as a correct logical notation, either in Frege's or Russell's sense or a correct philosophical account of adequate notation. Genuine 'logical syntax', she claims, is a matter of use. 'Of course', she adds,

> Wittgenstein does not say this. . . . In fact Wittgenstein seems to say the opposite in several retrospective remarks, where he appears to say that at the time of writing the *Tractatus* he held the goal of a complete analysis to be achievable and desirable (*Wittgenstein and the Vienna Circle* 42, 73ff, 182ff, 250). However, these remarks make clear that Wittgenstein always rejected as nonsensical the idea that logical analysis could specify the forms of elementary propositions either a priori or in general.
>
> ('The Uncaptive Eye', op. cit., pp. 87 and n. 9)

This is deconstruction with a vengeance. According to the *Tractatus* logical grammar consists of rules of logical syntax. In order to avoid philosophical mistakes 'we must make use' of such a sign language (*Tractatus* 3.325). He later explained that in the book 'I laid down rules for the syntactical use of logical constants' (*Wittgenstein and the Vienna Circle* 74). He introduced a notation for the logical constants (the T/F notation),

> which has the advantage of rendering some things more clearly recognizable. It shows for example what all propositions of logic have in common. . . . The multiplicity of my symbolic system is correct from the beginning, and for that reason I do not need Russell's syntactical rules.
>
> (*Wittgenstein and the Vienna Circle* 80)

Wittgenstein does not *appear* to say the opposite of the view Floyd ascribes to him, he *does* say the opposite – not only in the passages she cites from *Wittgenstein and the Vienna Circle*, but also in 'Some Remarks on Logical Form' (see note 34). It is true that he always thought that logic could not specify the forms of elementary propositions a priori. But *all* his remarks make clear that he thought that this *is* to be done, but: 'in a certain sense *a posteriori*' ('Some Remarks on Logical Form' 163) – for it belongs to 'the application of logic' (see below pp. 374–5).

34 Later Wittgenstein explained matters more explicitly. In 'Some Remarks on Logical Form' he wrote:

> The rules of syntax which applied to the constants must apply to the variables also. By syntax in this general sense of the word I mean the rules which tell us in which connections only a word gives sense, thus excluding nonsensical structures. The syntax of ordinary language, as is well known, is not quite adequate for this purpose. It does not in all cases prevent the construction of nonsensical pseudo-propositions. ... The idea is to express in an appropriate symbolism what in ordinary language leads to endless misunderstandings. That is to say, where ordinary language disguises logical structure, where it allows the formation of pseudo-propositions, where it uses one term in an infinity of different meanings, we must replace it by a symbolism which gives a clear picture of the logical structure, excludes pseudo-propositions, and uses its terms unambiguously.
>
> ('Some Remarks on Logical Form' 162–3)

35 The (constitutive) laws of contract look after themselves in as much as if one fails to observe them one has not made a wrong contract, rather, one has not made a contract at all. An invalid contract is no more a kind of contract than counterfeit money is a kind of currency. But that does not stop people from making invalid contracts when they fail to observe the laws of contract-formation.

There is another sense in which 'logic must look after itself', namely that logic cannot be *justified* by reference to reality.

36 Indeed, this was nothing new in Wittgenstein's reflections: ' "*p*" is true' says nothing else but *p* (*Notebooks 1914–16* 9, cf. 94, 112). On this too he never changed his mind (see *Philosophical Grammar* 123, *Philosophical Investigations* §136). It is surprising to see Ricketts attributing to the *Tractatus* a correspondence conception of truth ('Pictures, Logic and the Limits of Sense in Wittgenstein's Tractatus', op. cit., p. 64). This is mistaken. In so far as there is a correspondence conception of anything in the *Tractatus*, it is a correspondence conception of sense. The fact that Wittgenstein speaks of a proposition's agreeing with reality if it is true does not imply any commitment to a 'truth-relation' or 'correspondence-relation' between propositions and facts, of which being true consists. To assert that a proposition '*p*' agrees with reality is to assert that '*p*' says that *p* and it is in fact the case that *p*.

37 Diamond, 'Introduction II, Wittgenstein and Metaphysics', in *The Realistic Spirit*, op. cit., p. 18.

38 The verb '*erläutern*' and noun '*Erläuterung*' are not technical terms, but common or garden ones. The elucidations referred to in *Tractatus* 3.263 are precisely parallel to Russell's 'explanations' of indefinables in *Principia* *1. The sense in which the (pseudo-) propositions of the *Tractatus* elucidate (*Tractatus* 6.54) is quite different – they clarify the philosophical matters discussed in the book, *inter alia* by bringing one to apprehend that what the *Tractatus* tries to say cannot be said and that the attempt merely results in pseudo-propositions; and bringing one to understand that what cannot be thus spoken about is nevertheless shown by well-formed propositions.

39 For a detailed examination of the later fate of the various things which, according to the *Tractatus*, cannot be said but are shown by the forms of the propositions of language, see P.M.S. Hacker, 'When the Whistling had to Stop' (forthcoming). With respect to many of the salient points, the young Wittgenstein had indeed apprehended important truths, only 'through a glass darkly'.

40 Diamond, in 'Throwing Away the Ladder', op. cit., p. 179, takes this on the authority of Geach in his article 'Saying and Showing in Frege and Wittgenstein', op. cit. However, Geach presents no evidence for this claim. Conant similarly asserts it to be so, without presenting any textual evidence for the claim. That the showing/saying distinction derived from reflection on Russell's theory of types was already argued by J. Griffin in his *Wittgenstein's Logical Atomism*, Oxford, Oxford University Press, 1964, ch. 3 and further elaborated in Hacker, *Insight and Illusion*, op. cit., ch. 1. For a recent defence of this claim, see H.-J. Glock, *A Wittgenstein Dictionary*, Oxford, Blackwell, 1996, pp. 332–5.

41 Paul Engelmann, *Letters from Ludwig Wittgenstein with a Memoir*, L. Furtmüller (trans.) Oxford, Blackwell, 1967, p. 7. Note that Wittgenstein's expression is *'das Unaussprechliche'*, as in *Tractatus* 6.522 (there translated as 'things that cannot be put into words').

42 Engelmann, ibid., p. 85.

43 Engelmann wrote: 'The best way to approach an understanding of the *Tractatus* – and one that leads *in medias res* – is the way that Wittgenstein himself, steeped in these thoughts as he then was, took, almost as a matter of course, in the conversations at the start of our acquaintance'. Ibid., p. 100.

44 Ibid., pp. 97f.

45 See R. Monk, *Wittgenstein: The Duty of Genius*, London, Jonathan Cape, 1990, pp. 183f. and also his *Bertrand Russell, the Spirit of Solitude*, London, Jonathan Cape, 1996, p. 568.

46 The paper entitled 'Philosophy' from which this remark is taken was written in the summer of 1929.

47 Logic 'is prior to the question "How?", not prior to the question "What?".' This is explained in *Wittgenstein and the Vienna Circle* 54: 'A relation that says "how?" is external. It is expressed by a proposition. "Internal" – we have two propositions between which a formal relation holds'. Hence logic is prior to statements concerning external relations, and internal relations cannot be described.

48 L. Wittgenstein, 'Some Remarks on Logical Form', *Proceedings of the Aristotelian Society*, 1929, supp. vol. 9, pp. 163f. Subsequent references in the text are to the original pagination.

49 This modifies the position of the *Tractatus*, for Wittgenstein distinguishes here between complete and incomplete descriptions. To say that this line is longer than that one, or that this suit is darker than that one is to give incomplete descriptions. But, he claims, if we describe such states of affairs completely, the external relation disappears, and *no* expressible relation is left – only an ineffable internal relation between lengths or between colours (*Wittgenstein and the Vienna Circle* 55).

50 It is noteworthy that this remark signals the beginning of his move away from the *Tractatus* conception that ineffable necessities are shown by features of the symbolism to his later view that what seemed to be attempts to express ineffable necessities are no more than grammatical rules that owe no homage to reality.

51 Floyd remarks that 'It is one of the great myths of twentieth century philosophy that the early Wittgenstein was a "logical atomist"' ('The Uncaptive Eye', op. cit., p. 85). If this is a myth, it is one Wittgenstein accepted in 1929, for he wrote

> our analysis, if carried far enough, must come to the point where it reaches propositional forms which are not themselves composed of simpler propositional forms. We must eventually reach the ultimate connection of the terms, the immediate connection which cannot be broken without destroying the propositional form as such. The propositions which represent this ultimate connection of terms I call, after B. Russell, atomic propositions. They, then, are the kernels of every proposition, *they* contain the material, and all the rest is only a development of this material. It is to them that we must look for the subject matter of propositions.
>
> ('Some Remarks on Logical Form' 162f)

For further evidence regarding his own ideas about his earlier logical atomism, see above.

52 He is inaccurate here, since he was more careful in the *Tractatus* to distinguish fact from complex, and said that a fact consists of, or is constituted of, objects.

53 *Tractatus* 2.011.

BIBLIOGRAPHY

Primary sources

The Blue and Brown Books, Oxford, Blackwell, 1975 [1958].
Culture and Value, G.H. von Wright (with H. Nyman) (ed.), P. Winch (trans.), Oxford, Blackwell, 1980.
Geheime Tagebücher, Wilhelm Baum (ed.) (3rd edition), Vienna, Turia and Kant, 1992.
Last Writings on the Philosophy of Psychology Volumes 1 and 2, G.H. von Wright and H. Nyman (eds), C.G. Luckhardt and M.A.E. Aue (trans.), Chicago, Chicago University Press, 1982.
Lectures and Conversations on Aesthetics, Psychology and Religious Belief, C. Barrett (ed.), Berkeley, University of California Press, 1970.
Ludwig Wittgenstein: Letters to Russell, Keynes and Moore, G.H. von Wright (ed.), Oxford, Blackwell, 1974.
Ludwig Wittgenstein: Letters to C.K. Ogden, with Comments on the English Translation of the Tractatus Logico-Philosophicus, G.H. von Wright (ed.), Oxford, Blackwell, 1973.
Notebooks 1914–16, G.H. von Wright and G.E.M. Anscombe (eds), G.E.M. Anscombe (trans.), Oxford, Blackwell, 1961.
On Certainty, G.E.M. Anscombe and G.H. von Wright (eds), D. Paul and G.E.M. Anscombe (trans.), Oxford, Blackwell, 1969.
Philosophical Grammar, R. Rhees (ed.), A. Kenny (trans.), Oxford, Blackwell, 1974.
Philosophical Investigations, R. Rhees and G.E.M. Anscombe (eds), G.E.M. Anscombe (trans.) (revised edition), New York, MacMillan, 1958 [1953].
Philosophical Occasions: 1912–1951, J. Klagge and A. Nordmann (eds), Indianapolis, Hackett, 1993.
Philosophical Remarks, R. Rhees (ed.), R. Hargreaves and R. White (trans.), Oxford, Blackwell, 1975.
'Philosophy': sections 86–93 of the so-called 'Big Typescript', H. Nyman (ed.), C.G. Luckhardt and M.A.E Aue (trans.), *Synthese*, 1991, vol. 87, pp. 3–22 (reprinted in *Philosophical Occasions*).
Prototractatus – An Early Version of Tractatus Logico-Philosophicus, B.F. McGuinness, T. Nyberg and G.H. von Wright (eds), D.F. Pears and B.F. McGuinness (trans.), London, Routledge, 1971.
Remarks on the Foundations of Mathematics, G.H. von Wright, R. Rhees and G.E.M. Anscombe (eds), G.E.M. Anscombe (trans.) (revised edition), Oxford, Blackwell, 1978 [1956].
Remarks on the Philosophy of Psychology, vol. 1, G.E.M. Anscombe and G.H. von Wright (eds), G.E.M. Anscombe (trans.), Oxford, Blackwell, 1980.
Remarks on the Philosophy of Psychology, vol. 2, G.H. von Wright and H. Nyman (eds), C.G. Luckhardt and M.A.E. Aue (trans.), Oxford, Blackwell, 1980.

Tractatus Logico-Philosophicus, C.K. Ogden (with F. Ramsey) (trans.), New York, Routledge, 1922.

Tractatus Logico-Philosophicus, D. Pears and B. McGuinness (trans.), London, Routledge and Kegan Paul, 1961 [1922].

Wiener Ausgabe, vols 1–5, M. Nedo (ed.), New York, Springer-Verlag, 1995.

Wittgenstein and the Vienna Circle: Conversations Recorded by Friedrich Waismann, B. McGuinness (ed.), J. Schulte and B. F. McGuinness (trans.), New York, Harper and Row Publishers, 1979 [1967].

Wittgenstein's Lectures on the Foundations of Mathematics: Cambridge, 1939, C. Diamond (ed.), Hassocks, Sussex, Harvester, 1976.

Wittgenstein's Lectures, Cambridge 1930–32, From the Notes of John King and Desmond Lee, D. Lee (ed.), Oxford, Blackwell, 1980.

Wittgenstein's Lectures, Cambridge 1932–35, From the Notes of Alice Ambrose and Margaret MacDonald, A. Ambrose (ed.), Chicago, Chicago University Press, 1979.

Wittgenstein on Personal Experience 1935–36, C. Diamond (ed.; from notes by Margaret MacDonald), unpublished.

Zettel, G.E.M. Anscombe and G.H. von Wright (eds), G.E.M. Anscombe (trans.), Oxford, Blackwell, 1981 [1967].

Selected secondary sources

The works listed below were selected for their bearing on the approach to Wittgenstein's early and later philosophy displayed in Parts I and II of this volume. Included are works which develop the approach, discuss its ramifications and/or criticize some of its central tenets.

Affeldt, S.G., 'The Ground of Mutuality: Criteria, Judgment, and Intelligibility in Stephen Mulhall and Stanley Cavell', *European Journal of Philosophy*, 1998, vol. 6, pp. 1–31.

Albritton, R., 'On Wittgenstein's Use of the Term "Criterion"', in J. V. Canfield (ed.), *The Philosophy of Wittgenstein*, vol. 7, *Criteria*, New York, Garland Publishing Inc., 1986.

Anscombe, G.E.M., *An Introduction to Wittgenstein's Tractatus*, Bristol, Thoemmes Press, 1971.

—— *Collected Papers*, vol. 1, *From Parmenides to Wittgenstein*, Oxford, Blackwell, 1981.

—— *Collected Papers*, vol. 2, *Metaphysics and Philosophy of Mind*, Oxford, Blackwell, 1981.

—— 'The Reality of the Past', in Anscombe, *Collected Papers*, vol. 2.

—— 'Wittgenstein and Linguistic Idealism', in Anscombe, *Collected Papers*, vol. 1.

Cavell, S., 'The Argument of the Ordinary: Scenes of Instruction in Wittgenstein and in Kripke', in *Conditions Handsome and Unhandsome: The Constitution of Emersonian Perfectionism*, Chicago, University of Chicago Press, 1990.

—— 'The Availability of Wittgenstein's Later Philosophy', in Cavell, *Must We Mean What We Say?*

—— *The Claim of Reason: Wittgenstein, Skepticism, Morality and Tragedy*, Oxford, Oxford University Press, 1979.

—— 'Existentialism and Analytic Philosophy', in *Themes out of School*, San Francisco, North Point Press, 1984.

—— 'The *Investigations'* Everyday Aesthetics of Itself', in S. Mulhall (ed.), *The Cavell Reader*, Cambridge, Mass., Blackwell, 1996.

—— 'Knowing and Acknowledging', in Cavell, *Must We Mean What We Say?*

—— *Must We Mean What We Say? A Book of Essays*, Oxford, Oxford University Press, 1976.

—— 'Must We Mean What We Say', in Cavell, *Must We Mean What We Say?*

—— *A Pitch of Philosophy: Autobiographical Exercises*, Cambridge, Mass., Harvard University Press, 1994.

—— *This New Yet Unapproachable America: Lectures after Emerson after Wittgenstein*, Albuquerque, Living Batch Press, 1989.

Cerbone, D., 'Don't Look But Think: Imaginary Scenarios in Wittgenstein's Later Philosophy', *Inquiry*, 1994, vol. 37, pp. 159–83.

Cohen, T., Guyer, P. and Putnam, H., *Pursuits of Reason*, Lubbock, Texas Tech University Press, 1992.

Conant, J., 'How to Pass from Latent to Patent Nonsense: Kierkegaard's *Postscript* and Wittgenstein's *Tractatus*', *Wittgenstein Studies*, 1997, diskette 1, 11–2–97.TXT.

—— 'Kierkegaard, Wittgenstein and Nonsense', in Cohen *et al. Pursuits of Reason*.

—— 'The Method of the *Tractatus*' in E. Reck (ed.), *From Frege to Wittgenstein*.

—— 'Must We Show What We Cannot Say?', in Fleming and Payne (eds), *The Senses of Stanley Cavell*.

—— 'Putting Two and Two Together: Kierkegaard, Wittgenstein and the Point of View for their Work as Authors', in T. Tessin and M. von der Ruhr (eds), *Philosophy and the Grammar of Religious Belief*, London, Macmillan, 1995.

—— 'The Search for Logically Alien Thought: Descartes, Kant, Frege and the *Tractatus*', *Philosophical Topics*, 1991, vol. 20, pp. 115–80.

—— 'Throwing Away the Top of the Ladder', *Yale Review*, 1991, vol. 79, pp. 328–64.

—— 'Wittgenstein on Meaning and Use', *Philosophical Investigations*, 1998, vol. 21, pp. 222–50.

—— 'On Wittgenstein's Philosophy of Mathematics', *Proceedings of the Aristotelian Society*, 1997, vol. 97, pp. 195–222.

Cook, J., 'Human Beings', in P. Winch (ed.), *Studies in the Philosophy of Wittgenstein*.

—— 'Wittgenstein on Privacy', *The Philosophical Review*, 1965, vol. 74, pp. 281–314.

Coope, C., Geach, P., Potts, T. and White, R., *A Wittgenstein Workbook*, Berkeley, University of California Press, 1970.

Diamond, C., 'Frege and Nonsense', in Diamond, *The Realistic Spirit*.

—— 'How Old Are These Bones?: Putnam, Wittgenstein and Verificationism', *Proceedings of the Aristotelian Society*, 1999, suppl. vol. 73.

—— 'Inheriting from Frege', in T. Ricketts (ed.), The *Cambridge Companion to Frege*, Cambridge, Cambridge University Press, forthcoming.

—— 'Losing your Concepts', *Ethics*, 1988, vol. 98, pp. 255–77.

—— 'Ludwig Wittgenstein' and 'Wittgensteinian Ethics', in L. Becker (ed.), *Encyclopedia of Ethics*, New York, Garland, 1992.

—— 'Realism and Resolution: Reply to Warren Goldfarb and Sabina Lovibond', *Journal of Philosophical Research*, 1997, vol. 22, pp. 75–86.

—— *The Realistic Spirit: Wittgenstein, Philosophy and the Mind*, Cambridge, Mass., MIT Press, 1991.

—— 'Rules: Looking in the Right Place', in Phillips and Winch, (eds) *Wittgenstein: Attention to Particulars*.

—— 'Throwing Away the Ladder: How to Read the *Tractatus*', in Diamond, *The Realistic Spirit*.

—— 'What Does a Concept-Script Do?', in Diamond, *The Realistic Spirit*.

—— 'What Nonsense Might Be', in Diamond, *The Realistic Spirit*.

—— 'Wittgenstein', in J. Kim and E. Sosa (eds), *Companion to Metaphysics*, Oxford, Blackwell, 1995.

—— 'Wittgenstein and Metaphysics', in Diamond, *The Realistic Spirit*.

—— 'Wittgenstein, Mathematics and Ethics: Resisting the Attractions of Realism', in H. Sluga and D. Stern (eds), *The Cambridge Companion to Wittgenstein*, Cambridge, Cambridge University Press, 1996.

Dreben, B., 'Quine and Wittgenstein: The Odd Couple', in *Wittgenstein and Quine*, R. Arrington and H.J. Glock (eds), London, Routledge, 1996.

Dreben, B. and Floyd, J., 'Tautology: How Not to use a Word', *Synthese*, 1991, vol. 87, pp. 23–49.

Fleming, R. and Payne, M. (eds), *The Senses of Stanley Cavell*, Lewisburg, Pa., Bucknell University Press, 1989.

Floyd, J., 'On Saying What You Really Want To Say: Wittgenstein, Gödel and the Trisection of the Angle', in J. Hintikka (ed.), *From Dedekind to Gödel*, Dordrecht, Kluwer Academic, 1996.

—— 'Gödel et les mathématiques selon Wittgenstein, in E. Riga (ed.), Paris, TER, forthcoming.

—— 'The Uncaptive Eye: Solipsism in Wittgenstein's *Tractatus*', in L. Rouner (ed.), *Loneliness, Boston University Studies in Philosophy and Religion*, South Bend Ind., University of Notre Dame Press, 1998, pp. 79–108.

—— 'Wittgenstein on 2, 2, 2. . . : On the Opening of *Remarks on the Foundations of Mathematics*', *Synthese*, 1991, vol. 87, pp. 143–80.

Floyd, J. and Shieh, S. (eds), *Future Pasts: Perspectives on the Place of the Analytic Tradition in Twentieth Century Philosophy*, Cambridge, Mass., Harvard University Press, 1999.

Friedlander, E. 'Heidegger, Carnap and Wittgenstein: Much Ado about Nothing', in A. Biletzki and A. Matar (eds), *The Story of Analytic Philosophy*, London, Routledge, 1998.

Gerrard, S., 'A Philosophy of Mathematics Between Two Camps', in H. Sluga and D. Stern (eds), *The Cambridge Companion to Wittgenstein*, Cambridge, Cambridge University Press, 1996.

Goldfarb, W., 'I Want You to Bring me a Slab: Remarks on the Opening Sections of the *Philosophical Investigations*', *Synthese*, 1983, vol. 56, pp. 265–82.

—— 'Metaphysics and Nonsense: On Cora Diamond's *The Realistic Spirit*', *Journal of Philosophical Research*, 1997, vol. 22, pp. 57–73.

—— 'Wittgenstein on Understanding', *Midwest Studies in Philosophy*, 1992, vol. 17, pp. 109–22.

Gould, T., *Hearing Things: Voice and Method in the Writing of Stanley Cavell*, Chicago, University of Chicago Press, 1998.

Hertzberg, L., 'Acting as Representation', in K.S. Johannessen and T. Nordenstam (eds) *Wittgenstein – Aesthetics and Transcendental Philosophy*, Vienna, Hölder-Pichler-Temsky, 1981.

Hylton, P., 'Functions, Operations and Sense in Wittgenstein's *Tractatus*', in W.W. Tait (ed.), *Early Analytic Philosophy*, Chicago, Open Court, 1997.

Ishiguro, H., 'Use and Reference of Names', in Winch (ed.), *Studies in the Philosophy of Wittgenstein*.

—— 'Wittgenstein and the Theory of Types', in I. Block (ed.), *Perspectives on the Philosophy of Wittgenstein*, Cambridge, Mass., Harvard University Press, 1981.

Kenny, A., 'The Ghost of the *Tractatus*', in *The Legacy of Wittgenstein*, Oxford, Blackwell, 1984.

Kremer, M., 'Contextualism and Holism in the Early Wittgenstein: From *Prototractatus* to *Tractatus*', in *Philosophical Topics*, 1997, vol. 25, pp. 87–120.

—— 'The Multiplicity of General Propositions', *Nous*, 1992, vol. 26, pp. 409–26.

McDowell, J., 'Criteria, Defeasibility and Knowledge', in McDowell, *Meaning, Knowledge and Reality*.

—— 'Intentionality and Interiority in Wittgenstein', in McDowell, *Mind, Value and Reality*.

—— 'Meaning and Intentionality in Wittgenstein's later philosophy', in McDowell, *Mind, Value and Reality*.

—— *Meaning, Knowledge and Reality*, Cambridge, Mass., Harvard University Press, 1998.

—— *Mind and World*, Cambridge, Mass., Harvard University Press, 1994.

—— *Mind, Value and Reality*, Cambridge, Mass., Harvard University Press, 1998.

—— 'One Strand in the Private Language Argument', in McDowell, *Mind, Value and Reality*.

—— 'Wittgenstein on Following a Rule', in McDowell, *Mind, Value and Reality*.

McGinn, M., 'Between Elucidation and Therapy', in *Philosophical Quarterly*, 1999.

McGuinness, B., 'The So-called Realism of Wittgenstein's *Tractatus*', in Block, I. (ed.), *Perspectives on the Philosophy of Wittgenstein*, Cambridge, Mass., MIT Press, 1981.

Minar, E., 'Feeling at Home in Language (What Makes Reading *Philosophical Investigations* Possible?)', *Synthese*, 1995, vol. 102, pp. 413–52.

—— 'Paradox and Privacy: On Paragraphs 201–2 of Wittgenstein's *Philosophical Investigations*', *Philosophy and Phenomenological Research*, 1994, vol. 54, pp. 43–74.

—— *Philosophical Investigations Paragraphs 185–202: Wittgenstein's Treatment of Following a Rule*, New York, Garland, 1990.

Mounce, H.O., *Wittgenstein's Tractatus: An Introduction*, Chicago, Chicago University Press, 1981.

Mulhall, S., 'The Givenness of Grammar: A Reply to Steven Affeldt', *European Journal of Philosophy*, 1998, vol. 6, pp. 30–44.

—— *Stanley Cavell: Philosophy's Recounting of the Ordinary*, Oxford, Clarendon Press, 1994.

—— *On Being in the World: Wittgenstein and Heidegger on Seeing Aspects*, London, Routledge, 1990.

Palmer, A., *Concept and Object: The Unity of the Proposition in Logic and Psychology*, London, Routledge, 1988.

Phillips, D.Z and Winch, P. (eds), *Wittgenstein: Attention to Particulars*, New York, St. Martin's Press, 1989.

Putnam, H., 'Kripkean Realism and Wittgensteinian Realism', in A. Biletzki, and A. Matar, (eds), *The Story of Analytic Philosophy*, London, Routledge, 1998.

—— *Realism with a Human Face*, J. Conant (ed.), Cambridge, Mass., Harvard University Press, 1990.

—— *Renewing Philosophy*, Cambridge, Mass., Harvard University Press, 1992.

—— 'On Wittgenstein's Philosophy of Mathematics', *Proceedings of the Aristotelian Society*, 1996, suppl. vol. 70, pp. 243–64.

—— *Words and Life*, J. Conant (ed.), Cambridge, Mass., Harvard University Press, 1994.

Read, Rupert. '"The real philosophical discovery": A Reply to Jolley', *Philosophical Investigations*, 1995, vol. 18, pp. 362–9.

Reck, E. (ed.), *From Frege to Wittgenstein: Perspectives on Early Analytic Philosophy*, Oxford, Oxford University Press, 2000.

Reid, L., 'Wittgenstein's Ladder: the *Tractatus* and Nonsense', *Philosophical Investigations*, 1998, vol. 21, pp. 97–151.

Rhees, R., *Discussions of Wittgenstein*, London, Routledge, 1970.

—— 'The Philosophy of Wittgenstein', in Rhees, *Discussions of Wittgenstein*.

—— 'The *Tractatus*: Seeds of Some Misunderstandings', in Rhees, *Discussions of Wittgenstein*.

—— *Without Answers*, London, Routledge, 1969.

Ricketts, T., 'Frege, the *Tractatus*, and the Logocentric Predicament', *Nous*, 1985, vol. 19, pp. 3–15.

—— 'Frege's Foray into Metalogic', *Philosophical Topics*, 1997, vol. 25, pp. 169–88.

—— 'Objectivity and Objecthood: Frege's Metaphysics of Judgement', in L. Haaparanta and J. Hintikka (eds), *Frege Synthesized*, Boston, D. Reidel, 1986.

—— 'Pictures, Logic, and the Limits of Sense in the *Tractatus*', in H. Sluga and D. Stern, *The Cambridge Companion to Wittgenstein,* Cambridge, Cambridge University Press, 1996.

Sellars, W., 'Naming and Saying', in *Science, Perception and Reality*, London, Routledge, 1963.

Sluga, H., *Gottlob Frege*, London, Routledge and Kegan Paul, 1980.

Stone, M., 'Focussing the Law: What Legal Interpretation is Not', in A. Marmor (ed.), *Law and Interpretation: Essays in Legal Philosophy*, Oxford, Oxford University Press, 1994.

Stroud, B., 'Wittgenstein and Logical Necessity', in G. Pitcher (ed.), *Wittgenstein: The Philosophical Investigations*, Notre Dame, University of Notre Dame Press, 1966.

—— 'Wittgenstein's Philosophy of Mind', in Floistad, G. (ed.), *Contemporary Philosophy*, vol. 4, *Philosophy of Mind*, The Hague, Martinus Nijhoff, 1983.

Tait, W.W., 'Wittgenstein and the "Skeptical Paradoxes"', *Journal of Philosophy*, 1983, vol. 83, pp. 475–88.

Weiner, J., *Frege in Perspective*, Ithaca, NY, Cornell University Press, 1991.

—— 'Theory and Elucidation: The End of the Age of Innocence', in Floyd and Shieh (eds), *Future Pasts*.

Winch, P., 'Can we Understand Ourselves?', *Philosophical Investigations,* 1997, vol. 20, pp. 193–204.

—— *Ethics and Action*, London, Routledge, 1972.

—— *The Idea of a Social Science* (2nd edition), London, Routledge, 1990 [1958].

—— 'Judgement: Propositions and Practices', *Philosophical Investigations*, 1998, vol. 21, pp. 189–202.

—— 'Language, Thought and World in Wittgenstein's *Tractatus*', in Winch, *Trying to Make Sense*.

—— 'Persuasion', *Midwest Studies in Philosophy*, 1992, vol. 17, pp. 123–37.

—— 'True or False?', *Inquiry*, 1988, vol. 31, pp. 265–76.

—— *Trying to Make Sense*, Oxford, Blackwell, 1987.

—— 'The Unity of Wittgenstein's Philosophy', in Winch (ed.), *Studies in the Philosophy of Wittgenstein*.

Winch, P. (ed.), *Studies in the Philosophy of Wittgenstein*, London, Routledge, 1969.

INDEX